Complete Horoscope Interpretation
Putting Together Your Planetary Profile

Complete Horoscope Interpretation

Putting Together Your Planetary Profile

by Maritha Pottenger

International Standard Book Number 0-917086-81-3

Cover Design by Maria Kay Simms

Published by ACS Publications, Inc.
P.O. Box 34487
San Diego, CA 92163-4487

First Printing, June 1986
Second Printing, November 1987
Third Printing, October 1988
Fourth Printing, December 1990

Dedication

Dedicated with love to:

My mother, Dr. Zipporah Pottenger Dobyns, for all the reasons she already knows

My father, Dr. Henry F. Dobyns, for reasons we are both still discovering

Also by ACS Publications, Inc.

Acknowledgments

Each of us builds on our experience and understanding from others. In the world of ideas, it is often difficult to trace any true "history" of development. Everyone I have ever known has, in some measure, contributed to this book. However, some people deserve special mention.

★ My mother, Dr. Zipporah Dobyns, who invented the astrological alphabet (or "Zip Code") and more importantly, always encourages her children to seek alternatives, take charge of their lives and do the best they can with any given circumstances. Her support has been, and is, constant.

★ My brother, Rique, who undertook the incredible task of programming the computer to create Planetary Profiles — and succeeded with a result superior to any we had envisioned.

★ Marc Matz, who continues to offer the support only a lover can and teaches me more about projection than anyone else in our ongoing interactions.

★ Aline Kestenberg, who faithfully read the entire manuscript in its first draft and offered many useful suggestions for clarification and elaboration and has been unfailing in her support.

★ Jalien Shandler, who wrote most of the section on Sexuality, read the entire manuscript in its seventh draft, and sparked ideas, inspiration and alternatives with me, as well as being a loving friend.

★ Neil Michelsen, who asked me to write the text for a computerized natal interpretation that would **synthesize**, and believed it was possible even when I had doubts!

★ Linda Harris, Muriel Seed and Shioshya Wilson, who read portions of the manuscript and made helpful comments regarding organization, clarity and style.

★ My other family and friends who gave unstinting emotional support when dealing with the vicissitudes of a writer's schedule and moods as well as valuable feedback regarding their own Profiles — Anastasia Angelini, Jackie Siegel Bartelt, Marguerite Dar Boggia, Pamela Crozat English, Edna Good, Laurel Siegel Gord, Helen Kessler, E. Rosalind Philpot, Bill Pottenger, Mark Pottenger, Wayne Turner, Julie Webster, and Dave Yamauchi.

★ ACS staff who work very hard "behind the scenes" to make a book successful while the author gets the public recognition: Barbara Bethea, Mary Effington, Anna Mathews and Spencer See.

★ The many customers of Astro Computing Services who took the time to complete our feedback forms and give us useful information to further refine and improve our interpretations.

★ The Universe for providing this wonderful playground called Life for us to experience!

WHAT THIS BOOK WILL <u>NOT</u> DO FOR YOU

1. Teach you exact details such as this person is 6 foot three, has red hair and teaches karate in the suburbs.

2. Turn you instantly into a professional astrologer.

3. Make you a psychotherapist.

4. Solve all your problems (although it will offer an approach which can help turn problems into opportunities).

WHAT THIS BOOK WILL DO FOR YOU

1. Offer you a logical, coherent, easy-to-follow system for quickly spotting the major issues and themes in a horoscope.

2. Present you with a way to delineate charts "cold" — without preparation, without having to read various paragraphs in books — simply using your own logic and what is before you in the horoscope.

3. Give you some basic psychological concepts which can be extremely useful in working with people and what their charts indicate.

4. Allow you to enter a world view of hope and faith which assumes there are always positive options.

Contents

CHAPTER ONE

PHILOSOPHICAL FOUNDATIONS

For all of us, our worlds are an interaction between our perceptions and physical "reality." Our perceptions are molded and channeled by our interpretations, attitudes and assumptions about what is real and what is possible. When Charles Darwin and the crew of the *H.M.S. Beagle* anchored off the shore of Patagonia, they discovered the natives living there literally could **not see** the ship. Though the *Beagle* was only a quarter of a mile offshore, the natives could not imagine such a large vessel. Though they could perceive the smaller boats in which the crew rowed to shore, for the natives — the *Beagle* did not exist![1]

For many years, people were convinced that running a mile in four minutes was "impossible." After Roger Bannister broke the barrier, many more people followed course. Despite the old cliche that "Seeing is believing," it often seems more the case that people "see what they believe" rather than "believing what they see" (and similarly for what we "hear" and "feel").

It is not necessary that your philosophy parallel mine to use this book, but I believe it will be helpful for you to know what my basic assumptions are. The clearer my world view is to you as a reader, the easier it will be for you to decide what you wish to accept and what you do not. We all make models to approximate reality; I hope that you will find my models useful. I also hope each of you will improve upon them for your own use!

My World View

The following table is my modification of a handout I received through Jim Eshelman. I asked him who had originated it so I could give credit and he said he received it at a workshop from someone else who did not know who had created this wonderful model. If anyone out there does know, I would love to be informed! I find it an excellent summary of most of my assumptions about life.

---

1. LeShan, Lawrence, *Alternate Realities*. New York: Ballantine Books, 1976, pp.6-7.

THE RULES FOR BEING HUMAN

1. You will receive a body.
You may love it or dislike it, but it's yours for the entire term. (You can do more with it than you suspect.)

2. You will learn lessons.
You are enrolled in a full-time, informal school called life. Every day in this school you will have the opportunity to learn lessons. You may like the lessons or think them irrelevant or stupid.

3. There are no mistakes, only lessons.
All experiences are valuable for learning. Growth is a process of trial and error. We are all experimenters.

4. A lesson is repeated until it is learned.
A lesson will be presented to you in various guises until you have learned it. When you have learned it, you can go on to the next lesson.

5. Learning lessons does not end.
There is no part of life without lessons. If you are alive, you are learning.

6. Others are merely mirrors of you.
You cannot adore or detest something about another person unless it reflects to you something you adore or detest about yourself.

7. You have everything you need.
You have within you all the needed tools and resources for mastering life. The power and responsibility for your life are yours. Trust the answers within.

8. All your inner resources can be helpful.
Pain is not a necessary part of learning. Life can be an exciting uncovering, allowing more and more of your inner abilities.

For me, astrology is a symbolic blueprint of the human psyche. The patterns of the heavens are like a mirror, reflecting back for us our own potentials — strengths, weaknesses, abilities, talents and conflicts. I assume that there are positive options within every part of the horoscope and every part of the human psyche. A major characteristic of the best counselors is their ability to turn "negatives" into positives, to turn supposed liabilities into assets. By assuming that this is possible, I leave the door open for clients to change their attitudes.

INNER CONFLICTS

Although there are positive options, I do assume that human beings, by their nature, experience conflict. That is, none of us (on this plane of existence) is so highly evolved as to have our whole act together. We are all learning and growing. And the path of growth includes making peace between the various warring factions that often exist within our psyches. Ambivalence is very common and a very normal human reaction. We want something, but we don't. The challenge of our spiral of evolution is to find a synthesis, a middle position between our various drives and needs, to make room for all our potentials. That is, of course, a very long-term process. I believe we have more than one lifetime in which to complete it.

People set themselves up for problems by trying to ignore a part of their basic nature, by only expressing one side of their potential. Where astrology is helpful is in pointing out the issues to the client. Part of astrology is the art of self-acceptance. This model views all the twelve sides of life as potentially positive. Nothing needs to be "cut out" or rejected. Life is a quest for wholeness. When clients have discomfort or problems, examining the issues involved can help the clients to be more accepting toward their own natures. Sometimes, just allowing a denied side some small expression in their lives is enough to fix everything. Sometimes more effort and changes are necessary. It is inspiring to see a client make an absolute turnabout in life — simply by accepting a part of who s/he is. Realizing that none of these needs are "bad" gives everyone permission to find the most satisfying paths to meeting their various desires. For many people, having the astrologer confirm that certain parts of life **are** naturally contradictory, that ambivalence and feeling some inner conflict is **normal**, is a tremendous relief!

The Psyche's Defense Mechanisms

I find three concepts from clinical psychology helpful in looking at some of the ways we stop ourselves from becoming whole. One flight from wholeness is called **repression**. This refers to burying a basic part of who we are, a fundamental drive, within the unconscious. Once it is buried, we forget we buried it and have no conscious awareness of that part of our nature. A common outcome is physical illness. If we block a basic drive in our psyche, it can hit the physical body. Illness serves unconscious needs (discussed more fully in Chapter 16). For example, the individual who is extremely strong, competent and capable may have a hard time facing her vulnerable, dependent, childlike side. If she represses her need to sometimes lean on other people, physical illness can become her only route to being taken care of. (This is not the most comfortable way of getting closeness needs met, but no one ever accused the unconscious of being perfect — only of striving to fit in the missing parts.)

Another flight from wholeness is what psychologists call **projection**. In such cases, the mirror principle of life operates. We draw into our lives people who will manifest for us the missing pieces (the parts of our own nature which we are not facing). The major problem in such cases is that these other people whom we unconsciously attract tend to **overdo** whatever qualities we are **underdoing** in our lives. So, if we are strongly identified with a need to be free and achieving in the world, we may be denying our needs for emotional attachment. In such cases, we are likely to attract other people who are too dependent, too emotional, too possessive, too clinging, who seem to want to tie us down and hem us in. Our need to be needed and to be strong and responsible can keep on attracting victims, or weaker people who want to be taken care of. We get the closeness, but at what price?

The opposite side, of course, is the person totally identified with the desire for love, relationships, warmth and an emotional commitment. Such a person may be denying her needs for freedom, space and independence. She may unconsciously attract "free soul" types as lovers, people unwilling to settle down and be faithful. Or, she falls in love with married men (not really available, so she still has her freedom). Or, the only attractive people she knows live one thousand miles away (again, unconsciously retaining space and independence). There are lots of variations.

When projection is going on, the client need only realize that the other party is mirroring the client's own potential, in an exaggerated form. Once the client can integrate that quality, in a moderate fashion, balance is achieved and s/he no longer needs that external example. Of course, this is much easier to say than to do!

The attribute being mirrored is **not** negative; the other party is simply carrying it to an extreme. It is the task of the client to discover a fulfilling way of expressing that basic part of her nature, in moderation, in balance with her other needs.

It is also important to remember that projection is a two-way street. If one party is unconsciously denying one end of the polarity, the other party is probably unconsciously denying its opposite. If one projects freedom needs, the other projects closeness needs. It becomes a natural match; each finds someone to express what s/he will not allow him/herself to manifest! Both are teaching one another and both are learning. Neither one is "making" the other do anything. They are attracted to one another because they both have something to give and receive in the relationship.

Another concept borrowed from psychology is **displacement**. This simply refers to expressing a perfectly natural and positive drive at an inappropriate time or place. For example, there are times in life when being direct, honest, forthright and assertive is the only way to get what you want. There are other times when more tact, diplomacy or subtlety is called for. If we insist on being ruthlessly, bluntly, totally honest at all times, in all situations, we will create great pain for ourselves and others. However, if we always tell little white lies, avoid saying what we really mean, hint around rather than express our preferences, we will also create great pain for ourselves and others. Balance calls for some of each — depending on the circumstances.

LIFE IS WHOLENESS

I assume that the goal of life is learning — and that we are all here to learn. I assume that everything within our nature (and within our horoscopes) is **potentially** positive. We have only to create the needed balance and determine the appropriate circumstances for manifesting our various sides. The more we are able to integrate **all** that we are, the more comfortable we will be, the easier and faster the learning will be and the more satisfaction we will gain. My role, as an astrological counselor, is to assist my clients in accepting their potentials, in finding ways to turn "negative" attributes into positive ones, in learning to balance inner conflicts for optimum results.

THE GREAT DEBATE: FATE VERSUS FREE WILL

Fate and free will do not form a dichotomy in my view. Both are a part of life. However, I subscribe to a greater level of free will than many astrologers. In my opinion, very little is absolutely "set" in our lives, in the sense of being "fated" and immutable. I think the rock-bottom basics include such things as the physical laws of our universe (e.g., gravity, the necessity of breathing, eating and sleeping), but even these have been transcended, at certain times by some individuals. I prefer to operate under the assumption that I am not positive what, if anything, is fated. This always gives me the option of change and improved circumstances.

I do feel that very few precise events in life are "fated" in the sense of being foreordained when we came into life. However, there is a certain amount of interaction in life. If I come into (for learning purposes) a body with a predisposition toward high cholesterol and proceed to eat, drink and be merry with high-sugar, high-fat foods while getting very little exercise, I am setting myself up for an eventual heart attack. There will come a time when that result is, essentially, "inevitable" or "fated." But it is **my** action and attitudes which have created that. Had I chosen to act differently, I would have a different "fate."

The analogy I like best is that we are all afloat on the River of Life. Some of us are in rowboats. Some of us are in motorboats. Some of us are hanging on to a log, while others are floundering in the open River, swimming as best we can. Down the River is a waterfall. Those of us who have learned to swim or who have a boat and have learned to steer, have an excellent chance of going over that waterfall in an easy fashion — or even choosing to steer against the current for a time and bypass that waterfall by taking another byway on the River. Those of us clutching a log or adrift in the current are much more at the mercy of whatever comes down the River, whatever swift eddies carry us along.

I believe we are "fated" to face certain issues in each life by virtue of who we are. Our attitudes and actions create our *karma* and determine our fate. If we are of a quarrelsome nature, we will continue to get involved in fights and arguments until we change our nature. If we are excessively sweet and nice, we will continue to attract others who use and abuse our power against us, until we change our nature.

I do **not** believe the details are fated. I do not believe anyone **must** marry an alcoholic, lose a job, be chronically ill. I do believe that we attract events and situations that give us opportunities to become more of what we are capable of becoming. And, if we are stuck in a negative pattern (floundering in the River), we are likely to continue our same unhelpful reactions because they are familiar. But change is always an option. And *karma* is immediate. As soon as we change our actions and attitudes, we change our *karma*. Because **we** are different, we begin attracting different circumstances for learning.

What the horoscope offers us is a map of the basic psychological issues and principles we are facing and trying to balance. It does not reveal "fated" details which "must" happen. Any principle can have a whole **range** of possible details. But, if we understand the basic principle being dealt with, we can choose to operate with the more fulfilling (less frustrating) details available.

Let us take the simple example of a Mars/Saturn aspect. This could express, in terms of physical details, as:

1) breaking a bone (Saturn) while running (Mars)
2) getting a speeding (Mars) ticket (Saturn — dealing with the law)
3) building strong muscles (Mars) and firm bones (Saturn) with systematic (Saturn) exercise (Mars)
4) pioneering (Mars) a new career (Saturn)
5) having a fight (Mars) with the boss (Saturn)
6) feeling our body (Mars) is paralyzed (Saturn)
7) fear (Saturn) of taking action (Mars)
8) calcification (Saturn) in the muscles (Mars), e.g., gout, arthritis
9) high physical energy (Mars) put into material constructions (Saturn)
10) meeting the qualifications (Saturn) for an auto race (Mars)

and many, many other possible options.

Predicting any of these possible details (or others) is not going to be helpful to a client. If we are right, the client feels "stuck." It was "fated" and they do not believe they can change it. If we are wrong, it makes us and astrology look bad.

If we deal with the **psychological principles** which lie behind **all** the details, we can be helpful. We can encourage the client to work for wholeness, so that s/he can express positive, fulfilling details. I do not care **which** details my clients express and I am not about to guess them. I care that they understand the **issues** being faced, so that they can resolve them in a satisfying manner.

The principles of Mars and Saturn are to make peace between pure self-will ("I want to do what I want to do right now") and the realistic limits of the physical world's structure and the regulations of life, especially as personified in authority figures. Note the balance or imbalance in the ten (out of millions) possible details cited:

1) breaking a bone while running
   This is a case of overdoing the Mars principle and underdoing the Saturn

principle. If we are too set on what we want (Mars), we do not take reasonable, practical precautions (Saturn).

2) getting a speeding ticket

This is another case of excessive Martian expression with insufficient attention to Saturn. If we put our personal desires (Mars) above the law (Saturn), we get caught (not always on the human level, but faithfully on the cosmic level).

3) building strong muscles and firm bones with systematic exercise

This is a case of integrating the two principles. When we make a reasonable balance between personal, bodily expression (Mars) and the physical laws of life (Saturn), we can reap useful results.

4) pioneering a new career

Again, we have a balance of the two themes: drive (Mars) and discipline (Saturn), desire (Mars) and common sense (Saturn), confidence (Mars) and practicality (Saturn), initiative (Mars) and carry-through (Saturn).

5) having a fight with the boss

Here we have excessive expression of Mars principles, with not enough of Saturn principles. Personal self-expression (Mars) is allowed to overcome our practical dealing with the structure of the world (Saturn).

6) feeling our body is paralyzed

Here, excessive expression of Saturn principles and inhibition of Martian themes creates the problem. Our cautious, practical, limit-seeking side (Saturn) is allowed to overwhelm our expressive, spontaneous, confident side (Mars).

7) fear (Saturn) of taking action (Mars)

This is another case of too much on the side of Saturn principles and too little on the side of Mars principles. Our assessment of the world's blocks (Saturn) is weighted more heavily than our own ability and desire to act (Mars).

8) calcification in the muscles, e.g., gout, arthritis

Excessive rigidity and concern with limits (Saturn) can carry over to the physical level as well if we give it [limitation] more weight than our own desires and expression (Mars).

9) high physical energy put into material constructions

Again, a reasonable balance between self-will (Mars) and the practical restraints of the world (Saturn) can achieve much.

10) meeting the qualifications for an auto race

We face the laws (Saturn) and energetically (Mars) do as much of what we want (Mars) to do as we can within the limits of what is allowed (Saturn).

I am not saying that astrologers cannot or should not predict. I do believe some predictions are possible. The more we know of an individual's background, the more likely we will be able to choose the most probable detail for a given pattern. People do tend to continue along the track they have been taking. If we know someone has a history of fighting with authority figures, we can predict choice #5 above. If we are aware of someone's tendency to speed, we can suspect #2 may occur. If our client tells us he has just quit his job, #4 is a possibility, and so on.

The important question for me is: is a prediction helpful? Does it empower the client — or simply make me feel good to be so "right on"? I will often give examples of **possible** outcomes to clients, in order to illustrate the principles involved. When clients understand the issues they are facing, they can manifest many different details — including some which did not occur to their astrologer!

Clients given only one possibility tend to feel "locked in." If a "positive" prediction comes to pass, they are still stuck in a place of feeling it must have been ordained because the astrologer predicted it. If a "negative" prediction comes to pass, they feel trapped by a cosmos which dooms them to certain uncomfortable experiences. Over and over again, psychological research demonstrates that people are happiest and most successful in their lives when they **subjectively feel that they are in control and can DO something about their lives**. People are least happy and successful when they feel circumstances are beyond their control.

The self-fulfilling prophecy must also be considered. Clients who expect only one possibility are less likely to try alternatives. Clients who are given a world view of openness and choice are more likely to experiment and discover new ways of being and behaving, new paths to happiness. A basic principle for me is, **there is often more than one right answer** in any given situation.

I want the biggest, widest, most complete universe of choices for myself and my life, and believe my clients deserve exactly the same!

CHAPTER TWO

UNCOVERING THEMES IN DELINEATION

The major hurdle for students of astrology is "putting the pieces all together." Over and over, I hear students say, "I can look at this part of the horoscope by itself and that one by itself, but how do I combine three, four and even more!?"

Certainly a part of the solution is practice. Like anything else, the more we do, the better we get at it. A certain amount of integration comes simply from doing charts, charts and more charts!

However, the process of spotting major themes in a horoscope,[1] rather than bits and pieces, can also be aided greatly by the use of the **astrological alphabet** (also known affectionately as the "Zip Code"). This system enables the astrologer to quickly and easily pinpoint the most central themes in the nature of the client.

The concept of the astrological alphabet, as outlined by Dr. Zipporah Dobyns, is that astrology deals with twelve basic ways of being in the world, twelve fundamental human drives, twelve human needs and modes of operation. Each of the twelve is positive — no malefics. Each of the twelve is necessary — a part of being human. Each of the twelve if overdone, or expressed to the exclusion

---

1. If you prefer **not** to search for repeated themes yourself, you can order the "PP BOOK" option from Astro Computing Services, which allows you to use this book to make complete, synthesizing delineations of horoscopes without figuring out which themes are emphasized.

　　Available for $3.00 each, the "PP BOOK" report calculates the emphasis on all the letters of the alphabet, themes and aspects in each horoscope for which you provide the data. The report lists each significant focus (e.g., "There is a Letter 3 theme in "Identity," and gives the appropriate page numbers for you to read in this book ("See pages 107-108 in the *Complete Horoscope Interpretation* book.")

　　The computer will not **always** arrive at the same results as you might, as certain steps are ambiguous (e.g., how much weight to give a planet making a conjunction, based on the orb). However, the majority of the time, the computer answers will concur with those deriving from hand calculations — or the recommended quick scan of a horoscope. Thus it provides an excellent teaching tool.

　　The "PP BOOK" does **not** provide a listing of **each and every** astrological factor making up the significant themes. For that, you would order "PP WEIGHTS" (discussed in footnote #2 in Chapter 6).

of any of the other eleven — can be destructive. These twelve sides of life are mirrored in the horoscope by a planet, a house and a sign.

Following is a diagram of the astrological alphabet. (Note the inclusion of the "big four" asteroids and Chiron in the table. You can choose to ignore the asteroids and Chiron if you prefer not to work with them. The alphabet works with or without the asteroids!)

The Astrological Alphabet of Zipporah Dobyns

LETTER	PLANET	HOUSE	SIGN	ELEMENT	QUALITY
1	Mars ♂	1	Aries ♈	Fire	Cardinal
2	Venus ♀	2	Taurus ♉	Earth	Fixed
3	Mercury ☿	3	Gemini ♊	Air	Mutable
4	Moon ☽	4	Cancer ♋	Water	Cardinal
5	Sun ☉	5	Leo ♌	Fire	Fixed
6	Mercury ☿ Ceres ⚳ Vesta ⚶	6	Virgo ♍	Earth	Mutable
7	Venus ♀ Pallas ⚴ Juno ⚵	7	Libra ♎	Air	Cardinal
8	Pluto ♇	8	Scorpio ♏	Water	Fixed
9	Jupiter ♃ Chiron ⚷	9	Sagittarius ♐	Fire	Mutable
10	Saturn ♄	10	Capricorn ♑	Earth	Cardinal
11	Uranus ♅	11	Aquarius ♒	Air	Fixed
12	Neptune ♆	12	Pisces ♓	Water	Mutable

Venus and Mercury, in their own nature, are considered to be more like Letters 2 and 3, respectively. (Letters 6 and 7 are more fully described by the asteroids which are discussed in Chapter 3.)

The alphabet concept does **not** mean that signs, planets and houses are treated equally or said to be "the same." Dr. Dobyns states very clearly that planets are the most emphatic, important form of the astrological alphabet. (This is backed up by the research of the Gauquelins who find some significance to the placement of planets in the chart — and, to some degree, support for houses. They have yet to find statistical support for signs.) Dr. Dobyns weights aspects next in importance after planets, with houses third and signs last.[2]

What the theory of the Zip Code presents is that certain groups of planet/house/sign combinations share **themes**. They key into the same sides of life, the same ways of being in the world, the same basic motivational drives (but

2. The question of how much to weight various parts of the horoscope is a controversial one. I do not believe final answers are available as yet. In this book, I will follow the above sequence — planets, aspects, houses and signs in descending order. Figures will be offered for people who enjoy playing with numbers, but they are **not** intended to represent any kind of absolute. They are a "best guess" approximation based on my current knowledge.

a planet is a much stronger statement of the importance of that theme than a sign is). An awareness of the alphabet allows the astrologer to quickly spot repeated messages in the horoscope.

Spotting Themes

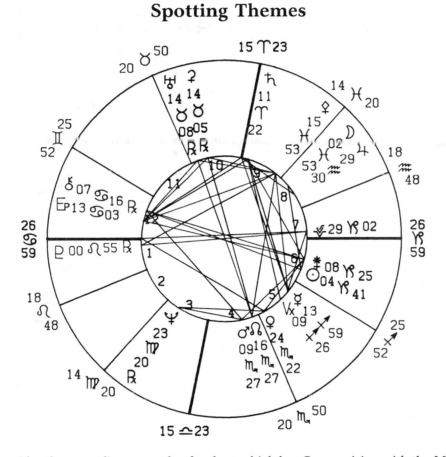

Consider the preceding example of a chart which has Cancer rising with the Moon in Pisces in the 8th house and Mars in Scorpio in the 4th house. The 1st house is occupied by Pluto in Leo. Why are we considering those particular factors? Because most astrologers agree that the rising sign and 1st house keys are symbolic of the person's basic identity, sense of self, spontaneous action in the world. With Cancer rising, the Moon is a ruler[3] of the 1st house while Mars is always

---

3. Beginners, please note that the planet associated with each sign of the astrological alphabet is, in mainstream astrology, called the "ruler" of that sign. E.g., Mars "rules" Aries, Venus rules Taurus, Mercury rules Gemini, etc. Venus and Mercury do double duty — each ruling two signs. When considering the facets of life connected to a given house of the horoscope, one factor to be integrated is the ruler of the sign on the cusp (boundary line) of that house. The planet which rules the sign on the cusp is assumed to represent additional information about the matters of that house.

the natural ruler of the 1st house (since Aries occupies the 1st house in the natural zodiac).[4]

It is important to remember that planets are considered from two **different** viewpoints. One viewpoint is the nature of the planet itself. The other viewpoint is a planet functioning as a ruler of a sign — in which case that planet is "standing in" for a certain letter of the alphabet, which is not necessarily the same as the planet's own nature. When we consider anything involving this 8th house, we have a Letter 4 theme because the Moon is there — and the Moon is Letter 4 **in its own nature**. We also have a Letter 12 theme because the Moon is in Pisces. However, in a chart with Cancer rising, the Moon rules the Ascendant [Letter 1]. Thus, the Moon is **also** a key to Letter 1 [by virtue of rulership]. Therefore, when summing the different forms of Letter 1, we would go the the Moon and add in Letter 8 [Moon in 8th house], Letter 12 [Moon in Pisces] and the nature of any planets conjunct or parallel the Moon. Note that we do **not** count the Letter 4 nature of the Moon in this case. We go to the Moon **only** in terms of its rulership of the 1st house. [The Letter 4 connection would have already been counted in terms of the Cancer rising.]

We are narrowing our search to these particular factors as we want to hone in on what is called "identity." If we were considering a factor such as "career," we would be focusing on other parts of the chart. At an initial glance, the placements of Pluto, Moon and Mars seem to have little in common (other than a fair amount of water[5] by either sign or house). However, using the astrological alphabet, it is immediately clear that there is a repeated theme of **Letter 8** in this chart where identity is concerned. Pluto — Letter 8 — is in the 1st house. The ruler of the 1st house (the Moon ruling the Cancer rising) is in the 8th house — Letter 8. The natural ruler of the 1st house (Mars) is in the 8th sign — Letter 8. We have a clear-cut, easily visible theme!

In the astrological alphabet, Pluto, Scorpio and the 8th house all point to themes of depth analysis, inward probing, investigation, emotional intensity, transformation, transmutation and issues around power, especially when sexual or financial areas are involved. Issues often revolve around learning what is enough and when to let go.

Recall that the Letter 8 theme is tied to identity in this particular example. In such a case, we would suspect that this person does a lot of looking inside, probing his/her inner motivations. We would anticipate strong sensuality and emotional intensity with the likelihood of a power drive and the potential of struggles with others until the sexual/financial area can be comfortably shared. Some of

---

4. Beginners: the "natural zodiac" refers to a horoscope in which the sign Aries occupies the 1st house of the chart; Taurus occupies the 2nd house; Gemini occupies the 3rd house, etc.

5. Astrology groups the planets/houses/signs in terms of four "elements" and three "qualities." The elements are fire, earth, air and water and occur in that order, repeating three times in the zodiac. Thus, Aries is fire; Taurus is earth; Gemini is air; Cancer is water and Leo begins fire again, etc. The qualities are: cardinal, fixed and mutable — in that order. More detailed descriptions of elements and qualities occur in Chapter 4.

the learning is likely to be around being able to release (emotionally, physically and spiritually). Death (one part of Letter 8) is the ultimate release on the physical level. But transformation and transmutation issues are also connected to Letter 8 — other paths to finishing up one chapter and moving on to another. We would expect an individual who is an instinctive investigator, drawn to a number of in-depth studies, and naturally inclined to probe the psyches of people nearby as well as his/her own. (Page 111 of Chapter 6 describes a Letter 8 theme in identity.)

Had Letter 8 been connected to other parts of the chart — e.g., career, children, relationships, etc. — we would look for Letter 8 themes in those areas. For example, Letter 8 connected to career would imply a need for depth investigation in the work — be it the detective, the researcher, the student of occult areas. Work involving sexual and/or financial areas would certainly be possible (sex therapist, accountant, tax lawyer, investment banker, etc.). Issues of release and letting go could emerge in the career (e.g., hospice worker) or simply the person's emotional intensity about the job and tendency to keep on hanging on in whatever s/he is doing. We would expect a worker who is determined, persevering, thorough and strongly involved on an emotional level with his/her career. (See also page 145-146 in Chapter 7.)

Similarly, if Letter 8 were tied to other areas of the chart, we would draw other conclusions. The Letter 8 theme is still there, but our interpretations are based on **where** in the chart it occurs. For example, if Letter 8 is strongly connected to money and financial areas, we would expect someone who hangs on to money and might have problems around releasing or letting go of it. Money could be a source of emotional security and could be used to obtain power in the world. (See also page 327 in Chapter 12.)

Three Uses of the Zip Code

Note that we use the astrological alphabet in **three** different ways. **One** use is to draw certain parameters in the chart — that is, to ascertain certain areas which will be examined for significance to various parts of life (e.g., identity, work, relationships, money, etc.). In our previous example, when seeking the themes which indicate ''basic identity,'' the Zip Code tells us to examine planets in the 1st house, the rising sign, placement of the actual ruler of the rising sign and the placement of Mars (natural ruler of the 1st house). This allows us to look at certain factors in the horoscope, without attempting to conceptualize the whole thing.

The logic of the Zip Code and its various mixtures leads naturally into the division of the horoscope into different areas. Once the concept of each of the twelve sides of life is clear (the topic in Chapter 3), it becomes easy to determine which of the various ''letters'' of the alphabet are involved in different life areas.

The **second** use of the Zip Code is to easily spot major themes in the given areas which we have defined. In our example, we saw a repeated theme of Letter 8 for the life area of identity. We might also discover, for example, a theme of parenting connected to relationships, security connected to money and freedom connected to parents. The most central issues in the nature are found again and again in the horoscope. Repetition of a theme assures us that it is truly important. The Zip Code allows us to spot such reiterations quickly and easily.

The **third** use of the Zip Code is with the chart as a whole. That will be the topic in a later section of this book. Initially, it is easier for the student to deal with limited areas rather than the whole horoscope. However, once the basic logic of the alphabet is clear, dealing with the chart as a whole also becomes very easy.

How to Use This Book

For the purposes of explanation, this book will first cover the various themes which can be spotted in a horoscope (whether in the chart as a whole or limited to certain areas). The alphabet, which is the logical basis of everything, will be our first focus — in Chapter 3. Then (in Chapter 4) we can consider various combinations of the alphabet which lead to other themes (e.g., freedom-loving, mental, security-oriented, etc.). Aspects and the search for themes through aspects are discussed in Chapter 5.

The middle chapters of this book are devoted to defining and giving examples of life areas, e.g., identity, work, relationships, etc. Chapter 6 covers the topic of identity, Chapter 7 delineates career, etc., through future trends in Chapter 17. Gaining an overview of the whole chart is the subject of Chapter 18, while additional counseling issues are covered in Chapter 19 and a brief summary is presented in Chapter 20.

Initially, the topics in Chapters 6 through 17 will be defined in detail in terms of all the various factors which must be considered in the horoscope in order to analyze each life area. (For example, to identify important motifs in the life area of relationships, we would examine the sign/house/aspects to Venus, the Descendant, the ruler of the Descendant, any planets in the 7th house and even more.) The use of the Zip Code allows the astrologer to include **all** the relevant factors (not overlooking anything) while screening out what does not pertain. Based on that perusal of significant factors, you will obtain a list of significant motifs for that life area — which could be a single letter of the astrological alphabet, a combination of two, or some other themes (such as elements, qualities, freedom, security, etc.). Aspects and nodes are also discussed.

The major portions of Chapters 6-17 provide summaries of the meanings of every possible motif — as manifested for that particular life area (such as the delineation for a Letter 1 theme in career, for a freedom theme in children, for a fire theme in parents, for a 1-10 combination in relationships, etc.). Delineations are supplied for each letter of the alphabet, for a number of themes (including elements, qualities, polarities and other themes such as security, risk, freedom, etc.), for combinations of two letters of the alphabet, for various positions of the nodes of the Moon, and for harmony and conflict aspects from one life area (such as identity) to any of the basic 12 letters of the Zip Code. Thus, this book can be used as a source for **summary delineations of the major themes in any horoscope, broken into the life areas discussed here**.

The "No Effort" Approach

For those individuals who do not wish to attempt the synthesizing approach presented here, the delineations within can also be matched with traditional "planets in signs" and "planets in houses" approaches. Appendix 2 demonstrates how to use this volume in that fashion. (For example, readers can begin by looking up the house and sign placements of each of their planets in Appendix 2 and they will be referred to the proper interpretations within various sections of this book.)

For readers who prefer to focus in terms of a life area (e.g., identity, career, etc.) rather than a planet, the following listing will be useful. Rather than becoming familiar with the factors involved in the various life areas (by working one's way through this book), you can use this list to quickly find the desired delineations within this text for any chart you wish to analyze.

If you are ready to learn a **complete** synthesizing approach, please skip the rest of this chapter, going directly to Chapter 3.

IDENTITY

Mars in **Aries** or **1st** house: Letter 1, page 107.
Mars in **Taurus** or **2nd** house: Letter 2, page 107.
Mars in **Gemini** or **3rd** house: Letter 3, page 107.
Mars in **Cancer** or **4th** house: Letter 4, page 108.
Mars in **Leo** or **5th** house: Letter 5, page 109.
Mars in **Virgo** or **6th** house: Letter 6, page 109.
Mars in **Libra** or **7th** house: Letter 7, page 110.
Mars in **Scorpio** or **8th** house: Letter 8, page 111.
Mars in **Sagittarius** or **9th** house: Letter 9, page 111.
Mars in **Capricorn** or **10th** house: Letter 10, page 112.
Mars in **Aquarius** or **11th** house: Letter 11, page 113.
Mars in **Pisces** or **12th** house: Letter 12, page 114.

Ascendant in **Aries** or **1st** house: Letter 1, page 107.
Ascendant in **Taurus** or **2nd** house: Letter 2, page 107.
Ascendant in **Gemini** or **3rd** house: Letter 3, page 107.
Ascendant in **Cancer** or **4th** house: Letter 4, page 108.
Ascendant in **Leo** or **5th** house: Letter 5, page 109.
Ascendant in **Virgo** or **6th** house: Letter 6, page 109.
Ascendant in **Libra** or **7th** house: Letter 7, page 110.
Ascendant in **Scorpio** or **8th** house: Letter 8, page 111.
Ascendant in **Sagittarius** or **9th** house: Letter 9, page 111.
Ascendant in **Capricorn** or **10th** house: Letter 10, page 112.
Ascendant in **Aquarius** or **11th** house: Letter 11, page 113.
Ascendant in **Pisces** or **12th** house: Letter 12, page 114.

Ruler of the **1st** house in **Aries** or **1st** house: Letter 1, page 107.
Ruler of the **1st** house in **Taurus** or **2nd** house: Letter 2, page 107.
Ruler of the **1st** house in **Gemini** or **3rd** house: Letter 3, page 107.
Ruler of the **1st** house in **Cancer** or **4th** house: Letter 4, page 108.
Ruler of the **1st** house in **Leo** or **5th** house: Letter 5, page 109.
Ruler of the **1st** house in **Virgo** or **6th** house: Letter 6, page 109.
Ruler of the **1st** house in **Libra** or **7th** house: Letter 7, page 110.
Ruler of the **1st** house in **Scorpio** or **8th** house: Letter 8, page 111.
Ruler of the **1st** house in **Sagittarius** or **9th** house: Letter 9, page 111.
Ruler of the **1st** house in **Capricorn** or **10th** house: Letter 10, page 112.
Ruler of the 1st house in **Aquarius** or **11th** house: Letter 11, page 113.
Ruler of the **1st** house in **Pisces** or **12th** house: Letter 12, page 114.

Sun in the **1st** house or **Aries**: read Letter 5, page 109.
Moon in the **1st** house or **Aries**: read Letter 4, page 108.
Mercury in the **1st** house or **Aries**: read Letter 3, page 107.
Venus the **1st** house or **Aries**: read Letter 2, page 107.
Mars in the **1st** house or **Aries**: read Letter 1, page 107.
Jupiter in the **1st** house or **Aries**: read Letter 9, page 111.
Saturn in the **1st** house or **Aries**: read Letter 10, page 112.
Uranus in the **1st** house or **Aries**: read Letter 11, page 113.
Neptune in the **1st** house or **Aries**: read Letter 12, page 114.
Pluto in the **1st** house or **Aries**: read Letter 8, page 111.
Ceres or **Vesta** in the **1st** house or **Aries**: read Letter 6, page 109.
Pallas or **Juno** in the **1st** house or **Aries**: read Letter 7, page 110.
Chiron in the **1st** house or **Aries**: read Letter 9, page 111.

WORK
Venus, Ceres, Vesta, MC or **Saturn** in **Aries** or **1st** house: Letter 1, page 140.
Venus, Ceres, Vesta, MC or **Saturn** in **Taurus** or **2nd** house: Letter 2, page 141.
Venus, Ceres, Vesta, MC or **Saturn** in **Gemini** or **3rd** house: Letter 3, page 141.
Venus, Ceres, Vesta, MC or **Saturn** in **Cancer** or **4th** house: Letter 4, page 142.
Venus, Ceres, Vesta, MC or **Saturn** in **Leo** or **5th** house: Letter 5, page 143.
Venus, Ceres, Vesta, MC or **Saturn** in **Virgo** or **6th** house: Letter 6, page 144.
Venus, Ceres, Vesta, MC or **Saturn** in **Libra** or **7th** house: Letter 7, page 145.
Venus, Ceres, Vesta, MC or **Saturn** in **Scorpio** or **8th** house: Letter 8, page 145.
Venus, Ceres, Vesta, MC or **Saturn** in **Sagittarius** or **9th** house: Letter 9, page 146.
Venus, Ceres, Vesta, MC or **Saturn** in **Capricorn** or **10th** house: Letter 10, page 147.
Venus, Ceres, Vesta, MC or **Saturn** in **Aquarius** or **11th** house: Letter 11, page 148.
Venus, Ceres, Vesta, MC or **Saturn** in **Pisces** or **12th** house: Letter 12, page 149.

Ruler of the **2nd**, **6th** or **10th** houses in **Aries** or **1st** house: Letter 1, page 140.
Ruler of the **2nd**, **6th** or **10th** houses in **Taurus** or **2nd** house: Letter 2, page 141.
Ruler of the **2nd**, **6th** or **10th** houses in **Gemini** or **3rd** house: Letter 3, page 141.
Ruler of the **2nd**, **6th** or **10th** houses in **Cancer** or **4th** house: Letter 4, page 142.
Ruler of the **2nd**, **6th** or **10th** houses in **Leo** or **5th** house: Letter 5, page 143.
Ruler of the **2nd**, **6th** or **10th** houses in **Virgo** or **6th** house: Letter 6, page 144.
Ruler of the **2nd**, **6th** or **10th** houses in **Libra** or **7th** house: Letter 7, page 145.
Ruler of the **2nd**, **6th** or **10th** houses in **Scorpio** or **8th** house: Letter 8, page 145.
Ruler of the **2nd**, **6th** or **10th** houses in **Sagittarius** or **9th** house: Letter 9, page 146.
Ruler of the **2nd**, **6th** or **10th** houses in **Capricorn** or **10th** house: Letter 10, page 147.
Ruler of the **2nd**, **6th** or **10th** houses in **Aquarius** or **11th** house: Letter 11, page 148.
Ruler of the **2nd**, **6th** or **10th** houses in **Pisces** or **12th** house: Letter 12, page 149.

Sun in the **2nd**, **6th** or **10th** houses or in **Taurus**, **Virgo** or **Capricorn**: read Letter 5, page 143.
Moon in the **2nd**, **6th** or **10th** houses or in **Taurus**, **Virgo** or **Capricorn**: read Letter 4, page 142.
Mercury in the **2nd**, **6th** or **10th** houses or in **Taurus**, **Virgo** or **Capricorn**: read Letter 3, page 141.
Venus the **2nd**, **6th** or **10th** houses or in **Taurus**, **Virgo** or **Capricorn**: read Letter 2, page 141.
Mars in the **2nd**, **6th** or **10th** houses or in **Taurus**, **Virgo** or **Capricorn**: read Letter 1, page 140.
Jupiter in the **2nd**, **6th** or **10th** houses or in **Taurus**, **Virgo** or **Capricorn**: read Letter 9, page 146.
Saturn in the **2nd**, **6th** or **10th** houses or in **Taurus**, **Virgo** or **Capricorn**: read Letter 10, page 147.
Uranus in the **2nd**, **6th** or **10th** houses or in **Taurus**, **Virgo** or **Capricorn**: read Letter 11, page 148.
Neptune in the **2nd**, **6th** or **10th** houses or in **Taurus**, **Virgo** or **Capricorn**: read Letter 12, page 149.
Pluto in the **2nd**, **6th** or **10th** houses or in **Taurus**, **Virgo** or **Capricorn**: read Letter 8, page 145.
Ceres or **Vesta** in the **2nd**, **6th** or **10th** houses or in **Taurus**, **Virgo** or **Capricorn**: read Letter 6, page 144.
Pallas or **Juno** in the **2nd**, **6th** or **10th** houses or in **Taurus**, **Virgo** or **Capricorn**: read Letter 7, page 145.
Chiron in the **2nd**, **6th** or **10th** houses or in **Taurus**, **Virgo** or **Capricorn**: read Letter 9, page 146.

RELATIONSHIPS

Venus, Pallas, Juno or Pluto in Aries or 1st house: Letter 1, page 179.
Venus, Pallas, Juno or Pluto in Taurus or 2nd house: Letter 2, page 181.
Venus, Pallas, Juno or Pluto in Gemini or 3rd house: Letter 3, page 182.
Venus, Pallas, Juno or Pluto in Cancer or 4th house: Letter 4, page 182.
Venus, Pallas, Juno or Pluto in Leo or 5th house: Letter 5, page 183.
Venus, Pallas, Juno or Pluto in Virgo or 6th house: Letter 6, page 184.
Venus, Pallas, Juno or Pluto in Libra or 7th house: Letter 7, page 185.
Venus, Pallas, Juno or Pluto in Scorpio or 8th house: Letter 8, page 186.
Venus, Pallas, Juno or Pluto in Sagittarius or 9th house: Letter 9, page 186.
Venus, Pallas, Juno or Pluto in Capricorn or 10th house: Letter 10, page 187.
Venus, Pallas, Juno or Pluto in Aquarius or 11th house: Letter 11, page 188.
Venus, Pallas, Juno or Pluto in Pisces or 12th house: Letter 12, page 188.

Ruler of the 7th or 8th houses in Aries or 1st house: Letter 1, page 179.
Ruler of the 7th or 8th houses in Taurus or 2nd house: Letter 2, page 181.
Ruler of the 7th or 8th houses in Gemini or 3rd house: Letter 3, page 182.
Ruler of the 7th or 8th houses in Cancer or 4th house: Letter 4, page 182.
Ruler of the 7th or 8th houses in Leo or 5th house: Letter 5, page 183.
Ruler of the 7th or 8th houses in Virgo or 6th house: Letter 6, page 184.
Ruler of the 7th or 8th houses in Libra or 7th house: Letter 7, page 185.
Ruler of the 7th or 8th houses in Scorpio or 8th house: Letter 8, page 186.
Ruler of the 7th or 8th houses in Sagittarius or 9th house: Letter 9, page 186.
Ruler of the 7th or 8th houses in Capricorn or 10th house: Letter 10, page 187.
Ruler of the 7th or 8th houses in Aquarius or 11th house: Letter 11, page 188.
Ruler of the 7th or 8th houses in Pisces or 12th house: Letter 12, page 188.

Sun in the 7th or 8th houses or in Libra or Scorpio: read Letter 5, page 183.
Moon in the 7th or 8th houses or in Libra or Scorpio: read Letter 4, page 182.
Mercury in the 7th or 8th houses or in Libra or Scorpio: read Letter 3, page 182.
Venus the 7th or 8th houses or in Libra or Scorpio: read Letter 2, page 181.
Mars in the 7th or 8th houses or in Libra or Scorpio: read Letter 1, page 179.
Jupiter in the 7th or 8th houses or in Libra or Scorpio: read Letter 9, page 186.
Saturn in the 7th or 8th houses or in Libra or Scorpio: read Letter 10, page 187.
Uranus in the 7th or 8th houses or in Libra or Scorpio: read Letter 11, page 188.
Neptune in the 7th or 8th houses or in Libra or Scorpio: read Letter 12, page 188.
Pluto in the 7th or 8th houses or in Libra or Scorpio: read Letter 8, page 186.
Ceres or Vesta in the 7th or 8th houses or in Libra or Scorpio: read Letter 6, page 184.
Pallas or Juno in the 7th or 8th houses or in Libra or Scorpio: read Letter 7, page 185.
Chiron in the 7th or 8th houses or in Libra or Scorpio: read Letter 9, page 186.

MIND

Mercury, Uranus or Jupiter in Aries or 1st house: Letter 1, page 223.
Mercury, Uranus or Jupiter in Taurus or 2nd house: Letter 2, page 223.
Mercury, Uranus or Jupiter in Gemini or 3rd house: Letter 3, page 224.
Mercury, Uranus or Jupiter in Cancer or 4th house: Letter 4, page 224.
Mercury, Uranus or Jupiter in Leo or 5th house: Letter 5, page 225.
Mercury, Uranus or Jupiter in Virgo or 6th house: Letter 6, page 225.
Mercury, Uranus or Jupiter in Libra or 7th house: Letter 7, page 226.
Mercury, Uranus or Jupiter in Scorpio or 8th house: Letter 8, page 227.
Mercury, Uranus or Jupiter in Sagittarius or 9th house: Letter 9, page 227.
Mercury, Uranus or Jupiter in Capricorn or 10th house: Letter 10, page 228.
Mercury, Uranus or Jupiter in Aquarius or 11th house: Letter 11, page 229.
Mercury, Uranus or Jupiter in Pisces or 12th house: Letter 12, page 229.

Ruler of the 3rd, 6th, 9th or 11th houses in Aries or 1st house: Letter 1, page 223.

Ruler of the 3rd, 6th, 9th or 11th houses in Taurus or 2nd house: Letter 2, page 223.

Ruler of the 3rd, 6th, 9th or 11th houses in Gemini or 3rd house: Letter 3, page 224.

Ruler of the 3rd, 6th, 9th or 11th houses in Cancer or 4th house: Letter 4, page 224.

Ruler of the 3rd, 6th, 9th or 11th houses in Leo or 5th house: Letter 5, page 225.

Ruler of the 3rd, 6th, 9th or 11th houses in Virgo or 6th house: Letter 6, page 225.

Ruler of the 3rd, 6th, 9th or 11th houses in Libra or 7th house: Letter 7, page 226.

Ruler of the 3rd, 6th, 9th or 11th houses in Scorpio or 8th house: Letter 8, page 227.

Ruler of the 3rd, 6th, 9th or 11th houses in Sagittarius or 9th house: Letter 9, page 227.

Ruler of the 3rd, 6th, 9th or 11th houses in Capricorn or 10th house: Letter 10, page 228.

Ruler of the 3rd, 6th, 9th or 11th houses in Aquarius or 11th house: Letter 11, page 229.

Ruler of the 3rd, 6th, 9th or 11th houses in Pisces or 12th house: Letter 12, page 229.

Sun in the 3rd, 6th, 9th or 11th houses or in Gemini, Virgo, Sagittarius or Aquarius: read Letter 5, page 225.
Moon in the 3rd, 6th, 9th or 11th houses or in Gemini, Virgo, Sagittarius or Aquarius: read Letter 4, page 224.
Mercury in the 3rd, 6th, 9th or 11th houses or in Gemini, Virgo, Sagittarius or Aquarius: read Letter 3, page 224.

Venus in the **3rd**, **6th**, **9th** or **11th** houses or in **Gemini, Virgo, Sagittarius** or **Aquarius**: read Letter 2, page 223.

Mars in the **3rd**, **6th**, **9th** or **11th** houses or in **Gemini, Virgo, Sagittarius** or **Aquarius**: read Letter 1, page 223.

Jupiter in the **3rd**, **6th**, **9th** or **11th** houses or in **Gemini, Virgo, Sagittarius** or **Aquarius**: read Letter 9, page 227.

Saturn in the **3rd**, **6th**, **9th** or **11th** houses or in **Gemini, Virgo, Sagittarius** or **Aquarius**: read Letter 10, page 228.

Uranus in the **3rd**, **6th**, **9th** or **11th** houses or in **Gemini, Virgo, Sagittarius** or **Aquarius**: read Letter 11, page 229.

Neptune in the **3rd**, **6th**, **9th** or **11th** houses or in **Gemini, Virgo, Sagittarius** or **Aquarius**: read Letter 12, page 229.

Pluto in the **3rd**, **6th**, **9th** or **11th** houses or in **Gemini, Virgo, Sagittarius** or **Aquarius**: read Letter 8, page 227.

Ceres or **Vesta** in the **3rd**, **6th**, **9th** or **11th** houses or in **Gemini, Virgo, Sagittarius** or **Aquarius**: read Letter 6, page 225.

Pallas or **Juno** in the **3rd**, **6th**, **9th** or **11th** houses or in **Gemini, Virgo, Sagittarius** or **Aquarius**: read Letter 7, page 226.

Chiron in the **3rd**, **6th**, **9th** or **11th** houses or in **Gemini, Virgo, Sagittarius** or **Aquarius**: read Letter 9, page 227.

CHILDREN AND CREATIVITY

Sun, Moon or **Ceres** in **Aries** or **1st** house: Letter 1, page 261.
Sun, Moon or **Ceres** in **Taurus** or **2nd** house: Letter 2, page 262.
Sun, Moon or **Ceres** in **Gemini** or **3rd** house: Letter 3, page 262.
Sun, Moon or **Ceres** in **Cancer** or **4th** house: Letter 4, page 263.
Sun, Moon or **Ceres** in **Leo** or **5th** house: Letter 5, page 264.
Sun, Moon or **Ceres** in **Virgo** or **6th** house: Letter 6, page 265.
Sun, Moon or **Ceres** in **Libra** or **7th** house: Letter 7, page 265.
Sun, Moon or **Ceres** in **Scorpio** or **8th** house: Letter 8, page 266.
Sun, Moon or **Ceres** in **Sagittarius** or **9th** house: Letter 9, page 267.
Sun, Moon or **Ceres** in **Capricorn** or **10th** house: Letter 10, page 268.
Sun, Moon or **Ceres** in **Aquarius** or **11th** house: Letter 11, page 269.
Sun, Moon or **Ceres** in **Pisces** or **12th** house: Letter 12, page 269.

Ruler of the **4th** or **5th** houses in **Aries** or **1st** house: Letter 1, page 261.
Ruler of the **4th** or **5th** houses in **Taurus** or **2nd** house: Letter 2, page 262.
Ruler of the **4th** or **5th** houses in **Gemini** or **3rd** house: Letter 3, page 262.
Ruler of the **4th** or **5th** houses in **Cancer** or **4th** house: Letter 4, page 263.
Ruler of the **4th** or **5th** houses in **Leo** or **5th** house: Letter 5, page 264.
Ruler of the **4th** or **5th** houses in **Virgo** or **6th** house: Letter 6, page 265.
Ruler of the **4th** or **5th** houses in **Libra** or **7th** house: Letter 7, page 265.
Ruler of the **4th** or **5th** houses in **Scorpio** or **8th** house: Letter 8, page 266.
Ruler of the **4th** or **5th** houses in **Sagittarius** or **9th** house: Letter 9, page 267.

Ruler of the **4th** or **5th** houses in **Capricorn** or **10th** house: Letter 10, page 268.
Ruler of the **4th** or **5th** houses in **Aquarius** or **11th** house: Letter 11, page 269.
Ruler of the **4th** or **5th** houses in **Pisces** or **12th** house: Letter 12, page 269.

Sun in the **4th** or **5th** houses or in **Cancer** or **Leo**: read Letter 5, page 264.
Moon in the **4th** or **5th** houses or in **Cancer** or **Leo**: read Letter 4, page 263.
Mercury in the **4th** or **5th** houses or in **Cancer** or **Leo**: read Letter 3, page 262.
Venus the **4th** or **5th** houses or in **Cancer** or **Leo**: read Letter 2, page 262.
Mars in the **4th** or **5th** houses or in **Cancer** or **Leo**: read Letter 1, page 261.
Jupiter in the **4th** or **5th** houses or in **Cancer** or **Leo**: read Letter 9, page 267.
Saturn in the **4th** or **5th** houses or in **Cancer** or **Leo**: read Letter 10, page 268.
Uranus in the **4th** or **5th** houses or in **Cancer** or **Leo**: read Letter 11, page 269.
Neptune in the **4th** or **5th** houses or in **Cancer** or **Leo**: read Letter 12, page 269.
Pluto in the **4th** or **5th** houses or in **Cancer** or **Leo**: read Letter 8, page 266.
Ceres or **Vesta** in the **4th** or **5th** houses or in **Cancer** or **Leo**: read Letter 6, page 265.
Pallas or **Juno** in the **4th** or **5th** houses or in **Cancer** or **Leo**: read Letter 7, page 265.
Chiron in the **4th** or **5th** houses or in **Cancer** or **Leo**: read Letter 9, page 267.

BELIEFS AND VALUES

Jupiter, Uranus or **Neptune** in **Aries** or **1st** house: Letter 1, page 301.
Jupiter, Uranus or **Neptune** in **Taurus** or **2nd** house: Letter 2, page 301.
Jupiter, Uranus or **Neptune** in **Gemini** or **3rd** house: Letter 3, page 302.
Jupiter, Uranus or **Neptune** in **Cancer** or **4th** house: Letter 4, page 302.
Jupiter, Uranus or **Neptune** in **Leo** or **5th** house: Letter 5, page 303.
Jupiter, Uranus or **Neptune** in **Virgo** or **6th** house: Letter 6, page 303.
Jupiter, Uranus or **Neptune** in **Libra** or **7th** house: Letter 7, page 304.
Jupiter, Uranus or **Neptune** in **Scorpio** or **8th** house: Letter 8, page 304.
Jupiter, Uranus or **Neptune** in **Sagittarius** or **9th** house: Letter 9, page 305.
Jupiter, Uranus or **Neptune** in **Capricorn** or **10th** house: Letter 10, page 305.
Jupiter, Uranus or **Neptune** in **Aquarius** or **11th** house: Letter 11, page 306.
Jupiter, Uranus or **Neptune** in **Pisces** or **12th** house: Letter 12, page 306.

Ruler of the **9th, 11th** or **12th** houses in **Aries** or **1st** house: Letter 1, page 301.
Ruler of the **9th, 11th** or **12th** houses in **Taurus** or **2nd** house: Letter 2, page 301.
Ruler of the **9th, 11th** or **12th** houses in **Gemini** or **3rd** house: Letter 3, page 302.
Ruler of the **9th, 11th** or **12th** houses in **Cancer** or **4th** house: Letter 4, page 302.
Ruler of the **9th, 11th** or **12th** houses in **Leo** or **5th** house: Letter 5, page 303.
Ruler of the **9th, 11th** or **12th** houses in **Virgo** or **6th** house: Letter 6, page 303.
Ruler of the **9th, 11th** or **12th** houses in **Libra** or **7th** house: Letter 7, page 304.
Ruler of the **9th, 11th** or **12th** houses in **Scorpio** or **8th** house: Letter 8, page 304.
Ruler of the **9th, 11th** or **12th** houses in **Sagittarius** or **9th** house: Letter 9, page 305.

Ruler of the **9th**, **11th** or **12th** houses in **Capricorn** or **10th** house: Letter 10, page 305.

Ruler of the **9th**, **11th** or **12th** houses in **Aquarius** or **11th** house: Letter 11, page 306.

Ruler of the **9th**, **11th** or **12th** houses in **Pisces** or **12th** house: Letter 12, page 306.

Sun in the **9th**, **11th** or **12th** houses or in **Sagittarius, Aquarius** or **Pisces**: read Letter 5, page 303.

Moon in the **9th**, **11th** or **12th** houses or in **Sagittarius, Aquarius** or **Pisces**: read Letter 4, page 302.

Mercury in the **9th**, **11th** or **12th** houses or in **Sagittarius, Aquarius** or **Pisces**: read Letter 3, page 302.

Venus the **9th**, **11th** or **12th** houses or in **Sagittarius, Aquarius** or **Pisces**: read Letter 2, page 301.

Mars in the **9th**, **11th** or **12th** houses or in **Sagittarius, Aquarius** or **Pisces**: read Letter 1, page 301.

Jupiter in the **9th**, **11th** or **12th** houses or in **Sagittarius, Aquarius** or **Pisces**: read Letter 9, page 305.

Saturn in the **9th**, **11th** or **12th** houses or in **Sagittarius, Aquarius** or **Pisces**: read Letter 10, page 305.

Uranus in the **9th**, **11th** or **12th** houses or in **Sagittarius, Aquarius** or **Pisces**: read Letter 11, page 306.

Neptune in the **9th**, **11th** or **12th** houses or in **Sagittarius, Aquarius** or **Pisces**: read Letter 12, page 306.

Pluto in the **9th**, **11th** or **12th** houses or in **Sagittarius, Aquarius** or **Pisces**: read Letter 8, page 304.

Ceres or **Vesta** in the **9th**, **11th** or **12th** houses or in **Sagittarius, Aquarius** or **Pisces**: read Letter 6, page 303.

Pallas or **Juno** in the **9th**, **11th** or **12th** houses or in **Sagittarius, Aquarius** or **Pisces**: read Letter 7, page 304.

Chiron in the **9th**, **11th** or **12th** houses or in **Sagittarius, Aquarius** or **Pisces**: read Letter 9, page 305.

MONEY

Venus or **Pluto** in **Aries** or **1st** house: Letter 1, page 324.
Venus or **Pluto** in **Taurus** or **2nd** house: Letter 2, page 325.
Venus or **Pluto** in **Gemini** or **3rd** house: Letter 3, page 325.
Venus or **Pluto** in **Cancer** or **4th** house: Letter 4, page 325.
Venus or **Pluto** in **Leo** or **5th** house: Letter 5, page 326.
Venus or **Pluto** in **Virgo** or **6th** house: Letter 6, page 326.
Venus or **Pluto** in **Libra** or **7th** house: Letter 7, page 326.
Venus or **Pluto** in **Scorpio** or **8th** house: Letter 8, page 327.
Venus or **Pluto** in **Sagittarius** or **9th** house: Letter 9, page 327.

Venus or **Pluto** in **Capricorn** or **10th** house: Letter 10, page 328.
Venus or **Pluto** in **Aquarius** or **11th** house: Letter 11, page 328.
Venus or **Pluto** in **Pisces** or **12th** house: Letter 12, page 328.

Ruler of the **2nd** or **8th** houses in **Aries** or **1st** house: Letter 1, page 324.
Ruler of the **2nd** or **8th** houses in **Taurus** or **2nd** house: Letter 2, page 325.
Ruler of the **2nd** or **8th** houses in **Gemini** or **3rd** house: Letter 3, page 325.
Ruler of the **2nd** or **8th** houses in **Cancer** or **4th** house: Letter 4, page 325.
Ruler of the **2nd** or **8th** houses in **Leo** or **5th** house: Letter 5, page 326.
Ruler of the **2nd** or **8th** houses in **Virgo** or **6th** house: Letter 6, page 326.
Ruler of the **2nd** or **8th** houses in **Libra** or **7th** house: Letter 7, page 326.
Ruler of the **2nd** or **8th** houses in **Scorpio** or **8th** house: Letter 8, page 327.
Ruler of the **2nd** or **8th** houses in **Sagittarius** or **9th** house: Letter 9, page 327.
Ruler of the **2nd** or **8th** houses in **Capricorn** or **10th** house: Letter 10, page 328.
Ruler of the **2nd** or **8th** houses in **Aquarius** or **11th** house: Letter 11, page 328.
Ruler of the **2nd** or **8th** houses in **Pisces** or **12th** house: Letter 12, page 328.

Sun in the **2nd** or **8th** houses or in **Taurus** or **Scorpio**: read Letter 5, page 326.
Moon in the **2nd** or **8th** houses or in **Taurus** or **Scorpio**: read Letter 4, page 325.
Mercury in the **2nd** or **8th** houses or in **Taurus** or **Scorpio**: read Letter 3, page 325.
Venus the **2nd** or **8th** houses or in **Taurus** or **Scorpio**: read Letter 2, page 325.
Mars in the **2nd** or **8th** houses or in **Taurus** or **Scorpio**: read Letter 1, page 324.
Jupiter in the **2nd** or **8th** houses or in **Taurus** or **Scorpio**: read Letter 9, page 327.
Saturn in the **2nd** or **8th** houses or in **Taurus** or **Scorpio**: read Letter 10, page 328.
Uranus in the **2nd** or **8th** houses or in **Taurus** or **Scorpio**: read Letter 11, page 328.
Neptune in the **2nd** or **8th** houses or in **Taurus** or **Scorpio**: read Letter 12, page 328.
Pluto in the **2nd** or **8th** houses or in **Taurus** or **Scorpio**: read Letter 8, page 327.
Ceres or **Vesta** in the **2nd** or **8th** houses or in **Taurus** or **Scorpio**: read Letter 6, page 326.
Pallas or **Juno** in the **2nd** or **8th** houses or in **Taurus** or **Scorpio**: read Letter 7, page 326.
Chiron in the **2nd** or **8th** houses or in **Taurus** or **Scorpio**: read Letter 9, page 327.

SEXUALITY

Venus, Mars, Sun or **Pluto** in **Aries** or **1st** house: Letter 1, page 352.
Venus, Mars, Sun or **Pluto** in **Taurus** or **2nd** house: Letter 2, page 353.
Venus, Mars, Sun or **Pluto** in **Gemini** or **3rd** house: Letter 3, page 354.
Venus, Mars, Sun or **Pluto** in **Cancer** or **4th** house: Letter 4, page 354.
Venus, Mars, Sun or **Pluto** in **Leo** or **5th** house: Letter 5, page 355.
Venus, Mars, Sun or **Pluto** in **Virgo** or **6th** house: Letter 6, page 356.

Venus, Mars, Sun or **Pluto** in **Libra** or **7th** house: Letter 7, page 357.
Venus, Mars, Sun or **Pluto** in **Scorpio** or **8th** house: Letter 8, page 357.
Venus, Mars, Sun or **Pluto** in **Sagittarius** or **9th** house: Letter 9, page 358.
Venus, Mars, Sun or **Pluto** in **Capricorn** or **10th** house: Letter 10, page 359.
Venus, Mars, Sun or **Pluto** in **Aquarius** or **11th** house: Letter 11, page 360.
Venus, Mars, Sun or **Pluto** in **Pisces** or **12th** house: Letter 12, page 361.

Ruler of the **2nd**, **5th** or **8th** houses in **Aries** or **1st** house: Letter 1, page 352.
Ruler of the **2nd**, **5th** or **8th** houses in **Taurus** or **2nd** house: Letter 2, page 353.
Ruler of the **2nd**, **5th** or **8th** houses in **Gemini** or **3rd** house: Letter 3, page 354.
Ruler of the **2nd**, **5th** or **8th** houses in **Cancer** or **4th** house: Letter 4, page 354.
Ruler of the **2nd**, **5th** or **8th** houses in **Leo** or **5th** house: Letter 5, page 355.
Ruler of the **2nd**, **5th** or **8th** houses in **Virgo** or **6th** house: Letter 6, page 356.
Ruler of the **2nd**, **5th** or **8th** houses in **Libra** or **7th** house: Letter 7, page 357.
Ruler of the **2nd**, **5th** or **8th** houses in **Scorpio** or **8th** house: Letter 8, page 357.
Ruler of the **2nd**, **5th** or **8th** houses in **Sagittarius** or **9th** house: Letter 9, page 358.
Ruler of the **2nd**, **5th** or **8th** houses in **Capricorn** or **10th** house: Letter 10, page 359.
Ruler of the **2nd**, **5th** or **8th** houses in **Aquarius** or **11th** house: Letter 11, page 360.
Ruler of the **2nd**, **5th** or **8th** houses in **Pisces** or **12th** house: Letter 12, page 361.

Sun in the **2nd**, **5th** or **8th** houses or in **Taurus, Leo** or **Scorpio**: read Letter 5, page 355.
Moon in the **2nd**, **5th** or **8th** houses or in **Taurus, Leo** or **Scorpio**: read Letter 4, page 354.
Mercury in the **2nd**, **5th** or **8th** houses or in **Taurus, Leo** or **Scorpio**: read Letter 3, page 354.
Venus the **2nd**, **5th** or **8th** houses or in **Taurus, Leo** or **Scorpio**: read Letter 2, page 353.
Mars in the **2nd**, **5th** or **8th** houses or in **Taurus, Leo** or **Scorpio**: read Letter 1, page 352.
Jupiter in the **2nd**, **5th** or **8th** houses or in **Taurus, Leo** or **Scorpio**: read Letter 9, page 358.
Saturn in the **2nd**, **5th** or **8th** houses or in **Taurus, Leo** or **Scorpio**: read Letter 10, page 359.
Uranus in the **2nd**, **5th** or **8th** houses or in **Taurus, Leo** or **Scorpio**: read Letter 11, page 360.
Neptune in the **2nd**, **5th** or **8th** houses or in **Taurus, Leo** or **Scorpio**: read Letter 12, page 361.
Pluto in the **2nd**, **5th** or **8th** houses or in **Taurus, Leo** or **Scorpio**: read Letter 8, page 357.
Ceres or **Vesta** in the **2nd**, **5th** or **8th** houses or in **Taurus, Leo** or **Scorpio**:

read Letter 6, page 356.

Pallas or **Juno** in the **2nd**, **5th** or **8th** houses or in **Taurus, Leo** or **Scorpio**: read Letter 7, page 357.

Chiron in the **2nd**, **5th** or **8th** houses or in **Taurus, Leo** or **Scorpio**: read Letter 9, page 358.

PARENTS

Sun, Moon, Saturn or **Ceres** in **Aries** or **1st** house: Letter 1, page 404.
Sun, Moon, Saturn or **Ceres** in **Taurus** or **2nd** house: Letter 2, page 405.
Sun, Moon, Saturn or **Ceres** in **Gemini** or **3rd** house: Letter 3, page 405.
Sun, Moon, Saturn or **Ceres** in **Cancer** or **4th** house: Letter 4, page 406.
Sun, Moon, Saturn or **Ceres** in **Leo** or **5th** house: Letter 5, page 406.
Sun, Moon, Saturn or **Ceres** in **Virgo** or **6th** house: Letter 6, page 406.
Sun, Moon, Saturn or **Ceres** in **Libra** or **7th** house: Letter 7, page 407.
Sun, Moon, Saturn or **Ceres** in **Scorpio** or **8th** house: Letter 8, page 407.
Sun, Moon, Saturn or **Ceres** in **Sagittarius** or **9th** house: Letter 9, page 407.
Sun, Moon, Saturn or **Ceres** in **Capricorn** or **10th** house: Letter 10, page 408.
Sun, Moon, Saturn or **Ceres** in **Aquarius** or **11th** house: Letter 11, page 408.
Sun, Moon, Saturn or **Ceres** in **Pisces** or **12th** house: Letter 12, page 409.

Ruler of the **4th** or **10th** houses in **Aries** or **1st** house: Letter 1, page 404.
Ruler of the **4th** or **10th** houses in **Taurus** or **2nd** house: Letter 2, page 405.
Ruler of the **4th** or **10th** houses in **Gemini** or **3rd** house: Letter 3, page 405.
Ruler of the **4th** or **10th** houses in **Cancer** or **4th** house: Letter 4, page 406.
Ruler of the **4th** or **10th** houses in **Leo** or **5th** house: Letter 5, page 406.
Ruler of the **4th** or **10th** houses in **Virgo** or **6th** house: Letter 6, page 406.
Ruler of the **4th** or **10th** houses in **Libra** or **7th** house: Letter 7, page 407.
Ruler of the **4th** or **10th** houses in **Scorpio** or **8th** house: Letter 8, page 407.
Ruler of the **4th** or **10th** houses in **Sagittarius** or **9th** house: Letter 9, page 407.
Ruler of the **4th** or **10th** houses in **Capricorn** or **10th** house: Letter 10, page 408.
Ruler of the **4th** or **10th** houses in **Aquarius** or **11th** house: Letter 11, page 408.
Ruler of the **4th** or **10th** houses in **Pisces** or **12th** house: Letter 12, page 409.

Sun in the **4th** or **10th** houses or in **Cancer** or **Capricorn**: read Letter 5, page 406.
Moon in the **4th** or **10th** houses or in **Cancer** or **Capricorn**: read Letter 4, page 406.
Mercury in the **4th** or **10th** houses or in **Cancer** or **Capricorn**: read Letter 3, page 405.
Venus the **4th** or **10th** houses or in **Cancer** or **Capricorn**: read Letter 2, page 405.
Mars in the **4th** or **10th** houses or in **Cancer** or **Capricorn**: read Letter 1, page 404.
Jupiter in the **4th** or **10th** houses or in **Cancer** or **Capricorn**: read Letter 9, page 407.
Saturn in the **4th** or **10th** houses or in **Cancer** or **Capricorn**: read Letter 10,

page 408.

Uranus in the **4th** or **10th** houses or in **Cancer** or **Capricorn**: read Letter 11, page 408.

Neptune in the **4th** or **10th** houses or in **Cancer** or **Capricorn**: read Letter 12, page 409.

Pluto in the **4th** or **10th** houses or in **Cancer** or **Capricorn**: read Letter 8, page 407.

Ceres or **Vesta** in the **4th** or **10th** houses or in **Cancer** or **Capricorn**: read Letter 6, page 406.

Pallas or **Juno** in the **4th** or **10th** houses or in **Cancer** or **Capricorn**: read Letter 7, page 407.

Chiron in the **4th** or **10th** houses or in **Cancer** or **Capricorn**: read Letter 9, page 407.

KARMIC CHALLENGES (GROWTH AREAS)

Saturn or the **south node** in **Aries** or **1st** house: Letter 1, page 434.
Saturn or the **south node** in **Taurus** or **2nd** house: Letter 2, page 434.
Saturn or the **south node** in **Gemini** or **3rd** house: Letter 3, page 435.
Saturn or the **south node** in **Cancer** or **4th** house: Letter 4, page 435.
Saturn or the **south node** in **Leo** or **5th** house: Letter 5, page 435.
Saturn or the **south node** in **Virgo** or **6th** house: Letter 6, page 435.
Saturn or the **south node** in **Libra** or **7th** house: Letter 7, page 435.
Saturn or the **south node** in **Scorpio** or **8th** house: Letter 8, page 436.
Saturn or the **south node** in **Sagittarius** or **9th** house: Letter 9, page 436.
Saturn or the **south node** in **Capricorn** or **10th** house: Letter 10, page 436.
Saturn or the **south node** in **Aquarius** or **11th** house: Letter 11, page 436.
Saturn or the **south node** in **Pisces** or **12th** house: Letter 12, page 436.

Sun conjunct **Saturn** or the **south node**: read Letter 5, page 435.
Moon conjunct **Saturn** or the **south node**: read Letter 4, page 435.
Mercury conjunct **Saturn** or the **south node**: read Letter 3, page 435.
Venus conjunct **Saturn** or the **south node**: read Letter 2, page 434.
Mars conjunct **Saturn** or the **south node**: read Letter 1, page 434.
Jupiter conjunct **Saturn** or the **south node**: read Letter 9, page 436.
Saturn conjunct **Saturn** or the **south node**: read Letter 10, page 436.
Uranus conjunct **Saturn** or the **south node**: read Letter 11, page 436.
Neptune conjunct **Saturn** or the **south node**: read Letter 12, page 436.
Pluto conjunct **Saturn** or the **south node**: read Letter 8, page 436.
Ceres or **Vesta** conjunct **Saturn** or the **south node**: read Letter 6, page 435.
Pallas or **Juno** conjunct **Saturn** or the **south node**: read Letter 7, page 435.
Chiron conjunct **Saturn** or the **south node**: read Letter 9, page 436.

Themes for All Life Areas

Using the letters of the alphabet derived from these lists, mix and match them to form any of the themes listed in Chapter 4. (Appendix 2 also provides a list of themes associated with each planet.) The interpretations for each alphabet combination are given in the appropriate chapters (e.g., Chapter 6 discusses identity).

Using the above listings will not give as comprehensive a delineation as would using this book as designed, but it will be an excellent introduction. It is my hope that readers would then be drawn to continue on and enhance their understanding of the search for themes within a horoscope. The process is really much easier than it seems at first glance.

By gaining a logical, working knowledge of the astrological alphabet, you will be able to quickly and easily spot the basic drives in any horoscope. By knowing where and how to look, what to ignore and what to consider, the astrologer can, indeed, read a chart "cold" — picking up major issues after only a few minutes study of the chart! The following chapters will demonstrate how to do that.

Bon voyage!

CHAPTER THREE

THE ASTROLOGICAL ALPHABET

Synthesis through Rapid Scanning

I want to stress that, in interpreting an actual horoscope, I would **not** sit with pencil and paper listing numerous factors, weighting them and coming up with averages and the most prominent themes. That is an exercise in boredom and self-punishment! What I actually do is quickly scan the horoscope, keeping in mind the sequence of weighting (planets most emphatic, then aspects, houses and signs), looking for any themes which are repeated. Depending on the individual chart, a theme which occurs three times may seem significant for that person, whereas another person may have themes repeating nine or more times!

If you like lists, they are an excellent way to practice the Zip Code initially, but please bear in mind the objective is a rapid scan which notes (mentally) the most repeated themes for each life area. The objective of the Zip Code is to **eliminate** pen, paper and calculations — not to proliferate them!

I hope no reader will be frightened away by the seeming masses of data (e.g., lists of factors to scan) presented in this book. With a little practice and familiarity, the process of quickly skimming a chart to seek the repeated messages takes only a minute or so for each life area. The astrologer's best tool is the tremendous synthesizing and integrating power of the human brain. Leave the means, averages and totaling of every single item to computers! That is what they do best. Use your intuitive, holistic, global intelligence to put the pieces together and come up with a sense of what is significant. It does **not** matter if you cannot cite every single factor that repeats a given theme. What matters is that you noted it in your once-over-lightly perusal.

Since so many factors are involved, the process may, at first, seem overwhelming. Remember, you are dealing with 12 basic life drives; that simplifies the matter considerably. The secret is to look for **themes**. By finding what is repeated in the horoscope, the astrologer organizes the information and can avoid feeling overloaded.

Weighting

Weighting will remain an intuitive act. If, for example, certain planets are prominent by aspects, I consider that an emphatic theme, even if not repeated in the chart in other ways. But I would want to see a theme based on signs repeated several times before considering it relevant. Thus, a close conjunction to Mars would show a major theme in terms of identity. (We would interpret the nature of the planet which is making the conjunction in terms of the person's self-expression.) A planet occupying the 1st house probably shows an important theme in the individual's sense of self. A sign (other than the Ascendant) occupying the 1st house shows a less important theme. (The Ascendant and Midheaven are important angles, which I treat much as planets, so I give them a lot of weight. Therefore the Ascendant and Midheaven signs are more significant than other signs on cusps or in the houses.)

Potential differential weightings of the various factors are discussed in each chapter, under the appropriate life areas, e.g., identity, work, etc. Please recall that these suggestions are exactly that. I do **not** possess "the word" on weightings. But regardless of differing weights, when themes are repeated, they are significant. **What is most important in the psyche will be reiterated in the horoscope**.

Letter 1: ♂, ♈, 1st house

Letter 1 of the astrological alphabet indicates pure self-will in action. This part of life says, "I want to do what I want to do **right now**!" It is spontaneous, impulsive, active, energetic, courageous and assertive. Tied to our basic health and vitality, it is a key to our ability to be ourselves and defend ourselves, including defending the physical body against hurt or invasion (disease). Issues around anger are quite possible when Letter 1 is prominent.

Direct and forthright, people who have this theme emphasized in their charts may find that the personal freedom to do one's own thing is a major issue. In some cases, individuals whose charts emphasize Letter 1 fall into, "If I can't have it my way, I won't play." They may run away or adopt a hermit role in order to live life, as much as possible, solely on their own terms.

The list of key words for Letter 1 includes many which are defined culturally as traditionally "masculine." Thus, it is easier for men to actualize those parts of their nature symbolized by Letter 1, as those attributes fit what society defines as masculine. Due to cultural pressures and conditioning, women are less likely to be comfortable with Letter 1 drives in their nature, even when strongly present. Assertion, directness, physical courage, spontaneous anger, vigorous action and putting one's self before others are often more of a challenge for women than men.

Letter 1 is our instinctive identity, our natural, spontaneous way(s) of being in the world. It indicates our **early** identity — that is, our tendencies and traits before we have fully incorporated the growth potential symbolized by our Sun and other parts of the chart. Depending on what is mixed with Letter 1, our spontaneous instincts may be very different. If we have a strong water theme — e.g., water planets in the 1st house or conjunct the Ascendant; water signs rising and/or in the 1st house; Mars conjunct water planets, in water houses or signs; Aries occupied by water planets or Aries in water houses — our natural, instinctive action may be to wait, play it safe, go inward. With fire connected to Letter 1, we are likely to be spontaneous, open and direct. With air connected to Letter 1, our basic tendency is to think, to communicate, to be logical and detached. With earth connected to Letter 1, our natural impulse is to be practical, grounded and deal with the physical world.

For most of us, identity is partially learned through **role models** — individuals we adopt as examples. Role models can be either positive or negative. If positive, we wish to emulate and imitate that individual; we admire the person and try to be like them. If negative, we wish to do the opposite of our role model. Whatever paths they pursued, we will move in the reverse; we will rebel. They are an example of what we do **not** want to do; whom we do **not** want to be.

A person's definition of self can be clarified by role models. Knowing about their potential in the horoscope helps us define more clearly the essence of the person involved. If, for example, Letter 1 is strongly mixed with Letter 4 or 10 (the parental letters), we would expect a parental role model. Mom or Dad (or the mother or father figure) would be a major influence for that individual. The person's actions would often be a repeat or an exact reversal of parental actions. In a very real sense, this person is finding him/herself **through** interactions with a parent. By clarifying and establishing areas of agreement/disagreement with that parent, the person gets a firmer sense of personal identity.

Whatever factors are mixed with Letter 1 in the horoscope are keys to basic identity and action. If parental letters are involved (4 and/or 10), the indications are that this person is an instinctive parent. Right from the beginning of the life, the person is likely to exhibit nurturing, sensitive, empathic, vulnerable, caretaking, emotional (Letter 4) behavior or responsible, practical, aware of limitations, solid, disciplined, self-denying, control-oriented (Letter 10) behavior. Letter 1 symbolizes doing what comes naturally.

Letter 1 in the chart is indicated by Mars, the 1st house and the sign Aries. To consider **all** forms of Letter 1, we would need to examine the planet Mars, including all conjunctions and/or parallels to Mars along with the house and sign position of Mars. We would look at **everything** connected to the 1st house. This includes the nature of any planets in the 1st house and the placement of the ruler of the rising sign: conjunctions or parallels, house, and sign.

I also consider the placement of rulers of other signs in the 1st house. I find it useful to consider not only the ruler of the sign on the cusp of a house, but also the rulers of **all** signs within a house. Thus, in the case of an interception, I am looking at the information from **three** rulers. (An interception occurs when one sign occupies two cusps, so that another sign is "squeezed out" or "squeezed in," having no cusp of its own.) For the house with an interception, I would look at: the ruler of the sign on the cusp, the ruler of the intercepted sign and the ruler of the sign which occupies the rest of the house (as well as planets actually in the house, signs in the house, aspects, etc.).

Still looking at all forms of Letter 1, we also include the Ascendant (rising sign) and any other signs (besides the rising sign) occupying the 1st house. We would check to see what houses are ruled by any planets in the 1st house. For example, if the Moon is in the 1st, where does Cancer fall in the chart? We would also look to see where the sign Aries is in the chart: what planets are within the sign of Aries, what cusp(s) Aries rules (tying that part of life to identity) and any houses Aries occupies.

For those who use the East Point and Antivertex,[1] the treatment here is to consider them variants of Letter 1. They are assumed to be **secondary** Ascendants, representing personal action and identity — but not as important as the actual Ascendant. Planets closely (within 3°) conjunct either of these angles (East Point or Antivertex) indicate important themes in the basic nature or self-expression of the individual, as if those planets conjuncted the Ascendant (only not quite as emphatic).

All of the above factors together become the sum of Letter 1 in the chart.

---

1. The Antivertex/Vertex axis and East Point/West Point axis are both formed by intersections of great circles (as are the Ascendant/Descendant and Midheaven/IC). These intersections points are called "angles" of the horoscope and are meaningful. The Ascendant is formed by the intersection of the rational horizon with the ecliptic in the east (the Descendant in the west). The Midheaven is formed by the intersection of the ecliptic with the Meridian above the horizon (the IC below the horizon). The Antivertex is formed by the intersection of the Prime Vertical with the ecliptic in the east (the Vertex in the west). The East Point is formed by the intersection in the east (West Point in the west) of the ecliptic with an unnamed great circle which passes through the east and west points of the horizon and the north and south poles of Earth.

In this book, the East Point and Antivertex are considered secondary Ascendants (Letter 1) while the West Point and Vertex are considered secondary Descendants (Letter 7).

TEST YOURSELF

The chart below has a repeated theme connected to Letter 1 which occurs in seven different ways. (It occurs eight times if you use co-rulers.)[2] What is the theme and how is it said?

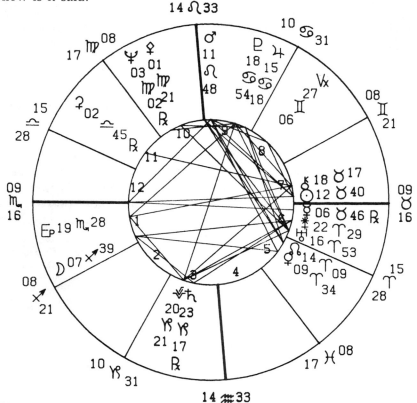

2. In the ancient days, astrologers could work only with the visible planets. The Sun and Moon were called "planets" and along with Mercury, Venus, Mars, Jupiter and Saturn, there were seven known planets. The two "lights" (the Sun and Moon) were assigned only one sign each to rule, while the other planets were associated with two signs each in terms of rulership. Thus, in the ancient world, Mercury ruled both Gemini and Virgo; Venus ruled both Taurus and Libra; Mars ruled both Aries and Scorpio; Jupiter ruled both Sagittarius and Pisces; Saturn ruled both Capricorn and Aquarius.

With the invention of the telescope and advanced theories of astronomy which could postulate where another planet ought to be, based on disturbances in the orbits of known planets, three additional planets came to light: Uranus, Neptune and Pluto. With time and observation, each of these three was assigned rulership of a sign. Thus, in modern times, Uranus rules Aquarius, Neptune rules Pisces and Pluto rules Scorpio. However, many people find it useful to retain the "old" rulers as "co-rulers" of a sign. Thus, where Scorpio falls in a horoscope, they consider **both** Pluto and Mars as having useful information about that life area.

Please note that co-rulers refer **only** to the process of consulting the placement (aspects, house, sign) of a planet in terms of a sign it rules elsewhere. One does **not** change the nature of the planet to fit co-rulers. Thus, Jupiter — in its own nature — is always Letter 9. Jupiter can be consulted (as a co-ruler) where Pisces appears in a chart (although Neptune is the primary referent), but aspects to Jupiter, and Jupiter in terms of blending its nature with the house and sign it occupies, remain Letter 9 always.

Although co-rulers "work" and offer additional insight, they are **not** essential. Beginners should feel free to ignore them!

ANSWER: The theme is Letter 9.
1. Mars (1) is in the 9th house (9)).
2. Pluto rules the Ascendant (1) and is conjunct Jupiter (9).
3. Pluto rules the Ascendant (1) and is in the 9th house (9).
4. Jupiter rules the Sagittarius in the 1st house (1) and is in the 9th house (9).
5. The 1st house (1) is occupied by [the Moon in] Sagittarius (9).[3]
6. The Moon is in the 1st house (1) and rules the 9th cusp (9) [opposite Vertex in Gemini].
7. The Antivertex (1) is in Sagittarius (9).
8. [Mars co-rules the Ascendant (1) and is in the 9th house (9).]

If you are not sure how we arrived at those answers, here is the complete listing of everything connected to Letter 1 in this chart. (This list is presented for learning purposes only. Once you are familiar with the Zip Code, you will **not** be making lists — except, perhaps, mentally. You will be quickly scanning the horoscope for repeated messages.)

We first consider **the planet Mars (Letter 1)** (weighting conjunctions to Mars most heavily, then house position, with sign position last). Mars is conjunct the MC (10), in the 9th house (9) in Leo (5).

Second, we would want to count **any planet conjunct and/or parallel the Ascendant (1), whether or not it is in the 1st house.** Here, we have none.

Third, we consider **anything in the 1st house (1) of the chart.** The planet in the 1st house (1) is the Moon (4). The sign of the Ascendant (weighted like a planet) is Scorpio (8). The sign which is occupied in the 1st house is Sagittarius (9).

Fourth, we must consider **rulers of the 1st house** (weighting their placements in terms of conjunctions most significant, then house position, then sign). Pluto rules the Ascendant so is a key to Letter 1 in this chart. (We counted Letter 8 already for the Scorpio Ascendant. We do not count it again when looking at the ruler — Pluto in this case.) Pluto is conjunct Jupiter (9), in the 9th house (9), in Cancer (4). In addition, we have Jupiter as a ruler of Sagittarius, which falls in the 1st house. Jupiter is conjunct Pluto (8), in the 9th house (9), in Cancer (4).
If we consider co-rulers, Mars is the co-ruler of Scorpio. Thus, we would look again to Mars, repeating Letters 10 (conjunction to the MC), 9 (9th house) and 5 (in Leo).

---

3. In this horoscope, the Moon is less than one degree from the 2nd house cusp. Many astrologers (including me) would consider the Moon as a key to the 2nd house **as well as** the 1st house. Having a planet near the cusp tends to tie the two houses together. We would also consider the Moon a key to Letter 1 **and** Letter 2, due to its placement. How close to the cusp a planet should be in order to be counted as occupying "both" houses in a sense is a matter of opinon. I tend to consider planets within two degrees of a cusp as having relevance to both houses.

Fifth, we would consider the **houses ruled by any planets occupying the 1st house** (since those planets are keys to Letter 1). Here, we have the Moon ruling Cancer, which falls on the cusp of the 9th (9) house.

Sixth, we consider **the sign Aries** (Letter 1). (We would weight planets occupying Aries most heavily, followed by houses being occupied.) The planets (and asteroids) occupying Aries are Venus (2), Uranus (11) and Juno (7). Aries occupies the 5th house (5) two times for the north node and Venus and Aries occupies the 6th house (6) twice with Juno and Uranus. Aries also falls on the cusp of the 6th house (6).

Seventh, we would consider the **East Point and the Antivertex** (weighting planets making conjunctions most heavily, followed by the house and sign placements of the East Point and Antivertex). In this case, neither auxiliary Ascendant makes any conjunctions to planets. The East Point is in the 1st house (1) in Scorpio (8). The Antivertex is in the 2nd house (2) in Sagittarius (9).

For the moment, ignore relative strengths. (For example, a planet occupying the 1st house is more significant than where the sign Aries falls.) Just simply totaling up all the scores, we have the following summary (for themes connected to Letter 1):

Letter 1: 1	Letter 7: 1
Letter 2: 2	Letter 8: 3
Letter 3: 0	Letter 9: 8
Letter 4: 3	Letter 10: 2
Letter 5: 4	Letter 11: 1
Letter 6: 3	Letter 12: 0

There is a clear emphasis on Letter 9! Letter 5 is in second place. Letters 4, 6 and 8 are in a tie for third. The other letters are probably not significant in their representation. Remember, we are **not** weighting any of these factors, in this list. We are counting simple repetitions — of any kind — of all our factors. Realizing that planets are the most emphatic statement, we would mentally give extra weight to Letter 4 (thanks to that Moon in the 1st house) and probably less weight to Letter 5 (which is mostly due to the sign (least emphatic) Aries occupying the 5th house two times when doing a quick, intuitive scan of the chart.

If you wish to jump ahead in interpretation, turn to page 111 of Chapter 6 (identity) and read the description for Letters 9.

Letter 2: ♀, ♉, 2nd house

Letter 2 is symbolic of our capacity to enjoy the physical, sensual world. This includes eating, drinking, smoking, making love, making money and creating beauty. A common motto for an emphasis on Letter 2 is: "If it feels good, do it!" Keywords for this side of life include sensuous, materialistic, hedonistic, placid, easygoing, comfortable and passive. Dr. Zipporah Dobyns gives us the image of Ferdinand the Bull sitting in the field and smelling the flowers. The focus is on life's pleasures. Depending on the individual, those pleasures could be sought through appetite gratification, sexual means, gardening, making money, collecting possessions, dancing, singing or other artistic pursuits, etc. The key is enjoyment.

Pure Letter 2 is laid-back and relaxed. It is practical and tends to be grounded, but — in its own nature — is not oriented toward hard work. The motivation is to enjoy the physical world. The orientation is to keep life attractive and pleasant.

Note that I do **not** connect Letter 2 to "values" as is done with the 2nd house by some astrologers. Monetary values and material comfort are definitely indicated by Letter 2. Spiritual values, however, are Letters 9 and 12. Morals, ethics and principles regarding our vision of the Absolute fall into Letters 9 and 12. Letter 2's focus is quite physical and finite. Thinking of Letter 2 as the "pleasure principle" directed at the material world works quite well.

Letter 2 in the chart is indicated by Venus, the 2nd house and the sign Taurus. (Remember that pure Letter 2 — Venus in Taurus in the 2nd house — is Ferdinand smelling the flowers. Many people think of Taurus as a charging bull. That **can** be the case with the Sun in Taurus. After all, the Sun is fire which brings themes of life, action, sparkle, zest and enthusiasm to whatever it occupies. Pure Letter 2 is more placid.)

To examine all forms of Letter 2 in a chart we would consider Venus (conjunctions or parallels, house, sign); any planets in the 2nd house (nature of the planets, conjunctions or parallels, signs); any signs in the 2nd house including the sign on the cusp; the rulers of the signs in the 2nd (conjunctions or parallels to rulers, house placement, sign placement); houses ruled by planets in the 2nd; any planets in the sign Taurus, plus in what houses and on what cusps Taurus falls in the chart.

TEST YOURSELF

The chart below has a repeated theme connected to Letter 2 which occurs in six different ways. What is the theme and how is it said?

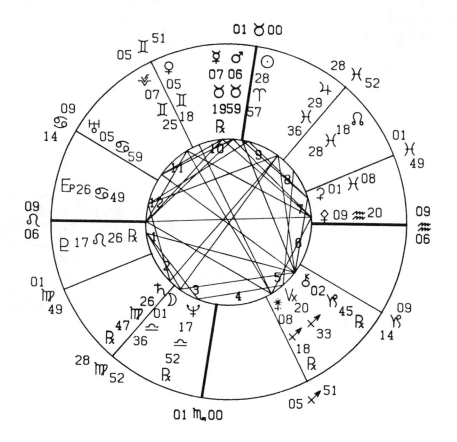

ANSWER: The theme is Letter 10.

1. Venus (2) is in the 10th (10).
2. The 2nd house (2) is occupied by Saturn (10).
3. Mercury rules the Virgo cusp of the 2nd (2) and is in the 10th house (10).
4. Taurus (2) occupies the Midheaven (10).
5. The sign Taurus (2) is occupied in the 10th house (10) [by Mars].
6. The sign Taurus (2) is occupied in the 10th house (10) [by Mercury].

   (Here we are counting Mercury "twice," but that is appropriate. We would consider **anything** occupying the sign Taurus wherever it falls in the chart when we are looking for themes. The fact that the sign Taurus is occupied (by Mercury) in the 10th house is a 2/10 theme (Taurus/10th house). Since Mercury is a ruler of the 2nd house in this case, we need to look at it from that perspective as well. Mercury in its own nature is Letter 3, but as ruler of the 2nd house, Mercury becomes a key to Letter 2 and in the 10th repeats the 2/10 theme.)

If you are not sure where those answers came from, here is a listing of **everything** connected to Letter 2 in this chart. First we consider the planet **Venus** (weighting conjunctions most, followed by house and sign placements). Venus is conjunct Vesta (6), in the 10th house (10) in Gemini (3). (If you don't use asteroids, ignore Vesta.) Next, we consider all **planets in the 2nd house**. Here, we have Saturn (10) conjuncting the Moon (4). Saturn is in Virgo (6). We must also look to **rulers of the 2nd house**. Virgo is on the cusp of the 2nd house and Virgo is the only sign in the 2nd since there is an interception (in the 3rd and 9th houses). Mercury rules Virgo. Mercury is conjunct Mars (1), in the 10th house (10) in Taurus (2). Mercury also widely conjuncts the MC (10) and the Sun (5). (Whether or not you count the conjunctions to the MC and the Sun depends on the orbs you use.)[4] Next, we consider the **houses ruled by planets in the 2nd**. Saturn is in the 2nd and rules the 6th (6). Then, we look to see **which planets occupy the sign of Taurus**. In this case, Taurus is occupied by the MC (10), Mars (1) and Mercury (3). [Unless otherwise indicated, Mercury will be taken, in its own nature, as primarily Letter 3. Venus will be assumed to be primarily Letter 2. This issue is discussed further in the sections on Letters 6 and 7.] We also look to see which **houses are occupied by the sign Taurus**. Taurus falls in the 9th (9) and 10th (10) houses in this chart.

Thus, our grand total for Zip Code factors connected to Letter 2 in this horoscope is:

Letter 1: 2	Letter 7: 0
Letter 2: 1	Letter 8: 0
Letter 3: 2	Letter 9: 1
Letter 4: 1	Letter 10: 5 or 6
Letter 5: 0 or 1	(depending on orbs)
(depending on orbs)	Letter 11: 0
Letter 6: 2 without asteroids,	Letter 12: 0
3 with asteroids	

Clearly, the dominant theme is Letter 10. (Letter 6 is in second place using asteroids. The combination of six and ten, as discussed in the next chapter, is a theme of work, practicality, discipline and a critical outlook.)

Letter 2 is **part** of the picture in money, career (earnings), sensuality and sexuality. If you wish to jump ahead in interpretation, you can read pages 124, 338, and 374 in Chapter 7 (work), 12 (money) and 13 (Sexuality), which discuss the

---

4. Beginners, hang in there! Aspects and the issue of orbs will be discussed in Chapter 5.

theme of "competence" (Letters 6 and 10) in these life areas. You can also read the individual discussions of Letter 6 and Letter 10 in each of those chapters (pages 144, 147, 326, 328, 356, and 359).

Letter 3: ☿, ♊, 3rd house

Letter 3 symbolizes our capacity to learn and to communicate with others. It is a key to the eye-mind-hand coordination. The interaction of thinking, sight and manipulation of the world through finger dexterity enhances intellectual development. Letter 3 also indicates how we learn and the people on whom we practice our early intellectual skills. This includes brothers, sisters, aunts, uncles and collateral relatives in general (other than parents). Neighbors and people near at hand are part of the picture. The major key here is vicinity or propinquity. When we are very young, we cannot usually go too far afield. So we practice our early learning, try out our new ideas, develop our verbal skills with whoever is right around and handy.

Letter 3 is our capacity for objectivity and detachment — looking at life from an intellectual rather than an emotional stance or distancing ourselves from what is going on as an observer rather than a direct participant. The mind symbolized here is the young mind wherein the curiosity is great and discrimination small. Like the baby who learns through putting objects in her mouth, the essence of Letter 3 knowledge is dipping and tasting, moving from flower to flower. Thus, it can be quite scattered and superficial at times. It includes the early learning environment and education through high school. Letter 3 is also a key to many varieties of communication such as magazines, newspapers, telephone, letters and teaching in general.

Since Letter 3 symbolizes other people (relatives, neighbors) as well as the early mental world of the person who owns the chart, there is an overlap. Certain qualities (indicated by Letter 3) can be expressed both by the individual whose chart it is and also by people close at hand. Because people have many different sides and needs which sometimes conflict with one another, it is common for us to make unconscious choices as to which qualities to express: "I will do this, but not that." Since the psyche strives for balance and wholeness, we then attract other people in our lives who can manifest those attributes which we are denying within ourselves. It is as if they will supply the missing pieces of the puzzle.

This process (of unconsciously attracting others to manifest parts of our own potential which we have disowned) is called **projection**. The only problem is, the more we deny a potential within our own nature, the more extreme a reflection we get from others. The more we project, the more exaggerated an example we see in the behavior of others.

One example was provided by a woman who had a 10th house stellium in Taurus and was expressing the earth part of her nature in traditional, positive ways. She worked as an accountant and was very dedicated, rational, grounded, responsible and hardworking. She also had Neptune in Libra in the 3rd. Despite the artistic potential of the Taurus stellium and the strongly aspected Neptune, she was not creating beauty (other than the beauty of balanced books). However, she had a highly artistic sister. Indeed, her sister had "always" been the artistic one — and she had "always" been the responsible one. Her sister was also living out other Neptune potentials — spacey, irresponsible and getting herself into situations where she ended up a victim. Guess who bailed the "Neptunian" sister out? You got it! The woman with the 10th house stellium was always there to shoulder the load.

These two sisters had a lovely division of labor. I like to imagine that the unconscious "dialogue" went something like this: Sister One: "I'm really skilled at being responsible, conscientious and careful. I feel uneasy about being sensitive, imaginative and open to the cosmos." Sister Two: "I love fantasy, flowing with life and creating beauty, but I'm not sure I want to really work and take care of myself." Sister One: "Let's make a deal! I'll express your responsibility potential for you if you express my imaginative potential for me." Sister Two: "Great idea. You're on!"

Each sister felt that the differing needs of practical versus idealistic, grounded versus imaginative, were too difficult to integrate. Each chose (unconsciously) to take one side of the polarity and (unconsciously) encouraged the other sister to express the other side. Between the two of them, they had it all. The problem was, they had **too much**. Sister One was overdoing the responsibility trip; Sister Two was overdoing the imaginative trip. They needed to learn from one another **positive** ways to integrate the missing qualities into their own lives. With projection, we learn through the mirror of the other person. The challenge, however, is not to do what they are doing. They are usually **overdoing** it. The goal is to manifest in a **moderate, satisfying** manner the drives which the other person is exaggerating for our learning.

Please note that projection is always a two-way street. The learning is mutual. If we are learning to manifest one quality, the person exaggerating that quality is learning another quality from us (which we are probably exaggerating).

Divisions of labor are extremely common in families. Psychologists and others have noted that siblings tend to "divide up the territory." If the firstborn is a "brain," the second-born may be a "jock," the third-born a "social butterfly," and so on. Most children want to be unique and achieve recognition. If an older sibling seems to have a certain part of life nailed down solidly and successfully, the tendency is to seek another area in which to succeed. (Some children assume that the positive options are all taken and may achieve recognition as the family "black sheep.") It is one thing to master certain skills when we are young and put off others. But it is another to continue denying a part of who we are. The more we cut off some of our own potential, the more exaggerated versions of it we will attract from other people, as our inner wisdom strives to bring in wholeness.

The astrologer must interpret horoscopes with care where other people are concerned. It is true that siblings and neighbors are illustrated by Letter 3. But if Letter 3 is explained as **only** being your "artistic sister" or "smart brother" or "nosy neighbor," the astrologer is doing the client a vast disservice. By encouraging projection, an astrologer makes it even harder for the client to get in touch with less developed sides of his/her nature. Our job is to help the client toward wholeness, to assist the client in discovering positive ways to manifest **all** his/her differing drives and needs.

Letter 3 is indicated in the chart by Mercury, the 3rd house and Gemini. To consider all forms of Letter 3 in a chart, we would look at Mercury (conjunctions or parallels, house, sign), all planets in the 3rd house, all signs in the 3rd house (including the sign on the cusp), the rulers of those signs in the 3rd (conjunctions or parallels, house and sign placement); houses ruled by any planets in the 3rd house; and any planets in Gemini plus where the sign Gemini falls on cusps or in houses.

TEST YOURSELF

The chart below has a repeated theme connected to Letter 3 which occurs in seven different ways. What is the theme and how is it said?

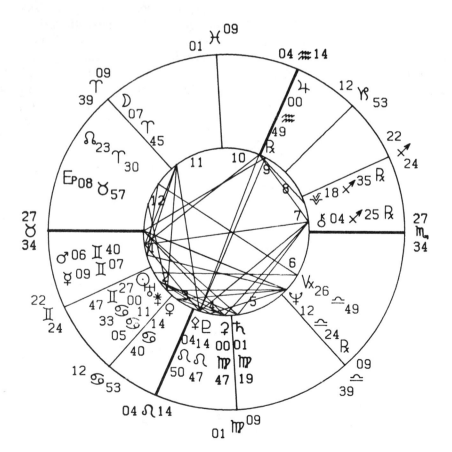

ANSWER: The theme is Letter 1.
1. Mercury (3) is conjunct Mars (1).
2. Mercury (3) is in the 1st house (1).
3. The 3rd house (3) is occupied by Venus which rules the Ascendant (1).
4. The 3rd house (3) is ruled by the Moon (Cancer cusp) which is in Aries (1).
5. Gemini (3) is occupied by the planet Mars (1).
6. and 7. Gemini (3) is occupied in the 1st house (1) **twice**.

Please note that this blend of Letters 1 and 3 can be considered from **two** perspectives. If we are looking at Letter 1 as a key to identity, we can say the person is identified with the mind, logic, detachment, learning and curiosity about many things (Letter 3). We would be aware of the possibility that a sibling or relative might be an important (positive or negative) role model. If we are looking at Letter 3 as one of our keys to this individual's intellectual and communicative abilities, we would say this individual is likely to be forthright, direct, spontaneous, open and could use words as a weapon (the tongue like a sword) — Letter 1. It is the same combination, but the conclusions we draw are based on the perspective we adopt!

If you wish to look ahead at the interpretation, page 107 in Chapter 6 (identity) discusses a Letter 3 theme. Since Letter 3 is **one** of the keys to the mind, you can also read page 223 in Chapter 9 (mind), which discusses a Letter 1 theme in terms of mental and communication skills.

Letter 4: ☽, ♋, 4th house

Letter 4 is our capacity for emotional closeness and attachment. It symbolizes both nurturance and dependency, our ability to care for others and to allow ourselves to be taken care of. It is the archetype of the traditional mother/child relationship. On the one hand, we have a desire to protect, feed, support and look after another human being. On the other hand we have emotional vulnerability, the need for protection and tender, loving care. Both the mother instinct and the neediness of a baby are a part of Letter 4. The caretaking needs of Letter 4 are not channeled solely into children. Many people are quite emotionally attached to pets or plants. The emotional security needs of Letter 4 can also be focused on food or collecting things.

It is not uncommon for people to have developed one part of Letter 4 at the expense of another. Some people are quite comfortable with nurturing, but have difficulty letting their guard down, allowing other people to comfort them. Some people find it easy to receive protection, but a challenge to look after and help others. And there are those who are uncomfortable with all forms of emotional attachment as well as those who are at ease both caring and being cared for.

Socialization plays an important role in our society. Many of the qualities defined traditionally as "feminine" fit into Letter 4. Women are commonly expected to be nurturing, emotionally supportive, but also somewhat childlike and dependent. Men are commonly expected to be strong, invulnerable and rational rather than emotional or sensitive. Thus, it is easier for women to express the sides of their nature shown by Letter 4. It is harder for men. Even if a man has a strong Letter 4 emphasis in his chart, he may be out of touch with that part of his nature. Quite often, men will project their Letter 4 qualities onto the women in their lives. Since the qualities of Letter 1 are a challenge for many women, a number of men and women have made the deal of: the man does Letter 1 for the woman and the woman does Letter 4 for the man. This is encouraged by societal roles and assumptions as well.

Carl Jung is one of the psychologists who commented on this "masculine/feminine" division. He noted that one of the tasks of individuation and growth is to incorporate **both** sides of this polarity. He also noted that this is a task many people do not undertake until mid-life. Today, more people appear to be facing the integration at an earlier age. Cultural awareness of sex roles has begun to counter the polarizing of "masculine" versus "feminine" within individuals and between the sexes. Healing the split is easier and quicker for individuals who have not spent forty years identified with only half of their human potential. Integrating Letter 4 themes into our lives means making room for fulfilling ways to experience emotional attachment, caretaking, vulnerability, softness, sensitivity, gentleness, empathy, concern, dependency and close, caring commitments.

Besides indicating our capacity to mother and be mothered, Letter 4 is a key to our early nurturing experiences and the person(s) who played the major role(s) as emotional caretaker(s). Letter 4 symbolizes home and family — both the home in which we grew up (family of orientation) and the home we build for ourselves as adults (family of procreation). Unconditional love is one side of Letter 4 — caring for another human being simply because they need the care, because they are, without that individual having to **do** anything. Thus, Letter 4 in the horoscope shows the parent or parent figure who gave us (or was supposed to provide) this early nurturing and unconditional support.

In traditional roles, Letter 4 is the mother or mother figure (whoever played the role regardless of biology). This can range from the birth mother to the father, an aunt, a grandparent, a sibling or someone else. The horoscope does not show a person's parent. It does reflect that person's **experience** of a parent, the perceptions and assumptions s/he is likely to make about that parent. Parents influence children, but children also elicit responses from parents and different children will have different relationships with the same parents. Their horoscopes will reflect these varied situations.

Many psychologists (Freud, Erikson, Bowlby) have remarked on the importance of a child's early experiences of emotional attachments. How we do (and do not) gain a sense of unconditional support from our caretakers and nurturing environment has a profound impact on our emotional security. Erikson labeled the task of the first stage of growth as developing a sense of trust or mistrust of the world — as a safe, protective, nurturing place or a threatening, depriving, frustrating place. Our early perceptions, assumptions and reactions tend to be carried into adulthood. Later emotional commitments (or lack of) are often a repeat of early attachment experiences.

Sometimes examining old feelings and frustrations can open up new opportunities for closeness. (We must also remember that children are not just blank slates. They elicit responses from parents. Children also **interpret** what happens.) In the end, **what** happens is immaterial. It is **how we feel** about events, our **perceptions and attitudes** that count. And we are in charge of those. We can always change perceptions and attitudes! In that regard, the past is **not** static. People perpetually rewrite history in terms of current experiences. As our ideas change, we have different feelings about what happened before.

For example, an indulged child often feels his/her early life was pleasant and easy. As that child grows older, however, s/he may come to resent that "easy" childhood for lacking opportunities for growth in competence and strength. "Loving, giving" parents may be redefined as "overprotective" and "encouraging dependency." Similarly, the child of a "harsh, regimented" upbringing may recognize that "punitive, critical" parents did provide opportunities for accomplishment and the development of self-reliance.

One study examined children from terrible backgrounds and environments (e.g., alcoholic parents, great poverty, schizophrenia in the family) with siblings who were incompetent, ill, psychologically disturbed and generally dysfunctional.[5] The researchers were curious as to why the children they studied were so "together": functioning well in school, socially adjusted, apparently happy — given such awful backgrounds. The investigators concluded that those children who were successful and created happy, nondestructive lives had an important, supportive figure — be it a parent, uncle, aunt, cousin, teacher, minister, neighbor, etc. It was noteworthy that **quality** mattered — not quantity — and what was most vital was the child's **own perception**. That is, this significant figure did **not** have to play a "major role" in the child's life in terms of hours spent together or events shared. What mattered was that the child **interpreted** that individual as a positive role model, paid attention to that person, and emphasized the helpful role of that individual in his/her life and development. Another major factor in the success of these children was their **perceived, subjective** power. They defined themselves as in control of their lives, and able to make a difference. Rather than feeling "stuck" or paying attention to the negative factors in their families and environments, these children would focus on what they **could** do — and would do it! Consequently, they tended to be very well liked by their schoolmates and friends and very approachable and friendly with adults. They made the most of their opportunities!

Besides indicating the unconditional love parent, Letter 4 can be a key to our

---

5. See, for example, "Superkids" by Maya Pines in *Psychology Today*, Vol. 12, No. 8, January 1979, pp. 52-63 and "Resilient Children, PT Conversation with Michael Rutter" in *Psychology Today*, Vol. 18, No. 3, March 1984, pp. 56-65.

country or homeland, the land in general, real estate, immovable possessions, our genealogical roots, history, antiques and inherited conditions. It is our emotional home, our source, our foundation.

Letter 4 in the horoscope is indicated by the Moon, 4th house and the sign Cancer. To consider all forms of Letter 4, we include the Moon (all conjunctions or parallels, house and sign placement); any 4th house planets; any 4th house signs; the rulers of the 4th house (conjunctions or parallels, house and sign placement); houses ruled by any planets in the 4th house; any planets in Cancer and where Cancer falls in the horoscope.

TEST YOURSELF

The chart below has a repeated theme connected to Letter 4 which occurs in six different ways. What is the theme and how is it said?

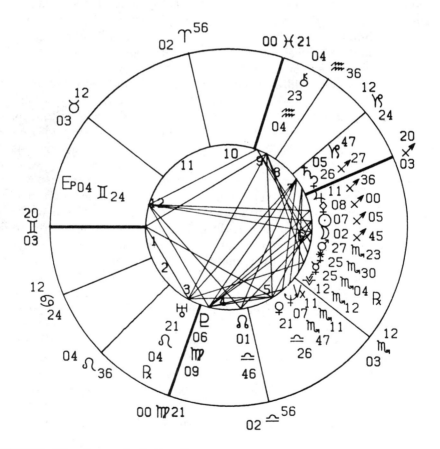

ANSWER: The theme is Letter 6.
1. The Moon (4) is in the 6th house (6).
2. Mercury, ruler of the 4th-house cusp (4) is in the 6th house (6).

3. The 4th house (4) is occupied by Pluto, which rules the 6th house (6).
4. The IC (4) is conjunct Pluto, which rules the 6th house (6).[6]
5. The cusp of the 4th house (4) is Virgo (6).
6. The 4th house (4) has a planet [Pluto] occupying the sign of Virgo (6).

Please note that this chart has a second theme connected to Letter 4 which occurs three times. That is Letter 8.
1. The 4th house (4) is occupied by Pluto (8).
2. The IC (4) is conjunct Pluto (8).
3. Mercury rules the 4th cusp (4) and is in Scorpio (8).

If you wish to look ahead in the interpretation Letter 4 is **one** of the keys to parents. Pages 406 and 407 discuss themes for Letter 6 and Letter 8 as far as parents.

Letter 5: ☉, ♌, 5th house

Letter 5 is a key to creativity, the urge to pour out into the world and do more than has been done before. It indicates our need to shine, to achieve recognition, to be noticed, applauded, loved and appreciated. With Letter 5, we seek the limelight; we gravitate toward center stage. A risk-taking capacity is part of Letter 5. We risk emotionally or physically, hoping that the rewards will be worthwhile. People may risk in loving and being loved (through romantic affairs or with children), in gambling and speculation, in investment (another way of gambling), in sales, promotional activities or entertainment (where ego and creativity are on the line). The rewards sought may be love, money, applause, attention or fame. By taking risks, trying to do more, we grow.

Letter 5 also represents the people in our lives associated with these activities: our children and lovers (where the relationship is intense and emotional but not committed to long-term). And it points to stockbrokers, entertainers, teachers and salespeople.

Self-esteem is the issue. We all need a sense of pride in ourselves. We need to feel good about who we are. Letter 5 in the horoscope is a key to where we need to feel proud of ourselves. It is important for us to be recognized and admired in those areas. We are ego-vulnerable where Letter 5 is concerned. We seek a sense of power and majesty. Letter 5 includes the symbols of the throne and scepter. We want to be dramatic and important where Letter 5 is concerned.

---

6. The angles of the horoscope — Ascendant, Descendant, Midheaven (MC) and IC (4th-house cusp) are important points. Aspects to them are as significant as aspects to planets. The Ascendant is another form of Letter 1; the Descendant of Letter 7; the IC is Letter 4 and the MC is Letter 10. I do not find the intermediate house cusps to have this degree of significance. However, planets conjuncting (within a degree or two) a house cusp, I do consider as having meaning for **both** houses, and tying the two houses together.

Some books suggest people with a Letter 5 emphasis are easily flattered. This can be the case. The more emphasis on Letter 5 in a horoscope, the stronger the drive for recognition within the individual. If such a person does not have an inner core of faith and security, s/he may look to other people to validate his/her existence and meaningfulness. Likewise, the person with inner security does not need to prove him/herself at the expense of others. It is the individual with a weak ego, with low self-esteem, who builds himself up at the expense of others, who attracts sycophants. Self-love must precede love from others. If I do not consider myself lovable, I will never believe other people do love me. I will be convinced they are out to get me, want something, are just liars, etc. If my self-esteem is firm, I find it easy to give love and to receive it from others.

Self-esteem can be enhanced through positive affirmations (giving our unconscious repeated, supportive messages), through paying attention to what we do well (rather than focusing on "errors") and through allowing other people's compliments to touch us. Creating something from our own center will often help build a healthy pride in who we are.

The thrill of passion is also a part of Letter 5 which symbolizes the orgasm. One forum of expression for Letter 5 drives is sex. For many people, sexual activities are the only times they experience a sense of power, esteem and importance. It is no surprise that sex is overused in our advertising and entertainment worlds. The excitement, drama and recognition associated with passion is used to sell a number of totally unrelated objects. Letter 5 represents both love and passion, but the two are not always linked in society.

The fiery, exuberant energy which is symbolized by Letter 5 can be summarized by the fact that the Sun (Letter 5) is a star. Letter 5 is our capacity to be a star, to light up the world around us and to bask in the warmth of other, appreciative stars.

Letter 5 in the horoscope includes the Sun, Leo and the 5th house. To examine all forms of Letter 5, we would include: the Sun (conjunctions and/or parallels to it, house and sign placement); rulers of the 5th house (conjunctions, parallels, house and sign placement); rulers of other signs in the 5th besides the sign on the cusp (conjunctions, parallels, house and sign placement); planets in the 5th house; signs in the 5th house; houses ruled by planets in the 5th house; planets occupying Leo; houses occupied by Leo, including any cusps. (We do **not** look to houses ruled by planets in Leo, as the chain has to stop at some point. Also, since the sign is the least emphatic of our factors, the nature of the planets occupying Leo would be most important, followed by the nature of the house which Leo occupies. Stretching to look at the houses ruled by planets in Leo is farther than necessary. However, as indicated, considering the nature of the houses ruled by planets falling in the 5th house **does** work.)

As with any letter of the astrological alphabet, look first to the planet (the Sun, in this case); then to the house (here, the 5th house), weighting first planets within the house, followed by rulers of the house; and finally consider the sign (Leo, here), including planets within that sign and the houses where the sign falls.

TEST YOURSELF

The chart below has a repeated theme connected to Letter 5 which occurs in four different ways. What is the theme and how is it said? (It is **not** the obvious theme of Letter 7 with Libra occupied four times in the 5th).

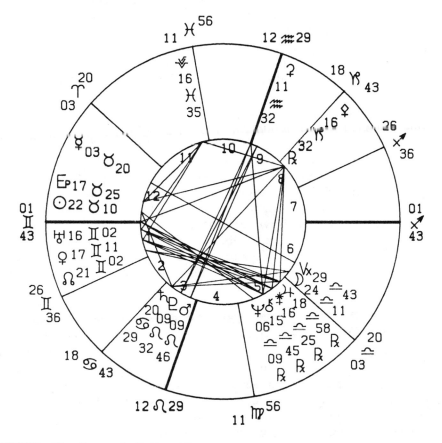

ANSWER: The theme is Letter 12.
1. The Sun (5) is in the 12th house (12).
2. The 5th house (5) is occupied by Neptune (12).
3. Mercury rules the 5th-house cusp (5) and is in the 12th house (12).
4. Leo (5) is occupied by Mars, ruler of the 12th house (12).[7]

If you wish to look ahead in the interpretation, turn to page 269 of Chapter 10 (children and creativity) as Letter 5 is one of the keys to this life area.

---

7. Note that Jupiter is not brought into the picture here. Jupiter is considered a co-ruler of Pisces. That means we look to Jupiter when we have Pisces involved in an area (after checking Neptune). We do **not** look to Jupiter when reading the 12th house.

Letter 6: ☿, ?, ⚕, ♍, 6th house

The keynote theme of Letter 6 is efficient functioning: both in the body (good health) and on the job. Dedicated to performing the task **well**, people with an emphasis on Letter 6 can be very pragmatic and capable. Skills associated with Letter 6 include analysis, discrimination, discipline and the ability to take things apart (mentally and physically) and put them back together in even better shape.

Letter 6 shows a critical capacity — an eye for flaws. By identifying mistakes, errors and shortcomings, the individual can improve the situation, person or product. The focus is on what is wrong in order to make it right. Of course, critical judgment can be overdone. Where Letter 6 is involved, people tend to turn that area of life into a job — flaw-finding and searching for problems to correct. If we turn our Letter 6 skills against ourselves or other people, overdoing the focus on what is wrong, the result can be highly uncomfortable. (This is most likely when Letter 6 is mixed with those parts of the chart which point to people. For example, Letter 6 mixed with Letter 1 shows a personal identification with the quest for mistakes, a tendency to be highly self-critical, a focus on one's own identity as the area to determine what is wrong.) The drive indicated by Letter 6 is highly effective if channeled into a working situation. But we set ourselves up for trouble if we try to turn the whole world into a job (nit-picking at everything) or focus our flaw-finding lens on areas of life where relaxing and letting life flow is much more appropriate.

Letter 6 represents, on the positive side, being conscientious, competent, well organized, sensible, dedicated, productive and thorough. The desire is to do a good job, to carry through on accomplishments until there is a tangible result. The person seeks a sense of achievement. With a Letter 6 emphasis, the person usually needs some kind of job or career. It does not necessarily have to pay. The essence is not remuneration, but rather the sense of a skilled craftsperson, of having done one's best. The "job" defined by Letter 6 is whatever we see as our task(s) in the world, our contribution to society, our productive outlet(s).

It is no accident that Letter 6 pertains to both work and health. How we feel about our jobs has a profound impact on our health. People who detest their work (but are afraid to leave it) will often get sick, as an (unconscious) escape from the job they cannot stand. If we really are sick (literally) of our work, it behooves us to either quit and find a new job, or find something we **can** enjoy about our work, so we don't continue making ourselves sick.

People whose charts show a strong focus on Letter 6 are more apt to get sick from **not** working. When the drive for productivity is particularly emphasized, the individual tends to feel guilty when not working. This can be a special challenge when Letter 6 is mixed with Letter 1 (identity) or 5 (self-esteem). Often, the person will feel: "I **should** be working." Excessive guilt and self-criticism can lead to illness. Or illness can be a way to gain attention (Letter 5).

Children with these mixtures need to be given opportunities to be productive.

They should be encouraged to undertake responsibilities (at their level) even at a young age. They need a sense of accomplishment, of being able to do something well. When their sense of identity (Letter 1) or ability to take pride in themselves (Letter 5) is tied to efficiency, they need a positive outlet, a way to feel useful. Too often, parents overprotect children, not giving them a chance to discover their own strengths. It is not uncommon for children with a Letter 6 emphasis mixed with 1 (and sometimes with 5) to be ill when young. When they are old enough to contribute, and discover things they can do well, they usually become quite healthy, and remain healthy as long as they do not try to retire completely. Such people need to maintain a productive outlet in order to feel good about themselves.

The strong drive for self-sufficiency and a sense of "If you want it done right, do it yourself" can also set up a person with a 1-6 emphasis for health problems. If minor aches and pains are ignored too long because the person only wants to acknowledge his/her capable side, they can evolve into major problems. Also, an overdevelopment of the productive function is often associated with discomfort around dependency. And becoming ill is a societally sanctioned channel for being dependent, for gaining some nurturing and tender, loving care. Generally, of course, this is an unconscious solution. Consciously these people want to be strong, competent and take care of themselves. But unmet closeness/dependency needs can lead to illness if not satisfied in other ways.

Successful integration of the drives symbolized by Letter 6 includes some kind of work or career which allows a sense of productivity, accomplishment and doing things well; appropriate attention to nutrition, exercise, rest and physical/emotional/intellectual/spiritual needs to maintain good health; limiting the flaw-finding lens to appropriate parts of life so that it does not spill over and affect those experiences that are meant to be fun.

Letter 6 is indicated by the 6th house and the sign Virgo in the chart. The planet Mercury is a ruler of Virgo as well as Gemini, but seems to fit into Letter 3 (in its own nature) more than Letter 6. Mercury tends to be more the scattered, insatiably curious, all-over-the-map mind of Letter 3 rather than the disciplined, organized, thorough and discriminating mind of Letter 6. But we still look to Mercury as the ruler of any Virgo in a chart.

For those who do not use the asteroids, you will have to decide whether you are seeing Mercury from a Letter 3 or a Letter 6 perspective when dealing with the question of how to count the nature of Mercury itself. One option is to assume that Mercury is Letter 3 when occupying air (like Gemini) houses and signs or fire (which is compatible with air). Mercury can be Letter 6 when occupying earth (like Virgo) houses and signs or water (which is compatible). In cases where the house and sign differ, you would have to choose. Dr. Dobyns weights houses more than signs (and I agree). Thus, a 10th house Mercury would be treated as a Letter 6 Mercury even if it were in a fire or air sign. Mercury in Aries in the 10th would thus be a 6-1-10 combination. (If you take Mercury as Letter 3 always and use the asteroids, Mercury in Aries in the 10th would be a 3-1-10 combination.) Just remember to still refer back to Mercury when looking at Virgo in the chart.

Those who use the asteroids can apply Ceres and Vesta to Letter 6. I am **not** suggesting Ceres and Vesta as rulers, however. Thus, Ceres and Vesta, in their own nature, apply to Letter 6 (with a Letter 4 overtone for Ceres and overtones of 8 and 10 for Vesta).[8] (The asteroids can be weighted half as much as planets if you wish.)

TEST YOURSELF
The chart below has a repeated theme connected to Letter 6 which occurs in six different ways (eight ways with asteroids). What is the theme and how is it said? (Mercury is in a water house, so I am calling it Letter 6 in this case.)

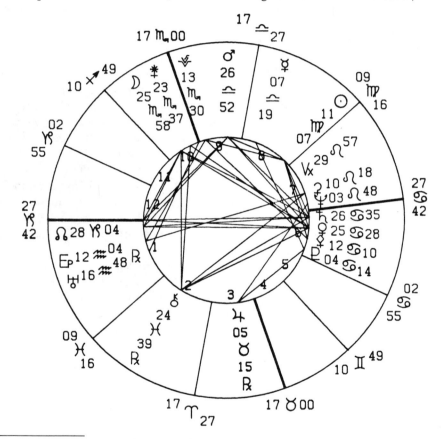

---

8. Ceres seems to be an "Earth Mother" figure, concerned with work for the sake of the people involved. Often drawn to the land and green, growing things, Ceres denotes the fertile side of Virgo and is a key to mothering, nurturing, protection of the young, etc. Ceres functions very well as a secondary key to the mother (or mother figure) after the Moon and is often prominent in current patterns when people are involved with birthing, adopting, or gaining children through marriage, grandchildren, etc. Vesta symbolizes the impersonal side of Virgo and is concerned with work for its own sake. Dedicated, disciplined, thorough and careful, Vesta can show tunnel vision. The work attitude may interfere with emotional relationships when Vesta is mixed with personal or interpersonal parts of the chart, and alienation is a danger. Efficiency is paramount for Vesta.

ANSWER: The theme is Letter 8.
1. Mercury (6) is in the 8th house (8).
2. The 6th house (6) is occupied by Pluto (8).
3. The 6th house (6) is occupied by Venus, which rules the Libra in the 8th house (8).
4. The Moon rules the 6th-house cusp (6) and is in Scorpio (8).
5. Virgo (6) is on the cusp of the 8th house (8).
6. Virgo (6) is occupied [by the Sun] in the 8th house (8).
7. Vesta (6) is in Scorpio (8).
8. The Moon rules the 6th house cusp (6) and conjuncts Juno in Scorpio (8).

There is also a secondary theme of Letter 10 connected to Letter 6:
1. Vesta (6) conjuncts the MC (10).
2. The 6th house (6) is occupied by Saturn (10).
3. The 6th house (6) is occupied by Pluto, ruler of the MC (10).
4. The Moon rules the 6th cusp (6) and is in the 10th house (10).
5. The Moon rules the 6th cusp (6) and make a conjunction (to Juno) in the 10th house (10).

As is discussed in Chapter 5 on page 83, this combination of 6-8-10 denotes strong obsessive-compulsive tendencies: thorough, careful, disciplined, hardworking, concerned with getting all the details correct, critical, concentrated. This theme is significant in the chart as a whole. Since Letter 6 relates to work and health, you could also read pages 145 and 147 in Chapter 7 (work) for Letters 8 and 10, plus pages 387 and 389 in Chapter 14 for Letters 8 and 10 in health.

Letter 7: ♀, ☿, ⚳, ♎, 7th house

Letter 7 symbolizes peer relationships, equalitarian interactions. This includes marriage, living together, therapeutic associations, lawyer-client relationships and any regular, ongoing, systematic, shared activities (even if time-limited) such as a weekly bridge club. The key here is the regularity of the associations. We form a relationship; we interact to meet each other's needs for a period of time. Letter 3 relationships are based on propinquity; Letter 7 relationships are ongoing commitments.

Peer relationships imply being on the same level but do **not** have to be harmonious. They **can** be, but Letter 7 also includes competitive relationships. (For a true contest, the opponents have to be near-equals in abilities. Otherwise, the winner and loser are a foregone conclusion. In competitive interactions, people win sometimes and lose sometimes.) Lawsuits are also represented by Letter 7 as are warfare and open enemies. This drive encompasses our need for one-to-one interactions, face-to-face exchanges with others.

Letter 7 also denotes a desire for balance and harmony. It is often connected to the arts, especially the visual arts (i.e., photography, architecture, graphics, interior decorating, painting) which involve a sense of line, form and space. These arts often involve stepping back (detachment) and looking at the creation with some space between — an air function, and Letter 7 is air.

If the desire for ease and harmony is carried too far, people with an emphasis on Letter 7 can be overly accommodating. They may too often put the needs of the other person ahead of their own. They may have trouble acting on their own, waiting always to **react** to someone else. The drive symbolized by Letter 7 is a seeking of pleasure with people. Some individuals may block their own assertion out of a desire for peace and beauty. Sometimes they will settle for the mere **appearance** of harmony, in which case they can appear hypocritical or too concerned with what other people think.

You will also find people with Letter 7 emphasized in their horoscope who are **intensely** competitive — even cutthroat. Their one-to-one interactions may be anything but sweetness and light. (Many lawyers and generals have Sun in Libra, for example.) The person who wants to "win" at any cost (whether in the courtroom, on the tennis courts or in courting a lover) has not learned the instinctive balance of Letter 7. This "contamination" of Letter 7 is one possible form with fire factors (especially the Sun or Mars) in the 7th house or in Libra. The self-orientation (of Mars) or desire for power and adulation (of the Sun) may override Letter 7's equality instincts. In such cases, personal relationships can become battlegrounds.

If not integrated, one possible form of 1/7 blends is: "I want my relationships only on **my** terms." And, remember, the Sun is part of our **growth potential**, what we are doing more of with age and maturity. The Sun in Libra has a growth goal of developing more balance. Evenhandedness is **not necessarily** present early in life (though it can be).

The focus with Letter 7 is on doing things with other people rather than alone. We can cooperate with teamwork or compete with others. Letter 7 can also denote a strong sense of justice. There is a marked desire for fair play. Evenhandedness is appreciated. If the need for "justice" is overdone, people's scorekeeping in relationships can reach ridiculous heights.

Part of the essence of Letter 7 is an objective look at relationships. As with all air, the goal is to accept and understand without having to change the other person. We are learning about ourselves and about life by observing significant others. We constantly confront our needs and theirs and seek a balance. Negotiation, compromise and the art of diplomacy can all be involved with Letter 7. One-on-one is the focus and we may be learning to be an equal, learning to compromise and/or learning to compete in a fair manner.

Letter 7 in the horoscope is indicated by the 7th house and the sign Libra. Venus is a ruler of Libra along with Taurus. In its own nature, Venus seems more Taurean (earthy, sensual, grounded), but it does rule Libra as well. With Taurus, Venus seeks pleasure from the physical world. A Libra Venus seeks pleasure with people.

Those who use the asteroids can assign Pallas and Juno to Letter 7. Pallas, in its own nature, seems Libran with overtones of Sagittarius or Aquarius for a decidedly transpersonal thrust. Justice is a strong theme and a prominent Pallas may be a key to politics. Relationships have more of a freedom overtone, more detachment. Juno, in its own nature, has Scorpio overtones, with an intensity and a focus on committed relationships. It works well as the "marriage asteroid" — a key to issues faced in partnerships as well as the type of partner one is likely to attract. Both can be keys to beauty, especially of the visual sort (graphics, architecture, modeling, interior decorating, photography, etc.).

Without the asteroids, you will have to decide on an individual basis whether a specific Venus ought to be counted as Letter 2 or Letter 7. Perhaps Venus in earth or water houses or signs could be assigned to Letter 2 while Venus in air or fire houses or signs could be seen as Letter 7.

Again, I still take Venus as the ruler wherever Libra falls in the chart. The asteroids do not rule Libra, but are Libran in their own nature. Venus does rule Libra, but one must decide whether a given Venus is more Taurean (2) or Libran (7) in its own nature.

To include all forms of Letter 7 in a horoscope, we would examine: Venus, Pallas and Juno (conjunctions, parallels, house and sign placements); planets in the 7th house; signs in the 7th house; rulers of the 7th cusp (with their conjunctions, parallels, house and sign placements); rulers of other signs in the 7th house; houses ruled by planets in the 7th house; planet occupying Libra in the horoscope and houses occupied by Libra in the horoscope.

TEST YOURSELF

The chart below has a repeated theme connected to Letter 7 which occurs five times (counting Venus as Letter 2). It has another theme connected to Letter 7 which occurs four times (counting Venus as Letter 7). What are the themes and how are they said?

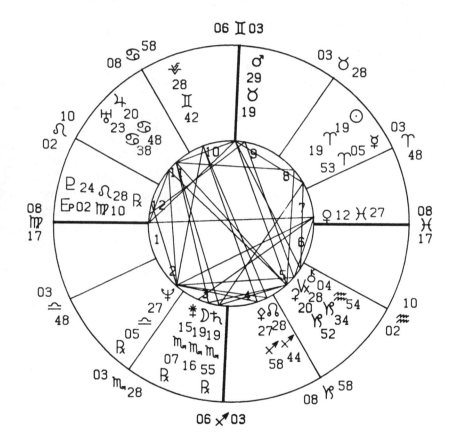

ANSWER: The first theme is Letter 2.

1. The 7th house (7) is occupied by Venus (2).

   (This would be considered 7/7 if Venus is counted as Letter 7 only.)

2. Neptune rules the 7th-house cusp (7) and is in the 2nd house (2).

3. Mars rules the Aries in the 7th house (7) and is in Taurus (2).

4. Libra (7) is on the cusp of the 2nd house (2).

5. Libra (7) is occupied [by Neptune] in the 2nd house (2).

   (This may appear to be counting Neptune twice, but is appropriate. We would count **any** planet or planets in the 2nd house which are in the sign of Libra since that is mixing Letters 2 and 7. In this case, Neptune happens to rule the

7th house, so must be counted from that perspective as well. If Aries were on the cusp of the 7th, Neptune would be counted only once — as the planet occupying Libra.)

ANSWER: The second theme is Letter 12.
1. Venus (7) is in Pisces (12).
2. The 7th house (7) has a Pisces (12) cusp.
3. The 7th house (7) is occupied by a planet in Pisces (12).
4. Libra (7) is occupied by Neptune (12).

If you wish to look ahead in the interpretations, pages 181 and 188 in Chapter 8 discuss themes connected to Letters 2 and 12 in relationships (since Letter 7 is one key to relationships).

Letter 8: ♇, ♏, 8th house

Letter 8 symbolizes the drive for self-insight, self-understanding and self-mastery, the urge to plumb the deepest recesses of our psyches. This grasp of hidden knowledge is gained partially through our intimate associations: the sharing of sensual, sexual and financial issues with other human beings. Letter 8 represents our mate and the process of learning about parts of ourselves through the mirror of another person. Intense emotions are being dealt with where Letter 8 is involved.

The drive to go inward, the probe for answers which Letter 8 denotes, can be channeled into occult studies, depth psychotherapy, detective work, insurance investigation or any kind of research. The quest is for root causes, for what lies below the surface. Determined to get to the bottom of things, relentless and unflagging, Letter 8 can indicate the most persistent, tenacious and thorough of bulldog approaches.

Completion is an important theme with Letter 8. Knowing when to let go, what is enough and when to release and move on can all be challenges for individuals with a strong focus on Letter 8. The ultimate form of physical release and moving on is death, which is a part of Letter 8. But deaths (and transformations) can take many different forms: the death of a relationship, of a lifestyle, of a physical body, etc. Letter 8 is involved with the closing of chapters and the transmutation of energies (on the physical, emotional, mental and spiritual levels). Like all water, Letter 8 shows the urge to hang on for security reasons. Sometimes people hang on to negative emotions — such as guilt, anger, jealousy, resentment, possessiveness — much too long. These emotions become like poisons in the body, leading to physical illness if maintained long-term. Part of the Letter 8 challenge is being able to release or transform and transmute negative emotions into positive energy, attitudes and actions. Forgiveness (of ourselves as well as others) is often a crucial act. Faith can also help to transmute negatives when we can "give it to God."

Joint finances and possessions of all sorts are associated with Letter 8. It is a key to any earnings which come through other people (e.g., government grants, welfare, inheritance, lotteries, return on speculation) or which are a payment of earlier efforts (royalties). It is also a key to anything we must or do pay to others (debts, taxes, spousal or child support, etc.). It includes possessions and money which belong to our partners (business, marriage, etc.) or are held by both of us. Joint pleasures are a part of the picture, so our handling of sexuality is an issue.

There is a drive for power and mastery indicated by Letter 8. The mastery can be self-directed or the individual can strive for power over others. In such cases, money and sex are common tools for manipulating and controlling people. Intimidation, power plays, threats, blackmail and other forms of emotional ploys (e.g., tears) all may be used by the person determined to have things his/her way. Power struggles, especially in close relationships, are not uncommon where Letter 8 is involved. Extremely dependent people may cling to others for support, or use indirect, manipulative means to get taken care of. The issues usually revolve around giving, receiving and sharing material pleasures and possessions. The challenge is for everyone involved to be comfortable while contributing and accepting financially and sexually and being able to compromise and share equally where the sense world is concerned.

Sensual/sexual blocks often point to a need to forgive the self for supposed "sins" (sometimes just the old image of sex as "dirty" is interfering). A "spirituality" which denies humans the right to enjoy the material world (including sex) can be part of the issue. We also have to believe that we **deserve** pleasure (which can be an extra challenge for people with pronounced Letter 6 or 10). Anger and resentment can be involved when lack of response is used to punish others as well as ourselves. The desire for self-control, if overdone, can block spontaneity and pleasure.

When the power is directed inward with self-mastery as the goal, it can also be carried too far. For some individuals, complete renunciation is the only path they know to "master" their sensual/sexual appetites. Celibacy, poverty or extreme self-denial may be the only answer such people see to their quest for self-control. An ascetic lifestyle, which deprives them of even reasonable pleasures, is sometimes chosen. This can include withdrawal from personal relationships. Rather than dealing with intimacy issues, such people choose to retreat, to "control" through avoidance. Eventually, individuals in that position will have to learn that mastery means being able to enjoy life **moderately** — without excessive indulgence but also without excessive denial.

Life is interconnected (as the water element teaches us). Letter 8 is a key to our ability to give, receive and share sensually and sexually, but those abilities are also affected by our self-esteem (Letter 5), ability to assert ourselves (Letter 1), etc. Life is a balancing act — striving toward positive expression of all parts of life.

Letter 8 in the horoscope is indicated by Pluto, the 8th house and Scorpio. (Mars can be utilized as a co-ruler of Scorpio, but Pluto is the primary ruler.) For all forms of Letter 8, we would examine: Pluto (conjunctions, parallels, house and sign placement); planets in the 8th house; signs in the 8th house; rulers of the 8th house (conjunctions, parallels, house and sign placement); houses ruled by planets in the 8th; planets occupying Scorpio and houses occupied by Scorpio.

TEST YOURSELF
The chart below has a repeated theme connected to Letter 8 which occurs in seven different ways. What is the theme and how is it said?

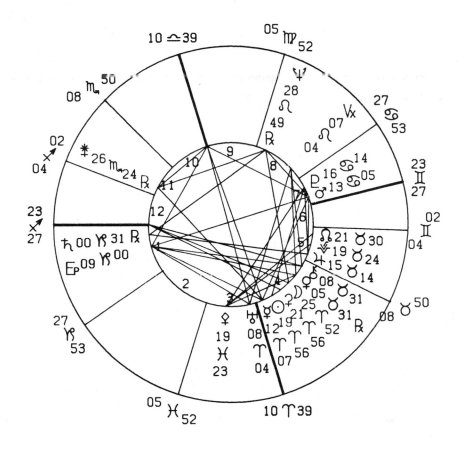

ANSWER: The theme is Letter 4.
1. Pluto (8) is conjunct Mars, which rules the 4th-house cusp (4).
2. Pluto (8) is in Cancer (4).
3. The 8th-house cusp (8) is ruled by the Moon which is in the 4th house (4).
4. The 8th house (8) is also ruled by the Sun which is in the 4th house (4).
5. The Virgo in the 8th house (8) is ruled by Mercury, which is in the 4th house (4).
6. The Virgo in the 8th house (8) is ruled by Mercury, which is conjunct the IC (4).
7. The 8th house (8) has Cancer (4) on the cusp.

If you wish to read ahead in interpretation, the Letter 4 theme in the area of sexuality (Chapter 13) is discussed on pags 354-355. The Letter 4 theme for money (Chapter 12) appears on page 325. (Letter 8 is one of the keys to both sexuality and handling of finances.)

Letter 9: ♃, ♐, 9th house

Letter 9 symbolizes our search for something more in life, our quest for meaning and understanding. Here we see our drive to grasp the meaning of the universe and why we are here, our urge to reach for something higher, to comprehend the ultimate in life. Our seeking may lead us into religion, philosophy, higher education (college level and beyond), spiritual studies, traveling to the ends of the earth or any arena which offers possible answers to the mysteries of life.

Letter 9 is a key to our ideals and our values, what we trust and where we put our faith. Depending on what is mixed with Letter 9, the horoscope may indicate faith in a bank account, in a marriage or other partner, in ourselves, in a Higher Power, in beauty or something else.

The major importance of the 9th and 12th houses is pointed out in the research of Michel and Francoise Gauquelin. They found planets in the 9th and 12th houses (plus 10° into the 1st and 10th) to be keys to major character traits and to occupational choices among highly successful people.

The 9th and 12th could be called houses of visualization. And what we value and visualize, we tend to create in our lives. What we define as ultimately important, we seek to manifest more and more of in our lives.

We can often idealize where Letter 9 is concerned. There is a "More is better" tendency with this side of life. Whatever we value most highly, we tend to pursue — sometimes to excess. Letter 9 is associated with exaggeration and overreach. We can easily overdo whatever we turn into an idol.

Part of the quest is for an intellectual understanding of life's meaning, so Letter 9 is a key to belief systems. But the quest is for concepts which we can verbalize, ideas which we can put into words and explain. There is a mental focus here along with the tremendous excitement of being a seeker and a searcher. Of course, if pleasure is made into an ultimate value, the individual may simply look for the best party, the ultimate high in sex, drugs or other material means rather than intellectual or spiritual paths.

In order to search, one must be free, so independence is an important component of Letter 9. People with a Letter 9 emphasis often want to be able to take off on a trip (mental or physical) at any time. Also, when ideals are excessively high, splitting the scene can be one way to escape or avoid the issue.

Letter 9 indicates our world view, our theories about the way life is (or ought to be), what we see as reality, what we accept as just and true. This is truth with a capital "T" — ultimate answers. With Letter 9, issues revolve around faith, trust, beliefs and values. Some people will have excessive faith and confidence — to the point of rashness (usually with a fire emphasis). Others will be facing the challenge of learning to trust and have faith (conflicts between Letter 9 and other parts of life) or to have a **reasonable** faith.

I call Jupiter "Great Expectations." And, like the Dickens novel, it does not always have a happy ending! Where Letter 9 is concerned, people often expect more, better, higher, faster than is really possible. Dreaming the impossible dream is one thing, but living chronically frustrated and disillusioned because your marriage/job/self/etc., does not measure up to perfectionistic standards is hardly worth it. We need **enough** faith in life and ourselves to cope, but not **too much**!

In the horoscope, Letter 9 is indicated by Jupiter, the 9th house and Sagittarius. All forms of Letter 9 would include: Jupiter (conjunctions, parallels, house and sign placement); Chiron [9] (conjunctions, parallels, house and sign placement); planets in the 9th house; signs in the 9th house; rulers of the 9th cusp (conjunctions, parallels, house and sign placements); rulers of other signs in the 9th house; houses ruled by planets in the 9th; planets occupying Sagittarius; houses occupied by Sagittarius.

---

9. Chiron, the planetoid orbiting between Saturn and Uranus, can also be considered Letter 9 in its own nature — with overtones of Letter 11. It seems to be a key to the search for truth — especially the willingness to go beyond traditional boundaries in that quest. It is often prominent in the charts of people who come from very nonintellectual backgrounds, but feel driven to read, to study and to pursue knowledge. Chiron also has a strong freedom theme and the issue of idealism, wanting more than is possible, is relevant.

TEST YOURSELF

The chart below has a repeated theme connected to Letter 9 which occurs in five different ways. What is the theme and how is it said?

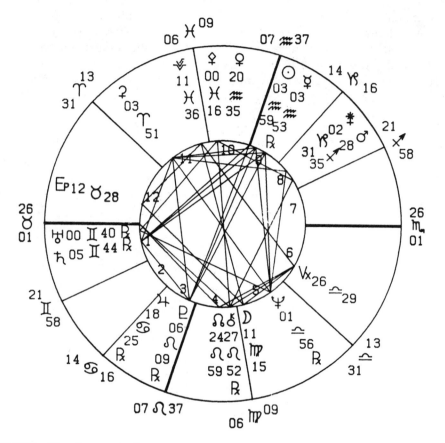

ANSWER: The theme is Letter 3.
1. Jupiter (9) is in the 3rd house (3).
2. The 9th house (9) is occupied by Mercury (3).
3. The 9th house (9) is occupied by the Sun which rules the Leo in the 3rd house (3).
4. The 9th-house cusp (9) is ruled by Saturn which is in Gemini (3).
5. The Aquarius in the 9th house (9) is ruled by Uranus which is in Gemini (3).

If you wish to look ahead in the interpretations, page 302 of Chapter 11 discusses the Letter 3 theme in terms of beliefs and values (an area where Letter 9 is one of the keys).

Letter 10: ♄, ♑, 10th house

Letter 10 represents our understanding of and relationship to the laws of the game of life. This includes natural, physical laws such as gravity, and cultural laws such as traffic signals. Also included are cosmic laws such as *karma*. *Karma* is simply cause-and-effect: "As ye sow, so shall ye reap." Our character, in the form of habitual attitudes and actions, creates our destiny. If we change our character, we change our destiny. For example: if we are using our Martian (Letter 1) side to start fights and arguments, or repressing it into headaches and sinus colds, or projecting it and attracting aggressive, violent people, we can choose to manifest our Letter 1 potential another way. We may take up racquetball, work out in a gym, play tournament chess, get involved in a competitive business or fight for a cause in which we believe. When we change our habitual pattern of acting and feeling, we change our destiny (our *karma*). We move from fights, colds or attacks to energy, vitality and achievements.

All rules and roles are part of the picture shown by Letter 10, even those roles which are unnecessarily limiting, such as stereotypes. Letter 10 also symbolizes those people in our lives who carry out the law — from the neighborhood police officer to the president of the United States. Our first authority figure, usually a parent, is shown by Letter 10.

The parent of Letter 10 is the conditional love parent, or reality parent. This is the parent who teaches the child about cause-and-effect, who works with consequences. "If you put your hand in the fire, it will get burned." (And the child with strong Letter 10 may well have to experience the burning him/herself. Letter 10 learns through experience and often prefers not to take someone else's word for it!) Letter 10 points to the parent who uses reward (and perhaps punishment). "I appreciate you when you pick up your toys." This parent teaches responsibility, practicality and sets limits. In traditional archetypes, this is the fathering role. However, the role can be played by either parent or both. It is quite common nowadays for parents to share the roles of Letters 4 and 10, or for a single parent to express both.

Letter 10 in the horoscope gives clues about our relationship to authorities and the powers that be. Initially, most of us experience Letter 10 themes as a sense of restriction, of being held back, inhibited, told "No." As we grow older, the challenge is to incorporate the power symbolized by Letter 10 into our own hands. Then we become capable, responsible movers, shakers and doers in society. At that level, Letter 10 becomes a key to our career, our professional role in society, our status, our reputation and ability to have an impact on the material world. It shows our executive drive and capacities to handle authority, power and responsibility.

When dealing with rules and limits, there are two basic extremes to which people can go. One extreme is to see more barriers than are there, to follow more rules than are needed, to unnecessarily restrict life. Many people operate under self-imposed blinders, not seeing opportunities, believing they are blocked, inhibited, unable to cope when there are actually many options open to them. Some feel so inadequate and helpless they do not even try. The other extreme is to refuse to recognize any rules at all, to deny even basic limits in life. Such people can fight the rules of society (through a life of rebellion or crime), can fight natural laws (not eating right, exercising, or getting enough rest so the logical consequence is physical problems), can chronically try to live life totally on their terms, unwilling to consider that certain basic parameters exist.

Let us look at the example of a young woman (32 years) who was informed in her regular checkup that her cholesterol count was much higher than it ought to be for good health. Her first reaction was anger (unwilling to accept Letter 10 limitations): "Why me? How could this happen? My family is long-lived and healthy. It isn't fair!" Her second reaction was self-blocking (excessive internal limitations): "Well, I guess I'll just have to live with it; I guess I'm stuck." Her third reaction was a realistic working within the limits of what is possible in the world. She established a new diet and began exercising regularly. Eight months later and 15 pounds lighter, she has a very healthy lifestyle and a much reduced cholesterol count.

This woman could have done the self-blocking in other ways. We can give up or cop out in numerous variations. She could have fought the limits in other ways (e.g., deciding to eat whatever she wished and "to h_____ with cholesterol"). She can also choose to fight the limits or give up again at any time. She is in charge of her reactions. (As a marvelous example of how our **perceptions** of events matter much more than the events themselves, this woman notes: "When I was first informed of my high cholesterol count, I considered it a **terrible** event — a nasty shock. Now, I consider it the best thing that could have happened to me! I'd been telling myself for years I needed to buckle down and exercise and that I ought to lose some weight, but I kept on procrastinating. It was only with the impetus of the cholesterol count that I finally actually **did** something. All I can say is, if my unconscious arranged that, I've got a really smart unconscious!")

The challenge represented by Letter 10 is to assess the rules of the game — in a very sensible, pragmatic fashion — and then to work responsibly **within** those rules to achieve as much as possible. By working **with** the natural consequences of life, we can accomplish much. The final, internalized form of Letter 10 is our own conscience. When we follow our conscience, we need no external rules or limits. We provide our own. The challenge is to make sure they are sensible and practical — neither too much nor too little.

Typical key words for a positive integration of Letter 10 include responsible, hardworking, thrifty, careful, cautious, disciplined, in control, executive drive, pragmatic, concerned with structures, rules, limitations and "appropriate" behavior.

Letter 10 in the horoscope includes Saturn (conjunctions, parallels, house and sign placement); planets in the 10th house; signs in the 10th house; rulers of the 10th cusp (conjunctions, parallels, house and sign placements); rulers of other signs in the 10th house; houses ruled by planets in the 10th house; planets occupying Capricorn; houses occupied by Capricorn.

TEST YOURSELF
The chart below has a repeated theme connected to Letter 10 which occurs four times. (One repetition is a very subtle variation which we have not discussed yet.)

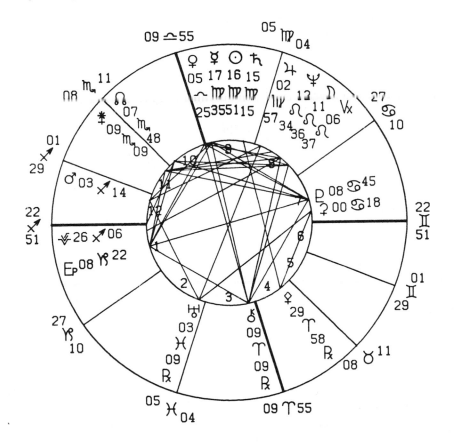

ANSWER: The theme is Letter 5.
1. Saturn (10) is conjunct the Sun (5).
2. Saturn (10) is conjunct Mercury, which rules the Gemini in the 5th house (5).[10]

---

10. It is true that there is only a little bit of Gemini in the 5th house, but the sign **is** present. We would not weight the Gemini very much in terms of letter 5, since it is an unoccupied sign and not even on the cusps of the house, but it is still one of the factors. In terms of consistency, we would consider the Gemini in the 5th as well as the Taurus in the 5th. (In this particular chart, Gemini is in three houses — falling on two cusps — 6th and 7th — plus that small section of Gemini in the 5th. This repetition of Mercury's involvement as ruler of Gemini is a little extra emphasis on the importance of Mercury in the chart.)

3. The MC (10) is conjunct Venus, which rules the 5th-house cusp (5).
4. The 10th house (10) and 5th house (5) are ruled by the same planet.

    (This is the subtle variation. Due to the double rulership of Venus and Mercury, there will always be at least two houses ruled by Venus and at least two by Mercury. That is a link, showing some commonality between the houses so ruled. Here it repeats the 10/5 theme.)

    If you wish to look ahead in the interpretations, Letter 10 is involved with work and also with parents. The Letter 5 theme for parents is discussed on page 406 of Chapter 15. The Letter 5 theme for career appears on page 143 of Chapter 7.

The Test Chart also has a secondary theme of Letter 9 connected to Letter 10:
1. Saturn (10) conjuncts Mercury, which rules the 9th cusp (9).
2. Saturn (10) is in the 9th (9).
3. Venus rules the MC (10) and is in the 9th (9).

Letter 11: ♅, ♒, 11th house

Letter 11 symbolizes our individualistic nature, originality and desire for what is new, different, progressive, unusual and future-oriented. Freedom is a theme, in order to go beyond old limits, to break new ground, to push past former boundaries. Here we have the theme of revolution, the electric excitement of discovery and unique solutions.

    Letter 11 is a key to anything new-age from astrology to the study of Zoroastrianism. It is associated with all kinds of new technology, including lasers, computers, spaceships and much more. Anything on the cutting edge of change can be a focus. The battle cry of Letter 11 is "Down with the old and up with the new." I was once given the definition of traditions as "dead people's rules" — surely a Letter 11 statement!

    Letter 11 is associated with openness and free circulation — whether that be the circulatory system of the body or the circulation of ideas in society. Clubs, groups, associations of all kinds fall into Letter 11. Friends and the widest circle of acquaintances are included. Indeed, Letter 11 encompasses all of humanity. This is the capacity to accept anyone and everyone on his/her own terms — provided we are given the same respect. Brotherhood, sisterhood, personhood, humanitarianism and tolerance are potential themes of Letter 11. The primary "hopes and wishes" of Letter 11 are freedom from constraint or restraint, openness to all ideas and possibilities, unlimited options and the detachment to accept almost anyone (sometimes with no real closeness to anyone either).

    Excessive forms of Letter 11 can be chaotic, rebellious, insistent on personal freedom without respect for the rights of others, excessively detached and objective or outright strange and weird. More balanced use of these themes can lead to tremendous inventiveness, great tolerance, an acceptance of people as they are, personal independence and a burning desire to go where no one has gone before, to open new vistas for humankind.

TEST YOURSELF

The chart below has a repeated theme connected to Letter 11 which occurs eleven or twelve times (depending on how you count Venus). What is the theme and how is it said?

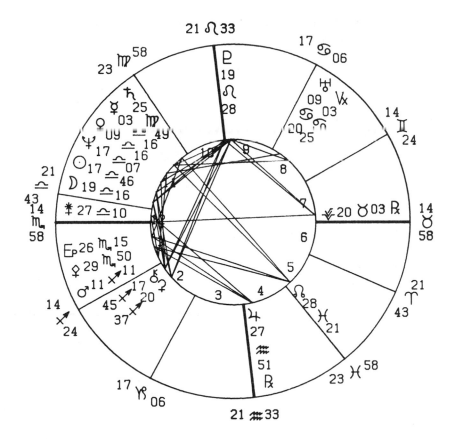

ANSWER: The theme is Letter 7.

1. The 11th house (11) is occupied by Venus (taking Venus as Letter 7).
2. The 11th house (11) is occupied by Venus, which rules the 7th-house cusp (7).
3. The 11th house (11) is occupied by Mercury, which rules the Gemini in the 7th house (7).
4. & 5. Mercury rules the 11th-house cusp (11) and conjuncts Venus which rules the 7th house (7) [natural and actual ruler].
6. Mercury rules the 11th cusp (11) and is in Libra (7).
7. Venus rules the Libra in the 11th house (11) and is in Libra (7).
8, 9, 10, 11 & 12. The 11th house (11) is occupied by five planets in the sign of Libra (7).

Since Letter 11 is one of the keys to the mind, a Letter 7 theme for that life area can be envisioned by reading page 226, in Chapter 9.

Letter 12: Ψ, ⧗, 12th house

Letter 12 represents the seeking of Oneness with the Whole, or cosmic consciousness. This is an experience of Union that goes far beyond words. The quest for connectedness to the Universe, identified by Letter 12, is explored by some people through great art, by others in mystical experiences, by others through religious conversions, by others through nature worship. The desire to merge or unite with a sense of ecstasy and inspiration leads some into drugs or other escapist routes. Here we have the quest for an emotional absolute, a utopia, a vision of infinite love and beauty.

Letter 12 denotes the ultimate unification experience. This merging recognizes that we are all One with no loss of individuality. The power and the glory of the experience are irreducible to verbal descriptions. An important part of Letter 12 seems to be our handling of faith, especially the ability to have faith in a Higher Power, to trust in the universe, to believe that life is ultimately good.

For the individual lacking basic faith (in his/her own capabilities or in the basic goodness of life), the confrontation with infinity (which is a part of Letter 12) can be overwhelming and frightening. This can result in individuals running away from life in some fashion. (They may be running from the simple vastness, from the incredible task of converting the ideal vision into a reality, or both.)

Some people contemplate the immensity of the universe and feel, "It is so infinite; I am nothing in comparison." Rather than being refreshed and inspired to be One with such grandeur, they feel terrified and insignificant. Others discover an essential vision, but despair of manifesting it on earth. Rather than face an imperfect physical plane, such people retreat into chronic fantasy, psychosis, sleeping a lot, daydreaming, alcohol and other drugs or any route which allows them to avoid looking at how less than ultimately lovely their lives are and how they are doing nothing about it. Rather than trying to improve the world, to bring their dreams into manifestation, these individuals look for a quick, easy, painless escape from a nonideal world.

Those people who have basic (unconscious, emotional) faith in themselves and the world are doing something to bring their visions down to earth. They may be inspired artists (whether professionally or as an avocation). They may be helpers, healers, saviors of others (professionally or informally). They may be mystics, meditators or supremely attuned to the world of nature. They may be drawn to spiritual studies. Whatever the path, these people have a connection to the cosmos. They have had (or believe they can have) peak experiences. They **know** — on a gut level, not on just an intellectual level — that life is good and that we are all one. They are working to spread the beauty, to share the goodness, to reconfirm the unity of all of humanity, all of the universe.

Letter 12 is indicated in the horoscope by Neptune, the 12th house and Pisces.

They all reflect our quest for the emotional ideal. Played out through roles of artist, helper and victim, they signify our journey to reconnect with all that is, to reexperience the ultimate ecstasy that comes from Oneness with the Whole.

TEST YOURSELF
The chart below has a repeated theme connected to Letter 12 which occurs four times. What is the theme and how is it said?

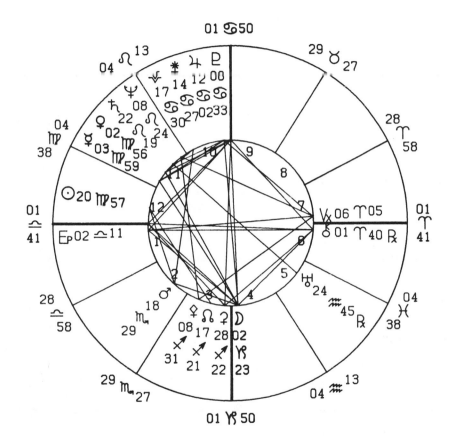

ANSWER: The theme is Letter 11.
1. Neptune (12) occupies the 11th house (11).
2. Mercury rules the 12th-house cusp (12) and is in the 11th house (11).
3. Venus rules the Libra in the 12th house (12) and is in the 11th house (11).
4. The 12th house (12) is occupied by the Sun, which rules the 11th-house cusp (11).
   Some people would consider Mercury as occupying **both** the 11th and 12th houses, since it is so close (within a degree) to the cusp. In such a case, that is another count for a link between Letters 12 and 11.

If you wish to look ahead in the interpretations, Letter 12 is **one** of the keys to beliefs and values. Page 306 of Chapter 11 discusses Letter 11 themes in that life area.

With a good background for identifying each letter of the astrological alphabet, you are now ready to look at themes and combinations involving more than one letter (in Chapter 4).

CHAPTER FOUR

THEMES

Naturally, themes tied to **one** letter of the astrological alphabet are only a small part of the picture. Quite commonly, themes will emerge which are **combinations** of the various letters of the alphabet — whether by twos, threes, fours, etc. Some combinations with which most astrologers are already familiar are those grouped as elements (fire, earth, air and water) and qualities (cardinal, fixed and mutable), but many other mixtures exist which are summarized in this chapter.

The Elements

The astrological alphabet can be divided into groups of four elements. Although ancient astrologers conceptualized the world as being made up of these four elements, modern astrologers use the concepts of the elements as another model for human motivations and behaviors.

When considering elements in a horoscope, it is vital **not** to count only occupied signs. Occupied houses are also an important part of the picture — and so are planets and aspects. **Fire** includes the Sun, Mars and Jupiter; the 1st, 5th and 9th houses; as well as Aries, Leo and Sagittarius. **Earth** includes Venus (as ruler of Taurus), Mercury (as ruler of Virgo), Ceres, Vesta and Saturn; the 2nd, 6th and 10th houses; as well as Taurus, Virgo and Capricorn. **Air** includes Mercury (as ruler of Gemini), Venus (as ruler of Libra) and Uranus; the 3rd, 7th and 11th houses; as well as Gemini, Libra and Aquarius. **Water** includes the Moon, Pluto and Neptune; the 4th, 8th and 12th houses; as well as Cancer, Scorpio and Pisces.

Planets (and aspects) are the most emphatic form elements can take. As an example, a Sun/Mars conjunction is a much stronger fire statement than the Sun in Aries, Leo or Sagittarius or the Sun in the 1st, 5th or 9th houses. Chapter 18 will consider element weighting and balancing for the chart as a whole. Until then, consider elements in terms of the life areas — identity, work, beliefs, etc. — with which you are particularly concerned. For example, suppose you are analyzing an individual's approach to work and success in the world. The handling of the material world is indicated by earth, so we would consider all forms of Letters 2, 6 and 10 in the horoscope.

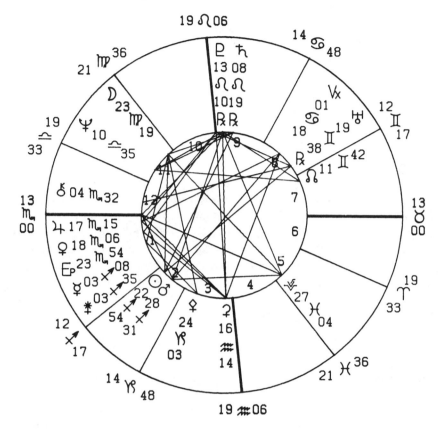

Above you see a sample chart. Looking at the 2nd, 6th and 10th houses, we see they are occupied by: the Sun (**fire**), Mars (**fire**), the sign Sagittarius (**fire**), the Antivertex (**fire**), Capricorn (earth), with Sagittarius (**fire**) also on the cusp of the 2nd; the sign Aries (**fire**) on the cusp with nothing in the 6th; the sign Leo (**fire**) on the cusp with nothing in the 10th. The fact that the Sun and Mars are conjunct (widely) and parallel one another adds to the fire emphasis as does Mars conjunct Antivertex (**fire** planets). Since the Sun and Mars fall in "work" houses, we would also look to see where Leo and Aries fall in this chart, as the Sun and Mars rule those signs. Leo falls in the 9th (**fire**) and 10th (earth) houses while Aries falls in the 5th (**fire**) and 6th (earth) houses. Considering the planets which are natural rulers of the earth houses, Venus (as a key to Letter 2) is in the 1st (**fire**), in Scorpio (water), conjunct Jupiter (**fire**) and widely conjunct the Ascendant (**fire**). Mercury (as a key to Letter 6) is in the 1st (**fire**), in Sagittarius (**fire**). If you use the asteroids, Mercury is conjunct Juno (air). With the asteroids, we also look to Ceres and Vesta as forms of Letter 6. Ceres is in the 3rd (air), in Aquarius (air), conjunct the IC (water). Vesta is in the 5th (**fire**), in Pisces (water). Our last earth planet is Saturn (Letter 10) which is in the 9th (**fire**) in Leo (**fire**), widely conjunct Pluto (water). The actual rulers of the earth houses in this chart are Jupiter which is in the 1st (**fire**), in Scorpio (water), conjunct Venus (earth) and the Ascendant (**fire**); Mars which is in the 2nd (earth), in Sagittarius (**fire**), widely conjunct the Sun (**fire**) and the Antivertex (**fire**); the Sun which is in the 2nd (earth), in Sagittarius (**fire**), widely conjunct Mars (**fire**). The earth signs are Taurus, Virgo and Capricorn. Taurus is not occupied. Virgo is occupied by the Moon (water) in the 11th (air). Capricorn is occupied by the Antivertex (**fire**) in the 2nd (earth) and by Pallas (air) in the 3rd (air). If we consider also the other signs present in the 2nd, 6th and 10th houses, we would look at Capricorn, Taurus and Virgo (all three earth). The rulers are Saturn in the 9th (**fire**), in Leo (**fire**) conjunct Pluto (water); Venus in the 1st (**fire**) in Scorpio (water), conjunct Jupiter (**fire**) and the Ascendant (**fire**); Mercury in the 1st (**fire**) in Sagittarius (**fire**) conjunct Juno (air).

We have counted over 50 factors in assessing the career potential, and more than 30 (over half!) of them are fire. Since the average would be about one-quarter, we clearly have a marked theme. (Without the asteroids, the percentage which is fire is even higher.) A reminder: this list is for practice and teaching. Do your scanning mentally to become comfortable with a rapid skim.

We can clearly assume that fire issues will be central in this person's handling of career needs. They would want excitement and action in their work. Restless and probably impatient, they would work best on their own, without supervision. They would be best off in a situation involving some physical activity and variety as they are unlikely to appreciate sitting still for long. Outgoing and expressive, they need work that gives them room to expand, to take risks and to gain feedback from others. They are likely to be confident and full of energy on the job. If carried too far, they could be rash, foolhardy and impulsive in their work. They might fight with people on the job, especially anyone who tried to tell them what to do or how to do it. They would be best off self-employed or with a boss who isn't around.

FIRE

♂, ☉, ♃, ♄, ♈, ♌, ♐, 1st, 5th, 9th houses

Fire (Letters 1, 5, 9) is spontaneous, creative and expressive. The essence of new beginnings, fire has the courage to risk, to take chances, to move into new directions. Naturally spontaneous, fire is outgoing and extraverted. Dynamic, dramatic, energetic, confident and eager, fire is drawn toward excitement. Feeling vital and alive is essential, and strong fire is often a key to great physical vitality, recuperative capacities and the ability to bounce back from almost anything. Optimistic, fire has great faith: in one's own abilities with Letter 1, in one's own power and will with Letter 5 and in a Higher Power with Letter 9.

EARTH
♀, ☿, ?, ⚷, ♄, ♉, ♍, ♑, 2nd, 6th, 10th houses

Earth (Letters 2, 6, 10) denotes practicality, realism, productive efforts and tangible results. Earth shows our relationship with the material world — both the capacity to enjoy it (Letter 2) and the ability to work productively within it (Letters 6 and 10). Earth's focus is on the physical world and attends to pleasures, possessions and measurable accomplishments. Earth is the silly putty we use to manifest our ideas (air), our feelings (water), and our creative impulses (fire).

AIR
☿, ♀, ♀, ⚹, ♅, ♊, ♎, ♒, 3rd, 7th, 11th houses

Air (Letters 3, 7, 11) signifies the objective, detached intellect. A key to our conceptual abilities, air denotes lightness, equalitarian relationships, thinking and perceptions. With air, we deal in mental models — maps to try to describe what we have experienced and done with fire and earth. The essence of air is to accept and understand — the appropriate path where other people are concerned. We learn to relate as equals, communicating and sharing ideas freely, without trying to change or make over the other individual.

WATER
☽, ♇, ♆, ♋, ♏, ♓, 4th, 8th, 12th houses

Water (Letters 4, 8, 12) symbolizes the unconscious mind. On the water level, we assimilate, incorporate and absorb. We take in our experiences and build them into automatic habit patterns, about which we no longer have to think consciously (which is air). Water is the universal solvent, and with water, we either enclose or are absorbed by something bigger. With Letter 4, we care for (as a parent) or are cared for and protected (as a child). With Letter 8, we share intimacy and a close relationship; we have a "we" attitude rather than an "I" attitude. With Letter 12, we are a part of the entire universe, experiencing the grandness and wonder of ultimate Oneness.

Water is a key to autonomic activities and times (such as sleep) when we turn off the conscious mind and allow the unconscious to take over. When processing on a water level, we instinctively seek safety and security to do the inner work. Water is sensitive, intuitive, empathic and psychic. Recognizing the oneness of all, there are no boundaries. Thus, some protection is essential, lest the person feel invaded, overwhelmed, trespassed by feelings and impressions of others. Water merges.

Element Combinations

The basic four elements can also be blended in six element combinations. Remember, we are talking about a lot more than just occupied signs! Element combinations can be emphasized in the following ways: (1) in terms of planetary combinations (e.g., strong, repeated contacts between fire and earth planets point to the fire/earth combination); (2) in terms of planet/house combinations (e.g., all the fire planets falling in earth houses and earth planets occupying mainly fire houses constitute fire/earth); (3) in terms of planet/sign combinations (fire planets in earth signs and earth planets in fire signs focus on fire/earth); (4) in terms of house/sign combinations (e.g., fire signs in earth houses or earth signs in fire houses signify fire/earth blends); or (5) in terms of combinations of any of the above (e.g., strong fire emphasis by house along with strong earth emphasis by sign).

The meaning of each combination follows logically from the two elements involved in the mixture. Imagining the physical manifestation of each combination can also help to conceptualize the themes involved.

FIRE/EARTH or MOLTEN LAVA

♂, ☉, ♃, ⚷, ♈, ♌, ♐, 1st, 5th, 9th houses with
♀, ☿, ⚳, ⚶, ♄, ♉, ♍, ♑, 2nd, 6th, 10th houses

The energetic drive of fire blended with the persistent achievements of earth can make for enduring accomplishments. This can be **the most** productive of all combinations. Able to "keep on keeping on," energetic and capable even when others have fallen aside, people with strong fire/earth combinations tend to be extremely high achievers. Usually, such people feel strong and are seen as strong by those around them.

But don't get in their way! Because they generally know what they want and have the power to go after it, these individuals can be very direct and single-minded in pursuing their goals. Some seem to operate as bulldozers in life and you may feel as if you've been run over if you get in front of a such an individual under full acceleration. After all, would you try to stop a molten lava flow?

If the fire emphasis is predominant, the person will be determined to live life the way **they** want to. Doing their own thing may be predominant, even at the expense of accomplishments. They probably want to be productive only on their own terms, in their own way. They are likely to seek lots of excitement. If the earth is predominant, the person will need measurable results and concrete attainments. If the earth side is so strong as to overwhelm the fire, the individual may even be blocked and depressed rather than pushing the world.

By blending the enthusiasm, confidence and pioneering spirit of the fire with the perseverance and patient thoroughness of the earth, they can create optimum results.

FIRE/AIR or HOT AIR BALLOONS
♂, ☉, ♃, ♭, ♈, ♌, ♐, 1st, 5th, 9th houses with
☿, ♀, ♀, ✳, ♅, ♊, ♎, ♒, 3rd, 7th, 11th houses

Life is often a party for fire/air people. Up, optimistic, extraverted and fun-loving, these people can be perennially on the move. Restless, they seek variety and new experiences. Often quite charming and verbally skilled, they make super sales-people and wonderful entertainers. On occasion, they can also succumb to the foot-in-mouth syndrome. Quick-witted and lively, they keep life interesting. Preferring to stay with their "high," they usually avoid being dragged down by life or other people. They can always leave if they feel things are getting too confined, stuffy or uncomfortable. They provide a lovely leavening for the seriousness of life.

FIRE/WATER or STEAM
♂, ☉, ♃, ♭, ♈, ♌, ♐, 1st, 5th, 9th houses with
☽, ♇, ♆, ♋, ♏, ♓, 4th, 8th, 12th houses

Fire and water are the two emotional elements, while earth and air are the cool, logical and rational elements. The more fire and water emphasis, the more likelihood the person will feel life very intensely. Fire tends to express, while water tends to hold back, so the balance will indicate the probability of more spontaneity or more playing it safe. With fire/water conflicts, the individual may exhibit mood swings, from incredible optimism and elation with the fire side to tremendous pessimism and depression with the water side. There can also be periodic emotional explosions, the water half holding back and holding in until the fire half finally blows the lid. Whiskey in the Old West was "firewater" and this blend can denote very volatile emotions.

If integrated, fire/water blends point to the warmest, most caring, involved individuals. By making a place in their lives for both spontaneous, direct expression of feelings as well as an inward exploring and introspection, these individuals can express the best of both worlds. They feel and are willing to get emotionally involved. They are intense, passionate and wholehearted in their response.

EARTH/AIR or DUST
♀, ☿, ?, ✳, ♄, ♉, ♍, ♑, 2nd, 6th, 10th houses with
☿, ♀, ♀, ✳, ♅, ♊, ♎, ♒, 3rd, 7th, 11th houses

Logical and rational, people with marked earth/air emphases appreciate the mind — both the logical, analytical, theoretical (air) mind and the practical, grounded, sensible (earth) mind. Earth/air blends are optimum for problem-solving and detached assessment of situations. Relatively unfeeling, the theme revolves around dealing sensibly and effectively with the physical world. The talents indicated by earth/air mixtures are essential for fields such as bookkeeping, research, accounting, computer programming, engineering, any kind of repair work, etc.

However, most people would not utilize their earth/air side while making love or cuddling a child or pet.

EARTH/WATER or MUD

♀, ☿, ⚳, ⚶, ♄, ♉, ♍, ♑, 2nd, 6th, 10th houses with
☽, ♇, ♆, ♋, ♏, ♓, 4th, 8th, 12th houses

Earth and water combine practical and nurturing/dependent themes. One potential is the mothers, fathers and saviors of the world — people combining empathy and pragmatism for optimum results by caring for others. Another option is an individual very seriously pursuing his/her own security needs. Since both earth and water are oriented toward safety and protection, the combination can be too serious and even depressive if overdone.

Inclined to support the status quo, earth/water individuals usually hang on to what they have. They help provide stability in life and society. Often quite protective and helpful, it is common for them to carry more than their share of the load and take on more responsibilities than necessary. They usually opt for conservation and security.

AIR/WATER or MIST

☿, ♀, ⚴, ⚵, ♅, ♊, ♎, ♒, 3rd, 7th, 11th houses with
☽, ♇, ♆, ♋, ♏, ♓, 4th, 8th, 12th houses

This is the most internal of the combinations. Where fire/earth demand action in the external world, air/water can be quite content to think, to drift, to dream and live in an inner world of their own. Since air and water blend the conscious and unconscious minds, the combination can be excellent for therapists and psychics, bringing the unconscious material into consciousness with the ability to communicate it. Empathy is marked, with the intuitive connections of water as well as the objective appreciation of other people's viewpoints which air has. Often highly creative and imaginative, air/water people can be perpetual observers and spectators of life, especially if the outer world seems threatening. Properly integrated, the imagery, creativity and inner knowing of water/air can be a great asset in many vocations and many interpersonal situations.

Qualities or Modalities

Astrology can also divide the twelve sides of life into three groups (of four each) called qualities or modalities. These can also be applied to groups of planet/house/sign. The qualities are **cardinal, fixed and mutable**. Every quality group has one each of the elements represented. Thus, there is one fire cardinal, one earth cardinal, one air cardinal and one water cardinal. And so on for fixed and mutable.

Remember in assessing qualities, as with elements, to consider the planet/planet combinations and occupied houses as well as occupied signs.

CARDINAL

♂, ☽, ♀, ⚴, ⚵, ♄, ♈, ♋, ♎, ♑, 1st, 4th, 7th, 10th houses

Strongly cardinal themes (Letters 1, 4, 7, 10) indicate the individuals are likely to learn through events. The school of experience is their best teacher. Unless they have gone through the hard knocks themselves, they often do not learn what is necessary. The tendency is for that area of life (where cardinality is emphasized) to be active and full of events.

The people may **not** feel they initiate these happenings, but they still tend to attract crises into their lives. It is as if they learn only through doing. The major struggle is to balance four large corners of their lives: self-assertion, home and family or domestic needs, partnership and career. They may feel that one part of life continually takes away from another. They may feel torn between these different areas. They may feel that their supply of time and energy is less than they need to meet all their commitments.

Psychologically, this is the struggle among individual freedom, nurturance or dependency, equality and control. People may project or repress any one (or more) of the corners involved, developing the appropriate illness or attracting the appropriate individuals from whom they can learn about the corner they are denying.

Once they make peace, highly cardinal individuals create space in their lives to have hobbies and personal interests where they answer only to themselves; a home and family or nest of some sort (pets are one possibility) where they can protect and be protected; an equalitarian sharing of intimacy with at least one other person; and an arena in the outside world where they are in charge, making things happen. They can express each side of their nature in times and places which are fulfilling rather than frustrating.

This is not to say life becomes ideal. People with strong cardinal emphasis are likely to be reworking the balance lifelong. Day to day, they decide how much time and energy to devote to self-development, domestic needs, partnership desires and achievement drives. Daily, they assess the division and decide anew how to structure their lives.

FIXED

♀, ☉, ♇, ♅, ♉, ♌, ♏, ♒, 2nd, 5th, 8th, 11th houses

Strong fixity (Letters 2, 5, 8 and 11) points to individuals who have marked sensual needs. The material world of money, possessions and pleasures is an important experience for them. The challenge is to be able to give, receive and share comfortably with others. Some people retreat into complete asceticism and withdrawal, believing that is the only way to control their appetites. Some overindulge (whether in food, drink, sex, money, etc.). Some bounce from feast to famine, excesses to extremes of self-denial.

Since inner struggles are often mirrored in the outer world, fixed people tend to attract associates with the same conflicts. So, they can fight (with parents, partners, coworkers, children, friends) about the handling of money, resources, sexuality and material pleasures. Too often, one person identifies with the indulgence; the other identifies with the control end and they have chronic battles over who is right. (They both are.) Finding the middle ground of integration is not always easy.

Willfulness tends to be strong. Fixed people are highly resistant to the influence of others. It is not that they will not change. They can be **very changeable** if Letters 5 and 11 are strongly involved, but **only on their own terms**. They are determined to live their lives in their own way and may even take actions which are the proverbial "cutting off your nose to spite your face" in attempting to prove that they — and only they — are in charge and making their own decisions.

MUTABLE
☿, ? ⚷, ♃, ♅, ♆, ♊, ♍, ♐, ♓, 3rd, 6th, 9th, 12th houses

Mutable (Letters 3, 6, 9, 12) individuals are usually skilled at adapting to the situation. They are able to bend rather than break. Willing to learn vicariously, they need not undergo the crises of the cardinals nor the power struggles of the fixed individuals to figure out what is needed in their lives. Often highly mental, people with a mutable emphasis tend to be versatile with multiple interests. Finding a focus (among their many talents) may be a challenge. Perfectionism is often an issue for strongly mutable people as well, since Letters 9 and 12 (both mutable) are seeking an infinite ideal. Establishing value hierarchies ("this is more important than that"), making choices among multiple options ("I will do this before that") and appreciating the journey toward perfection (not demanding we arrive immediately) can all help mutable individuals cope more effectively in the world.

Polarity Themes

Astrology deals with six basic polarities: six pairs of natural oppositions which can be indicated by houses or signs. (Except for the Sun, Venus and Mercury, any planet could conceivably oppose any other planet, and they will denote one or two of the six basic polarities by house and sign placements.)

Oppositions point to natural partnerships. The two ends of a polarity are **complementary**. Each supplies something the other lacks. The two together do much more than either separately. Zip Dobyns uses the analogy of the human, opposable thumb. The opposable thumb is one thing which distinguishes humans from other primates. Monkeys and apes have a "thumb" which rides uselessly beside the other fingers. Humans, however, can bring the thumb and a finger **from opposite sides** to meet **in the middle**, together accomplishing much more than either could separately. This principle also underlies many of our tools such as pliers, tweezers, vise, etc. Such joint accomplishment is the goal of all polarities — a middle ground synthesis.

NODES OF THE MOON

Every individual has at least one polarity present in his/her chart, and usually two, by virtue of the nodes of the Moon. The nodes are **always** opposite one another and point to polarity issues in the life through the house and sign they occupy. (If the houses and signs repeat the same two letters of the astrological alphabet, that is a reiterated theme and important to note.)

The nodes are less important than planets; they represent points where the Earth and the Moon's orbits intersect. Like the Moon, the nodes are keys to our emotional needs, nurturance, dependency and our bonds to other people. If you want to fit them into the Zip Code, you can think of them as another form of Letter 4. I view them in the birth chart as primarily indicators of polarity issues. (In synastry work — comparing the charts of two or more people for potential compatibility — aspects to the nodes are often keys to relationships having a strong emotional impact.)

In this book, various nodal polarities will be discussed in those sections where they seem appropriate. The section on nodes will follow a discussion of alphabet themes in the text. Following is a brief summary of the six polarities. Remember that these can be emphasized through planets, houses and signs as well as the nodes of the Moon.

1-7, ♂-♀ or ♀ or ⚹, ♈-♎, 1st-7th houses

This is the basic self-versus-other polarity. Here, we are learning to balance what we want with the needs and desires of another person. Assertion meets accommodation as we strive for a balance. The challenge is to sufficiently satisfy our own desires without either overwhelming the other person or allowing the other to ride roughshod over our preferences. Appeasement is not a solution; neither is aggression. Compromise is indicated. Balance is the key.

2-8: ♀-♇, ♉-♏, 2nd-8th houses

This polarity manifests on the inner level as self-indulgence versus self-control. Where Letter 2 would happily eat, drink and be merry unto oblivion, Letter 8 strives for self-mastery, self-discipline and self-control. The resultant ambivalence can sometimes manifest in life as feast versus famine (around food), excessive drinking versus going on the wagon (around alcohol), extravagance versus penny-pinching (around money), sex versus celibacy, or other arenas of appetite indulgence versus appetite control. The challenge is to find a middle ground — to be able to enjoy the sensual, sexual, material world without being ruled by it but also not totally denying physical pleasures.

It is quite common for people to become uncomfortable with such an inner struggle and unconsciously project one end of the seesaw. In such cases, they attract into their lives other people to live out one side of the struggle. So, one person expresses the dieting side; another expresses the overeating side. One partner spends too much; the other partner is a miser. A parent represses his/her sexuality; a child is promiscuous. And so on. The more imbalance, the more extremes exhibited in the lives of the people involved.

With such outer polarizations, it is common for the people involved to point the finger and declaim that "if only that other person would change, everything would be fine!" Alas, if the other person **does** change, all too often the first person merely finds a new partner for the seesaw. The solution is to change **within**. Once we are more balanced internally, we no longer need to attract the external conflict from which to learn. We can draw in equally balanced people, with whom more comfort and mutual pleasure is possible.

3-9: ☿-♃ or ♄, ♊-♐, 3rd-9th houses

This polarity is often expressed in the mental arena. It is commonly present among people who spend their lives learning, teaching others and often traveling for knowledge (mentally if not physically). The perpetual quest for understanding is a major motivation.

However, two kinds of knowledge are being pursued. One is knowledge for its own sake, curiosity about the here-and-now world right around us. This is the kind of intellectual understanding which allows us to relate to people near-at-hand, to share a vocabulary and world view with relatives and neighbors. It enables us to function in the daily world, to fit into consensual reality. It is Letter 3 knowledge and has an immediate, short-range, indiscriminate focus.

By contrast, Letter 9 knowledge is more pointed. The quest is for answers about life's meaning, for an understanding of why we are here and what life is all about. The focus is long-term, on ultimate directions and perceptions. The concern is around ideas and ideals which may not have immediate (or any) relevance to day-to-day functioning. As a key to our idealization and visualization, it is what we are bringing into being, making a reality. It is the basic assumptions by which we run our lives, but unconcerned with petty details.

Thus, the challenge is to balance the two — enough awareness of long-range views to have a plan, to have goals and a vision of the future to pursue, but also enough common sense and understanding of the people and things around us to relate in the everyday world and communicate effectively. With this questioning combination, people often spend much time reevaluating their goals and values, seeking additional variety in the mental world and testing long-range ideas and ideals against the day-to-day needs of existence.

4-10: ☽-♄, ♋-♑, 4th-10th houses (Parental Polarity)

The polarity involved here is usually met first through our parents for here we face the issue of balancing conditional and unconditional love. Letter 4 represents pure caring, support, looking after and nurturance (which one need not earn; it is given because one **is**). Letter 10 represents learning through experience, through trial and error. Reward and punishment are used to mold our behavior, to help us fit into the limits and expectations of a society involving other people.

An excess of the energy depicted by Letter 4 can result in spoiled adults, who expect the world to do everything for them. An excess of the energy depicted by Letter 10 can result in inhibited, blocked adults who feel unlovable because they are judged only in terms of performance and fear no one would love them just for themselves. The challenge of child-rearing is to provide sufficient unconditional love to give the children a firm sense of trust in the world as a nurturing place and in themselves as lovable people, but sufficient conditional love so that they can develop self-discipline, a conscience and the ability to delay gratification appropriately.

The challenge of becoming adult is to develop a sense of being lovable within a realistic perspective that considers the expectations of others in the world we share. The goal is to have an inner core of trust in one's self as valuable and worthwhile, trust in the world as basically supportive with sufficient practicality and responsibility to do one's share of the work in the world and not expect that people will inevitably do what feels best to us. The task of adulthood is to develop these capacities regardless of the kind of parenting we had. And, in the end, we have the only power. Our attitudes, interpretations and assumptions determine how we feel and react much more than any overt events.

As we grow older, we meet the 4-10 polarity in another form, through the balancing of domestic (home, emotional) versus career (practical, status-oriented) issues. The goal, of course, is to maintain both emotional attachments (with a home and "family" in some form — remember, friends, pets, etc. can be family) as well as objective achievements (a career, contribution to the outer world). We learn to balance warmth and pragmatism, empathy and discipline, absorption and limitation.

5-11: ☉-♅, ♌-♒, 5th-11th houses

This polarity deals with the blending of our hearts and our heads. Where Letter 5 is passionate, emotional and spontaneously expressive, Letter 11 is detached, intellectual and aloof. Letter 5 indicates our desire to love and be loved, our creative outlets including children and our need for self-esteem, for pride, for being special in some way. Letter 11 denotes our desire for freedom, individuality and openness to all humanity; it shows our equalitarian capacities, our ability to relate to everyone on an equal level, to truly believe in equal opportunity.

Letter 5 shows our need for close, loving ties with a few other people. Letter 11 shows our need for relating to all people, understanding and accepting them without being emotionally involved. With Letter 11, we can relate as friends, acquaintances or members of a group; we do not have to have deeper feelings involved.

If we set these parts of life at odds with one another, we will indeed feel torn. Our minds war with our passions. Our children compete with our friends for attention. Our humanitarian concerns seem to draw us away from those we love — or vice versa. The challenge is to keep room for both. Our objectivity and detachment can give us a tolerance and openness our lovers and children will appreciate. Our outside involvements make us more interesting people to relate to. Similarly, our ability to love and care intensely gives us an emotional understanding of tolerance and humanitarian ideals that goes much deeper than an intellectual concept. We have room for both self-esteem and a sense of equality with all others. Our passion fuels our commitments to organizations and friends. Our hearts provide energy and drive to pursue goals carefully thought out by our heads.

6-12: ☿ or ⚳ or ⚶-♆, ♍-♓, 6th-12th houses

The confrontation of the real and the ideal is a focus for this polarity. Our vision of infinite love and beauty (Letter 12) faces the nitty-gritty reality of the world (Letter 6), especially in terms of our need to function effectively on the job and in our bodies. Without the dream of Letter 12, Letter 6 is in a squirrel cage, compulsively doing things "just right" with no real sense of meaning or understanding. Without the practicality of Letter 6, Letter 12 can be lost in the clouds, fantasizing grandly with no real accomplishment.

The integration marks practical idealists, realistic mystics, helpers and healers who do a great job, and marvelous artists and craftspeople. In its highest manifestation, the 6-12 blend is the old saw of inspiration (12) and perspiration (6) combined for optimum results!

A Potpourri of Themes

A number of other possible themes which are mixtures of different letters of the alphabet are available. The following are those themes I have found most useful in working with charts. Other potential themes exist and can be conceptualized by the working astrologer. Some of the themes listed here have large areas of overlap (e.g., obsessive-compulsive with the work/competence theme) but still some demarcations between them. Feel free to elaborate or condense as the spirit moves you!

FREEDOM

♂, ♃, ⚷, ♅, ♈, ♐, ♒, 1st, 9th, 11th houses

The need to be free, independent and not tied down is indicated by Letters 1, 9 and 11 of the astrological alphabet. They point to a seeking of liberty, an avoidance of restrictions or commitments. Depending on the other keys involved, the freedom theme could be manifested mainly in personal relationships (footloose and fancy-free), in job situations (often self-employed, or with a boss who does not closely supervise, or quitting and getting fired from the frustrations of feeling hemmed in vocationally), in beliefs (resistant to anyone else's beliefs, unwilling to accept any dogmas, oriented toward openness and exploration of ideas) or other areas.

"No man is an island," but people do vary in their needs for independence. Each of us must choose when, where and how much to express our needs for liberty and doing our own thing in the world.

CLOSENESS

☽, ☉, ♀, ⚴, ⚵, ♇, ♋, ♌, ♎, ♏, 4th, 5th, 7th, 8th houses

Letters 4, 5, 7 and 8 show the human need for close, emotional attachments. They are connected to a desire for a mate, home, family and children — or some kind of emotional support system. (Friends can play the role of family. Pets can meet the needs served by children, etc.) The yearning here is to share feelings with others, to care for and to be cared for, to love and to be loved. Letter 4 is the nurturance/dependence polarity; Letter 5 is the desire to pour out into the world (including through love) and get a response; Letter 7 is the desire to communicate and share space with another human being, and Letter 8 is the quest for a mate, someone to share the sensual/sexual/material world for mutual pleasure. All seek a connection to other beings. That bond can be very pleasant, cooperative and rewarding, but it can also be competitive and challenging. There is a need for people, an attraction toward interactions, but that is not inevitably easy and flowing.

An overdose of closeness can be suffocating to even the most loving of relationships. "Clutchy," possessive and smothering interactions do not build further intimacy. Too much other-directedness is not healthy for self-esteem and assertion needs. The need for love is as universal as the need for air and food, but each person finds his/her own ways, means, methods and amounts of giving and receiving love, of sharing life with other human beings.

ARTISTIC

♀, ⚴, ⚵, ☉, ♆, ♉, ♌, ♎, ♓, 2nd, 5th, 7th, 12th houses

Beauty and aesthetics are important parts of life. Letters 2, 7 and 12 are especially connected to the appreciation and creation of beauty in the world. Letter 2 is most associated with tactile forms of beauty, e.g., sculpture, fabrics, pottery, etc. Letter 7 is a major key to the visual arts, e.g., architecture, design, photography, painting, graphics, etc. Letter 12 is most flexible and adaptable, symbolic of almost any kind of artistic effort. Letter 5 is a major indicator of creative efforts, the need to pour out into the world and receive a response. If Letter 5 is mixed with any of the other three beauty letters, self-expression in an aesthetic mode is likely.

Naturally, if misdirected, such potentials could express as too much concern with appearances, an excessive need for pleasure and beauty (and avoidance of conflict), a self-centered desire for pleasure or a passive attitude which waits for someone else to make everything lovely. If personal responsibility is accepted, the individual is likely to both appreciate and create beauty in the world.

IDEALISTIC
4, ♄, Ψ, ♐, ♓, 9th, 12th houses

Our search for more, our yearning for something Higher, our quest for meaning in life, are denoted by Letters 9 and 12. Both point to, in some fashion, our seeking of God. Letters 9 and 12 are connected to idealization and visualization. Whatever we set up as the greatest good or an ultimate value, we tend to pursue and actualize in our lives. Letter 9 is our pursuit of an intellectual absolute; Letter 12 is our quest for an emotional absolute.

In both cases, it is quite common to want more than is possible. Where the Infinite is the standard, how can anything measure up? Wherever Letters 9 or 12 are involved in the horoscope, they point to an area we can easily idolize, ending up disappointed and disillusioned. Sometimes, we end up losing whatever (or whomever) we have put up on a pedestal in order to realize that it — a relationship, a job, a child — is not the Infinite for which we yearn.

People need something to reach for, a goal, an inspiration. The challenge is to look for our sense of ecstasy, our connection to something Higher, our ultimate understanding, in areas of life that **are** infinite (such as art, nature, religion, spiritual endeavors), and not expect godlike perfection from ourselves, our loved ones or limited parts of our lives.

Letters 9 and 12 are both connected to idealization and visualization — the quest for something more. The search is on a more traditionally intellectual plane with Letter 9 (answers to the meaning of the universe) while on a more emotional/intuitive plane with Letter 12 (merging with all there is in the universe). However, in both cases, we are dealing with the theme of **images, dreams and visions**. In both areas, we are facing questions of "What if?" I think of Letters 9 and 12 as areas of imagination, visualization and — potentially — actualization. It is quite true that thoughts/attitudes/emotions lead to physical results. What we idealize, value and focus on often in our thoughts/feelings, we tend to create as a reality in our world. Thus, it is no surprise to me that the Gauquelins found planets residing in the 9th and 12th houses to be fundamental, **keynote** indicators of profession and character in highly successful people. Their visualizations led to manifestations!

OBSESSIVE-COMPULSIVE
☿, ♁, ⚸, ♇, ♄, ♍, ♏, ♑, 6th, 8th, 10th houses

Letters 6, 8 and 10 all share an obsessive-compulsive theme. They all symbolize the potential of depth, concentration, organizational skills, obsessiveness, concern with details, thoroughness and perseverance. Such a theme in a chart can be great for research, graduate school, business or any activity that requires a careful, painstaking and disciplined approach. But, if clients are using their obsessiveness in their relationships (picking at a partner) or with their children (criticizing a child and trying to make him/her over) or with themselves (obsessing over every little error), there is a problem. It is not that the obsessive-compulsive ability is bad; it is simply that the clients are applying it to uncomfortable areas in their lives. If they channel those skills instead into careers, mental concentration, fix-it projects or other physical, task orientations — there need not be any difficulties!

COMPETENCE (WORK)

☿, ⚳, ⚶, ♄, ♍, ♑, 6th, 10th houses

Letters 6 and 10 apply to the drive to be efficient, practical, productive, sensible and work successfully in the world. Both are oriented toward searching for flaws in order to improve the current situation. Both tend toward a critical, judgmental attitude. Both tend to be cool, calculating and logical rather than emotional.

The flaw-finding lens of Letters 6 and 10 is oriented toward discovering what is wrong in order to fix it and make it better. This can be extremely valuable on the job or wherever the orientation is toward the physical world and a task of some kind. However, if this critical analysis is channeled against people, it can be a problem. Whether the issue is self-criticism (Letters 6 and/or 10 mixed with Letters 1 and/or 5), criticism in close relationships (6 and 10 mixed with 7 and 8), the danger is that the focus on what is wrong will create barriers in the closeness and caring between the people.

This can be an issue with parents (4 and 10), with children (5 and, to a lesser extent, 4), with partners (7 and 8) or almost anyone. The challenge is to keep relationships, (air), as arenas where we accept and understand without trying to change — the essence of air — while channeling our needs to critically analyze and make over (earth) into earth arenas (such as careers and physical tasks).

MIND/COMMUNICATION

☿, ⚳, ⚶, ⚴, ♃, ⚷, ♅, ♆, ♊, ♍, ♎, ♐, ♒, ♓,
3rd, 6th, 7th, 9th, 11th, 12th houses

The mental arena is symbolized by both air (Letters 3, 7 and 11) and mutables (Letters 3, 6, 9 and 12) in the horoscope. Air applies especially to the logical, linear (left-brain) kinds of thinking. It denotes our capacity for detachment and objectivity. Mutables denote our mental flexibility and adaptability. They point to vicarious learning, through observing and listening to other people. With all four elements present in the mutables, we can use the mind for expression (fire) with Letter 9, for tangible results (earth) with Letter 6, for objective understanding (air) with Letter 3 and for intuitive insights (water) with Letter 12.

The water form of wisdom is not what most people think of when considering intellectual prowess. Thus, many would exclude Letter 12 from a mental theme, or give it less weight. Our society is very biased in favor of left-brain (linear) insights. The more global, intuitive approach has been derided and minimized. However, it is just as essential, although often overlooked, because its understanding may not come through words, or through concepts easily expressed.

I include all mutables and air in the arena of the mind, but you can limit the focus to certain parts if you prefer to hone in on one or another kind of thinking.

RELATIONSHIPS

♀, ⚴, ⚵, ♇, ♎, ♏, 7th, 8th houses

Letters 7 and 8 point to our one-to-one interactions with other people. They indicate our need for face-to-face interchanges. This includes the potential of projection — facing parts of our own nature through the mirror of another person. The focus includes partnerships such as marriage, living together and business partners. It also includes any regular, systematic, ongoing relationships such as counselor-client. Cooperative relationships are one option, but competitive relationships are another. Competition is still a face-to-face, one-to-one interaction. In competition, we build our strength and test our abilities against those of another individual. With Letters 7 and 8, we are learning to share equally with other people, to relate fairly, to take turns, to know when to compete and when to cooperate.

SECURITY

♀, ☽, ☿, ⚳, ⚶, ♇, ♄, ♆, ♉, ♋, ♍, ♏, ♑, ♓, 2nd, 4th, 6th, 8th, 10th, 12th houses

Earth and water, in general, point to security needs. Both elements are keys to the desire to conserve, to care for, to preserve. Somewhat serious, people with an earth/water emphasis tend to be supportive and helpful; they are often found in nurturing roles. One danger is overdoing the rescue role and ending up carrying too much of the load of people around them. Or, if earth/water people take themselves and life too seriously, they can feel depressed and anxious. Then the water need for emotional attachment can lead to wanting other people to care for them. Generally, the compassion of water mixed with the practicality of earth points to very caring and capable individuals.

Earth and water have an investment in the past — water for emotional reasons (attachment) and earth through the desire to preserve past efforts and productivity. These elements suggest someone inclined to first try methods which have worked before, to follow traditional routes. Protectiveness is a common theme and earth and water usually eschew taking chances. Letter 12 is a possible exception. When the individual with strong Letter 12 has faith in a Higher Power, nothing else is needed. Like the Christians in the dens of lions, such individuals can face anything without fear. (When lacking faith in a Higher Power, Letter 12 individuals can be the most insecure and anxious of all.) However, the other earth and water letters (2, 4, 6, 8 and 10) are usually oriented toward safety, protection, care, caution, preservation and maintenance of the status quo.

RISK/CREATIVITY/CHANGE
♂, ☉, ♃, ♴, ♅, ♈, ♌, ♐, ♒, 1st, 5th, 9th, 11th houses

Fire and Letter 11 are the major risk-takers in the zodiac. Water and earth, in general, are oriented toward preservation and safety. Fire and air are more concerned with variety and something new. However, Letters 3 and 7 denote sufficient concern for the people near-at-hand not to get too caught up in taking chances. Fire thrives on excitement and is the essence of outthrust and creativity. Letter 11 is drawn to the new and the different. Letters 1, 5, 9 and 11 have the physical and intellectual courage to live life on the edge, to go for it, to risk in order to gain a desired reward, to push forward into unknown territory.

Naturally, anything can be carried to an extreme. Excessive expression of the drives denoted by Letters 1, 5, 9 and 11 can be rash, foolish and create a life of constant uproar and chaos. Yet being alive involves risks and change. Each person must seek his/her own, personal balance between too many chances and too much caution.

POWER
☉, ♇, ♄, ♌, ♏, ♑, 5th, 8th, 10th houses

And what of a power theme? Most astrologers correlate a drive for control, authority and an impact on the world with Sun, Pluto, Saturn (5, 8 and 10) plus their houses and signs. Certainly, mixtures of 5, 8 and 10 (such as the traditional Saturn or Pluto in the 10th) **can be** dictatorial and authoritarian. But that does **not** have to be bad! Power is neutral; the question is what the person does with it. An intense power drive can be the energy behind success in competitive sports, reaching the top in the business world, fighting for a worthy cause and defending the rights of everyone to a place in the sun.

People who have an instinctive power drive had better not ignore it; it will **not** go away. Repression will lead most likely to illness. Projection can attract other people who are power-hungry; while with displacement the individual may unconsciously fall into power struggles with the people s/he **wants** to cooperate with (such as loved ones). Encourage clients to channel that forcefulness into arenas that will be satisfying for them and the other people in their lives!

PERSONAL
♂, ♀, ☿, ☽, ♈, ♉, ♊, ♋, 1st, 2nd, 3rd, 4th houses

The zodiac can be envisioned as an evolutionary spiral or the human cycle of birth to adulthood. The first four houses and signs (and the planets ruling them) refer to the **personal** side of life, or the child. We begin with Letter 1, with simple being and action. "I am me; I do what I want when I want." We proceed to Letter 2, where we meet the physical world and seek to enjoy it through pleasures, appetite indulgence and beauty in tangible form. Next comes Letter 3, where we step back and look at the situation from a detached, objective viewpoint. Here, we strive to share the experience with those near at hand, to communicate our knowledge and understanding and gain theirs. With Letter 4, we absorb and assimilate the experience, make it ours on the unconscious level, where it becomes a part of our emotional foundation and support. Here too, we seek emotional security from life — the protection to meet our basic needs and desires, the safety to master our tasks thus far.

No matter what our age, we never lose the "child" needs (and rights) to be who we are, to enjoy ourselves and our world, to satisfy our curiosity and exercise our mind, and to seek emotional security and support.

INTERPERSONAL
(☽), ☉, (☿, ?, ⚵), ♀, ♀, ⚹, ♇, (♋), ♌, (♍), ♎, ♏,
(4th), 5th, (6th), 7th, 8th houses

The next four houses and signs (and their rulers) symbolize our capacity for adult relationships. Here, we go beyond personal needs and desires to interact on an equal basis with the people around us. We learn to work and to do our share while compromising and cooperating with those around us. At times, we may compete as well, but the basic focus is on one-to-one exchanges with other people. Our awareness of others and exchanges with them stimulate our development of the capacities to love, to achieve, to balance and to share.

In terms of its feeling-tone, Letter 6 is somewhat of an anomaly. Although connected to face-to-face interactions, its basic milieu is the workplace. Thus, its focus is cool and practical, while Letters 5, 7 and 8 all have emotional and feeling overtones. Also, Letter 4, although very personal in its search for security and safety, can also be interpersonal, in its nurturing care for others.

Thus, Letter 4 can be considered both personal and interpersonal, and Letter 6 is interpersonal, but lacks the strong emotional connection associated with 4, 5, 7 and 8. (See also the "closeness" theme discussed above.)

TRANSPERSONAL
♃, ⚷, ♄, ♅, ♆, ♐, ♑, ♒, ♓, 9th, 10th, 11th, 12th houses

The last four houses and signs (and their rulers) point to relationships with the world at large. Here, we face issues of the greatest good for the greatest number, relating to the establishment, to society, to people as groups rather than individuals. Letters 9 through 12 are keys to our ideas and ideals, long-range goals, handling of global perspectives, awareness of history and ability to see the whole.

A wider perspective can be very valuable in working with large issues and concerns, but the aloofness of the overview can be a drawback if carried into too much of one's life. Concern for the world as a whole and its problems is intended as a balance to personal needs and interpersonal sharing. One is not intended to overshadow or deny the other.

UNFINISHED BUSINESS

Wherever we are meeting other people, we are learning about ourselves. The people around us mirror back to us some of our own, unactualized potentials. We generally attract (unconsciously) individuals to express the sides of our nature with which we are least comfortable. They "do it for us" in a sense. However, if we continue to let them "do it for us," they will usually overdo and carry to an extreme what can be a very positive side of life. It is almost as if their exaggeration is designed to make it easier for us to identify the themes involved.

Finding ourselves repeating certain patterns and attracting the same sorts of people over and over again is an important message. We need to look at the behavior of such a person, figure out what that individual is **over**doing, and express the energy **in moderation** in our own lives.

For most of us, the first opportunities for learning through others come through our families. The family is like a crucible that sets a mold for later relationships. Often, we do not complete the learning, so continue to attract other people (friends, mates, children) to mirror back those qualities with which we are still having trouble. The mold repeats until we master those attributes.

The horoscope is a wonderful guide for indicating the potential of repeated projections. We can note the potential by watching the mixtures in the horoscope of the letters involved with various people.

Parents and Partners

☽, ♄, ⚳, ♋, ♑, 4th, 10th houses with ♀, ⚴, ⚵, ♇, ♎, ♏, 7th, 8th houses

Since parents are shown by Letters 4 and 10 and partners are indicated by 7 and 8, a mixture of 4 and/or 10 with 7 and/or 8 shows a blend of parent and partner themes. This denotes the potential of meeting unfinished business with Mom or Dad through later partnerships. The individual may "marry" Mom or Dad figuratively — picking someone who elicits the same kinds of feelings, the same kinds of reactions as s/he had with his/her parents — until the issues are resolved. Or, we can pick partners who set us up in the role of "Mommy" or "Daddy" rather than an equal partner. Another option is having a partnership relationship with our own parents — perhaps even so fulfilling, we are disinclined to seek other partnerships. The main theme is that parental issues are mixed with partnership ones, and unfinished business (feelings, attitudes, perceptions) from our relationship to our parents could easily spill over and affect our partnerships. We need to be clear and make sure we are expressing the potentials in a manner which is satisfying to us and the partner.

Siblings and Friends

☿, ♊, 3rd house with ♅, ♒, 11th house

We can also mix Letter 3 with Letter 11. Since Letter 3 designates siblings (and other relatives) while Letter 11 points to friends in general, this can indicate siblings who become friends, friends who are treated more like family (a brother or sister). We could end up in groups or associations with people who remind us of an early relative. They may appear to act "just like" a brother or sister we did not get along with. They may push the same buttons an aunt or uncle did. The challenge is to face those issues left over from the past in the current relationship in such a way as to gain resolution and mastery of the conflicts. If, for example, we always felt overshadowed by a "brighter" sibling, we are likely to continue to attract associates who seem "brighter, more capable, etc." until we master our feelings of inadequacy and come to appreciate our own uniqueness and the fact that we are irreplaceable. If we can come to see differing forms of intellect, various kinds of understanding, we are more likely to value our own mental approach and fall less often into the comparison trap.

Summary: Repeated Projections

When issues in the horoscope are mixed with the following areas, we **may** relive certain early reactions and feelings — until we master the issues involved. The following people may be significant in our learning experiences:

Letter 1: grandparents
Letter 2: parents of friends
Letter 3: siblings, cousins, aunts, uncles, nieces, nephews, neighbors
Letter 4: mom or dad (the nurturing parent or parental figure)
Letter 5: children or lovers
Letter 6: colleagues and coworkers
Letter 7: partners of all kinds, close friends, grandparents
Letter 8: mates, parents of friends
Letter 9: grandchildren, professors, religious figures, in-laws
Letter 10: dad or mom (the reality or rulemaker parent or parental figure), authorities including boss on the job
Letter 11: friends, acquaintances, foster children, step-children, children of others, humanity at large
Letter 12: inmates, institutionalized individuals, fantasy figures

Each time we meet the same issue, we have an opportunity to learn, a chance to master the situation. We can incorporate new ways of being, interacting and feeling. We can release old ideas, images and impressions. We can remove the "mask" of the past from the present and live fully in the now, rather than reacting to present-day people as if they were figures from our past. We can complete our "unfinished business" and move on to new challenges and opportunities in life!

Alphabet Themes by Twos

Often, the major motifs in a given life area seem to be two (or several) letters of the astrological alphabet. Many of the alphabet combinations by twos repeat themes already discussed. Following is a list of the categories into which each "combination by two" can be fit. The themes are listed in approximate order of importance. In some cases, a significant conflict will be indicated (e.g., security versus risk) which necessitates the blending of two separate themes. You can use this list as a reference to read in more detail about the various combinations by two in the chart.

Abbreviated summaries for **all** the combinations by twos are also given in Chapters 6, 7, 8 and 9 — for identity, work, relationships and mind. Themes by twos for other sections can be extrapolated from these.

1-2:   Personal, Fire-Earth
1-3:   Fire-Air, Personal
1-4:   Freedom vs. Closeness, Fire-Water, Cardinal
1-5:   Fire, Risk
1-6:   Fire-Earth
1-7:   Polarity, Fire-Air, Personal vs. Interpersonal, Cardinal
1-8:   Fire-Water, Personal vs. Interpersonal, Freedom vs. Closeness
1-9:   Freedom, Fire, Risk
1-10:   Fire-Earth, Personal vs. Transpersonal, Cardinal
1-11:   Freedom, Fire-Air, Risk
1-12:   Fire-Water, Personal vs. Transpersonal
2-3:   Personal, Earth-Air
2-4:   Personal, Earth-Water, Security
2-5:   Fixed, Security vs. Risk, Fire-Earth
2-6:   Earth, Competence
2-7:   Artistic, Earth-Air
2-8:   Polarity, Earth-Water, Fixed
2-9:   Fire-Earth, Personal vs. Transpersonal
2-10:   Earth, Security, Competence
2-11:   Fixed, Security vs. Risk, Earth-Air
2-12:   Artistic, Earth-Water, Personal vs. Transpersonal
3-4:   Personal, Air-Water
3-5:   Fire-Air
3-6:   Mutable, Mind, Earth-Air
3-7:   Air, Personal vs. Interpersonal
3-8:   Air-Water, Personal vs. Interpersonal
3-9:   Polarity, Mutable, Fire-Air, Mind
3-10:   Earth-Air, Personal vs. Transpersonal
3-11:   Air, Personal vs. Transpersonal, Mind

3-12:   Mutable, Air-Water
4-5:   Closeness, Fire-Water
4-6:   Earth-Water, Security
4-7:   Closeness, Cardinal, Air-Water
4-8:   Water, Closeness
4-9:   Fire-Water, Interpersonal vs. Transpersonal, Freedom vs. Closeness,
          Security vs. Risk
4-10:   Polarity, Parents, Water-Earth, Security, Cardinal
4-11:   Air-Water, Security vs. Risk, Freedom vs. Closeness
4-12:   Water
5-6:   Fire-Earth
5-7:   Fire-Air, Closeness
5-8:   Power, Fire-Water, Fixed
5-9:   Fire, Risk
5-10:   Power, Fire-Earth, Interpersonal vs. Transpersonal
5-11:   Polarity, Fire-Air, Freedom vs. Closeness, Fixed, Risk
5-12:   Fire-Water, Interpersonal vs. Transpersonal
6-7:   Earth-Air
6-8:   Obsessive-Compulsive, Earth-Water
6-9:   Mutable, Competence (Real) vs. Idealistic, Fire-Earth, Mind
6-10:   Competence, Earth, Obsessive-Compulsive
6-11:   Earth-Air, Mind
6-12:   Polarity, Mutable, Earth-Water
7-8:   Relationships, Air-Water, Closeness
7-9:   Fire-Air, Interpersonal vs. Transpersonal
7-10:   Cardinal, Interpersonal vs. Transpersonal, Relationships vs. Work
          (Competence), Air-Earth
7-11:   Air, Relationships vs. Freedom
7-12:   Artistic, Air-Water, Interpersonal vs. Transpersonal
8-9:   Fire-Water, Interpersonal vs. Transpersonal, Freedom vs. Closeness
8-10:   Obsessive-Compulsive, Power, Earth-Water, Security
8-11:   Security vs. Risk, Interpersonal vs. Transpersonal, Freedom vs.
          Closeness, Air-Water, Fixed
8-12:   Water, Interpersonal vs. Transpersonal
9-10:   Transpersonal, Fire-Earth, Competence (Real) vs. Idealistic
9-11:   Freedom, Risk, Transpersonal, Fire-Air, Mind
9-12:   Idealistic, Fire-Water, Transpersonal, Mutable
10-11:   Transpersonal, Earth-Air
10-12:   Transpersonal, Competence (Real) vs. Idealistic, Earth-Water
11-12:   Transpersonal, Air-Water

   This list is not exhaustive; it is merely a summary I have found useful in my work. Similarly, this chapter could not include all possible themes — merely those which I have found most helpful and most common in my work with astrology.

You can deduce themes of your own, based on a familiarity with the principles of the astrological alphabet. For example, the future theme is discussed in Chapter 17. One could also extrapolate a "past" theme — those letters of the astrological alphabet most associated with past, what has been before, the foundations of what we have now. Most astrologers associate all the water letters — 4, 8 and 12 — with the past, as well as Letter 10 which has much to do with consequences of past actions.

A theme which I use sometimes (in terms of basic identity or work) is that of possible mechanical skills. This is indicated by combinations of Letters 1 (metal tools and weapons), 3 (eye-mind-hand coordination), 6 (critical eye, instinct for taking things apart) and 11 (new technology). People with such mixtures, especially the planetary combinations which are the most emphatic form (e.g., Mercury/Mars/Uranus contacts), have much potential skill with mechanical things and an intuitive sense of how things work and what is necessary to make physical objects function more efficiently.

Naturally, other themes exist as well. I hope you will feel free to expand on this collection of themes with your own experience, logic and intuition.

CHAPTER FIVE

ASPECTS

Aspects refer to the angular distance between two planets (or points, such as the Ascendant and Midheaven). Aspects underline certain themes by emphasizing various planets, or combinations of planets. In considering aspects, the basic rule of thumb is: the closer the orb, the more important the aspect. **All** 1° orb aspects are important. Aspects up to a 3° orb are often important. After that, much depends on the context of the chart.

Orb refers to the issue of how much leeway we can allow and still consider that a given aspect exists. A conjunction, for example, is an aspect of 0° — the planets are (theoretically) in the same degree of the same sign. However, almost any astrologer would agree that two planets within a degree of each other are conjunct. Most astrologers would feel that two planets within three degrees are conjunct. Some astrologers will allow a conjunction (between the Sun and Moon) up to 15° away!

There are no "final truths" on orbs. The closer the orb, the more important the aspect. But, how far afield one should go and still count the aspect is an individual question. For the beginner who has not yet decided on orbs, I would suggest you play with the following orbs: conjunction — 6°; square, trine or opposition — 5°; sextile or quincunx — 3°; octile, tri-octile or semisextile — 1°. Do **not** feel bound by them. Experiment, and be willing to use smaller or larger orbs with any chart or as it feels appropriate.

Some of the questions you can ask yourself, when considering aspects with somewhat wide orbs, include:

A. Does the wide orb aspect **repeat a theme** already said in other ways? If so, you can probably count it. If it does not repeat a theme, the aspect is probably not significant.

B. Does the wide orb aspect tie into a major configuration (such as grand square, T-square, grand trine, etc.)?[1] Involvement with other closer aspects tends to "tighten" seemingly wide orbs. Thus, the **rolling conjunction** principle: with planets at 5°, 8°, 12°, 16°, and 19° of a sign, we have a "rolling conjunction" where they are all considered conjunct each other. (Normally, one would not "count" a conjunction from 5° to 19° of a sign. But here, due to the other planets in the middle, it "works.")

C. Are there a lot of tight, close aspects in the chart? If so, you do not need to go far afield, stretching your orbs. There is already plenty to work with, using narrow orbs.

When considering the chart as a whole (see also Chapter 18), the ideal would be to sum all aspects (giving less weight to wider aspects).

The following aspects are in general use in astrology:
conjunction 0°, semisextile 30°, octile 45°, sextile 60°, square 90°, trine 120°, tri-octile 135°, quincunx 150° and opposition 180°.[2] These aspects are based on relationships in zodiacal longitude, using the ecliptic. Many astrologers also use two aspects called parallel and contra-parallel which are based on declination, using the equator.[3]

Harmony Aspects

Harmony aspects (e.g., the grand trine) indicate parts of our own nature which are in agreement, work easily together, tend to reinforce and support one another. A smooth, easy flow sounds lovely, but remember, such a pattern can be a key

---

1. Beginners, a "T-square" involves at least three planets. Two form an opposition, while the third is square both ends of the opposition. (If lines were drawn between the planets, a "T" would be formed.) A "grand cross" or "grand square" involves four planets, all square and opposite one another. They form the corners of an imaginary square or cross. A "grand trine" involves three planets, all trine one another. Imaginary connecting lines would form a triangle.

   Suggested orbs (to start playing with) for major configurations is six degrees. Intepretations for these configurations are found in Chapter 18 (overview).

2. Beginners, learning your elements and qualities will help you to spot aspects. Any planets near to the same degree (regardless of sign) form aspects to one another. If they are one sign away, the aspect is a semisextile. Two signs is a sextile; three is a square; four is a trine; five is a quincunx and six is an opposition. (The exceptions are planets very late or very early in a sign. For example, a planet at 29 degrees of Leo is trine a planet at 1 degree of Capricorn, even though they are "five" signs away, they are really only 121 degrees apart, which is about four signs.)

   Another way to spot aspect is that all the elements trine one another (fire trines fire; earth trines earth, etc.). All the qualities square or oppose one another (cardinal is square and opposite other cardinals, etc.). Earth and water are either sextile or opposite one another. Air and fire are either sextile or opposite one another. If you memorize the six basic oppositions in astrology, the quincunxes are just one side of an opposition. Octiles and tri-octiles are harder to spot visually, as they involve 1½ or 4½ signs, but can be learned with practice. (Again, planets late in one sign or early in another will not fit this description. The final judgment is the exact number of degrees involved in determining an aspect.)

3. Parallels occur when two planets are within one degree of one another in declination, both north or both south. Contra-parallels occur when two planets are within one degree of one another, one north and the other south declination. Most astrologers agree on a strict one-degree orb for declination aspects.

to excesses. If several sides of our basic nature are all in agreement about what to do, it becomes easy to overdo in that area!

Thus, fire trines can represent too much in the area of self-confidence, going after what you want, optimism and initiative. There is nothing (outside of a Sun/Jupiter/Mars conjunction) so suggestive of personal power, drive and confidence as a grand trine among the fire planets (Sun, Mars, Jupiter). Trines involving fire houses or fire signs repeat such themes. People with earth trines (with planets the most emphatic statement) can overdo in practicality, hard work, responsibility, carrying the load, being serious. Air trine individuals can carry detachment, intellectualization and logic to an extreme. Water trines may show an overdose of sensitivity, empathy and openness on the psychic level to the whole world. Again, these are areas of potential talent; just don't get carried away!

Sextiles also show harmony between the life area under consideration and the themes indicated by the planets making the sextiles, but are not as emphatic as trines. The signs involved in sextiles are usually compatible (fire with air or earth with water). Thus, they reinforce one another's tendency toward stability and status quo (earth/water) or change and motion (fire/air). Semisextiles indicate a very slight potential harmony. Their potential is that of stepping stones. Each of the neighboring signs builds on the foundation of the one preceding it.

Conflict Aspects

Conflict aspects (square, opposition, octile, tri-octile and quincunx) are keys to parts of our psyche which do not blend easily and naturally. We have to pay attention in order to combine them; it does not simply flow. We need some effort and discipline to do these parts of life together. Once we make that integration, we are more versatile, talented and able to handle a wider variety of themes in life. Until we can make the combination, we tend to feel frustrated, blocked, torn between conflicting and contradictory needs. There is often ambivalence involved where challenging aspects are a key: "I want it, but I don't want it." The compromise position involves some of both sides (or all three sides with a T-square; all four with a grand cross). This can mean a compromise position (a little of each) or choosing different times and places in our lives to live out the various options.

For example, the inner tension between Mars, Moon, Venus (as ruler of Libra) and Saturn; or between 1st, 4th, 7th and 10th houses; or between Aries, Cancer, Libra and Capricorn, is the struggle between our needs for freedom, closeness, equality and control. This manifests on the outer level as choosing among self-development, home and family, a partnership and a career in the outside world. Time and energy commitments to each area must be weighed. We must make compromises to have room in our lives for all of them. If we try to choose any one corner at the expense of any other, we pay a price. And yet, blending self-assertion and personal needs with the desire for emotional closeness, caring and interdependency is not easy. It takes effort, attention and concentration. It may be we meet our freedom needs more in certain contexts with certain people and handle our closeness needs more in other situations, with different people. But both must be met.

Squares, oppositions and quincunxes are more emphatic than octiles and tri-octiles, but an exact octile is a stronger statement than a wide square. Quincunxes may be among the most challenging of aspects as the signs involved have nothing in common. With a square or opposition, the signs involved usually share a quality. In addition, the six polarities (oppositions) in astrology point to natural partnerships — parts of life that need one another and are complementary. Octiles and tri-octiles, like quincunxes, are where we seek to combine very different sides of our nature. Such aspects point to the need for attention and discipline, to consciously make room for both in our lives.

Delineating Aspects: Conjunctions

When focusing on one specific life area, first include only conjunctions involving that area. Conjunctions indicate mixtures — that the parts of life symbolized by the planets conjuncting one another are automatically blended. You do not get one without the other. They may blend easily (especially if the planets are sextile or trine in the natural zodiac) or with inner conflicts (more likely if the planets are square, opposite or quincunx in the natural zodiac). However, with a conjunction, the themes are inextricably bound to one another. The goal is to find a positive blend.

If, for example, you are analyzing the area of long-term relationships (Letters 7 and 8), you would include the nature of any planets making conjunctions to Venus or Pluto (plus Pallas and Juno if you use the asteroids). You would also include any conjunctions to rulers of the 7th and 8th houses. Any conjunctions **in** the 7th or 8th houses would be automatically tallied when you looked at what was occupying those houses. All of these aspects would be added to other factors making up Letters 7 and 8 in the chart to sum the relationship potential. In most cases, that sum will include some inner conflicts and ambivalences that need to be faced and mastered.

Themes through Aspects Other Than Conjunctions

Consider all the aspects (other than conjunctions) to that life area you are delineating (e.g., Letters 7 and 8). Group these aspects into harmony (trines, sextiles and semisextiles) or conflict (octiles, tri-octiles, squares, oppositions and quincunxes) and look for themes. Let us continue with the example of delineating someone's prospects for relationships. Suppose a woman has Venus quincunx **Saturn**, Pluto in the 7th square Mercury in the **10th**, Neptune in the 8th octile the **Midheaven**, and the ruler of the 7th tri-octile the ruler of the **Midheaven**.

This would give us a theme of Letter 10 in conflict with the relationship arena. We can interpret this as a challenge to integrate her equality/sharing needs with her control/power needs. We can see the potential of time/energy conflicts between relationships and work. We can see the call to balance beauty, ease and aesthetics with functionality, pragmatics and hard work. It is clear that these differing drives can also supplement one another, but only if the individual turns them into complementary rather than conflicting desires. And that takes time, attention and discipline.

Still looking at the same area, suppose that Venus trines the ruler of the **4th**, the **Moon** sextiles Pluto, and Neptune is in the 7th trining Saturn in the **4th**. Here we have a repeated theme of Letter 4 in harmony with the relationship area. This suggests the individual could easily blend her dependency/nurturance needs with her equality needs. It implies that compromise and taking turns between partnership and domestic duties could be handled with relative ease. It shows the potential for easy flow between partners and a parent. It indicates the potential that a feeling for beauty could help build a sense of emotional security and safety. It connotes that her feelings for her nest would assist in relating as an equal and sharing a commitment to another person.

As with this example, so with any horoscope, we seek the **repeated themes** in order to know what is important.

Themes Repeated by Aspects: An Alternative

Another way to search for themes in the horoscope is discussed in Appendix 2. This approach requires an understanding of all of the themes associated with each of the planets (and houses and signs). Such a listing is provided in Appendix 2 for each of the planets (and can be used for the house and sign associated with each planet in the natural zodiac). For example, Mars — and the 1st house and Aries — contribute to the themes of fire, cardinal, risk-taking, freedom and personal.

Aspects in a certain life area (or in the chart as a whole) can be scanned, bearing in mind the possible themes involved. Harmony aspects imply more ease in combining themes (although we still have to make the effort) and conflict aspects suggest we have to work harder at making a place in life for the varied themes involved. As always, we look for themes which come up again and again, by repeated involvement of the planets, houses and signs which contribute to those themes.

For example, the Moon contributes to the themes of water, cardinal, closeness, personal, security and parents. (The 4th house and Cancer contribute to these same themes.) Pluto contributes to the themes of water, fixed, closeness, security, power, obsessive-compulsive and relationships. (The 8th house and Scorpio contribute to these same themes.) Thus, many aspects in a horoscope which involve Moon, Pluto, 4th house, 8th house, Cancer and Scorpio would highlight those themes. Harmony aspects would suggest the common themes are easy to express: water, closeness and security (although they might be overdone). Conflict aspects imply some need for compromise in differing areas. The fixed theme might be at odds with the cardinal; the parental theme might not blend easily with the relationships theme; the closeness theme might be at war with the obsessive-compulsive focus, etc. The challenge is to make room for all sides in the life.

Basically, the approach is to constantly seek what themes are repeated, and to ask ourselves which motifs are relatively easy to combine and which ones might be difficult to blend. We are constantly seeking the commonalities and the contrasts between the themes represented by the planets/houses/signs emphasized by aspects. As always, the most important issues will emerge again and again.

CHAPTER SIX

IDENTITY

Following are interpretations of the various themes (element, quality, alphabet, other themes, nodes, aspects) as applied to the life area of identity. Remember that this focus in the horoscope reflects the client's basic sense of self, the client's way of being in the world. It may seem particularly apropos of his/her younger self as it ties into early self-expression, spontaneous actions, the way people came into life, the reactions and interactions which come most naturally to them. As individuals grow and evolve, they modify and overlay these basic tendencies. But the themes, in some permutation, remain.

The Factors

As indicated in the discussion of the astrological alphabet, the concept of identity can be summarized with all forms of **Letter 1**.[1] Astrologically, this means we would examine:

GROUP I
Any conjunctions to the planet Mars (the nature of the planet making the aspect, e.g. a Mars/Saturn conjunction shows a Letter 10 theme for identity)

---

1. If you prefer **not** to search for repeated themes yourself, you can order the "PP BOOK" option from Astro Computing Services (PO Box 16430, San Diego, Ca 92116), which allows you to use this book to make complete, synthesizing delineations of horoscopes without figuring out which themes are emphasized.

   Available for $3.00 each, the "PP BOOK" report calculates the emphasis on all the letters of the alphabet, themes and aspects in each horoscope for which you provide the data. The report lists each significant focus (e.g., "There is a Letter 3 theme in "Identity," and gives the appropriate page numbers for you to read in this book ("See pages 107-108 in the *Complete Horoscope Interpretation* book.")

   The computer will not **always** arrive at the same results as you might, as certain steps are ambiguous (e.g., how much weight to give a planet making a conjunction, based on the orb). However, the majority of the time, the computer answers will concur with those derived from hand calculations — or the recommended quick scan of a horoscope. Thus it provides an excellent teaching tool.

   The "PP BOOK" does **not** provide a listing of **each and every** astrological factor making up the significant themes. For that, you would order "PP WEIGHTS" (discussed in next footnote).

Any conjunctions to the Ascendant (the nature of the planet making the aspect, thus Pluto conjunct the Ascendant is a Letter 8 theme for identity)

Any conjunctions to the ruler of the Ascendant (If, for example, Cancer is rising, the Moon conjunct Jupiter is a Letter 9 theme for identity. Note that we do **not** count the Letter 4 theme **at this point**. It will be counted when we consider the rising sign.)

Any conjunctions to the rulers of other signs in the 1st house (If, for example, Sagittarius is rising and 5 degrees of Capricorn fall in the 1st house, we consider conjunctions to **both** Jupiter, ruler of Sagittarius, and to Saturn, ruler of Capricorn, as keys to identity. If Jupiter conjuncts Pluto while Saturn conjuncts Venus, we have themes of Letter 8 and Letter 2 for identity.)

Any conjunctions to the East Point or Antivertex (the nature of the planet making the aspect, so that Mercury conjuncting the East Point highlights Letter 3 for identity while the Sun on the Antivertex points to a Letter 5 theme in identity)

GROUP II

Any planets in the 1st house (the nature of the planets, e.g., Uranus in the 1st house is a Letter 11 theme for identity)

The Ascendant sign (e.g., Virgo rising is a Letter 6 theme for identity)

GROUP III

Any parallels to the planet Mars (the nature of the planet making the aspect)

Any parallels to the Ascendant (the nature of planet making the aspect)

Any parallels to the ruler of the Ascendant

Any parallels to the rulers of other signs in the 1st house

Any parallels to the East Point or Antivertex

The placement of Mars by house (e.g., Mars in the 5th house is a count for Letter 5 connected to identity)

The placement of the ruler of the Ascendant by house

The house placement of the ruler of any additional signs in the 1st house

The house placement of the Antivertex

The house placement of the East Point

The house(s) which have the signs on their cusps ruled by any planet(s) in the 1st house, e.g., if Jupiter is in the 1st, on what house cusp does Sagittarius fall?

The house(s) occupied by signs ruled by any planets making conjunctions to Mars, the Ascendant, the Ascendant ruler, other 1st house rulers, the East Point or the Antivertex. E.g., if Mars conjuncts Saturn, in what houses does Capricorn fall?

Any planets in Aries — the nature of the planet

GROUP IV

The sign of Mars

The sign of the Ascendant ruler

The sign of the ruler of any additional signs in the 1st house

The sign of the East Point
The sign of the Antivertex
Any signs in the 1st house which are occupied by a planet (the nature of the sign)
Aries on any house cusp(s) — the nature of the house
Any additional (unoccupied) signs in the 1st house

How to Weight the Factors

Please note that the factors are rank ordered (in chunks) according to their weighting. That is, planets (and angles) are most significant, so we consider first any conjunctions to Mars, the Ascendant, rulers of the Ascendant, rulers of the 1st house, the Antivertex and the East Point. Houses come next in weighting, so we look to the nature of the planets in the 1st. The Ascendant is a key angle, so its sign gets a lot of weight. Parallels are less emphatic than conjunctions, so they are considered next, followed by house placements and rulerships for important factors. Last, we consider signs, beginning with planets (most important) which occupy signs and ending with empty signs (unoccupied signs in a house we are examining).

If you want to use exact figures, a suggested weighting scale is given in the appendix — with worksheets for the various areas.[2] The worksheets can serve as a check to be sure you have looked at all the relevant factors. It could be helpful to use each worksheet **once** to practice looking for **all** the relevant factors in the chart. After that, however, I recommend the right-brain scanning method — unless you adore details and lists. If you do use the worksheets, do **not** assume they can pin the horoscope (or the person) down to exact numbers! Weighting factors is a very controversial area, and no one has "final" answers.

---

2. You can also obtain a listing of **all** the astrological factors which compose those letters of the Zip Code determined to be significant in a horoscope. This makes an excellent teaching tool and a valuable resource to check yourself against when practicing with the Zip Code.

Astro Computing Services, PO Box 16430, San Diego, CA 92116, has calculated 28,000 horoscopes and established averages and standard deviations for the scores of each letter of the astrological alphabet, each theme, and the conflict and harmony aspects to each life area.

Astro's report, called "PP WEIGHTS," will list those letters of the astrological alphabet which are one standard deviation or more above the mean — and list **all** the astrological factors which point to each significant letter of the alphabet. These weightings will also compare each individual's score on the various themes (e.g., risk-taking, artistic) to the means and standard deviations to determine which themes are significant.

Averages are established for aspects as well in order to note conflict or harmony in the different life areas.

The results obtained by Astro's "PP WEIGHTS" will not **always** coincide with those you determine by a quick scan and intuitive judgment, or by use of the worksheets. Certain of the steps (e.g., how much to weight a planet based on orb) are ambiguous, so different results can occur. However, most of the time, Astro's answers will confirm those you could obtain in working with the Zip Code. Furthermore, the **complete** listing of relevant factors is an excellent teaching tool.

Ask for "PP Weights." The price, as of December 1985 is $5.00

Use Your Right Brain

One of the amazing abilities of the human brain is its capacity for synthesis. You can scan the horoscope for the **entire** list of identity factors in just a couple of minutes, mentally noting any repeated themes. Such a method is **much** superior to an arbitrary weighting for each factor. **Whenever** a theme is repeated more than the other themes, it is important. Depending on how much you want to fine-tune your analysis, you can include **any** motif which is repeated in the horoscope, or you can consider only the two or three motifs which have the most repetitions.

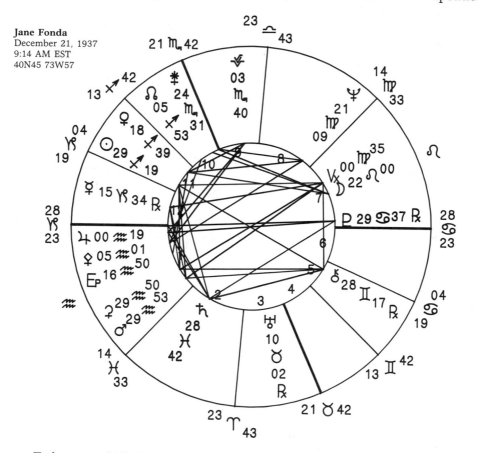

Jane Fonda
December 21, 1937
9:14 AM EST
40N45 73W57

To become skilled at delineating a chart ''cold'' (without prior study), become familiar with all the factors for each life area (based on a solid knowledge of the Zip Code). This enables you to spot the key issues in each area with a few minutes of scanning the chart.

The following list cites all of the identity factors for Jane Fonda's chart (which will be used as an example throughout this book). Note that a **quick scan** reveals

Letters 1, 3, 6, 9 and 11 are repeated most often. You do **not** need to make such lists. You can simply mentally note the repetitions as you examine a horoscope.

GROUP I
Conjunctions to ♂: ♄ (Letter **6**)
Conjunctions to Ascendant: ♃ (Letter **9**)
Conjunctions to Ascendant ruler: none
Conjunctions to other 1st house rulers: none
Conjunctions to East Point: none
Conjunctions to Antivertex: ♂ (Letter **1**) and ♄ (Letter **6**)

GROUP II
Planet(s) in 1st house: ♃ (Letter **9**), ♀ (Letter **7**), ♄ (Letter **6**), ♂ (Letter **1**)
Ascendant sign: ♑ (Letter **10**)

GROUP III
Parallels to ♂: none
Parallels to Ascendant: ♃ (Letter **9**), ♌ (Letter **4**)
Parallels to ruler of Ascendant: none
Parallels to other 1st house rulers: none
Parallels to East Point: none
Parallels to Antivertex: none
House of ♂: **1**
House of Ascendant ruler: **2**
House of other 1st house ruler(s): **3** and **8**
House of Antivertex: **1**
House of East Point: **1**
Cusp(s) ruled by planet(s) in 1st house: **11, 3**
Cusp(s) ruled by planet(s) conjuncting ♂, Ascendant, East Point, Antivertex, Ascendant ruler or other 1st house rulers: **3** [Mars conjuncts the Antivertex and rules the 3rd cusp.]
Planet(s) in Aries: none

GROUP IV
Sign of ♂: ♒ (Letter **11**)
Sign of Ascendant ruler: ♓ (Letter **12**)
Sign of other 1st house ruler(s): ♉ (Letter **2**) and ♍ (Letter **6**)
Sign of East Point: ♒ (Letter **11**)
Sign of Antivertex: ♓ (Letter **12**)
Occupied sign(s) in 1st house: ♒ (Letter **11**) and ♓ (Letter **23**)
Aries on a house cusp: **3**
Unoccupied sign(s) in 1st house: ♑ (Letter **10**)

We would read page 107 in this section regarding Letter 1 in Ms. Fonda's identity. The repetitions suggest a strong focus on being herself and doing her own thing, which might easily include physical activity (Letter 1); a focus on the mind and communication (Letter 3); an identification with work, efficiency, practicality and doing things well (Letter 6) with possible self-criticism; a concern with truth, ideals, justice and expansion in life (Letter 9); a strong streak of personal independence, uniqueness, rebellion and originality (Letter 11).

Certainly Ms. Fonda is know for her level of physical activity (Letter 1), her communication skills (Letter 3), her hardworking attitude (Letter 6), her ideals (Letter 9) and her unconventionality (Letter 11). Astrologers familiar with the work of the Gauquelins note that Jupiter is in the "zone of power" associated with actors and politicians! The rising Jupiter near her Ascendant also suggests enlarging tendencies. In discussing her books and videotapes, Ms. Fonda noted: "I had no idea how it all would just take off. I've got an **expansionist nature**, so I just started doing it, and one thing led to another." (p.9, *Los Angeles Herald Examiner*, September 13, 1985 [emphasis added]).

TWO SHORT CUTS

For quickness and ease of use, especially for people becoming familiar with the alphabet, you can limit your initial scan to factors in Groups I and II, adding Groups III and IV later.

Or, you can utilize Appendix 2 as a "cookbook" assist, reading different sections of this text based on the placements of each planet in a horoscope. For example, looking up Jane Fonda's Sun in the 11th house in Sagittarius, Appendix 2 would direct you to read Letter 11 in children (page 269), Letter 11 in sexuality (page 360), Letter 11 in future (page 113 visualizing ahead), Letter 5 in mind (page 225), Letter 5 in beliefs (page 303), Letter 5 in future [page 109, thinking ahead], Letter 9 in children (page 267), Letter 9 in sexuality (page 358) and Letter 9 in future (page 111 looking forward). You could then continue by reading the appropriate sections for the Moon and other planets. As you read along, repeated letters will become obvious.

Although the "cookbook" approach will yield useful information, I highly recommend that you practice the quick-scanning method of synthesis. Checking a list of factors takes only a minute or two with a little practice and the rewards are great. You can be confident that the themes you see repeated **are** significant.

Alphabet Combinations by Twos

Each pair of the letters of the astrological alphabet can be considered as a couple. Shorthand summaries of each combination of two letters of the alphabet form another section in this chapter. In the case of Ms. Fonda, we could look at every combination of two in the above factors: 1-3, 1-6, 1-9, 1-11, 3-6, 3-9, 3-11, 6-9, 6-11 and 9-11. (If that seems an overabundance, we can limit our perusal to the

1-6, 1-9 and 6-9 combinations, as Letters 1, 6 and 9 were our strongest themes.)
If you wish to look ahead, the 1-6 and 1-9 combinations are on page 115.

Themes

Themes can be ascertained by two methods. One approach is to consider **only**
those letters determined to be significant, and see what themes they can combine
to make. By that process, we would note a strong **freedom** theme in Jane Fonda's life area of identity: Letters 1, 9 and 11 are all prominent. Observers of Ms.
Fonda's life would generally agree she is highly independent and self-directed.
We can read about the freedom theme on page 122.

A second approach to spotting themes is to examine the totals for each letter
of the alphabet and compare the scores for various themes to what would be "average" or expected. For example, the freedom theme is the total of Letter 1, 9 and
11. You will need to do some rough arithmetic here, or get an intuitive impression. If a theme involves three (out of twelve) letters of the astrological alphabet,
you would expect it to have about ¼ of the total score. So, if the amount for those
letters seems appreciably more than ¼ of the total, count that as a theme — and
read the appropriate section.

In addition, when searching for themes, give extra weight to like planets in
aspect to one another. For example, Mars, Jupiter and Uranus are the four freedom planets. Any aspects between Mars, Jupiter and Uranus add to the freedom
theme. (Ms. Fonda's Mars makes a close semisextile to her Jupiter.)

Also give extra weight to like houses and like signs. Thus, Mars, Jupiter or
Uranus occupying the 1st, 9th or 11th house or Aries, Sagittarius or Aquarius would
give extra weight to the freedom theme for each occurrence. In Ms. Fonda's case,
both Mars and Jupiter occupy a freedom sign (Aquarius) as well as a freedom house
(the 1st). "Let freedom ring" is an extremely apt motto for her!

Aspects

Quickly scan all aspects other than conjunctions or parallels, grouping them according to harmony (sextile, trine, semisextile) and conflict (octile, tri-octile, square,
opposition, and quincunx). In considering each aspect, weight the nature of the
planet most heavily, followed by the house and the sign. Note both the house
occupied by that aspected planet and the house that planet rules through the sign
on the cusp. For example, Jane Fonda's Mars (an identity factor) makes the following **close** harmony aspects:
• sextile the Sun (5) in the 11th (11) in Sagittarius (9); the Sun rules the 7th (7)
• semisextile Jupiter (9) in the 1st (1) in Aquarius (11); Jupiter rules the 11th (11)
• trine Vesta (6) in the 9th (9) in Scorpio (8)
• trine Chiron (9) in 5th (5) in Gemini (3)

Mars makes the following **close** conflict aspects:
- octile Mercury (3) in the 12th (12) in Capricorn (10); Mercury rules the 5th and 8th (5)(8)
- quincunx Pluto (8) in the 7th (7) in Cancer (4); Pluto rules the 10th (10)

You can probably tell, by glancing through, which letters of the alphabet have lots of conflict to them and which have quite a bit of harmony. Read the appropriate interpretations based on your aspect scanning. If we considered all of Ms. Fonda's identity factors, the letter with the highest degree of harmony — weighting the nature of the planet most, then the ruler, then the house occupied, then the sign occupied — would be Letter 5. The letter with the highest degree of conflict would be Letter 8. Ms. Fonda is noted for her high degree of fiery energy in self-expression, with strong dramatic potential mirroring the harmony to Letter 5. This also implies a relative ease in being herself, being creative and having children. The conflict to Letter 8 implies that fitting in a mate is not always easy. Her spontaneous side (Letter 1) may be at odds with her need for depth (Letter 8). Power struggles over money, sex and possessions are possible — until the intense emotions of a 1-8 conflict are integrated.

An alternative approach to spotting aspect themes is discussed in Appendix 2.

Interpretations: Identity

Once you have pinpointed the significant themes (using the right-brain scanning method, the left-brain worksheets or Appendix 2 methods), all the interpretations (for identity) are given here.

The order of the delineations is: (1) individual letters of the astrological alphabet, (2) alphabet combinations by twos, (3) nodes of the Moon, (4) elements, (5) qualities, (6) additional themes, e.g., freedom, and (7) aspects.

Initially you may wish to make up a quick list of the emphasized themes when you complete your scan of a life area such as identity. For example:

Identity for _____

Most emphasized letter(s) of the astrological alphabet: _____
Most emphasized polarities: _____
Placement of nodes by house: _____
Placement of nodes by sign: _____
Element emphasis (if any): _____
Element combination emphasis (if any): _____
Quality emphasis (if any): _____
Any emphasized themes: _____
Significant conflict to _____ (letter of the alphabet)
Significant harmony to _____ (letter of the alphabet)

Read the appropriate delineation(s) within each of these groups.

ALPHABET THEMES

Letter 1: "I am Me."

There is usually a strong sense of personal freedom, independence and often a "loner" tendency within you. High vitality and lots of physical energy are common; sports often provide an outlet. Moving physically helps cut down on any restlessness. Waiting tends to frustrate you; impatience is quite possible. If carried to an extreme, impulsiveness is one potential. You prefer to go your own way and will resist being controlled, manipulated or told what to do by others. You cherish your liberty.

There is often a "self-centered" focus which can vary from a positive awareness of one's own needs and desires to disregard of the feelings of others in one's pursuit of what one wants.

You tend to be direct and spontaneous. What people see is what they get. This is not necessarily assertive action; your most spontaneous response may be careful analysis and discrimination or an inward probing of feelings. The trend is for you to express easily your natural instincts. You probably prefer the straight line to the convoluted path.

Open and forthright, you are capable of great bravery and have a natural ability to pioneer, breaking new ground in a number of areas.

Letter 2: "I enjoy the physical world."

Beauty, sensuality and material possessions, may all be a part of your basic identity. Whether you seek to be physically attractive yourself, surround yourself with lovely objects, collect possessions, amass money or indulge in a number of sensual pleasures, all the material goods in life contribute to your sense of self.

Artistic talent is quite possible, but so is overindulgence — whether in food, drink, smoking, sensuality or simple materialism. You tend to want to stay comfortable, secure and easygoing. A bit of laziness and passivity is possible.

When you are contributing to your own security, beauty and pleasure in life, people usually find you very attractive and easy to be with. You can be quite accepting, allowing people to be whoever and however they wish.

Letter 3: "I think, conceptualize and communicate."

Your mind is your primary identification. You see yourself as a thinking, communicating person. Curiosity is generally strong and you are drawn to learn (and often talk) about almost anything. The intellect could be quite sharp. You may use words as a weapon and usually think on your feet. Debate and extemporaneous speeches come quite naturally to you.

A sibling or other collateral relative (aunt, uncle, cousin) could have been a role model for you. Role models can be positive or negative; we may want to be similar to that person, or we may want to be the exact opposite. If there was such a role model, the person taught you (through doing it right **or** through doing it wrong) about mental quickness, communications and the ability to think logically. Whether we get the positive or negative model, the learning is there for us.

Verbal skills are often marked with this combination. Some people may find you **too** articulate. Easily bored, you prefer to avoid routines and seek constant mental stimulation and challenges to stretch your mind. Ideas and concepts excite you.

Letter 4: "I care for and am cared for."

Closeness is an important identity issue in your life. You may be inclined to nurture and "mother" others, or seek people who will take care of you. Often, pets can serve to receive your caring and give unconditional acceptance in return. You might even be very emotionally invested in caring for plants. (The opposite extreme is avoiding all forms of dependency like the plague.)

Your mother (or another potential nurturing figure) is suggested as an important role model for your own identity. That parental individual had a large impact on your ability to handle intimacy and emotional closeness with others. If your mother (or parental figure) is a positive example, you tend to emulate her; if you view her as a negative example, the tendency is to do the opposite of whatever she did. But she is often the measure, the standard — either of what **to** do, or of what **not** to do.

It might be advisable to examine carefully your current attitudes and reactions to your parents (parental figures), especially your mother. If you are still trying to "earn" their love, or prove something to them or get back at them, it behooves you to release the past and move on. In short, if you still have "unfinished business" with either or both parents around the issues of closeness and caring; if you are still replaying old feelings, reacting in old, familiar patterns — you are curtailing your present and future through your entrapment in the past.

Inner ambivalence is likely with this combination. Your desire for independence, space or freedom, may often feel at odds with your yearnings for close, emotional attachments. You may feel torn between independent action and involvement with a nest — home and family. Emotions are likely to be strong, but you may sometimes feel torn between open, direct expression of how you feel versus waiting, holding back until you are sure it is safe to reveal your inner sensitivities. Mood swings are possible: feeling high and optimistic — and then swinging into pessimism and a more depressed state.

Usually very warm and caring, you are capable of firm commitments, but probably want to be involved with people on your own terms. The mothering role is often important to you, so children, pets or someone to nurture are commonly a part of your life.

Letter 5: "I draw excitement, drama and applause through my creative efforts."

You have strong creative needs — to pour out into the world, to do more than has been done before. In some way, you need to feel your power in the world. Feedback is usually important. You may seek the limelight in some fashion, enjoy the appreciation others give to your efforts, or simply savor your own pride in your accomplishments. Children can be one focus of your need to create, but many other options exist.

It is possible that you are quite comfortable with good self-esteem, but it is also possible that you are ego-vulnerable, placing too much importance on the opinions of others. Love, admiration, approval, attention and emotional response are probably very basic needs for you. Pride may be quite marked.

When you feel secure and act naturally, you often come across as magnetic, dynamic, exciting, charismatic and energetic. You have a flair for dramatics and may be drawn to the theater, promotional work, charades or other forms of "onstage" activities. When overdone, you can be arrogant, grandiose and overbearing. Of course, your "royal" manner is, at times, simply a cover-up for inner insecurities.

When insecure, you can also "hide your light under a bushel" — afraid to risk exposure lest you be laughed at. Ridicule is one of the hardest things for you to cope with. Generally, you detest "losing" on any level and sometimes choose not to try rather than chance not being a winner.

Sports, sales, public relations, the performing arts, teaching, advertising, gambling, investments, speculation and other risky activities can provide outlets for your natural persuasive abilities, courage and urge to do more than has been done before.

Letter 6: "I function efficiently in my work and health."

This combination mixes personal identity and self-expression with work and health. The blend can manifest as "I am what I do" or "I will work **only** on **my** terms, **my** way, when I want and how I want!"

If you are expressing the first variation, you are likely to be practical, hardworking, analytical and capable. Because what you do is central to who you are, there is the potential of falling into a workaholic stance. Try to remember that there is more to life than a career! Playing is as important as working. If you get carried away with your desire for productivity, illness can become the body's path to taking a vacation. Efficient functioning is a prominent need in your psyche, but don't overdo it!

There is a tendency toward a performance orientation — judging yourself in terms of what you have accomplished — which needs to be kept in check. This combination is prone to flaw-finding and there is a real danger of excessive self-criticism. The "work attitude" (nit-picking, judgmental, looking for what is wrong in order to fix it) is extremely useful **on the job**. However, when it is self-directed, it is generally quite uncomfortable. Remember to count your good points as well as your "bad" ones — and that "good" and "bad" are often relative. A seeming weakness can become your greatest strength.

If you are expressing the second variation, you are likely to feel dissatisfied with most "ordinary" jobs. You tend to be restless and work only on your own terms. This is an excellent combination for the entrepreneur — or anyone having real control over when and where they work, but is not easy if economics demand you take orders and function according to someone else's rules. At times, illness may be an unconscious escape hatch — to avoid feeling guilty about not working or not accomplishing a task you detest. Compromises must be made — between efficient functioning and acting as you please!

Because children have few outlets for productive achievements which contribute to society, this combination sometimes indicates ill health when the person is young. Usually, once the person is old enough to **do** something, to be effective in the world, the individual regains the natural state of good health. That is likely to continue unless you decide to retire completely. A sense of **some kind** of productive effort is essential for feeling positive about yourself. You do not necessarily have to be paid in money for your labors, but the sense of good craftsmanship, of having done something **well**, is vital to your well-being.

Much of the focus of the identity is on efficient functioning — both on the job and in the body. Health can become an issue. The challenge is to do what you are capable of — efficiently and effectively, without being too hard on yourself physically or emotionally, but also without demanding a career be just exactly what you want. Paying one's dues — doing what is necessary while still finding room to do some of what **you** want to do on the job — is called for.

Letter 7: "I interact with others."

Personal relationships are important as you discover many facets of yourself through interactions with other people, especially partners and close friends. Your relationships may be cooperative and harmonious, competitive or helping/healing, but there is a learning through sharing. Artistic talent — especially a feeling for space, harmony, design and fashion — is quite likely. Graphic arts, painting, photography, dancing, interior decorating and design are a few of the many potential artistic pursuits. Music is also an option.

Although one-to-one interactions are an essential form of expression for you, there is usually some ambivalence between the "loner" role and the "togetherness" scene. You may bounce from one to the other; you may repress or project one end onto partners. You can also integrate, creating a life with some time for yourself, your own interests and hobbies, not having to answer to anyone else — but also time to share, to relate, to be on an equal level, to meet intimately with others.

Letter 8: "I pursue a deeper understanding of myself and life."

Probing beneath the surface comes naturally to you. Eschewing superficialities, you tend to question and examine, rarely accepting the first response, but searching for root causes and issues. Your relentless delving into motivations is as much self-directed as other-directed. You tend to play therapist to yourself continually: wondering, questioning, examining and digging at your desires, needs, and wishes. You seek a sense of self-mastery and can even go to extremes of self-denial if you feel that is the path to self-control.

An intense ambivalence lies within you. Some of your deepest learning and truest understanding is gained through relationships, especially with a mate. Learning to give, receive and share pleasures, money, sexuality and material possessions is an essential part of your evolution. Yet, you also have a great need for alone time — to search within, to process, to work over things in your mind and gut. You may feel torn between the roles of ascetic withdrawal versus sensual sharing.

The issue of power compels you. Analyzing and understanding your own power and the power of others is central to your search. Differentiating between power over people, over emotions, over sensuality, is part of the struggle. You may engage in power struggles, often drawing intense, strong people into your life in order to trigger your own power-oriented potentials and learn through the confrontation. Indirect power-seeking — manipulation, whether through guilt, tears, threats, etc. — can also be an arena for coming to terms with who you are and how you wish to relate to others, especially those with whom you are most intimate. Forgiving (yourself and others) and letting go may be challenges.

Gifted with the potential for much focus and concentration, you can exhibit a bulldog tenacity, relentlessly pursuing your objectives to the end. Because you can be systematic, organized and thorough, your talents often shine in the business world or any arena calling for thoroughness, discipline and careful attention.

Letter 9: "I seek constant expansion."

Your life is a quest for something more. A perpetual restlessness is likely which may draw you into physical travel or simply into ceaseless mental exploration through reading, studying, teaching and learning. Areas of particular interest are often philosophical, religious, spiritual or anything concerned with the question of the meaning of life. Perpetual parties are another option if you define having fun as your ultimate goal in life.

The ideals for self are often high. This can manifest as two extremes. One variant is "I am God. I have the right and power to do as I please. The world ought to recognize how great and wonderful I am and give me exactly what I want." A subset of this variant is the missionary type — an individual **convinced** that his/her version of truth is **the truth**, and everyone else had just better accept and follow it. Whether missionaries preach one form of morality, one form of religion, a scientific materialism or any other version of what life means, the common theme is their conviction that they have **the answers** and that only their answers are correct.

The other extreme is the person who feels, "I **should** be God. So, if I am not perfect, I am nothing." Such individuals have a standard for themselves which is **so** high, they can probably never achieve it. For them, one motto is, "I'll be God tomorrow." If we castigate ourselves for not being ideal yet, we are unlikely to get much fun or fulfillment out of our existence. If we can allow ourselves to be human, working **toward** perfection, we can enjoy the journey of life.

Your optimism and faith can be decided assets, as long as you keep your ideals reachable.

Letter 10: "I work with what is possible in the world."

Dealing with the limits of the world is a significant issue in your life. Rules, regulations, order, predictability and systematization all have an important place in your basic identity. One option is the highly effective, competent, achieving individual who is accomplishing all that s/he can within the limits of physical reality. Such people are often highly responsible, authoritative and tend to have positions of power in the world. Their careers tend to be central in their identity; they often have a sense of being whatever it is they do.

Other alternatives include overdrive and self-blocking. Overdrive sorts are continually butting their heads against stone walls, fighting against the limits. That could range from fighting authority figures (from father onward) to fighting against time (never enough time to do all they feel they should) to fighting practical, material limits (trying to get by with insufficient rest, nutrition, etc. — pushing their bodies too hard); to fighting against cultural regulations ("I'm going to do what I want to do; to heck with what anybody thinks!") to literally breaking the laws of the land (criminals).

Self-blockers go to the other extreme. They give up, often before even beginning. Convinced they would just fail, they may not even try. Overly susceptible to criticism (self-directed and from others), feeling inadequate, believing other people will stop them, judge them, put them down, the self-blockers simply declare themselves out of the running by refusing to even attempt anything. Rather than risk performing in a way that would fall short of their harsh, inner standards, they bow out altogether.

Overdrive people emphasize self-will over practical limits. Self-blockers emphasize restrictions and inhibitions over self-expression. The middle ground is to be able to do what one wants (most of the time) within a context of rules, regulations, other people's needs and the laws of the physical world we live in. Then you can be incredibly effective.

Usually, the example of the father or father figure is very important. Dad tends to be a role model — positive or negative — of what we want to be, or what we don't want to be. Sometimes the father provides the first criticism, harsh judgments, rejections. Sometimes the father is a highly productive individual. Sometimes Dad retreats into self-blocking. Regardless of the route taken by the authority figure, the individual must still choose, for him or herself, between practical accomplishments, overdrive and self-blocking. Unfinished business with father can sometimes delay integration. For example, some people are still trying to "beat" father, prove they are "better" than he is (usually into overdrive). Some are still seeking approval, affection, "You did well" from Dad, rather than "You could have done better" or other put-downs. Some see their fathers as so successful that they decide they can never compete, never measure up — so retreat into self-blocking.

The golden mean is to be able to determine what is truly possible in this world and achieve what we want within that context. Constantly striving for something that just goes against the grain of physical reality or cultural rules is often frustrating. Constantly perceiving limitations, restrictions and blocks where none really exist is also frustrating. We are all subject to certain "rules" in life; the quest is to correctly identify the essential rules and work within them, while also ascertaining which "rules" are unnecessary (can be broken) or simply our own, inner limitations (which we can evolve beyond).

Letter 11: "I am an individualist."

Uniqueness is essential to you. You are an individual and do not want anyone else to forget it. People who try to label you, stereotype you, confine you to any handy pigeonhole are in for a surprise. Indeed, you may sometimes delight in shocking people — doing or saying something that upsets their ncat, tidy, little world and forces them to examine their assumptions.

Personal freedom is very important to you; you resist being tied down to one person, one situation, one choice. For you, there are always alternatives, other options. You may be skilled at brainstorming and problem-solving because you are able to achieve a broad perspective and can think of nontraditional, innovative and inventive approaches to the situation. Of course, sometimes that manifests as you being just plain **weird**. Overdone originality can become eccentricity and irresponsibility. People with this blend have been known to rebel simply for the sake of rebelling to prove they are not "predictable."

Humanitarian causes, justice, equality may all appeal to you. You have also been known to deal better with people on a broad, impersonal level (where you still have your liberty) than in a one-to-one relationship (where your sense of freedom may be threatened). Detachment comes easily for you. You tend to have a wide circle of friends and acquaintances. You are often able to relate to anyone in the whole wide world; however, that relationship is usually more mental and casual than deep and emotional. Generally tolerant, you are better than most people at judging people by who they are, rather than skin color, religion, political persuasion, sex or other stereotypic labels.

Anything that is new, different, on the cutting edge of change, will often appeal to you. Generally, the future calls to you. Freedom of movement and action are also positives in your book. Consequently, aviation, the space program, computers, lasers, new technology and innovations of all sorts may be arenas which have your attention and involvement.

Letter 12: "I seek infinite love and beauty."

Your personal expression needs to be involved with a beautiful dream. Major roles range from artist to savior to victim. You may be physically beautiful, or seek it in the world. You may create beauty artistically (and also share it with others). You may be a helper and a healer of other people — whether professionally (psychotherapist, doctor, astrologer, etc.) or on an informal basis (providing tea, sympathy and assistance to anyone having problems). If carried to an extreme, the role of savior can become victim — when you give too much, sacrifice your own needs in attempting to help others. The world needs saints, but the role of the saint, when carried too far, leads to martyrdom and even death. This combination can indicate extreme personal idealism, the desire to always be spiritual, loving, helpful, beautiful, etc.

Victims share the same desires for an ultimate in life. But they perceive the world as ugly rather than beautiful, so victims are looking for an escape. To run away from an imperfect world (and to banish the awareness that they are not doing anything to change that world), victims may go to alcohol, drugs, fantasy, psychosis, sleeping all the time or any other escapist route. One of the most effective ways to alter a victim role is to help the victim turn from being a victim to being a savior. Alcoholics Anonymous and other self-help groups utilize this switch all the time. Fighting for a worthy cause is often an optimum way to balance your (sometimes conflicting) drives of self-assertion and self-sacrifice. Just be sure you can allow others their own causes too!

You are more prone than most people to fall into seeing life through rose-colored glasses. You **want** everything to be ideal, beautiful and loving, so sometimes you pretend it is! This misty-eyed idealism can also lead you into appearing very mysterious or not quite comprehensible to other people. You have a talent for illusions which can be of great value in sales, drama, magic shows, advertising, writing and other avenues. Or, you can be the most dramatic martyr around.

You tend to have very high standards for your personal behavior. Sometimes this is a problem as you end up following a pattern of "Perfect or not at all." You may be inclined to wait **until** you are perfect, or the situation is ideal, before acting. Unless you work effectively to create the desired environment, you might wait a long time.

Sensitive, imaginative and intuitive, you are able to act on your "inner wisdom." This often unconscious knowing can be a source of strength, faith and assistance in your creation of heaven on earth. As long as your fantasies, dreams and visions are backed by some realism and plain hard work, you can achieve truly beautiful and loving results.

ALPHABET COMBINATIONS BY TWOS

When identity is tied to two letters of the astrological alphabet, the following keywords would apply:

1-2...strength, determination, willpower, awareness of personal wants and needs; possible self-indulgence; natural sensuality.

1-3...mental and verbal swiftness, keenness, possibly aggression, good coordination, expressiveness, mental alertness.

1-4...inner ambivalence between freedom and closeness; need to blend liberty and emotional attachment, self-expression and desire for home, family, nest.

1-5...sparkle, dash, verve, excitement, action, vitality, life; fun, spontaneity accentuated; tendency to go full charge into life.

1-6...productivity, extreme competence, possibly overachieving; need to be wary of overdoing self-criticism. Often medical, healing interests/skills are present.

1-7...inner ambivalence between doing one's own thing and sharing the world with someone else; need to blend self-assertion and self-effacement in reasonable balance.

1-8...inner conflict between doing your own thing and facing your depths through sharing the physical, sensual, sexual world with someone else.

1-9...optimism, faith, confidence; possibly rash and foolhardy; tendency to act on faith; personal concern with truth and the meaning of life.

1-10...inner ambivalence between self-will and the limits to one's will (what is possible in the physical world). Need to balance spontaneous action with cautious productivity.

1-11...an emphasis on freedom, liberty and independence. Tremendous need to be your own person, do your own thing; resistance to strings from others.

1-12...a need to blend self-assertion and self-sacrifice without going to extremes on either end; energetic pursuit of beauty, ideals, dreams all healthy outlets.

2-3...pleasure from things and communication; focus on possessions and people near at hand; rational and practical more than emotional and intuitive.

2-4...strong tactile orientation; natural cuddler, snuggler; desire for physical and emotional security; may be a collector; pleasure from possessions and home.

2-5...inner conflict between desire for security and gambling instincts. Sensual/sexual nature usually strong; may feel torn between indulgence of self versus indulgence of loved ones.

2-6...may work at pleasure or find pleasure in work. Needing tangible accomplishments.

2-7...artistic talent and a strong feeling for beauty; the appreciation of aesthetics is a natural part of who you are; you may be physically attractive as well.

2-8 . . . inner conflict between self-indulgence versus self-control; possibly feast versus famine tendencies — whether around food, making love, alcohol or other physical appetites.

2-9 . . . an inner pull between pleasure from the material world and the search for something higher; need to reconcile sensual and spiritual natures.

2-10 . . . strong business talent, ability to be pragmatic and highly capable; may be tension between ambitious nature and desire to kick back and enjoy.

2-11 . . . inner tension between stability and desire for change; need to balance your innovative side with your desire for predictability and status quo.

2-12 . . . a strongly aesthetic nature, with potential talent in the arts; ability to create beauty and pleasure from all the senses as well. Relaxed, can be passive.

3-4 . . . both objectivity and subjectivity; logic and intuition; importance of family background in who you are; focus on a home with communication; security through your mind.

3-5 . . . a vibrant, magnetic, entertaining conversationalist and bon vivant; natural ability to take the stage and please everyone around you; childlike.

3-6 . . . an inner conflict between quantity versus quality; wanting to know a little about everything must be balanced with need to do things **well** and thoroughly.

3-7 . . . sociability, people-orientation, concern with ideas, communication and interactions; logical, rational, curious about people; natural mixer.

3-8 . . . an inner conflict between skimming the surface and probing the depths; need to choose when to be a butterfly and when to be a miner.

3-9 . . . intellectual curiosity, a mind constantly on the go and often itchy feet too; constant travel — either mentally, physically or both; learning and teaching too.

3-10 . . . an inner conflict between lighthearted approach and serious attitude; need to blend casual and committed orientations for optimal results.

3-11 . . . tremendous desire for variety and constant new and different stimulation; mind must be active; detest being bored; need constant challenges.

3-12 . . . inner ambivalence between merging with something Higher and communicating and interacting with the people near at hand. Make room for both.

4-5 . . . incredible warmth, natural nurturance, great capacity to love and be loved; usually strong desire for home, family, emotional attachments. Caring! May be highly creative.

4-6 . . . preference for the known, conventional and secure; steady work and home life desired. Avoid extremes of doing too much for others or allowing others to do too much for you.

4-7...inner tension between desire for an enveloping, encompassing relationship versus desire for an equalitarian, sharing relationship with some space.

4-8...intense, emotional nature with very deep feelings; much going on beneath the surface that will not be revealed to the world. Figuring out your roots is important.

4-9...inner struggle between desire for roots, security and nest versus the pull to explore the world, seek answers, broaden your horizons. Do both somehow!

4-10...a sense of inner tension between time/energy commitments to home and family versus career and success in the outside world; dominance versus dependency; control and authority versus support and compassion.

4-11...inner ambivalence between close, emotional ties and free, self-expression unbonded to anyone else; learning to be yourself and be vulnerable with another.

4-12...sensitive, naturally empathic, quite possibly intuitive; tendency to take things deeply to heart — may be easily hurt. The mother/savior quality can be very nurturing of others or seeking someone to be all-caring for the self.

5-6...personal pride through work accomplishments — self-esteem measured by productivity; potentially **very** competent. Balance self-criticism with self-aggrandizement.

5-7...a natural stage presence, love of fun and talent for amusing and entertaining others; can be the life of the party; sometimes **too** other-directed, approval-seeking or too tied to winning, coming out ahead.

5-8...a strong power drive, but a dilemma over how much to turn inward (self-control) and how much to express outward in relationships.; learning to share power in love relationships without manipulation or intimidation.

5-9...great dynamism, energy, enthusiasm; ability to excite others; natural sales person; skill in arousing emotions; great self-confidence, optimism, faith.

5-10...a power drive, but torn between power as a source of joy versus power as a responsibility; zestful pursuit of control versus dominance as a necessary, unenviable role. Balancing love needs with achievement needs.

5-11...balancing the mental approach with the emotional; making room for friends and lovers; keeping space in life for independence and love relationships.

5-12...incredible dramatic talent — ability to almost "cast a spell" on your audience; great actors, actresses, salespeople, promoters or martyrs.

6-7 . . . work and relationships both important to identity — may work with people, but don't turn relationships into a job (with judgmental attitudes).
You can be very practical about people.

6-8 . . . tremendous ability to focus, concentrate, organize and handle details;
business skills; talent for thoroughness and careful work; can be
obsessive.

6-9 . . . inner push/pull between the ideal (vision of what life ought to be) versus the real (nitty-gritty aspects of life); need for idealism and realism
to support each other — not fight.

6-10 . . . tremendous focus on work, achievement, "I am what I do;" danger of
being much too hard on yourself; tendency to feel overly responsible,
do more than your share.

6-11 . . . inner struggle between need for change, innovation and variety versus
the desire to get all the details right and be thorough. Integration is
necessary.

6-12 . . . learning to balance the search for a beautiful dream with a pragmatic
assessment of the physical world. Inspiration and perspiration combine
for best results.

7-8 . . . identification with partnership — learning who you are through interaction with others. Beware of giving away all your power or fighting to
keep it all in your hands; a compromise is necessary.

7-9 . . . natural charm and charisma; often attractive to others; may be passion
for justice and fair play which can express as a competitive nature.

7-10 . . . an inner conflict between equality and control; may also be expressed
as a struggle between time/energy commitments to relationships versus career; both are essential.

7-11 . . . associations with others are important; communication and interaction,
especially with friends, vital to who you are; open, tolerant, rational.

7-12 . . . strong feelings for beauty, personal expression through aesthetic channels very possible; diplomacy a likely skill; may idealize relationships
or overvalue harmony and ease.

8-9 . . . a depth quest for knowledge and understanding of yourself and the
universe; a mind of both depth and breadth; could be a bit fanatical at
times where beliefs are concerned.

8-10 . . . tremendous willpower, focus, concentration and follow through; natural
business acumen; good ability to handle resources; power-oriented.

8-11 . . . an inner struggle between power, focus, concentration and hanging on
versus equality, variety and moving on to something new and different.
Balance!

8-12 . . . strong, intense emotions which you tend to reveal to very few; seeking
a sense of union and intuitive understanding in relationships; may
withdraw when situations seem less than ideal.

9-10 . . . reaching for the stars with the ability to make your dreams come true. If the practical and visionary are not blended, you could be chronically frustrated, wanting more than you accomplish.

9-11 . . . an orientation toward independence — relating easily to large, abstract concepts and ideals; often committed to social justice; could be active in changing society.

9-12 . . . high ideals, expectations and goals; searching for the best in life. May sometimes be dissatisfied or talk yourself into seeing a more ideal picture than is really there. Keep your dreams grounded. Focus on faith.

10-11 . . . a need to blend the conventional and the unconventional, learning when to play by the rules and when to break them; getting the best from traditions as well as progress.

10-12 . . . an awareness of how the world could be improved; either working to change it for the better or seeking an escape from the current unsatisfactory state.

11-12 . . . a natural bent for humanitarian ideals, utopian inclinations. Great theorist; visionary, but may be somewhat impractical; concerned with large-scale issues.

NODES OF THE MOON

Since the Letter 1 is a key to identity, the placement of the nodes of the Moon in Aries/Libra or the 1st house/7th house has special importance for the issue of identity and self-expression. Other nodal placements are more significant in different life areas and will be discussed accordingly. For example, the nodes across Taurus/Scorpio or 2nd house/8th house are discussed in Chapters 12 (money) and 13 (sexuality).

Across Aries/Libra or 1st/7th Houses

You are facing polarity principles of doing your own thing versus maintaining an ongoing relationship. The struggle may be between the single lifestyle versus committed relationships. You might feel torn between assertion and effacement. You could go to extremes of giving away personal power or holding incredible power over someone else. You may vacillate between open, spontaneous, direct expression of anger and a tactful, diplomatic approach. Personal freedom and liberty could vie with needs for an affectionate bond and a loving relationship.

Feelings of not measuring up could be an inhibiting factor. You may be too hard on yourself or excessively judgmental of others. (You could also attract partners who are self-critical or harsh toward you.) Inadequacy feelings can complicate the sharing of power in a relationship.

Integration requires a secure sense of your own rights and abilities balanced with an appreciation of the rights and abilities of other people. Cooperation and compromise enable you both to get most (or all) of what you want within a relationship. A clear sense of who you are and what you want in relationships is a first step to obtaining your desires.

ELEMENT EMPHASIS

Fire
♂, ☉, ♃, ♅, ♈, ♌, ♐, 1st, 5th, 9th houses

Full of vim, vigor and vitality, you can be a real ball of fire! Although society is sometimes less than encouraging toward the free expression of fiery dynamism, you have the potential to be active, expressive, vibrant, lively and on the go. You probably hate repetition. Eager to do something and then move on to the next challenge, your enthusiasm can be contagious for the people surrounding you.

Usually direct and straightforward, you tend to know what you want and go after it. Rarely a shrinking violet, you do not need to be second-guessed; you'll tell people (or make very clear with your actions) exactly how you feel. Your physical energy level is often higher than most people's and impatience may be an issue. Sports, working out or other muscle-moving activities can help channel all your energy. But you may direct your marked creativity into intellectual, aesthetic or emotional activities rather than physical.

Sometimes your confidence, zest and natural optimism can lead you into risky situations; you can be a bit impulsive. But your love of life and full-speed-ahead attitude usually keep everything exciting and alive for you and anyone in your circle.

Earth
♀, ☿, ?, ⚷, ♄, ♉, ♍, ♑, 2nd, 6th, 10th houses

Practical, productive, efficient, oriented toward dealing with physical reality and the material world, you generally prefer tangibles to abstractions. Work and accomplishments are usually quite central to your sense of self, your need to achieve. You may even feel guilty for "sloughing off" when not working.

You prefer situations and circumstances which involve measurable, definable results. Emotions, theories, ideas and intuitions are less satisfying for you to deal with than known quantities and objects. You appreciate the security of knowing how things work and may put a lot of attention to figuring out the "rules" and "laws" behind whatever interests you (be it a physical object, a person, a situation or a society).

Essentially a realist, one of your best assets is the ability to face facts and deal with life as it is (as opposed to how we wish it were).

Air
☿, ♀, ♀, ⚷, ♅, ♊, ♎, ♒, 3rd, 7th, 11th houses

A natural thinker and communicator, you are identified with your mind. Ideas, concepts and information exchange are natural focuses in your self-expression. Conceptualizing is an instinctive response for you and theories come easily.

You may very well have a flair for equalitarian relationships. It tends to be easy for you to accept and understand people — on their own terms, not trying to change them. You usually enjoy the intellectual stimulation that other people bring.

Occasionally, your logical and rational skills may lead you into overintellectualization or rationalization, but generally your fine mind is a decided asset.

Water
☽, ♇, ♆, ♋, ♏, ♓, 4th, 8th, 12th houses

A deeply feeling person, you usually prefer **not** to wear your "heart on your sleeve." Though you can be immensely caring and concerned, you are unlikely to reveal the depths of your emotions to most people. Only someone in a very close and committed relationship would have any idea of the intensity of your emotions, and even then you would probably keep some things secret.

Probably blessed with some intuitive ability, you can sense with an "inner knowing" certain actions which are just right. (Be sure, however, you can distinguish between that inner knowing and simple fantasy.) Perceptive, sensitive, often empathic, you can tune into others and also apprehend the basic patterns of life, businesses, relationships or other processes.

For interpretations of element combinations (e.g., Fire-Earth, Fire-Air), see pages 73-75 of Chapter 4 (themes).

QUALITY EMPHASIS

Cardinality
♂, ☽, ♀, ♀, ⚷, ♄, ♈, ♋, ♎, ♑, 1st, 4th, 7th, 10th houses

You tend to learn through experience. Consciously or unconsciously, you attract events into your life (or directly create them) which will result in life structure changes. The ensuing crises are often periods of great personal growth for you.

Part of the issue is that you are striving to express four very different needs within your nature, and they may seem very much at odds with one another. You need somehow to create space in your self-expression to be: 1) free and independent; 2) warm, close, loving and emotionally attached; 3) equalitarian and sharing lightly with some space and detachment; and 4) responsible, in control with some authority and power. The balance is not easy to make and takes continuous adjustment and readjustment but each side is a necessary part of who you are.

Fixed
♀, ☉, ♇, ♅, ♉, ♌, ♏, ♒, 2nd, 5th, 8th, 11th houses

Faithful and loyal, you are dedicated to completing your commitments. A major strength lies in your desire to master and control your own life. You are determined to be yourself and highly resistant to any outside attempts to change or influence you. Resolute and capable of being quite stubborn, you steadfastly pursue your own course in life.

Naturally sensual, you may feel torn in your handling of the physical world. It is quite possible that you enjoy the indulgences of eating, drinking, making love, making money, smoking or satisfying other appetites, yet a sense of self-control and self-mastery may also be important to you. Achieving a balance is the challenge.

Because you are probably ambivalent in these areas, you could easily attract people into your life who share that ambivalence. Then you would engage in power struggles (over sex, money, etc.) — each trying to prove to the other that his/her way is the **right** way. Learning to compromise is part of the name of the game. The more you balance within, the easier balance becomes outside.

Mutable
☿, ♀ ♀, ♃, ♀, ♆, ♊, ♍, ♐, ♓, 3rd, 6th, 9th, 12th houses

You are likely to be adaptable, flexible and multitalented. Often interested in a myriad of subjects, you may have trouble choosing which one (or several) paths to pursue among your many options. You could scatter, spreading yourself too thin in trying to learn and know everything.

Ideals or expectations are often an issue. Wanting more than is possible (from yourself, from a career, from a person or elsewhere) is quite likely. You may set unreasonably high standards. Deciding where to seek perfection in life is important. Nature and spiritual answers may offer the infinite; human beings rarely do.

The mind is generally very important; you enjoy exploring ideas, reading, discussing, gaining and sharing information. Just remember that you cannot expect yourself (or anyone else) to know it all or to always have the right answer.

THEMES

Freedom
♂, ♃, ♀, ♅, ♈, ♐, ♒, 1st, 9th, 11th houses

There is a strong freedom theme in your basic makeup. This indicates an intense need to be yourself, be original, unique and not like anyone else. You are likely to resist being pinned down and tied down by anyone. Natural self-expression becomes important; the "yes man" role does not appeal. You like going your own way.

Closeness or Interpersonal

☽, ☉, ♀, ⚴, ⚵, ♇, ♋, ♌, ♎, ♏, 4th, 5th, 7th, 8th houses

There is a strong closeness theme in your basic identity. This indicates an involvement with other people on a face-to-face level, from family, mate and work associates to anyone seen on a systematic basis. The focus is on relating as an equal, learning to compromise, cooperate and compete fairly with those around us as well as being able to nurture and be nurtured. If unbalanced, you may be too other-directed needing other people in order to act. Or, you could be learning when to compete, when to cooperate and when to compromise. (Competing with members of our own team is rarely advisable.) You might overdo dependency or overdo taking care of others.

Sharing and exchanges with other people are extremely important and a significant center of your evolving in life. Warmth, caring and the ability to love may be quite marked. However, your associations with others can be competitive as well as harmonious. You are learning about yourself through interacting with others, but it is not necessarily all sweetness and light. Indeed, if you feel those around you are getting **too** close, you may choose to retreat within yourself for a time. You need some alone time to process your inner reactions to all this interchange.

Strong family connections are one way to meet your need for attachment. Pets may also be sources for a caring exchange. Sharing, intimacy and one-to-one relationships matter to you.

Artistic

♀, ⚴, ⚵, ☉, ♆, ♉, ♌, ♎, ♓, 2nd, 5th, 7th, 12th houses

There is a strong artistic theme within you. This can be real talent for creating beauty as well as a natural feeling and appreciation for the aesthetic. Expression can range over many areas — from the beauty of nature, of painting, photography, dancing, sculpture, handicrafts, to creating a meal that is a work of art, making a lovely garden, sewing exquisite clothes or other forms of expressing a feeling for harmony, grace, design and balance.

Idealistic

♃, ⚷, ♆, ♐, ♓, 9th, 12th houses

There is a strong idealistic theme within your nature. This can be expressed as high personal standards for your behavior or as feeling that you have a lot to measure up to. Your life can be guided by a sense of inspiration from above. You may also demand more than is reasonable of yourself **or** feel that you already are perfect and need expect nothing more. A seeking, a sensing, a yearning for something more in your own life and behavior is important.

Obsessive-Compulsive

☿, ⚳, ⚶, ♇, ♄, ♍, ♏, ♑, 6th, 8th, 10th houses

There is a strong theme of focused attention within your basic makeup. This shows potential talent for organization, efficiency, thoroughness, the handling of details, willpower and determination to do things well. If carried too far, it can be picky, critical, judgmental, annoying and practically drive other people crazy. Be sure your penchant for details and desire to have things just right has a positive outlet.

Competence

☿, ⚳, ⚶, ♄, ♍, ♑, 6th, 10th houses

The work you do plays a central role in who you are. One option is feeling that you are what you do — your work defines your identity. Another option is demanding work that is totally on your terms — your identity defines your work. You may refuse to consider jobs that seem uninteresting, or simply not what you want to do at the moment.

With the first option, your desire to contribute and do something in the real (i.e., physical) world, can lead to feeling guilty when you are not being "productive." There is a tendency to turn yourself into a job, being judgmental and nit-picking — searching for all your faults so that you can make yourself over and even better.

Sometimes, inadequacy feelings could block you from what you are capable of accomplishing; fear of not measuring up may stop you from taking the first step. You might also put off finishing something, continually "improving" it and doing it over and over again, rather than risking feeling it does not measure up if you announce it as completed. You could fall into illness on occasion — as an unconscious escape from feeling guilty about not doing "enough."

With the second option (defining your work by what you want), you may put a great deal of energy into your career — as long as things are going your way. A danger is that you will refuse to work if you feel that the job is passe, boring, or not fitting your current needs. If it is not on your terms, you may refuse to do it.

You have an excellent practical, realistic approach, but remember to count your assets as well as your flaws and remember to express yourself through your work without demanding everything be exactly as you want it. You are capable of achieving much through hard work, high energy, dedication, enthusiasm, discipline, confidence, pragmatism and a concern for getting it right!

Mental Stimulation

☿, ⚳, ⚶, ⚴, ♃, ⚷, ♅, ♆, ♊, ♍, ♎, ♐, ♒, ♓, 3rd, 6th, 7th, 9th, 11th, 12th houses

The world of the mind is vital to your identity. Primarily, you see yourself as a thinker and communicator. Ideas and people are important to who you are. You wish to relate to others easily and casually, on a peer level. Concepts appeal to you, and your mind is generally active and involved with whatever is going on.

When carried too far, you can seem scattered to others because you want to know so many things. Because your mind is usually quick, other people may not always follow your thinking or speech. Remember to be clear and do not jump too rapidly from one idea to another.

Relationships
♀, ♀, ⚹, ♇, ♎, ♏, 7th, 8th houses

There is a strong relationship theme in your basic nature: learning through other people. This can be a comfortable, peer exchange with mutual pleasure and sharing. Or, it can be competitive, game-playing, with contests to see who can get one-up on the other. You learn much about yourself through observing and interacting with other people.

Security
♀, ☽, ☿, ♀, ⚹, ♇, ♄, ♅, ♂, ♋, ♍, ♏, ♑, ♓, 2nd, 4th, 6th, 8th, 10th, 12th houses

You have a strong need for security in terms of your basic self-expression. Less inclined to rock the boat, you tend to seek out the safest path, take the tried-and-true variation and generally go with the known, the predictable, the status quo. Both physical and emotional security seem bulwarks in an increasingly changing and challenging world.

If you have not yet gained a sense of inner power, you may be focused largely on self-protection with a guarded attitude. If you have actualized some of your internal strengths, you may well be helping other people to feel safe, secure and cared for.

Risk/Creativity/Change
♂, ☉, ♃, ⚷, ♅, ♈, ♌, ♐, ♒, 1st, 5th, 9th, 11th houses

You have a strong need for risk, change and creativity in terms of your basic self-expression. Inclined to take chances, to lay it on the line, to play the odds (and even go against the odds), you are seeking to expand your options and widen your horizons. (In excess, this includes running away when you don't like where you are.) Independence of action in order to pour out from your own center is vital. You recognize that some kind of gamble is often necessary to go beyond what has been done before.

Parents
☽, ♄, ⚷, ♋, ♑, 4th, 10th houses

A parent or parents probably had an important impact on your basic identity. As positive or negative examples, their roles were useful in you learning about yourself. How you express your needs for nurturing and being nurtured, responsibility, authority, power and control is probably related to their examples. In dealing with the realistic limits of the world (including societal roles and rules), you may still be reacting to some old parental inputs. Be sure you have made peace with them (in terms of your inner feelings, not necessarily with them in person) and can be your own master.

Power
⊙, ♇, ♄, ♌, ♏, ♑, 5th, 8th, 10th houses

There is an intense power drive in your basic nature. This can express as a determination to run your own life, a need to win, and/or a desire to be on top and in charge. Directing the competitive zeal into sports, games, business or fighting for causes helps cut down on conflicts in other areas of life. If not positively channeled, the need to win can lead to power struggles, fights and unpleasantness with people you prefer to cooperate with. Your determination to have things "right" often means having them **your** way. You need a place to put your full power out onto the world — to strive, to push, to win, to run things exactly as **you** want — with end results that are positive and affirming for everyone concerned.

Personal
♂, ♀, ☿, ☽, ♈, ♉, ♊, ♋, 1st, 2nd, 3rd, 4th houses

You are likely to be very aware of what you want and need in life, preferring to be yourself, enjoy yourself, satisfy your curiosity and find some form of emotional security. Probably fairly secure in your basic sense of self, you tend to be clear about who you are and your personal needs. If carried to an extreme, this can manifest as selfishness or self-centeredness. But, in moderation, this indicates a good capacity to know yourself and satisfy your basic desires in life.

Transpersonal
♃, ⚷, ♄, ♅, ♆, ♐, ♑, ♒, ♓, 9th, 10th, 11th, 12th houses

You are likely to feel a part of something beyond just your own, personal self. Whether that connection is to humanity, to God, to a political or social cause or simply a sense of unity with Life, you tend to operate from a broad perspective. Your life is likely to center around a search for truth, a confrontation of cultural and societal rules and regulations, a tolerance and humanitarian outlook for all peoples or a sense of connectedness to the Universe. Rather than focusing on your individual needs, you probably include questions of the greatest good for the greatest number and a historical perspective. Some sense of how decisions and choices impact the world and what they might imply for other people or society at large is central to who you are.

Long-range goals, values and ideals are in your awareness. If carried to an extreme, your broad perspective could inhibit intimate one-to-one relationships or cripple your ability to meet your own needs. When in balance with the rest of life, this ability to see the overview and context of life simply adds a richer dimension to your experience.

ASPECTS

Harmony to Letter...

1: Your sense of identity and natural self-expression tend to flow easily within you. You basically agree on who you are and what you want in the world. You generally work with yourself and support the different facets of your being. The necessary confidence and assertion to express yourself lie at your fingertips. Because there is inner agreement, you may sometimes go overboard in doing what comes naturally to you, but basically, you support yourself and can balance inner ambivalences.

2: Your sense of identity and natural self-expression tend to flow easily with your physical desires and pleasures. You can usually determine what you want and pursue it in the world. You are able to comfortably enjoy physical pleasures (e.g., eating, drinking, money, sensuality) and feel good about yourself. Expressing beauty and/or sensuality comes naturally.

3: Your sense of identity and natural self-expression tend to flow easily with your desire to think and communicate. Your mental capacities assist you in expressing yourself and asserting yourself in the world. You are able to communicate who you are fairly easily. You generally know how to get along with the people in your immediate environment. You may have had a positive relationship with a brother, sister, aunt, uncle or neighbor who played a supportive role in encouraging you to do what you want and to be yourself.

4: Your sense of identity and natural self-expression tend to flow easily with your desire for warmth, family, emotional closeness and commitment. You may still have to do a little work to keep room for your desires for liberty and self-expression along with close relationships, but the desire is there to have both. The potential of harmony with your own nurturing instincts and dependency needs is strong. You probably learned, while still fairly young, to create space in your life for both assertive action as an individual and caring, compassionate involvement with other people.

5: Your sense of identity and natural self-expression tend to flow easily with your desire to be noticed and significant in the world. This indicates some natural charisma, drive and a potential "star" quality. Self-confidence and self-esteem are usually good. You know how to express yourself and can easily pour out into the world. If backed up by strong fire in the rest of the chart, you may sometimes be **too** expressive, impulsive, self-oriented. When balanced, the likelihood is of an instinct for drama, action and the willingness to take personal risks to be who you are and seek recognition from others.

6: Your sense of identity and natural self-expression tend to flow easily with your need to do something well. This indicates a good potential for endurance as well as initiation. You can get excited about projects and still carry through. You may have to deal with a little inner tension between an urge to rush forward and a desire to deal thoroughly with the details, but you can find a reasonable middle ground. Your practicality and realism can assist you in being yourself and doing your own thing.

7: Your sense of identity and natural self-expression tend to flow easily with your desire for partnership. You want to be yourself and also to share your life with someone else. This is a good potential for being able to cooperate, share, negotiate, compromise and meet in the middle with another human being. If not integrated, you may initially go through stages of competition, too much accommodation and/or too much aggression as you learn to balance your personal needs with those of another.

8: Your sense of identity and natural self-expression tend to flow easily with your desire for depth understanding. Your need to probe deeper and figure out root causes supports your self-expression and actions in the world. The more fully you explore your own inner depths, the freer you feel to be yourself. Some of this understanding is intuitive and may be difficult to articulate, but you can instinctively act on it even when it is beyond words.

9: Your sense of identity and natural self-expression tend to flow easily with your search for the truth and ultimate meaning. Your seeking of answers about the meaning of life encourages you to feel more confident about who you are and your right to be yourself in this world. The more you learn and discover about reality, the more you appreciate the freedom to do your own thing. Faith, confidence, zest and enthusiasm are likely to be high.

10: Your sense of identity and natural self-expression tend to flow easily with your awareness of structure and the rules of the game. You are capable of doing all that you can within the limits set by our physical existence. You know when to push and when to be cautious; when to go full speed ahead and when to apply the brakes. You may occasionally overdo the drive side or overdo the sense of restrictions but have the ability to be highly capable.

11: Your sense of identity and natural self-expression tend to flow easily with your sense of uniqueness. You thrive on being yourself and not like anyone else. Personal liberty and independence come naturally to you. You instinctively make your own path in life. Friends can be a source of support to you; they reinforce your need to do your own thing. Progressive ideas and involvements probably appeal to you.

12: Your sense of identity and natural self-expression tend to flow easily with your yearning for something Higher in life. Your faith and trust in the universe affirm your personal self-expression. Your sense of harmony with the infinite aids your courage and self-confidence.

Conflict to Letter...

1: Your sense of identity and natural self-expression tend to conflict within you. It is possible you feel torn — as if you are several different people, with varying needs which are sometimes in conflict with each other. You may feel ambivalent about how much to express, how to handle your anger, when and where to assert yourself. You could sabotage yourself at times. The more fully you explore the various facets of your identity, the easier it will become to express your different sides in fulfilling ways in your life.

2: Your sense of identity and natural self-expression tend to conflict with your desire for physical possessions, pleasures and indulgences. You may have to work a little to make peace between your sense of who you are and your need to enjoy the world of money and the senses. Keep room for both personal freedom and independence of action as well as the capacity to enjoy (moderately) the material goods and pleasures of life.

3: Your sense of identity and natural self-expression tend to conflict with your ability to think and communicate. This could express as occasionally feeling blocked in expressing yourself, misunderstood, or having trouble conceptualizing the way you would like. Your detached, objective side may be in conflict with your impulsive, instinctive side. As you pay attention and create opportunities to be yourself naturally — doing your thing in the world and still being a thoughtful, expressive individual — the tension will dissipate. Sometimes a sibling or early relative acts out the part of your nature which is at odds and you could have conflicts with that individual, especially around issues of who you are and how you think and communicate. As you resolve the inner struggle, the outer one will ease.

4: Your sense of identity and natural self-expression tend to conflict with your desire for emotional closeness and security. Your need for free self-expression and independence may conflict with your desire for a home, family and a warm sharing. This struggle was probably initially experienced through your relationship with your mother or mother figure. She could have seemed too into her own thing (selfish, gone, angry, etc.) or too clingy, possessive and ''clutchy'' as you worked to find a balance between a caring relationship and personal liberty. As you find an internal integration, your relationship with her can also improve.

5: Your sense of identity and natural self-expression tend to conflict with your desire to shine and be significant. You may feel conflicted about where and for what you want attention. You may sit on your charisma and inhibit your natural ability to take center stage. You might also overdo and demand constant limelight and applause from others. The issue revolves around being who you are naturally **and** gaining love, admiration and positive feedback from others.

Check for the Following Conditions

If Saturn, Vesta, South Node, Virgo or Capricorn is in the first house, add the following material:
You are probably harder on yourself than is called for. You tend to block your own ability to be significant because you are too self-critical. Since you judge yourself harshly, you are reluctant to chance being judged by others. Consequently, you do not give them much of a chance to admire or appreciate you. Start counting your assets and forget most of the flaws! (You are probably overemphasizing your faults anyway.) Love yourself more and you'll discover others around eager to love you also.

If there is a lot of fire in the chart, add the following material:
You tend to have lots of energy, drive and enthusiasm. Sometimes you can get carried away with your excitement and get involved with things you later regret. You tend to take many things personally and come from a stance of how you will be affected. This can result in extreme self-consciousness and discomfort or a naive egotism which may be a bit off-putting to others. Yet your zest for life and living can be very exciting to others if you are willing to share the fun!

6: Your sense of identity and natural self-expression tend to conflict...

Check for the Following Conditions

If there is a heavy fire or air emphasis, use this paragraph:
...with your desire to do the job well. Details may bore you; ordinary routine may seem uninteresting; perhaps your work incites no enthusiasm within you. You may wish to move on quickly and feel constrained by the inertia of your colleagues. You may crave excitement and feel bogged down by the necessary duties of life. The challenge is to integrate your quick, confident, zestful side with your cautious, careful and painstaking side.

If there is a heavy earth or water emphasis, use this paragraph:
...with your desire to do the job well. Your need to take care of business may conflict with your natural confidence and courage. You may hold yourself back from spontaneous expression because you are concentrating on getting the job done right. Efficiency appeals to you and may win out over spontaneity and pure zest for living. Strike a happy medium between a dedicated, disciplined focus on work and an impulsive, outgoing leap into life.

If there is a relative balance of elements, use this paragraph:
...with your desire to do the job well. You may feel torn between immediate action and a patient dealing with all the details. Efficiency may vie with

spontaneity as you strive to balance your desire to move on to the next challenge with your need to be productive and effectively complete each project.

7: Your sense of identity and natural self-expression tend to conflict with your desire for a close partnership. Partially, you are facing yourself through relationships and learning about who you are through the people you interact with. Extremes (by you or them) of assertion or appeasement are to be avoided. The goal is sharing — with neither you nor the other party having too much of the power or initiative in the relationship. You may feel torn between your wish to go it alone and the pull of an attachment to someone else. Keep room for both modes in your life.

8: Your sense of identity and natural self-expression tend to conflict with your desire for depth understanding and exploration. Power and control issues may surface — both in relationships and within your own being where physical pleasures are concerned. You may find yourself attracting people you end up struggling with over issues of sensuality and possessions. Or, you may spend time feeling torn between indulgence (in food, drink, sex, spending money, or other material pleasures) and self-control. Seek a happy medium within yourself and share the power in relationships.

9: Your sense of identity and natural self-expression tend to conflict with your desire to search for the ultimate truth and meaning in life.

Check for the Following Conditions

If there is heavy fire or air, use this paragraph:
You probably have great vitality, enthusiasm, faith and trust in the world and yourself. Your natural optimism will carry you through many situations. Sometimes your zest and impulsiveness can be excessive, however. If you feel you have the ultimate answers, you could come across as a missionary to others on occasion. Beware of trying to do more than is possible. Give yourself time to reach your goals, remember that no one is perfect and that truth is a process not a product.

If there is heavy earth or water, use this paragraph:
You are likely to have some doubts where ultimate meaning is concerned. Or, perhaps your beliefs are in conflict; you may have contradictory values. Your ideals and expectations could be excessive. It is important to have something to reach for, but do not forget that you (and other people) are human. Develop a firm sense of faith and trust in the universe so that you can relax after doing your part.

If there is a relative balance of elements, use this paragraph:
You may be feel torn around values, truth, faith and aspirations. You could vacillate between excessive faith and confidence versus trying to do everything

yourself and expecting more than is reasonable. Clarifying your long-range goals, values, ethics and moral principles could be quite helpful. You may be struggling with contradictory values; establishing priorities can make life easier.

10: Your sense of identity and natural self-expression tend to conflict with your perception of the rules of the game (of life). You probably first faced this conflict between self-will and authority in your relationship to your father or father figure. With him, you had an opportunity to practice the balance between drive and discipline; realism and impulsiveness; enthusiasm and concrete achievements. The more you made peace between your **inner** father (the need to be aware of the structure of the world and work within it) and your own sense of doing what you want in the world, the more likely you would be to have a comfortable relationship with your actual father (or father figure).

Check for the Following Conditions

If there is heavy earth or water, use this paragraph:
It is possible that you feel blocked, inhibited, criticized or put down by those around you and/or circumstances. Your harshest critic is probably internal. Focus on your accomplishments and forget about shortcomings for a time. Do what you can within the realistic parameters of your present situation and strive to do more and more. You tend not to believe you can do something until after you have done it. Be willing to try; you'll discover you are much more capable than you gave yourself credit for being.

If there is heavy fire, use this paragraph:
It is possible that you have a tendency to push the world, to try to always do what you feel is important, to test the limits. You may sometimes butt your head (metaphorically) against Life's regulations in the form of time (only 24 hours in a day), social roles and rules, societal laws and the natural laws of our physical universe (needing to eat, sleep, etc.). Balance your enthusiasm and energy with a pragmatic assessment of what is possible.

11: Your sense of identity and natural self-expression tend to conflict with your desire for uniqueness. You may feel frustrated in your desire to be free, different, unusual. Perhaps the independence you find is not what you wanted once you achieve it. Perhaps you are seen as an individual in an area where you would rather be one of the gang, while your cherished uniqueness in another area is not noticed. Perhaps you inhibit your love of liberty and originality for fear of not being liked, being criticized or other concerns. Cherish your specialness; there is no one else like you in this world. You are irreplaceable.

12: Your sense of identity and natural self-expression tend to conflict with your yearning for something Higher. You may feel torn between the pursuit of your own, personally-centered actions versus merging with the universe through great art, healing activities, mystical experiences or other ways of seeking union. You may at times feel lost in the immensity of the cosmos, overwhelmed by infinity. You may also feel incredibly confident, with the power of the universe behind you. Work to achieve a balance between action as a single, lone human and feeling a part of a "cause," a religion, a movement or something larger than yourself.

CHAPTER SEVEN

WORK AND CAREER OPTIONS

Following are interpretations of the various themes (element, quality, alphabet, other themes, nodes, aspects) as applied to the life area of work and career.

This section addresses the client's handling of the physical, material world. This includes some kind of job, career, means of earning a living or area of competence. This section also looks at the client's orientation toward the "real" (physical) world. (See also Chapter 12 on money.)

Astrology does not say an individual would be uniquely suited for one specific career; most people have aptitudes in a number of different areas. Astrology mirrors inner motivations and drives which function best in certain kinds of fields, certain working environments. Knowing ourselves better enables us to choose careers which are most fully satisfying.

The Factors

In considering work potentials indicated by the horoscope, we would include **Letter 2** (which encompasses earning money as well as other pleasures), **Letter 6** (efficient functioning on the job as well as in the body) and **Letter 10** (power, responsibility and authority including the ability to pursue a career).[1]

---

1. If you prefer **not** to search for repeated themes yourself, you can order the "PP BOOK" option from Astro Computing Services (PO Box 16430, San Diego, Ca 92116), which allows you to use this book to make complete, synthesizing delineations of horoscopes without figuring out which themes are emphasized.

Available for $3.00 each, the "PP BOOK" report calculates the emphasis on all the letters of the alphabet, themes and aspects in each horoscope for which you provide the data. The report lists each significant focus (e.g., "There is a Letter 3 theme in "Identity," and gives the appropriate page numbers for you to read in this book ("See pages 107-108 in the *Complete Horoscope Interpretation* book.")

The computer will not **always** arrive at the same results as you might, as certain steps are ambiguous (e.g., how much weight to give a planet making a conjunction, based on the orb). However, the majority of the time, the computer answers will concur with those derived from use of the worksheets — or the recommended quick scan of a horoscope. Thus it provides an excellent teaching tool.

The "PP BOOK" does **not** provide a listing of **each and every** astrological factor making up the significant themes. For that, you would order "PP WEIGHTS" (discussed in next footnote).

Astrologically, this means we would examine:

GROUP I
Any conjunctions to the planets Venus (as ruler of Taurus), Mercury (as ruler of
   Virgo) and Saturn as well as the asteroids Ceres and Vesta. (We would consider
   the nature of each planet making the conjunction.)
Any conjunctions to the MC (the nature of the planet making the conjunction)
Any conjunctions to the ruler of the Midheaven
Any conjunctions to the rulers of the 2nd and 6th cusps
Any conjunctions to the rulers of other signs in the 2nd, 6th or 10th houses

GROUP II
Any planets in the 2nd, 6th and 10th houses (the nature of the planets)
The sign of the MC
Any planets within two degrees of the 2nd, 6th and 10th houses, but occupying
   the 1st, 3rd, 5th, 7th or 11th houses. [Note that planets conjuncting the MC
   from the 9th house are already counted in Group I.]
Any planets occupying Gauquelin sectors (in 9th or 12th houses or within the
   first 10 degrees of the 1st or 10th houses)

GROUP III
Any parallels to the planets (or asteroids) Venus, Saturn, Mercury (if desired), Ceres
   or Vesta (if desired)
Any parallels to the MC (nature of the planet making the aspect)
Any parallels to rulers of the 2nd, 6th or 10th cusps
Any parallels to rulers of other signs in the 2nd, 6th or 10th houses
The placement of Venus, Saturn, Mercury (if desired), Ceres and Vesta (if desired)
   by house
The placement (by house) of the rulers of the 2nd, 6th and 10th cusps
The house placement of the rulers of any additional signs in the 2nd, 6th or 10th
   houses
The house(s) which have the signs within them ruled by any planet(s) in the 2nd,
   6th or 10th houses, e.g., if the Moon in in the 2nd, in what houses does Cancer
   fall?
The house(s) which have the signs within them ruled by any planets conjuncting
   Venus, Mercury (if desired), Saturn, plus Ceres and Vesta (if desired). For ex-
   ample, if Saturn conjuncts Pluto, in what houses does Scorpio fall?
Any planets in Taurus, Virgo or Capricorn — the nature of the planet(s)

GROUP IV
The sign of Venus, Mercury (if desired), Saturn, Ceres and Vesta (if desired)
The signs on the cusps of the 2nd and 6th houses
The signs of the rulers of the 2nd, 6th and 10th cusps
The signs of the rulers of any additional signs in the 2nd, 6th and 10th houses

Any signs in the 2nd, 6th & 10th houses which are occupied by a planet (the nature of the sign)
Any additional (unoccupied) signs in the 2nd, 6th and 10th houses
Any planets in Taurus, Virgo and Capricorn — the nature of the house occupied
Taurus, Virgo and Capricorn on any house cusp(s) — the nature of the house

How to Weight the Factors

Please note that these factors are rank ordered (in chunks) according to their weighting. That is, planets (and angles) are most significant, so we consider first any conjunctions to Venus, Saturn, Vesta, Ceres (and Mercury if we take it as a Virgo Mercury). Then we consider rulers of the 2nd, 6th and 10th houses. Houses come next in weighting, so we look to the nature of the planets in the 2nd, 6th and 10th and then house placements for important factors. The research of the Gauquelins has demonstrated the importance of certain planetary placements within the "Gauquelin sectors," as keys to profession, so a separate area in the interpretation section lists those associations. Last, we consider signs.

If you want to use exact figures, a suggested weighting scale is given in the appendix — with worksheets for work and the other various life areas.[2] However, the right brain scanning of the horoscope is recommended, which does not require lists.

THREE SHORT CUTS
For quickness and ease of use, especially for people becoming familiar with the alphabet, I suggest focusing initially on factors in Groups I and II.

For example, since Jane Fonda's (see next page) Ceres (key to work) closely conjuncts Mars, we would read the interpretation for Letter 1 in this "Work" section.

---

2. You can also obtain a listing of **all** the astrological factors which compose those letters of the Zip Code determined to be significant in a horoscope. This makes an excellent teaching tool and a valuable resource to check yourself against when practicing with the Zip Code.

Astro Computing Services, PO Box 16430, San Diego, CA 92116, has calculated 28,000 horoscopes and established averages and standard deviations for the scores of each letter of the astrological alphabet, each theme, and the conflict and harmony aspects to each life area.

Astro's report, called "PP WEIGHTS," will list those letters of the astrological alphabet which are one standard deviation or more above the mean — and list **all** the astrological factors which point to each significant letter of the alphabet. These weightings will also compare each individual's score on the various themes (e.g., risk-taking, artistic) to the means and standard deviations to determine which themes are significant.

Averages are established for aspects as well in order to note conflict or harmony in the different life areas.

The results obtained by Astro's "PP WEIGHTS" will not **always** coincide with those you determine by a quick scan and intuitive judgment, or by use of the worksheets. Certain of the steps (e.g., how much to weight a planet based on orb) are ambiguous, so different results can occur. However, most of the time, Astro's answers will confirm those you could obtain in working with the Zip Code. Furthermore, the **complete** listing of relevant factors is an excellent teaching tool.

Ask for "PP Weights." The price, as of December 1985 is $5.00

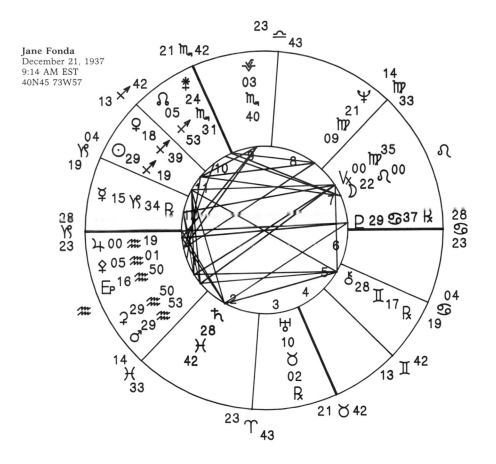

Jane Fonda
December 21, 1937
9:14 AM EST
40N45 73W57

Once you are familiar with Groups I and II, you can move on to incorporate factors from Groups III and IV as well, seeking the those themes which are again repeated. For example, Letter 11 is connected to work by the following: Venus in the 11th; Ceres in Aquarius, Aries in 2nd ruled by Mars which is in Aquarius, Sagittarius in 10th ruled by Jupiter which is in Aquarius, Taurus is occupied by Uranus, Capricorn falls in the 11th house [as well as in the 12th], and three keys to work make conjunctions in Aquarius (Ceres to Mars; Jupiter ruling the Sagittarius in the 10th conjuncts Pallas, and Mars ruling the Aries in the 2nd conjuncts Ceres).

An alternative approach is to use Appendix 2. If we examine Ms. Fonda's Saturn (one key to career), we find it in the 2nd house in Pisces. Appendix 2 refers us to the appropriate pages for Letter 10 in work, money, sexuality, beliefs and future, along with Letter 2 in work and parents plus Letter 12 in work and parents. If we are focusing only on career (work), we note career themes on pages 141 (Letter 2), 147 (Letter 10) and 149 (Letter 12). Then, look to see what is listed in terms of work for each of the other planets.

Another option is to use the placements illustrated in the listing within Chapter 2. The "work" listing in Chapter 2 would refer the reader immediately to the appropriate delineations to read for the placements of Venus, Saturn, Mercury, Ceres, Vesta and the rulers of the 2nd, 6th and 10th houses (all keys to career).

Themes

Themes can be ascertained by two approaches. One method is to combine the totals for those letters of the alphabet determined to be significant based on the steps above. In Jane Fonda's horoscope, for example, we have noted a Letter 11 theme and might suspect a Letter 7 theme with Juno conjunct the MC. Letters 7 and 11 share the theme of **air**. Ms. Fonda is known for her political activism and writing as well as her work as an actress. Communication, people and ideas are central to her work.

A second method for seeking themes is to sum **all** the scores for all 12 letters of the alphabet, and look to see which combinations have an above average emphasis. For example, the air theme is the total of scores from Letters 3, 7 and 11. You will need to do some rough arithmetic here, or get an intuitive impression. If a theme involves three (out of twelve) letters of the astrological alphabet, you would expect it to have about ¼ of the total score. So, if the amount for those letters seems appreciably more than ¼ of the total, count that as a theme — and read the appropriate section.

In the case of Ms. Fonda, Letter 7 is repeated by: 10th house Juno (7), 6th cusp (Cancer) ruled by Moon which is in 7th (7), Scorpio MC ruled by Pluto which is in 7th (7) and conjuncts the Descendant (7), MC conjuncts Juno (7), and the 10th house Sagittarius is ruled by Jupiter which conjuncts Pallas (7).

When searching for themes, we give additional weighting to like planets in aspect to one another. For example, Mercury, Pallas, Juno and Uranus are the air "planets" (plus Venus when Venus is a Libra rather than a Taurus Venus). Any aspects between Mercury, Pallas, Juno and Uranus add to the theme of equality and objectivity (air). Ms. Fonda has Mercury parallel Venus, Pallas octile Venus, Uranus widely trines Mercury and Uranus widely squares Pallas.

We would also give extra weight to these factors in each other's signs and/or houses. Ms. Fonda has Pallas in Aquarius and Uranus in the third house — instances of the air factors backing each other up.

A quick glance at the number of movies Ms. Fonda has done, the video cassettes she has made, her books, and the causes for which she has lectured and demonstrated reveals the importance of communication in her life. She has done the speaking, writing, teaching and has the constant involvement with people which air can indicate. Her equalitarian instincts (associated with air) are strongly marked.

Lawrence Guiles notes in his biography (*Jane Fonda: The Actress in Her Time*) that during the 1970s she was often on the road, from demonstration to demonstration, with very little sleep, but always ready to talk and share, no matter how large or small the group of people. She is eager to share knowledge and information with anyone and everyone. The wide dissemination associated with air also fits the fact that Ms. Fonda's videos appear in so many bookcases across America and her name often appears on the list of ten most admired American women.

Letter 7 is often associated with lawyers (one-to-one interactions and confrontation through the courts) and politicans (who depend on other people to vote for them). Letter 11 is symbolic of legislative bodies, from Congress down to city councils. When 7, 9 and 11 are emphasized in a chart, there is often a passion for justice, equality and fair play. Ms. Fonda's political activism has ranged from movies with a message (*The China Syndrome*) to political demonstrations, to influencing elections to the Santa Monica City Council on a local level and, of course, her husband's position of Assemblyman in the California state legislature. She uses her career (including the money she makes) to further her vision of justice, equality and fair play. And it may be that her high visibility through social causes also contributes to her career. People sometimes go to films because the actors are controversial.

Aspects

Quickly scan the aspects other than conjunctions or parallels, grouping them according to harmony (sextile, trine, semisextile) and conflict (octile, tri-octile, square, opposition and quincunx). In considering each aspect, weight the nature of the planet most heavily, followed by the house and the sign. Note both the house occupied and the cusp ruled by the planet being aspected.

For example, Ms. Fonda's chart has the following **close** harmony aspects to Saturn:
• sextile the Ascendant (1) in Capricorn (10)
• sextile Jupiter (9) in the 1st (1) in Aquarius (11); Jupiter rules 11th (11)
• trine Pluto (8) in the 7th (7) in Cancer (4); Pluto rules the 10th (10)
• trine Juno (7) in the 10th (10) in Scorpio (8)
• square the Sun (5) in the 11th (11) in Sagittarius (9); Sun rules 7th (7)
• square Chiron (9) in Gemini (3) in the 5th (5)

Mentally sum all "conflict" aspects for each letter of the astrological alphabet and sum the "harmony" aspects for each letter of the alphabet.

Here again, you can probably tell by glancing through, which letters of the alphabet have lots of conflict to them and which have quite a bit of harmony. If you feel any group of aspects has an emphasis on one or more letters of the alphabet, read the appropriate interpretation. (In Ms. Fonda's case, we might suspect that conflict to Letter 5 — her need to shine and be significant, her desire to sway people emotionally — might sometimes be an issue for her in working successfully and competently. Biographies report that Ms. Fonda had a strong ambivalence about being onstage. For many years, she did not trust her own abilities, was quite self-critical and unsure of her talent. She was drawn to the limelight, yet also afraid of it. Even today, she talks as if she prefers acting a role in front of others to being herself. "On television, I'm me and I just don't like to see me being me. My dad always felt I went into acting for that reason, to hide behind masks of other people. I just hate the way I come across as a person when someone's on television asking me questions about myself. I always think, 'Why did I say that? Why did I have to talk too much? I should have revealed less or . . .' "[*Los Angeles Herald Examiner*, p.9])

Initially you may wish to make up a quick list of the emphasized themes when you complete your scan of a life area such as work (career). For example:

Work for _____

Most emphasized letter(s) of the astrological alphabet: _____
Most emphasized polarities: _____
Placement of nodes by house: _____
Placement of nodes by sign: _____
Element emphasis (if any): _____
Element combination emphasis (if any): _____
Quality emphasis (if any): _____
Any emphasized themes: _____
Significant conflict to _____ (letter of the alphabet)
Significant harmony to _____ (letter of the alphabet)

Interpretations: Work

ALPHABET THEMES

Letter 1: The Solo Worker

"I'll do it **my** way!" is your song. You function best in situations where you can do your own thing. Owning your own business is excellent, but you can also do well running your own division or section of a larger company. Basically, you need room in your job to work undisturbed. You tend to do your best when on your own. Having other people around is just a distraction and you usually dislike taking orders from anyone else.

You have a pioneering spirit and can operate well in a trailblazing capacity. Your courage and willingness to lay it on the line can break into territory where others fear to tread. If carried too far, of course, these qualities can indicate rashness, impulsiveness and a self-centered drive to have everything on your own terms.

Physical activity is important; you should not settle for a job where you sit at a desk all day. You need some movement and changes of scene. You do not enjoy repetition. You are at your best when doing something **once** and then moving on to new areas to conquer. If you are out of touch with your own strength, assertion and independence, you may find yourself surrounded by coworkers and bosses who are aggressive, argumentative, selfish and iconoclastic and who pick fights. Anger could be an issue on the job.

Potential talents include mechanical ability, medical skills, sports, the "killer instinct" for competitive fields and a high energy level for working at what **you** want to do.

Letter 2: Working for Pleasure

You have the potential of really enjoying your work. This mixture can indicate the possibility of pleasure coming through work. You know how to gain satisfaction from what you do. If carried too far, your relaxed easygoing attitude could be a problem — you might expect the work to always be enjoyable, or be too relaxed about performing your duties. However, this usually just indicates someone who values comfort on the job.

For best results, you need a working environment where you feel at ease. A moderate temperature, comfortable chair, aesthetically appealing surroundings and pleasing colleagues all pay big dividends where you are concerned. You also expect tangible rewards (a good salary) from your career.

If you are not in touch with your sensual nature, you could find the people with whom you work too indulgent, lazy, laid-back, satisfied and stuck in a rut. They might strike you as excessively concerned with security and finding the easy way. (Whatever we underdo, those around us will tend to overdo.)

You could be involved in providing comfort and/or beauty to other people. Any career in the aesthetic area is possible (painting, dancing, sculpting, poetry, decorating, makeup, fashion, hairdressing...). So is work involving basic material resources and possessions (banking, commodities, providing goods which assist creature comforts) and sensuality (massage, physiotherapy, acupressure...). But part of your skill lies in finding pleasure through whatever tasks you perform and in appreciating the rewards of whatever accomplishments you make.

Letter 3: Working Logically

You work best with your mind. Thinking and communicating is your forte. Curious and eager to learn more, you are best off in a field which offers a lot of variety — either something new and different to learn all the time, or new people to meet, or new places to go and see. Your interests are often varied and you may be overextended, trying to do too many things. Multiple careers are not uncommon (sequentially or even juggling two or three at one time).

Physical labor is not your style. Ideas and people offer a forum for your talents. You have a facility for language and relating to others which can express in numerous fields. Possibilities range from the skilled secretary, receptionist, telephone operator to the professor, teacher (from elementary school to college), writer, lecturer, salesperson, songwriter, etc. Fairly often, this combination symbolizes good coordination and fine eye-mind-hand dexterity which is useful for tasks as varied as typing, playing a musical instrument, the professional magician, a dealer in Las Vegas, etc. Sometimes the work involves other family members, such as brothers, sisters, aunts, uncles, cousins and so on.

You are able to be flexible in your work, easily moving from one project to another. You do not take anything too seriously, being able to detach and view the whole situation objectively. This attitude, if overdone, could become flippant and careless. If you are out of touch with this side of your nature, your colleagues and/or boss might seem cool, scattered, superficial, gossipy, flighty or talkative. Your light touch, objective, detached mental approach and easy camaraderie with those around you generally make for work full of information exchange and sociability.

Letter 4: Work of Substance

Security — physical and emotional — ranks high as a focus in your career. This can range from nurturing and protecting people or animals to providing the basic needs of life (food, shelter, clothing). You see work as a source of security and sustenance for yourself and are also likely to provide reassurance or support to others.

Areas of expertise can range from the housekeeper, nanny, governess and/or cook to the real estate agent, clothing manufacturer, buyer, restaurateur, hotel owner or worker, contractor, builder, architect, etc. Caring for animals is an option — as a vet, dog groomer, zookeeper or ecologist. Working with the public is also quite possible as is a career involving women. Since the "home" in some fashion is commonly involved, this can include businesses being operated out of the home, a homemaking career, real estate, home appliances, a military career oriented toward protecting the homeland, genealogy which traces family roots and work that is done at home (such as the author working on his/her word processor).

There is a tendency to form closer than usual ties to coworkers. You may find yourself mothering them or being mothered in some fashion by them. The desire is for some emotional closeness and caring — not just an aloof task orientation. If these qualities are carried to excess, you may experience colleagues as too dependent and needy or smothering and intrusive in their efforts to be emotionally involved with you.

When home is the focus of work and effort, often the nurturing is directed only toward close friends and family. You may retreat into the nest as a security measure and not be very involved, as far as work endeavors are concerned, with the outside world.

Your mother (or mother figure) is a role model, positive or negative, for your attitudes about working and being effective in the world. If positive, you tend to emulate her approach. If negative, you take the opposite position. This can indicate a family business, working with/for one or both parents. It can also simply point to mother as an influence over what you define as doing a good job, performing well. Usually mother's example is by being efficient, capable, a hard worker or the exact reverse (inefficient, inadequate, perhaps ill or otherwise unable to cope with reality). Either way, the focus in the relationship revolved around the proper way to deal with the physical, nitty-gritty world.

You have the ability to be both pragmatic and helpful in your approach to productivity.

Letter 5: Work of Significance

You need to shine in your work! In some way, your career should involve being onstage, the center of attention and receiving admiration, appreciation and applause in some form. It is a place to allow expression of your creativity. It is a place to gain self-esteem and a healthy sense of pride in your accomplishments. We all need appreciation, but be sure you are not too dependent on other people responding to and approving of what you do. Feeling good about yourself only because you have "performed" well on the job is an uncomfortable state of affairs. If you are too ego-vulnerable, you may fear trying certain things, because you hate to "lose" and would rather not try (at times) than risk being laughed at or put down. If you trust in your natural magnetism and drive, you can accomplish much.

Potential talents range from teaching, acting, sales, promotion, advertising to the entertainment world in any form, or speculation and gambling. You have an instinct for risk-taking in your work, an urge to somehow expand, hit the "big time," do more than has been done before. Whether you risk money (gambling and speculation), your ego (entertainment), or your time and persuasive ability (sales, teaching), the hope is that you will get a bigger and better return on your investment!

One possible way to express your creativity is through having and raising children. You could make a career out of working with children (your own or other people's). Your urge to pour out in the world can express through love as well as other emotionally exciting avenues.

Since it is essential for you to be important in your work, you do not function as comfortably in a subsidiary position. You are best off running the show. Your natural dynamism makes you less inclined to wait in the wings while others direct the action. If you deny this part of your inner motivations, you will continually attract prima donnas, people who refuse to ever get offstage, self-centered egotists who believe the whole world revolves around them.

You prefer excitement and action in your work. This may mean you are reluctant to settle for an "ordinary" job or something less than the best. Carrying through on boring details is **not** your forte; you prefer to delegate that to someone else. Your most significant talent is the ability to touch the inner child in all people. You can get other people excited and involved. This gives you ability in working with children in many fields (teaching, coaching, Little League...), in recreation (getting people to loosen up and have fun) and in any kind of promotional or creative field. Your dramatic instincts help you to sway people and have an impact.

Letter 6: Working Hard

You expect work to be work — requiring discipline, dedication, pragmatism and concentration. You are usually a conscientious and careful worker, doing your very best to do a **good job**. Efficiency and productivity are important to you. One of your talents is analysis and discrimination. You are skilled at picking an object or situation or person apart to discover all the flaws. The goal then is to put it back together, working even better than before. (This is much easier to accomplish with things than people. The critical eye can be a liability where relationships are concerned.)

Your organizational skills, thoroughness and penchant for handling details in a logical, systematic fashion make you a tremendous asset in almost any field requiring focus, concentration and productivity. Almost any business could benefit from your skills and many scientific fields are possible careers as well, especially those involving research. Areas requiring logical analysis, such as computer programming, are likely bets. Your interests often involve medicine, health, healing and nutrition, so those fields may also appeal.

Your standards for work are often exacting and you may feel, "If you want it done right, do it yourself." Another possibility is the tendency to get obsessed with little details: "I'll keep on and on until I get it right" (but there is always another flaw). An alternative is, "I won't do it unless it is just right." If you are expressing the first potential, you commonly carry more than your share of the load. You are an employer's dream as you are perfectly happy to carry out your duties (at whatever level of the hierarchy) for the pure satisfaction of having done them **well**. When you retire, they usually hire three people to replace you.

With the second and third options, you may have trouble getting things done — either endlessly procrastinating in an attempt to have everything absolutely perfect or simply refusing to attempt projects which you feel will have results below your standards. Of course, there is always the middle ground — an individual doing all that is possible, working hard enough (but not too hard) and knowing when is enough in terms of critical judgment.

Two extremes you need to avoid. One is the workaholic. Because you want to do everything well, you can end up trying to do it all and can work long hours. If this is carried to an extreme, your body may break down as the only way to get you to take a vacation! The opposite end is the person who is obsessed with inefficient functioning, often with health problems. This can be connected with an obsessive need to do it **right** in the work and a fear of failure. Unconsciously, if we are sick, we can get out of feeling guilty about not working. In such cases, finding **something** you can do — and do well for the sense of skilled craftsmanship — will often help to improve the health.

Usually, you are an excellent, dedicated and effective worker whose major flaw may be working too much. Remember there are other parts of life!

Letter 7: People-Work

People are your focus. Your work needs to involve relating to others and associations. The loner approach is not for you. Rather, you need someone with whom to share, or someone with whom to compete, but you function best in the relationship mode.

Potential careers include such possibilities as a counselor, lawyer, consumer advocate, personnel administrator, astrologer or any position which incorporates one-to-one interactions. The focus is on a peer exchange — whether cooperative or competitive. This can even include making a career out of marriage or a succession of business partnerships. You might also work with a marital partner (or meet him/her through your work).

An alternative is pursuit of your aesthetic interests. Talent in the areas of photography, graphics, interior decorating, design, fashion, painting and any of the visual and fine arts is possible. Music is an option. Vocations such as modeling where the beauty comes through your own appearance are also possible. The aesthetic could even be combined with the feeling for people in fields such as art therapy. Balance and harmony are important in both the artistic and the people fields.

Generally, you are oriented toward an attractive, easy working environment, and not noted for a willingness to sweat hard or labor arduously. Usually, you are inclined to seek out the path of least resistance, the easiest way to accomplish what is needed. This can include charming other people into doing some of it on occasion. However, your basic sense of fair play tends to keep you from taking too much advantage of others. You may sometimes lean, but are usually willing to take turns.

If you are not comfortable with these facets of your nature, you may face them through people you work with. You could view colleagues as competitive and combative. Or, you might perceive them as too other-directed, needing other people in order to act. The easygoing, "let's not work **too** hard" approach might be played out by someone around you on the job.

You can be very appealing, attractive and diplomatic when you choose. Using your grace and charm in interacting with others or to create more beauty in the world is likely.

Letter 8: The Persistent Worker

Your orientation is to probe beneath the surface, to uncover what is hidden and reach a depth understanding of the situation. You can utilize a bulldog tenacity in your work and have an immense capacity for concentration, focus and follow through. Determined and resolute, you may stop at nothing to achieve your goals.

Skilled with details and with an instinct for handling money, you are often found in financial fields — from accounting to tax law to government grants to the IRS to investment counseling and loan officers. Your investigative nose may lead you into fields of insurance investigation, detective work or research of any kind. Your tremendous organizational skills and thoroughness make you an asset in almost any kind of business.

Depth psychotherapy is another option. You tend to probe psyches (your own and other people's) as an avocation if not as a vocation. With your ability to be cold-blooded when called for, you can be an excellent surgeon or medical technician. You value self-control and refuse to allow yourself to be squeamish.

The handling of joint resources, possessions, pleasures and sensuality is one where you have a practical approach. So you can be found in fields such as massage and physical therapy, marriage counseling, sex therapy, budgeting, purchasing or any vocation in which you help people to be practical and organize their money, resources, possessions or pleasures. Since you are dealing with shared resources and support from other people, fields such as politics (depending on people to vote for you) are possible. Inheritance may also figure in your sources of income.

You function best in an environment which is under your control. Indeed, you could even become a bit obsessive about having every detail **just so**. If possible, seek a position of authority as you may very well resent taking orders from above. Negative uses of your power drive could lead to confrontations, battles, power struggles or manipulation, blackmail and intimidation. (If you are denying your need for control, you may attract others who express a dominating drive in excess.)

You tend to be drawn to areas where intense emotions are aroused which can be very exciting and stimulating as long as you handle them carefully. Your intuition may also be useful in your work.

Letter 9: Working for MORE

The central drive in your career area is the reach for something higher. This can range from seeking the best party, the most fun, the jolliest companions to searching for the Ultimate Truth to understand and know the secrets of the universe. The latter quest can lead you into religion, philosophy, spiritual studies, education and travel as potential vocations. Teaching, publishing, the law (especially the judiciary where moral principles and a sense of justice is involved) and writing might all appeal. Whether you choose the role of professor or guru or travel consultant or globe-trotter or professional hedonist, the central theme is looking for something **more** in life — maybe over the next hill, in the next book, at the next party.

This inner restlessness can sometimes lead to job-hopping. You may go from one job to the next, each time hoping that **this** one will have the perfect hours, with the perfect pay, with the perfect coworkers, etc. When it is not ideal, you either leave (or unconsciously set yourself up to be fired) to continue the quest.

Another option is trying to do your work perfectly — never making a mistake. Setting that kind of impossible standard for your performance is an incredible demand. You are likely to end up disappointed when you turn out to have some shortcomings, or afraid to even try — for fear your successes will not match the grandiose image you have for them. Keep your dreams and ideals; we all need something to reach for. Just make sure that some of them are attainable.

It is also possible you value the work ethic, that doing a good job becomes paramount with you. Your career and handling of the physical world may be a major, important issue for you. Your sense of ultimate meaning and what really matters may be tied to your ability to succeed in the "real world." As long as this is in balance with other parts of life, you are just likely to push yourself to accomplish all you can. If you overvalue one part of life, it can become too much of a focus for you, with corresponding deprivation in other areas.

The idealism of this combination can also be expressed through work that makes the world more perfect. Whether you choose to inspire other people (religion), teach them so that they can improve their situations (education), provide justice (the courts of law) or offer a sense of meaning through art, nature, good works — the common thread is a desire to uplift and improve humankind through your efforts.

Letter 10: The Structured Worker

An awareness of and ability to get to the bottom line is one of your assets. Practical, sensible, reality-oriented, you pay attention to the essentials and can screen out wishful thinking or excessive dreaminess. Your emphasis is on survival — what is necessary. This includes skills at figuring out the rules in a given environment. You are aware that every arena has its own limitations and restrictions. Part of your function is to pinpoint the "laws" for where you are and work realistically within them.

An excessive focus on the limits can result in feeling inhibited, blocked and held back. By focusing on what **could** be a problem, or where a restriction **might** exist, you can create a barrier in your mind. Then, you can become afraid to even try accomplishments which are perfectly reasonable. Or, you could obsess about doing things in just the right way, thus delaying achievements through nit-picking. Part of the challenge is separating basic constrictions (which must be obeyed) from apparent limitations. Acumen is essential.

Your attitudes about work and success are likely to be strongly influenced by a father or father figure. The authority parent was either a positive (admired, emulated) or negative (you went the reverse) role model for your own concepts and opinions about what work is, what entails doing a good job, standards of performance and success. Father may have worked hard and been practical and sensible. He could have been a workaholic. He could have fallen into self-blocking — believing he was more limited than he actually was. Whatever his actions, he brought your attention to the area of reality-testing and figuring out what is possible in the world and then **doing** it!

There is a natural executive ability here, a tendency to work one's way to the top. You are willing to pay your dues and usually put in a lot of hours and plain, old hard work to achieve a position of authority. Your skills can be useful in any business field or any vocation requiring a practical assessment of the situation. If you drive yourself too hard, your health might suffer as a sign to slow down. If you are feeling inadequate, demanding more than is reasonable of yourself, illness can offer you an unconscious way out of feeling guilty. But the general tendency is to be very conscientious, super responsible (often doing more than your share of the work), hardworking, ambitious and effective.

Letter 11: The Unconventional Worker

There is something unusual about your work — either the job itself, the way you do your job, your style of working or the environment on the job. You are drawn to something out of the ordinary as one way of expressing your uniqueness and individuality. If carried too far, your desire to march to a "different drummer" could lead to constant job turnover as you are unwilling to accept discipline or order at work. If your need for liberty is curtailed, you may unconsciously attract sudden changes, shifts or abrupt surprises (including being fired) in your work — to provide the variety and stimulation you crave.

New technology is a potential area of interest for you, so computers, lasers, aviation or anything on the cutting edge of change is a potential career involvement. You have a strong need for freedom in your work which can lead to vocations in the air or simply a lot of change, variety and independence in when, where and how you do your work. Some would call it erratic; you tend to call it interesting. Routine usually bores you.

Ideally, your mind needs to be stimulated by your work. You can be very original, inventive and creative in your activities and need a sense of challenge from your career. If you feel you've got it all down and know it all already, you will not want to hang around. Changes of scene help keep the situation from becoming stale.

You can be a bit of a rebel. You tend to operate as a "friend" to everyone at work; that is, you feel they are all your peers. You do not set the boss up above you — nor anyone else; your approach tends to be equalitarian. If you feel too claustrophobic about rules and regulations hemming you in, you are tempted to just split — or say or do something a bit shocking to the people around you. Many times, you can get away with being a little "kooky" or "eccentric," but keep it within bounds! Astrology, being a field full of eccentrics with an unusual approach outside society's rules, is another potential vocation.

If you are uncomfortable with your needs for freedom and uniqueness while on the job, you may find colleagues to express those drives for you. In such cases, they will seem chaotic, confusing, erratic, irresponsible, unpredictable and upsetting. It's more fulfilling to express your own needs for liberty, openness and the unusual in some comfortable, helpful fashion. You can make a significant contribution through being open, flexible and willing to try a variety of options, exploring the new ideas which occur to you.

Letter 12: The Visionary Worker

This theme tends to be lived out in three major roles: the professional artist, the professional helper and/or the professional victim. All are seeking their own version of the beautiful dream, infinite ecstasy. The artist is inspired by a cosmic vision and is trying to bring it into being here on Earth. The helper/healer/savior has utopian ideals about the best of all possible worlds and is striving to help create that here on Earth, by assisting others in leading more fulfilling and fulfilled lives. The victim also has a dream but is unwilling or feels unable to do anything about it. So, the victim retreats (into drugs, alcohol, illness, fantasy, sleeping all the time, etc.) to escape from the fact that the world is **not** perfect and s/he is not doing anything to change it!

The artist could function in any of the beauty fields — including creating it with his/her own body or through any art form. Besides standard "beauty" fields such as painting, photography, music, design and singing, other forms of the aesthetic could be expressed. The world of film, enacting fantasies and offering ideal visions, might be a focus. Beauty can also be expressed with food, clothing, cosmetics or even landscape gardening. The possibilities are endless. The savior could be in the medical, counseling, astrological or any other vocation which involves assisting people in living more satisfying lives. The victim could choose any form of escapism. A temptation professional helpers have to resist is becoming too involved with the saving role. Sacrificing too much turns the savior into victim. Knowing how much to give, when to give and how to give are important.

The yearning for a connection to the Infinite is tied to your handling of the physical world. This can manifest as the search for the perfect job (with disillusionment when it is less than ideal and perhaps going from job to job — hoping the next one will be more ideal). Or, the person may attempt to be godlike and perfect — never making a mistake, an inhuman demand. One victim variation is waiting for God to do the work — expecting somehow that everything will fall in your lap like manna from heaven! Other alternatives include a career that satisfies your ideals, that improves the world and an idealization of doing a good job.

The worst of this combination is never being satisfied because the real world falls short of your inspired vision. The best of this combination is continually working, on a practical level, to help create your beautiful dream and make it an actuality.

ALPHABET COMBINATIONS BY TWOS

1-2 . . . a need to have your work under your own, personal control; desire to accomplish when, where and how you choose; resistance to outside authority; strong, determined; desire for comfort and excellent recompense on the job. Laid-back style may vie with high energy.

1-3 . . . a flexible approach to the job and strong need for variety in the working environment and tasks; much energy for communication, information exchange. Coordination and dexterity may be excellent.

1-4 . . . an inner struggle between work which allows you freedom and independence versus work which satisfies emotional needs and a desire for security. May need to balance compassion and competition.

1-5 . . . desire for exciting work! There is also a need for movement on the job; reluctance to settle for something ordinary; much vitality, enthusiasm, charisma to offer through career.

1-6 . . . a strong focus on productivity, accomplishment and general competence with a tendency to measure yourself by what you do. You may be overly harsh in judgments of your achievements or demand that the work be on your terms. The combination calls for integration of self-will with practical necessities.

1-7 . . . learning how to balance the power between you and others through your work; a career which involves relating to people so you can integrate doing your own thing with accommodation.

1-8 . . . a desire for power and control through your work in the world; talent in fields involving medicine, assertion, business; learning to balance direct confrontation with more subtle forms of power-seeking.

1-9 . . . an orientation toward fun, humor, verve and action on the job. Restless, you are inclined to continually expand occupational horizons and need new challenges or else have a tendency to leave (or get fired) due to boredom.

1-10 . . . a need to balance your way of doing things with the rules (especially the boss's rules). You may push too hard for what you want or give up too soon on what you could do. Integrate your wants and needs with the structure of your working environment.

1-11 . . . a desire for freedom of action; preference for independence in your work; inclination to leave if you are feeling confined in career; can be innovative, creative.

1-12 . . . a preference for work which advances your personal ideals, your own vision; could be an aesthetic or healing career; energetic search of something inspiring through your vocation.

2-3 . . . pleasure through communication in your work; potential of working in fields creating beauty through language (music, song writing, lecturing); casual, comfortable attitude about work.

2-4 . . . a career in fields involving basic security and resources (banking, land, commodities, food . . .); desire for security and stability in the job.

2-5 . . . ambivalence between a career involving a steady, dependable situation and income versus a career involving risks, excitement and possibly making it big in the world.

2-6. . .a focus on work satisfaction, pleasure through doing a good job; tendency to value established routines, honing your skills to even more efficiency.

2-7. . .careers involving pleasure and/or beauty. Also, an easygoing, comfortable attitude about working (maybe **too** laid-back) is likely; focus on harmony at work.

2-8. . .excellent business skills, especially in fields involving finances. Talent in physical manipulation is also possible (e.g., massage, physiotherapy). The mixture suggests a grounded approach to work; seeking security in your vocation.

2-9. . .an inner struggle between tangible, earth-centered work versus a more philosophical, abstract career; integrating spiritual and material needs on the job.

2-10. . .a practical, grounded, reasonable approach to work. Sensible and stable, you tend to be a good, steady worker who values the rewards of success.

2-11. . .an inner conflict between work which is routine and predictable with a stable base versus work which is full of challenges, change, and allows you to be original. Integrate.

2-12. . .a desire for smoothness and ease on the job; potential talent in beauty fields; can operate as peacemaker, source of grace and harmonizing; may avoid unpleasantness.

3-4. . .working with the mind and emotions; could convey ideas to public, communicate feelings through the work, articulate security needs; often family-oriented career.

3-5. . .a talent for communication and persuasion; natural for sales, promotion, advertising, con artistry, teaching and entertaining; charismatic communication.

3-6. . .a strong need for mental involvement in the work. You probably have a talent for details, yet a breadth of interest can lead you to scattering and becoming overextended. Decide what to do well and what to dip into because you are curious.

3-7. . .a people involvement in the work; naturally sociable with a flair for communication and meeting people on their own level; open, at ease.

3-8. . .a need to compromise between a depth approach and a "once-over-lightly" style in your work. Both modes can be helpful. Good analytical skills are likely.

3-9. . .mental agility and verbal skills; excellent potential for any work involving communication, information exchange and travel; social flow very smooth; restless, variety-oriented.

3-10. . .you are trying to blend the butterfly (casual, playful) role with that of the ant (dedicated, serious) in your work; potential for mental quickness and perseverance.

3-11. . .a need for great variety in your work — changes of routine, environment, people, etc., all helpful. A mental focus for the career is likely; communication skills.

3-12 . . . the need to focus carefully on priorities in your work as it is easy for you to scatter your forces due to multiple interests; versatile, adaptable, flexible.

4-5 . . . tremendous warmth and caring to devote in the work; can be a career involving nurturance (e.g., homemaking, nanny); emotional bonds on the job.

4-6 . . . a supportive, caretaking attitude; inclined to carry the troubles of others directly through the work or through looking after those you work with.

4-7 . . . a vocation involved with people. You may feel some conflict between relationships with colleagues and family commitments; desire to share in both arenas.

4-8 . . . the potential of intuition furthering your career; a sensitive perception and ability to tune into other people. Skills in dealing with money, resources are likely.

4-9 . . . an ambivalence between work that allows you to stay close at home (literally and emotionally) versus work that allows you to go far afield.

4-10 . . . an inner conflict between time and energy commitments to a career, success and worldly ambitions versus caring involvements with a home, family, close emotional relationships. You may turn family or caretaking into career; could work out of your home.

4-11 . . . balance the desire for emotional security in the work versus the drive for change, innovation and originality. Both friends and family can contribute to success.

4-12 . . . a preference for a sheltered work situation. You could be sensitive and somewhat retiring in terms of handling the real world; gentle, potentially very giving. You might sacrifice too much; don't martyr yourself in your vocation.

5-6 . . . a go-getter; potentially very dynamic, productive and successful. You can combine tremendous confidence and enthusiasm with great practicality.

5-7 . . . an instinctive flair for persuading people. Your natural charisma can be a vocational asset in many fields; sociable, outgoing and expressive at work.

5-8 . . . a drive for control, power and authority in the vocation; intense emotional reactions to the working environment; strong, self-willed, persevering.

5-9 . . . the desire for exciting, active work which is on a grand scale; ambitious, unlikely to settle for the mundane; great confidence, enthusiasm, zest.

5-10 . . . a drive for power through the career; natural inclination to positions of authority; struggle between immediate desires versus carefully working your way up.

5-11 . . . learning to balance your emotional, approval-seeking side with your rational, objective side through your work; integrating intensity and detachment.

5-12...incredible dramatic talent; natural persuasive abilities; a spellbinder; skills in sales, entertainment, comedy, promotion, advertising, politics, etc.

6-7...a good capacity for logic and cool intellectual assessment in the vocation. You may sometimes delay as you seek to collect every bit of relevant information to make the optimal choice.

6-8...excellent analysis, critical judgment, thoroughness and attention to detail; fine business skills; careful, disciplined worker; sometimes obsessive.

6-9...applying the mind in the work. There may be tension between aspirations and applications — wanting success faster or to occur more perfectly than is likely.

6-10...a potential workaholic situation: tremendous dedication, discipline and determination to do things well. You could succumb to doing more than your share. Illness is possible if your standards are too harsh — if you push yourself too much. You might also stop yourself from doing some things for fear of not measuring up ("If I can't do it perfectly, I won't do it at all."). Keep moderate.

6-11...inner tension between your skills with details and organization versus your desire for variety and change in the working environment. Make room for both.

6-12...the potential of some restlessness in the work area. You need to integrate your vision of what you want on the job with self-discipline to achieve it lest you succumb to chronic dissatisfaction that the job is never ideal.

7-8...talent for working with people; careers involving relationships to others, ranging from marriage, the law, counseling, personnel, astrology, etc.

7-9...social skills and instinctive magnetism. There is often a strong sense of justice, so involvement with law, courts, politics, social causes possible. Bringing together people and ideals in the work is likely.

7-10...a potential conflict between relating as an equal partner versus relating as an authority figure on the job. You are balancing work and relationship needs.

7-11...intellectual, communication skills. Objectivity can be an asset in your work; talent for dealing with groups of people; an innate sense of fair play.

7-12...potential for involvement in aesthetic fields; appreciation of beauty, grace, harmony and ease in the work. You may be inclined to look for the easy way on the job.

8-9...your career tends to arouse strong feelings. You may be determined to achieve the best, but could be aiming for more than is reasonable. Tremendous drive is indicated.

8-10...great organizational skills, management abilities, talent for focus, follow through and disciplined effort. A pragmatist, you probably seek security and power through the vocation.

8-11 . . . learning to balance your desire for variety and change in your work with your desire for a stable, secure position. There is a pull between the power role versus an equalitarian attitude.

8-12 . . . potential of guidance from your own "inner wisdom" in your work. You have a natural affinity for what lies beneath the surface; sensitive to "the vibes."

9-10 . . . high expectations coupled with an awareness of the flaws in your work can lead to much accomplishment or chronic dissatisfaction if you focus on flaws instead of assets.

9-11 . . . an impulse toward work in a progressive, future-oriented field. Natural optimism encourages you to grow, change and expand in your career; may be humanitarian work.

9-12 . . . idealism in your work. This could express as a search for the perfect job, a value placed on the work ethic, trying to do your work perfectly or working to improve the world.

10-11 . . . combining the old and the new, the conventional and the unconventional in your work. Deciding which rules to follow and which to break vocationally is part of the focus.

10-12 . . . reconciling the starry-eyed idealist and hard-nosed pragmatist within you. Somehow your vocation must allow scope for both your visions and your practicality.

11-12 . . . an attraction toward transpersonal work, vocations involving humanity, the future, principles, ideals and abstractions. You are a potential visionary.

GAUQUELIN SECTORS

The research of Michel and Francoise Gauquelin uncovered certain planetary placements as significant (in odds many times against chance) for those highly successful in various professions. This does not mean that every person who does very well in a given profession has that placement. Nor does it mean that every person having a particular planetary placement automatically pursues a certain career. It does mean that achieving people in those careers have that configuration much more often than would be predicted by chance.

The "Gauquelin sectors" in a horoscope are made up of zones of 40 degrees. One significant zone, in respect to career, is the thirty degrees behind the MC (roughly equivalent to the Placidian 9th house) and ten degrees past the MC (into the 10th house). The other significant zone is thirty degrees behind the Ascendant (roughly equivalent to the Placidian 12th house) and ten degrees past the Ascendant (into the 1st house). Planets in these Gauquelin sectors tend to be associated with certain professions among highly successful people.

The planetary configurations discovered in the charts of highly successful people are:

• **Moon** in a Gauquelin sector — writers and politicians

• **Saturn** in a Gauquelin sector — scientists and physicians

• **Jupiter** in a Gauquelin sector — politicians, actors, journalists, playwrights and military men

• **Mars** in a Gauquelin sector — athletes, physicians, military men, scientists and businessmen

NODES OF THE MOON

The following nodal placements are especially relevant in career issues. Other nodal placements are discussed in other chapters (as are polarities).

Across Cancer/Capricorn or 4th/10th Houses

A likely balancing act for you is the tension between desires for a home, family and nest versus desires for success and achievement in the outer world. Commitments of time and energy to the domestic versus the career areas must be considered. You may feel one arena takes you away from the other. Feelings of inadequacy or insecurity at either end could tempt you to ignore that side of the polarity and not deal with it. Part of the issue is proving your competence in both areas, not sacrificing one for the other.

This ambivalence can manifest as dividing your life into sections, e.g., concentrating on a career for a few years, then concentrating on your home life. You could also blend the two, as in working out of your home (e.g., writers), having a family business which involves domestic issues at work, working in a field that relates to home or nurturing feelings (e.g., land, real estate, food) or literally working on your home (refurbishing, etc.).

On the psychological level, you are striving to integrate a need for emotional closeness (dependency and/or nurturance) with a drive to be responsible and in charge. Compassionate caring must be balanced with hard-nosed realism. Emotions and pragmatism call for integration. The gentle touch and the iron fist must be blended.

Across Virgo/Pisces or 6th/12th Houses

You are probably balancing the real and the ideal in terms of your work. The combination can be a restless one, with the potential of you going from job to job in search of a more ideal situation. One potential is the search for a perfect career, with resultant frustration and disillusionment with the flaws of each position you take. Another possibility is getting caught up in the desire to perform your work perfectly, without any mistakes. That is a hopeless task as we are all human.

Feelings of inadequacy can complicate the struggle. If you are excessively hard on yourself, you may stop before you even start, afraid to attempt **any** work situation as you feel sure you would **not** perform perfectly. Or, you can be needlessly self-critical when you make mistakes, unable to fill the role of saint. Or, you could decide to wait **until** you find the perfect job, or until you know you can do everything ideally— and never accomplish anything!

Other alternatives include some kind of blend of your need to be competent and capable with your desire to do something higher, more ideal, more beautiful. This can include working in fields involving beauty or aesthetics in some fashion. It can encompass helping/healing work or any job which leaves the world a better place than it was previously. Your work needs to **mean** something to you. A job which is simply a job will be frustrating to you.

The challenge is to ground your ideals, so that you can feel you are beautifying or improving the world in some way, uplifting our current state of existence, but also getting some concrete, real-world results in what you do.

ELEMENT EMPHASIS

Fire

♂, ☉, ♃, ⚷, ♈, ♌, ♐, 1st, 5th, 9th houses

You need excitement in your work. Restless and mobile, you fare best in situations where you can move around. Sitting at a desk all day is not your favorite activity. Changing scenes and changing people help too.

Often dissatisfied with an "ordinary" job, you tend to seek a sense of conquest through your work. Great at initiation and inspiring others, you may have less concern for carrying through and following up. Your talent lies in getting the ball rolling, leaving others to finish up as you progress to another project. Energetic and active, you can go through work like a buzz saw if it is important to you. But, when you feel your duties are beneath you, the tendency is to leave the situation rather than hang around and work it out. Personal freedom is very important. If you have a boss, it had better be someone who will refrain from breathing down your neck. You function best with lots of space and room to do your thing.

If you are out of touch with this side of your nature, you are likely to attract it (in excess) in coworkers, colleagues and bosses. They could seem hyper, rash, impulsive, fiery, impatient and insistent on personal liberty.

Earth

♀, ☿, ⚳, ⚵, ♄, ♉, ♍, ♑, 2nd, 6th, 10th houses

You need concrete results in your work. Dealing with physical objects or products or having clear-cut measurements and standards is extremely gratifying. You need to see the manifestations of your accomplishments. Knowing you have done well means less to you than having a tangible outcome to look at or seeing measurable indications of what you have done.

Stability appeals to you and you are less inclined to rock the occupational boat than some. Practical attainments and realism matter a great deal to you; you value your success and the material goods that it can bring you. Sometimes you may work too hard, caught up in the need to be productive. Dedicated and enduring, you have the capacity to keep on striving long after others have fallen by the wayside. You like to finish up and you work best when you can see, hear or feel directly the results of what you have done.

If you are not in touch with this part of your nature, you may meet it (in excess) through the people you work with. They could seem too materialistic, boring, stodgy, hardworking, unchanging and concrete.

Air

☿, ♀, ⚴, ⚵, ♅, ♊, ♎, ♒, 3rd, 7th, 11th houses

You need interactions with people and ideas in your work. Theories and abstractions appeal to you. Often your career will involve communication, writing, teaching or exchanging information with other people. Finger dexterity is also possible. Socially oriented, you need to be involved with others on the job. Don't get stuck in a corner with only machines to talk to! You need conversation as much as your daily bread.

Your attitude on the job is equalitarian and you tend to work easily with others. However, bosses could find you a bit difficult at times, as you tend to come from a peer position. You expect everyone to relate on your level and usually treat others equally. Logic, detachment, objectivity and the capacity to take things lightly are all potential skills in your career.

If you are out of touch with these potentials within your own nature, you are likely to attract colleagues and bosses who will overdo these themes. They might seem too talkative, too detached, cool, aloof or objective in an uncomfortable fashion.

Water

☽, ♇, ♆, ♋, ♏, ♓, 4th, 8th, 12th houses

You need a feeling connection with colleagues and/or your career. You may find yourself emotionally involved with those who share your working environment. You could play a nurturing, protective role or attract coworkers who seem to want to take care of you. There may be a higher degree of intimacy and emotional attachment than is usual in your working environment.

You have deep security needs, both on the physical and the emotional level. Your career partly serves your need for money in the bank and the sense of a solid foundation which you can trust. But you also seek a sense of connection through your work. Your career may involve delving into the underlying order in life (e.g., geology, physics, chemistry) or anything to which you can make a personal commitment, feel a sense of attachment to. You can also do well in fields providing basic material security to others — food, shelter, clothing and just about any business realm.

If you are not in touch with this side of your nature, you are likely to attract it (in excess) through those people who work with you. They may seem overly sensitive, vulnerable, clinging, dependent or possessive. They may value security very highly and have deep, intense emotions which are often held inside.

Fire-Earth

♂, ☉, ♃, ♄, ♈, ♌, ♐, 1st, 5th, 9th houses &
♀, ☿, ?, ♥, ♄, ♉, ♍, ♑, 2nd, 6th, 10th houses

Productive, efficient, capable, responsible and driving, you have zest, confidence and enthusiasm matched by endurance and perseverance. Tremendously capable, you generally accomplish a great deal. Sometimes you may push too hard and alienate those around you or go full speed ahead toward a goal only to decide (when you get there) it wasn't really what you wanted. Take time to smell the flowers.

If this part of your personality is disowned, you may attract colleagues who carry it to an excess. They could seem hard-driving, competitive and willing to step on anyone to get the job done.

Fire-Air

♂, ☉, ♃, ♄, ♈, ♌, ♐, 1st, 5th, 9th houses &
☿, ♀, ♀, ✴, ♅, ♊, ♎, ♒, 3rd, 7th, 11th houses

Entertaining and optimistic, you are a natural salesperson, an instinctive promoter. You have great talent for any area requiring verbal skills and natural confidence. Able to make people laugh and with a trust in the future, you gravitate easily to fields involving advertising, selling or persuasion.

You expect to enjoy your work and function best in a lighthearted environment. If your coworkers get too serious, you may resort to jokes, comedy or simply leave the scene rather than come off your natural high. Fun-loving and sociable, you like to interact with others on the job and prefer situations that are constantly changing. You enjoy the challenge of the new and routine bores you. Like a rolling stone, you operate well in careers which involve a lot of variety.

If this side of your nature is not acknowledged, you may attract colleagues who will manifest it for you (in an excessive manner). They could seem too lighthearted, flippant and devil-may-care. They may not take much seriously. They may be erratic and unpredictable.

Fire-Water

♂, ☉, ♃, ♄, ♈, ♌, ♐, 1st, 5th, 9th houses &
☽, ♇, ♆, ♋, ♏, ♓, 4th, 8th, 12th houses

Intense and emotional, you work best on projects where your feelings are deeply involved. Your career must involve your heart for best results. A casual approach does not suit you. You may sometimes be led, by inner wisdom, into direct action — later discovering your intuitive impulse was exactly the right thing to do at the time. Detachment and logical analysis are more likely to come after the fact. First, you understand issues on the gut level.

The strength and depth of your emotional responses can sometimes seem overwhelming to those around you. Mood swings are possible, ranging from incredible optimism to the depths of depression. You might also feel torn between spontaneous expression of your emotions versus a holding back until you feel it is safe to share.

If you are out of touch with this side of your nature, you are likely to meet it (in excess) through colleagues, coworkers and bosses. They could seem extremely emotional, torn between outward expression and an inward searching and processing. They might swing from extreme optimism to great pessimism. They could be extremely warm, caring people.

Earth-Air

♀, ☿, ⚳, ⚶, ♄, ♉, ♍, ♑, 2nd, 6th, 10th houses &
☿, ♀, ⚴, ⚵, ♅, ♊, ♎, ♒, 3rd, 7th, 11th houses

Logical and practical, theoretical and grounded, your mental faculties can be a tremendous asset in your work. Oriented toward rationality and an intellectual approach, you can remain calm, cool and collected in a vocational crisis. Your powers of analysis, discrimination and intellectual understanding can be helpful in a number of fields. Your basic approach is sensible.

An excellent problem-solver and efficiency expert, you have a talent for figuring things out and making them work in an improved fashion. It is not that you are uncaring or unemotional; it is merely that you value efficiency on the job and prefer to keep feelings out of it.

If you are not in touch with this part of your nature, you could attract it (in excess) from the people with whom you work. They could seem cold, calculating, uncaring and only concerned with the bottom line.

Earth-Water

♀, ☿, ⚳, ⚶, ♄, ♉, ♍, ♑, 2nd, 6th, 10th houses &
☽, ♇, ♆, ♋, ♏, ♓, 4th, 8th, 12th houses

A natural caretaker, you may be drawn to situations where you can serve and succor other people. Often in the helping professions, you tend to be emotionally involved, but also looking after others in a very practical manner. Your combination of empathy and pragmatism makes for a real need to improve people's lives.

A potential weakness is your need to be needed. You tend to take your job very seriously and could be prone to depression or feeling overwhelmed at times. You can carry the load for other people, doing more than your share if you aren't careful. You are capable of balancing compassion with common sense! Physical and emotional security are likely to be important to you. If your safety seems at stake, you may focus totally on self-protection, with little concern for others. Your potential for constructive caring is excellent, but it is likely to be self-directed until you feel secure in your own, inner strength.

If you are out of touch with this part of your own nature, you are likely to experience it (in excess) through colleagues. They may seem too serious, overly protective, too concerned with taking care of others, insecure, or very stable and grounded but not much fun.

Air-Water

☿, ♀, ⚴, ⚵, ♅, ♊, ♎, ♒, 3rd, 7th, 11th houses &
☽, ♇, ♆, ♋, ♏, ♓, 4th, 8th, 12th houses

An idea person, you have a rich, creative imagination which can make wonderful contributions to your work. Incredible fantasies abound within you and you may be sharing your inner world in a number of artistic, intellectual, theoretical or inspirational fields. Skilled at blending the conscious with the unconscious, you are a natural psychotherapist. Writing and teaching are also common fields.

Your basic instinct is to use the mind and emotions; you do not enjoy physical labor. Some might call you lazy; you simply prefer to work with ideas and principles rather than physical objects and sweat. Because you enjoy your internal creations, it is easy for you to withdraw, especially if the working environment seems unpleasant. You can adopt an "I'm not here" attitude that almost makes you invisible to the people around you when you choose to avoid confrontations or controversy. Sensitive and often poetic in your outlook, you generally take the easy road.

If you are out of touch with these potentials within you, colleagues and bosses are likely to overdo them for you. They might seem spacey, hard to reach, lost in their own little worlds, drifting and dreaming through life. Imagination can be strong, but practicality may be weak.

QUALITY EMPHASIS

Cardinal

♂, ☽, ♀, ⚴, ⚵, ♄, ♈, ♋, ♎, ♑, 1st, 4th, 7th, 10th houses

You work best by learning through experience. Others can offer insights and advice, but you learn more by trying and doing than by listening to other people's instructions, reading, attending classes, etc. It is not that such information is useless to you. Rather, it means little until you apply it in your own way and experience how you would express the knowledge. A common result is that you unconsciously draw events and situations (even crises) into your life which offer you opportunities to learn by doing. Sometimes, this can feel like the School of Hard Knocks, but it can also allow you to take shortcuts in developing your vocational skills.

Part of the issue is an inner ambivalence as to your true "calling." You are likely to be torn between putting energy into a career in the outside world versus a home and family versus a significant partnership versus self-development and expression. You may feel you are juggling very different needs and rarely have time to satisfy all.

This conflict can unconsciously attract events and crises into your life. Periodic changes in your life structure, including career, are likely. As you recognize your own internal need for events and happenings from which you can learn, it will become easier to deliberately create events which you desire, rather than just reacting to things which seem to be coming from outside (and are a manifestation of your unconscious needs). If for example, we are feeling confined, frustrated and hemmed in on the job (our needs for self-expression not being satisfied), we can set ourselves up to be fired — unconsciously gaining the freedom we want. If we deliberately create space and independence in our working environment, we may discover other options.

Fixed

♀, ☉, ♇, ♅, ♉, ♌, ♏, ♒, 2nd, 5th, 8th, 11th houses

You want your work under your own control. You see your vocation as a potential area of strength and power. You are unwilling to be dominated by the boss or anyone else in the working environment and can slip into power struggles if you feel someone is trying to control you or tell you what to do. Self-willed and determined to do things your way, you can move mountains in your career (or waste time with jockeying for positions of dominance).

You are best off in a highly competitive working environment — whether through business, sports or fighting for a cause. Your natural power drive needs an outlet through the career, lest it all go into fights with coworkers. The drive to have an impact on the world can be a great motivating factor in your accomplishments. Just be sure you are pushing where you want to push and not fighting the people on your own team!

If you are out of touch with this side of your nature, you are likely to feel the people around you are carrying it to an extreme. They may seem hopelessly stubborn, power-hungry and utterly determined to have their own way. Competitiveness may get out of hand.

Mutable

☿, ⚳ ⚶, ♃, ⚷, ♆, ♊, ♍, ♐, ♓, 3rd, 6th, 9th, 12th houses

You need to get beyond the myth of a single job for a lifetime. It is unlikely that one career will satisfy your multiple interests and diverse talents. You are quite likely to have several different careers, sequentially — or even more than one at a time! You do not have to be in a field for 50 years to make a difference. Whether you choose a vocation for 5 years or 20 years, doing your best is what matters.

Because you have a wide variety of abilities, you may initially feel scattered and have trouble settling on one career. After you make a choice, give yourself permission to be flexible. You are never locked in! Try to avoid perfectionistic standards. You are unlikely to find the perfect job and it is probably not possible for you **never** to make a mistake in your work. Take satisfaction in doing your best for the moment, working toward perfection and knowing that you can change your career (or working environment, or associates and responsibilities) at any time.

If this side of who you are is denied, you are likely to discover it (in excess) through colleagues. They could seem flighty, constantly changing jobs, erratic, scattered or hopelessly idealistic.

THEMES

Freedom
♂, ♃, ♄, ♅, ♈, ♐, ♒, 1st, 9th, 11th houses

You prefer to work your own way, with considerable independence. Although you can cooperate with others, you are not terribly skilled at taking orders. Having your own area to pursue your job is the best. You need room for change, innovation, variety and a sense of newness and challenge in your work environment.

Closeness or Interpersonal
☽, ☉, ♀, ☿, ⚸, ♇, ♋, ♌, ♎, ♏, 4th, 5th, 7th, 8th houses

Your work situation ought ideally to involve relationships with others. This can range from working with your own family (homemaker, family businesses) to working for the families of others (nanny, housekeeper, governess) to situations involving emotional warmth and exchange (counseling) to a sense of commitment and caring with your colleagues. Competitive businesses are also quite possible, since competition involves one-to-one interaction. Personal, face-to-face interchanges as a regular part of your job are best.

Artistic
♀, ☿, ⚸, ☉, ♆, ♉, ♌, ♎, ♓, 2nd, 5th, 7th, 12th houses

You have aesthetic talents and appreciation which could contribute to a work situation. Your sense of balance, harmony, grace, line and form can be an asset. Your career may involve beauty fields (e.g., design, fashion, architecture, photography, painting, sculpture, modeling, cosmetology, hairdressing, buying for clothing stores, etc.) or balance (e.g., music, mathematics, accounting).

Idealistic

♃, ⚷, ♆, ♐, ♓, 9th, 12th houses

There is an idealistic theme connected to your work. You can look for the ideal job (perfect hours, perfect pay, perfect colleagues) and never be satisfied or spend your life changing jobs, each time hoping the next one will be **the** one. Or, you can try to do your work perfectly and be hard on yourself for making a mistake, for being human. Another possibility includes working to make a more perfect or more ideal or more beautiful world. Alternately, you may idealize the work ethic and believe that doing a good job is an ultimate value.

How you choose to blend the search for something ultimate with your career is up to you, but they are tied together.

Obsessive-Compulsive

☿, ⚳, ⚵, ♇, ♄, ♍, ♏, ♑, 6th, 8th, 10th houses

There is an obsessive-compulsive theme connected to your work. This shows considerable talent for any business field. You are likely to have organizational skills, a penchant for details, a natural thoroughness and dedication to doing things well and taking care of business. The bottom line is important to you. A sense of order is usually strong.

If carried too far, you can get caught up in the petty details of your job and lose sight of the bigger picture. You can become compulsive about getting it right and so be afraid to move onward. Your desire for efficiency can degenerate into a critical, judgmental attitude which can be counterproductive. If handled effectively, however, this talent is an asset in your rise to the top.

Competence

☿, ⚳, ⚵, ♄, ♍, ♑, 6th, 10th houses

Basically, you expect your work to be work. That is, your attitude is practical and realistic and you expect to put in some effort on the job. You do not expect it to be easy or a cinch. As a consequence, you sometimes do more than your share of the load as you naturally attract responsibilities. Dedicated and disciplined, you are usually highly efficient. You can slip easily into being a workaholic and have to remind yourself to take vacations.

An alternate (or additional) potential is becoming obsessed with getting things done **right**. This can lead to an excessive concern with petty details and procrastination in terms of completing projects. You could end up refining and retuning small parts of your projects, never quite satisfied, never quite willing to declare yourself finished — because what you have done is not yet totally perfect.

Your focus on the flaws can be a problem if you let your criticism get out of hand. But — in the proper time and place — your ability to analyze and discriminate can be a real asset that improves every project you are involved with.

If you feel nonproductive, illness can be a potential escape from feeling guilty about not accomplishing what you feel you ought.

For you more than for most people, how you feel about what you do has a profound impact on your health. The happier you are with your achievements in terms of a career or job, the healthier you are likely to be.

Mental Stimulation
☿, ?, ⚴, ♀, ♃, ⚷, ♅, ♆, ♊, ♍, ♎, ♐, ♒, ♓, 3rd, 6th, 7th, 9th, 11th, 12th houses

You need a job which involves your mind and gives it an opportunity to stretch and grow. You get bored easily with routine situations and environments. Keep room to move around mentally and physically so you have new situations and new people to interact with.

Any field which involves ideas and people will help to channel the strong intellectual emphasis for your career. Information exchange of any sort is also excellent.

Relationships
♀, ♀, ⚶, ♇, ♎, ♏, 7th, 8th houses

You need to work with people. It can be in a cooperative, harmonious, sharing mode or in a competitive, testing style, but interaction is essential. A solitary environment or a situation with machines is not for you. Interchange with other human beings is important to you.

Fields such as personnel work, counseling, consulting, law, secretarial, hostessing, are quite likely. Anything which makes people your project is appropriate.

Security
♀, ☽, ☿, ?, ⚴, ♇, ♄, ♆, ♂, ♋, ♍, ♏, ♑, ♓, 2nd, 4th, 6th, 8th, 10th, 12th houses

You need a sense of security through your work. This usually includes a regular paycheck, a sense of stability, standard hours and a secure situation. You will generally prefer the known to the unknown where jobs are concerned and opt for the sure money in the bank rather than risking more on something which may not pan out. You want to know that you can depend on your vocational situation.

Risk/Creativity/Change
♂, ☉, ♃, ⚷, ♅, ♈, ♌, ♐, ♒, 1st, 5th, 9th, 11th houses

You are willing to take risks in your career. If a change may bring greater rewards, you will try it. You may gamble a sure situation on the chance of something better. Your hours may be irregular, you may be self-employed, your paychecks could be erratic or other parameters of your career could be uncertain. You are likely to prefer situations allowing your creativity to flourish, which means a certain degree of independence. (If overdone, you could simply split from job situations which you perceive as too confining.) You tend to attract nonstandard situations.

Parents
☽, ♄, ♆, ♋, ♑, 4th, 10th houses

Your attitudes about work, productivity and what entails doing a good job are probably influenced by your parent(s). This can be through a positive or a negative role model (wanting to be like them or the opposite in terms of how they handled the real world). But much of your feelings about and approach to the workaday world is molded by them. You could even be involved in working with them in a family business. But, in some way, your sense of productivity is a reaction to their measurements.

One of the issues you are facing is the balance between emotional needs and achievement needs. Your drive for productive accomplishments must be integrated with your desire for a nest which provides a sense of safety, an emotional haven. Domestic and career issues both call for attention. You are learning, through your job, to make peace between the authority (hard-nosed, realistic) approach and the supportive, nurturant approach to the world.

Power
☉, ♇, ♄, ♌, ♏, ♑, 5th, 8th, 10th houses

You want control over your career and working environment. You function best in situations where you have the power over what happens on the job; you do not take orders comfortably. Ideally, you need a career which gives you opportunities to go all out to win and be on top. Your competitive zest needs an outlet in the business world or fighting to win in some arena. Otherwise, you may end up in power struggles with bosses, coworkers and the people around you on the job.

Personal
♂, ♀, ☿, ☽, ♈, ♉, ♊, ♋, 1st, 2nd, 3rd, 4th houses

You want your work to be done on your own terms. Control of your working environment is important to you and you often prefer to labor alone, so others do not interfere. You will tend to gravitate toward situations where you have a great deal of personal authority over what you do.

You work because of personal needs. It could be that you feel driven to be productive, or perhaps you just enjoy the security and material possessions that a good job can insure. The focus though is on self-satisfaction through what you do — not trying to please others or fit an abstract concept. Basically, you work for yourself — if not literally, certainly emotionally.

Transpersonal
♃, ⚷, ♄, ♅, ♆, ♐, ♑, ♒, ♓, 9th, 10th, 11th, 12th houses

You operate best in a career that affects the world at large or has some sort of higher purpose or meaning. This can range from politics, to metaphysics, to education, to group activities, to new-age occupations to economics. The key is that you want your work to matter, to be significant, to more than just yourself. You may wish to change the structure of society (or certain parts of it). You may wish to illuminate, inspire, inform or otherwise uplift people.

Your work may involve humanitarian principles, ideals or broad, philosophical issues. You prefer a wide perspective.

ASPECTS

Harmony to Letter . . .

1: Your desire to be productive, make money and handle the physical world is in harmony with your basic energy, vitality and self-expression. You can put enthusiasm and vigor into your work which enhances your efficiency. Your skilled performance with the material realm supports your self-confidence and initiative.

2: Your desire to be productive, make money and handle the physical world is in harmony with your potential for gaining material resources and pleasures. You have the capacity to be successful because you are willing to work hard and can be realistic. There is also a good potential for enjoying your work, experiencing your career as a source of pleasure and satisfaction.

3: Your desire to be productive, make money and handle the physical world is in harmony with your ability to think and communicate. Your intellectual skills support your practical grasp of realities. Your facility with the people near at hand promotes success on the job. Your pragmatic abilities reinforce your objective, reasoning capacities.

4: Your desire to be productive, make money and handle the physical world is in harmony with your desire for emotional and physical security. You are capable of building a firm foundation in life, with the physical and the emotional resources to provide a sense of safety for you and those closest to you. You can be pragmatic as well as warm, realistic as well as caring. You know how to balance career necessities with domestic needs. Your compassion can assist your career and your strength in dealing with the outer world helps you to look after those dearest to you.

5: Your desire to be productive, make money and handle the physical world is in harmony with your desire to shine and be significant. Your professional success can be assisted through your charisma and magnetism. Your instinct for taking risks can reap favorable results where work in the world is concerned. Your zest and enthusiasm promote increased success and your realistic achievements can allow you to gain the favorable attention you desire.

6: Your desire to be productive, make money and handle the physical world is in harmony with your need to be efficient and capable. You can be a dedicated and persevering worker, ever ready to do what needs to be done. You may sometimes work too hard or too much as you are inclined to feel other people will not do the job as well as you yourself. Disciplined and thorough, your care and concern with good workmanship pay dividends in material success.

7: Your desire to be productive, make money and handle the physical world is in harmony with your desire for relationships. Your productive role in the world can also support and enhance your people associations. Your need for interaction with others harmonizes well with your motivation for efficiency. Work and partnerships can reinforce one another. You can be supportive of a partner's career and vice versa. Good potential for business relations.

8: Your desire to be productive, make money and handle the physical world is in harmony with your desire for depth understanding. Your thorough investigation and analysis of the world can lead to more practical attainments in the world. Your ability to share the physical world comfortably with others is enhanced by a realistic attitude. Your probing analysis assists your successful completion of projects. Support from others may contribute to your career.

9: Your desire to be productive, make money and handle the physical world is in harmony with your desire for ultimate meaning and understanding of life goals. Your visionary side helps to inspire your productive efforts and gives a sense of purpose to your accomplishments. Your attention to practical needs grounds your search for something more and helps to bring your long-range goals to fruition. Your optimism supports your career achievements.

10: Your desire to be productive, make money and handle the physical world is in harmony with your sense of responsibility and desire for power and control. You can achieve much in life because you are willing to work for it. You figure out the system and work within its rules to reach the top. Your willingness to take responsibility and to be capable reinforces your ability to rise to the top of your field.

11: Your desire to be productive, make money and handle the physical world is in harmony with your sense of individuality and uniqueness. Your work reinforces your sense of being not like anyone else. You can find new avenues, unusual methods or interests in your concern with worldly success. Your inventive, original approach can assist you in your career achievements.

12: Your desire to be productive, make money and handle the physical world is in harmony with your sense of union with something Higher in life. You are able to operate successfully in the pragmatic physical world as well as the idealistic, inspired realms. Your dreams give inspiration to your everyday accomplishments and your practical, productive efforts supply grounding for your cosmic conceptions.

Conflict to Letter...

1: Your desire to be productive, make money and handle the physical world may be at odds with your basic sense of identity and self-expression. You may feel torn between doing what you want and doing what you feel is your duty or a necessity. Instinctive action may war with detailed planning. Free flow could be at odds with a focused concentration. When spontaneity and discipline are optimally combined, you can be highly effective.

2: Your desire to be productive, make money and handle the physical world may be at odds with your potential enjoyment of material resources and pleasures. You may feel torn as to which physical indulgences matter most to you (e.g., eating, drinking, smoking, making money, making love, etc.). You may feel a conflict between work and pleasure; duties and enjoyment. If you overvalue hard work and productive efforts, you could unconsciously end up earning less than you deserve because you expect to have to work for it! Integration means enjoying all aspects of the physical world — career achievements as well as physical pleasures, productivity along with indulgence.

3: Your desire to be productive, make money and handle the physical world may be at odds with your ability to communicate casually and your mental capacities. Perhaps you are torn between a serious versus a flippant approach to your job. Or, you may feel your work does not allow you the scope to be a thinking person. You may feel stifled in saying what you are thinking in your current working environment. It could take extra effort to create a space for productive attainments which also includes room for you to think, share ideas and talk things over easily with others.

4: Your desire to be productive, make money and handle the physical world may be at odds with your desire for a home, family, nest, security and emotional warmth. You may feel your caring side is at odds with your pragmatic, performance-oriented side. You may be struggling between a desire to go within and deal with matters of feelings versus a need to accomplish in the outer world. You may feel success leaves no room for emotional relationships and needlessly give up (either relationships or the pursuit of success). You **can be** highly successful and simultaneously highly compassionate.

5: Your desire to be productive, make money and handle the physical world may be at odds with your desire for excitement, drama and living life on the edge in some way. You may feel your risk-taking needs are at odds with the desire for a stable career which will provide financial security. The challenge is to integrate your need for admiration, attention and emotional response into your work in some way, rather than keeping them at odds with one another. Your vitality and sparkle can enhance your success.

6: Your desire to be productive, make money and handle the physical world may be at odds with your need to be efficient, productive and thorough.

Check for the following conditions:

If there is heavy air and fire
You may be inclined to dislike jobs you experience as boring and routine. Dealing with the nitty-gritty details could be a challenge. Learning to work steadily and patiently may not come easily, but is — at times — necessary. Your challenge is to ensure that you are sufficiently practical, cautious and capable in your work without losing your zest and liveliness.

If there is heavy earth and water
You may be inclined to take your job and yourself too seriously and probably carry more than your share of the load at work. You could even be a workaholic type, feeling "If you want it done right, do it yourself!" If you push yourself too hard, health problems could result from overwork or an unconscious escape from feeling guilty about not doing "enough." The challenge is to be truly realistic (not pessimistic) and know where your responsibilities end. Doing your job is appropriate, but do not do everyone else's as well!

If there is relative balance of elements
You are striving to do a good job without going to extremes. Avoid an excessive workaholic focus. Too much concern with getting the details right could lead to procrastination as you strive endlessly to get everything just so. Or, you might stop yourself from trying, for fear your efforts will not be good enough. You are capable of much accomplishment; stay practical, reasonable and moderate in your approach to achievement.

7: Your desire to be productive, make money and handle the physical world may be at odds with your desire for a long-term partnership. You may feel a conflict between your need to work and your need to relate. You could experience your work as pulling you away from a close relationship or vice versa. The challenge is to make room in your life for both success in a career and the maintenance of a long-term, caring partnership.

8: Your desire to be productive, make money and handle the physical world may be at odds with your desire for a depth understanding of life. You may feel torn between a need to get the job done and a desire to thoroughly understand the situation, delving deeply for answers. Your analytical drive could sidetrack you from doing what is necessary. Or, you might avoid essential investigation in your concern for efficiency. Balance productivity with an essential grasp of the basic issues.

9: Your desire to be productive, make money and handle the physical world may be at odds with your desire for a sense of meaning and purposefulness in life. Your ideals might be at odds with your work. Perhaps you feel success and ethics do not mix. Perhaps your moral principles conflict with some of your essential responsibilities on the job. Perhaps your work feels too mundane and your spiritual side experiences dryness as a result. Perhaps you simply expect more than is reasonable of yourself as a worker. The challenge is to integrate your search for meaning with your need to do something well in the world.

10: Your desire to be productive, make money and handle the physical world may be at odds with your handling of power, control and authority issues. It could be that you have an intense need to dominate the working environment and strive to get or stay on top. You could be experienced as critical, judgmental and harsh as a result. Or, you might get involved with people whom you experience as hard, unyielding and into a power trip. The goal is to be practical and realistic about what you can do and cannot do. Carry out your appropriate responsibilities — neither too much nor too little.

11: Your desire to be productive, make money and handle the physical world may be at odds with your desire for variety, change, innovation and something new.

Check for the following conditions:

If there is heavy fire and air
You might feel that your work is stifling and uncreative. You may yearn for changes and feel hemmed into a boring situation due to security needs, desire for money, a sense of responsibility, etc. You may, consciously or unconsciously, attract changes or upsets into your working environment simply because you are feeling frustrated. Look for a constructive way to integrate your needs for freedom and variety into your working situation.

If there is heavy earth and water
You could feel that you function best with a certain order and systematization in your work. Changes and alterations might upset you. Innovation can be helpful but you must make peace between your desire to do something step-by-step in a logical sequence and the need for occasional creative leaps.

If there are relatively balanced elements
You are facing the issue of conventionality versus unconventionality; stability versus change or freedom versus structure in your work. Whether the conflict is around your duties, your hours, your environment, your authority or other areas, the challenge is to make room for both practical accomplishments with some lasting result as well as a sense of openness and ability to carry out your responsibilities in your own, unique fashion.

12: Your desire to be productive, make money and handle the physical world may be at odds with your desire to tune into the infinite in some fashion. Your idealism may be at odds with the work you do. Perhaps you feel that the pragmatics and the ethics of your career clash. Perhaps your vision of something ultimately lovely conflicts with your practical, everyday duties. Faith and fear may war with one another over the appropriate approach to take. Integrate your discipline and thoroughness on the job with your inspiration and inner wisdom for best results.

CHAPTER EIGHT

RELATIONSHIPS

This section applies to your close, personal relationships with other people. This includes marriage and living together, but also close friendships, business partnerships, therapeutic relationships. Any systematic, ongoing, regular interaction with other people is a part of this arena. The issues revolve around not just a verbal and emotional sharing of yourself with others and relating to others, but also the capacity to share the physical world (money, possessions, sexuality, pleasures) with intimates in a mutually satisfying manner.

This chapter will focus on committed one-to-one relationships. Parental relationships are covered in Chapter 15. Children are discussed in Chapter 10. Relationships dealing with the workaday world fall into Chapter 7. Here, we will be examining potentials for close, intimate associations.

A basic issue in relationships is: what are we expressing, allowing and manifesting of our various potentials and what are we denying, holding back of who we could be. Whatever potentials we restrict within ourselves, we tend to unconsciously attract those qualities from other people. The problem is, the more we look for something "outside," in that other person, the more we tend to get an extreme — an exaggerated version of that potential.

Everyone in our lives is teaching us something about ourselves. If I am out of touch with my need for independence, I attract excessively independent people. They are providing the examples, the role models, for me to learn how to be independent. The goal is not for me to be like those other people. Those individuals are probably **too** independent. Whatever quality we deny, other people tend to manifest in excess, in extremes. So, the challenge is not to become **like** that other person, but rather look at the quality the person is exhibiting (in extreme form) and figure out positive, fulfilling ways to manifest it in our lives.

Because we are all complicated people, wc often have contradictory needs and desires. Our motivations may be mixed. In such cases, it is very easy to identity with one part of who we are, and disown another side of our being. In any situation of inner conflict, several options exist. We can 1) repress, 2) project,

3) displace, 4) bounce from one extreme to the other, 5) always want what we don't have because our timing is off, or 6) integrate.

Consider the example of the freedom versus closeness conflict — a common dilemma for a large majority of the Western world. Most of us want the independence and space to be who we are, do as we please, without too much interference from others. We would like to be able to go our own ways often, not having to be concerned with the needs and desires of other people. Yet, most of us also want close, caring relationships. We want to love and be loved, to share commitments with people near and dear to us. This creates an inner conflict. It is extremely difficult to be totally close and totally free simultaneously.

When we repress, we bury one of our basic desires and motivations in the unconscious. Generally, it is hidden so well we forget we ever felt that way. However, the drive does not go away; it simply works from underground. The unconscious does its best to bring that denied quality into our lives. If all else fails, the ultimate result of continued repression is physical illness. The energy hits the physical body and the appropriate problem manifests. Dependency needs which are not being met or acknowledged can often end up as stomach problems (ulcers, colitis, etc.). Frustrated freedom needs can manifest as headaches, minor accidents (cuts, burns), sinus colds. Facing and dealing with our various psychological needs helps to maintain good health (along with proper diet, exercise, rest, faith and a positive attitude).

Projection is another tool the unconscious uses to help us recognize a part of our own nature which we are busily denying. With projection, we unconsciously are drawn to people who will "live out" whatever we are choosing not to face within ourselves. The problem is, when we get someone else to "do it for us," they usually overdo it! It is as if Life operates as a fun house mirror, exaggerating and blowing things out of proportion — perhaps so we will notice. With projection, we get what we want (unconsciously), but before we knew we asked for it (consciously)!

With freedom/closeness struggles, if we consciously identify with the closeness side and project the freedom side, then we tend to attract and be attracted by the classic "free soul" types — the traditional bachelor or bachelorette who does not want to get married or be tied down to a relationship. Another pattern is falling in love with a married person (who, of course, is not really available) or falling in love with someone in another city, state or country (too far away to have a close, regular commitment). Or, we can love several people simultaneously, insuring that we will not be totally tied to any one of them. Somehow or other, we manage not to be able to maintain a one-to-one attachment. We may even always fall in love with the one who will leave us. Somehow, the only exciting people are the ones who do not **want** a relationship.

What happens is that our psyches are always striving for balance. So, if we overemphasize one side of our being consciously, our unconscious seeks the opposite extreme. As long as we consciously cling to the idea of closeness, our unconscious will continue to present us with the freedom, space, independence and detachment that we also want, but are unaware of on the conscious level.

The reverse happens as well, naturally. If we consciously identify with a desire to remain free, unshackled, able to go our own way and make our own path, but deny a need for closeness and emotional sharing, then we will project the latter and unconsciously attract other people to do it for us. This can range from very dependent, "clinging vine" sorts of individuals, to outright victims who look to us to meet their every need. Sometimes an unacknowledged "need to be needed" promotes situations such as the sudden invalidism of someone in the family who we "have" to take care of — just as we were about to take off on our trip around the world. And, if we are the strong, invulnerable, "I can handle anything" sort of person, sometimes getting sick ourselves is the only way we know of to **be** taken care of. If we cannot allow ourselves any other sort of vulnerability, then illness can be a perfect (albeit unconscious) path to getting some needed nurturance. However, it is also very common for people who are out of touch with their desire for close, emotional sharing to attract people who are **too** dependent, possessive, overly concerned with togetherness.

Displacement is another potential when we have an inner conflict. This simply means expressing a perfectly natural and okay part of who we are in a time and place where the result is less than optimal. For most people, freedom needs are comfortably expressed in personal hobbies, interests and solitary activities. Closeness needs are met through intimate associations with other people. If we demand to be totally free when interacting with those near and dear to us and seek some unconditional support and assistance when trying to handle something that is our personal responsibility, we may be in for some discomfort. The challenge of integration means not only being all that we are capable of being, but also choosing the appropriate times and places to express our myriad ways of being in the world.

Another variation is the person who lives life jumping from one end of the seesaw to the other. Such individuals go wholeheartedly into their freedom sides, eschewing all relationships, proclaiming the sanctity of individualism, asserting the superiority of being single. They then become lonely and rush into relationships. Successfully submerging themselves in their partners, they are almost swallowed up. Becoming claustrophobic, they run away from the relationship and retreat into solitude once more. Loneliness returns in full force, propelling them toward another too close, too absorbing relationship. They can continue flipping from one extreme to the other as a lifelong pattern until they learn to compromise, to find a middle ground.

A common problem, on the road to integration is for people to discover that their timing is out of sync. Consider the couple who have both acknowledged their freedom/closeness conflicts and are working to make room for both needs in their lives. The issue is that when she wants to be close, he wants to be free. And when she wants to be free, he wants to be close. More work remains to be done on both their parts. Since the end result of such a conflict is space and detachment, it is likely that both parties still have more need for separation than they realize. It is also possible they do not really want the relationship. Of course, no relationship is optimally balanced. There will inevitably be times when one party wants more freedom or more closeness than the other. The question is one of degree. Are both people reasonably happy with the balance **most** of the time?

There are people who have been able to integrate these inner ambivalences. They have arranged their lives to have times and places for both independence and emotional attachments. They avoid extremes on either end, instead seeking a middle ground most of the time. They communicate clearly with loved ones to resolve issues as early (and easily) as possible. They acknowledge their inner conflicts, which is the first step to finding solutions. They realize that life is a process, where new answers are found as old issues reform in new disguises. They know that each variation of integration will become outmoded as they change and grow and are open to discovering new ways of relating and balancing with one another.

The Factors

Close, intimate associations are indicated by **Letters 7** (peer relationships) and **8** (shared resources, pleasures, sexuality, money) of the astrological alphabet.[1]

Thus we will include the following:

GROUP I
Conjunctions to Venus (ruler of Libra) and Pluto
Conjunctions to the Descendant
Conjunctions to Pallas and Juno (Libran asteroids)
Conjunctions to the rulers of the 7th and 8th cusps
Conjunctions to the rulers of any other signs (occupied or unoccupied) in the 7th and 8th houses
Conjunctions to the West Point (auxiliary Descendant)
Conjunctions to the Vertex (auxiliary Descendant)

---

1. If you prefer **not** to search for repeated themes yourself, you can order the "PP BOOK" option from Astro Computing Services (PO Box 16430, San Diego, Ca 92116), which allows you to use this book to make complete, synthesizing delineations of horoscopes without figuring out which themes are emphasized.

Available for $3.00 each, the "PP BOOK" report calculates the emphasis on all the letters of the alphabet, themes and aspects in each horoscope for which you provide the data. The report lists each significant focus (e.g., "There is a Letter 4 theme in "Relationships," and gives the appropriate page numbers for you to read in this book ("See pages 182-183 in the *Complete Horoscope Interpretation* book.")

The computer will not **always** arrive at the same results as you might, as certain steps are ambiguous (e.g., how much weight to give a planet making a conjunction, based on the orb). However, the majority of the time, the computer answers will concur with those derived from use of the worksheets — or the recommended quick scan of a horoscope. Thus it provides an excellent teaching tool.

The "PP BOOK" does **not** provide a listing of **each and every** astrological factor making up the significant themes. For that, you would order "PP WEIGHTS" (discussed in next footnote).

GROUP II

Nature of any planets in the 7th and 8th houses
Nature of any planets in the 6th or 9th houses which are within two degrees of the 7th or 8th cusps
Descendant sign

GROUP III

Parallels to Venus, Pluto, Pallas, Juno, Descendant, 8th cusp ruler, Descendant ruler, Vertex or West Point
House placements of Venus, Pluto, Juno and Pallas
House placements of the rulers of the 7th and 8th cusps
House placements of rulers of any other signs in the 7th and 8th houses
Nature of the house(s) ruled by any planets in the 7th and 8th houses
Houses ruled by planets forming conjunctions to Venus, Pluto, Pallas, Juno, Descendant, Descendant ruler, 8th cusp ruler, West Point or Vertex
Nature of any planets in Libra or Scorpio
Houses occupied by any planets in Libra or Scorpio
Houses with Libra or Scorpio on the cusp

GROUP IV

Sign placement of Venus, Pluto, Juno and Pallas
Sign placement of the rulers of the 7th and 8th cusps
Sign placement of rulers of any other signs in the 7th and 8th houses
Sign on the cusp of the 8th house
Sign of the West Point
Sign of the Vertex
Signs occupied in the 7th and 8th houses
Signs unoccupied in the 7th and 8th houses

If you want to use exact figures, a suggested weighting scale is given in the appendix — with worksheets for the various areas.[2]

---

2. You can also obtain a listing of **all** the astrological factors which compose those letters of the Zip Code determined to be significant in a horoscope. This makes an excellent teaching tool and a valuable resource to check yourself against when practicing with the Zip Code.

Astro Computing Services, PO Box 16430, San Diego, CA 92116, has calculated 28,000 horoscopes and established averages and standard deviations for the scores of each letter of the astrological alphabet, each theme, and the conflict and harmony aspects to each life area.

Astro's report, called "PP WEIGHTS," will list those letters of the astrological alphabet which are one standard deviation or more above the mean — and list **all** the astrological factors which point to each significant letter of the alphabet. These weightings will also compare each individual's score on the various themes (e.g., risk-taking, artistic) to the means and standard deviations to determine which themes are significant.

Averages are established for aspects as well in order to note conflict or harmony in the different life areas.

The results obtained by Astro's "PP WEIGHTS" will not **always** coincide with those you determine by a quick scan and intuitive judgment, or by use of the worksheets. Certain of the steps (e.g., how much to weight a planet based on orb) are ambiguous, so different results can occur. However, most of the time, Astro's answers will confirm those you could obtain in working with the Zip Code. Furthermore, the **complete** listing of relevant factors is an excellent teaching tool.

Ask for "PP Weights." The price, as of December 1985 is $5.00

A SHORT CUT

For quickness and ease of use, especially for people just learning to use the alphabet, I suggest limiting your focus to the factors in Groups I and II initially. (An alternative is to use Appendix 2 as described in Chapters 6 and 7.)

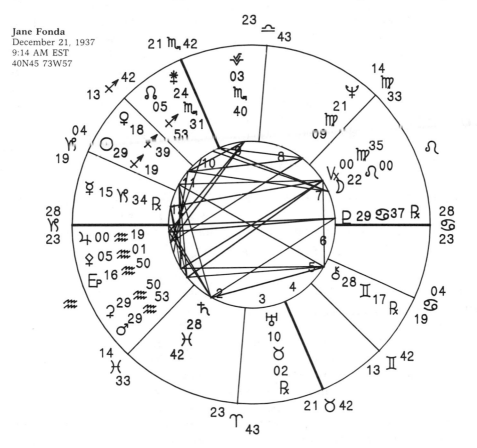

Jane Fonda
December 21, 1937
9:14 AM EST
40N45 73W57

For example, since Pluto closely conjuncts the Descendant (in the 7th house) in Jane Fonda's chart, we would suspect that Letter 8 could point to important issues in her relationships. With the Moon in the 7th house, Letter 4 might also be an important factor in her relationships. Additional possibilities include Letter 12 (Neptune occupies the 8th), Letter 9 (Pallas conjuncts Jupiter) and Letter 10 (Juno conjuncts the MC). If a letter appears more than once in Groups I and II, it is definitely significant: read that interpretation.

Once you have mastered the factors in Groups I and II, include Groups III and IV. If factors in Groups III or IV repeat a letter suggested once by Group I or II, it confirms that letter's significance. For example, in the Fonda horoscope, Venus is in Sagittarius (9), the 8th house Libra is ruled by Venus which is in Sagittarius (9), Scorpio is occupied in the 9th house (9), Libra is on the cusp of the 9th

(9), the nodes of the Moon [keys to relationships] parallel Jupiter (9) and Pallas conjuncts Jupiter (9). These seven repetitions support a Letter 9 focus in Ms. Fonda's relationships (pages 186-187).

Letter 4 is repeated six times in Ms. Fonda's relationship arena: the 7th house Moon (4), 7th house is occupied by a planet in Cancer (4), Descendant is in Cancer (4), Pluto is in Cancer (4), the West Point widely conjuncts the Moon (4), and the Descendant makes a conjunction in the sign of Cancer (4). Thus, we would also read the Letter 4 theme for Ms. Fonda's relationships (pages 182-183).

The combination of Letters 4 (home) and 9 (truth, the open road) can often point to tension between roots and adventures. Individuals may go on the road and feel at home anywhere, and/or have lots of books, philosophical discussions and idealistic issues within their home. Ms. Fonda has demonstrated several sides of the attachment versus liberty conflict of 4-9 (page 193) in her relationships.

Themes

Themes can be ascertained by two methods. One approach is to examine only those letters of the alphabet determined to be significant, based on the above. If we look at Ms. Fonda's houses of relationships (the 7th and 8th), one obvious theme is that all three water planets are present! The Moon (4) and Pluto (8) fall in the 7th, while Neptune (12) occupies the 8th house. This suggests a strong focus on deep feelings in relationships, seeking a "soul mate" sense, a merging or union with the partner. Water wants to absorb or be absorbed. When water is well integrated, nonverbal communication is excellent and tuning into one another psychically is common.

Of course this strong desire for intimacy would not be easy to blend with the emphasis on freedom we found in the identity section! That could be one reason Ms. Fonda did not marry until she was almost 28 (late for her generation). (Before taking the plunge, she made statements to the effect that marriage was "obsolete.") It would not be easy for a person strongly identified with Letter 11 and Letter 1 to risk losing that independence in the absorbing, unifying, blending focus of watery relationships! We might expect both attraction toward — and fear of — the "oneness" urges of water.

A second approach to spotting themes is to get a rough total for all of the letters of the alphabet, and see which combinations appear to have an above average emphasis. For example, the water theme is the total of scores from Letters 4, 8 and 10. You will need to do some rough arithmetic here, or get an intuitive impression. If a theme involves three (out of twelve) letters of the astrological alphabet, you would expect it to have about 1/4 of the total score. So, if the amount of those letters seems appreciably more than 1/4 of the total, count that as a theme — and read the appropriate section (page 202 in this case).

In addition, when searching for themes, give additional weighting to like planets in aspect to one another. For example, the Moon, Pluto and Neptune are the water planets. Any aspects between the Moon, Pluto and Neptune add to the focus on water in a chart. Ms. Fonda has the Moon semisextile Neptune.

Also give extra weight to like houses and signs. Thus, the Moon, Pluto or Neptune occupying the 4th, 8th or 12 houses or Cancer, Scorpio or Pisces would give extra weight to the theme of water for each occurrence. Ms. Fonda has Neptune occupying the 8th house and Pluto occupying Cancer.

Aspects

Quickly scan all aspects other than conjunctions or parallels, grouping them according to harmony (sextile, trine, semi-sextile) and conflict (octile, tri-octile, square, opposition and quincunx).

In considering each aspect, weight the nature of the planet most heavily, followed by the house and the sign. Note both the house occupied and the cusp ruled by the planet being aspected.

For example, Ms. Fonda has only a wide trine to the Moon from her Venus (as far as harmony aspects). She has the following **close** conflict aspects to her Venus:

- square Neptune (12) in the 8th (8) in Virgo (6); Neptune rules 2nd (2)
- octile Pallas (7) in the 1st (1) in Aquarius (11)
- octile Vesta (6) in the 9th (9) in Scorpio (8)

You would also examine the aspects to Ms. Fonda's other relationship factors — Pluto, Pallas, Juno, planets in and ruling the 7th and 8th houses. Then, you make an intuitive judgment of whether any letters of the alphabet have lots of conflict to them or have quite a bit of harmony. If we examine all factors, we find strong conflict between Letter 1 and relationship factors, confirming the freedom (1) versus closeness (7 and 8) struggle we suspected earlier.

Another approach to spotting themes is discussed in Appendix 2.

Interpretations: Relationships

ALPHABET THEMES

Letter 1: Assertion Vs. Accommodation — Owning Your Own Power

The issues revolve around identity and self-expression within the context of a relationship. Freedom of action is often an issue. Space, independence and a sense of separateness may be important. One question is how much you feel confident, in touch with, aware of and able to express your own, personal power and ability to be who you are, act as you choose. There are six major variations of actions among people who share this theme. The first three most people find somewhat uncomfortable; the last three are usually more fulfilling.

The first three variations involve a sense of vulnerability, people who are out of touch with their own power, feeling at the mercy of what others could or would do to them. They experience other people as having the power to use or abuse them, accept them or reject them, allow them to act or prevent them from acting. Coming from such a position of powerlessness, one variation is the doormat. Such people try to please and appease others. "Tell me what to do; tell me how to be so that you will like me." They try to "psyche" other people out; figure out what is desired and provide it. The unconscious (or partially conscious) hope is: "If I do what they want, I won't get hurt." Yet, as long as people experience the power as **external** rather than **internal**, they will fear what others **might** do. The extreme form of the "doormat" is found in people so out of touch with their own power, that they stay in abusive relationships, afraid or feeling unable, unwilling, or undeserving of seeking something better.

A second variation could be summarized as, "I'll get you first." The feeling is still one of vulnerability. The assumption is that other people are threats, so the individual acts to "wipe out" the other people for fear they might hurt him/her. The motto is: "The best defense is a good offense." Actions against others can range from mental denigrations to verbal attacks to actual physical violence in extreme forms. (Hitler and Jim Jones were extreme examples of this theme.)

A third variation is to seek safety through withdrawal. These people feel fearful of what others might do to them, so they avoid others. They withdraw from personal relationships, shut themselves away in a shell. Like the old Simon and Garfunkel song, they pretend: "I am a rock; I am an island." They try to convince themselves they do not need anyone, but strive to keep the world at arm's length, lest they be hurt.

The fourth variation involves simple compromise. The individual gives up some of the power. The other party in the relationship gives up some of the power and they meet in the middle. They compromise and cooperate. They negotiate to reach a mutually satisfying plan of action. Neither gets **exactly** and **totally** what they want, but both get a reasonable solution.

A fifth variation is healthy competition. Such people find and develop their power to act in the world and assert themselves through competitive activities. When structured, with rules and regulations so no one gets hurt, such an outlet can be very positive. Competitive sports, games and business allow an individual to test strength and power against the abilities of someone else. Note that a contest has to be between equals or near equals in order to be a true contest. If the people involved are of extremely disparate abilities, everyone knows beforehand who will win and who will lose; there is no contest. Competition involves the experience of both winning (and the other person is still okay) and losing (and discovering we are still okay). We build our strength through the challenging of another individual.

A sixth variation is to establish relationships of a helping/healing nature. Working with people we perceive as "weaker" or "needy" in some way allows us a position of strength. We are less likely to feel vulnerable or threatened when dealing with people who come to us for help. This enables the person to deal with issues of power, assertion and self-expression in the context of relating, without feeling overwhelmed by others.

The key issue within all these variations is the question of discovering ways in which **each person** in the relationship can be free to express who and what s/he is, naturally, spontaneously, without fear. If one person has all the power in the relationship, there is no balance. The person projecting (unconsciously giving away) that power needs to reclaim it. The person trying to run the whole show needs to get in touch with his/her ability to be vulnerable, receptive, sharing rather than unilaterally demanding "my way."

Other overlapping issues include freedom, courage, the ability to take risks, self-assertion and independence of action. Unless we are confident of our own strength and power, we may fear to act, to assert ourselves, to take chances, to be who we are. However, if we have an overdeveloped sense of independence, freedom and self-expression, we may have difficulties making commitments, sharing and compromising. If we identify with one extreme, we are likely to attract the opposite extreme in our relationships.

Staying in the middle, with a relationship which allows some space, independence, separateness between the parties can help to integrate the freedom and closeness needs. Sharing the power is a goal. If each person appreciates his/her own being and feels comfortable with manifesting that, the relationship is more likely to be balanced, with each able to be themselves and allow the other to also be who s/he is.

Letter 2: "There are no rocks in the River of Love."

The focus is on a beautiful relationship. This can range from a focus on the superficial, physical appearance of the other individual (or others paying attention to our appearance) to a fairy tale assumption that the course of "true love always runs smoothly" with no fights, arguments, hassles, etc. There is often a seeking of comfort — both materially in terms of money, possessions and physical pleasures and also psychologically in terms of not making waves.

The question is whether this seeking of beauty and comfort is a mutual creation or whether one party expects the other to provide it all. This can range from the search for a rich spouse who will support us in the style to which we wish to become accustomed to the quest for a fellow hedonist with whom to eat, drink and be merry.

If we deny a part of ourselves too much, expecting it from someone else, we usually get it in an excessive form. If we seek money, we may get it — and a partner who is stodgy, boring, routine, stable and totally unexciting. If we seek sensuality, we may get it — and a partner who is into pleasure but does not want to work. If we seek physical beauty, we may get it — and a partner who is simply a pretty package with little else to share.

Where both parties in the relationship are contributing to the creation of beauty, stability, pleasure and comfort, the association tends to be quite easygoing and accepting. Seldom do these people push each other. They are content to be who they are and allow the other person to be who s/he is, as well. Sensual indulgences, art, beauty, possessions and financial resources are all potential focuses in the relationship and mutual pleasure is the norm.

Letter 3: A Mental Relationship

Here the focus is on a meeting of the minds before anything else. The issues revolve around communication, intellect, varied interests and a cool, detached ability to look into anything and everything. People who share this energy tend to have very mental relationships. There is generally a lot of conversation, frequently a love of sharing trivia. They may take classes together, travel with one another, lend each other books and stimulate one another's minds in all ways. The first attraction is usually on the intellectual level.

If one party is projecting onto the other, however, the result is generally someone who does the thinking and/or talking for the other party. So, the "strong, silent" type unconsciously chooses a quick, articulate butterfly to express for him/her. The problem is, sooner or later, the "strong, silent" type feels the butterfly is **too** scattered, **too** talkative (or perhaps gossipy, superficial) and ought to listen more! Similarly, if we choose someone (unconsciously) to think for us, usually we end up annoyed with their obsession with logic, analysis, etc.

Detachment is often an issue — the ability to be objective and to laugh at life, not taking it too seriously. If we have not fully developed these qualities in our own being, we may be annoyed when partners, friends or associates demonstrate them to excess. What seemed initially an attractive flightiness degenerates into a disgusting lack of thoroughness, organization and followthrough.

Stimulation is often an issue. There is an attraction to constant activity in the life — something new to learn or experience all the time. We can consciously, deliberately create such an environment, or we can depend on others to provide the stimulation for us. In that case, however, we may be sometimes upset and disturbed by their timing and choices of new and different activities.

In terms of old patterns, we are often facing issues that we faced earlier in our lives with a brother, sister, aunt, uncle, cousin or other collateral relative (excluding mother and father). If you feel "stuck" in a pattern, examine your early home life. Try to figure out if there is someone your current partner/friend/associate reminds you of. They may not act or look the same, but the key is you feeling the same kinds of feelings as you felt before. If so, go back to that early relationship (in your mind) and try to resolve those old issues. Do any necessary forgiving. Realize that you did the best you knew how at that time and you are a different person now. Release and let go so you can move forward. The issues will still generally revolve around detachment, objectivity, the mind, the ability to communicate (or not), the light touch and the capacity to flit from flower to flower. Figure out how to express those qualities in ways which make you happy.

Letter 4: Sharing the Mothering

The issues here revolve around nurturance and dependency. The focus is on emotional closeness and vulnerability, caring for and being cared for. When balanced, we are comfortable in both roles: able to nurture as well as be nurtured. Until we find a balance, we may experience discomfort with both our nurturing potential and our dependency needs. We could go to the extremes of operating (unconsciously) as a baby looking for a mother (attracting people who try to take care of us) or a mother looking for a baby (attracting people who expect us to take care of them).

If we are able to take turns — sometimes being supported emotionally; other times supporting — there is a built-in equality and balance. If we play "mother" and attract "babies," sooner or later we usually get tired of carrying all the emotional load or the "baby" gets tired of not having any of the power.

There can be unfinished business with mother or the mother figure — the person who played the role (or was supposed to play the role) of unconditional love parent in our life. All children need unconditional love when very young: "I love you because you are. You do not have to **do** anything to earn my love." If we did not get the kind of unconditional love we wanted when young, we may spend time later searching for that loving mother we feel we never had — or searching for someone to whom we can be that loving mother we always wanted. When there is a tremendous amount of pain tied into the nurturing we did (or did not) receive, we may avoid dependency as much as possible, for fear of being hurt again.

Clarifying old issues with a parent (or parental figure) can help clear out unnecessary complications in present relationships. We cannot change the past, but understanding and forgiving the past (forgiving **ourselves** as well as others) often clears the way for changing the future.

Family is often quite important. Besides the potential of mothering or being mothered by a spouse, this combination can also indicate a close, ongoing relationship with one's own parents. In adulthood, children may become like partners to their parents. Many of your emotional needs could be met through family. Pets and plants can also serve to satisfy people's needs to care for and to feel that their existence matters. Sometimes, animals are much freer with unconditional love than people! The basic focus is on emotional warmth and attachment in close associations.

Letter 5: Wish Upon a Star

Applause, admiration, approval and attention are focuses in our relationships. Whether we are seeking someone we can applaud, admire and assume is fantastic, or we want someone who will give us that wonderful recognition and appreciation, the drive is for intense, exciting, charismatic interactions. The most positive form is a mutual fan club: two people, each fully behind the other, each fully supportive, admiring, convinced the other can do and be whatever s/he desires.

Where projection is involved, we can play the role of the Star and the Little Gray Mouse. The Star is always onstage, constantly demanding applause, discontented with any role but that of royalty. Often majestic, commanding with great stage presence, the Star can and does regularly sway people emotionally. Stars make great salespeople, advertisers and promoters. The Little Gray Mouse finds a Star because s/he is out of touch with his/her own ability to be charming, dramatic and magnetic. So, the Little Gray Mouse vicariously enjoys all the attention which the Star garners. However, unless the Little Gray Mouse eventually learns to sometimes be a Star and the Star learns to take a turn **off**stage, the inevitable happens: 1) the Little Gray Mouse gets tired of applauding and leaves to either find a new star **or** develop his/her own Star potential; 2) the Little Gray Mouse does such a **good** job of applauding that the Star leaves because "Why should such an exciting person as me hang around such a dull person as you!?"

We all need the limelight somewhere in life — a place to shine; a place to be significant; to earn the appreciation, admiration and approval of others. But self-appreciation and approval must come first. If we are only dependent on others admiring us, we can easily fall into the rug ("walk on me") syndrome — trying always to please others, not feeling validated unless others approve. Or, we can act overbearing and arrogant to hide the inner insecurity of wondering if we really are okay. Part of the theme here is self-esteem. We need to like ourselves as well as be liked and admired (in some arenas) by others.

Seen from another viewpoint, this theme is a mixture of partnership with child energies. We can choose to share a childlike enthusiasm, spontaneity, joy, zest for life and openness to new experiences with our partners. We can treat children like equals. Indeed, our own children may fill some of our relationship needs, becoming more like partners as they move into being adults. We can also attract associates who are childish and self-centered, demanding all the attention and applause. Or, we can act the part of the child. We can also have a child that reminds us of a partner. (If we liked the partner, we will probably enjoy the child. If we did not like the partner, we will be bothered by the same qualities in the child.) But the basic issues revolve around the capacity for excitement, liveliness, admiration and esteem in relationships.

Letter 6: Working at Relationships

You have an interface of work and partnership. This can be manifested in several ways. You may work with a partner — having a task orientation or shared career as well as an emotional/romantic commitment. You may meet close friends/partners through your work. You may have a very pragmatic, practical, critical approach toward partnerships with a focus on productivity, concrete results and discipline. You may make partnership into a job or career or turn your partner into a job (trying to make him/her over). You may attract (projection) partners who are workaholics, critical, realistic, disciplined, etc. Your career may involve relating to people, e.g., counseling, personnel work, lawyer-client relationships, and so on. All are potential variations. The expressions you choose are up to you.

The work attitude (critical, flaw-finding, disciplined) can be an asset when utilized in moderation. But applied indiscriminately to relationships, it is more likely to wreak havoc. One pitfall to avoid is setting up work in opposition to relationships — as if one had to choose between a career or job and an association.

Part of the issue here is the ability to do the necessary, but often boring, details which get the job done. This can be a focus in relationships. Who does the "servicing" of the relationship? Who is the one usually applying the self-discipline? Is one party working more than another? Is one person (regardless of sex) playing the Earth Mother role? Is one party a workaholic? (If so, projection is likely. The workaholic needs to learn to relax and enjoy life more and the other party needs to learn more discipline and willingness to be dedicated.)

A potential focus in the relationship is around health and illness. One partner might express the extreme of inefficient functioning with many health problems, while the other party works and carries the load of taking care of business. Illnesses can be compounded by feelings of guilt and frustration around not doing things well. Making sure each partner has his/her own arena to be productive helps immensely. Sidestep tendencies to criticize one another excessively. Focus on working **together**.

The best thing about this combination is when you really commit to a relationship, you are usually willing to **work at it**. Least prone to fairy tale images, you are most likely to see what is there, in yourself and the other person, and deal with it in a practical, grounded manner.

Letter 7: Even Steven Only

Equality is the name of the game. You may seek it through negotiation and cooperation. You may seek it through competition or something approaching open warfare. You need to be on an "even keel" with the one you share your life with. Indeed, scorekeeping is a potential — where either or both partners keep a running tally in their heads of who has scored "points" over the other (by making a decision, winning an argument, etc.). As soon as one party gets a few points ahead, the other makes a determined effort to "even up the score." Your strong sense of fair play can also lead to very cooperative relationships on even terms.

Aesthetics are often a draw. Whether you are attracted to an artist or artistic type, are involved with beauty yourself, seek a physically attractive partner or simply enjoy going to art museums and galleries, the need is for some interaction with balance, grace, harmony and beauty in the life. At times, the concern with appearances can be carried too far. Then the potential of obsessions such as "keeping up with the Joneses" or "What will the neighbors think?" arises. Loveliness and charm on all levels appeal.

Usually partnership is important. If this need is projected, you may unconsciously attract people that always seem marriage-oriented. They continually push for a commitment, for a legal bond or tie, while you want to hang loose and see how things go.

If the need for balance is carried to an extreme, any sort of inequality in the relationship can bother you. If you seem to love the other party less, or the other person seems to love you less, that can become a great concern. Your sense of justice wants to keep things as "fair" as possible in the relationship. Relationships that are 50/50 are usually preferred, and much mutual enjoyment, love and harmony are possible.

Letter 8: Intense Intimacy

You are pulled toward intense emotional involvements, depth investigation and self-transformation and mastery through the mirror of another person. More than any other blend, this combination emphasizes the reality of projection: we meet and have the chance to recognize unactualized parts of our own nature through the people closest to us. Such relationships can be extremely therapeutic, where we probe the very depths of our being.

Power over shared resources and pleasures is often a focus. Learning how to give, receive and share pleasures can be a challenge. Some people have difficulty giving; others find it hard to receive, while still others do not yet know how to share. And many people do get intensely emotionally involved when money and sex are the issues. If negatively handled, power plays, manipulation (tears, threats, guilt trips) and domination are all potentials — whether you are the perpetrator or the recipient. Jealousy and possessiveness are possible, when the power is turned outward to try to control others rather than inward to control the self.

Being able to let go in relationships is often a challenge. You may hold on to people and associations too long. Learn to recognize the signs of death in an association — when it is time to move on for new learning. Sometimes what needs to be released is simply old emotions. There is often a tendency to cling to guilts, resentments, angers, old negative emotions. If dwelt on for too long, they can lead to physical problems. Forgiving and releasing is an important skill.

You have tremendous potential power on the emotional level. Channeled inward, it can lead to incredible alterations of your psyche on the deepest levels. But do not overcontrol yourself. Self-denial is another extreme to be avoided. People may respond instinctively to the sense of emotional intensity and seething that you can emote. Seek others who are willing to go as deep as you are; superficialities will only bore you. You can be as exacting and demanding of yourself as others — constantly probing, examining and looking for deeper answers.

Letter 9: Beware Idolatry

This is a "perfect" partner blend. Unfortunately, it does not guarantee that you will **find** the "perfect" partner, just that you are likely to seek him/her! The search for the ultimate ideal mixed with people associations can manifest in several ways. One variant is the student looking for the guru: seeking the wise sage with all the answers to the universe, the meaning, the truth and the light. Of course, we can also play the guru looking for the student to sit at our feet and drink up our

words of wisdom. Another variant is to go into the Church, literally or figuratively, because no human being is good enough. So, one can "marry God." Another
option is simply to keep on searching for that great ideal and never finding it.
That would not bother you too much, since you also have some strong freedom
needs. Keeping the standards so high that no one measures up enables you to retain your independence! Another possibility is attracting victims who expect you
to meet all their needs, to show them the way to enlightenment (or at least,
perpetual happiness). Of course, that is a seductive trap, since they are never happy, no matter what you do.

Sharing the search for an ultimate is another potential path. You may enjoy
studying with a partner, traveling together, meditating with one another, having
a joint spiritual endeavor. You may look to religion, philosophy, science, education, nature, God or other avenues for the final answers about the meaning of
life and why we are here. Shared ideals can lead to shared inspirations. There
is the potential of tremendous joy, enthusiasm, excitement here. That feeling of
being "on top of the world" is quite possible: optimistic, idealistic, philanthropic
and generous. Just make sure your feet are on the ground when you head is in
the clouds.

When the idealism is shared, you think your partner is the absolute best and
s/he feels equally positive about you!

Letter 10: Marriage is Forever

Although it is not uncommon for you to hesitate — thinking long and hard before
committing yourself to a relationship — once you have made that commitment,
you seldom give up. Indeed, sometimes you stay in relationships long "dead,"
still struggling to make it "work out." Your sense of duty and responsibility can
be overdone.

The issues here revolve around responsibility, power, control and authority.
When those qualities are seen as external (in other people), the tendency is to
avoid or delay relationships — for fear of being hurt, dominated, rejected, criticized,
controlled, etc. Or, we can project those qualities, but look for the "good father" —
stable, dependable, hardworking, who will take such good care of us. The trouble is, "good fathers" usually end up in control and the "child" in the relationship generally comes to resent that. If we internalize those qualities of discipline,
authority, power and realism, we can share them in our relationships for mutual
support, practicality, contributions and responsibilities. Or, we can overdo those
qualities, in which case we attract weaker people who lean on us, expecting us
to carry the whole load, putting us into that "father figure" role.

The key is for **both** parties to work, be pragmatic, be disciplined (reasonably
so), conscientious, careful and dedicated. If one person is doing it all, that party
usually ends up a workaholic, critical, dominating and/or excessively serious.

Unfinished business with the father or father figure is often played out through
close relationships. The father or father figure gives us our first experience of

conditional love: "I love you because you performed properly. You did the 'right' thing." We need that reality parent in order to learn the rules and roles of society, to live with other people. But, if we continue to experience the power externally, we will simply get new "fathers" from time to time who limit, restrict and control our lives. One key is to become our own father, while being able to share the responsibility with someone close. We can both work, both be dedicated, both have a career and contribute to society. Each partner finds in the other a solid source of strength and support.

Letter 11: Pals

You are ready to be partners with friends and friends with partners. Indeed, you are capable of being friends after a romantic relationship has ended. You know how to make the transition. You can also allow a platonic friendship to grow into something deeper.

Freedom, independence, uniqueness, originality and space are issues. When shared, both people are individuals, respecting each other's needs for room in the relationship. They often have separate interests, hobbies, friends, activities, and are **not** a "do everything together" couple. They enjoy their individual lives and then coming together to share. They accept and understand one another — without having to change the other person. The cardinal sin is boredom; that can be used as an excuse to find someone new and different. If you project your need for freedom, then attracting the classic "free soul" who is unwilling to commit is quite possible.

Another potential projection is when one person is overdoing the need for uniqueness and originality for the other. In that case, the first person is likely to be weird, strange and even flaky. Irresponsibility is possible. Some people will use their relationships as a channel for rebelling against the world and/or their parents. So they deliberately pick partners/close friends from a very different background/race/creed, etc. There is a big difference between appreciation of someone's uniqueness and valuing that person as a special human being (who happens to have a different religion or skin color) versus choosing to relate to someone on the basis of their different religion or skin color because that will shock others.

The most positive form of this blend is partners who are best friends — truly open and accepting of whatever the other person is, enjoying learning, growing and stretching their limits through one another.

Letter 12: Fantasy?

The search is for that "made in heaven" relationship — a seeking of infinite Love and Beauty through human interactions. So often, the dream is not redeemable in the real world. More positive options include seeking that wonderful experience **with** someone else (not expecting them to provide it). People can merge with the

Infinite through art, beauty, nature and religious or spiritual experiences. Shared ecstasy can be achieved (or fantasies and illusions can be shared).

Less fulfilling routes include spending one's life on a quest for Prince or Princess Charming — who either does not exist or seems to be found repeatedly, only to turn out flawed later on. Repeated involvements with the "ideal mate" do not always teach the lesson; sometimes people continue to believe that "**this** one is the magic one!" Or, we can attract victims — whether drug addicts, alcoholics, down and out sufferers who look to us to save them, succor them, rescue them, and turn their world into a lovely, rosy glow. The task, of course, is not possible, but if we need to be needed, we may try — for a time. (Then, of course, we end up feeling victimized by the victim!)

Some people "marry God" because no one else is good enough. We all need relationships, we all need that yearning for something higher, a sense of emotional connection to the Infinite. Seeking the infinite **with** other human beings is much easier to manage than expecting another human being (or ourselves) to **be** infinite and perfect.

Other forms of projection include attracting artists or people involved in helping and healing others. As long as both parties can manifest some of their idealism in healthy ways in the relationship, it can be a most beautiful, loving and inspiring association.

ALPHABET COMBINATIONS BY TWOS

The following are shorthand summaries of relationship combinations for two letters of the astrological alphabet. The summaries below depict characteristics that your partner(s) might exhibit. The alternative possibility is that you yourself can behave in alignment with such characteristics in your relationships. Remember, the ideal is to **share** the themes involved. If either partner denies a potential within him/herself, the other partner is likely to **overdo** that potential. Seek a moderate middle ground.

1-2: Your relationships are dealing with the issue of personal needs. Your partners could be strong, determined and in touch with what they want. They might also be **too** self-oriented, self-indulgent, lacking in empathy for others. You are learning together about when to put yourself first and the importance of enjoying life.

1-3: Handling assertion and the mind are issues in your relationships. Your partners could be bright, quick-witted and expressive. They might be cutting, ironic, sarcastic. They are probably active and restless. An energetic exchange of ideas is quite possible.

1-4: You and your partners may be torn between self-development and the establishment of a nest. You are trying to balance personal needs for freedom with needs for emotional closeness and sharing. You could experience partners as too free (not there when you needed them), too close (smothering, possessive) or both until you learn balance.

1-5: Zest, joy, vitality and confidence are important issues in your relationships. Your partners could be excitement addicts of some sort — pursuing the adrenaline rush of being onstage, gambling , living life to the full in some fashion. If overdone, they could be impulsive, foolhardy, overconfident or self-centered. Sharing the limelight and the fun pays great dividends.

1-6: You and your partners are facing themes of free, spontaneous expression versus careful, painstaking dedication to detail. If not integrated, any of you may vacillate from nit-picking to letting it all hang out and may over-do either end. If integrated, you could all be energetic, competent workers.

1-7: Your relationships are dealing with the dilemma of balancing self-will with the rights and desires of another person. If you manage to integrate asser-tion and accommodation, you can create a model partnership. If not, there is still an opportunity to learn about making peace between the need to be yourself and the need to compromise with another for a relationship.

1-8: You and your partners are facing issues around self-restraint and the ability to share the material/sensual world with each other. One option is power struggles or manipulation, especially around money, possessions or sex. Another possibility is discovering the importance of self-mastery and plumbing the depths of the self out of respect for the rights of others.

1-9: Energy, vitality, freedom, creativity and the ability to take risks are possi-ble focuses in your relationships. Your partners may be lively, lighthearted, witty on-the-go people. They could be active in sports or otherwise on the move. Self-confidence and extraversion are likely to be high. If they carry their freedom needs to an extreme, they might not be around much. Share the liveliness, humor and spontaneity.

1-10: You are working on the balance between doing what one wants versus working within the realistic limits of the world. If integrated, you and your partners are probably extremely capable, achieving people. If still strug-gling, either of you could succumb to giving up (not attempting the possi-ble) or trying too hard (and hitting the stone wall of reality).

1-11: Your relationships are teaching you about freedom. If this is done in a comfortable sense, you enjoy your partner's uniqueness and independence and they encourage you to do your own thing. If they overemphasize this side of life, you may feel they are erratic or you could experience them as off into their own pursuits even when you want them.

1-12: Your relationships are arenas for blending the urge for spontaneous, per-sonal action with the desire to merge with the universe. Fighting for causes, active creation of beauty and energetic pursuit of ideals are all possibilities. So is the perennial victim. Your partners offer you examples of what **to** do or what **not** to do in blending self-assertion and self-sacrifice.

2-3: Your relationships are probably oriented toward comfort and easy interac-tion. Relatives could be important. The general theme is laid-back and casual. If carried too far, partners might be self-indulgent, lazy or gossipy and superficial. If moderately expressed, you are likely to have an easygoing, affectionate relationship.

2-4: Security, emotional and physical, would be important in your relationships. Partners could provide a stable, secure setting with warmth and affection. They could also seem stodgy, possessive, stuck in the past, indulgent or overly materialistic. Usually, your home base is an important source of support for you.

2-5: Your relationships are arenas for balancing risk-taking instincts with needs for stability and security. Partners could overdo either side, or spend time fighting, especially in areas involving money, possessions and sexuality. Your relationships are teaching you about willpower and determination.

2-6: Your partners are sharing themes of work, practicality and dealing with the real world with you. Their attitudes about effectiveness and pragmatism need to be balanced with yours. If overdone, you may feel they are too concerned with the bottom line, too focused on getting and having things in life. If moderate, they give a good example of relaxed efficiency.

2-7: Your partners are dealing in some way with issues of beauty, comfort, ease and harmony. They might be artistically talented, easygoing, uncomfortable with confrontation or place a high value on pleasure. Their examples teach you what to do and what not to do in facing your own needs for grace, balance and enjoyment in life.

2-8: Your relationships are mirroring the dilemma of self-indulgence versus self-control, whether primarily around food, drinking, sexuality, spending money, saving money or other avenues of appetite control. Partners could fall into power struggles with you over these issues. You have the opportunity to learn moderation through the interactions.

2-9: Your relationships may be divided between material pleasures versus ethical, spiritual, religious or philosophical principles. Partners may be trying to balance physical goods and enjoyments with the reach for meaning and a higher purpose in life. You have the option to integrate these drives.

2-10: Achievement, making something of oneself in the outer world, monetary success and a practical, realistic approach to life are probably significant issues in your relationships. If overdone, you may feel that partners are too grounded, boring, predictable, controlling or acquisitive. If shared, you both work to build a better, more effective relationship.

2-11: You are learning to balance the need for stability with the need for change and alterations in your relationships. Partners could carry either behavior to an extreme and seem stodgy and stuck-in-the-mud or erratic, irresponsible and weird. Their example can help you learn to integrate these drives.

2-12: Your partners may have an instinctive feeling for beauty. They are likely to appreciate the finer things in life (good food, drink, pleasant surroundings) and may have excellent taste. They could also be self-indulgent, lazy and inclined to seek the easiest way out. They are probably teaching you about ease and comfort.

3-4: Your place could be a center for relatives and neighbors to gather in. Issues

of closeness and communication are important in your relationships. Partners could be very warm, friendly and easy to talk to — or too clingy, protective, dependent, casual and undisciplined.

3-5: Your partners could be a lot of fun — lighthearted, entertaining, sociable
with natural dramatic talent. If they carry this theme too far, you may
experience them as acting more like children than adults — possibly self-
centered, wanting to play rather than do their duties, casual and carefree
rather than serious. Sharing the lightness and the laughs means you can
enjoy interacting with one another.

3-6: Your partners may be presenting an example of the dilemma between
multiple interests and the desire to do things really well. The opportunity
for learning by you is there whether they integrate these needs; are too
scattered and superficial; or are too focused on the flaws, critical and
needing to get things just so. Communication and shared ideas are essential for you.

3-7: Your partners are probably very social people, interested in ideas and people. They are helping you deal with the mind and tongue and might be
natural communicators. If overdone, they could be too detached, logical
and objective (lacking warmth), too gregarious, excessively other-oriented
or superficial.

3-8: Your relationships are presenting you with a learning ground for the issue
of breadth versus depth. Partners (and you) may be struggling to blend
the desire to explore all ideas, understand everything, versus the need to
concentrate in a very intense manner on one area. The casual, light touch
needs to be blended with the intent, obsessive focus.

3-9: Probably very mental, flexible, adaptable and curious, your partners may
be continually studying, teaching, learning, communicating or traveling.
Your relationships present an opportunity to deal with your own intellect
and restlessness. The potential of being too diversified is here. Having
priorities is essential.

3-10: Your partners have the capacity to be very cool, rational and objective.
They are learning to balance a casual, lighthearted style with a serious
approach. Their example — positive or negative — helps teach you about
your own ability to be detached, logical and realistic.

3-11: Your partners could be friends with you, respecting your independence.
There is the potential for much ease in communication and interchange,
a mutual acceptance. They are likely to treat you as a peer, an equal. If
carried to an extreme, you may feel they often leave you to your own
devices while doing their own thing, or are too intellectual and not emotional enough.

3-12: Your partners could have a wide variety of interests and talents. If not
able to establish clear values and priorities, they could be confused, unclear
or overextended. You are learning (through their positive or negative example) how to integrate an awareness of the everyday world of people

around you with the inspiration and pull from above of something more.

4-5: Your partners could be extremely warm, loving and family-oriented. They are probably highly emotional. If they overdo this theme, they might try to control and dominate through emotional manipulation and dramatization. They might appear very needy emotionally. There can also be a very great love bond with this combination.

4-6: Your partners are exposing you to principles of work and nurturance. They could be dedicated caretakers — even too protective, inclined to do everything themselves. The opposite extreme is partners who are dependent, expecting you to be realistic and look after them. A more comfortable blend is partners who are efficient as well as warm, caring as well as capable. The goal is mutual support.

4-7: You and your partner are facing the question of how much closeness you wish in your relationship. On the one hand, you would like a sense of union, a merging, a total interdependence. On the other hand, you would like an innate sense of equality, a feeling of some space and separation. Making the balance is an issue for both of you.

4-8: Through your partners, you are learning about unconscious motivations, depth understanding and emotional needs. They are probably very intense, but rather unrevealing of what is going on inside them. They may be inclined to mull things over before reaching decisions. Security could be an issue for both of you, and facing your inner depths.

4-9: You and your partners are trying to balance the desire for a nest with the pull toward the open road. You may try to bring the world into your home (books, philosophical discussions, religion) or your home into the world (trailers, trips, etc.). You are integrating the same pull — between independence (to search for the truth) and emotional commitments (e.g., home and family). You or a partner could overdo one end or the other until balance is reached.

4-10: You are facing the seesaw between unconditional love and acceptance versus conditional love which teaches realism and consequences. ("I love you when you are good.") Partners could overdo either side — being too protective or too judgmental, critical, harsh. You are learning through relationships to balance emotional security needs with practical, survival, reality needs.

4-11: Your relationships are probably featuring the conflict between staying within the nest and pursuing something unique, unusual or progressive in the world. Freedom drives have to be integrated with needs for an emotional commitment. You could experience partners as overdoing either side — too much closeness (clingy, possessive, dependent) or too much freedom (erratic, irresponsible, flighty).

4-12: Your partners are probably very sensitive, intuitive, gentle individuals. They might operate from the role of a nurturing, protective helper or from the role of a dependent, helpless victim. Whatever the model, you are

facing issues of empathy, emotional support, caring and a psychic connection to others.

5-6: Your relationships are teaching you about the blend between being creative
and achieving practical results. If partners overdo one side, they could be
selfish, intent on their own needs or too concerned with gaining attention, applause or power — riding roughshod over people in their path. If
they overdo another side, they might be too focused on the end product
to enjoy the process of creating it. You and your partners can be highly
capable people who accomplish a lot, combining self-confidence with
pragmatic discipline.

5-7: Your partners are probably very sociable, fun-loving and charismatic. They
could have a lot of charm and appeal. If they depend too much on their
magnetism to get by, they could be a bit impractical. Through relationships you are learning about relaxing, enjoying life and looking on the
bright side of things.

5-8: Your partners are probably very intense, emotional people who could feel
torn between expressing their deep feelings and keeping them inside. They
are likely to have a drive for power and might fight with you over money
issues or around questions of sexuality and possessions. Control and approval are probable issues in your relationships.

5-9: Themes of energy, action, vitality, charisma and courage are important
in your relationships. A partner's desire for excitement could lead to some
risk-taking activities. Your partners are probably restless and eager to keep
moving. If they overdo these themes, they could be careless, overly optimistic, foolhardy and carried away with grand schemes and dreams of
an impractical nature. They might come across as simply self-centered and
solely intent on doing what they wanted to do. Share the zest.

5-10: Your partners probably have a drive for power, authority and control. If
handled wisely, they provide a role model for having an impact in the
world. A less comfortable lesson could involve power struggles with them,
learning your own strength through combat and competition. Success and
winning would be a major value.

5-11: Your relationships are seeking to strike a balance between needing emotional warmth, loving response and admiration versus wanting logic, rationality and detachment. Partners or you might feel torn between loved
family members and friends. Partners offer an example (positive or
negative) for integrating freedom and closeness needs, the pull of the head
and the heart.

5-12: Your partners could be extremely dramatic and persuasive. They could
live on a "larger than life" scale, blowing everything up. They are probably very emotionally intense. If not handled, they could be volatile —
even explosive at times. The drama could go into playing the victim or
martyr role — or be used positively to persuade, entertain and involve
others. Your own instinct for showmanship, your idealism and your search

for something more in life, need constructive outlets.

6-7: Your partners are probably rather cool, calm and collected. They know how to be logical and objective. Sometimes, they may weigh things overlong, trying to reach the absolute **best** decision. Generally, they are oriented toward the rational. If excessively so, you might long for more warmth. You are facing issues of practical empathy and realistic caring in your relationships.

6-8: Your relationships are dealing with the issues of discipline, exactitude, carefulness, perseverance and practicality. Your partners could be very organized, systematic, thorough and precise. If carried to an extreme, they could be obsessive-compulsive in their outlook or behavior. Moderate attention to detail by both of you can reap excellent results

6-9. In your relationships, you are striving to integrate a desire for precision, discipline, hard work and attention to detail with a search for something higher, a theoretical understanding of life's meaning, or a desire for something more. The result could be a practical achievement of your dreams or an underlying dissatisfaction with the quality of life and tendency to criticize its lack of perfection. Either you or a partner could be practical idealists — or continually disappointed that life was not the way you wished it would be.

6-10: Your relationships are facing (positively or negatively) issues about work, pragmatism and achievement. Partners could be workaholics and **too** oriented toward doing a good job. They could be blocked, inadequate people so that you ended up working and being realistic to cope for them. Their attitudes about what entails success and achievement offer learning for you.

6-11: You are learning to integrate themes of freedom, spontaneity and openness with discipline, attention to detail and concentration. Partners might seesaw between a picky focus on petty issues to an erratic, unpredictable cutting loose. You both need a place for originality and and a place for discipline.

6-12: Your relationships are trying to balance the search for a beautiful dream with an awareness of what is possible and the flaws of the world. Options include you or partners going in and out of jobs, being a victim, feeling dissatisfied with the state of the universe — or actually grounding your visions in a realistic manner. Your or partners might seem impossible to please — with perfectionistic standards and excessively high expectations. Common integrations include artists and craftspeople, helpers and healers — anyone making dreams real.

7-8: Your partners are probably focused on relationships and value interactions with people. If overdone, they may be more committed to wanting a relationship than you are. They could treat you as an equal with room to be yourself and relate as a peer. Competition could also be a factor in your relationship. Through them, you are learning about equality and sharing.

7-9: Your ideals and sense of right, wrong and ultimate reality could be focuses in your relationships — along with expectations and fun. Your partners are probably extraverted, optimistic and socially oriented. They could have a strong sense of justice and fair play, to the point of being highly competitive. Together, you are learning to enjoy life within a common ethical and value framework.

7-10: You are striving to balance the push/pull between success in the outer world and sharing in a committed relationship. Partners might feel torn between equality and control; a career and a partnership. They could bounce from treating you as an equal to trying to dominate. Balance is essential.

7-11: A mental focus is important in your relationships — with a need for space as well. Your partners have the capacity to be quite bright, communicative, accepting and tolerant. Naturally objective, they might treat you as a good friend as well as a partner. If carried too far, this detachment could be a way for them to do what they want while avoiding emotional commitments. Another option is developing your mind and independence in reaction to partners who denied their own capacities for objectivity and equality. Usually, however, there is a sense of openness and easy communication.

7-12: Your partners might have strong aesthetic leanings. Artistic appreciation and talent could come through them. They would be drawn toward harmony, grace and ease. If they fall into expecting the universe to provide, they could be charming and pleasant but not very inclined to work hard. Pleasure, beauty and the desire for a smooth flow in relationships is likely.

8-9: Your partners are probably emotionally intense, perhaps with feelings held back and then exploding out periodically. They are learning to make peace between a natural outpouring and a tendency to internalize feelings, to search within for answers. Your relationships are teaching you about self-control, understanding your inner depths, and a search for truth and meaning in life.

8-10: Your partners are probably extremely disciplined; they could even go to extremes of self-denial and excessive control. Power would be important to them. Unless channeled into the world, they might overcontrol themselves or others. Dominance could be an issue in your relationship. They also have much to teach you about organization, thoroughness, concentration and willpower.

8-11: You and your partners are seeking to find a balance between the need for security (especially financial and material) and the need to be original, innovative and creative. They might feel tension between their desire for power and their equalitarian nature. You are facing these dilemmas through their example and your interactions.

8-12: Perceptive, very likely psychic, your partners could be highly sensitive people with much happening below the surface. Nonverbal communication is quite possible with each of you tuning into the other (in a positive and/or negative fashion). Unconscious motivations could play a major role in the relationship. Uncovering hidden desires and supporting your inner wisdom is important.

9-10: Your partners are capable of seeing the big picture. They may have an awareness of larger issues and influence your world view, your perception of reality. Inclined to expect a lot, they could achieve many dreams or live perennially frustrated because nothing was as ideal as they wished. You are learning to balance the ideal and the real in your relationships.

9-11: Freedom is vital in your partnerships — especially the intellectual freedom to explore new ideas (and possibly new horizons as well). Partners may not want to be tied down and probably encourage you to be independent partially to give them room in pursuing their own interests. If their need for space is overdone, you could experience them as cold and unavailable when you want warmth.

9-12: Your feelings about partnership are likely to be strongly connected to your perception of the absolute in life — truth, the infinite, ultimate meaning and inspiration. Your partners could be visionary, idealistic, religious, perfectionistic or victims unhappy with the state of their lives (including missing or absent partners). You may want more than is possible from them or vice versa. Searching for the Highest in life together — rather than either one expecting the other to **be** "everything" for him/her usually works the best.

10-11: Your relationships are teaching you about the integration of conventionality with unconventionality; freedom with discipline; adherence to tradition with breaking the rules. Whether partners overdo one side or the other — or reach a healthy integration — they offer you an opportunity for learning about how to handle (or how not to handle) those themes.

10-12: You and your partners are attempting to make peace between the real and the ideal. In its highest form, this means bringing your visions to Earth and concretizing them. In less comfortable applications, you or partners may be critical of people or situations that do not measure up to your expectations, or any of you may give up and not try, for fear the result will be less than ideal.

11-12: This combination suggests partners with a perspective much broader than the home and family; you could share a transpersonal orientation and humanitarian instincts. Your partners could also be simply confused with their own little world so that you experienced them as not there (physically or just psychologically) in the home. They are teaching you about integrating (or not blending) freedom needs and the pull of a vision.

POLARITIES

1-7: ♂-♀ or ⚵ or ⚶, ♈-♎, 1st-7th houses

You are likely to be facing a polarity: the balance between self-assertion and accommodation or aggression and appeasement. You are learning to make room for both self-will and the needs and desires of another person. You are practicing negotiation, interaction between two people so that both of you get your needs met.

Until integration is achieved, you may vacillate between excessive aggression or extreme energy and pursuit of your own desires, to playing doormat and giving away all the power to someone else. If you deny the potential of either end within yourself, you will attract partners who **overdo** that basic theme — mirroring it back to you. The middle point allows you to be strong and also sharing; independent but also committed; self-expressive but also loving.

2-8: ♀-♇, ♉-♏, 2nd-8th houses

You are probably facing a polarity: the internal balance between self-indulgence and self-control. The usual battlegrounds involve food, sex, drinking, money or other sensual pleasures. The seesaw option can find us swinging from feast to famine around food; total abstinence to rampant indulgence around sex or alcohol; extremes of spending or saving with money.

Because external conflicts often feel subjectively easier to cope with than internal struggles, it is common for people to attract partners who share these issues. Then they can practice finding a balance by nagging each other about their weight, or about smoking or drinking, or by fighting about money. Once we make the internal balance, the external is easy.

3-9: ☿-♃, ♊-♐, 3rd-9th houses

You could experience seesaw swings between long-range and short-range views. The issue revolves around how much to focus on the here-and-now, right around you reality versus putting your sights on what lies ahead, a future vision, a dream to shoot for. The present and future can vie with one another. Current understanding may be at odds with an inspired quest. You could go to an extreme with either position, or attract partners who overdid one side or the other.

Both viewpoints tend to value mental stimulation, studying, learning, traveling and information exchange, so all of that can be important in your relationships. A sharing of ideas is vital. Try to keep equal time for both your perception of immediate concerns and your grasp of ultimate objectives.

4-10: ☽-♄, ♋-♑, 4th-10th houses

You are probably facing the polarities of conditional and unconditional love in your relationships. These seeming opposites are also parental archetypes. The unconditional theme is the traditional "mothering" role of supportive, warm and loving caretaking. You may seek to act in this way toward partners, or attract partners who try to nurture you. The conditional theme is the traditional "fathering" role of being strong, capable, responsible, hardworking and putting importance on performance — doing the job well. You may seek to be a source of strength, power and authority for your partners, or attract people who try to play that role in your life. It is possible that you could overdo either approach: the warm, nurturing one or the judgmental, performance-oriented one. You might also attract partners to play either end of the seesaw. Integration involves a blend of caring and pragmatism, warmth and practicality, emotions and realism. It also means being able to take turns playing the "parent" role in a peer association, so that neither partner has all the authority or power all the time. You share strengths. (See also the Parents and Partners theme.)

5-11: ☉-♅, ♌-♒, 5th-11th houses

The likely issues here are the balance between the head and the heart or intellect and emotions. A related issue is the tension between freedom needs and desires to love and be loved. Within your close relationships, you are seeking to integrate the desire to be unique, bright, intellectual and independent with the need to be appreciated, admired, passionate and committed to a close association. You could bounce from one extreme to the other — cool, aloof and detached one moment, passionately exciting and excited the next; calm and rational one moment, intensely emotionally involved the next. You might decide retaining your personal liberty and not being like anyone else are the most important things in life, only to change you mind and feel that having someone to love, look up to and applaud you is an essential ingredient.

You could also attract partners who play out either side of this polarity for you. If you identify with one side, they will typically express the opposite extreme. You play hot; they play cold (or vice versa). You play emotional; they play intellectual. You play equalitarian and we are all equal; they play King (Queen) of the Mountain and "I'm better than anyone else." And so on, until both of you learn to reach a balance and to share both kinds of expression in a happy medium.

6-12: ☿ or ⚵ or ♀-♆, ♍-♓, 6th-12th houses

The conflict between a beautiful dream of infinite love and perfection versus the basic, practical details of everyday life with its physical limitations and regulations may be an issue in your life. The ideal confronts the real as you strive to blend the two comfortably. You could express either extreme in your relationships: spacey, visionary, seeking a lovely, seductive ultimate in your partner, dreaming of oneness, playing savior or victim, searching for a godlike figure and an experience of ultimate ecstasy **or** critical, judgmental, focusing on the flaws, aware of the partner's shortcomings, work-oriented and only concerned with the bottom line of doing the job right. You might also attract partners who manifest either of these extremes.

The goal is to blend the two positions into a reasonable synthesis, whereby you and a partner are doing all that you can, in a realistic and practical fashion, to create a loving, idealistic relationship: moving together toward a vision, but neither one expecting the other to provide heaven on earth for him or her.

NODES OF THE MOON

The following nodal placements are particularly relevant in the area of relationships.

Across Aries/Libra or 1st/7th Houses

You are probably facing a polarity: independent action versus operating in tandem. A common result is restlessness in relationships. You are likely to feel ambivalent about relating, unsure if you would rather be part of a team or on your own. Your needs for liberty may conflict with your desires to share.

You might overdo either end of the seesaw — giving in too much to other people or being too self-centered and set on having things **your** way. You could go from relationship to relationship (or attract people who go from one person to the next) in a reaction to your inner ambivalence.

The issue of sharing power in a relationship may be complicated by feelings of inadequacy and insecurity. It is quite possible that either you or your partner (or both) are self-critical and overly hard on yourselves. Before you can really establish a relationship, you need to know (at least somewhat) who you are. Before you can fully experience an identity, you have to accept yourself (rather than rejecting parts as not good enough). Self-appreciation may be an important order of business for you and your significant others.

Integration of this polarity entails you being able to pursue independent paths for yourself as well as make a commitment to a long-term relationship. Freedom and closeness needs are balanced in whatever fashion you decide (as long as there is at least a little of each). The goal is a harmonious blending of self with other in a mutually satisfying sharing.

Across Taurus/Scorpio or 2nd/8th Houses

This nodal polarity can also be very significant in relationships, but is manifested primarily through issues of money, sensuality and sexuality. Thus it is discussed in detail in Chapters 12 (money) and 13 (sexuality). However, the "Polarities" section within this chapter can be applied to any nodal placement.

ELEMENT EMPHASIS

Fire

♂, ☉, ♃, ⚷, ♈, ♌, ♐, 1st, 5th, 9th houses

Excitement is the name of the game. Restless and active, you dislike being still when something could be happening. Sometimes your relationships become an arena for testing your courage and taking risks. Consciously or unconsciously, you attract people who give you opportunities to be brave, spontaneous, open and expressive. If you are projecting your abilities, your associates will overdo these qualities — as an exaggerated mirror to show what you are learning about through them.

The thrill of an adrenalin rush draws you onward. If you do not arrange for fulfilling, satisfying forms of excitement and drama in your life, you may attract dangerous, disheartening forms of stimulation. Sexual passion is one of many avenues to experience that joie de vivre, that buoyant, top-of-the-world feeling that you seek so often. You need to feel vital and alive when involved with other people.

Earth

♀, ☿, ⚳, ⚶, ♄, ♉, ♍, ♑, 2nd, 6th, 10th houses

The "real world" is your focus in relationships. Whether you share that with a partner, or look for a partner to "do it for you," the emphasis is on work, responsibility, resources, stability and dealing with practical, tangible results. Abstractions mean less to you than what you can touch and experience directly. Money, possessions, and power over the physical world are important experiences for you.

If this energy is shared, you may be working with a partner, pursuing tasks, careers, investments, and earnings together. If you are projecting, you may be looking for someone else to be dependable, stable, hardworking and practical. If so, your friends and partners will end up overdoing those qualities. Your approach is pragmatic. Love is shown and judged by what is done more than what is said.

Air

☿, ♀, ⚴, ⚵, ♅, ♊, ♎, ♒, 3rd, 7th, 11th houses

Communication and objectivity are issues. A joint mental bent is quite possible. You may enjoy talking, sharing thoughts, writing and exchanging information with partners. If projected, you may look to others to think, talk and explore the intellectual world for you. But they will end up seeming too abstract, detached or logical for you. A mutual experience means both parties are in touch with their reasoning capacities; both value their minds; both enjoy communicating and both are capable of viewing life from an objective, detached, impersonal viewpoint.

Your orientation is toward equalitarian relationships. You prefer to meet your partners on the same level as you inhabit. But you are willing to compete as well as cooperate. You tend to be social and enjoy people and ideas.

Water

☽, ♇, ♆, ♋, ♏, ♓, 4th, 8th, 12th houses

Feelings and sensitivity reign supreme. You are probably dealing with your own inner depths and those of a partner. The potential of an instinctive understanding is good. You may have the capacity to "tune in" psychically to those near and dear to you. Wordless communication is quite possible. If you project the sensitivity and emotionality, you will attract partners who seem excessive in those respects.

Extremes to be wary of include overvaluing your own intuitive capacity or depending too heavily on the empathy of others. The first can lead to you believing you understand something about the other person without checking it out. You **could** be wrong! Feelings are not infallible. The second could lead to you expecting other people to "mind read" you — to know what you are thinking and feeling without you having to say anything. Intuition, sensitivity and caring are very valuable; just balance them with a little logic and rationality.

Fire-Earth

♂, ☉, ♃, ⚷, ♈, ♌, ♐, 1st, 5th, 9th houses &
♀, ☿, ⚳, ⚶, ♄, ♉, ♍, ♑, 2nd, 6th, 10th houses

A major theme in your relationships is having an impact on the world. You may be extremely strong, driving and effective in your handling of partnerships, striving to produce exactly the results that you desire. You may also attract powerful, capable people as potential partners. If you project your own strength, you could even experience them as overwhelming.

Working together is an option, channeling that ambition, determination and energy to be movers, shakers and doers in the outside world. Or, you could simply focus much of your attention on creating the most effective partnership possible. However you handle the issue, you will not be unmoved by your relationships. They will affect you profoundly.

Fire-Air

♂, ☉, ♃, ⚷, ♈, ♌, ♐, 1st, 5th, 9th houses &
☿, ♀, ⚴, ⚵, ♅, ♊, ♎, ♒, 3rd, 7th, 11th houses

You are looking for a good time in your relationships — to be able to laugh, to play, to have fun! You may find it quite easy to entertain yourself and others, having a natural sparkle and charisma. Amusing and sociable, you could easily attract people who want to share your optimistic attitude toward life.

If you project this part of your nature, you will attract happy-go-lucky types who are constantly on the move and enjoying life. They may be hard to pin down or depend on, but always good for a chuckle. Such partners can bring out your inner child and help you be carefree and casual in relationships.

Fire-Water
♂, ☉, ♃, ♅, ♈, ♌, ♐, 1st, 5th, 9th houses &
☽, ♇, ♆, ♋, ♏, ♓, 4th, 8th, 12th houses

Emotionality is a keynote in your relationships. The potential is there for tremendous warmth and caring. An intensity of feelings is likely. You tend to attract relationships which will arouse the depths within you and the other party. There may be an internal struggle between expressing feelings and holding back for security reasons. Try to keep room for both your spontaneous forms of expression as well as your more cautious mode.

If you are out of touch with this volatile side within your own nature, you may attract partners subject to extreme mood swings. Or, you may simply get involved with incredibly intense, deeply emotional individuals who take everything to heart. Your relationships may not always be easy, but they are not likely to be casual.

Earth-Air
♀, ☿, ?, ⚶, ♄, ♉, ♍, ♑, 2nd, 6th, 10th houses &
☿, ♀, ?, ⚳, ♅, ♊, ♎, ♒, 3rd, 7th, 11th houses

You are dealing with themes of logic and pragmatism in your relationships. You can be very analytical and sensible in your approach to partnerships, carefully figuring out the optimum choices. At times, people might even see you as cold-hearted because you value the rational so much.

If this side of your nature is projected, you are likely to attract other people who carry this theme to an extreme. They might be aloof, intellectually detached and concerned more with logic than feelings. Their practicality could bury the romance in a mass of facts and figures. They could be great at doing useful things for you, but inept when it comes to a gentle touch, loving look or romantic whisper in your ear.

Earth-Water
♀, ☿, ?, ⚶, ♄, ♉, ♍, ♑, 2nd, 6th, 10th houses &
☽, ♇, ♆, ♋, ♏, ♓, 4th, 8th, 12th houses

Compassion and helpful assistance are themes within your relationships. This is a common combination for anyone in the helping/healing professions whose work involves assisting people in bettering their lives. The key issue is being able to save people professionally without trying to also save them on the personal level.

If the need to be needed is too strong, you could attract people in your partnerships who expect to be taken care of — alcoholics, fantasizers, people into escaping reality in some way. Your caring and willingness to help can lead you to be sucked into a savior role which doesn't work when the basic relationship is supposed to be equalitarian. It's okay to give at the office, but remember to both give and receive at home.

Conversely, if you are out of touch with this side of your nature, you could attract "Mother Earth" types (of either sex) who will try to look after you and make it all better. You may unconsciously draw in potential partners who aspire to a saving and helping role and set you up to play the victim or the individual needing assistance. Nurturing is all very well and good within a relationship — as long as it is shared. Neither party should be doing all the caretaking within a peer relationship.

Air-Water

☿, ♀, ⚴, ⚵, ♅, ♊, ♎, ♒, 3rd, 7th, 11th houses &
☽, ♇, ♆, ♋, ♏, ♓, 4th, 8th, 12th houses

It is likely that relationships have been an important topic in your own inner world of thoughts and fantasies. You may spend a lot of time envisioning your ideal relationship or having imaginary dialogues with the "perfect partner" in your head. Your rich, creative imagination can be a source of inspiration and assistance in sharing your life with someone else. This blend shows the ability to bring together conscious reasoning with unconscious knowing to create a more perfect whole. This mixture of right and left brain approaches can help you build beautiful relationships.

If carried too far, you may prefer to simply dream about relating without ever dealing with the day-to-day grind of living with another person. Thinking about how it **might** be could feel preferable to coping with how it **is**. If projected, you could attract nebulous, hard to pin down, spacey partners who never seem quite all there or who are off into their own little fantasy worlds and not really making a connection in the here and now.

QUALITY EMPHASIS

Cardinal

♂, ☽, ♀, ⚴, ⚵, ♄, ♈, ♋, ♎, ♑, 1st, 4th, 7th, 10th houses

Your chart suggests some strong inner conflicts known as the Cardinal Dilemma. This refers to certain basic motivations which often feel contradictory. You are striving to make peace between your needs for freedom, closeness, equality and control. Finding a balance point, a middle ground is not always easy. Sometimes you have to express one part of your naturc in one area of your life and another side of who you are in a different area of your life.

You need all four corners of this dilemma; they are all a part of you. First is the freedom to be yourself, to not answer to anyone else, to be alone (at times) doing what you want to do, unconcerned about others, to be able to assert your own wants and needs. Second is the ability to share emotional closeness with other people, especially through a home and family (a nest); to be able to care for others and be cared for by them; to be vulnerable and nurturing. Third is the ability to be an equal, to relate on a one-to-one level with other human beings; the ability to accept others as they are without having to change them, to compromise, harmonize and make sure both your needs and theirs can be met in a relationship. Fourth is the ability to be in control. The executive drive to run the show must be satisfied somewhere, often through a career or task in the outer world. The need is for structure, rules, organization and predictability.

You are learning to balance, integrate and satisfy these diverse sides of yourself, each in a fulfilling way in your life. If you project any corner of this dilemma, you will attract others who overdo that energy. If you repress one side of who you are, physical illness could manifest. Denying your freedom needs can lead to sinus colds, headaches or minor cuts, burns, accidents. Repressed yearnings for closeness can manifest as stomach problems. Frustrated desires for equality are sometimes connected to kidney problems and the handling of sugar in the body. Control and responsibility issues may be mirrored by back difficulties, premature crystallization (gout, arthritis, etc.) and stress to the knees or hearing.

Doing the "right" thing in the "wrong" place can result in you trying to control where equal relating is more appropriate, or doing your own thing when responsibility would be more productive, or looking for nurturance when you are on your own, etc. Flipping from one side to another, without a middle ground can also be dizzying. The challenge is to create times and places in your life for each part of who you are to be able to manifest positively, in ways which will affirm and support you and those close to you.

Fixed
♀, ☉, ♇, ♅, ♉, ♌, ♏, ♒, 2nd, 5th, 8th, 11th houses

You are facing your strength, determination, perseverance and steadfastness through your relationships. You and your partners are likely to share themes around living life on your own terms, not subject to the influence of others. Sometimes, you may feel others are trying to get you to behave in a certain way even when they are not. You are prone to seeing power plays, which do not always exist.

In relationships, issues around sensuality, sexuality and money often surface. There is the danger of power struggles in your close associations, particularly around who earns it, who owns it, who spends it, who enjoys what? Learning to share the power over the material, physical, sensual world is not always easy. If you project the power, you may get involved with others who try to manipulate or dominate you. If you hang on totally to the power, you may be unwilling to do things any way other than your own.

Part of the ambivalence where resources are concerned may relate to an inner struggle between self-indulgence versus self-control. If you are not sure how much **you** want to indulge your appetites, doing what feels good versus maintaining a sense of control and self-mastery, it is easy to externalize the conflict. Thus, you identify with one end of the seesaw and attract partners who identify with the opposite end of the seesaw. Then you can fight about spending versus saving, or sex versus celibacy, or smoking versus not smoking, drinking versus not drinking and so on. Once we recognize the ambivalence is **internal**, we no longer need the external struggle in order to learn and grow.

Sensuality is usually very important in your relationships and needs an appropriate focus and expression. The material world can provide much pleasure as long as we remain masters and not obsessive victims of our desires.

Another issue revolves around the tension between security versus risk or stability versus change. A part of you is emotionally tied to the status quo, enjoys a rut as long as it is comfortable and hates to rock the boat. But another part of you loves to gamble, appreciates the thrill of living life on the edge and feels making changes is the most exciting thing in life. So, you strive for a balance in your life. If you project one end of this dilemma in your relationships, you could attract a partner to play one side, while you play the opposite end. Then you can fight about it. One can argue for the tried, true, safe and boring. The other can argue for the new, exciting but risky. Once you integrate the struggle within (yourself), the struggle without (in relationships) is no longer necessary.

Mutable
☿, ♇ ⚷, ♃, ♵, ♆, ♊, ♍, ♐, ♓, 3rd, 6th, 9th, 12th houses

Your relationships are providing an opportunity to confront the conflict between your ideals and your vision of reality. Steering between the Scylla of excessive perfectionism and the Charybdis of destructive criticism is a challenge. You may manifest the idealism and/or pragmatism yourself, or attract others who will express those qualities for you. The optimum result is creating the best possible relationship. Pitfalls to avoid include the search for the perfect (nonexistent) partner; repeatedly "falling in love" only to find the Prince/Princess is a frog, and trying again over and over; relating only to God because no human being is ideal enough; playing savior to others by attracting victims (alcoholics, drug addicts, people not living up to their full potential) to "rescue"; putting lovers/partners up on pedestals. The challenge is to maintain high goals, values and ideals in and for relationships, without demanding inhuman perfection (for yourself, partners or the relationship).

Mental stimulation and involvements are important. You may find it easy to scatter your forces with multiple interests, but you need associates who will share your involvement in many and varied areas. Multiple partners are an option, as you tend to get bored easily. Also, your high standards, if excessive, can mean that no one measures up for long.

You learn very well vicariously. You do **not** have to experience everything directly yourself. Through books, observation and discussion, you can avoid many of the painful processes others get through the school of hard knocks. You tend to be flexible and adaptable to others and diverse situations.

THEMES

Freedom
♂, ♃, ♭, ♅, ♈, ♐, ♒, 1st, 9th, 11th houses

You prefer to keep your options open, not be tied down in a committed relationship. You may relate to people more on an impersonal, abstract level, or in groups rather than regularly in a one-to-one setting. You can resent others putting "strings" on you and have the opinion that you can always leave if a relationship becomes "heavy" or confining. You function best with a lot of space and independence. Being a "couple" often seems limiting to you. Cherishing your individuality, you may resist being labeled or lumped with another person, no matter how much you value them.

If you are living out your needs for liberty through someone else, the other party is likely to be overdoing that energy: perhaps just classically unwilling to be attached; perhaps married; living a distance away or just emotionally detached — in some way not really available.

Freedom of action, the ability to pursue your dreams, ideals, visions and aspirations in whatever directions they take you, the expression of your own uniqueness are all important to you. Remaining friends with a partner, each allowing the other much flexibility in the relationship, allows intimacy as well as independence.

Closeness or Interpersonal
☽, ☉, ♀, ♀, ⚶, ♇, ♋, ♌, ♎, ♏, 4th, 5th, 7th, 8th houses

Emotional attachments are the cement that holds your life together. For you, a relationship includes commitment, preferably on a deep level. Love is central in your universe and that usually includes a home and family, although pets and/or plants can also serve to meet your needs to be needed and to feel your existence matters. Sharing appeals to you. The search is for that sense of uniting and merging with another human being — for the high that comes through love given and received.

If this theme is projected, you may attract people (or pets) who seem excessively dependent. They may appear overly emotional, too sensitive, too vulnerable and needy. Their other-directedness could offend you, until you come to terms with your own need for intense, feeling involvements.

Warm and loving, you seek people to share feelings of intimacy, closeness and union.

Artistic

♀, ⚵, ⚶, ☉, ♆, ♉, ♌, ♎, ♓, 2nd, 5th, 7th, 12th houses

There is a theme of beauty in your relationships. Expression can include: choosing physically attractive partners, attracting partners who expect you to always look lovely, getting involved with artists or expecting love to be beautiful, flowing, harmonious and comfortable.

The key is being able to share an appreciation of the aesthetic with your partners. This can include creating beauty together (with drawing, painting, sculpture, cooking, gardening, architecture, design, sewing or other activities which allow a sense of the aesthetic). It can include enjoying the beauty of nature with one another or each of you feeling the other is a vision. A positive side is a sense of grace and harmony inherent between the two of you.

Less positive forms occur when one partner is expecting the other to somehow provide all the loveliness within the relationship. Then, either person may discover s/he has chosen a pretty package with very little inside or may insufficiently value the other person due to the exterior appearance. Either partner could deny his/her own artistic talent, convinced that the other one is truly the artist. Either one could expect more than is reasonable from the partner in terms of always agreeing, being accommodating, sweet, kind, loving, etc. True love's course does **not** always run smoothly — and that can be a shock to people who define love as always pleasant and easy. But a shared focus on harmony can lead to a truly beautiful relationship.

Idealistic

♃, ⚷, ♆, ♐, ♓, 9th, 12th houses

There is a theme of idealism in your relationships. Expression can range from believing your partner is perfect; choosing a partner who believes s/he is perfect; having many relationships in the hopes that the **next** one will be ideal; avoiding relationships because you fear they will not be ideal; attracting partners who expect you to be perfect; or a relationship where both people are constantly creating a more ideal, better situation.

The key is to search for the ideal together, without either person expecting the other to "play God" to him or her. Looking for Prince or Princess Charming usually leads to disillusionment and disappointment. Trying to be someone's all in all commonly results in savior/victim relationships. Idealizing someone a little bit is one thing; it is helpful to not focus too much on a partner's faults. But putting someone up on a pedestal, making a person more than human is asking for trouble in relationships which are supposed to be equalitarian. If God is the role model, few people will measure up! (And the result can also be loneliness if the person is seeking more than is humanly possible in relationships.)

So, search together for the beautiful dream. Together, create a more ideal world, a more rewarding relationship, a more satisfying sharing.

Obsessive-Compulsive

☿, ⚳, ⚶, ♇, ♄, ♍, ♏, ♑, 6th, 8th, 10th houses

There is an obsessive-compulsive theme in your relationships. This can range from a determination to arrange your relationships, organizing them to be **just so**, to attracting other people who are compulsive in your relationships. Your attitude could be an extreme focus on control and getting all the details right or you might draw in other people manifesting that approach.

The key is to focus the obsessive-compulsive talent (ability to handle details, organized, thorough, able to concentrate) in areas where it will be helpful (e.g., keeping track of anniversaries, remembering what your partner likes, handling the physical aspects of the household). If you let the compulsive spirit spill over into the personal side of the relationship (whether it is your obsessiveness or that of your partner), it is likely to be less comfortable. Either of you could feel turned off by your partner's petty insistence on having certain details right, excessive concern with certain little items, unwillingness to stray from the straight and narrow course, desire for control and having his/her own way in the situation.

Competence

☿, ⚳, ⚶, ♄, ♍, ♑, 6th, 10th houses

This theme shows a good capacity for working with people professionally but has the danger of criticism and judgment being a problem in personal relationships. This can be expressed as fault-finding by you toward others, or you could attract others who are nitpicky and spend time cataloging your flaws. If these attributes are projected, one partner could be a workaholic, or put everything into a career. Sometimes, there is a pull between the desire for accomplishment through applied efforts in the world, and closeness in a sharing relationship.

The task orientation needs to be kept where it is suitable and appropriate: directed toward the physical world, work and accomplishments. We can work at making relationships better, as long as we do not fall into making the association into a **job** — involving discrimination, critical judgment and a focus on what is wrong (in order to fix it and make it better).

It is quite possible that you could work with partners, having associations that involved business as well as romance, meet partners through your work and work at building a good relationship.

Mental Stimulation

☿, ⚳, ⚶, ⚴, ♃, ⚷, ♅, ♆, ♊, ♍, ♎, ♐, ♒, ♓,
3rd, 6th, 7th, 9th, 11th, 12th houses

Relationships to you involve ideas and people — often, the more, the better. When your mind is not being stimulated, you tend to feel bored and turned off. Communication is a necessary ingredients in your associations. Sharing of ideas, books, classes, travel and all forms of broadening, strengthening and utilizing the mental faculties tend to appeal.

If this drive is projected, you could attract people who are excessive in these respects — ranging from being scattered (multiple interests), overly logical, objective, detached and rational; too talkative or appearing to be extremely brilliant. (Just remember, you have to be as bright as they are to be capable of appreciating their brilliance.)

Whether you enjoy word games, reading, studying, taking classes together or sharing other forms of mind-stimulation, the key is a social and mental exchange in your relationships.

Relationships
♀, ☿, ⚴, ♇, ♎, ♏, 7th, 8th houses

There is a strong theme of relating in your chart. This can be expressed as a desire for partnership — by you and/or the people you attract. (If you also have strong freedom needs, for example, you may get involved with people that always want to marry and settle down while you are trying to keep your options open.) The need for interaction can be satisfied through cooperation and harmonious activities — but also through competition. You have a strong need to meet people on their own level. Your sense of justice and fair play is usually strongly developed.

Security
♀, ☽, ☿, ⚶, ⚳, ♇, ♄, ♆, ♂, ♋, ♍, ♏, ♑, ♓,
2nd, 4th, 6th, 8th, 10th, 12th houses

There is a strong theme of security in your relationships. If it is shared, you are likely to choose situations where both you and your partner have a sense of stability, predictability and knowing what is coming next. You will be able to depend on one another and feel safe in the relationship. If these needs are projected, you may attract partners who overdo this theme. They could seem too stodgy, too concerned with keeping life safe and predictable, boring, stuck in the mud and overly materialistic or safety-oriented. Another potential is that your partners would expect **you** to be the safe, secure, stable figure for them.

The key is for both people to contribute to the sense of commitment and safety within the relationship. If either party is responsible for more than his/her share of providing security, problems can arise. When one person plays the role of "**the rock**," s/he usually ends up a millstone — around your own neck or that of the partner. If both people are solid and dependable — they lean on one another and support each other's strength rather than one grinding the other to pieces with endurance.

Risk/Creativity/Change

♂, ☉, ♃, ⚷, ♅, ♈, ♌, ♐, ♒, 1st, 5th, 9th, 11th houses

There is a strong theme of creativity and risking in your relationship. You are seeking change, innovation, the new, the sense of gambling with life, hoping for a significant payoff. If the risk-taking is shared with a partner, you can both enjoy living life on the edge. You may take a lot of chances with each other and in your relationship, make many changes, allow a lot of space and freedom — but appreciate the excitement, aliveness and zest this brings to you.

If one person is expected to express the risking nature for both of you, that one person is likely to overdo it. S/he could be extremely foolhardy, irresponsible and just get carried away with enthusiasms or inspirations. A willingness to gamble in life can be downright dangerous in some situations. The speculative spirit needs to be handled with care.

Whether the risks you take and the creative outlets you choose are more physical, monetary, emotional, mental, spiritual or otherwise, the need to "go for it" is there! The urge to try for more than has been done in the past — in the hopes that the result will be even more in the future — is very prominent in terms of your relationship needs.

Parents and Partners

☽, ♄, ⚳, ♋, ♑, 4th, 10th houses

The tendency is to meet old issues (leftover from mother, father or both) with partners. It is easy to feel the same feelings, replay the same games, until we learn what is necessary to finish up and move on. Issues tend to revolve around nurturance, dependency, responsibility and control. Until integrated, you may attract people who try to "mother" you or expect you to "mother" them in the relationship. Or, you may get involved with dominating, controlling "father" types or draw in irresponsible individuals who expect you to be "father" — strong, practical, carrying the whole load of the relationship.

The goal is to be able to **take turns** parenting each other in the relationship. You can both be nurturing, helpful, considerate, able to do your share and contribute equally to the building of a satisfying association.

Power

☉, ♇, ♄, ♌, ♏, ♑, 5th, 8th, 10th houses

Power issues are being faced through your one-to-one relationships. One potential is attracting partners as strong as you are and together changing the world and yourselves. Another possibility is attracting people who seem very masterful and dynamic, only to end up feeling dominated and controlled as they overdo the power principle. Another option is getting involved with individuals who set you up in the role of authority figure, where you have all the power — but also the responsibility and carry the load for the relationship.

Your capacity for dominance, control, competitiveness and drive needs positive channels in the outside world or your relationships might be marred by power struggles. You could find yourself fighting, arguing and engaging in direct (or manipulative) power struggles with those near and dear to you. Competition could win out over cooperation. Find some way to ''win'' **together** with your partner — neither one at the expense of the other. Set up win/win situations where you both are happy; avoid win/lose choices.

Personal
♂, ♀, ☿, ☽, ♈, ♉, ♊, ♋, 1st, 2nd, 3rd, 4th houses

You are learning about personal needs through your relationships. This could be through a shared focus. Both you and your partner might enjoy doing your own thing and then getting together later to share. You could both be skilled at knowing what you want and pursuing it in the world.

It could also be that you are learning to put yourself first by watching your partner's example. You could attract people who are very self-oriented (even selfish) and concentrating on doing what they want. Through observing them, you can learn to give yourself priority more often and do as you please. The more you allow others to overdo in manifesting this theme, the more likely they will step on you or in some way take advantage. The issue revolves around appreciating yourself sufficiently to make satisfying your needs important, while still being willing to compromise within the context of a relationship.

Transpersonal
♃, ⚷, ♄, ♅, ♆, ♐, ♑, ♒, ♓, 9th, 10th, 11th, 12th houses

You are learning to blend the need for one-to-one relationships with the impulse to affect the wider world. This can lead to associations which leave their mark on the world, such as through friendships, groups, organizations, social causes, a strong career and so forth. You could make changing relationships your field, e.g., counseling, healing. The tendency is to somehow expand or stretch an ''ordinary'' relationship so that it encompasses more inclusive issues and concerns than just the two of you. This can include fighting for justice together, political action, etc.

If this theme is projected, you may feel your partners are too caught up in making history, changing the world or looking at the big picture to really relate to you. It is possible you feel neglected, as if you take second place to the state of humanity. The overview must be balanced with current concerns and immediate, face-to-face intimacy.

Freedom Versus Closeness

♂, ♃, ⚷, ♅, ♈, ♐, ♒, 1st, 9th, 11th houses Versus
☽, ☉, ♀, ⚳, ⚵, ♇, ♋, ♌, ♎, ♏, 4th, 5th, 7th, 8th houses

Ambivalence reigns within you, as you experience strong desires for both independent action and close, emotional attachments. You are striving to find a comfortable blend of your drives for both love and liberty. You are dealing with the freedom/closeness dilemma and could succumb to repressing, displacing or projecting either drive.

Solutions include having **moderation** of both participation and solitary pursuits; self-assertion and sharing; intimacy and independence or expressing the various sides of your nature at different times and places in your life.

ASPECTS

Harmony to Letter . . .

1: There is potential harmony between your desire for equality, for sharing your life with another and your urge for self-expression and doing your own thing. You can be yourself and still maintain a committed relationship with another human being.

2: There is potential harmony between your desire for equality, for sharing your life with another and your desire to enjoy physical indulgence. You can enjoy the world of people as well as the world of appetites and possessions. Mutual pleasure-seeking is possible.

3: There is potential harmony between your desire for equality, for sharing your life with another and your need to learn and communicate. Partners can stimulate your thinking and vice versa. Intellectual exchange can be a significant part of your relationships.

4: There is potential harmony between your desire for equality, for sharing your life with another and your yearning for emotional security. Your home base can help solidify a partnership; your ability to relate as a peer is bulwarked by a sense of inner safety and protection.

5: There is potential harmony between your desire for equality, for sharing your life with another and your need to seek the limelight. Your charisma and magnetism can help keep relationships interesting and committed. Your ability to take turns being onstage and being off keeps potential self-centeredness in check.

6: There is potential harmony between your desire for equality, for sharing your life with another and your drive for competence and productivity. Your realistic approach helps ground and stabilize your relationships while your sense of justice and fair play assists you in working productively with others.

7: There is potential harmony within you regarding the nature of partnership and sharing. You are fairly clear about what you want in relationship to other people. You know when to cooperate, when to compete, when to accommodate and when to assert in relationships.

8: There is potential harmony between your desire for equality, for sharing your life with another and your need to delve deeply for thorough understanding and analysis of life. Giving, receiving and sharing pleasures and possessions in an intimate context is easier for you than for most people.

9: There is potential harmony between your desire for equality, for sharing your life with another and your pursuit of ultimate truth and the understanding of life. Your ethical and philosophical principles assist and affirm your relationships and vice versa.

10: There is potential harmony between your desire for equality, for sharing your life with another and your pragmatic, achieving side. Your career aspirations can support your partnership(s) and vice versa.

11: There is potential harmony between your desire for equality, for sharing your life and your needs for individuality and uniqueness. Friendships and partnerships can intermix as you are more fully yourself and simultaneously more committed to relationships.

12: There is potential harmony between your desire for equality, for sharing your life and your need to search for something Higher in life. Faith supports your partnerships and your relationships affirm your quest for something Higher.

Conflict to Letter. . .

1: There is potential conflict between your desire for equality, for sharing your life and your needs for self-expression and assertion. You may feel torn between going it alone versus doing things together; between pleasing yourself versus giving in to the other person; between freedom and involvement; between direct, spontaneous action and the zigzags of negotiation and compromise.

2: There is potential conflict between your desire for equality, for sharing your life and your capacity for physical possessions and pleasures. You may experience partnerships as interfering with your sensual satisfactions. You may feel looking after material goods takes time and energy away from emotional commitments. Financial conflicts within your relationships are possible. Harmonize.

3: There is potential conflict between your desire for equality, for sharing your life and your need to think and communicate. You could experience your partnerships as interfering with your pursuit of information and exploring of the mind. You might feel your easy flow of communication is a barrier to emotional closeness, or experience communication blocks in relationships. Keep room for intellectual detachment and exploration as well as emotional commitments.

4: There is potential conflict between your desire for equality, for sharing your life and your need for emotional closeness and security. You may feel torn between an absorbing, merging relationship versus a more open, casual commitment. Being a peer may vie with acting like a nurturing parent or child within the partnership. Or, you could feel torn between partners and children. You can all take turns caring for each other if willing.

5: There is potential conflict between your desire for equality, for sharing your life and your urge to shine and be center stage. Who gets to be the star and when may be an issue in your relationships. Either you or your partner may feel overwhelmed by the other's dynamism and charisma or simple arrogance. Shared admiration works best.

6: There is potential conflict between your desire for equality, for sharing your life and your urge to function efficiently in the world. You may feel that love needs conflict with work needs, either in your actions or those of your partner (or both). A work-oriented attitude (looking for defects) can wreak havoc in close relationships. Keep flaw-finding attitudes on the job and practice acceptance in relationships.

7: There is potential ambivalence around your definitions of equality, sharing and one-to-one relationships. You may feel torn between cooperating, competing, giving in, asserting and other ways of relating. Other people are likely to be important in your life, but you may not be sure exactly what you want from or with them. Clarify your feelings to help create optimum associations.

8: There is potential conflict between your desire for equality, for sharing your life and your need for depth answers and understanding. Your probing for answers might lead at times to withdrawal from others or other people could experience your need to know as intrusive. Differing sexual needs and styles are a possibility. Your willingness to confront even unpleasant ideas and issues must be balanced with your desire for harmonious emotional attachments.

9: There is potential conflict between your desire for equality, for sharing your life and your search for meaning, truth and ultimate answers in life. Spiritual/religious/ethical quests may take you away from partnerships or vice versa. Perfectionistic standards may be an issue in your relationships. Beware of looking for God in a partner or attracting people who put you in an all-powerful role. Neither of you is responsible for making everything ideal for the other party, but together you can cocreate your own "heaven."

10: There is potential conflict between your desire for equality, for sharing your life and your need for control and authority. The role of executive vies with the role of partner. Career and relationship demands on time and energy may compete with one another. You may feel torn between relating as a peer versus maintaining a position of power and dominance. Or, you could attract people dealing with that issue. Find a compromise position.

11: There is potential conflict between your desire for equality, for sharing your life and your desire for uniqueness and individuality. Your urge for freedom competes with your pull toward committed relationships. Individualism confronts the couple mentality. You are striving to balance the need to share with the need to go your own way and express your unique being.

12: There is potential conflict between your desire for equality, for sharing your life and your yearning to experience infinite love and beauty. Your urge to merge with something Higher could pull you away from relationships (or vice versa). Your seeking of an ultimate might make associating with mere human beings a challenge. Avoid the extremes of savior/victims involvements while channeling your idealism into a constructive role in your relationships.

CHAPTER NINE

MIND AND COMMUNICATION

This section is concerned with the way you relate to your thinking processes and how you communicate. Thoughts, speech and writing are some of the ways in which we share information. Reading, listening and teaching are other options. Here the focus is on the collection and exchange of ideas and the process through which we engage in this interchange.

The Factors

In considering potentials for the mind and communication styles as indicated by the horoscope, we would include all air (objective, reasoning capacity) and mutables (flexible, adaptable, mental rather than physical approach). This encompasses: **Letter 3** (young, curious mind, learning to learn & communicate) **Letter 7** (ability to relate as a peer, share ideas with others) **Letter 11** (comprehension of humanity as a whole, progressive ideas) **Letter 6** (analytical, flaw-finding mind, mental discrimination) **Letter 9** (philosophical mind, search for meaning and understanding) **Letter 12** (intuitive understanding, inner wisdom, connection to universal knowledge).

Mercury comes in twice, of course — through its rulership of both Gemini and Virgo. This is apt as Mercury, more than any other planet, is a key to the reasoning mind. I do also include the asteroids Ceres and Vesta with Letter 6, as additional keys, pointing particularly to the ability to focus, concentrate and work well with details.

I consider Letters 7 and 12 as secondary keys and weight them less than Letters 3, 6, 9 and 11. Letter 7 is the least detached and objective of the air letters and Letter 12 is more a nonrational grasp of life — which most people think of as emotional rather than intellectual. Within Letter 7, I feel that Venus represents sensuality, pleasure and affection. Venus mirrors feelings — not thoughts. So, I consider the 7th house and Libra (secondarily) for intellectual matters — but eliminate Venus. Similarly, the asteroid Juno seems to point to the more emotional, relationship-oriented side of Libra. Pallas, however, has overtones of Sagittarius and Aquarius along with Libra and seems tied into perception. Thus, Pallas — which is assigned primarily to Letter 7 — can operate as a secondary key here to the mental processes.[1]

Astrologically, this means we would examine:

GROUP I

Any conjunctions to the planets Mercury, Jupiter and Uranus, plus the asteroids Ceres and Vesta

Any conjunctions to Neptune or Pallas [½ weight] (We would consider the nature of the planets making the conjunctions.)

Any conjunctions to the rulers of the 3rd, 6th, 9th and 11th houses

Any conjunctions to the rulers of the 7th and 12th houses [½ weight]

Any conjunctions to the rulers of other signs in the 3rd, 6th, 9th or 11th houses

Any conjunctions to the rulers of other signs in the 7th or 12th houses [½ weight].

GROUP II

Any planets in the 3rd, 6th, 9th and 11th houses (the nature of the planets)

Any planets in the 7th and 12th houses (the nature of the planets) [½ weight]

Any planets within two degrees of the 3rd, 6th, 9th, or 11th house cusps, but inside the 2nd, 4th, 5th, 8th, or 10th houses (the nature of the planet)

GROUP III

The placement of Mercury, Jupiter and Uranus by house

The placement of Ceres and Vesta by house

House placements of rulers of the 3rd, 6th, 7th, 9th, 11th and 12th cusps

The placement of Pallas (for Libra) and Neptune by house [½ weight]

Houses ruled by planets making conjunctions to Mercury, Jupiter, Uranus, Pallas, Ceres, Vesta or Neptune

Planets parallel Mercury, Jupiter, Uranus, Pallas, Ceres, Vesta or Neptune

Planets parallel to rulers of the 3rd, 6th, 7th, 9th, 11th or 12th cusps

---

1. If you prefer **not** to search for repeated themes yourself, you can order the "PP BOOK" option from Astro Computing Services (PO Box 16430, San Diego, Ca 92116), which allows you to use this book to make complete, synthesizing delineations of horoscopes without figuring out which themes are emphasized.

Available for $3.00 each, the "PP BOOK" report calculates the emphasis on all the letters of the alphabet, themes and aspects in each horoscope for which you provide the data. The report lists each significant focus (e.g., "There is a Letter 2 theme in "Mind," and gives the appropriate page numbers for you to read in this book ("See pages 223-224 in the *Complete Horoscope Interpretation* book.")

The computer will not **always** arrive at the same results as you might, as certain steps are ambiguous (e.g., how much weight to give a planet making a conjunction, based on the orb). However, the majority of the time, the computer answers will concur with those derived from use of the worksheets — or the recommended quick scan of a horoscope. Thus it provides an excellent teaching tool.

The "PP BOOK" does **not** provide a listing of **each and every** astrological factor making up the significant themes. For that, you would order "PP WEIGHTS" (discussed in next footnote).

Any planets in Aquarius, Virgo and Gemini and Sagittarius — the nature of the planet

Any planets in Libra or Pisces — the nature of the planets [½ weight]

GROUP IV

Any planets in Aquarius, Virgo and Gemini and Sagittarius — the nature of the house occupied

Any planets in Libra or Pisces — the nature of the house occupied [½ weight]

Aquarius, Virgo and Gemini and Sagittarius on any house cusp(s) — the nature of the house

Libra or Pisces on any house cusp(s) — the nature of the house [½ weight]

The sign of Mercury, Jupiter, Ceres, Vesta and Uranus

The sign of Neptune and of Pallas [½ weight]

The sign of the rulers of the 3rd, 6th, 9th and 11th cusps

The sign of the rulers of the 7th and 12th cusps [½ weight]

The signs of the rulers of any additional signs in the 3rd, 6th and 9th and 11th houses

The signs of the rulers of any additional signs in the 7th and 12th houses [½ weight]

The signs on the cusps of the 3rd, 6th, 9th and 11th houses

The signs on the cusps of the 7th and 12th houses [½ weight]

The house(s) which have the signs on their cusps ruled by any planet(s) in the 3rd, 6th or 9th or 11th houses, e.g., if the Moon in in the 3rd, on what house cusp does Cancer fall?

The house(s) which have the signs on their cusps ruled by any planet(s) in the 7th and 12th houses [½ weight]

Any signs in the 3rd, 6th, 9th and 11th houses which are occupied by a planet (the nature of the sign)

Any signs in the 7th and 12th houses which are occupied by a planet (the nature of the sign) [½ weight]

Any additional (unoccupied) signs in the 3rd, 6th, 9th and 11th houses

Any additional (unoccupied) signs in the 7th and 12th houses [½ weight]

You can add up the totals of the above factors for each letter of the astrological alphabet. Forms are given in the appendix for your use.[2]

---

2. You can also obtain a listing of **all** the astrological factors which compose those letters of the Zip Code determined to be significant in a horoscope. This makes an excellent teaching tool and a valuable resource to check yourself against when practicing with the Zip Code.

Astro Computing Services, PO Box 16430, San Diego, CA 92116, has calculated 28,000 horoscopes and established averages and standard deviations for the scores of each letter of the astrological alphabet, each theme, and the conflict and harmony aspects to each life area.

Astro's report, called "PP WEIGHTS," will list those letters of the astrological alphabet which are one standard deviation or more above the mean — and list **all** the astrological factors which point to each significant letter of the alphabet. These weightings will also compare each individual's score on the various themes (e.g., risk-taking, artistic) to the means and standard deviations to determine which themes are significant.

(footnote continued on next page)

A SHORT CUT

For quickness and ease of use, especially for people just learning the alphabet, I suggest limiting the focus initially to factors in Groups I and II, or using the procedures outlined in Appendix 2 (and Chapters 6 and 7).

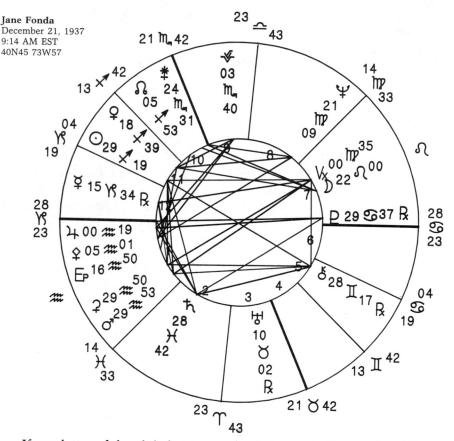

Jane Fonda
December 21, 1937
9:14 AM EST
40N45 73W57

If any letter of the alphabet is represented once in Groups I and II, consider it as probably significant. (If that letter is repeated in Groups I and II, it is definitely important.) For example, Jane Fonda's 3rd house is occupied by Uranus, suggesting that a Letter 11 theme may be important as far as her mind. The conjunction of

2. (continued from previous page)
    Averages are established for aspects as well in order to note conflict or harmony in the different life areas.
    The results obtained by Astro's "PP WEIGHTS" will not **always** coincide with those you determine by a quick scan and intuitive judgment, or by use of the worksheets. Certain of the steps (e.g., how much to weight a planet based on orb) are ambiguous, so different results can occur. However, most of the time, Astro's answers will confirm those you could obtain in working with the Zip Code. Furthermore, the **complete** listing of relevant factors is an excellen. teaching tool.
    Ask for "PP Weights." The price, as of December 1985 is $5.00

Ceres to Mars (1) suggests a Letter 1 theme may be significant. (Jupiter occupying the 1st house and Mars ruling the 3rd while occupying the 1st repeats the Letter 1.)

Ms. Fonda's willingness to speak out for what she believes definitely supports Letters 1 and 11. Indeed, her commitment to causes has sometimes led her to make statements which she later regretted. The "impulsive" potential of Letter 1 (page 223) has been manifest on occasion. One suspects that Ms. Fonda's defense of the North Vietnamese in the 1970s is something she would prefer to forget. Fortunately, her concern for the truth leads her to acknowledge and correct most errors. As Fred Guiles quotes in his biography of her: "Did I say THAT?" can be her rather appalled recognition of her tongue sometimes outracing her mind (p. 279 of *Jane Fonda: The Actress in Her Time*).

If a letter of the alphabet is represented only once in Groups I and II, check to see if it is repeated in Group III or IV. If so, consider that letter significant. In Jane Fonda's case, we see the following repetitions of Letter 1: the 3rd house Uranus rules Aquarius which falls in the 1st (1), 3rd cusp is Aries (1), Jupiter occupies the 1st (1), Pallas occupies the 1st (1), Jupiter conjuncts the Ascendant (1) and Jupiter is parallel the Ascendant (1). In addition, all the Aquarian placements in the 1st house repeat Letter 1. Jupiter is counted in the 1st several times: a key to the mind in its own nature, as a actual ruler of the 11th, as a planet in Aquarius and as a planet conjuncting Pallas. We must bear in mind that the Letter 1 theme for mind works two ways: (1) suggesting an expressive, courageous, direct, personally-centered approach to thinking and communicating with potential rashness or impulsivity and (2) linking identity (Letter 1) with the mind. The latter emphasizes that Ms. Fonda is, first and foremost, a communicator, that her natural instinct is to think, to talk, to exchange ideas and give and receive information.

In examining Groups III and IV, also look for any letters of the alphabet which occur six or more times. Consider them significant and read the appropriate interpretations. For example, the Letter 11 theme is repeated in Groups III and IV with: 3rd house occupied by Uranus (11), Jupiter in Aquarius (11), Pallas in Aquarius (11), Ceres in Aquarius (11), 3rd cusp ruled by Mars in Aquarius (11), 3rd house Taurus ruled by Venus in the 11th (11), 9th house Libra ruled by Venus in the 11th (11), 11th house Sagittarius ruled by Jupiter in Aquarius (11), Sagittarius occupied (twice) in the 11th (11, 11), Jupiter conjunct Pallas in Aquarius (11) and 3rd house ruler (Mars) conjunct Ceres in Aquarius (11). Thus, we assume Letter 11 is a significant focus in Ms. Fonda's mental and communication style (an appropriate focus for an activist and such a liberal person as Ms. Fonda). Ms. Fonda well expresses the progressive, future-oriented, individualistic, original thinking of a Letter 11 theme for the mind.

Themes

Themes can be ascertained in two ways. One approach is to consider **only** those letters determined significant with the above work and check to see what themes they combine to form. In Ms. Fonda's case, Groups I and II suggest we consider

Letters 9, 1, 6 and 7 as possibilities. Groups III and IV emphasize Letters 5, 11 and 9. Blending the two groups gives us themes of fire (1, 5, 9), freedom (1, 9, 11), and risk (1, 5, 9, 11) as potential themes.

A second approach to spotting themes is to examine the totals for **all** the letters of the alphabet and determine which combinations have an above average score. You will need to do some rough arithmetic here or get an intuitive impression. If a theme (e.g., risk — Letters 1, 5, 9 and 11) involves four (out of twelve) letters of the astrological alphabet, you would expect it to have about ⅓ of the total score. So, if the amount for those letters seems appreciably more than ⅓ of the total, count that as a theme — and read the appropriate section.

When searching for themes, give additional weighting to like planets in aspect to one another. For example, Mars, the Sun, Jupiter and Uranus are the four planets associated with risk-taking. Any aspects between Mars, the Sun, Jupiter and Uranus add to the potential of a willingness to take chances, be creative and make changes. (Ms. Fonda has a semisextile between the Sun and Jupiter, a sextile from the Sun to Mars and a semisextile from Jupiter to Mars. If Chiron is included with Letter 9, Chiron is closely opposite the Sun, quincunx Jupiter and trine Mars.)

Also give extra weight to like houses and like signs. Thus, Mars, the Sun, Jupiter or Uranus occupying the 1st, 5th, 9th or 11th houses or Aries, Leo, Sagittarius or Aquarius would give extra weight to the risk-taking theme for each occurrence. (In Ms. Fonda's case, Jupiter occupies Aquarius and the first house, the Sun occupies Sagittarius and the 11th house and Chiron occupies the 5th. I think most people would be willing to rate Ms. Fonda's communication style as one willing to take risks!)

Aspects

Quickly scan all aspects other than conjunctions or parallels, grouping them according to harmony (sextile, trine, semisextile) and conflict (octile, tri-octile, square, opposition and quincunx). In considering each aspect, weight the nature of the planet most heavily, followed by the house and the sign. Note both the occupied house and the cusp ruled by the planet being aspected. For example, Mercury (one "mind" factor) in Ms. Fonda's horoscope makes no close harmony aspects. (It has a wide trine to Uranus and a wide trine to Neptune.) It makes the following close conflict aspects:

- octile Mars (1) in the 1st (1) in Aquarius (11); Mars rules 3rd (3)
- octile Ceres (6) in the 1st (1) in Aquarius (11)

After examining aspects to the other "mind" factors, you would make an intuitive judgment of whether any letters of the alphabet have lots of conflict to them or have quite a bit of harmony. If you feel any group of aspects has an emphasis on one or more letters of the alphabet, read the appropriate interpretation. (With the Mercury aspects alone, we might suspect that Letter 1 issues could point to conflicts for Ms. Fonda — perhaps speaking too quickly, impulsively, or being too forceful in expressing what she thinks.) An alternative approach to aspects appears in Appendix 2.

Interpretations: Mind and Communication

ALPHABET THEMES

Letter 1: The Verbal Duelist

Quick-witted, you are seldom at a loss for words. Talented at extemporaneous speeches, you can also be a skilled debater. At times, you may use words as weapons: biting, ironic, sarcastic, sardonic — aggressing verbally. Your sharp tongue has probably made some opponents regard testing your mettle as a worthy battle, while others just slink away. You tend to be expressive and may fall into "**My** way of thinking is the only possible way of thinking" because it seems so "natural." Remember, other people will have alternative points of view.

Spontaneous and direct, you usually say what you mean and mean what you say. Sometimes, the result is a bit too impulsive. "Be sure your mind is in gear before putting your mouth in motion," as the old proverb says! Your ability to think and to speak are probably essential parts of who you are. You tend to think of yourself as a bright and articulate person. Word power often comes naturally.

Exciting and even aggressive topics can interest you. If you are a reader of fiction, adventure stories are likely to appeal. The thrill of action, combat and self-expression in the world are all likely to be important themes for your mental explorations. But since the world of the mind is central to your identity, you could explore anything and everything as far as interests and intellect. You could easily be a voracious reader since thinking and communicating are essential in your life and your mind could be drawn to literally **anything**. Insatiably curious, you may have driven parents, teachers or friends crazy with wanting to know the "why" of everything. Your keen mind is ready to go in all directions.

Letter 2: The Comfortable Communicator

Communication, to you, should be comfortable and easy. You prefer to avoid stress and strain. Since you have a keen aesthetic sense of the beauty of words, some potentials include poetry or simply a flowing use of language. If comfort and ease are overvalued, you may stick to predictable, known paths of interaction, simply because you do not want to bother to learn another way.

Your mind can be quite thorough and practical. At times, you may be a bit plodding, tending to keep on going in the same direction, until you get somewhere. It is wise to occasionally change course. Your opinions are generally deep-rooted and usually not subject to much outside influence. A pragmatist, you want to put the mind to use, to help you enjoy the physical, material world. Abstract theories have little appeal. You are more likely to seek ways and means to gain more beauty, comfort and pleasure in your life, through your mind or tongue.

Words and concepts can feed your natural sensuality. You may enjoy thinking, talking or reading about sensual/sexual pleasures, including good food, drink, etc. Money may also be a topic of interest in your reading and discussions. If you indulge in fiction, you probably prefer happy endings.

Letter 3: The Inquisitive Investigator

Insatiable curiosity is a likely attribute. Facile, you can talk to almost anyone about almost anything. Constantly picking up on little gems of information, you can be an avid trivia collector. Since much of your learning comes through the spoken word, you are also eager to pass on your own knowledge that way. Sometimes you talk too much and do not listen enough. But you often prefer gaining understanding through listening to someone rather than reading or going out and doing.

Fairly detached and often logical, you can appear rather cool and unfeeling to some. You find it easy to avoid emotional entanglements when you stay with your observer role. Due to your endless curiosity, you can end up skimming the surface, becoming scattered and superficial. Articulate and expressive, others often envy your "gift of gab."

When you do read, it might be for short periods of time. You could prefer magazine articles or short stories to long books. Or, you may go quickly from one thing to the next intellectually, never staying too long with one topic. Variety and constant mental stimulation are essential to you. Since you can become interested literally in **anything**, your taste in literature is likely to be quite varied.

Letter 4: The Thinking/Feeling Mix

This combination suggests a blend between the intellect and the emotional security needs. One potential is the person who does not utilize pure, logical analysis. Intuitive perceptions and emotional reactions are utilized as much as rationality.

Another option is the person for whom the mind is a source of emotional security. You may rely on your intellect and thinking abilities as the basic bedrock of your life. Your mind is the foundation on which everything else is laid. In such a case, you may depend on rationality or logic to provide your basic safety and protection in life. Beware of being disappointed if you rely solely on your intellectual skills.

Protectiveness is often a part of the communication style — self-protection and/or looking after others. When you are feeling nurturant, you follow the "If you cannot say anything good, don't say anything" rule and can be quite silent. Generally, for you, ease in communication is tied to emotional security. When and where you feel safe, you can be quite open and talkative. Otherwise, you may, literally, never open your mouth! Usually close family situations are where you feel most secure.

Your mother or mother figure could have been an important role model (positive or negative) for your approach to the world of the mind.

Reading can be a form of security for you — especially indulged in at home (not at the library) where you can retreat into your own little world. Cookbooks or gourmet magazines are one possibility — or simply reading at the dinner table (and breakfast and lunch). Other intellectual interests might include business publications which offer the potential of increasing your nest egg. Home-oriented, you may enjoy home-improvement manuals, fix-it instructions, manuals for sewing, knitting, crocheting, etc. However, if you are into feeding your mind (which is likely with this combination), you may be open to **any** form of intellectual sustenance.

Letter 5: The Entertainer

Your mind is a source of self-esteem; you need to feel proud of your ability to think and speak. Sometimes this expresses as a large vocabulary (or excessive pomposity); sometimes as cracking lots of jokes or making lots of puns; or simply being the life of the party. In whatever fashion, you need to be noticed for your mind and verbal skills. Admiration for your intellect is important.

The sales field is a natural one for you. Exuberant and majestic, you tend to present everything in a vibrant, exciting, larger-than-life manner. You can easily sweep others along into your enthusiasms. A natural promoter, your excitement is contagious. With excellent dramatic instincts, you can talk people into things. This does sometimes lead to exaggeration, however. You use your mind and tongue to achieve an adrenaline rush, the thrills, the "highs" that mean so much to you.

If a reader, your tastes in literature are likely to run to drama. Plays may appeal and films may be an enjoyable recreation for you. A fascination with famous individuals, including movie stars, is possible. You might enjoy reading or talking about grand schemes, great dreams that paid off for people. Majestic undertakings are likely to excite you. Intellectual involvements can be a forum for your creative expression and keep your life stimulating.

Letter 6: The Wordsmith

Words, for you, are tools. They can be utilized to make life function more efficiently. They may very well be a part of your career and work in the world. You tend to be quite analytical and nit-picking in your mental approach, ready to pick things apart and find all the flaws. The end goal, of course, is to put them back together in even better shape. However, sometimes you get stuck in the critical mode and forget to move on to improving the situation. The criticism can just as easily be self-directed as other-directed.

Often, you are unforgiving of your mistakes, feeling they reflect an inner incompetence. Learning self-forgiveness is important. Remember, if you did it right the first time, you haven't learned anything. It is only when we make a mistake and then do **better**, that we know we have grown and learned! Your communication style is toward functionality. If you see conversation as useful and productive, you will participate. If not, you will remain silent.

Reading may very well be a form of self-improvement for you. Technical manuals of all kinds are a likely focus, as you seek means to raise your competence level and skills. Sometimes various handicrafts appeal to your desire to do something with your hands which is useful. You may also be a general "fixer-upper," teaching yourself minor repairing skills as you maintain the physical surroundings. (You enjoy the thrift of saving money from repair bills and the competence of being able to improve your physical environment.) Anything which enhances your job skills is a probable attraction; you often read material which is directly involved with your field of endeavor. Self-help books could appeal. Your desire for improvement could lead to an interest in anything you believe will sharpen your mind.

Letter 7: The Diplomat

Words, for you, are a bridge to other people. They spark the relating instinct and get people involved with one another. Sometimes that involvement is cooperative and harmonious; other times it may be highly competitive. But the theme is a give and take between people, a back and forth, a sharing interaction. You prefer to have a peer, someone on your level with whom to bat the conversational ball back and forth. Innately sociable, you would rather discuss than monologue.

When you are in your appeasement mode, you can be too concerned with protecting the other person's feelings. This can lead to "little white lies" which lead to big bloopers as one lie begets another. Or, you may simply avoid arguments as unpleasant. Tact and diplomacy are probably skills for you; just use them at the appropriate time and place.

Any literature which appeals to your basic desire for balance is a possibility. This can range from pleasure in studying mathematics to enjoyment of manuals on fashion and design. The visual aspect is often important to you, and books on fine photography, architecture or other aesthetic forms may fill your needs. Beauty and appearance are often a concern and you could collect manuals on makeup, hair, exercise, clothes, personal appearance and creating an attractive "look." Love and affection are other possible topics of interest, so romances or books about relationships may occupy your shelves. If the competitive spirit predominates, law books may abound or books which teach expertise in whatever activity you currently want to win. You may hone your skills (through reading) in a variety of competitive events, from aikido to tennis; from backgammon to bridge; from poker to Ping Pong, etc.

You look to your mind to bring pleasure, beauty and relationships into your life.

Letter 8: The Relentless Researcher

Intense and all-absorbing, you rarely give up on an issue. With bulldog tenacity, you have been known to wear a subject to death, simply refusing to release it and go on to something else! With excellent analytical and organizational skills, you can be a superlative researcher. Obsessive, with a talent for details, you are well qualified to put the pieces together in a number of areas. Rarely content to accept the surface meaning, you tend to probe ever deeper, looking for root causes and underlying meanings.

Gifted with a sharp tongue, you rarely use it indiscriminately. Often, you intuitively sense the weakest link or the chink in the armor of another person. You tend to utilize that knowledge when it is most effective. By avoiding a "scatter gun" attack, you save your put-downs for really crucial moments and often have an overwhelming impact. People tend to love or hate your mind and communication style. Few are indifferent.

Your interests are usually drawn to subjects of depth, and your reading material tends to be serious and multilayered. Occult topics may hold your interest, but a concern with monetary issues is also a likely focus. When researching an area of interest, you are likely to be incredibly thorough and intense in your pursuit of knowledge. Investigation often appeals to you, so detective stories or murder mysteries are one way to unwind. Themes of transformation often appeal greatly to you, drawing you to literature discussing great life crises and turning points. Death is one such turning point and you probably enjoy thinking and reading about people who master life's great challenges, including overcoming death.

Your mind is deep and you are willing to go to the limit in seeking answers.

Letter 9: The Sage

Philosophical, questioning, searching and seeking, the quest for meaning is a fundamental part of your mental life. Understanding why we are here and what life is all about drives you to study, learn, travel, teach, take classes, read and search for knowledge in all areas of the globe, with all peoples. Universal understanding is a goal — the desire to fathom life's existential issues. Religion, spiritual studies, philosophy, science or other belief systems may attract you with an offer to help comprehend life's mysteries.

Usually blessed with a keen sense of humor, you can be quite entertaining — and even a prankster on occasion. Quick-witted, when misapplied, you can run the smoothest of cons. Truth may be a central issue in your communications. Extremes range from "foot in mouth" bluntness to a carefree stretching of the facts to fit your fancy. The middle ground is an appreciation of honesty without overdoing it. Usually very articulate, you are capable of expanding knowledge in a variety of areas. Another skill is the ability to see the wide perspective, the long-range view. Generally optimistic, you tend to assume that things will work out for the best — sooner or later. Sometimes, however, you become impatient when it is not sooner!

Reading is often a major activity and pleasure for you. For recreation, travel brochures or books about someone's journeys and discoveries are a good bet. Spiritual essays, philosophical tracts, religious ideas or anything oriented toward a search for the meaning of life is also a real draw for you. Humorous books are another potential recreation; you like to laugh. Your reach for something more is partially channeled through the world of the mind.

Letter 10: The Solid Citizen

Responsible, patient, thorough, painstaking, you are very disciplined in your mental approach. Solid and realistic, you probably prefer to work with tangibles and physical facts; abstractions are less significant in your mind. You have a facility for critical evaluation. Sometimes this leads to an excess of judgment. You can be very inhibited in your verbal and intellectual expression because you believe your thinking and/or speaking is not "good enough." Occasionally, there are literal blocks to communication (e.g., stuttering, phone phobias), usually related to too much self-criticism. Fear of failure and brooding about making a mistake can become a self-fulfilling prophecy. Your awareness of "the rules" and other people's expectations might also stop you on occasion from expressing what you feel is "not proper."

Your strengths include an excellent ability to face facts and deal with the world as it really is. You often have an instinctive grasp of power relations and tend to utilize the mind as a tool in your ambitions, wanting to reach a position of more control and authority. Willing to hang in there and expend whatever effort is necessary, you can be highly successful because you persevere.

Your taste in literature is often practical. If you read, it is probably material you feel will enhance your career or your ability to cope with life. You may read as a means to gain power and authority. Often status-oriented, you may pursue good literature as much because it is approved as because you enjoy it. History may appeal as could tomes discussing basic structures (e.g., the economic or political system). Pragmatic, you are likely to pursue the written word which seems useful to you. Work-related subjects may be devoured, with "fun" stuff left at the bottom of the heap. Your approach to the world of the mind is probably strongly influenced by your father or father figure (like him, or the exact opposite).

Your career could easily involve the mind, or thinking and communicating can be seen as a major life-task. In such a case, you may read faithfully and regularly because mental involvements feel like survival needs. Communication may seem like a responsibility and you can be very dedicated to your intellectual duties.

Letter 11: The Unconventional Thinker

Innovative, inventive and original, you think for yourself and refuse to accept other people's dogmas. Sometimes your rebelliousness (mental and/or physical) can go to the extremes of recalcitrance or chaos. Usually you just insist on making up your own mind and following your own ideas. Creative, you can be an excellent problem-solver and brainstormer because you are capable of coming from a unique perspective. Rather than remaining stuck in traditional ways of thinking, you have a freshness, an ability to stand the situation on its head and conceptualize new solutions.

Often very bright, you can be hard for other people to follow; the more you pursue your own, unique style of thinking and communication, the more risk that some people will not understand what you mean. Progressive, unusual, avant-garde ideas tend to attract you. Friends are often a source of intellectual stimulation; you enjoy batting ideas back and forth. Unconventional in your thinking, you have been known to say some things more for the shock value than anything else. You will pursue knowledge in any area. Open-minded, you are willing to go beyond ordinary limits in the pursuit of understanding.

The literature which draws you tends to be unconventional and forward-looking. Science fiction is one likely field. Technical material, especially involving computers, new-age knowledge, space age or other futuristic ideas can be a focus of your attention. Astrology is certainly one of several potential involvements for your freewheeling mind. Anything unusual or individualistic could draw your attention.

Letter 12: Intuitive Understanding

Imaginative and sensitive, your thinking has a large share of intuition and feelings mixed in. Generally blessed with a creative imagination, you may be drawn to many artistic fields: films, poetry, painting, writing fiction, music, song writing, etc. Your fantasy skills are strong. Daydreaming is probably a hobby of yours, and some of your best ideas can come to you in that waking/dreaming twilight zone. Just be sure you can distinguish achievable fantasies from those that are pure wish fulfillment.

Able to blend the rational with the nonrational and the conscious with the unconscious, you can be a superb psychotherapist, an inspired artist, a persuasive advertiser or enter any other field which allows your imagination full rein and blends conscious reasoning with unconscious "knowing." Your perspective is toward the infinite. Sometimes this leads to dissatisfaction, when the human world does not match the ideal vision you have within. Rather than running away from an ugly reality (into fantasy or other escapes), the best path is to help bring that more ideal vision into existence on the physical plane. Helping, healing activities or artistic, aesthetic achievements can help achieve that goal.

ALPHABET COMBINATIONS BY TWOS

1-2: Your identity is tied to your ability to think and communicate. You tend to go your own way where concepts are concerned and may be surprised to discover other people do not think as you do. You can use your mind as a source of strength and to make your life comfortable.

1-3: Your mind is likely to be quick, sharp and lively. You are probably quite articulate and skilled with word play. Mental games may appeal to you and you know how to use words as weapons. Easily bored, you seek constant mental challenges.

1-4: You are torn between spontaneous, natural expression and holding back for fear of hurting someone. You may vacillate between sharp words and extreme compassion. You enjoy thinking for yourself, yet you want your words to bring people closer.

1-5: Quick on the trigger, you can fall into impulsive speech and exaggeration. Easily excited, you tend to express your ideas with drama and energy. You can get very fired up about something and your enthusiasm is usually contagious. Once you've sold the ideas to others, you are ready to move on to something new.

1-6: Quick-witted and sharp, yet precise, you can accomplish a great deal with your mind. But there is potential conflict between your impulsive need to communicate and your desire to figure out everything and get it just **right** before saying anything. Spontaneity and exactitude must be blended.

1-7: You tend to think in terms of polarities; rarely do you see one side of a question without an awareness also of the other. At times this double vision can seem a handicap as you try to separate your point of view from someone else's and clarify what you really think.

1-8: An incisive mind is likely with a biting tongue possible as well. Intolerant of obfuscation, you tend to cut to the very heart of the matter under discussion. You may experience some tension between your desire for fast processing of thoughts and ideas versus your drive to understand the deepest levels of meaning.

1-9: Bright, quick, articulate and witty, other people sometimes have trouble keeping up with your rate of thought and/or speech. Noted for "telling it like it is," you are not always tactful. Concepts excite you and you can easily get other people stirred up too, but you are ever eager to move on to the next new idea.

1-10: You are likely to be contending with two very different head spaces: one feeling that you can conquer anything with your mind and the other feeling inhibited, limited and that your mental facilities do not measure up to your internal standards. You are capable of achieving much through the intellect and communication. Relax and give yourself a break.

1-11: Freedom of thought is especially important to you. You insist on thinking for yourself and resist the pronouncements of others. At times, you may be prone to making shocking statements to help show people you make your own rules mentally. You may be quite original and inventive.

1-12: You are dealing with two different modes of understanding. One part of you trusts only in experience, personally doing it yourself in order to learn. Another part of you seeks insight through the intuitive, opening up to an instinctive **knowing** beyond words and concepts. You need both personal discovery and sensitivity to your inner wisdom.

2-3: Your approach to the mental world is light and comfortable. You can enjoy playing with words, but do not get serious. When communication or thinking becomes arduous, you are likely to seek an easier path. Often, the people and situations right around you are the most interesting to you.

2-4: Somewhat reticent, you know more than you tell. You use your mind and style of communication to protect your security and that of others. Consequently, you will rarely speak up if you believe someone might be hurt by what is said. You strive to keep conversations smooth and easy.

2-5: Two different styles of thinking and communication appeal to you. On one hand, you prefer to keep familiar pathways of logic, dependability, and follow lines that have worked before. On the other hand, you are oriented toward risking a novel approach in order to go after a bigger impact on the world.

2-6: Your mental approach is based on logic, rationality and what works in the physical world. Fundamentally pragmatic, you seek ideas that are functional, that serve some purpose. Talk, too, where you are concerned, must be useful. Otherwise, your attitude is: why say it!

2-7: Your thinking can sometimes seem like a work of art. You have a natural affinity for grace and beauty in language. As a conscquence, you tend to avoid unpleasant topics and can be a master diplomat when you choose. Since your thoughts usually flow smoothly and easily, you may be inclined to "shine it on" if it appears a lot of mental effort will be called for. You expect sweetness and light.

2-8: You are likely to experience ambivalence between a desire to go placidly along your normal mental ruts, comfortable, at ease and feeling fine versus a need to investigate, probe the depths, ask penetrating questions and generally uncover what is hidden. Your desire for intellectual discipline may clash with the pleasure you take in being relaxed and easygoing in your thinking.

2-9: You may feel torn between channeling your intellect toward material fulfillments, possessions and pleasures versus spiritual, ethical and religious aspirations and goals. People may be surprised that you think and speak so quickly on some occasions, yet very deliberately on others.

2-10: Careful, cautious and logical in your thinking, you work best with a linear approach. Common sense tends to appeal to you and you prefer any practical analysis to intuition. You trust the real (i.e., physical) world. You may apply your mind and communication skills in your career.

2-11: You may have an inner conflict. On the one hand, you enjoy following comfortable patterns of thinking, familiar ways of analyzing. On the other hand, you like to be original and innovative. In sharing ideas with others, you may feel torn between a laid-back, easygoing style of communication versus being unique, rebellious and even shocking in your expressions.

2-12: You may have great talent for creating pretty word pictures, whether through poetry or other mediums. You can intuitively tune into what will sound the most harmonious and graceful. Harshness of thoughts or tongue may turn you off; euphony appeals. You prefer to concentrate on the pleasant, eschewing the uncomfortable in hopes it will go away.

3-4: Family probably influences your thinking and perceptions a lot. Relatives could be role models (positive or negative) for your mind and communications. You are likely to gravitate toward conversations involving people and situations near at hand. Immediate concerns command your attention.

3-5: Vivacious and versatile, you have a skill for making people laugh. Able to enjoy the world of the mind and tongue, you may be quite facile with language and easily able to persuade others. Entertaining and fascinating, you can touch the child within everyone around you.

3-6: Quantity versus quality is a dilemma you face in terms of thinking. On the one hand, you are interested in everything, curious and want to explore and study it all. On the other hand, you seek a thorough, exacting knowledge of each subject, complete in itself. A compromise is called for.

3-7: A people person, you do well in communications of all sorts and are oriented toward interactions with others. Objective, logical and detached, you can play it cool when needed. With a fine rational mind, you know how to meet people on their level and find it easy to relate to others.

3-8: Your mental approach is sometimes a contradiction. Although insatiably curious and drawn to investigate a multitude of areas, you also seek a depth understanding of each subject. The pull between a once-over-lightly approach versus an intense, probing scrutiny is quite strong.

3-9: Restless, you are likely to be traveling constantly — mentally if not physically, always on a trip. Ever curious, ever interested in all that goes on around you, seeking knowledge from all sources is your forte. Your role is the perpetual student and the natural teacher.

3-10: Rationality is your style — a logical fact-finding and summing up of information. You do not cloud your mind with emotional attitudes and prejudices; you cherish the attitude of detachment and objectivity. Sometimes you may feel ambivalence between your lighthearted style and your tendency to take the intellect very seriously.

3-11: Casual and carefree in your mental approach, you probably have an excellent mind but do not get overly serious about it. You can cheerfully thumb the nose or say something outrageous if you feel that is needed. Objectivity comes easily to you. Sharing ideas with friends and exchanging information is very important.

3-12: Inclined to be scattered in your thinking, your handicap is a desire to know and understand everything. By trying to absorb too much information, you can become confused and overloaded. Keep clear standards about what is most essential for you to learn and ignore the rest. A great creative imagination and talent in fantasy is likely.

4-5: Objectivity is less important to you than emotional warmth. Home and family are primary concerns and important topics of conversation for you. Feelings may win over logic. You can communicate with great intensity and have a strong emotional impact on others.

4-6: Your mind is oriented toward service or caretaking in some way. This can range from finishing people's sentences for them to practically adopting anyone who sounds needy. If you feel insecure, you are likely to clam up as a self-protective measure. Safety is an issue in your communications.

4-7: Relationships are very important to you. Your thinking and communication are most likely to revolve around those closest to you. On the one hand, you are attracted to openness, ease and an equalitarian exchange of ideas. On the other hand, you are drawn to a protective, cautious style of interaction which will take care of everyone's feelings. Some middle ground is essential.

4-8: A deep mind is likely. Although you are probably somewhat reticent, there is much intellectual exploration going on which you may not share easily with others. Your search for answers, especially those meanings that are hidden, is a major part of your intellectual style. You learn partially through solitude and through this seeking.

4-9: You may feel torn between an interest in broad, philosophical questions versus an involvement in home and family issues. Whether to put your mind and attention more on the domestic front or the wider world could be an inner conflict. Similarly, your style of communication could vary from "no holds barred" bluntness to a protective, quiet support.

4-10: Both parents were likely to have an impact on your mind and thinking. Your style of communication is probably strongly influenced by them — similar or the opposite. You are striving to blend a "cold, hard facts" approach to thinking and communicating with a warm, protective style. (See also Parental theme.)

4-11: Intuitive perceptions are quite possible, but you may feel ambivalent over balancing your two kinds of intuition. One sort is flashes that take you from A to L instantly without everything in between. The other kind is a nonverbal knowing, an inner feeling that is not clearly explicable. Both can be helpful.

4-12: Sensitive, perceptive and quite possibly psychic, you understand things not just through your rational mind. Feelings can be just as important to you as logic. Silence is often valued as you are protective of yourself and others. You would often rather say nothing than risk hurt to yourself or someone else.

5-6: Energetic and efficient in your thinking and communication, you can use your intellectual abilities to achieve in the world. Able to excite people with concepts but also get solid work done, your combination of talents can be quite mentally productive.

5-7: Charm and charisma are two of your assets and you generally exhibit good communication and persuasive skills. Oriented toward fun and ease, you are not inclined to pursue arduous thought but can often be relied upon to provide entertaining and enjoyable ideas.

5-8: The mind is a source of power for you, a tool for making your mark in the world. A natural drive to control and dominate intellectually could result in intimidation of others or overcontrol of yourself if mishandled. Your communication style tends to be intense with people reacting either very negatively or very positively. You seldom go halfway.

5-9: A quick mind and tongue are common with this combination. You are naturally drawn to exciting topics, stimulating conversations and ideas which are progressive, new, creative or forward-going. You abhor mental stagnation and constantly seek new challenges to your mind and ability to speak.

5-10: Your mind feeds your ambitions. You expect your intellectual capacities to advance you in the world and can use communication skills to further your position. Your logic, rationality and ability to plan offer support for your power drive and desire to succeed.

5-11: You may be subject to an inner struggle in terms of your style of thinking. You can be quite detached, objective and rational and yet you also have a very intense, emotional side which demands decisions based on the heart. Your communication style may also vary from cool, calm and collected to volatile, vibrant and vivacious. Both can be useful, depending on circumstances.

5-12: Naturally dramatic, you tend to think of things in a **big** way. Often a talented entertainer, you can be an extremely skilled host or hostess. You can create fascinating, scintillating conversations and ideal party environments. Sometimes your instinct for exaggeration can make it hard to deal with the ordinary drudgery of life. You might prefer to live on a grand scale. You tend to think big, talk big and act big whenever possible. Because you can be very persuasive, you can get other people to go along with your enthusiasms. Just be sure the cause is worthy of all that excitement and drama.

6-7: Logical, rational, sensible, practical and grounded, you use your mind as a tool in your pragmatic assessment of the world and other people. Detached and objective in your approach and your style of communication, you can usually figure out the most helpful step to take and do it.

6-8: Thorough and exacting in your thinking, you want everything in its place intellectually. Your reading and learning is often oriented toward material achievements. At times, your desire for exactitude can lead to obsessing over certain concepts, stopping you from getting as much done as you could. You can be very organized and systematic in your thinking.

6-9: An active and restless mind is indicated, with tension between your capacities for abstractions, theories and visions versus your pragmatic approach. You may feel torn between fantasy and a focus on real-world issues. Your intellectual interests are likely to be extremely broad and your standards very high. If you keep on trying to learn everything or feeling you have to know everything, you will live chronically frustrated. Remember, life is a process.

6-10: Your approach to ideas tends to be pragmatic: will it work? Often your reading and studying is work-oriented with materials which will advance your career. Practical and realistic, you usually prefer sensible conversations which serve a purpose. Chatter for its own sake is meaningless to you. You expect to put your mind to work in the world.

6-11: A finely honed and original mind is quite possible. You may have an inventive streak backed by a talent for analysis and picking things apart. The combination can lead to real mental attainments and creations if you avoid falling into a conflict between your free-ranging intellect and your need to focus on the details. Exploration and exactitude can be supportive of each other; they need not conflict.

6-12: A multiplicity of concepts is often running through your head. Both imaginative and rational, you can combine intuitive and logical thinking for best results. However, you may sometimes feel torn between your desire to fantasize and your need to deal with practical results in the world. Keep room for both functionality and beauty in your mental pursuits.

7-8: Other people spark ideas and conversation for you. Usually interaction is preferable to a vacuum where you are concerned. Much learning comes through your relationships. People associations may be important topics of discussion or reading as well. Sometimes you can be too accommodating in talking with others, but the mutual feedback process is very valuable.

7-9: Lively and extraverted, you can be very entertaining and enjoy a variety of conversations. Justice and fair play are often important topics. A search for meaning and truth may pervade your mental pursuits. The best and the brightest often appeal to you in relationships, seeking to satisfy your restless need for more knowledge, more understanding.

7-10: You may sometimes feel torn between a mental and verbal style that stresses self-control and reticence versus accommodation, association and free give-and-take. Both your relationships and your career are likely to be important focuses for your mind and conversations, so you may at times feel torn between the two, trying to make priorities in time and energy commitments.

7-11: Sociable and people-oriented, you thrive on interaction with others. Relationships are mentally stimulating and you enjoy exchanging information and ideas with other people. Logical and rational, you can be an excellent rationalizer, intellectualizer or simply a skilled theoretician. Grasping abstract concepts comes easily to you.

7-12: With both fantasy and logic at your fingertips, you can create many beautiful images. Language can be flowing and a work of art with you. At times, the desire for ease and harmony could lead to being **too** diplomatic (e.g., evasive or untruthful). Your intuitive perceptions about others can be useful in psychotherapy or other healing work. Sometimes you may prefer the "head trip" to reality because it is smoother. Your talents can give much to others if you are willing to share.

8-9: Your thinking is inextricably mixed with your feelings. Logic is **not** your sole measure; emotions count. You may be torn between your urge to spontaneously express and your desire to protect yourself and others by holding in. This could come across as erratic communication to others — fiery and expressive one moment and clamming up or retreating into silence the next. Find a balance between hiding every single reaction inside versus letting it all hang out.

8-10: Careful, thorough and painstaking in your mental analyses, you are not about to blow the whole thing by impulsive speech. Cautious and somewhat reticent in your communications, you want to be sure you have everything in order before saying anything. You could use the mind as a weapon — a tool for power, or simply be very interested in different forms of mind control (e.g., meditation). Your approach to the intellect is disciplined.

8-11: Your mind may have a scientific bent, interested in a depth understanding of life's processes. You could feel some inner conflict around verbal expression, with a part of you wanting to play with words and enjoying discussions with anyone about anything while another part of you prefers to lie back, take everything in, mull it over and then speak pithily — but with great control — to evoke the responses you desire.

8-12: There are depths to your mind that many people never dream of! With a probing, seeking intellect, you search for answers and a sense of understanding the basic meaning and purpose of life. Your inner investigation is often not a topic of conversation (except to someone **very** near and dear). With most people, you can practice the "Silence is golden" technique which works very well. They do not know your soft spots and you need not reveal your deepest feelings.

9-10: Issues revolving around ethics versus pragmatics or other forms of idealism versus the real world are likely to be important to you. Avoid overvaluing either side — your high standards and expectations **or** your need to achieve in the physical world. Avoid chronic disillusionment or dissatisfaction that life is never as perfect as it **ought** to be, but find some reasonable, practical way to ground some of your dreams and bring them to earth in a manifest form.

9-11: Lively and generally articulate, you can be a natural entertainer. Quick-witted and often quick-tongued, you are usually drawn to new, original pioneering and creative concepts. Sometimes, you get carried away with your enthusiasms, before thinking things completely through. Just be sure you have done your homework! Your verbal skills could be an asset in many communication fields, and you are usually quite persuasive. Fun-loving and optimistic, you tend to prefer topics that are "fun" and keeping the conversation moving. One subject pales quickly for you; variety is a necessary spice in your mental life.

9-12: Mental issues revolve around ideals and expectations. Do not demand more than is reasonable of yourself (be it trying to learn everything about everything, wanting to never make a mistake, etc.). Maintaining goals is essential, but do not be too hard on yourself if you do not reach them immediately.

Clarifying priorities may be essential. Sometimes what your rational ("head") side wants seems in conflict with your feelings ("heart"). Find compromises to meet your varying needs. A strong mental focus is indicated, but also the potential of being overextended. You will always be learning; give yourself time and support on the journey toward infinite understanding.

10-11: Logical and rational, you can be an excellent problem-solver. Able to be sensible and objective, you can rise above the emotional trauma of many situations. Blessed with a long-range view and a sense of perspective, you are less likely to get hung up in small details or petty personal issues.

You may sometimes spend too much time dealing with abstractions and not getting down to cases. Once you apply yourself, your pragmatic assessments tend to be quite useful and ground your theorctical understandings. You can grasp the big perspective, not just on a theoretical level, but in ways that make a real difference in the world.

10-12: You are likely to think about the flaws of society and what can be done to correct them. With a marked awareness of the world's shortcomings motivating an inspired vision of possible improvements, you can be a source of great good to the world. If you get carried away with focusing on the imperfections, you may get stuck in negativity or become fearful to try anything — lest it not measure up to your great expectations. But if you blend your practical ideas with your visionary concepts, the result can be of value to you and the world.

11-12: Gifted with a marvelous creative imagination, you can blend the conscious and the unconscious, the intuitive and the rational for optimum results. Inclined to deal with concepts on a large scale, you are often concerned with transpersonal issues (be they political, economic, religious or otherwise involving a focus wider than purely personal needs). You can sometimes get lost in your own inner thoughts and feelings and forget to make contact or communicate clearly with those about you. Do not get too abstract. Use your insights to make a difference.

POLARITIES

1-7: ♂-♀ or ⚵ or ⚴; ♈-♎; 1st-7th houses

You are probably facing an inner ambivalence between free, open expression of what you want and think versus empathy and tuning into the desires of others. This can be making the balance between talking and listening, between asserting your conversational rights and those of another person, between your interests and those of a partner, etc. An enjoyment of communication is likely, but you may be integrating the push/pull between self versus other as far as intellectual exchanges. Avoid the extremes of pushing your ideas too hard **or** giving in too much to what other people think. Seek a middle ground.

You could easily have an instinct for polarities and make an excellent debater, with the capacity to see both sides of an issue. Harmony and balance usually matter to you, and you are likely to try to keep exchanges "even" and "fair" as you strive to divide up the intellectual and communication "pie" into equal slices. Taking turns is a natural compromise.

2-8: ♀-♇; ♉-♏; 2nd-8th houses

You may be struggling to balance your intense need to delve into the deeper meaning of things with your desire to lay back and seek easy, comfortable interchanges. One side of you is dedicated to a disciplined pursuit of knowledge with a willingness to confront unpleasantness in conversations. Another side of you would prefer to coast along in familiar mental territory and have easy, relaxing interactions with other people. Balancing your desire for pleasure from the mind with your desire for control and power over your intellectual prowess is one of the tasks.

Your style is more likely to be reticent than highly expressive. Your comfort-loving side would rather not risk disturbing someone, while your analytical, probing side is often turned inward with self-analysis. However, when you do decide to contribute to the conversation, it is usually worth listening to and often highly insightful.

3-9: ☿-♃ or ⚷; ♊-♐; 3rd-9th houses

You have the potential to be a perpetual student, teacher and traveler as you explore the mental (and often physical) world for answers. Generally insatiably curious, you may study anything (and everything). Eager to talk to others, you learn through conversations as well as books, seminars, trips and interactions with people. You can be quite articulate and may have skills in communication fields. Usually expressive, you can be quite verbal at times. Fortunately, your hunger for learning leads you to listen sometimes as well as talk!

Because your interests are often broad, you may be scattered, with too many subjects to cover any thoroughly. Sometimes, you could feel torn between investigating the people and things right around you in the here and now versus seeking answers about ultimate meaning and truth in a long-range or final sense. Everyday bits of information fascinate you as well as philosophical issues and ideals.

Your mind is likely to always be on the go and you may be physically restless as well. Knowledge is a lifelong quest for you.

4-10: ☽-♄; ♋-♑; 4th-10th houses

Silence may indeed be golden where you are concerned. Before speaking you may ask, "Is it helpful? Is it caring? Is it correct?" If the answer to any of those questions is no, you are likely to refrain from talking. Being accurate matters to you and you could sometimes inhibit yourself from expressing ideas which are valuable, because you fear not measuring up and are self-critical of your intellectual prowess. Anxiety about making a mistake may slow down your thinking processes.

You are also striving to balance your inner compassion with your concern for precision and accuracy. On the one hand, you are unwilling to shade the truth at all, believing that facts are facts and facing reality is the best course. On the other hand, you have a natural feeling for people and would prefer that nobody be hurt by what is said. So, you are striving to integrate your pragmatic side with your empathic side. A middle position allows you to be realistic while still kind.

5-11: ☉-♅; ♌-♒; 5th-11th houses

You are working to balance two different kinds of thinking and speaking. You can be the passionate persuader, swaying people with heartfelt expressions and emotionally laden words. You can incite, excite and move people with your ideas and language. (If overdone, you could appear bombastic, arrogant and exaggerative.) You are also able to be amazingly objective, coolly aloof and detached. You may offer logical reasons and rational explanations for any number of ideas. (If carried too far, you could intellectualize anything and have an infinite number of rationalizations and excuses.)

You might feel torn between listening to your feelings, versus trusting your head alone. Integration is necessary, but fiery intensity and cool logic are not always easy to combine. Once blended, this can be quite an articulate combination. Usually able to make people laugh, you can be quite an entertainer if you choose. A natural promoter, you provide the buyer with sensible reasons along with emotional persuasions. Friends, lover and children are especially likely to share your mental involvements and spark ideas with you.

6-12: ☿ or ♃ or ♆-Ψ; ℳ-ℋ; 6th-12 houses

You are striving to integrate two opposite ways of thinking and speaking. One impulse is to be exact, painstaking, cautious, careful and express pinpoint accuracy in your communications. Ever alert for a mistake, you would rather say nothing at all than risk being wrong. This side of you considers thinking and speaking as a job and works hard at improving efficiency in those areas. At times your critical eye leads to some inhibition, as you fear not measuring up to your demanding standards. The opposite impulse is a desire to let your thinking and communicating just flow. Beautiful language may well appeal, and a poetic style is quite possible. This side expresses by tuning into life intuitively and is drawn to fantasy.

When these two sides are integrated, you manifest the best of logic and intuition, the left and right brains, inspiration and discipline. Communication fields are a good bet and you could be a skilled writer. You will need to blend your realistic, functional side with your imaginative, dreamy side. Often a highly mental, curious, exploratory combination, you may be overextended because you cannot learn everything — though you would probably like to try!

NODES OF THE MOON
The following nodal placements are particularly relevant to the life area of the mind.

Across Gemini/Sagittarius or 3rd/9th Houses

A potential conflict here is between long-range goals, ideals, visions and dreams versus short-term interests and involvements. It also might involve the tension between pursuing knowledge in a haphazard manner, indiscriminately curious versus pursuing knowledge which adds to your sense of perspective on the meaning of life. A balance must be attained between dealing with everyday issues, consensual reality and the people around you versus confronting questions of ultimate meaning, direction and purpose in life. Immediate communication about concrete ideas may be at odds with a desire to engage in long, philosophical discussions about truth.

The combination tends to indicate a highly mental focus. This is a pattern found often among students, teachers and travelers, especially people who are engaged in lifelong learning. Until the seesaw is balanced, however, you could seem scattered to those about you as you bounce from one idea to the next, from the short-term reality to the long-term dreams. When someone asks a simple question, an extensive philosophical dissertation is probably not appropriate. However, if someone is floundering in an existential dilemma, a flip response avoiding the issue is not a solution. Both forms of communication are necessary in life. Both approaches can be useful.

Sometimes a sense of mental inadequacy may be an issue. You may not trust your ability to think, conceptualize, dream or communicate. You may inhibit your abilities through excessively high standards. You could be comparing yourself against someone else whom you see as much more competent intellectually. Commonly, this pattern indicates a fine (but restless) mind. However, you must come to terms with your different interests and pursuits and accept the fact that this part of your life will never be perfect. That is, you will never know it all, learn it all, be able to communicate everything. With that acceptance, there often comes great joy from many mental (and sometimes physical as well) journeys in pursuit of knowledge.

ELEMENT EMPHASIS

Fire
♂, ☉, ♃, ⚸, ♈, ♌, ♐, 1st, 5th, 9th houses

Knowledge is exciting for you. You seek to continually expose yourself to new experiences. Since you learn by doing, direct action is preferable to reading about something or trying to pick it up from someone else. Your patience is limited; if you cannot learn something quickly, you would rather move on. You can also succumb to speaking impulsively. Generally, your thought processes are swift. You may feel intolerant when others cannot keep up with you. Sometimes, however, you leap to conclusions far beyond what is justified by the data.

Often blessed with a ready wit, you can be the life of the party, the super salesperson or the favorite professor who knows how to liven up a lecture with humor. Usually quick-tongued and often sharp tongued, you are generally ready with words and a good extemporaneous speaker.

Earth
♀, ☿, ?, ⚴, ♄, ♉, ♍, ♑, 2nd, 6th, 10th houses

Practical and grounded, you want to put ideas to use in the world. It is not enough to just **know** something. For you, the important question is: "What can I **do** with this?" or "How can I **use** this knowledge?" Specifics appeal to you. For you, the "real world" is physical, concrete knowledge. There is usually a right answer and a wrong answer in your book. And each question is only supposed to have one right answer.

At times, your efficient, productive emphasis can lead to an excess of criticism — either self-directed, turned against others or both. Analysis, discrimination and figuring out a more efficient approach are great talents; just be sure you direct your strengths at improving the world of things. Few people appreciate being "made over" — no matter what the motivation.

Your verbal style tends to be somewhat reticent. Generally, you speak only when you see it as serving some useful purpose. If it is a task or assignment, however, you will do your dedicated best.

Air
☿, ♀, ♀, ⚹, ♅, ♊, ♎, ♒, 3rd, 7th, 11th houses

Ideas and communication are second nature to you. Mental pursuits appeal and you are eager to share the world of the mind with friends and loved ones. Bouncing ideas back and forth, stimulating each other's creativity are pastimes you enjoy immensely. You like to theorize and can go off on interesting tangents sometimes. One idea leads to another and you may occasionally forget to tie the whole, lovely, mental superstructure to something solid and realistic. One word also can lead to another. Generally quite verbal, you can be verbose if you get carried away with the flow.

A past master at intellectualization and rationalization, you usually have reasons for everything and rarely miss out with your excuses. You tend to rely heavily on logic and rationality and may have to work at communicating with emotional people. Of course, when you are detached (which is potentially quite often), you do not particularly care about how others feel. You can be quite articulate and very bright. Just remember to use your talents with caring and wisdom.

Water
☽, ♇, ♆, ♋, ♏, ♓, 4th, 8th, 12th houses

You may not learn so much as absorb — sometimes without even thinking about it. Like a sponge, you pick up many things from the physical environment and people around you. Often intuitive, you may get impressions or have a sense of **knowing** something — without knowing how. Once you develop a clear differentiation between true, psychic understanding and wish fulfillment or fantasies, you will be able to rely on your intuitive perceptions. Some knowledge, which appears psychic, is merely an unconscious processing of many, small clues picked up subliminally. Such information can be quite valuable.

Your verbal style tends to be silent. You value security and will not expose yourself without a good reason. In an environment where you feel safe, you can be quite talkative. Otherwise, you tend to clam up, figuring if other people do not know what is going on inside, there is less chance you'll be hurt.

You can be extremely perceptive, but rarely share all your understandings. People are sometimes surprised when they discover your hidden depths.

Fire-Earth
♂, ☉, ♃, ⚴, ♈, ♌, ♐, 1st, 5th, 9th houses &
♀, ☿, ⚵, ⚶, ♄, ♉, ♍, ♑, 2nd, 6th, 10th houses

Productive and capable, you expect to put your mind to use in the world. It is not enough to say something; you want to do something as well. Both actions and words are important to you; you prize results and are willing to get in there and produce some of them. Other people find it difficult to sidetrack you once you get an idea, as you are driving and determined.

If your innate confidence and enthusiasm fights your need to check things out and make sure they are right, you could be pulled between spontaneity and discipline. However, if you harness the fire of your native optimism and excitement to the engine of your willingness to work and get the job done, you can manifest almost any idea you come up with. You may bowl people over.

Fire-Air
♂, ☉, ♃, ♄, ♈, ♌, ♐, 1st, 5th, 9th houses &
☿, ♀, ⚷, ⚳, ♅, ♊, ♎, ♒, 3rd, 7th, 11th houses

Sociable, extraverted, outgoing and expressive, you can be the life of any party if you choose. Naturally articulate and verbal, you know how to use words. Often entertaining and witty, you can share ideas in a way that is both entertaining and informative. Fun-loving and optimistic, you tend to prefer "up" topics to "down" ones and like to keep things lively. A bit of a rolling stone mentally, you can get bored and want to move on when a concept has been kicked around for awhile. Because your mind tends to be quick (and often your tongue as well), other people may not always keep up with you.

New ideas come naturally to you and you could be quite a pioneer in coming up with original, creative concepts. Sometimes, you rush into a concept half-cocked, but your excitement is contagious and it is easy to draw people along with you. Just be sure you've done your homework too! Communication fields offer you great opportunities as you have good persuasive skills.

Fire-Water
♂, ☉, ♃, ♄, ♈, ♌, ♐, 1st, 5th, 9th houses &
☽, ♇, ♆, ♋, ♏, ♓, 4th, 8th, 12th houses

You do not operate solely on logic. Your thinking tends to be very influenced by your feelings which are quite intense. Your emotional reactions make a big difference in how you communicate. You are probably torn between expressing your natural instincts versus waiting to make sure it's safe to say what you think. As a consequence, people may sometimes see you as erratic — blowing off steam at one moment and clamming up the next. Even when you do not express them, however, you have strong feelings and are reacting to what is happening.

Because you can be in touch with your inner wisdom, you will sometimes act on it from an intuitive space without a logical or rational explanation for what you are doing. Your first instinct is sometimes right on — even if it isn't "rational." Just be sure you can distinguish between inner wisdom and wishful thinking!

Earth-Air

♀, ☿, ⚳, ⚶, ♄, ♉, ♍, ♑, 2nd, 6th, 10th houses &
☿, ♀, ⚴, ⚵, ♅, ♊, ♎, ♒, 3rd, 7th, 11th houses

Logic and rationality are central to your intellectual experience. You are usually pragmatic rather than intuitive, sensible rather than emotional. Often talented with facts and figures, you can bring order out of chaos and be an excellent problem-solver. Your cool, calm and collected style of communication and thinking can be very helpful, especially in situations where feelings are getting out of hand.

You may sometimes be a bit torn between the theoretical side of life and the practical applications, but usually you find a happy medium of understanding the concept in theory but also working to find a useful outlet in real life.

Earth-Water

♀, ☿, ⚳, ⚶, ♄, ♉, ♍, ♑, 2nd, 6th, 10th houses &
☽, ♇, ♆, ♋, ♏, ♓, 4th, 8th, 12th houses

Your mind is oriented toward security and preserving what has gone before. You see the value of many traditions and strive to keep what is useful and worth retaining. Somewhat serious, you are inclined to take many things on your shoulders and can end up feeling and acting responsible for many duties that are not truly yours.

Your communication style tends to be rather reticent. You are quite sensitive to the power of words to do damage and tend to remain silent rather than risk hurting others or being hurt yourself. You also feel that speech should be useful. If you do not see any purpose to be served by talking, you are unlikely to speak up.

Air-Water

☿, ♀, ⚴, ⚵, ♅, ♊, ♎, ♒, 3rd, 7th, 11th houses &
☽, ♇, ♆, ♋, ♏, ♓, 4th, 8th, 12th houses

You tend to have a very rich inner life and vivid imagination. All kinds of fantasies are at your fingertips with potential talent for poetry, creative writing or any field requiring imagination. You are able to blend the conscious with the unconscious mind which makes an excellent combination for any kind of psychotherapy, counseling, healing or communication work.

You have your own little world inside your head which is not always easy for other people to enter. Sometimes they may feel as though you are not really "there" with them. Strive to externalize some of your thoughts and feelings. Sharing with others can lead to further enrichment of their lives and yours. Beware of living too much in the head; sometimes it is a temptation that leads to avoiding work or practical accomplishments because mind games are so much easier. You can handle both reality and fantasy.

QUALITY EMPHASIS

Cardinal
♂, ☽, ♀, ☿, ⚹, ♄, ♈, ♋, ♎, ♑, 1st, 4th, 7th, 10th houses

Yours is often the school of "hard knocks." Truly, for you, experience is the best teacher. Though you are capable of learning from others or through observation, somehow it never quite "sticks" with you as thoroughly as when you experience the situation directly and deal with your own actions.

Crises may bring out the best (and the worst) in you, but often it seems to take an event to crystallize your opinions or attitudes about something. Knowing through doing is very much your style. Abstract knowledge means little to you. "Real world" information that you can depend on is what matters.

Fixed
♀, ☉, ♇, ♅, ♉, ♌, ♏, ♒, 2nd, 5th, 8th, 11th houses

You want control over your mind and communications and tend to resolutely continue along whatever mental paths you have chosen to trod. With a great strength of will and mental discipline, your mastery of ideas, concepts and communicative skills can be amazing. Persistent and steadfast, it is quite difficult to turn you aside once you have made up your mind about something. Remaining true to your own ideas can be both a strength and a weakness.

Somewhat resistant to the inputs of other people, you probably do not wish to be influenced by what others think or say. You are determined to find your own way, be true to your own thinking. Sometimes, you become very fixed in your opinions, because you are digging in your heels against being moved by anyone else or because your way of thinking just seems so normal and natural, it is hard to imagine other points of view. People may perceive you as closed-minded. Learning to bend a little, to consider another perspective, to wander away from the path as you have determined it, may take a little work but is worth it.

You have great powers of concentration and are capable of a single-minded focus on a project to the very end. Able to screen out what you view as unimportant information, you can accomplish prodigious amounts of mind-work. You exhibit great control over your intellectual environment.

Mutable
☿, ♐, ♇, ♃, ♇, ♆, ♊, ♍, ♐, ♓, 3rd, 6th, 9th, 12th houses

Interested in everything, your mind is probably lively and curious. With a multiplicity of interests and talents, your first challenge is finding a focus. Which one (or several) of your many potentials do you develop more fully? Beware of frittering away life as a dilettante or "Jack (Jill) of all trades."

Often, your standards are very high — perhaps unreasonably so. You can be hard on yourself — never satisfied, because your performance always could have been better, faster, higher, sooner, improved in some fashion. Allowing yourself to be human may be a lesson for you to learn. Be sure you can appreciate the journey toward achievement, as well as the actual fruits.

Your keen intellectual capacities support almost any kind of mental work. Teaching, learning, traveling, lecturing, writing and many other "mind" careers are possible. This combination can show skills with languages, picking them up rather easily. You may even have a great talent for mimicry and adopting accents.

You can also learn well vicariously — watching others, but not having to experience the traumas yourself. Books, seminars, anything that stretches your brain, will often appeal.

THEMES

Freedom
♂, ♃, ♄, ♅, ♈, ♐, ♒, 1st, 9th, 11th houses

More than most people, you cherish thinking for yourself. Unwilling to accept other people's authority in terms of ideas and concepts, you insist on making your own exploration and decisions. Often rebellious in your outlook, you do not automatically believe that just because you hear it or read it makes it so. Personal experience is your ultimate test.

With a free-ranging mind, you often are drawn to areas and ideas which are unconventional. Your speech also tends to be forthright and direct. Your communication style is open and you are more likely to say something than withhold it, figuring that honesty is generally the best policy. Sometimes this is not appreciated by others. Because your mode of thinking and speaking is generally very unique, you can be quite distinctive.

Closeness or Interpersonal
☽, ☉, ♀, ☿, ⚹, ♇, ♋, ♌, ♎, ♏, 4th, 5th, 7th, 8th houses

You are inclined to temper your logic with feelings and emotional reactions. Cold, hard facts alone are insufficient in your opinion. How facts are going to affect people is important to you and you weigh your words with that in mind. Empathic and concerned with others, you can be an excellent diplomat, choosing expressions that will be the most soothing to the people involved.

A caring, concerned person, your feelings usually reflect in your voice. You may have difficulty in coming across as objective or detached, because you tend to be emotionally involved with the subject.

Artistic

♀, ⚴, ⚵, ☉, ♆, ♉, ♌, ♎, ♓, 2nd, 5th, 7th, 12th houses

You have the potential for a real flow and grace with language. This can include appreciation for beautiful words in such areas as poetry, lyrics and creative writing. You can create a melodious mode of expressing yourself and make communication into a work of art.

You tend to prefer thinking and discussing ideas that are pleasant and may have difficulties around confrontation. Your preference for harmony can lead to avoidance of what you see as ugly or even to laziness if you expect other people to always create the beauty for you. You can charm people with your thoughts and words if you choose.

Idealistic

♃, ⚷, ♆, ♐, ♓, 9th, 12th houses

You place a high value on the mind; thinking and communication are very important to you. Because of this, you may — at times — expect more than is reasonable in the mental realm. You often are trying to reach the unreachable stars in some sense. This could be attempting to learn everything about everything; overextending yourself and feeling scattered with all you are trying to learn and understand. It may be that no matter how much you know, you are never satisfied and keep on pushing yourself to learn more. Goals are important and necessary, but remember to enjoy the journey toward ultimate understanding as well!

Sometimes part of the problem is that your head goals conflict with your heart goals. One form of this is the struggle between truth and compassion, where the head may call for truth at any cost while the heart demands that caring and concern for the other person moderate what is said.

An important part of this mental focus is using your mind to understand your place in the universe, to seek a sense of meaning and purpose in life. The quest for answers about the infinite is central in your intellectual explorations.

Obsessive-Compulsive

☿, ⚳, ⚶, ♇, ♄, ♍, ♏, ♑, 6th, 8th, 10th houses

Pinpoint accuracy is your forte. Cautious, exacting, precise and detail-oriented, you have great qualifications for the researcher, organizer, efficiency expert par excellence. Determined to gain a **thorough** knowledge of whatever interests you, you can become compulsive in your obsessive seeking of all the facts.

With an innate skill for flaw-finding and hard-nosed analysis, you can be too critical at times — of yourself as well as others. Sometimes you may feel inadequate intellectually, because your standards are so very demanding. Dedicated and persevering, you rarely release an idea once involved.

Competence
☿, ?, ♥, ♄, ♍, ♑, 6th, 10th houses

You may very well work with your mind — in a field involving the intellect and/or communication. Ideas and people are likely to be central in your career. Your mental approach tends to be practical, realistic and grounded. You seek to constantly improve the efficiency of your mind through analyzing shortcomings. Beware of overdoing your critical standards. If you are too harsh in your judgments, you may inhibit yourself from thinking and communicating (for fear of making a mistake, of not doing it "right") in circumstances which you could have handled very well. If you turn thinking or speaking into a "job," it may seem an awesome task. Remember to be productive and efficient; don't get stuck at the flaw-finding level.

Mental Stimulation
☿, ?, ♥, ♀, ♃, ♇, ♅, ♆, ♊, ♍, ♎, ♐, ♒, ♓, 3rd, 6th, 7th, 9th, 11th, 12th houses

The mind, ideas, concepts, communication and peer relationships are strongly emphasized. Interactions in the mental world are very important. Sharing ideas with friends, partners and people around you is a vital activity. Information exchange is quite natural to you. Teaching, learning, traveling and experiencing are all forms of gathering more knowledge. Your mind is constantly active. You might even have trouble sleeping at night sometimes when you are caught up in a cycle of thoughts around thoughts.

Usually bright, articulate and expressive, you find the realm of the mind infinitely fascinating.

Relationships
♀, ♀, ✳, ♇, ♎, ♏, 7th, 8th houses

Sociable and outgoing, you are naturally oriented toward relating with others. Exchanges tend to flow smoothly as you have an instinctive empathy for the other person's point of view. Since your associations are a major focus, you will often find yourself talking about a relationship, relationships in general or the other person's relationships. You tend to particularly seek a sense of balance and even handedness in relationships. Occasionally, your competitive spirit may lead you to be more cutting than you would generally. You could enjoy winning arguments and promoting your ideas.

More often, however, your need for other people can lead you to be too accommodating and too willing to give in to the other person's point of view. It is all very well to learn from others, but do not sell your own opinions short. You need intellectual stimulation from those with whom you associate.

Security
♀, ☽, ☿, ⚷, ⚶, ♇, ♄, ♆, ♅, ♋, ♍, ♏, ♑, ♓, 2nd, 4th, 6th, 8th, 10th, 12th houses

Your mind is often applied to seeking security in the world — physical and emotional. You value ideas that will give you stability and dependability. You are a bit more inclined to trust the traditional and what has worked in the past. The deeper the waters, the less likely you are to rock the boat.

Your communication style is likely to be somewhat quiet and sensible. If there is no good reason to say something, you would rather remain silent. Speech, for you, should be compassionate and serve a purpose. Hurtful comments and chatter for its own sake do not appeal.

Risk/Creativity/Change
♂, ☉, ♃, ⚴, ♅, ♈, ♌, ♐, ♒, 1st, 5th, 9th, 11th houses

Your mind is open to the new, the innovative, the progressive. You may enjoy gambling on new ideas and spend pleasurable hours speculating about what you will do if you "hit it big" with your latest project. An independent thinker, you can be extremely creative with your mind. Naturally optimistic and hopeful, you tend to assume that what you believe in will work. You are a bit more inclined to trust something that looks promising, that will expand on the past, than the old way of doing things.

Your communication style is likely to be expressive and outgoing. You tend to enjoy speaking and may be a bit better at talking than listening. Often articulate and verbally skilled, you can be an excellent communicator and natural teacher. It is easy for you to convey ideas and share information.

Parents
☽, ♄, ⚷, ♋, ♑, 4th, 10th houses

Your mental outlook and conception of thought are much influenced by your parent(s). Whether they were bright and articulate themselves or not, their attitudes had a strong impact on how you feel about your intellectual capacities and abilities. Your communication style is likely to be measured against their standards (either like them or the exact opposite).

If you saw them as smart, expressive and intelligent, you may have appreciated that and be striving to emulate them. If you felt they overdid it, you could have experienced them as too detached, too cool and intellectual when you wanted emotional warmth. It is also possible that they were negative role models in the sense that you tried to do the opposite of them and developed your own intellectual capacities because you felt they had neglected theirs. But what you view as thinking, verbal skills and mental capacities is largely a reaction to how they handled that area of life.

Power
⊙, ♇, ♄, ♌, ♏, ♑, 5th, 8th, 10th houses

You want control over your mental processes and concepts. Inclined to be resistant to the ideas of others, you usually trust your own conclusions. Mind control (through meditation, hypnosis, guided imagery or other techniques) is often of interest to you. Since you view the intellect as a tool for gaining authority in life, you are willing to discipline it accordingly. Your urge for dominance can be channeled into mental pursuits.

Personal
♂, ♀, ☿, ☽, ♈, ♉, ♊, ♋, 1st, 2nd, 3rd, 4th houses

You are likely to have a good grasp of what you want and need in life. It is easier for you than some to define and delimit what you desire. You can focus on personal issues. Staying in the here and now comes fairly naturally to you. Topics of most central importance to you are likely to range around your own desires, home, family and interactions with people near at hand.

Transpersonal
♃, ⚷, ♄, ♅, ♆, ♐, ♑, ♒, ♓, 9th, 10th, 11th, 12th houses

You may find yourself easily drawn into concerns which affect the world or humanity as a whole. Your mind has a transpersonal bent — which could manifest as a religious theme, a commitment to ecology, an analysis of our economic system, activity in politics or some other focus dedicated to large-scale issues. Your impulse is to bring a wider perspective into any discussion, to expand the horizons, to help other people see the long-range implications and repercussions. You want people to deal with the whole beyond the parts, to see the interconnections.

ASPECTS

Harmony to Letter...

1: There is potential harmony between your manner of thinking and communicating and your sense of identity. You can be direct in expressing what you want and are usually clear about your desires. Your intellectual skills support your ability to be yourself. You are likely to be articulate and intellectually and/or verbally skilled.

2: There is potential harmony between your manner of thinking and communicating and your appreciation of beauty, aesthetics, comfort and physical pleasures. Your mental abilities may be a source of income for you or provide basic physical security and comfort to your life. You may work with beautiful language — through songs, poetry, music or other modes. Pleasure in sharing information and ideas is likely.

3: There is a marked emphasis on the mind, with excellent potential for skills in communication. Curiosity is likely to be strong. You have talent for relating easily to those people around you. Your casual, carefree approach to interacting helps other people to relax. Full of questions, you are always learning more. Trivia collection may be a habit of yours. Teaching is another potential ability.

4: There is potential harmony between your manner of thinking and communicating and your sense of emotional security. You may rely on intellectual prowess to provide a sense of safety. Your early home environment could have encouraged the development of your mind. You can communicate very well about issues which are deeply emotional.

5: There is potential harmony between your manner of thinking and your ability to be significant in the world. You may utilize your mental faculties to obtain recognition and applause from others. Your creative enthusiasm could assist your mastery of intellectual realms. You can communicate with flair and drama.

6: There is potential harmony between your manner of thinking and communicating and your need for exactitude. Your analytical capabilities can assist you in selecting logical, rational options. Information exchange is enhanced as you can combine a casual curiosity about everything with a disciplined pursuit of precise answers and thorough explanations. Writing is one potential, as is any productive output from your mental abilities.

7: There is potential harmony between your manner of thinking and communicating and your desire to share with others. Your sense of fair play enables you to take turns talking and listening. Relationships may support your intellectual activities and your exploration of concepts draws you into more interaction with others.

8: There is potential harmony between your manner of thinking and communicating and your desire for depth understanding of life. Given to probing deeply, your delving for root causes encourages constant intellectual growth and transformation. You use your mind as a tool for self-insight and self-mastery.

9: There is potential harmony between your manner of thinking and communicating and your ideals about life. Your search for answers to the meaning of the universe leads you to explore the mental world even more. Your curiosity and openness to ideas leads you to explore many paths. One possibility is the perpetual student/teacher/traveler.

10: There is potential harmony between your manner of thinking and communicating and your drive to achieve in the outer world. Your ambitions and aspirations help fire your intellectual explorations and your mind is an important tool in your material achievements.

11: There is potential harmony between your manner of thinking and communicating and your facility for unusual approaches. Your individuality and inventiveness assist you in original conceptions. Your desire to share ideas and stimulate minds affirms your personal uniqueness.

12: There is potential harmony between your manner of thinking and communicating and your connection to the universe. Your rational, logical conceptions can be assisted by intuitive insights. Your psychic openness is probably balanced by an awareness of consensual reality and the demands of your surrounding environment and associations.

Conflict to Letter...

1: There is potential conflict between your manner of thinking and communicating and your self-expression.

Check for the following conditions:

If there is heavy water and earth:
You may inhibit yourself from saying what you are thinking at times, usually due to self-doubts, fear of criticism or an overly serious approach. Often, you think too long, hesitating to communicate what is going on until it is sometimes too late. Trust yourself and share your concepts freely; you and those around you will learn much!

If there is heavy fire and air
You may sometimes be more expressive than is in your best interests. You tend to "let it all hang out" which can lead to challenges with other people. You may not always think before speaking. Spontaneity is a wonderful quality, but temper it with some tact and awareness of your impact on other people. You can be extremely articulate and may use words as weapons — biting, ironic, sarcastic. Put your verbal skills to good use.

If there is a relative balance of elements
You may be torn between inhibition and expression, sometimes holding back from what you wish to think and other times blurting out more than is wise. You may rush into some situations without thinking them through and delay yourself at other times, trying to find an intellectual answer when simple action is what is needed. Balance communication and mental needs with self-expression, spontaneity and independence needs.

2: There is potential conflict between your manner of thinking and communicating and your appreciation of physical pleasures. You may feel the mental and material are at odds in your life and be torn between emphasizing the intellect versus enjoying the senses.

3: There is potential ambivalence within you around issues of thinking and communicating. You may feel torn between different styles of speaking or expressing yourself — or how much (or little) you should say. You may be at odds over divergent thoughts, concepts or ideas. Casual curiosity and lighthearted seeking and exchanging of information may be sources of conflict in your life. You could feel scattered if you spread yourself too thin trying to cover the waterfront with your interests and involvements. Mental stimulation is important to you, but don't get carried away.

4: There is potential conflict between your manner of thinking and communicating and your desire for emotional security. You may feel your intellectual needs pull you away from home and family or vice versa. It could appear that you are having to make choices between thinking and feeling. The challenge is to balance information exchange and emotional commitments.

5: There is potential conflict between your manner of thinking and communicating and your need for attention and admiration from others. You may sometimes inhibit yourself from speaking because you fear the reactions of other people. Or, you may find yourself grandstanding in ways that are not wise, gaining center stage through methods whereby you feel not very bright. Your need for self-esteem can harmonize with your desire for intellectual involvements. Create comfortable ways to shine through your mental prowess and utilize your enthusiasm to further your intellectual explorations.

6: There is potential inner ambivalence in the area of handling mental interests, pursuits and communication. One side of your nature is calling for indiscriminate inquiry into everything while another side demands a thorough and complete examination of each small area. The dilemma of quantity versus quality faces you in your intellectual endeavors. Establish priorities so that you can feel comfortable doing some things well and thoroughly while other involvements are haphazard, for fun.

7: There is potential conflict between your light, casual approach to exploring ideas and your desire for empathy and a significant connection to other people. Your flippancy may vie with your drive for emotional commitments. You may feel at odds between knowledge for its own sake versus knowledge which assists your relationships. Keep room for both.

8: There is potential conflict between your detached, casual curiosity about life and your desire for deep, penetrating analysis. Your mental approach may range from flippant to super serious; superficial to incredibly intense. You may feel torn between garnering vast bits of trivia from all over, versus obsessing and ruminating deeply over one facet of your investigations. Both casual detachment and intense scrutiny have their place; maintain a balance in your approach.

9: There is potential inner ambivalence about your handling of intellectual issues and communication. You may feel torn between short-range and long-range views of life. You may find the search for truth and meaning pulls you away from everyday experiences and the people right around you — or vice versa. Curiosity for its own sake vies with the mind applied to a quest for higher meaning. A mentally restless combination, you may be constantly on the go; keep clear priorities to avoid feeling overextended and dissatisfied because you cannot know and understand it all.

10: There is potential conflict between your manner of thinking and communicating and your drive for productive performance in the world. Your stern standards may inhibit you from expressing casually and naturally. You might clam up, fearing criticism (from yourself and/or others). You may channel your mental explorations only into certain approved directions. Perhaps you feel a casual, easygoing approach to learning will restrict your accomplishments in the world. Practicality is a useful addition to pure curiosity, but do not overdo the limits you place on your mental explorations and expressions.

11: There is potential conflict between your manner of thinking and communicating and your drive for individuality and uniqueness. You might go far beyond standard boundaries in exploring concepts and expressing ideas. Or, you could inhibit yourself from sharing your inventive thoughts, fearing the people around you would not understand. Potentially a highly innovative and inventive mind is yours; just be sure you can communicate your unusual ideas with those around you.

12: There is potential conflict between your manner of thinking and communicating and your intuition and inner knowing. Your logic and intuition may be in conflict. You could feel scattered at times, wanting to know and absorb everything on all levels. Your conscious and unconscious understanding may be at odds with one another. Balance rationality and psychic understanding for best results.

CHAPTER TEN

CHILDREN AND CREATIVITY

This area of the horoscope applies to your capacity for doing more than has been done before. It points to creativity — or, more generally, zest — both on the physical level, through procreation and artistic pursuits, and on the emotional and mental levels through coming from your own unique center. During such an act, people tend to feel vital and alive — all the juices are flowing. There is a sense of excitement, of expansion, of pushing back the boundaries of life.

To create, to push boundaries, requires the ability to take risks. The gambler, the speculator, the investor, all need the courage to put their money on the line in hopes of a bigger return. The race car driver, hang glider, acrobat and similar people need courage and steady nerves to stretch their physical capacities to the limit. Some of the essence here is the thrill of an adrenaline rush. For many people a major outlet for the feelings of power, of aliveness, of excitement, comes through sexual acts. And for most of us, the tremendous buildup of falling in love, being in love and loving is a major component of stimulation in our lives. Love can be the ultimate risk.

This is the urge for ego-expansion, in whatever way we fulfill that need. It is connected to self-esteem; everyone needs a sense of pride in his/her actions and the ability to feel good about what we are doing in life. This section will discuss some of the themes around your self-esteem, pride in yourself and ability to create, including potentials around children. Having children is one form of creativity, but remember that many other forms exist as well. For some people, pets or plants, rather than children, are recipients of nurturing and loving energy.

Some potential areas of talent will be mentioned. It is important to remember that these are only **potential** and only examples. There is not room to cover all possible skills; the examples are merely to spark your thinking. Every person will **not** express creatively in the examples given, but the listed areas of ability are likely places for an individual seeking a creative outlet to begin exploring.

When our needs for appreciation or esteem are not being met properly, we may project certain attributes onto lovers and/or children and meet these qualities through them. Thus, the following section will also include some options around love relationships. When reading about "children," think also in terms of your own, inner child — the playful, spontaneous, naturally creative, expressive and intuitive part which each of us has. Our inner child deserves the same love, respect and support as do outer children.

The Factors

Astrologically, the major association with creativity (of which having children is one form) is **Letter 5**. Letter 5 is our capacity to pour out into the world from our own center, including childbirth. (Letter 4 and Ceres represent the ability to care for the children once they are here.) However, to some extent, **all of fire** is involved with the creative picture. Fire is the initiating element. Fire begins; it symbolizes the first, creative spark. Because the planets are the strongest form, I would tend to include both Mars and Jupiter (but not their houses and signs) as keys to creativity.

Letter 11, concerned with originality and inventiveness, is also very creative. But it can be internal (air). We will be focused on creative **expression** — which implies more fire, so I would include the planet Uranus only. Thus, the keys to creativity in a pure sense would be **Mars, Jupiter, Uranus** and all forms of **Letter 5** (Sun, Leo, 5th house).

Where children are concerned, we must bring in Letter 4 (involved with caretaking) plus the 11th house — a key to other people's children, stepchildren and foster children. (Since signs are the weakest form of the alphabet, I would include Uranus and the 11th house as keys to alternate ways of being a parent — but not Aquarius.) So we must include all forms of **Letters 4 and 5 plus Uranus and the 11th house for children**.

This section will combine children and other forms of creativity in the interpretations, but you can separate them in your own work.[1]

This means we include the following factors for creativity [with additional factors for children in brackets]. For children, use the entire list of factors.

---

1. If you prefer **not** to search for repeated themes yourself, you can order the "PP BOOK" option from Astro Computing Services (PO Box 16430, San Diego, Ca 92116), which allows you to use this book to make complete, synthesizing delineations of horoscopes without figuring out which themes are emphasized.

Available for $3.00 each, the "PP BOOK" report calculates the emphasis on all the letters of the alphabet, themes and aspects in each horoscope for which you provide the data. The report lists each significant focus (e.g., "There is a Letter 3 theme in "Children and Creativity," and gives the appropriate page numbers for you to read in this book ("See pages 262-263 in the *Complete Horoscope Interpretation* book.")

The computer will not **always** arrive at the same results as you might, as certain steps are ambiguous (e g., how much weight to give a planet making a conjunction, based on the orb). However, the majority of the time, the computer answers will concur with those derived from use of the worksheets — or the recommended quick scan of a horoscope. Thus it provides an excellent teaching tool.

The "PP BOOK" does **not** provide a listing of **each any every** astrological factor making up the significant themes. For that, you would order "PP WEIGHTS" (discussed in next footnote).

GROUP I

Any conjunctions to the Sun, Mars, Jupiter or Uranus
Any conjunctions to the Moon or Ceres [children]
Any conjunctions to the ruler of the 5th cusp
Any conjunctions to the ruler of the 4th or 11th cusps [children]
Any conjunctions to the ruler of any occupied signs in the 5th house (other than the sign on the cusp)
Any conjunctions to the rulers of any occupied signs in the 4th or 11th houses (other than the signs on the cusps) [children]
Any conjunctions to the ruler of other signs in the 5th house
Any conjunctions to the rulers of other signs in the 4th or 11th house [children]

GROUP II

Any planets occupying the 5th houses
Any planets occupying the 4th or 11th houses [children]
Any planets occupying the 6th house within two degrees of the 5th cusp
Any planets occupying the 3rd house within two degrees of the 4th cusp [children]
Any planets occupying the 10th or 12th houses within two degrees of the 11th cusp [children]

GROUP III

Parallels to the Sun, Mars, Jupiter, Uranus or rulers of the 5th
Parallels to the Moon, Ceres or rulers of the 4th or 11th [children]
Placement of the Sun, Mars, Jupiter and Uranus by house
Placement of the Moon and Ceres by house [children]
Placement of ruler of the 5th cusp by house
Placement of the rulers of the 4th and 11th cusps by house [children]
Placement of ruler(s) of other signs in the 5th by house
Placement of rulers of other signs in the 4th and 11th by house [children]
House(s) ruled by any planets occupying the 5th house
House(s) ruled by any planets occupying the 4th or 11th houses [children]
Planets occupying Leo
Planets occupying Cancer [children]

GROUP IV

Sign placement of the Sun, Mars, Jupiter and Uranus
Sign placement of the Moon and Ceres [children]
Sign placement of the ruler of the 5th cusp
Sign placement of the rulers of the 4th and 11th cusps [children]
Sign placement of ruler(s) of other signs in the 5th house
Sign placement of rulers of other signs in the 4th and 11th houses [children]
Signs occupied by planets in the 5th
Signs occupied by planets in the 4th and 11th [children]
Houses with Leo on the cusp

Houses with Cancer on the cusp [children]
Houses occupied by planets in Leo
Houses occupied by planets in Cancer [children]

Factors appear in their approximate order of importance, weighting planets, houses and then signs. If you want to use exact figures, a suggested weighting scale is given in the appendix — with worksheets for children, creativity and the other various life areas.[2]

A SHORT CUT
For quickness and ease of use, especially for people just learning to use the alphabet, I suggest focusing first on Groups I and II.

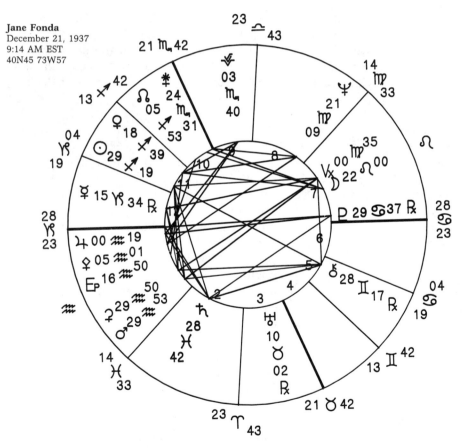

Jane Fonda
December 21, 1937
9:14 AM EST
40N45 73W57

2. You can also obtain a listing of **all** the astrological factors which compose those letters of the Zip Code determined to be significant in a horoscope. This makes an excellent teaching tool and a valuable resource to check yourself against when practicing with the Zip Code.

Astro Computing Services, PO Box 16430, San Diego, CA 92116, has calculated 28,000 horoscopes (footnote continued on next page)

If any letter of the alphabet is represented once in Groups I and II, consider it as probably significant. (If a letter is represented twice in Groups I and II, it is definitely significant.) For example, Jane Fonda's Ceres closely conjuncts her Mars and is in the 1st house, so we would suspect a Letter 1 theme might be important in regard to children.

Once you are comfortable with the factors in Groups I and II, go on to include Groups III and IV. Check to see if factors in Groups III or IV repeat any letters appearing once in Group I or II. In Ms. Fonda's case, the placement of Jupiter in the 1st house (1) repeats a Letter 1 theme for creativity. (Since Jupiter rules the 11th cusp, we count it twice.) The Letter 1 themes points to strong creative needs as a basic part of the identity, which can be expressed through having children. However, with the freedom needs symbolized by Letter 1, the individual may delay having children — or choose to express creatively in other ways. In Ms. Fonda's case, she had her first child at age 30.

You can also examine Groups III and IV for any letters of the alphabet which repeat several times. For example: Cancer is on the Descendant (7), Cancer is occupied in the 7th house (7), Leo is occupied in the 7th house (7), the 5th house Cancer is ruled by the Moon in the 7th (7) and the 11th house Sun rules the 7th (7). This supports the Letter 7 theme suggested by Jupiter conjunct Pallas (7) plus an 11th house Venus (2 or 7) and the Sun parallel Venus (2 or 7).

Ms. Fonda seems to communicate easily with her children. Her attitude is equalitarian (7) and they may enjoy a sense of partnership (7) with her. The Letter 7 theme suggests aesthetic interests and/or beauty could carry on in the children as well. Often, with Letter 7 involved, children stay in touch with parents and have lots of contact and interaction, even in adulthood. The ongoing relationship (7) is important. Of course, the Letter 7 theme in terms of creativity also indicates Ms. Fonda has talent involving aesthetics, beauty and appearance (7) or relating to people (including politicians). Much natural charisma and charm is likely.

---

2. (continued from previous page)
and established averages and standard deviations for the scores of each letter of the astrological alphabet, each theme, and the conflict and harmony aspects to each life area.

Astro's report, called "PP WEIGHTS," will list those letters of the astrological alphabet which are one standard deviation or more above the mean — and list **all** the astrological factors which point to each significant letter of the alphabet. These weightings will also compare each individual's score on the various themes (e.g., risk-taking, artistic) to the means and standard deviations to determine which themes are significant.

Averages are established for aspects as well in order to note conflict or harmony in the different life areas.

The results obtained by Astro's "PP WEIGHTS" will not **always** coincide with those you determine by a quick scan and intuitive judgment, or by use of the worksheets. Certain of the steps (e.g., how much to weight a planet based on orb) are ambiguous, so different results can occur. However, most of the time, Astro's answers will confirm those you could obtain in working with the Zip Code. Furthermore, the **complete** listing of relevant factors is an excellent teaching tool.

Ask for "PP Weights." The price, as of December 1985 is $5.00

Themes

Themes can be ascertained by two methods. One approach is to examine **only** those letters judged to be significant by the above procedures, and determine what themes can be created by combining those letters. In the case of Ms. Fonda, Letters 5 and 7 come through strongly for children and creativity, with a lesser focus on 11, 3, 9 and 1. This suggests a possible air (3, 7, 11) or fire (1, 5, 9) focus.

A second approach to spotting themes is to examine **all** the letters, deciding which combinations of letters have above average scores. You will need to do some rough arithmetic here, or get an intuitive impression. If a theme involves six (out of twelve) letters of the astrological alphabet, you would expect it to have about 1/2 of the total score. So, if the amount for those letters seems appreciably more than 1/2 of the total, count that as a theme — and read the appropriate section. The theme for "Mind/Communication" involves letters 3, 6, 7, 9, 11 and 12, so we would expect them to be about 1/2 of the total. If these scores are appreciably higher (and most of them are), we can suspect a mind/communication theme for Jane Fonda in the area of children and creativity.

This is reflected in Ms. Fonda's current concern with education (her latest focus along with her politician-husband, Tom Hayden). In a 1986 interview, Jane Fonda emphasized the importance of keeping our educational system top-notch, so our children can compete in any markets in the world and understand all areas. Since she is strongly identified with the role of thinker and communicator, it is natural for Ms. Fonda to emphasize intellectual skills in her children and others. Mental development is a key issue for her with children.

When searching for themes, give additional weighting to like planets in aspect to one another. For example, Ms. Fonda also has a theme of "closeness" (Letter 4, 5, 7 and 8) in terms of children and creativity. The closeness planets are the Moon, the Sun, Venus (as ruler of Libra), Pallas, Juno and Pluto. Aspects between them emphasize the theme of emotional attachments and caring. (Ms. Fonda has the Sun parallel Venus, Sun quincunx Pluto, Sun contra-parallel Pluto, Venus octile Pallas, Pluto widely opposite Pallas and Pluto widely trine Juno.) Also give extra weight to like houses and like signs. The Sun, Pluto, Pallas, Juno or Venus occupying the 4th, 5th, 7th or 8th house, or in Cancer, Leo, Libra or Scorpio would give extra weight to the theme of closeness. In the case of Ms. Fonda, the Moon is in the 7th and in Leo, Pluto is in the 7th and in Cancer and Juno is in Scorpio. Being a good mother, being available to her children and sharing warm, caring feelings is a priority for her. Despite a busy life and demanding schedules, she maintains close family connections.

Aspects

Quickly scan all aspects other than conjunctions or parallels, grouping them according to harmony (sextile, trine, semi-sextile) and conflict (octile, tri-octile,

square, opposition and quincunx). In considering each aspect, weight the nature of the planet most heavily, followed by the house and the sign. Count the nature of the house ruled by the planet (its sign on the cusp) as well as the house occupied by that planet. For example, the Sun is one creative factor. In Ms. Fonda's chart, the Sun makes the following **close** harmony aspects:
• sextile Mars (1) in the 1st (1) in Aquarius (11); Mars rules 3rd (3)
• semisextile Jupiter (9) in the 1st (1) in Aquarius (11); Jupiter rules 11th (11)
• semisextile the Ascendant (1) in Capricorn (10)
• sextile Ceres (6) in the 1st (1) in Aquarius (11)

The Sun makes the following **close** conflict aspects:
• square Saturn (10) in the 2nd (2) in Pisces (12); Saturn rules 12th and 1st (12)(1)
• quincunx Pluto (8) in the 7th (7) in Cancer (4); Pluto rules 10th (10)
• opposite Chiron (9) in the 5th (5) in Gemini (3)

After examining the aspects to all the creative factors, make an intuitive judgments as to whether any letters of the alphabet have lots of conflict to them or have quite a bit of harmony. If you feel any group of aspects has an emphasis on one or more letters of the alphabet, read the appropriate interpretation. In Ms. Fonda's case, for example, we might suspect that harmony to Letter 11 could end up significant. This highlights her originality, suggesting she can easily be creative in a unique manner. Her freedom side blends well with her creative needs. Personal creativity could affect and be affected positively by group endeavors, humanitarian causes and progressive ideals. Being friends with her children may come easily. Her children may support her individualistic rebellious side and her originality may enhance her relationships with her kids.

Interpretations: Children and Creativity

ALPHABET THEMES

Letter 1: Flair

There is often an instinctive sense of showmanship, a natural flair for dramatics. Talent for films, charades or other performing arenas is likely. Public relations, promotion, advertising or sales may be areas of talent, with a flair for having an emotional impact on other people. A feeling for fire may be present with affinity for metal etching, woodburning or glassblowing. Projects that can be finished quickly are usually preferred. Energetic, active dancing can be an outlet, including aerobics. Risky businesses or pleasures may appeal, as the fire need for excitement is high. Or, the thrills may be sought through torrid love affairs which burn out as quickly as they began. A basic part of the identity is the need to expand, to do more than before.

Because there is often a desire to be creative on your own terms and in your own ways, you might delay having children, not wanting your freedom to be curtailed. Or, if your needs for activity, excitement and independence are projected, lovers and children are the likely people to act out the drives we deny within ourselves. Possibilities can include people who are **too** free and easy, too eager to do their own thing and go their own way. We may see our children as rebellious, acting-out kids (as they overdo the assertion we deny within ourselves). We may be attracted to exciting, dramatic individuals, who provide the vitality and aliveness which we seek. The child within us is fun-loving and spontaneous. The more we accept him/her, the more we can feel comfortable and have positive relationships with our own children. The less comfortable we are with our inner child, the less easy to accept similar qualities in our actual children.

If these themes are integrated, parents and children often play very well together. Both can be spontaneous, dramatic, magnetic and joyful individuals. Creative acts which gain one the center stage are particularly likely, such as the performing artist. Love relationships are usually very important.

Letter 2: Gusto

Creativity is experienced as a source of pleasure or perhaps revenue. This can range from the artist who makes a living through creative acts (or the gambler, speculator, investor, risk-taker, who expands on what was to create what can be). It can include the hedonist who values more and more of physical pleasures and possessions. The orientation is more toward security and safety than major risks, however. The satisfactions in life are sought through comfort, indulgence and ease. With your natural sensuality, the tactile involvements of sculpture, pottery, fabrics or even making teddy bears could appeal. Music (singing and playing), gardening and cooking are other possible forums for creative expression.

In relationships with children, there can be too much comfort, with the danger of spoiling the child. If the pleasure is shared equally, there is lots of affection between parents and children, with a mutually accepting relationship.

If the above is projected, lovers and/or children may overdo stability, predictability, stubbornness, materialism, desire for ease, laziness or self-indulgence. We may see them as set in their ways, rigid, self-centered or boring and routine.

If these themes are integrated, there is much pleasure, love and affection shared. Physical appetites may be a focus in the relationship (enjoying eating, drinking together) and touch is often an important way of communicating. The people involved know they can depend on one another to be there when needed.

Letter 3: A Scintillating Mind

Pride is taken in the mind, especially in the ability to think and to speak. This can even go overboard into "showing off" with language — whether with multisyllabic words, puns, sharing founts of knowledge, etc. Such individuals are seeking recognition through their mental prowess. Sales and promotional abilities are likely to be marked with a flair for emotional use of language.

Finger dexterity may be quite marked, with skills for puppetry, quick sketches or caricatures, magic shows, card tricks or other nimble activities. Communication arenas (broadcasting, public speaking, disc jockeying, news reporting, photojournalism, neighborhood grapevine, informal or formal teaching) may appeal to you.

Children tend to be verbal and often quite bright. Communication is usually important in the family. If these qualities are projected, the parent may experience offspring as excessively detached, flighty, curious, scattered or superficial. If shared, collecting information may be one form of family fun. Mental games are often a form of recreation.

The creative zest is easily expressed through language and the mind. This can range from the witty professor, the quick-witted salesperson, the skilled comedian, the facile interpreter. Word play appeals.

Letter 4: Love

You are capable of tremendous warmth and emotional attachment. Your home, family and domestic scene may be sources of pride and self-esteem. Usually a devoted and loving parent, you feel strongly about those closest to you and express yourself largely through nurturing activities. This can include a strong emotional connection to pets and/or plants in addition to (or instead of) your own family. Vocations such as parenting, midwifery, coaching may appeal. You tend to seek recognition and appreciation through caretaking activities, dependency and/or nurturance.

A feeling for water may be present with an affinity for water ballet, synchronized swimming, collecting sea shells, painting with water colors or breeding tropical fish. Creative nurturance may be expressed through cooking, doll-making, knitting, sewing, crocheting and maintaining a "homey" atmosphere.

You have an instinctive connection to the child within yourself and other adults; this can lead to a strong, loving bond to other people, an ability to laugh and play together, a natural expressiveness. You are seeking to synthesize your public and private sides — the need for the limelight with your need for a nest, a place to retreat from the world.

If you are comfortable with both your protective and your vulnerable sides, you are likely to be a very supportive parent, with a strong intuitive understanding of your children. There may very well be a psychic connection and an ability to understand one another on a nonverbal level. If you are feeling ambivalent and conflicted about your emotional needs, your children will reflect that inner struggle. You could be overly protective and smother your children with your omnipresent concern. You could look to your children to provide you with security, reassurance, emotional support and the nurturance you want in life.

Unfinished business with your own mother might be faced through your children. This can include feeling your own mother is like a child, requiring your care. It can include seeing your mother as childlike — spontaneous, fun-loving, dramatic and possibly self-centered, demanding, needy. It can include having children whom you try to mother unconditionally, giving them all the loving support you **wish** you had gotten from your own mother. It can include looking to your children to provide the emotional reassurance and protection that you feel was missing in your early life.

The children are likely to be very sensitive, emotional and involved with issues of nurturance and dependency. The more balanced you are — able to both give and receive emotional support — the more balanced the children are likely to be.

Where children are not a part of the picture, you need an outlet for some of the warmth and caring in your nature. Animals are one possibility, or supportive activities, where you "do for" others.

Letter 5: Excitement

Dramatic flair and an instinctive stage presence are likely. Public recognition, approval and admiration are important. You seek the limelight in some fashion. The urge to expand yourself into life in some way is strong. An instinctive risk-taker, you seek to pour out into the world and receive favorable feedback — some kind of rewarding response. One variation is gambling and speculating (including on the Stock Market) — investing money, hoping for a bigger return. Another possibility is pouring yourself into love relationships and/or children, hoping they will love you in return and make you proud of them. Entertainment fields (acting, directing, filmmaking or editing, circus performing or directing charades), public relations and promotional activities may help satisfy your need to have an impact, to persuade and sway people with your charisma.

A very strong love bond with children is quite possible. Children may be seen as a joyful expression of your creativity and a source of fun. Playing together is likely, enjoying spontaneous, fun, expressive pastimes. You could create new games together. You are likely to take your children's actions as a reflection on yourself and must beware of putting your ego on the line as a result of their actions. As much as you may love them, as much as they may mirror some of your own nature, they are their own people.

If you are uncomfortable with your need for response from others (whether love, money, admiration, approval, etc.), you are likely to have children dealing with the same issue. One possibility is constant power struggles over who gets to be the star, each attempting to upstage the other. Another potential is self-centered, egotistical children who overdo the need for attention from others (thus pointing to your tendency to underdo this side of life). Or, your children might feel overwhelmed by your natural magnetism and extroversion and retreat into a wallflower role, feeling they cannot compete with you for applause. The issues revolve around pride (and shame), attention (and being ignored), self-esteem (and lack of it). Keeping a healthy outlet for both your creativity — need to shine and be proud of yourself — as well as for the creativity of your children leaves room for everyone to grow, to do more than they have done in the past.

Letter 6: Doing it RIGHT

Being efficient and productive is a source of pride for you. You appreciate feedback on what a good job you have done. For you, realism and practicality are noteworthy qualities. You seek recognition for your accomplishments. Whether or not you are paid for your efforts, you would like acknowledgment of your tasks and functions. Whatever you feel your contribution is, you strive to make it carefully and to perform it as well as possible.

Your precision and eye for detail could express in calligraphy, drafting, architecture and design, anatomical sketches or medical illustrations. Often skilled mechanically or with handicrafts, you could make models, miniatures, sew, quilt or have ability in numerous crafts. Writing is another possible talent.

Besides needing strokes around your work, you may seek recognition for an efficient body in terms of health. (Or, you may try for the limelight by focusing on your **ill** health and your **in**efficient bodily functioning.)

Your attitude toward parenting is practical and goal-oriented. You want to do it right and do it well. In order to accomplish this, you often focus on the existing flaws — so that you can improve the situation. If carried too far, this critical attitude can be a problem. You might be too judgmental — of yourself as a parent or of the children as children. Remember that everyone involved is human and makes mistakes! Too much of an orientation toward performance will kill spontaneity and the fun in a relationship.

This combination can also show a family business — literally working with the kids. Or, careers involving other people's children (coaching, nanny, governess, teacher, housekeeper, recreation director, etc.) are possible. The work may deal directly with children or simply require that childlike magnetism, spontaneity and joy which is helpful in sales, promotion, advertising and entertainment.

One danger to guard against is turning your critical eye against your creative side. Whether you are expressing through love, sexuality, persuading others, gambling or other forms of dramatic outpouring, nothing dampens enthusiasm more than a judgmental attitude, a focus on performance. Some parts of life are meant to be unrehearsed. Fun is usually best the first time around!

Letter 7: People Play

Other people are a potential source of joy. Your dramatic instincts and natural charisma emerge especially in close relationships. Some of the zest and enthusiasm could go into intense competition, a desire to play one-up to those around you. But a cooperative sharing of the stage, a willingness to take turns being important, is also quite possible. Often, there is a strong feeling for beauty and aesthetic talent (especially in the performing arts) is quite likely.

With an instinct for balance and harmony, you could be drawn to music (singing, playing, composing). Your visual sense may be quite developed, with talent for decorating, photography, fashion design, painting, architecture, flower arranging and color analysis. Your personal appearance may be a source of pride (or shame) to you with style a concern. Ego needs are partly met through the way you look. Relationships are generally very important. Love is a major focus.

Where children are involved, the theme revolves around equality and sharing. This can indicate a very comfortable, easygoing, harmonious relationship where you are a relaxed, accepting and affectionate parent and the children respond in kind. The peer relationship could also be played out through competition, however. Communication is usually important. Shared aesthetic interests can be a strong bond between you and your children — or simply a mutual desire for harmony. Be sure a need for pleasant interactions does not lead to avoiding issues that must be faced. The children could be very attractive physically, artistically talented and/or charming, pleasant, compatible.

This can be a highly entertaining combination — the life of the party on occasion. You have a talent for getting an emotional response from others. People may not always like you, but they rarely ignore you. You know how to make an impact. If you are frustrated and conflicted about your need to shine, you are likely to attract associates who will overdo that part of life for you — too dynamic, too exciting, too self-oriented, too hyper, too much into laughing, loving and playing all the time. The liveliness and funlovingness of your nature needs a constructive, enjoyable outlet.

Letter 8: Self-Control

You pride yourself on your ability to control your own life (or feel inadequate due to a loss of control). The theme revolves around power. You have tremendous potential, strength, drive and intensity. With you, extremes are easy. Fiercely emotional, you often operate from an all-or-nothing framework. Capable of the deepest commitment and love to another human, you can also ruthlessly cut yourself out of any relationship if you feel it is over. (If you are not in touch with your own strength and power, you may experience other people as doing the cutting off, or feel you have to withdraw to protect yourself.)

You are likely to see your area of soul growth as involving depth understanding and mastery. This can range from psychotherapy, to occult studies, to researching hidden areas, to any kind of investigation which takes you beneath the surface of the subject. But the end goal is an intuitive understanding of the buried essences of your own soul. Inner searching may lead you to meditative music, the study of magic, Rolfing, psychodrama or the urge to walk on fire in your pursuit of self-mastery. Your natural sensuality could be channeled into massage, chiropractic or other healing arts.

To fully explore your depths, you need another person — a mate — with whom to interact. For you, love relationships are intense; nothing lighthearted and superficial will do. All or nothing at all is very much your attitude.

This same emotional fervor exists where children are concerned. You are deeply connected to any children, with a strong, nonverbal bond between you. Tuned into one another, you can generate tremendous love (and tremendous hate) between you. Rarely is the relationship tepid. Because you are learning how to use your power wisely, you are likely to have children facing that same issue. Together, you will learn to sidestep power struggles with each other and turn the power inward for self-mastery and self-control. But even here, both you and the children must avoid the extreme of overcontrol — the ascetic self-denial and inhibition that carries the desire for mastery too far. Similarly power over others (whether through confrontation and direct power plays or through emotional blackmail and manipulation) must be eschewed and power over self pursued.

On the highest levels, you experience your children as co-therapists, as you stimulate one another to probe your darkest recesses, look even where you would rather not and face your own Shadow, making room in life for all your potentials. Constant self-transformation and transfiguration can be a source of incredible joy in your life.

Letter 9: Up, Up and Away!

Fun and games time! Restless and ready to move, this is a combination eager to express. Pride and self-esteem are tied to the mental world, especially to the search for the truth. Optimism is often high and there tends to be a feeling of openness for something more. The sense is one of expansiveness. Grandiose ideas and projects may appeal as you want to do things in a **big** way! Each project may beget a new project, in an endless spiral of more and more activity. You could become carried away with your enthusiasms and get overextended.

Verbal skills are quite possible and this is a natural teacher/preacher combination with the desire to seek the limelight through conveying truth, ideals, inspiration, philosophy, religion, to other people. You might look to education (through degrees), travel, spiritual quests or religious principles for a sense of self-esteem and importance. This blend tends to go overboard on faith and may speculate too much too fast, trusting that all will work out in the end. The natural optimism and self-confidence in the area of risk-taking and self-expression could be overdone, even to the point of physical danger if excessive. Promotion comes naturally and humor could express in comedy acts or cartooning. Writing talent is likely and journalism may also appeal.

Where children are concerned, issues involve ideals, ideas and our quest for meaning in life. One variation is the individual who makes children into an ultimate value. In such a case, if one is good, more is better and the person may have lots of children. Another variation is the person who wants to be the perfect parent of perfect children in a perfect world and chooses **not** to have children if that ultimate vision is impossible. Parents may expect more than is humanly possible of children; children of parents; or parents of themselves. Mutual idealization can occur, with the parent feeling the children truly are perfect and the children returning the favor to the parent. Mutual disappointment can also happen when people discover the shortcomings of each other and their idol falls off his/her pedestal. Sharing the drive for something higher allows parents and children to pursue the truth together, whether in studies, travel, religious or spiritual pursuits, or simply having a lot of great parties. The focus is on a shared quest for whatever the people define as the ultimate, the most important, the most vital in their lives — that which provides meaning.

Letter 10: Success Equals Power

Self-esteem is measured through success and achievements in the outer world. Pride is based on accomplishments and handling responsibilities. Approval and admiration are often sought through a career and ambitions may be high. Since self-worth is being based on performance, there is the danger that you may become self-critical and feel inadequate when you judge your performance as below standard. Conversely, when you achieve successes, you are likely to feel great joy. Success breeds more success and you could end up glorying in power and reaching for the heights. Avoid both extremes: self-critical denials and put-downs as well as overreach and excessive ambition. You usually feel a strong accountability for your actions. You are quite prepared to accept the credit and the blame.

As well as natural talent for business, you can be creative in areas requiring careful attention to structure: sculpting, woodworking, glassblowing, working with crystals or building doll houses (and construction in general). You enjoy having tangible output from your creativity.

Issues with children revolve around duty, responsibility, hard work and realism. Your attitude toward parenting tends to be serious, dedicated, concerned about doing it right. This can be channeled into a critical, judgmental attitude — toward yourself as a parent or toward the children. A performance orientation can be helpful in terms of a responsible attitude, but don't overdo it. One extreme is the parent who is overly responsible, tending to carry the world on his/her back. Such a parent may even have children with special problems, which further encourage the taking up of their burdens.

A challenge with this combination is to be **clear** about who ought to do what in the relationship. A parent who does **too much** for the children ends up with spoiled children who do not know their own strength since Mommy or Daddy did everything for them. A parent who demands heavy responsibilities from children before they are capable of handling them ends up with scared, inadequate children who feel no matter what they've done, it is not enough — children who expect to fail.

This blend is also common in family businesses or where the work involves the children. Channeling the work (critical) attitude into shared tasks is usually more comfortable than having it affect the emotional side of relationships.

Issues with father (revolving around the handling of power, responsibility, control and authority) are likely to be faced again through children. If you have lots of unresolved feelings about your father, you may meet him again — in a sense — through one of your children. The challenge is to be able to set realistic limits for your children, providing them with a firm foundation of rules without being restrictive, and encouraging them to develop their own capacities to be strong, powerful and effective in the outer world.

Letter 11: Unique and Irreplaceable

You pride yourself on being different in some way. Your uniqueness is a form of asserting individuality and expressing your own, special essence. At times, you may even engage in behavior which is shocking to other people as a way to flaunt your unconventionality, or a means of impressing upon them that you **are** yourself and not anyone else. If carried too far, acts of rebellion, anarchy and chaos may appeal. In moderate form, you can be highly creative, innovative and expressive, open to exploring new options. Risk-taking comes naturally, although much of it may occur mainly in the mind. Often future-oriented and progressive, you glory in breaking old barriers and setting new records.

Your creative efforts will be unique and individualistic. You may be drawn to avant garde music or art, or simply your very own, personal taste. Telecommunications, radio and TV are possible attractions, along with laser art, holography or other artistic uses of new technology. Coming from your own center is vital.

Your relationships to children include issues around freedom, eccentricity and experimentation. Sometimes people with this combination choose not to have children — as they fear a family would curtail their personal freedom. Those who do have children usually encourage the children to be independent, thus gaining much liberty for themselves. Often, children are treated as friends and peers with much communication, tolerance, openness and mutual acceptance. Parents who are still torn between the parental role and a need for personal freedom may experience that ambivalence through their kids. Parents who overdo the need for family closeness will feel their children are rebellious, erratic, too independent, too detached, too aloof. The children may engage in shocking activities. Parents who overdo the need for independence will believe their children are tying them down, hemming them in, preventing them from being themselves. In the relationship, both parties must make room for personal self-expression and independent action as well as loving and being loved. Both the mind and the heart need an outlet. Neither cool, detached intellect nor passionate, intense yearning stands alone.

Letter 12: Magic!

Tremendous magnetism and stage presence are likely. Natural dramatic talent is combined with the ability to cast an illusion, to persuade people to see what you wish them to see. Such skills mark the best actors and actresses — and the most dramatic martyrs! Abilities exist for any entertaining, persuasive, selling field. Self-expression may be tied to the role of artist, savior or victim. Being a victim can be a major production. But the creative, inspired artist is equally likely. And, the charismatic, helpful healer is another potential. The urge is to do more in reaching toward the heights in life. The spiritual calls for attention. The personal ego seeks to merge with the Infinite, to find ultimate Oneness (through utopian idealism, artistic expression or escapist paths).

Specific skills may include dancing, music (singing, dancing, composing), makeup, costume design, magic shows, animation, filmmaking and much more. Almost any artistic expression is possible with this combination.

In terms of children, issues revolve around the handling of idealism, the urge for infinite love and beauty. This can indicate a mutual admiration society, where parents and children idolize and idealize one another. If overdone, mutual disillusionment is a possibility. Sharing aesthetic pursuits, spiritual quests, religious ideals, utopian dreams are other potentials. If the urge to play God is carried too far, or one person puts another into the position of playing God, savior/victim relationships are possible. These usually end in discomfort when either the savior tires of doing all the work or the victim tires of having none of the power. (But unless each has learned to channel that search for the Infinite into a reasonable area, the victim will simply attract a new savior and the savior a new victim.) Parents and children both need a sense of inspiration and uplifting in their lives — but neither should expect the other to provide that Infinite experience. Looking for God in nature, spiritual quests, religious experiences, mysticism or other unlimited avenues is more ultimately satisfying than trying to play God for someone else or expecting another person to be more than human.

ALPHABET COMBINATIONS BY TWOS
Refer to Chapter 8 (Relationships) and read the appropriate **Combinations by Two** (pages 189-197) in terms of children and lovers rather than partners.

POLARITIES

1-7: ♂-♀ or ⚳ or ⚴, ♈-♎, 1st-7th houses

Polarities are important in your love relationships. You have a need for balance and strive to keep things equal. This can lead to accommodating too much or being ultracompetitive in an effort to "even the score." A passion for fair play can be helpful; just use it wisely. You find it easy to see the opposite point of view.

Your creative talents could go into ideas, relationships or straight into action. Sometimes there is grace and skill in physical movement with this combination — such as dancing, skiing, skating, water ballet, etc. You are learning to balance personal preferences in creativity with what other people like and admire.

Assertion must be integrated with accommodation, without an overdose of either. You could fall into giving up your power and feeling like a doormat in your love relationships, or fighting to get your power back, or withdrawing from the whole situation. You could attract lovers and/or children who tend to give away their own power. The issues of compromise, competition and dealing with people on a fair, equitable level are central with those you love. If you have trouble reaching an inner harmony, your lovers/children could end up on the opposite end of the seesaw from you: whatever you de-emphasize, they overdo. Share the possibilities for best results.

2-8: ♀-♇, ♉-♏, 2nd-8th houses

Issues of self-indulgence versus self-control are significant in your love relationships. Because you are ambivalent about the degree of self-control you wish to manifest over your own appetites, you tend to get involved with people who are also ambivalent. The focus can vary — on eating, drinking, smoking, making or spending money, or other forms of gratification. However, the issues remain around how much to indulge and how much to control one's appetites.

If you identify too strongly with one end, you are likely to draw in lovers and/or children who will manifest the other end to an extreme. Then you could end up in power struggles or simply nagging each other a lot about drinking less, quitting smoking, dieting or other forms of sensual discipline. Issues with kids and lovers revolve around being able to give, receive and share pleasure comfortably in an intimate context with others. As you achieve an inner balance, equal sharing with your external relationships becomes more comfortable and easier.

Talent in areas involving sensuality (e.g., sculpture, pottery, sewing, fashion, makeup, dancing, music) is quite possible. You have a good capacity for discipline and dedication to back up your appreciation of beauty. Your own taste is very strong and may not always fit other people's styles. Persevering, you are likely to finish projects you start.

3-9: ☿-♃ or ♄, ♊-♐, 3rd-9th houses

Mentally versatile, you could exhibit talent in a number of mental arenas, including — but not limited to — speaking, writing, teaching, advertising, selling and religious or spiritual work. The short-range view and long-range goals are both calling for attention. You need to establish priorities. Make choices between time/energy commitments to immediate gratification and a focus on exchanging ideas and information with the people and questions going on right now versus pursuing goals for the future which could be very meaningful but have little immediate application. Small-scale issues and large-scale ones must be balanced.

Interactions with loved ones are likely to involve a mental focus, with a need for constant learning, information exchange and intellectual stimulation. You could trade roles of teacher and student often.

You are also confronting the pull between your lighthearted, casual side versus your desire for understanding the meaning and significance of life. If you are uncomfortable with this dichotomy, you could attract loved ones to play out one end of the polarity for you. They might overdo either side — the casual, flippant side or the philosophical, questing side. Through your interactions with lovers and/or children, you are learning to make room for both.

4-10: ☽-♄, ♋-♑, 4th-10th houses

In loving and being loved, you are learning to balance unconditional acceptance with a concern for performance. You may feel torn between coming across as a warm, loving, supportive person versus a stern, authority figure with certain expectations and demands. Part of this dilemma is balancing emotional needs with pragmatic, physical (survival) needs. It also means establishing priorities between home and family versus work and career as focuses for your creative efforts. You can give much to both, but need a balance.

As a parent, you could integrate these themes and provide the total support and love needed when your children are very young, converting to more and more of a reality focus as they get older. It is also possible you might overdo either side. Too much focus on doing what is right can lead to criticism, harshness and feelings of inadequacy, failure. Too much taking care of can lead to dependency and the person never knowing his/her own strength if someone else always did it. If you underdo one side, lovers and/or children are likely to overdo it.

A balance of warm, compassionate caring with sensible, realistic assessments helps both you, children and other loved ones cope successfully with life.

(See also the Parental theme.)

5-11: ☉-♅, ♌-♒, 5th-11th houses

You are facing a polarity in your love relationships of heart versus head. You may be torn between thinking and feeling. You can be very rational, objective and detached at times, but you also get caught up in intense, emotional reactions. Somehow, the two must be balanced in your relationships with lovers and/or children and in your creative efforts.

Part of the conflict can also express as a pull between being a unique, independent individualist versus loving and being loved. You may have some original and inventive instincts, yet you want people to like and admire what you do. You need attention, applause and approval from those you care about, yet you also enjoy a sense of aloofness, going your own way, relating to humanity more than close, intimate associations. The passionate lover must be blended with the detached humanitarian.

It is not uncommon with this combination for people to delay long-term love relationships and having children. Often they are ambivalent about giving up their freedom, so put off final commitments.

If you project any end of these conflicts, you will probably attract lovers/children to overdo them. They could be so cool and detached you get turned off — or able to rationalize and intellectualize anything. They could be so emotional, dramatic and inclined to exaggerate situations, that you are wary of listening to their version. With them, you are learning to balance detachment and drama, excitement and intellect, passion and rationality, objective and subjective, head and heart.

6-12: ☿ or ♀ or ♀-♆, ♍-♓, 6th-12th houses

This is a common polarity for artists and craftspeople of all kinds (as well as helpers and healers). The ideal and beautiful is brought down to earth and made real (or we constantly seek more "Heaven on Earth" than is possible). A talent for creating things which are useful as well as attractive is likely.

When it comes to loving, you are striving to integrate a search for the beautiful dream with the nitty-gritty reality of the world. Visions confront practicalities as you figure out how to reach for the stars without falling flat on your face.

When your idealism and pragmatism complement and supplement each other, you work in a disciplined manner to create the best possible relationships with lovers and/or children. You are willing to face facts, but do not get caught up in pickiness. You are seeking an ideal, but do not get lost in the clouds. You could be the most inspired of creative artists as well.

If you are not able to blend these two drives comfortably, you could end up swinging from one extreme to the other: fantasy to critical judgment. Those you love might also manifest either side for you — too concerned with a quest for something infinite or too focused on flaws and what is wrong. The starry-eyed idealism can result in disillusionment in love when we discover the other person is not perfect, or that true love does not always run smoothly. Some people simply keep their relationships on a fantasy level, waiting for that ultimate person who never comes. Others get involved in relationships where one person plays God to the other — trying to save someone from drugs, alcohol or other escapist paths.

But an excess of reality can be just as painful. The person who sees only the bottom line in relationships can be experienced as cold, critical, unloving, judgmental and nit-picking. A disciplined attitude can be helpful, but love requires also some idealism and romanticism to appreciate the other person despite imperfections.

Balancing these two themes in interactions with loved ones gives you the opportunity to make the most of love — having a vision toward which you work effectively, bringing your dreams to earth.

NODES OF THE MOON
The following nodal placements are particularly relevant in the areas of children and creativity.

Across Leo/Aquarius or 5th/11th Houses

There is likely to be a inner push/pull between your urges for freedom and your desire for emotional closeness. You might delay long-term love relationships or having children because you are unsure you want to confine yourself, or fear a threat to your personal liberty. Or, you could become involved with people who already have children, who meet your needs for attachment, but without the same responsibility as starting from scratch with your own. Another option is foster children or caring for needy children of the world in some way. You might also encourage your own children to develop independence, partly to ensure you have an opportunity to pursue your own interests.

If you are still ambivalent about your inner balance between independence and commitment, you are likely to attract lovers and children with the same inner conflict. Then, you could play out opposite ends of the seesaw, until you both learn to balance. One overdoes the freedom side ("I don't need you. Leave me alone to do my thing. I'm off — good-bye.") and the other overdoes the closeness side ("I need you. I care about you. I want to be with you."). Extremes include people who leave or run away (excessive freedom) or people who are clutching and possessive (excessive closeness). Integration allows everyone room to express both sides, in different times and places in life.

This combination can be a highly creative one, with a sense of individuality and uniqueness backed up by the zest to pour out and do something in the world. However, feelings of inadequacy may complicate the issue. It is quite possible you are unduly critical of your creative efforts, judging them more harshly than anyone else. You may hide your light under the proverbial bushel and be afraid to let your natural flair out. Sometimes you create something, only to hide it away or destroy it, because it does not meet your critical standards. Or, you do not trust your own taste, because it is sometimes different than the norm. Fear of measuring up could also inhibit you in the choice of having children or not — and in how you relate to them if you do have children. Allow space in the relationship for everyone to be him/her unique self. Don't pressure yourself or any children with critical judgments or fears of inadequacy.

When balanced, this can be a very joyful, creative, expressive, fun-loving combination, with the ability to optimally blend zest and intellectual analysis, passion and objectivity, expression and observation, intense relationships and casual friendships.

Across Cancer/Capricorn or the 4th/10th Houses

You are probably dealing with some ambivalence between warm, nurturing support versus a practical facing of the facts. On the one hand, you can care very deeply about your family, but you also want to enhance personal responsibility. You may sometimes feel torn between how much you should stress compassion versus competence or emotional support versus self-sufficiency. You are likely to have children facing the same kinds of issues, so you can learn together to share conditional and unconditional love.

Beware the extremes of doing so much for your children that they feel smothered and unable to cope on their own — or expecting so much from them in the way of performance that they feel you only love them for what they can do. Responsibilities need to be shared lest you fall into carrying too much of the load, or unconsciously encouraging your children to take up burdens that seem too heavy for you. Mutual caretaking and dedication to getting the job done works best.

This ambivalence might also express as inner tension between home and family commitments versus work in the outer world. You may feel torn between time and energy demands of the domestic versus the career front. You could experience your job as taking you away from your family or vice versa. Some people manage to combine the two by working from the home (author, homemaker, housekeeper, consultant, astrologer, etc.), having a family business or treating co-workers like family. (It is also possible your own family feels like a "job" which could seem a bit uncomfortable to them.) Some people devote themselves solely to the family for a time, and then solely to their career. Others, juggle both simultaneously. Many options are available. You need both an objective sense of achievement and close, caring involvements with other people. How you choose to create the balance is up to you.

ELEMENT EMPHASIS

Fire
♂, ☉, ♃, ♄, ♈, ♌, ♐, 1st, 5th, 9th houses

Creativity is high and the need for excitement is strong. You can be vibrant, intense, vital and dynamic. An innate optimism pushes you on to try, to dare, to go where others would not. Courage — mental, spiritual and emotional as well as physical — is a theme. Any activity which gives you that feeling of coming alive may appeal. Sexual energy is often high, but other highly exciting forms of recreation and creation are also common. You need to be noticed and are usually in the forefront of any action.

There is an instinctive urge to do more than you have done in the past, with a desire not to repeat yourself. Consequently, you are on an eternal quest for new worlds to conquer. This can range from physical exploits, to emotional, loving highs, to spiritual thrusts toward higher consciousness. The reach is upward and outward for more. The drive is strong; impatience is likely. You are eager to do, to move, to act, to feel, to get the blood rushing through your veins with a new excitement!

If these themes are projected onto children and/or lovers, you will attract people to live out this vitality and drama for you. They may be extremely magnetic types, easily drawing other people to them. They may seem histrionic and exaggerative if they overdo the need for excitement and liveliness. You could experience them as self-centered and demanding, wanting everything on their own terms, if they carry the confidence of the fire to an extreme.

If these themes are shared, you can have a lot of fun with one another, constantly spur each other on to greater and greater exploits, and encourage one another to do more and more. (Just keep a little caution to temper the courage as needed.)

Earth

♀, ☿, ⚳, ⚶, ♄, ♉, ♍, ♑, 2nd, 6th, 10th houses

The zest and enthusiasm in your nature is likely to be channeled into concrete accomplishments. There is a desire to pour out into the world, not just on the emotional level, but also having an impact on the physical plane. This often means great productivity. Excitement comes through achievements in the real world. You seek recognition through **doing**.

Since you tend to judge yourself in terms of what you make a reality, there is some danger of stifling your own creativity through critical assessments. At times you may be too hard on yourself, inclined to reject your efforts, even when other people might value them. Your desire to do things well can set up an inhibition whereby you stop yourself from trying (or put down your attainments) for fear of failure or not measuring up to your internal standards.

If this side of your nature is projected into children and/or lovers you could attract people who are very physically oriented. This could range from individuals you see as excessively materialistic or hedonistic to careful, dedicated, productive people intent on making their mark in the world. If the work attitude is overdone, criticism could be a problem in your love relationships — whether you are judging others or being judged by them. You might see them as simply boring and too predictable in their need to always deal with the "bottom line" (i.e., physical, material reality). Part of the challenge is channeling the need to have an impact — the need to manipulate — into the physical plane and not into the emotional side of love relationships.

If this theme is shared with the people close to you, it is likely you will enjoy doing things together. Working with your own children — formally or informally — is quite possible, or sharing any form of realistic, practical task orientation. You can enjoy the physical, sensual world together and get mutual satisfaction from your successes.

Air

☿, ♀, ⚴, ⚵, ♅, ♊, ♎, ♒, 3rd, 7th, 11th houses

Your creativity is largely channeled into verbal and mental areas. A quick, bright mind is likely and usually you are quite articulate as well. Your facility with words can be helpful in a number of areas, plus you can just be a lot of fun for the people around you. A natural entertainer, you know how to turn a phrase, make people laugh, spark the enthusiasms of those about you. You tend to expect attention and applause as a result of your intellectual abilities.

Mental sports and word games may appeal as forms of recreation and you are likely to seek constant expansion of your intellectual horizons. The use of the mind and communication are important in your love relationships. You need someone with whom you can share the mental realm and especially someone who you feel is an equal. You are likely to want to treat both lovers and children as peers. Authority trips have little appeal where those you love are concerned.

If these issues are projected into children and/or lovers, you may attract people to manifest your intellectual, communicating or detached side. This can range from very bright individuals to garrulous people. Often you will experience an overdose of this issue in your love relationships. If you are out of touch with your own objective capacity, you may feel your loved ones are **too** detached, too cool, aloof and unemotional. Or, they may simply be too talkative or more concerned with intellectual issues than you would like. You could even go so far as to deny your own capacity to think and believe that your children/lovers are much brighter than you.

The key is sharing these themes so that you can easily relate together. Communication often flows fairly easily as you all tend to enjoy sharing and meeting on a peer level. You have the ability to treat your children as partners and friends more than as kids and this can be appreciated by them. Intellectual arguments, mental games, word play and exchange of information can all be rewarding activities between you and your loved ones.

Water
☽, ♇, ♆, ♋, ♏, ♓, 4th, 8th, 12th houses

Your excitement and enthusiasms come through deep emotions and an exploration of the inner world. Your feelings are very intense and you may experience, simultaneously, the urge to "let it all hang out" with the urge to go inside, keep it to yourself and work it out internally. Balancing the need to thrust outward with the drive to probe inward may take a little effort. Your road to center stage or achieving the limelight comes through your deepest emotions and intensity of response.

You can be extremely intuitive and may be drawn to understanding things which are not easily communicated by the conscious, rational mind. Listening to your inner wisdom can be very helpful, but you must be able to distinguish between that inner knowing and pure fantasy. Much of your creativity lies in the nonrational arena, dealing with emotional and spiritual issues more than conscious, logical ones. There is strength on the global, intuitive (right brain) side.

If these themes are projected, you may attract lovers and/or children who are extremely sensitive, inward and deeply emotional. They could overdo the tendency to hold things back and keep feelings inside. They could depend too heavily on intuition over rationality or simply be very easily hurt by the world. Dependency and nurturance would be issues with these individuals and part of the challenge is to be able to care for them (and allow them to care for you when appropriate) without one person ending up carrying more than his/her share of the emotional load in the relationship.

There is the potential of a very deep, nonverbal, psychic connection between you and loved ones. You could know, instinctively, how to tune into one another and at times may even seem to read each other's minds. But this natural empathy can be extremely positive or negative depending on how you handle it. Usually, your love relationships are very intense. Rarely are they lukewarm. But the potential of great rewards is present. You have much warmth and caring to share.

Fire-Earth

♂, ☉, ♃, ⚷, ♈, ♌, ♐, 1st, 5th, 9th houses &
♀, ☿, ⚳, ⚶, ♄, ♉, ♍, ♑, 2nd, 6th, 10th houses

You have the capacity to know what you want and pursue it unswervingly. Drive plus dedication can accomplish a tremendous amount and you have both. Although emotional responses are important to you and you need feedback and appreciation, you will not be content with feelings alone. You want some solid achievements to look to and feel proud of. Your creativity lies in having an impact on the world and you strive to reach the heights.

You can turn your work into play because you enjoy accomplishment so much. Just be sure that the work attitude doesn't disturb times when you really want to play. Critical judgment is rarely helpful when you are making love or involved in pleasant recreation.

If the above themes are projected, you may experience children and/or lovers as ambitious, driven personalities. You may feel overwhelmed by their need to be important, to make their mark in the world. Their ability to single-mindedly focus on getting the job done could bother you. Learning to share that desire for effectiveness can be very helpful. Then you can work together, to create an end result desired by all.

Fire-Air

♂, ☉, ♃, ⚷, ♈, ♌, ♐, 1st, 5th, 9th houses &
☿, ♀, ⚴, ⚵, ♅, ♊, ♎, ♒, 3rd, 7th, 11th houses

Lighthearted and fun-loving, you know how to love life and can help other people appreciate its pleasures as well. An instinctive entertainer, you usually enjoy communication, amusement and interaction with other people. Your creative zest often shows in quickness of wit and mental skills. Facile, flexible, optimistic and able to weigh a number of options, you can get center stage through your use of the mind.

If you unconsciously seek other people to express this side of your nature, you are likely to experience your lovers and/or children as flighty, erratic, restless, foolishly optimistic and excessively concerned with having a good time. You may decry their lack of seriousness or condemn their sense of humor. Laughing and loving together is your best bet. Share the fun! Kick back and relax; you can truly enjoy it.

Fire-Water
♂, ☉, ♃, ⚷, ♈, ♌, ♐, 1st, 5th, 9th houses &
☽, ♇, ♆, ♋, ♏, ♓, 4th, 8th, 12th houses

Intense and emotional, your deepest feelings are tied up with your need to achieve recognition and approval. Needing a response and feedback from others, you may feel very vulnerable having to risk the loss of other people's appreciation. Your ego needs to be fed, but it can seem very scary to lay it on the line. You may even vacillate between overconfidence and tremendous fear and anxiety. You may swing from great faith in your abilities and talents to severe doubts.

People tend to have strong reactions to you; rarely are they neutral. Because your feelings run so deeply and strongly, you tend to elicit intense responses from others. One of your skills is getting people emotionally involved. But if you fear your own emotions, this can occur in a manipulative manner rather than through direct routes.

If you project your need for intensity, sensitivity, and a deep, emotional connection, you may draw in people who are overdoing that side of life. Lovers and/or children may be volatile, have incredible mood swings, be prone to strong emotional reactions (and consequently illogical at times), and yet be capable of tremendous warmth and love. Mutual caring is the best answer — each of you supporting and nurturing the other but also able to receive from the other person so that a sense of equality is maintained. You can feed each other's excitement, whether sexual, emotional, spiritual, etc., and help one another find the maximum satisfaction possible. This can be the most deeply caring of all combinations.

Earth-Air
♀, ☿, ?, ⚸, ♄, ♂, ♍, ♑, 2nd, 6th, 10th houses &
☿, ♀, ⚥, ⚹, ♅, ♊, ♎, ♒, 3rd, 7th, 11th houses

You need appreciation for your logic and practicality. Your ability to add things up and get the right answer is an asset that cries for recognition. A source of self-esteem for you is through productive efforts and sensible plans. You can be admired for your ability to be objective and detached rather than getting caught up in an emotional morass.

If these qualities are manifested through your children (and/or lovers), they may strike you as excessively cool, aloof and uncaring. You may yearn for a more emotional response for them and feel frustrated with their focus on the practicalities of life. They may come across more like scientists running an experiment than loved ones at times.

If these attributes are shared, both you and those you love can enjoy the world of the mind and senses. Facing facts can be helpful in getting what you want out of the world and detachment helps to balance emotion. You can enjoy thinking, communicating, working and being effective together. You can treat one another as equal contributors in the world.

Earth-Water

♀, ☿, ⚳, ⚵, ♄, ♉, ♍, ♑, 2nd, 6th, 10th houses &
☽, ♇, ♆, ♋, ♏, ♓, 4th, 8th, 12th houses

You may take pride in being solid and responsible. Love might be linked to safety. If you are feeling insecure, you are likely to seek protection from others and may screen out anything other then your needs. If you are aware of your strength, you are likely to seek self-esteem partially through the caretaking role. You may have a tendency to carry the world on your back, easily absorbing the trials and tribulations of others. If not guarded against, you could attract lots of people who need to be taken care of (including lovers and/or children with special problems and special needs). Nurturing is a wonderful expression of human caring, but be sure that you are not solely the one giving. Be able to receive as well. Balancing nurturance and dependency may be a challenge.

If these issues are projected, you could attract children that overdo either the caretaking role or the role of needing to be taken care of. They may come across as little mothers or fathers even when young. Or, they may seem handicapped, needing lots of assistance to cope with life.

Sharing this supportive, protective, looking after energy can result in relationships of mutual giving, mutual support and a great deal of dependability.

Air-Water

☿, ♀, ⚴, ⚵, ♅, ♊, ♎, ♒, 3rd, 7th, 11th houses &
☽, ♇, ♆, ♋, ♏, ♓, 4th, 8th, 12th houses

Your creative imagination and fantasy are potential sources of self-esteem and ego gratification. You can be noted for the rich inner world to which you possess the keys. Blessed with the capacity to tune into unconscious as well as conscious material, you can blend the two for optimum results very impressive to others. This combination of the intuitive with the rational can be helpful in many circumstances. You have the ability to use both logic and an inner knowing.

If you meet these qualities first through your loved ones, they may seem a bit spacey or hard to reach. It would be as if they are in their own little worlds, which do not always connect to the ones inhabited by other people. They may be very bright, imaginative and talented but inclined to drift and dream through life without doing a lot.

Sharing these themes means that your love relationships have elements of fantasy and that you can use both a nonverbal, intuitive connection to those you love as well as a rational, logical understanding of them. You can meet each other both in the mental and in the emotional world and make peace between the two arenas. You can dream together, share fantasies and indulge in lots of fun "head trips" with each other. A rich inner world can creatively enliven your outer world experiences of one another.

QUALITY EMPHASIS

Cardinal
♂, ☽, ♀, ☿, ⚹, ♄, ♈, ♋, ♎, ♑, 1st, 4th, 7th, 10th houses

You are likely to feel ambivalent about the sources of your self-esteem. Part of you would like recognition for your own individual efforts and development; part wants love and admiration for your commitment to your family; part wants attention through a career in the world and part of you seeks approval for your efforts as a partner in a significant relationship. You may feel like a juggler as you strive to make room for all your needs and desires. Since you have varied sources of ego-gratification, you need to diversify your activities, keeping room for all.

This inner conflict can be reflected in your children. Initially, it may simply be a question of whether or not to have children — whether you are willing to give up your freedom and commit time and energy that would otherwise go into your work and/or relationship(s). If you do choose to have children, you are likely to be torn between a desire to share warmth and closeness with them versus a need to be doing your own thing in the world and with other people besides your family.

Achieving a reasonable balance allows you freedom to pursue your own interests and hobbies, emotional sharing with your family, equality with your partner and a place in the world to exercise your need to achieve. If you are still torn, you may be controlling where equality would suit better, dependent where independence would be more appropriate, task-oriented where caring would be helpful, etc. The key is making room in your life for freedom and closeness; equality and control; dominance and dependency. This also means the space to be an individual, part of a family, a partner and a worker.

Since your lovers and/or children tend to mirror this conflict, you could easily end up on opposite ends of the seesaw. When you want freedom, they clutch and cling. When you want closeness, they push away and are off into their own activities. Learning to compromise — allowing all people to be both cool and caring as well as committed and free — is helpful. The more you balance your inner conflict, the easier outer differences become to handle.

Fixed

♀, ☉, ♇, ♅, ♉, ♌, ♏, ♒, 2nd, 5th, 8th, 11th houses

Strong, persistent and blessed with considerable willpower, you usually know what you want and are able to pursue it resolutely. You probably have a natural sensuality and a good capacity to enjoy the world's physical pleasures. Other people may notice you for your charisma, hedonism, talent with handling material resources or ability to manipulate the world. You have an instinctive drive for power which needs a productive outlet in the world. Otherwise, you may find yourself becoming caught up in power struggles with people you would prefer to cooperate with.

You may feel torn between security needs and the desire to gamble, speculate, go for broke to bring off a coup. This tension between stability and change or taking chances and playing it safe could be expressed in many areas. It is especially likely to be a factor in your attitudes toward the handling of money, possessions and sexuality. You may go from one extreme to the other.

It is also quite possible that you will attract lovers and/or children who have a similar conflict. Then, you could end up fighting with one another about who earns the money, who spends it, what it gets spent on, spending versus saving, who enjoys what in terms of sex and other physical, sensual issues. The more you reach an inner balance, the easier an outer balance is to achieve.

It is quite likely that your lovers and/or children will be as strong-willed and intense as you are. None of you is amenable to being told what to do. You may all have to learn to share and to compromise. Try to make your sensual exchanges and monetary decisions cooperative, involving teamwork rather than a power struggle with everyone out to "win."

Mutable

☿, ⚳ ⚴, ♃, ⚷, ♆, ♊, ♍, ♐, ♓, 3rd, 6th, 9th, 12th houses

You may pride yourself on your flexibility or adaptability. You could achieve recognition through your ability to learn vicariously, through observation of others, not having to endure traumas yourself. Often quite versatile, you may gain applause through a number of different talents, many involving the mind or a feeling for beauty.

Because you are multitalented, you may initially have trouble choosing in which area(s) you wish to excel. You could easily scatter your forces and try to be great at **everything**. You may attempt more than is possible at times.

Similar themes exist for lovers and/or children. You are likely to attract people who are also quite bright and multifaceted. Sometimes they may be hard to pin down. You may expect more than is reasonable of them and vice versa. Establishing priorities and value hierarchies in your love relationships can be very helpful.

THEMES

Freedom

♂, ♃, ⚷, ♅, ♈, ♐, ♒, 1st, 9th, 11th houses

There is a strong freedom theme which shows a need for space in your love relationships. One form of this is expressing your uniqueness in some creative fashion, pouring out from your own center to do something in the world which will bring you recognition and applause. You need some room to pursue your enthusiasms and excitements in life. You thrive on activities that make you feel vibrant, alive and able to do what you want. Sometimes this combination indicates such a premium placed on liberty, you choose not to have children, lest they tie you down.

If this sense of fun and liveliness is shared with your loved ones, you will give one another plenty of independence and spend some time apart, pursuing your own interests and hobbies. You can also share some of the excitement, stimulation and sense of fun that comes with going in new directions and taking risks.

If you are not aware of your own needs for liberty, you could attract lovers and/or children who are overdoing that side of life. With lovers, that could include getting involved with people who are not really available (e.g., married, living a long distance away, unwilling to commit, determined to be independent) up to and including falling in love with the one who will always leave you. With children, that can include kids that are very independent, run away from home a lot (literally or figuratively) and constantly push for more space, feeling confined by you.

The more you can express your own needs for independence, the easier that will be to share with others in a comfortable exchange. Then you can feed each other's excitement and applaud one another as you reach greater and greater heights in your own areas of exploration.

Closeness or Interpersonal

☽, ☉, ♀, ⚴, ⚵, ♇, ♋, ♌, ♎, ♏, 4th, 5th, 7th, 8th houses

Your potential arenas of creativity are quite varied. You may be a people person, exuberantly expressing your love and caring. Your courage and willingness to risk could be directed towards doing your all for family and loved ones. You might be an intensely warm, supportive, involved individual, constantly striving to expand the options and opportunities of those to whom you are attached. Your zest to create more could be channeled into the home. You could also be a healing professional, using your people skills in your vocation. If you do not find people sufficiently rewarding, you may look to pets or plants to supply the recognition, attention and positive feedback that is essential for your being.

One-to-one relationships are likely to be a focus, but these could be competitive as well as cooperative. You could find yourself drawn to the thrilling blood rush of competitive sports, the adrenalin high of arguing in court, the excitement of beating out another company in the business world, the satisfaction of winning a game, selling more than your fellow salespeople or other avenues to achieving recognition, applause and reward through competitive interactions.

You may very well have artistic or aesthetic outlets for your creativity, especially those involving a feeling for line, space, harmony and balance. Interior decorating, graphics, photography and similar fields are potential areas of talent. Of course, your passion for balance could also go into fighting for equality, justice or fair play in a number of areas.

If you are out of touch with these sides of your nature, you could attract lovers and/or children who overdo the themes. They may seem clinging, possessive, histrionic, competitive in a cutthroat manner, beautiful, artistic, evenhanded or appeasing. They would act as a mirror for you — reflecting less developed parts of your nature just as you reflect less developed parts of their natures for them.

If you are able to share this desire for closeness with others, that leaves room for both of you to care and be cared for, for everyone to be both protective and vulnerable, giving and receiving in the relationship. Such relationships can be very warm, caring and mutually supportive, with equality preserved by taking turns. You may feel great closeness with your children and lovers.

Artistic

♀, ⚴, ⚵, ☉, ♆, ♉, ♌, ♎, ♓, 2nd, 5th, 7th, 12th houses

There is a strong artistic theme in your horoscope which shows the ability to create beauty. Your sense of aesthetics can be a source of pride and self-esteem. There is the potential of recognition and appreciation of your creative efforts.

Your talents could lie in many areas. The traditional arts — drawing, painting, sculpture, music — are certainly possible. But other fields, such as fashion, design, photography, architecture, interior decorating, creating meals as works of art, designing a lovely garden, and more, are possible. There is a strong feeling for beauty, an aesthetic appreciation. Some people may express this talent through collecting beautiful things, but the ability is there to create as well as enjoy beauty.

If you project such talents, you may become involved with lovers who are performing artists or into the aesthetic realms in some fashion. Or, you could simply fall in love with people who are very beautiful physically. You might also attract children who are concerned with appearance, artistically talented or very visually oriented. The more this theme is shared between you and your loved ones, the less likely any one of you is to overdo in this area.

Idealistic

♃, ⚷, ♆, ♐, ♓, 9th, 12th houses

Creativity is probably an important value for you. It is likely that somc form of pouring out into the world, doing more than you have done before, is a major focus for you. One variation comes through loving and being loved, although your inspired, creative, exciting side could also go into sales, promotion, advertising, artistic endeavors, aesthetic outlets, etc.

If your high expectations are channeled toward love relationships, you are probably searching for an ideal. This can lead to great demands placed on yourself as well as those you care about. The tendency is to want your loving to be perfect and few human beings are able to measure up to an infinite standard.

One danger is never being satisfied with yourself as a lover, with the other person as a lover or with children as children. Somehow, no one fits your fantasy of what they **ought** to be like. So, you live chronically disappointed. Another danger is falling in love repeatedly, each time believing you have found the ideal individual, only to be disappointed later when that person turns out to be all too human with flaws and shortcomings. Another side is persuading yourself that everything **is** perfect and refusing to see other people as they really are — continuing to relate to your fantasy lover rather than the real thing.

Alternatively, you could attract people who think they are perfect and expect you to treat them like demigods. Or, you could draw in individuals who play a savior/victim game — whether they select you as victim to their savior or savior to their victim role. And, some people eschew love relationships and/or children completely, taking the attitude of "Perfect or not at all." They refuse to get involved until they find that ideal, ultimate person (who does not exist).

A helpful route is to search together, with loved ones, for something to make the world more ideal, to inspire each other, to stir one another's emotions, or to give a sense of something Higher to life. You may find a shared spiritual quest very exciting. You may enjoy fighting for causes together. You could have a deep religious connection. Many variations can work as long as the search for God is channeled into a direction that is infinite and not into expectations of other human beings.

Obsessive-Compulsive
☿, ♃, ♆, ♇, ♄, ♍, ♏, ♑, 6th, 8th, 10th houses

There is a theme of compulsive attention to details, focus and concentration where your creative power is concerned. This can indicate the potential of attention and recognition being achieved through your talent for organization and thoroughness. You may be admired for your ability to carry through and complete projects effectively.

These skills are also a factor where love relationships are concerned. You are likely to be dealing with issues of concentration, discipline and practicality where loved ones are concerned. If these qualities are shared, you may simply be very pragmatic and work hard with one another. You can attend easily to tasks and do what needs to be done. You are likely to see one another clearly (without rose-colored glasses) and be dedicated to building a solid relationship. You could organize and arrange the details of your relationships to exactly fit your standards and sense of what is practical.

If anyone carries these attributes to an extreme, then criticism, nitpickiness, obsessiveness and an orientation toward the real world could create difficulties in the relationship. You might feel criticized by lovers and/or children or feel very critical toward them. Any of you might be too concerned with the exact little details of who did what, when and where and might lose the spontaneity and fun of the relationship. You could be so concerned with getting it **right** that you are afraid to love, afraid to have children or express creatively in other channels. A hard-working, disciplined approach could be carried to the extreme of blocking feelings and creating a sense of inadequacy.

It's great to be effective, but remember to have fun too!

Competence

☿, ⚳, ⚵, ♄, ♍, ♑, 6th, 10th houses

There is a strong theme of productivity in your drive for recognition. This suggests you are likely to make an impact in the world and achieve attention through your material accomplishments. Some kind of physical, concrete manifestation of your talents is suggested. You can take pride in a sense of doing things well and getting things done. Potential talent in business or any field which requires awareness of the bottom line is likely.

Where love relationships are concerned, this implies a very practical, realistic attitude. You expect love to require a certain amount of work and are willing to be disciplined and dedicated. This can be helpful in that you don't believe in fairy tale endings, but the work attitude can be a problem if carried too far. Then it leads to criticism, judgment, assigning labels of "right" and "wrong" and a focus on changing and manipulating the world (which can include other people) rather than understanding and accepting others.

If this attitude is overdone (whether by you, or by lovers and/or children), there can be hassles in the relationship. Any party might feel blocked, inhibited, afraid to try lest s/he be put down, criticized or judged as inadequate. This fear of failure can lead to actual failure and even more insecurity if not nipped in the bud. Few things inhibit the fun of loving (including lovemaking) more than a sense of judging or being judged on one's performance.

Reality is great, but keep room for some fantasy and fun too!

Mental Stimulation

☿, ⚳, ⚵, ⚴, ♃, ⚷, ♅, ♆, ♊, ♍, ♎, ♐, ♒, ♓,
3rd, 6th, 7th, 9th, 11th, 12th houses

You need to be admired and appreciated for your mind. Part of your self-esteem and ego is connected to your ability to think and communicate. You are probably skilled with words and talented intellectually and may be achieving the attention you seek through that arena.

In terms of love relationships, intellectual stimulation is very important. You need lovers and/or children with whom you can talk, discuss, argue, exchange information and share ideas. A sense of mental compatibility is vital. A shared appreciation of the intellectual world helps tremendously. Naturally equalitarian, you seek people who will relate on your level and find it easy to talk to most people.

If this quality is projected, you could attract lovers and/or children who express your mental needs for you. They could be very bright, very articulate, extremely adaptable and versatile, but you could even deny your own intellectual abilities while appreciating theirs. Just remember, it takes talent to recognize talent! If they overdo this theme, they could be good at intellectualizing and rationalizing life, always having an excuse or an explanation, but rarely relating on a feeling level.

Usually, this combination indicates a good potential for sharing easily with others, for a comfortable give-and-take in relationships.

Relationships
♀, ☿, ⚷, ♇, ♎, ♏, 7th, 8th houses

You are seeking a sense of drama, excitement and aliveness through your close partnerships. This can be a shared experience, where you each applaud, admire and appreciate one another, spurring each other on to greater and greater moments of achievement. Sharing and interacting provides you with that sense of vitality and importance. The involvement with others could be competitive as well as cooperative. Indeed, the zest of competition may set your blood singing at times. But the urge is to seek out one-to-one confrontations with others as a way of gaining a sense of who you are and what is important about you.

Potential creativity lies in areas involving balance and harmony (ranging from fields as diverse as the law; visual arts such as photography, design, architecture, painting, etc.; music; and counseling or helping activities). Your inspiration often comes from deep within and intense emotions can be an energizing source of creative efforts and accomplishments. In whatever ways you choose to pour out into the world, you can put your full heart into it.

If these qualities are projected, you may experience your children and/or lovers as expressing the competitive urge, zest for cooperation, artistic talent, intense emotionality or passion for equality that you deny within yourself. They may strike you as overdoing these qualities, or carrying them to an extreme, but the example is there.

You could very well treat your children more like partners than kids, seeing them as equals, assuming that you are all in this together. There is a natural ability to relate as a peer with your children, to meet them on their own ground. It is also possible that your partner could strike you as a child. (On the positive side, your partner could be fun-loving, charismatic, exciting and dramatic. On the negative side, s/he could seem self-centered, egotistical and emotionally demanding.) You may experience yourself as meeting a partner through your children in the sense of having a child that reminds you of a spouse. Whatever you most liked and disliked in the spouse will be there again in the child, giving you a second chance to come to terms with those themes.

Generally, the orientation is toward pleasure and sharing in love relationships.

Security
♀, ☽, ☿, ?, ⚴, ♇, ♄, ♆, ♉, ♋, ♍, ♏, ♑, ♓, 2nd, 4th, 6th, 8th, 10th, 12th houses

Your desire for security (physical and emotional) is at odds with your instinct for taking chances. You may feel torn between the grand gesture (which may or may not pay off) and the tried-and-true path.

This conflict is likely to be mirrored by your lovers and/or children. That is, they will feel the same tension between sticking to the status quo versus taking a risk for something bigger and more rewarding. Commonly, the ambivalence will express as power struggles between you — especially over money, sex or the handling of physical resources and possessions. It is often easier to experience a conflict externally than internally. As you and your lovers/children become more balanced in your own attitudes about stability versus change, you will agree with one another more in your interactions. Outward battles merely reflect the inner struggle.

Deciding how much you want to earn, how much you want to spend and for what, what you enjoy in terms of sensual and sexual pleasures, and being very clear about it will help to resolve the issues. Facing your own ambivalence and leaving room for both some security and some risk-taking will also aid the process.

Risk/Change/Creativity
♂, ☉, ♃, ⚵, ♅, ♈, ♌, ♐, ♒, 1st, 5th, 9th, 11th houses

You have a strong need to move forward, to look to the future, to anticipate something better. Highly creative, you are usually willing to initiate changes in order make your life more exciting and fulfilling. Your gambling instincts are probably strong — whether expressed through money, commodities, relationships, vocations or other areas. The desire is to take the plunge, hoping for a bigger return that the rewards will justify the risks. This attitude goes hand in hand with a natural optimism and tendency to trust the future. You also probably enjoy the thrill of taking life to the limit and the excitement of speculation and creativity.

If you look to other people to satisfy this need within you, it is likely you will attract lovers and/or children who are big risk-takers. Whether they gamble with money, goods, love, their bodies or other resources, the willingness to take a chance is there. Courage is generally high and a strong sense of confidence is likely. If they express this to an extreme, they may be rash, foolhardy, impulsive and inclined to push their luck beyond the point it is wise. You may find yourself trying to tone down their forays into making it big, their independence or their creativity. Either party could choose to run away if the situation is not to their liking.

The key is to share that desire for excitement, stimulation and the rush of adrenalin. You need some activities to get your blood moving, to feel turned on by, but you can choose those pastimes that will be most personally satisfying and will meet your need to make changes without going overboard. Plus, if you and your loved ones back each other up, you establish some emotional security in the middle of your wildest speculation.

Parents
☽, ♄, ♃, ♋, ♑, 4th, 10th houses

Your attitudes about being significant, important, loved and appreciated are significantly affected by your experience of your parent(s). At least one parent was, positively or negatively, a role model for being a star. This could have been a dramatic, magnetic, exciting, fun-loving parent with whom you had a strong, loving bond. It could also have been a childish, self-centered, egoistic parent who constantly demanded attention, control and dominance over everything. Another alternative is a parent who becomes like a child to you, in that you end up caring for the parent, looking after him/her as if that person were your child. Whether the model of your parent(s) was comfortable or not, the parent(s) taught you about being in the limelight and gaining recognition and approval.

The pattern continues with your own children, if you choose to have them. That is, you could easily have a child who reminds you of one or both parents. In a sense, it would be like meeting your mother or father again through your children. If you felt a lack of nurturant caring (the traditional mothering quality) or responsible looking after (the traditional fathering quality) with either parent, you could face similar feelings with your own children. The danger is relating to a child as if that child were your parent, rather than seeing him/her as an individual. Finishing old business with parents, releasing any leftover feelings, forgiving them and yourself for any unpleasant interactions, can help insure a positive relationship with your own children.

Of course, if you had the warm and loving experience with your own parents, it is easier to create the same context with your kids. There is a strong potential for being a very responsible parent, caring deeply about what happens to your children. Just don't get **too** serious about it. Remember to relax also.

Power
☉, ♇, ♄, ♌, ♏, ♑, 5th, 8th, 10th houses

You are dealing with issues of power, authority and control through your love relationships. You have a strong need to pour out from your own center, in your own way. You need love, admiration, limelight and appreciation for your special qualities and for your ability to be significant and impact the world. Ideally, you have a mutual admiration society with those people close to you. Less ideally, you may be trying to control (or being controlled by) children and/or lovers through power plays, manipulation or other ploys to take charge. Focusing on teamwork, winning together, helps minimize the potential of one person "winning" at the expense of a loved one. Keep room for everyone to feel applauded and have places in life to compete, to wholeheartedly throw yourselves into winning, which will not impact negatively on those you love.

Personal
♂, ♀, ☿, ☽, ♈, ♉, ♊, ♋, 1st, 2nd, 3rd, 4th houses

There is an intense need to express creatively from your own center. Whether that is poured out more into artistic, writing, entertaining pursuits, or more into loving and being loved is up to you. The need is for personal self-expression that gains you attention and positive feedback.

Putting the self first is also likely to be an issue with children and/or lovers. You may be learning how to make your needs a priority (in which case the people around you will role model assertive, confident, self-centered behavior — perhaps in excess). Or, you could be learning to moderate your own needs. But the issue of knowing what you want and feeling free to directly pursue it will be significant in your close love relationships.

Transpersonal
♃, ⚷, ♄, ♅, ♆, ♐, ♑, ♒, ♓, 9th, 10th, 11th, 12th houses

You may feel pulled to direct your creativity toward large-scale issues. This could range from a focus on various social causes to a soul-searching quest for the "best" utopia. The urge is to come from your own center with the enthusiasm, energy and persuasiveness to make changes which will alter society in some way. You need an impact not just on the people right around you, but also on the world as a whole.

This transpersonal focus could be a bit of a challenge in close love relationships. Children and/or lovers may feel that your involvements in the wider world pull you away from home, family and partnership concerns. Or, if this theme is projected, you may resent the demands that societal concerns make on the time and energy of your children and/or lovers. The challenge is to integrate the love function on all levels — personal, one-to-one as well as *agape* (love which envelops people in general).

Freedom Versus Closeness
♂, ♃, ⚷, ♅, ♈, ♐, ♒, 1st, 9th, 11th houses Vs.
☽, ☉, ♀, ☿, ⚵, ♇, ♋, ♌, ♎, ♏, 4th, 5th, 7th, 8th houses

You are balancing freedom and closeness needs in your love relationships. Keep room for liberty as well as attachment. If you disown either side, you will attract an exaggerated version from lovers and/or children. Rather than warm and loving, they will seem clutching and possessive. Rather than independent, they will seem unavailable and uncaring. Compromise; make room for both.

Security Versus Risk

♀, ☽, ☿, ?, ♢, ♇, ♄, ♆, ♅, ♋, ♍, ♏, ♑, ♓, 2nd, 4th, 6th, 8th, 10th, 12th houses Vs.
♂, ☉, ♃, ♦, ♅, ♈, ♌, ♐, ♒, 1st, 5th, 9th, 11th houses

You are facing issues of stability versus change through your love relationships. Part of you wants to keep everything safe, secure and predictable. Another part wants to take risks, upset the apple cart, try whatever is new and different. You may feel the conflict around the handling of money or possessions, around sexual expression, around relating to your children, around the lover(s) you choose or around other arenas.

Because you are divided within, you are likely to attract other people who also feel ambivalent. It becomes easy to adopt opposite points of view and fight about the issues. You could slip into power struggles with lovers and/or children as an unconscious way to deal with the inner conflict. Balancing the inner struggle helps to take care of the outer differences.

ASPECTS

Harmony to Letter . . .

1: Your creative spirit is potentially in harmony with your basic identity and self-assertion. Your zest, enthusiasm and sense of fun support your ability to be yourself. Whether expressed through procreation (having children) or creation (mental, emotional or physical) — your impulse to pour into the world and receive positive feedback for your creations is strong.

2: Your creativity is potentially in harmony with your desire for pleasures and material security in life. You may have to compromise between your desire to take chances, breaking new ground and your need for life's basic comforts, but the ability to blend the two is there. Artistic talent is possible; so is skill in investments. Whether through children, finances or other areas, you can bring together risk-taking and common sense for optimum results.

3: Your zest and enthusiasm feed your mind and vice versa. Mental acrobatics are possible, as are playfulness and a spirit of fun. Your natural creativity (including potential involvements with children) is enhanced by your communication and intellectual skills. Your logic and rationality support your childlike enthusiasm and ability to take risks.

4: Your creativity is enhanced by your warmth and caring. A very loving combination, this is a natural for strong involvement with a home and family. Having and caring for children can be one form of creative expression, but involvements with the business world, commodities, land and the public are also possible. Your ability to be onstage, risking or attracting the limelight complements your basic emotional security needs.

5: Your creativity is marked and your zest and enthusiasm for life can be a decided asset in any endeavors. Able to come from your own center and express in a spontaneous, engaging manner, you can easily gain attention and positive feedback from others. Whether you express your talent through children, artistic creations, speculation, investments, promotion or other channels of personal expression, one of your greatest gifts to others is the ability to fling yourself full force into living, drawing others along with your excitement.

6: Your creative spirit is in potential harmony with your need to do something well in life. Your risk-taking abilities enhance your practical accomplishments; your pragmatism complements your zest and spontaneity. You can harmonize working and having children; you are capable of blending the two easily. Your sensible side and your enthusiastic side work well together.

7: Your creative urges are in potential harmony with your desire for partnership, equality and harmony. One option is a natural reinforcement between the roles of partner and parent — each supporting the other. Artistic talent is also likely and persuasive abilities are possible. Your zest and enthusiasm help maintain excitement in your relationships, while your need for balance makes sure no one gets too self-centered.

8: Your creative spirit is in potential harmony with your desire for depth knowledge. You can easily juggle the roles of mate and parent, keeping room for intimacy with a spouse as well as with children, but also maintaining a corner of solitude to explore your deeper Self. Your enthusiasm and intensity complement one another.

9: Your quest for meaning in life is in potential harmony with your creative spirit. Your zest and need for excitement can assist your search for Ultimate Truth. Your faith in life and optimism support you in taking risks and reaping the rewards of allowing your natural charisma and dynamism to express.

10: Your creative urges are in potential harmony with your sense of responsibility. You are able to blend spontaneity and discipline for impressive accomplishments. Capable of combining roles, you can pursue a meaningful career while still being a successful, dedicated parent. Hard work grounds your inspirations and makes them real.

11: Your creative urges are in potential harmony with your need to be free and individualistic. Uniqueness comes naturally to you in some form of creative expression — whether through children, art, investments or other forms of pouring out into the world and hoping for a return. You know how to be friends with those you love.

12: Your creative spirit is in potential harmony with your quest for infinite love and beauty. This can indicate strong artistic talent. Dramatic ability is likely to be strong as well. Idealism supports your love relationships and your sparkle and zest energize you in the search for a Higher meaning.

Conflict to Letter . . .

1: Your creative spirit may be in conflict with your basic identity and self-assertion. Demands from lover(s) and/or children could compete with doing what you want in the world. Simply doing your own thing may be at odds with your desire to do something bigger and more impressive than ever before. Keep room for both self-expression and self-expansion through doing more than has been done before, creating anew.

2: Your creative urges need to be balanced with your desire for pleasure, security, ease and comfort. You may feel your preferences are at odds with you children's. You could feel torn between laying back and enjoying the world versus taking chances in order to make a splash and be noticed in some way. Compromise between stability and excitement needs.

3: Your creative urges may be at odds with your desire for logic, rationality and objectivity. You may feel torn between detachment and excitement, the need to be passionately involved, perhaps with loved ones, versus the need to step back and look at things from a cooler perspective. You may have to compromise between demands on your time and energy as a parent versus desires to explore the intellectual world.

4: Your creative impulses may be at odds your desire for a nest and emotional security. Home and family demands may compete with your need to do something significant, something worthy of notice and applause. Safety needs (drawing inward in a protective way) may clash with the desire for spontaneity and expression. Both are necessary.

5: There is potential conflict in the area of creativity and your risk-taking capacity. This could be due to a sense of inadequacy, blocking yourself. You might feel torn between differing kinds of creativity (e.g., having children, artistic expression, promotional strategies, etc.) or unsure in your self-esteem. Conflicts with children or around the question of having children (or otherwise expressing your inner spirit) could be an issue. Support your creative potentials; love yourself.

6: There is potential conflict between your creative urges and your need to analyze and find the flaws in order to improve upon life. Your critical judgment may block your creativity, with fears of inadequacy or failure. You may be overly hard on yourself. Your zest and enthusiasm may be at odds with your desire to do things well and thoroughly. Combine spontaneity and patience for best results.

7: There is a potential conflict between your creativity and your desire for equality and sharing. These could express as making time and energy divisions between a partner and your children. It could indicate a strong competitive spirit with a need to be as noteworthy as anyone around you. It may point to the need to make peace between full-throttle enthusiasm and an approach which balances and weighs all the pertinent facts. Make your two sides partners — not opponents.

8: There is potential conflict between your enthusiastic, exciting side and your desire for self-control and self-mastery. Intense passion is likely, but you may feel torn between wearing your heart on your sleeve versus not revealing your inner feelings. Your could feel pulled between the needs of children versus the needs of your mate. Concentrate on teamwork rather than power struggles.

9: There is potential conflict between your ideals and your creative impulses. You may feel at odds with lover(s) and/or children around ethics or moral principles. Your quest for higher knowledge may pull you away from love relationships or vice versa. Your expectations may be higher than are reachable for human, loving relationships. Aim high, but not impossibly so.

10: There is a potential conflict between your creative urges and your need for responsible, solid achievements in the world. You may feel torn between the time and energy demands of a career versus those of being a parent. You could feel a pull between love needs versus work needs. Your enthusiasm, energy and dynamism can complement your cautious realism if you integrate them.

11: Your creativity is potentially at odds with your desire for freedom and independence of action. This could manifest as a reluctance to be tied down by children — or by other forms of creative expression. It might indicate a fear of — or an excessive emphasis upon — uniqueness in your personal expression. You need to pour out from your own center, in your very own way, and receive attention and admiration for your individuality.

12: Your creative urges are potentially in conflict with your quest for cosmic consciousness. This can be an extremely dramatic combination, with the ability to emotionally sway and persuade others. Artistic talent is also quite possible, as are promotional and sales abilities. The challenge is to blend human love relationships (including with children) with the quest for something Higher in life. Beware of expecting too much from those we love (or them from us), but also avoid settling for a life devoid of inspiration and the connection to something Infinite.

CHAPTER ELEVEN

BELIEFS AND VALUES

This section addresses your underlying assumptions about life, truth, reality, morality, ethics and beliefs. One's world view is reflected in religion, philosophy, science, education, spiritual precepts or other systems which offer a sense of meaning, an explanation of why we are here and where we are going.

We all live our lives based on certain assumptions about what is real, what is worth pursuing, what is important and what is possible. A sense of faith can be a major bulwark and support in living; it can also be a burden and a barrier if we have excessive faith (and are foolhardy) or place our faith in the wrong areas (such as expecting other human beings to be perfect and godlike). When we turn a small **part** of life into "God," we risk feeling lost — or that life has no meaning — when that part of life is transformed or proves to be limited rather than infinite.

This area of the chart mirrors the issues you are dealing with in terms of your belief systems and values. They could be firmly and solidly based, or you could have a situation of too much faith, too little faith or faith in inappropriate areas. By your awareness of the basic issues and drives, you can choose to express those motivations in a manner most satisfying and fulfilling for you.

The Factors

Astrologically, we are especially concerned with those keys to the infinite and the search for meaning. This includes **Letter 9** (a key to religious or spiritual ideals, the pursuit of the truth), **Letter 12** (the quest for cosmic consciousness, universal understanding) and **Letter 11** (hopes and wishes, future orientation). Letter 11 could be given half the weight of Letters 9 and 12, since the beliefs of Letter 11 are more intellectual, while those of Letters 9 and 12 are more emotional.

Usually the latter are more deeply rooted and more powerful. (Chiron is included with Letter 9 — having having also overtones of Letter 11.)

Thus, we examine:[1]

GROUP I
Conjunctions to Jupiter, Neptune and Chiron
Conjunctions to Uranus [½ weight]
Conjunctions to rulers of the 9th and 12th cusps
Conjunctions to ruler of the 11th cusp [½ weight]
Conjunctions to rulers of other signs in the 9th and 12th houses
Conjunctions to rulers of other signs in the 11th house [½ weight]

GROUP II
The nature of planets in the 9th and 12th houses
The nature of planets in the 11th house [½ weight]
The nature of planets within two degrees of the 9th and 12th houses, even though
occupying the 8th, 10th or 1st houses

GROUP III
Parallels to Jupiter, Neptune or Chiron
Parallels to Uranus [½ weight]
Houses ruled by planets forming any conjunctions to Jupiter, Neptune or Chiron
Houses ruled by planets forming any conjunctions to Uranus [½ weight]
House placements of Jupiter, Neptune and Chiron
House placement of Uranus [½ weight]
House placements of rulers of the 9th and 12th cusps
House placements of the ruler of the 11th cusp [½ weight]
House placements of rulers of other signs in the 9th and 12th houses
House placements of rulers of other signs in the 11th house [½ weight]
Houses ruled by any planets occupying the 9th and 12th houses
Houses ruled by any planets occupying the 11th house [½ weight]

---

1. If you prefer **not** to search for repeated themes yourself, you can order the "PP BOOK" option
from Astro Computing Services (PO Box 16430, San Diego, Ca 92116), which allows you to use
this book to make complete, synthesizing delineations of horoscopes without figuring out which
themes are emphasized.

Available for $3.00 each, the "PP BOOK" report calculates the emphasis on all the letters of
the alphabet, themes and aspects in each horoscope for which you provide the data. The report
lists each significant focus (e.g., "There is a Letter 10 theme in "Beliefs and Values," and gives
the appropriate page numbers for you to read in this book ("See pages 305-306 in the *Complete
Horoscope Interpretation* book.")

The computer will not **always** arrive at the same results as you might, as certain steps are ambiguous (e.g., how much weight to give a planet making a conjunction, based on the orb). However,
the majority of the time, the computer answers will concur with those derived from use of the
worksheets — or the recommended quick scan of a horoscope. Thus it provides an excellent teaching
tool.

The "PP BOOK" does **not** provide a listing of **each and every** astrological factor making up
the significant themes. For that, you would order "PP WEIGHTS" (discussed in next footnote).

Planets occupying Sagittarius or Pisces
Planets occupying Aquarius [½ weight]

GROUP IV
Sign placements of Jupiter, Neptune and Chiron
Sign placement of Uranus [½ weight]
Sign placements of rulers of the 9th and 12th cusps
Sign placement of ruler of the 11th cusp [½ weight]
Sign placements of rulers of other signs in the 9th and 12th houses
Sign placement of rulers of other signs in the 11th house [½ weight]
Signs on the cusps of the 9th and 12th houses
Sign on the cusp of the 11th house [½ weight]
Houses occupied by planets in Sagittarius or Pisces
Houses occupied by planet(s) in Aquarius [½ weight]
Signs occupied in the 9th and 12th houses
Signs occupied in the 11th house [½ weight]
Other signs (unoccupied) in the 9th and 12th houses
Other signs (unoccupied) in the 11th house [½ weight]

How to Weight the Factors

Please note that these factors are rank ordered (in chunks) according to their weighting. If you want to use exact figures, a suggested weighting scale is given in the appendix — with worksheets for career and the other various life areas.[2]

A SHORT CUT
For quickness and ease of use, especially for people learning to use the alphabet, I suggest focusing initially only on Groups I and II.

---

2. You can also obtain a listing of **all** the astrological factors which compose those letters of the Zip Code determined to be significant in a horoscope. This makes an excellent teaching tool and a valuable resource to check yourself against when practicing with the Zip Code.

    Astro Computing Services, PO Box 16430, San Diego, CA 92116, has calculated 28,000 horoscopes and established averages and standard deviations for the scores of each letter of the astrological alphabet, each theme, and the conflict and harmony aspects to each life area.

    Astro's report, called "PP WEIGHTS," will list those letters of the astrological alphabet which are one standard deviation or more above the mean — and list **all** the astrological factors which point to each significant letter of the alphabet. These weightings will also compare each individual's score on the various themes (e.g., risk-taking, artistic) to the means and standard deviations to determine which themes are significant.

    Averages are established for aspects as well in order to note conflict or harmony in the different life areas.

    The results obtained by Astro's "PP WEIGHTS" will not **always** coincide with those you determine by a quick scan and intuitive judgment, or by use of the worksheets. Certain of the steps (e.g., how much to weight a planet based on orb) are ambiguous, so different results can occur. However, most of the time, Astro's answers will confirm those you could obtain in working with the Zip Code. Furthermore, the **complete** listing of relevant factors is an excellent teaching tool.

    Ask for "PP Weights." The price, as of December 1985 is $5.00

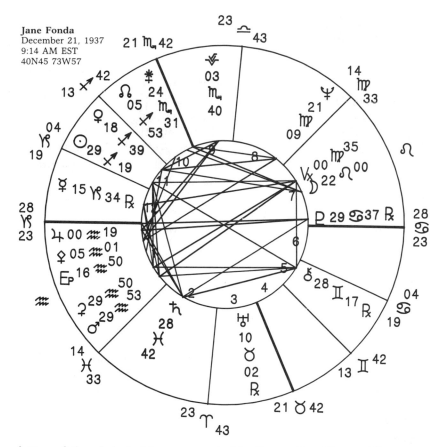

Jane Fonda
December 21, 1937
9:14 AM EST
40N45 73W57

If any letter of the alphabet is represented in Group I or II, consider it as prob-ably significant. (If that letter is repeated in Groups I and II, it is definitely signifi-cant. Read the interpretation.)

Looking at Groups I and II in the example chart of Jane Fonda, Jupiter con-juncts Pallas, giving us a Letter 7 theme (but only ½ weight since Pallas is an asteroid). Jupiter also rules the 11th house (which gets partial weight for goals and beliefs). The 9th house is occupied by Vesta (½ weight), giving us a Letter 6 theme. The 11th house is occupied by the Sun (Letter 5) and Venus (Letter 2 or 7). The 12th house is occupied by Mercury, supplying a Letter 3 or 6 theme. Thus, we have possible themes of 2, 3, 5, 6 and 7.

Once factors in Groups I and II are very familiar, add Groups III and IV. If any of the letters from Groups I and II are repeated in Groups III and IV, con-sider them confirmed and read the appropriate section. In the case of Ms. Fonda, a different picture emerges when we consider **all** the factors. Letter 1 emerges as the most significant: Jupiter in the 1st (1), Aquarian Mars (1), four Aquarian placements occupying the 1st house (1)(1)(1)(1), Jupiter conjunct the Ascendant (1), Jupiter parallel the Ascendant (1), Pisces in the 1st (1) and we return to Jupiter's

1st house placement with its rulership of the Sagittarius in the 11th. The Letter 1 focus points to the central role beliefs and values play in Ms. Fonda's life. Her basic identity (1) is tied to her beliefs, values and ideals. They permeate everything she does, all actions she takes. They are a vital core of who she is and a major definition for her sense of self.

The Letter 1 component also warns of the danger of a "true believer" — someone who feels "my beliefs are the only right, true and just beliefs." Such assumptions were the basis of many wars. We would expect Jane Fonda to express her beliefs openly, directly and assertively (Letter 1). We might also suspect she could aggressively (Letter 1) push her belief system on the world or impulsively and forcefully present her ideals.

In examining Groups III and IV, also look for any letters of the alphabet which occur five or more times. Consider them significant and read the appropriate interpretations. For example, in the Fonda horoscope, the Letter 11 theme is repeated by: Jupiter in Aquarius (11), 9th house Libra ruled by Venus in the 11th (11), Sagittarian Sun in the 11th (11), Sagittarius on 11th cusp (11), Sagittarian 11th cusp ruled by Jupiter in Aquarius (11), Jupiter conjuncts Pallas in Aquarius (11).

The Letter 1 theme appears on page 301 ("I will find Truth — MY WAY") with Letter 11 on page 306 ("The Original Thinker").

Themes

Themes can be ascertained by two methods. One approach is to examine only the emphasized letters of the alphabet and see which themes are suggested by combinations of the emphasized letters. In the case of the Fonda example, with both Letter 1 and Letter 11 emphasized, we might suspect a **freedom** and/or a **risk-taking** theme could emerge. (Freedom includes Letters 1, 9 and 11. Risk-taking includes Letters 1, 5, 9 and 11.)

A second method of searching for themes involves looking at the totals for **all** letters of the alphabet. Since the freedom theme involves 3 out of the 12 letters, we would expect the scores for 1, 9 and 11 to be about 1/4 of the total of all scores. You can either do some rough arithmetic or get an intuitive impression. If the amount for the freedom letters seems appreciably more than 1/4 of the total, count that as a theme — and read the appropriate section (page 312).

When searching for themes, give additional weighting to like planets in aspect to one another, e.g., the Sun, Mars, Jupiter and Uranus are the four risk-oriented planets. Any aspects between the Sun, Mars, Jupiter and Uranus add to the focus on independence and liberty. (In the case of Jane Fonda, the Sun sextiles Mars and Mars is semisextile Jupiter. If Chiron is included, as partaking of both Letters 9 and 11 we see Sun opposite Chiron, Mars trine Chiron and Jupiter quincunx Chiron.)

Also give extra weight to like houses and like signs. Thus, the Sun, Mars, Jupiter or Uranus in the 1st, 5th, 9th or 11th house or in Aries, Leo, Sagittarius or Aquarius adds weight to the theme of change, creativity and a willingness to take chances. Ms. Fonda has Mars in a risk-oriented house (1st) and sign (Aquarius). Jupiter occupies a restless house (1st) and sign (Aquarius) as well. The Sun falls in a future-oriented sign (Sagittarius) as well as house (11th), while Chiron in the 5th backs up the creativity and willingness to lay beliefs on the line.

Ms. Fonda's handling of beliefs and values certainly reveals an independence of mind. Her liberal approach would be considered rebellious by many. She is noted for "marching to a different drummer." She has taken risks on behalf of her beliefs and values and puts a high priority on independence of thought and action — for others as well as for herself. She has also paid the price for her risk-taking and independence of mind. Conflicting ideals about the Vietnam War were another source of tension between Ms. Fonda and her father. She failed to win approval for a seat on an Arts Council in the State of California as many politicians viewed her as radical and inflammatory. Yet she has continued to stand up for her beliefs and remains very direct about her values and goals.

Aspects

Quickly scan all aspects other than conjunctions or parallels, grouping them according to harmony (sextile, trine, semisextile) and conflict (octile, tri-octile, square, opposition and quincunx). In considering each aspect, weight the nature of the planet most heavily, followed by the house and the sign. Count both the house occupied by the aspected planet and the house cusp it rules. For example, Jane Fonda has the following **close** aspects to her Jupiter (a beliefs factor) in terms of harmony:
• semisextile the Sun (Letter 5) in the 11th (11) in Sagittarius (9); Sun rules 7th (7)
• semisextile the Antivertex (1) in the 1st (1) in Pisces (12)
• semisextile Mars (1) in the 1st (1) in Aquarius (11); Mars rules 3rd (3)
• semisextile Ceres (6 — ½ weight) in the 1st (1) in Aquarius (11)
• sextile Saturn (10) in the 2nd (2) in Pisces (12); Saturn rules 12th and 1st (12)(1)

Her **close** conflict aspects to Jupiter include:
• opposite Pluto (8) in the 7th (7) in Cancer (4); Pluto rules 10th (10)
• quincunx Chiron (9) in 5th (5) in Gemini (3)
• square Vesta (6 — ½ weight) in the 9th (9) in Scorpio (8)

(We have already considered conjunctions in the earlier search for themes, so need not include them here.)

Make an intuitive judgment of whether any letters of the alphabet have lots of conflict to them or have quite a bit of harmony. In the Fonda example, we might suspect that harmony to Letter 1 is significant, while conflict to Letter 8 is also suggested. (Naturally, we would first see if the other factors — Uranus, Neptune, rulers of the 9th, 11th and 12th, etc. — repeat what seems implied by the Jupiter aspects.) Certainly, Ms. Fonda's beliefs and values are central to her sense of self (Letter 1). She constantly acts (1) on her principles! Her ideals and perfectionism could be barriers to successful intimacy. The fact that she and her current mate (Letter 8), Tom Hayden share basic beliefs and values suggests this marriage is likely to be enduring. Because her beliefs are such a core part of her being (Letter 1), a mate (Letter 8) who doesn't share them would be a source of conflict.

If you feel any group of aspects has an emphasis on one or more letters of the alphabet, or a theme, read the appropriate interpretation.

Interpretations: Beliefs and Values

ALPHABET THEMES

Letter 1. I Will Find Truth — MY WAY

You tend to trust action and your own experience. Usually disinclined to accept the dogmas or traditions of other people, you will seek out a direct, personal experience of truth or the meaning of life. Your values revolve around self-expression, assertion and being true to one's self. As a result, you might be very strong, active, courageous and in touch with who you are and what you want. Or, you could see your goal as reaching that state of freedom to be yourself with no strings, no inhibitions from others.

You can be very active in your pursuit of ultimate knowledge — whether through traveling, studying, religious pursuits, spiritual quests or other avenues to figuring out the answers of the universe. One potential danger is the role of missionary. If you believe you have found the **final** truth, you may slip into the position of a true believer and aggressively push your version of religion/spirituality/science/the answers to life upon other people. The result could be religious arguments (even minor wars!), heated philosophical discussions, conflicts over whose version of reality is more correct. You need a faith that makes sense to you personally, but remember to allow other people room to have beliefs and perceptions different from yours.

Letter 2: The Pleasure Principle

Comfort ranks high on your list of priorities. Part of your quest in life is to be able to enjoy the material, sensual world. The full satisfaction of your appetites can be a goal. This might be channeled toward food, drink, sex, making money, collecting possessions or creating beauty in the world. The theme is appreciation of the material side of life. Pitfalls include turning money or sex or some other physical pleasure into God. This leads to overindulgence in that area since it is valued excessively. The end result is usually the loss of whatever we idolize, as a path to discovering that object is not God — not infinite nor infinitely satisfying. Physical resources satiate physical needs; spiritual needs must be met elsewhere.

In religious or spiritual pursuits, the preference is for stability and security. You seek a meaning you can rely on. A world view of beauty and grace appeals to you. You prefer the world to flow easily and harmoniously. This relaxed perspective can be helpful in liking life. If carried too far, it could lead to laziness, stolidity and avoidance of confrontations. The best potential is for an affectionate relationship to the world — experiencing the Universe as basically good, well-meaning and satisfying.

Letter 3: Knowledge Over All

Much of your faith lies in the mind. Objectivity, rationality and the capacity to communicate are likely values for you. You tend to trust the intellect over the emotions and look to knowledge to understand the meaning of the universe.

People ties can also be important. Often, a relative (brother, sister, aunt, uncle, cousin) has a strong influence on your perceptions, your version of reality.

You tend to be curious about spiritual/religious systems and enjoy philosophical conversations. It is likely that you have studied a number of different approaches to life's meaning and constantly discover more questions. Your basic beliefs are probably somewhat eclectic — borrowing a little from here, a little from there. You see some logic and interest in a number of different inspirational systems and use a combination to form the basis of your faith.

You are more inclined than most to have a light touch where your basic assumptions are concerned. In your view, God most definitely has a sense of humor!

Letter 4: Caring and Commitments

Family and emotional support are fundamental underpinnings for your life. A sense of connection to other people (and/or pets) is vital. Warmth, caring, protection and nurturance rank high on your list of priorities. Your ideal is an exchange of caretaking energy, with you giving in your areas of strength and receiving in vulnerable areas. However, you may sometimes fall into playing a parenting role to those around you — carrying too much of the emotional burdens. Or, you could succumb to the temptation to seek out a Cosmic Womb — where you can feel totally nourished, protected and cherished.

Your beliefs and attitudes are likely to be strongly influenced by the perceptions of one parent, most likely mother (or mother figure). She could be a positive or negative role model. With the first, you would seek to emulate her. With the second, you would do the exact opposite of what she did; she would be your example of everything **not** to do. Her version of truth, reality, religion, ultimate meaning, has a significant impact on what you trust, value and expect from the Universe.

Security, roots and tradition are often important and you may be content with the faith of your ancestors. Generally, your vision of the Universe is of a warm, nest-like experience — a sense of reassurance and caring. Often your own family is a strong source of support and reassurance for your faith (or you seek such a home base).

Letter 5: A Zest for Life

Doing more than you have done before is a primary motivation. Life is often viewed as full of exciting opportunities. Love is usually central in your values and you can be quite a romantic. Your urge is for expansion into the world, pouring out from your own center to receive a response from others. This feedback could be in the form of love, admiration, money or applause. You may also place a high value on power — having an impact on people.

A key ingredient in your expectations is the enhancement of self-esteem. You need to be center stage in some way, in the limelight, receiving support, attention, appreciation. You are probably drawn to belief systems which allow you room to shine, which are magnetic, dynamic and exciting. You enjoy a show and even a spectacle!

If you are still uncomfortable with your natural charisma, you may choose to be inspired and swept away by others. You may attract dynamic, "live wire" religious leaders who easily sway the emotions of their followers. That "starring" quality needs an outlet in your faith and beliefs.

You may place a premium on taking risks. Since you value life on a grand scale, you are willing to gamble, to take chances, hoping for a rewarding response! You tend to have an underlying optimism, a sense that things will be even better tomorrow.

Letter 6: The Pragmatist

You are most likely to trust and believe in hard work and anything you can see, hear, touch and measure. Dealing with the "real" (i.e., physical) world is generally a priority. You tend to put your faith in doing a good job and taking care of business. This sometimes means you do most of the work, because you are more satisfied with your manner of accomplishments than anyone else's.

You are not inclined to value the purely mystical; you seek illuminations that are functional — that can be put to use in the world. A motto for you might be: "But what can you **do** with it?" Efficiency is very important to you and you value whatever will get the job done the most competently.

Your expectations of efficiency carry over into health as well and you generally keep good health as a major goal. You tend to appreciate all the puritan virtues — thrift, responsibility, practicality, productivity, caution, etc. The usual result is a pragmatic faith — based on what "works" for you.

Your concentration and focus on doing things well can sometimes lead to excessive flaw-finding and nit-picking. It may be a challenge for you to be able to "Let go and let God" as you tend to want to fix any little thing that goes wrong and you can almost always find another fault to be improved! But your general focus on practical accomplishments usually serves you well as you can handle almost anything which comes up.

Letter 7: The Arbitrator

You have a well-developed sense of fair play and could easily devote yourself to the cause of justice. Equality, balance and harmony are likely ideals for you to espouse. Cooperation and compromise could be the name of the game where you are concerned. One-to-one interactions are likely to be a priority in your life.

Because your standards are so high where relationships are concerned, you may sometimes have difficulties finding a satisfactory situation. It is possible you will feel no one measures up to what you are seeking. Or, you may attract people who expect more than is reasonable of themselves or of you. Student/guru relationships are also possible with one person playing the role of the wise teacher and the other the role of the naive, eager student. Just remember, no person can provide all the answers or meaning to life for another individual. If you overvalue the other person or the relationship, you may be too accommodating, too willing to give in. Compromise is all well and good, but playing doormat does not lead to healthy associations. Finding a partner to share your quest for ultimate meaning is likely to be more satisfying than looking to someone else to supply your meaning in life or trying to be "everything" for another person.

Because you value evenhandedness, you can sometimes succumb to a competitive urge. You might tend to "keep score" in relationships and may be overly concerned with evening things up.

Beauty, grace and aesthetic appeal are also likely priorities in your world view. Appearances can be very important to you. You prefer the world to run smoothly, comfortably without any unpleasantness.

Letter 8: The Pursuit of Self-Mastery

Your goals in life include reaching a deep understanding of your own psyche. Self-mastery and self-control are important to you. Power, especially over the realm of appetites and possessions, is a value. Since this is a central issue for you, you could feel torn between a strong, determined pursuit of money, sex and material goods versus the path of asceticism and withdrawal.

Religions or spiritual paths which emphasize the opposition of spiritual and carnal within the human animal are likely to appeal to you. You might also feel drawn to systems like Tantric Yoga, where the physical feeds the spiritual and vice versa. It is easy for you to go to extremes in your attempt to balance sensual pleasures with inspirational pulls.

Looking beneath the surface of life is important to you. You may mistrust surface appearances and tend to continually dig deeper. Naturally questioning, you can be relentless in your pursuit of the truth. Occult studies or any "hidden" knowledge is likely to attract you. Similarly, you can make a lifelong study of yourself, probing your deepest motivations, seeking a full understanding of your inner depths. You trust perseverance, self-control, insight and power over the material world.

Letter 9: Faith Can Move Mountains

Naturally optimistic, you often have great confidence and faith in the Universe. Inclined to trust that everything will work out fine, you may rush in where angels fear to tread.

A subscriber to the "More is better" theory, you can easily fall prey to excesses. If you decide that the truth is an ultimate value, you can be the bluntest, most ruthlessly honest person around. If you see good times as the meaning in life, you could go from party to party. If you decide the path to Nirvana is through Tibet, you are off. If you feel that education is the answer to all your problems, you may pursue degree after degree. Whatever you believe in, you tend to go all the way. In your worship of an ideology, beware lest you arrogantly suppress alternate points of view. You can slip into making final pronouncements about the meaning of life (which you may regret later). You can appear (and be) the most self-righteous and dictatorial of true believers in your certainty of faith.

Moderation may be a challenge for you. It is easy for you to expand a small part of life, to turn it into an idol, overvaluing it. Maintaining a perspective and a sense of appreciation for the different sides of life will help you sidestep the dangers of overoptimism, impulsive faith and an arrogant assumption that you have all the answers that matter.

In its highest form, the potential here is of a constantly expanding, growing faith, an innate trust in the Universe with the flexibility to continue seeking further answers.

Letter 10: The Realist (Sometimes, The Pessimist)

Your faith is likely to have undergone some heavy-duty questioning. It is quite possible that you have had periods of agnosticism or atheism, wondering if there were any meaning to life. You may be inclined to a very pessimistic outlook, perhaps even depressive, although you may label your attitude realistic. Generally, you are likely to trust the physical universe and are less inclined to believe in that which you cannot measure, feel, hear, see or touch. Materialism may be your religion, at least for a time. You place importance on being realistic and pragmatic, i.e., successfully changing the physical world to suit your desires and needs.

A sense of structure, orderliness and predictability may be priorities. You are likely to seek a well-defined, clearly described truth. You probably want to know exactly what "the rules" of life are so you can cope most effectively.

You may put your faith in power, especially power in the world. Status, ambition, the need to achieve, could be motivators for you. Generally, success in your career is a major goal.

Your belief system is, in some major way, influenced by a parent, probably father or father figure (who could have been an uncle, grandfather or even mother operating as the authority). His attitudes about what to trust, value and pursue as an ultimate in life had a great impact on your decisions about what really matters. He could have been a positive or a negative role model in terms of faith and values, but either way the impact is there.

You tend to place a high value on the work ethic. Usually responsible, cautious, careful, conscientious and disciplined, you believe that being practical will lead to solid accomplishments and it usually does.

Letter 11: The Original Thinker

Your approach to religious or spiritual beliefs is likely to be unconventional. Quite often, you rebel against the faith in which you were raised. You need to find your own answers, pursue your own version of truth and the meaning of life.

Generally resistant to dogmas, you seek a sense of openness and flexibility in your belief systems. Hierarchies turn you off and excessive rigidity just incites you to shocking behavior and/or statements. You may enjoy upsetting other people's assumptions about reality.

You place a high value on the mind, particularly the ability to be original and think for yourself. Friends can influence your basic assumptions about the world, but no one can tell you what to believe. You will find your own path(s).

You tend to place your faith in progress, change and the future. Usually you believe that justice, fair play and equal opportunity are vital components of life. If it comes to a question of traditions or the old versus innovations and the new, you will usually side with innovation. You may be involved with group political action.

Detachment and objectivity appeal to you, and you may be skilled at rationalization or intellectualization. You place a premium on individuality and unique self-expression, yet can simultaneously support communal concepts such as the idea of Spaceship Earth (all working together for mutual support). You probably value freedom and uniqueness.

Letter 12: The Natural Mystic

You have an intuitive understanding of the Oneness of all life. On a gut level, you can tune into the connections between all humans. Personally, the sense of union with something Higher is something you tend to seek lifelong.

This "urge to merge" can be manifested in several ways. One potential is the nature mystic who feels the pulse of all life through the oceans or forests or the grandeurs of nature. Another possibility is the inspired artist, who tunes into a higher vibration and then tries to bring that vision into some kind of earthly form or expression. Another potential is the healer, who senses the true oneness of humanity and seeks to succor others because the pain of another person is, in a very real way, the pain of the healer as well. Another possibility is adopting a victim role, looking to alcohol, pills, fantasy, sleep or some other escape to supply the sense of ultimate ecstasy that is yearned for.

There is a natural mysticism here, an instinctive understanding that life is more than just the material world. But the pull of the Higher Self can be expressed in a number of positive ways — or lead to the person running into their own dream world because they will not face the fact that our current world is not yet perfect, ideal and ecstatic. The vision of something more, something Higher, can lead to a deep, abiding faith which is a bulwark throughout the life, or to a search for the Cosmic Santa Claus who will make everything like a beautiful dream for us!

ALPHABET COMBINATIONS BY TWOS

Refer to Chapters 6 (pages 115-119) and 9 (pages 230-237) and read the appropriate **Combinations by Two**, thinking in terms goals, values and basic beliefs.

POLARITIES

1-7: ♂-♀ or ⚴ or ⚵, ♈-♎, 1st-7th houses

Torn between trusting yourself or other people more, you may swing from one extreme to the other. You might put too much faith in your own abilities and actions and then fall into overidealizing others, expecting them to be perfect.

Your understanding of life's meaning and purpose will come largely through interactions with others. The give and take between you and another person stimulates and helps develop your grasp of cosmic patterns and deeper truths.

2-8: ♀-♇, ♉-♏, 2nd-8th houses

You are making a balance between your need for physical indulgence and your desire for self-mastery. Power is something you appreciate, and you evince great determination to run your own life. However, you may feel torn between using your will and drive to pursue material pleasures in the world versus turning that power inward to control and understand yourself. You need to explore both areas — your inner being and the myriad material sources of enjoyment in the world.

You may sway from overdoing, overindulging and thinking that physical possessions, appetites and pleasures are all that matter to withholding and inhibiting in the name of self-control, adopting an ascetic role. Strive for balance.

3-9: ☿-♃, ♊-♐, 3rd-9th houses

Ideas are a major source of faith for you. You trust the mind, the ability to think, communicate and share concepts. Restless and curious about the meaning of life, you are likely to be engaged on a lifelong quest for "The Truth." A sense of openness is often a priority; you expect to keep on learning and growing.

You are learning to balance priorities between long-range goals and values versus short-range needs and necessities. Both are essential for getting what you feel is important in life.

4-10: ☽-♄, ♋-♑, 4th-10th houses

Security and tradition are important to you. A family religion may very well appeal, perhaps even the faith of your forebears. You seek a sense of safety through your religion/science/philosophy/world view. Family values are likely to rate high on your scale.

(See also the Parental theme.)

5-11: ☉-♅, ♌-♒, 5th-11th houses

Open, creative, exploratory, you are likely to be breaking new ground in your search for life's meaning(s). Discontent with the status quo can lead to you looking ahead or in unusual areas for answers. You tend to trust the new, progressive and forward-going in life. You may feel torn between trusting your intellectual assessment of what matters versus the impulses of your heart. Balancing the mind and emotions in matters of belief could be an issue for you.

6-12: ☿ or ♆ or ♃-♆, ♍-♓, 6th-12th houses

You are likely to be facing an inner crisis in faith. Part of you has an intuitive sense of connection to something Higher — a natural, unconscious faith. Another side of you is totally grounded in the material world, looking only for physical (i.e., measurable) explanations. The intuitive and the concrete aspects of your nature require some middle ground of integration.

NODES OF THE MOON
The following nodal placements are particularly relevant in the area of beliefs and values.

Across Gemini/Sagittarius or 3rd/9th Houses

You may feel torn about ultimate beliefs and values. You are likely to do a lot of questioning, wondering, seeking and inquiring in a quest to figure out the meaning of life. You may vacillate between a vast, philosophical perspective and a focus on the mundane, everyday attributes of living. You could be torn between making short-term versus long-term goals a priority. You may be unsure what to trust and value in life or lack faith in almost everything. (Excessive faith and trust is the flip side and just as dangerous.)

Feelings of inadequacy may complicate the issue. Sometimes early self-doubts about your mental prowess are a problem. You may underrate your mind or ability to conceptualize. You may pressure yourself to find "final" answers when each "answer" brings new questions. Seeking, searching, traveling, studying and discussing with others are all likely to contribute to your quest for meaning.

If you have balanced this polarity, you probably know that your seeking and searching will be a lifelong pattern. Every answer brings you new questions, but you enjoy the gathering and exchange of information, while accepting that the final, absolute truth may not be attainable at this time.

Across Virgo/Pisces or 6th/12th Houses

The polarity here is between spiritual aspirations and inspirations versus a focus on the physical details of life. You may feel torn between an instinctive attraction toward a sense of faith and a deep need to be practical and grounded in the material world. You could swing to either extreme: getting lost in fantasies, dreams, visions, the immensity of the universe or concentrating totally on putting all the pieces together and a disciplined, practical approach to life.

The challenge is to integrate your competent, capable, physical bent with your imaginative, visionary capabilities. You need a sense of faith to give meaning and purpose to your everyday activities but enough pragmatism to get things done in the real world. If you have balanced this polarity, you are likely to express both sides through such fields as the talented artist or craftsperson, the healer, the helper, the practical idealist and the realistic mystic.

Feelings of inadequacy could create problems at either end. If you lack trust in your own abilities, you may be afraid to try; you could give up sooner than is necessary in attempting projects. If you lack trust in the Universe, you will feel overly responsible and try to do everything yourself (not trusting others to do as well). Then you end up feeling burdened and pressured. If you feel overwhelmed by the infinite cosmos, you may retreat into concentrating solely on the material world as a solution for your anxiety. If you are too concerned with getting things done **just so**, you may have difficulty relaxing and allowing life to flow at times.

Faith in yourself and also in a Higher Power allows you to do all that you can do in a reasonable, competent fashion to get the job done and then trust that the Universe will take care of the rest.

ELEMENT EMPHASIS

Fire
♂, ☉, ♃, ♄, ♈, ♌, ♐, 1st, 5th, 9th houses

Your faith and optimism tend to be high. Whether you place your trust in yourself and/or a Higher Power, the basic thrust is toward doing more. There is an underlying need for expansion, to go further than you have gone before. Impatience is possible with the feeling of: "The universe should recognize me and my needs **now**." You are likely to value action, initiative, courage, risk-taking, open confrontation and the pursuit of new challenges.

Earth
♀, ☿, ?, ♀, ♄, ♂, ♍, ♑, 2nd, 6th, 10th houses

You can carry practicality to the ultimate extreme. Your values are solidly based in the material world. You trust what is tangible and measurable. You usually seek to achieve in a career and appreciate your ability to manipulate the physical world. Disinclined to take anything "on faith," you want a world view that makes sense, that "works," that is useful on a pragmatic level.

Air
☿, ♀, ♀, ✳, ♅, ♊, ♎, ♒, 3rd, 7th, 11th houses

You are most likely to trust the intellect. Thinking, communicating and sharing ideas are probable values. Preferring to be objective, you are likely to consider a number of points of view in formulating your basic belief system. You will listen to many opinions and perspectives and base your beliefs largely on logic and rationality.

Water
☽, ♇, ♆, ♋, ♏, ♓, 4th, 8th, 12th houses

Your faith is likely to come from a deep level within your psyche. Tuning into your Higher Self, perhaps unconsciously, leads to an implicit understanding of the meaning of life. You may not always be able to put your intuitions into words, but you can feel a sense of connection to the Universe on a gut level. Sometimes you may rely too much on feelings.

Fire-Earth
♂, ☉, ♃, ♂, ♈, ♌, ♐, 1st, 5th, 9th houses &
♀, ☿, ?, ♀, ♄, ♂, ♍, ♑, 2nd, 6th, 10th houses

You probably value energetic accomplishments. Your priorities are a blend of self-expression and productivity. The combination can be highly effective. If the fire side wins out, you may simply care most about doing exactly as you please in life. If the earth side wins out, you may put your faith in concrete achievements and responsibility. Together, drive and perseverance can move mountains if you choose.

Fire-Air
♂, ☉, ♃, ♂, ♈, ♌, ♐, 1st, 5th, 9th houses &
☿, ♀, ♀, ✳, ♅, ♊, ♎, ♒, 3rd, 7th, 11th houses

You value having fun. Your vision of a deity is likely to be a Being with a sense of humor — perhaps even a practical joker! You usually see life as arranged for us to enjoy and do your best to carry forward that vision.

Fire-Water
♂, ☉, ♃, ♂, ♈, ♌, ♐, 1st, 5th, 9th houses &
☽, ♇, ♆, ♋, ♏, ♓, 4th, 8th, 12th houses

You value intense emotions and heartfelt responses. Your vision of a deity is likely to be a Being of tremendous passion, caring and depth of feelings. You may trust emotional reactions (soul responses) more than pure rationalizations or intellectual explanations.

Earth-Air
♀, ☿, ♀, ♀, ♄, ♉, ♍, ♑, 2nd, 6th, 10th houses &
☿, ♀, ♀, ♀, ♅, ♊, ♎, ♒, 3rd, 7th, 11th houses

You value logic and practicality. Your vision of a deity is likely to be a Being who is sensible, grounded and operates on the basis of the mind. You trust objectivity and rationality. You may mistrust emotional reactions. You seek intellectual understanding and common sense in life.

Earth-Water
♀, ☿, ♀, ♀, ♄, ♉, ♍, ♑, 2nd, 6th, 10th houses &
☽, ♇, ♆, ♋, ♏, ♓, 4th, 8th, 12th houses

You value practical helpfulness. Your vision of a deity is likely to be a Being who is compassionate and effective, caring and motivated to assist troubled people. You are inclined to take your beliefs seriously and seek security in your world view.

Air-Water
☿, ♀, ♀, ♀, ♅, ♊, ♎, ♒, 3rd, 7th, 11th houses &
☽, ♇, ♆, ♋, ♏, ♓, 4th, 8th, 12th houses

You value understanding — both on the rational and intuitive levels. Your vision of a deity is likely to be a Being who is infinitely insightful, naturally blending the intellectual and the psychic for an optimum mix. Your goals probably include seeking a combination of conscious and unconscious knowing in your own life.

QUALITY EMPHASIS

Cardinal
♂, ☽, ♀, ♀, ♀, ♄, ♈, ♋, ♎, ♑, 1st, 4th, 7th, 10th houses

Your priorities are mixed and you may spend time feeling torn between conflicting needs. You are likely to value liberty as well as emotional attachments; home and family as well as work in the outside world. You may sometimes wonder if there is room in your life for everything that is important to you. All are necessary; the key is finding a balance most satisfactory to you.

Fixed
♀, ☉, ♇, ♅, ♉, ♌, ♏, ♒, 2nd, 5th, 8th, 11th houses

You are likely to value power and the control of your own life. Usually faithful and loyal, you probably believe in carrying through on one's commitments and finishing up what is started. Resistant to outside influences, you are disinclined to adopt a faith that puts you in a highly vulnerable position. Naturally sensual, you may feel a struggle between your physical, material needs and your spiritual aspirations. Yet they can support one another if you work for integration. You need to choose your own path; no one else can lead you. A major strength is your faith in your own inner answers; this becomes a weakness if your version of the truth is allowed to become self-righteous.

Mutable
☿, ?, ♀, ♃, ⚷, ♆, ♊, ♍, ♐, ♓, 3rd, 6th, 9th, 12th houses

Flexible, adaptable and curious, you have probably explored a number of potential world views. What you trust and value is likely to change over time, as you learn, study, read and watch other people. The seeking of knowledge and understanding is a high priority, but you probably will never feel you have enough, always wanting more. You may sometimes fall into perfectionism in your beliefs and expectations — demanding more than is reasonable, from yourself, loved ones, a deity or other sides of life. Learn to have aspirations without expecting to reach them all immediately.

THEMES

Freedom
♂, ♃, ⚷, ♅, ♈, ♐, ♒, 1st, 9th, 11th houses

The freedom to search for the truth is one of your highest values. Placing a priority on liberty, you seek a sense of personal independence and the ability to roam the world and search anywhere for life's meaning. Inclined to reject the dogmas of other people, you need to find your own sense of what the universe is all about.

Closeness or Interpersonal
☽, ☉, ♀, ☿, ✳, ♇, ♋, ♌, ♎, ♏, 4th, 5th, 7th, 8th houses

Emotional attachments are a major part of your value system. You probably place a priority on closeness and relating to others. You may idealize this area and want more than is possible, but are motivated to create the best possible relationships. Your belief system is likely to have compassion, caring, love and connecting as prominent values. Family is usually quite important.

Artistic
♀, ☿, ⚸, ☉, Ψ, ♉, ♌, ♎, ♓, 2nd, 5th, 7th, 12th houses

Beauty is a part of the cosmic scheme for you. Often, you feel a connection to the Universe through great art, nature or some part of life which evokes strong aesthetic reactions in you. Because you tend to value grace, balance and harmony, you may sometimes avoid unpleasantness and refuse to deal with it in life. You prefer life to flow smoothly and easily.

Idealistic
♃, ⚷, Ψ, ♐, ♓, 9th, 12th houses

Seeking the Highest comes naturally to you, with an instinctive reach upward. Not willing to settle for anything limited, your belief system needs to be truly infinite. Idealistic, with a pull toward the infinite, you can be a natural mystic. You may also feel your understanding is never broad or encompassing enough. You strive for something more than simple human comprehension.

Obsessive-Compulsive
☿, ⚵, ⚶, ♇, ♄, ♍, ♏, ♑, 6th, 8th, 10th houses

Precise and exacting, you seek an explanation for life that is logical and coherent. Your analytical approach is ready to poke holes in any belief systems that do not hang together. Inclined to get involved with petty details, you can sometimes lose sight and appreciation of the Whole because you are so caught up in figuring out one small part. You expect your faith to make sense.

Competence
☿, ⚵, ⚶, ♄, ♍, ♑, 6th, 10th houses

Solid accomplishments are what you value. Your faith is usually in the physical, the measurable. A pragmatist, you may or may not accept any meaning beyond the material. You expect hard work to lead to success and generally put your trust in doing things well.

Mental Stimulation
☿, ⚵, ⚶, ♀, ♃, ⚷, ⛢, Ψ, ♊, ♍, ♎, ♐, ♒, ♓, 3rd, 6th, 7th, 9th, 11th, 12th houses

You probably consider God's greatest gift to humankind is the human brain with its capacity for communication. Your beliefs are subject to much questioning, discussing, studying and seeking answers through reading, learning, interacting with others. You are likely to trust the intellect most and could reject the concept of a Higher Power if you cannot rationalize it to yourself. Yet you usually are drawn to thinking and talking about this area. Your curiosity is aroused.

Relationships
♀, ☿, ⚸, ♇, ♎, ♏, 7th, 8th houses

Your values are tied to people and often influenced by them. You do not operate in a metaphysical vacuum, but find your concepts stimulated by the thoughts of others. (You may share beliefs harmoniously, or engage in sharp, competitive debates about reality.) Your goals, ideals and standards for relationships tend to be exceptionally high. You may aim for more than is possible in that area and/or attract partners who expect more than is reasonable from you. Beauty is often a significant value in your belief system, as well as grace, harmony and interaction.

Security
♀, ☽, ☿, ⚴, ⚸, ♇, ♄, ♆, ♉, ♋, ♍, ♏, ♑, ♓, 2nd, 4th, 6th, 8th, 10th, 12th houses

Your faith rests in security and safety. You are likely to be drawn to a religious/spiritual/scientific belief system which offers a sense of predictable understanding and a firm foundation on which to rely. You seek the known and the stable and value the comfortable and familiar.

Risk/Creativity/Change
♂, ☉, ♃, ⚵, ♅, ♈, ♌, ♐, ♒, 1st, 5th, 9th, 11th houses

You put your trust in a sense of optimism, faith and the willingness to go for more! Courageous and forward-going, you tend to seek out constant challenges and opportunities to grow and expand in understanding. Generally pioneering in your beliefs, you are unlikely to accept the status quo. Creative and expressive, you will not be bound by old limits. You tend to rock the religious (spiritual/scientific) boat in your search for further insight into the meaning of life.

Parents
☽, ♄, ⚴, ♋, ♈♑, 4th, 10th houses

Your faith is profoundly influenced by your parent(s). This can include a conservative approach to religious/spiritual/scientific matters, carrying on the traditions of your forebears. It can simply mean that your parents' actions and attitudes had a strong impact on your vision of what life is all about. You could take them as negative role models and go in the opposite direction from them. But they are a likely standard of comparison (what you want or what you don't want) for your own ethics, values, beliefs and faith.

Power
☉, ♇, ♄, ♌, ♏, ♑, 5th, 8th, 10th houses

Power is likely to be an issue in your basic beliefs. You may trust and value strength, authority and control. While you might not say that "Might makes right," you are likely to feel that a position of strength beats vulnerability any day. You may make the achievement of a high level of dominance in life a long-range goal.

Control of your own life probably ranks high on your list of priorities. Vulnerability may be avoided as a seeming weakness. Wherever you define a lack, need or flaw, you are likely to seek immediate improvement and mastery.

If not personally identified with a need for power, your concept of a deity is likely to revolve around that issue. Omnipotence is truly a central theme for you — both in your personal actions and within your vision of reality.

You may need to clarify your ethics and moral principles about what kinds of power you trust and value and what kinds you abhor. Keep room for your own strength as well as faith in a Higher Power. Balance ethics and power urges.

Personal
♂, ♀, ☿, ☽, ♈, ♉, ♊, ♋, 1st, 2nd, 3rd, 4th houses

Your beliefs are your own and you are unlikely to be strongly inclined to accept other people's versions of reality. Getting what you want in the world is generally a priority. You are here first to please yourself. This does not mean you are automatically self-centered, but it does imply that your goals, values and ideals revolve first and foremost around your place in the scheme of things.

Transpersonal
♃, ⚷, ♄, ♅, ♆, ♐, ♑, ♒, ♓, 9th, 10th, 11th, 12th houses

Your world view tends to be broad and fairly inclusive. You like to understand things from a wide perspective. Unwilling to tie yourself down to one approach or one version of the truth, you are usually open to input from a number of different sources. You seek answers which are relevant not just to you personally, but also to the world as a whole and other people. You look for meanings that can contribute to society and people at large.

ASPECTS

Harmony to Letter...

1: There is potential harmony between your highest values and personal action. Your beliefs are likely to support your ability to be yourself and pursue your own interests. Your sense of faith and trust help you to maintain your freedom and independence.

2: There is potential harmony between your highest values and your ability to enjoy the material world. Your comfort and predilection for ease reinforce your vision of reality. Your belief system is likely to support your ability to enjoy money, possessions and sensual pleasures.

3: There is potential harmony between your highest values and your intellectual capacities. Your beliefs and world view are likely to support your ways of thinking and communicating. You know how to balance short and long-term goals for optimum results. Ideas fly; you probably have a very active mind.

4: There is potential harmony between your highest values and your desire for emotional closeness. Shared faith and congruent beliefs are a likely connection to those with whom you share a home. Your emotional security is enhanced by a sense of the meaning of life and your reaching out for more in life is balanced by a secure foundation.

5: There is potential harmony between your highest values and your need to pour out into the world, receiving positive feedback. Your ethics, goals and values assist you in finding positive avenues to gain self-esteem through your creative efforts. Your natural dynamism and magnetism supports your search for meaning. Your dramatic instinct can further your ideals.

6: There is potential harmony between your highest values and your desire to do a good job in life. You are capable of working in a situation that furthers your goals, ideals and visions of what life is all about. Your work can further your dreams while your dreams help inspire you to work more effectively.

7: There is potential harmony between your highest values and your need for equality, harmony and balance in life. Your sense of justice and fair play is likely to be strong. Agreeing on priorities and goals comes easily with partners.

8: There is potential harmony between your highest values and your desire for depth analysis and knowledge. Breadth and depth complement one another as you seek an understanding of life encompassing both a broad perspective and an intense scrutiny. Your capacity for self-control enhances your pursuit of the truth and your priorities in life probably encourage self-insight.

9: There is potential harmony in the area of your goals, values and beliefs. This suggests you can make priorities rather easily and go from one goal to another without great tension. Your faith and optimism are likely to be high, as you have inner agreement about what really matters in life.

10: There is potential harmony between your highest values and your drive for responsibility, authority and power in the world. Your ideals can enhance your career achievements and your worldly ambitions can support your sense of moral principles. Pragmatism and idealism can be blended very well by you; optimism and pessimism mesh for best results.

11: There is potential harmony between your highest values and your desire for uniqueness and individuality. Your drive for independence supports your search for something more in life. Your moral principles and ethics affirm your personal uniqueness and freedom.

12: There is potential harmony between your highest values and your quest for merging with the Infinite. Idealism is likely to be strong as you seek ways to manifest your dreams on earth. Helping, healing and artistic paths are all potential avenues for you manifesting your reach upward.

Conflict to Letter...

1: There is potential conflict between your faith and self-assertion. Extremes could range from excessive confidence (to the point of rashness) to fear of doing what you want, due to basic anxiety and insecurity (with a lack of faith in the universe). Make room in life for a sense of meaning, purpose and reaching for something more while still being able to be yourself and express naturally in the world.

2: There is potential conflict between your highest values and your desire for physical possessions, money and sensual pleasures. You may feel torn between "spiritual" and "carnal" desires as you reconcile the more earthy side of your nature with your aspirations and dreams. Avoid of the extreme of foolishly wasting substance and finances on impractical schemes, but also eschew a retreat into spirituality that denies the essential physical reality of life. Pleasure is an appropriate experience — in moderation.

3: There is potential conflict between your highest values and your ability to be objective and communicate easily with those around you. Grandiose ideas may separate you from people in your immediate environment. Excessively high expectations can make communication a chore. Mental restlessness and talent is likely. Maintain space in your life for both the inspiration from above and the ability to relate in the here and now.

4: There is potential conflict between your highest values and your ability to maintain close, committed relationships, including a home base. Your search for answers may simply take you away from home a lot, or bring much seeking and questioning into your home. Your desire for more can be at odds with your need for emotional security and safety. Keep room for both.

5: There is potential conflict between your highest values and your need to shine in the world. Your principles and ethics may be at odds with your desire to be a star. Your quest for something more in life may clash with loving and being loved. You need emotional response and admiration from others in life as well as a sense of meaning and purpose in terms of an ultimate perspective.

6: There is potential conflict between your highest values and your desire for practicality and sensible accomplishments. Idealism wars with realism as you seek to bring your dreams down to earth. Avoid starry eyed fantasy, but also eschew the extreme of drudgery with no sense of purpose or inspiration. Practical idealism works the best.

7: There is potential conflict between your highest values and your desire for one-to-one relationships with others. A strong sense of justice and fair play is likely, but you may feel expectations are an issue in your partnerships. Beware of demanding too much of others or attracting others who demand too much of you. Channel the reach for the Infinite into spiritual, religious, artistic or helping activities; practice acceptance and tolerance for human relationships.

8: There is potential conflict between your highest values and your desire for self-insight, self-mastery and self-control. Your reach upward and outward may conflict with your probing inward and downward. Extraversion and introversion vie for priority. Beware of using excessive ideals to cut yourself off from relationships (because you are not perfect or the other person is not). Balance the quest for something more with the need for a depth sharing in an intimate context.

9: There is potential conflict in the area of faith, values, goals and beliefs. You may lack faith (in yourself or a Higher Power), have excessive faith (rash, foolhardy), faith in inappropriate areas (looking to a human being to satisfy all your needs) or simply conflicting values. Examination, clarification and the establishment of value hierarchies can work wonders.

10: There is potential conflict between your highest values and your awareness of what one can do, cannot do and must do in life. Optimism may be at odds with pessimism as you strive to balance a freewheeling faith that everything will be okay with a cautious pragmatism that insists on expecting the worst. You **can** be a highly effective visionary — grounding your dreams in real accomplishments if you make peace between your reach for more (avoid excessive demands) and your practical abilities (avoid excessive criticism).

11: There is potential conflict between your highest values and your rebellious, innovative and inventive side. Your desire for independence and uniqueness could lead you to an excessively individualistic (even chaotic) approach to belief systems. You might refuse to make priorities or establish long-range goals lest they somehow "pin you down." Another option is stifling your individuality with an exaggerated importance placed on one version of "the Truth." You need room for both faith and independence in life; doing your thing but being able to trust all will work out once you've done what you can.

12: There is potential conflict in the area of your beliefs, values and moral/religious/spiritual systems. Your conscious and unconscious faith may be at odds. You may accept certain principles on one level, but attract opposite experiences due to unconscious ambivalences. Excessive idealism could be an issue, or simply lack of clarity among your many beliefs and goals. Systematizing and organizing your thinking about what is ultimately most important and meaningful in life is likely to bring the best results.

CHAPTER TWELVE

MONEY

This chapter will not tell you when you are likely to win the lottery or come into an inheritance. It might, however, help you to come to terms with some of your ideas and anxieties about money, and perhaps even clear away some blocks that have been preventing you from making more of the treasured stuff or from enjoying what you do have.

The Factors

Money and movable possessions are associated with **Letter 2** when we refer to direct earnings and personal property. (Of course, Letter 2 is pleasure from the material world in general and is **not** limited to money alone, encompassing also sensuality, beauty, artistic pursuits and other material pleasures.) **Letter 8** refers to return on investments, delayed earnings (such as royalties) and joint finances and possessions (with a partner, family, friend, etc.).

Note that Jupiter is **not** considered a "money planet." Jupiter is a key to our ultimate values. Whatever we turn into an ideal, we tend to pursue in life, wanting more and more. **If** Jupiter is connected to finances (e.g., conjunct or parallel Venus or Pluto, occupying the 2nd or 8th houses, in Taurus or Scorpio, ruling the 2nd or 8th houses or signs in those houses, conjunct or parallel any rulers of the 2nd or 8th), the individual **may** turn money (or pleasure) into "God" and pursue more and more financial gain. If the dollar is considered an ultimate value, how can one ever have enough? (Another option when Jupiter is mixed with money factors is to spend one's resources on the pursuit of the truth — putting money into education, books, seminars, travel, churches, spiritual explorations, etc.). Thus for money, we consider:[1]

GROUP I
Conjunctions to Venus (as ruler of Taurus) and Pluto
Conjunctions to the rulers of the 2nd and 8th cusps
Conjunctions to rulers of other signs in the 2nd and 8th houses

GROUP II
Planets in the 2nd and 8th houses
Planets within two degrees of the 2nd and 8th houses even though occupying the
  1st, 3rd, 7th or 9th houses

GROUP III
Parallels to Venus, Pluto, ruler(s) of the 2nd house, ruler(s) of the 8th house
House placements of Venus and Pluto
House placements of rulers of the 2nd and 8th cusps
House placements of rulers of other signs in the 2nd and 8th houses
Houses ruled by planets in the 2nd and 8th houses
Houses ruled by planets making any conjunctions to Venus, Pluto, 2nd house rulers
  or 8th house rulers
Planets in Taurus or Scorpio
Houses occupied by planets in Taurus or Scorpio

GROUP IV
Sign placements of Venus and Pluto
Sign placements of rulers of the 2nd and 8th cusps
Sign placements of rulers of other signs in the 2nd and 8th houses
Signs on the cusps of the 2nd and 8th houses
Houses with Taurus or Scorpio on the cusp

---

1. If you prefer **not** to search for repeated themes yourself, you can order the "PP BOOK" option from Astro Computing Services (PO Box 16430, San Diego, Ca 92116), which allows you to use this book to make complete, synthesizing delineations of horoscopes without figuring out which themes are emphasized.

　　Available for $3.00 each, the "PP BOOK" report calculates the emphasis on all the letters of the alphabet, themes and aspects in each horoscope for which you provide the data. The report lists each significant focus (e.g., "There is a Letter 1 theme in "Money," and gives the appropriate page numbers for you to read in this book ("See pages 324-325 in the Complete Horoscope Interpretation book.")

　　The computer will not **always** arrive at the same results as you might, as certain steps are ambiguous (e.g., how much weight to give a planet making a conjunction, based on the orb). However, the majority of the time, the computer answers will concur with those derived from use of the worksheets — or the recommended quick scan of a horoscope. Thus it provides an excellent teaching tool.

　　The "PP BOOK" does **not** provide a listing of **each and every** astrological factor making up the significant themes. For that, you would order "PP WEIGHTS" (discussed in next footnote).

Signs occupied by planets in the 2nd or 8th houses
Unoccupied signs in the 2nd or 8th houses

How to Weight the Factors

Please note that these factors are rank ordered (in chunks) according to their weighting. If you want to use exact figures, a suggested weighting scale is given in the appendix — with worksheets for money and the other various life areas.[2]

A SHORT CUT
For quickness and ease of use, especially for people just learning to use the alphabet, I suggest beginning with factors in Groups I and II.

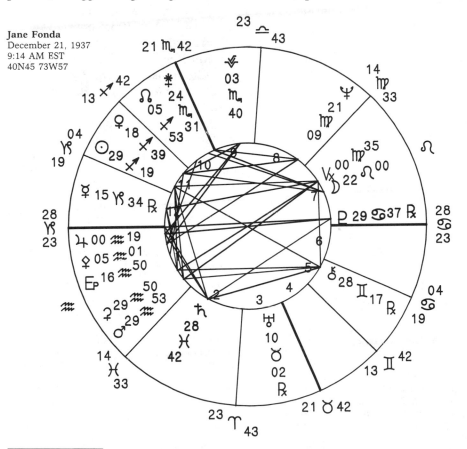

Jane Fonda
December 21, 1937
9:14 AM EST
40N45 73W57

---

2. You can also obtain a listing of **all** the astrological factors which compose those letters of the Zip Code determined to be significant in a horoscope. This makes an excellent teaching tool and a valuable resource to check yourself against when practicing with the Zip Code.

Astro Computing Services, PO Box 16430, San Diego, CA 92116, has calculated 28,000 horoscopes (footnote continued on next page)

If any letter of the alphabet is represented once in Group I or II, consider it as probably significant. (If one letter is represented twice in Groups I and II, it is definitely significant.) For example, in the Fonda chart, the Aries falling in the 2nd house is ruled by Mars, which conjuncts Ceres, giving us a (half-weight) focus on Letter 6. (We must always remember that Ceres can also be a key to mother or a mother figure. Ms. Fonda received a substantial trust from her mother's estate.) Also, the 8th house is occupied by Neptune (Letter 12) while the 2nd is occupied by Saturn (Letter 10).

Thus, we would suspect we may be looking at the interpretations for Letters 10 and 12 (and possibly 6) within this "Money" section.

Once you are familiar with Groups I and II, move on to Groups III and IV. If factors in Groups III and IV give at least one more repetition of a letter suggested by Groups I and II, consider that confirmation and read the appropriate interpretations (pages 324-329). In Ms. Fonda's case, Letter 10 is repeated by the ruler of the 8th cusp, Mercury, falling in Capricorn (10), Scorpio occupied (by Juno) in the 10th house (10) and Scorpio on the Midheaven (10). Letter 12 is repeated by Mercury (ruling the 8th) occupying the 12th house (12), the 2nd house being occupied by a planet in Pisces (12) and the fact that Saturn (in the 2nd) rules the 12th (12). Meanwhile, Letter 6 is repeated by the ruler of the 2nd, Neptune, in Virgo (6), Scorpio being occupied by Vesta (6) and the 8th cusp having Virgo (6).

In examining Groups III and IV, also look for any letters of the alphabet which occur five or more times. Consider them significant and read the appropriate interpretations. For example, a Letter 9 theme is repeated in the Fonda chart: Venus is in Sagittarius (9), Scorpio falls in the 9th house (9), the 8th house Libra is ruled by Venus, which is in Sagittarius (9), Jupiter (9) is in a Gauquelin sector and Scorpio is occupied in the 9th (9). Thus, we would also read the interpretation for Letter 9 in this section.

Both Letters 9 and 12 **can** point to great wealth (although they can also simply point to dreaming about great wealth and not doing anything). The inclusion of Letters 6 and 10 implies much hard work and the probability of success (unless self-critical tendencies are overdone).

---

2. (continued from previous page)
   and established averages and standard deviations for the scores of each letter of the astrological alphabet, each theme, and the conflict and harmony aspects to each life area.

   Astro's report, called "PP WEIGHTS," will list those letters of the astrological alphabet which are one standard deviation or more above the mean — and list **all** the astrological factors which point to each significant letter of the alphabet. These weightings will also compare each individual's score on the various themes (e.g., risk-taking, artistic) to the means and standard deviations to determine which themes are significant.

   Averages are established for aspects as well in order to note conflict or harmony in the different life areas.

   The results obtained by Astro's "PP WEIGHTS" will not **always** coincide with those you determine by a quick scan and intuitive judgment, or by use of the worksheets. Certain of the steps (e.g., how much to weight a planet based on orb) are ambiguous, so different results can occur. However, most of the time, Astro's answers will confirm those you could obtain in working with the Zip Code. Furthermore, the **complete** listing of relevant factors is an excellent teaching tool.

   Ask for "PP Weights." The price, as of December 1985 is $5.00

Themes

Themes can be ascertained by two approaches. One method is to examine **only** those letters of the alphabet which are emphasized and determine which themes can be made from combinations of those letters. In the case of Jane Fonda's chart, we have already noted that both Letters 6 and 10 look significantly above average in emphasis, so we would suspect a "work/competence/practical" theme here. Her biographies constantly stress her dedication, discipline and willingness to work hard for what she earns.

It is interesting to note that her "idealistic" letters, 9 and 12, also rank as significant (even **more** significant than 6 and 10 in terms of weighting). We might anticipate a "real versus ideal" or "visionary versus pragmatist" inner conflict (part of the 6-12 polarity) to be resolved around her handling of finances. Fred Guiles' biography of Ms. Fonda suggests that her idealism (Letter 9 and 12) led to her being taken advantage of financially by certain groups. Mr. Guiles also suggests that she became more practical with age, and less likely to be duped by so-called "worthy causes" wanting her money (and fame). He describes her as very generous with money, but wanting to know where every penny goes: an appropriate blend of the "real" and "ideal" themes.

Ms. Fonda also has a strong focus on three out of four (9, 10, 12) of the transpersonal factors where money is concerned. She is definitely known for giving money to causes and campaigns (including her husband's) which she feels will change the world and make it better.

A second approach is to figure out the totals for **all** the letters of the alphabet and then estimate which combinations have an above average emphasis. For example, the practical (or work or competence) theme is the total of scores from Letter 6 and 10. (To a certain extent, all of earth and water are more practical — with air and fire less so. However, the prime pragmatics of the zodiac are marked by an emphasis on Letters 6 and 10.) You will need to do some rough arithmetic here, or get an intuitive impression. If a theme involves two (out of twelve) letters of the astrological alphabet, you would expect it to have about 1/6 of the total score. So, if the amount for those letters seems appreciably more than 1/6 of the total, count that as a theme — and read the appropriate section (pages 338-339).

When searching for themes, give a little extra weight to like planets in aspect to one another. For example, Ceres, Vesta, (Mercury, if read as a Virgo Mercury) and Saturn are the practical "planets." Any aspects between Ceres, Vesta, (Mercury) and Saturn add to the practical theme. In Fonda's case, Saturn has a semisextile to Ceres while Mercury has a close octile to Ceres and Ceres trines Vesta.

Also give extra weight to like houses and like signs. Thus, Ceres, Vesta, Mercury and Saturn occupying the 6th or 10th houses or Virgo or Capricorn would give extra weight to the practical theme for each occurrence. Fonda has Mercury in pragmatic sign (10).

Aspects

Quickly scan all aspects other than conjunctions or parallels, grouping them according to harmony (sextile, trine, semisextile) and conflict (octile, tri-octile, square, opposition, quincunx and contra-parallel).

In considering each aspect, weight the nature of the planet most heavily, followed by the house and the sign. Count both the house occupied and the cusp the aspected planet rules.

For example, in Fonda's horoscope, a money factor, Pluto, is making the following **close** harmony aspects:

- trine Saturn (10) in the 2nd (2) in Pisces (12); Saturn rules the 12th and 1st (12)(1); Pluto makes the following **close** conflict aspects:
- quincunx the Sun (5) in the 11th (11) in Sagittarius (9); the Sun rules the 7th (7)
- quincunx Mars (1) in the 1st (1) in Aquarius (11); Mars rules the 3rd (3)
- opposite Jupiter (9) in the 1st (1) in Aquarius (11); Jupiter rules the 11th (11)
- quincunx Ceres (6 — ½ weight) in the 1st (1) in Aquarius (11)
- quincunx the Antivertex (1) in the 1st (1) in Pisces (12)
- contra-parallel Mercury (3) in the 12th (12) in Capricorn (10); Mercury rules 5th and 8th (5)(8)
- contra-parallel Venus (2) in the 11th (11) in Sagittarius (9); Venus rules the 4th and 9th (4)(9)

Make an intuitive judgment of whether any letters of the alphabet have lots of conflict to them or have quite a bit of harmony. Here, we would want to consider the other keys to money, besides Pluto. So far, we suspect Letters 1 and 11 may end up important in terms of conflict. (Note, we can assume conflict to freedom a theme, even if we do not count Letters 1 and 11 individually as dominant. You can extrapolate your own interpretations for the various themes and other combinations in the Zip Code.) If you feel any group of aspects has an emphasis on one or more letters of the alphabet, read the appropriate interpretation (pages 341-345).

Interpretations: Money

ALPHABET THEMES

Letter 1: The Free Spender

Money, sensuality and beauty are all potential forums for self-expression. The active pursuit of beauty (e.g., skating, dancing, diving, swimming, *Tai Chi*) is one potential. This combination usually indicates the ability to be comfortable with one's self — to like who you are. If overdone, self-indulgence (in food, alcohol, spending money, collecting possessions, smoking, drugs) is possible. Pleasure is sought through direct, spontaneous action — doing your own thing.

Spending habits are usually open. Impulsiveness can be a problem. Usually, if you like it, you buy it.

You can be very active in pursuit of material gain, as long as it is what you want. You follow your own rules in making and spending money and break those "rules" if you feel like it.

Letter 2: The Pleasure-Seeker

Comfort, security and stability appeal to you. You tend toward a predictable pattern in your handling of finances and resources. Often, you enjoy possessions. Sensuality is generally high — whether expressed through food, alcohol, spending money, smoking or other forms of physical pleasure. Aesthetic talent is a potential. Very often, the instinct for beauty is strong. You may be skilled in music, painting, sculpture, design, decorating, gourmet cooking, landscape gardening or other areas which allow scope for an aesthetic appreciation and a strong tactile sense.

Expenditures tend to be for items that will bring pleasure, ease and/or beauty into your life.

Letter 3: MINDing Your Money

You are curious and articulate about finances — your own and other people's. Analyzing monetary patterns is second nature to you. Economics may appeal — or simply discussing the neighbors' spending habits. Your mind and money are intertwined. This ranges from earning your income through mental pursuits (e.g., talking, writing, teaching, selling) to spending money on intellectual goods (e.g., seminars, trips, classes, books). You look to the mind as a source of potential pleasure. Since you tend to think about your expenditures, you are not prone to impulsive purchases, but you are an excellent rationalizer. Once you have bought it, you can cite innumerable reasons for having done so!

Letter 4: Safety First

Money, security, stability and predictability are sources of emotional support for you. Safety, for you, lies in a protected bank account (or several). Very often, you collect things. Possessions help you to feel secure. Having a lot of things around can be a sort of protection. Be wary of turning things — including food — into a major source of security and emotional support. Overeating is a potential here — or overindulging in any form of security-seeking. Find a source of emotional support that does not depend on outside, physical forms.

Your mother's example in handling money and resources is important in your experience. She is a role model — positive or negative. You may be like her — or trying to do the opposite — but there tends to be a lot of comparing of your behavior with hers. Consciously select the behaviors you wish to keep and those you do not. Otherwise, you may get caught up in old, automatic actions that are not in your best interest. Sometimes Mother is directly involved in your finances — as a source of support, or someone you spend money on. Resources may also go toward food or anything which contributes to the home environment. Family, pets, or anything which you want to take care of, can be a major source of income or outgo.

Letter 5: The Speculator

Money, for you, is fun! A natural risk-taker, you enjoy laying things on the line financially, and hoping for a bigger return. Looking for that grand payoff often appeals. You may dream a lot about "hitting it big" — through sweepstakes, lotteries, the tables at Vegas, a real estate "killing" or some other sudden windfall. You usually believe that money is made for spending — preferably with the maximum possible enjoyment.

Playing with money is a common pursuit. This can range from gambling, speculation and investment, to spending lots on recreation and other "fun" activities, to just "blowing" it on an extravagant purchase periodically. Children can also be recipients of your funds. Often generous, you are usually willing to share what you have with others. An innate optimism makes you feel you can always get more. Sometimes, you can even be a bit of a show-off with your resources — trying to impress people with your importance. Usually, you are fun to be with because you enjoy indulging and your excitement is contagious.

Letter 6: The Economist

Money for you, is a serious business. It may even be a career! Working in the banking, investment, accounting or money-related fields is entirely possible. This can include involvement with government funds and taxes. (Health fields are also a likely bet.)

Your focus is on efficiency. A skilled budgeter, you concentrate on getting the most out of your dollar. Often parsimonious, you have been known to comparison shop, making sure you get the best deal in town. Thrift can be your middle name. Since you tend to view earning a living as something requiring dedication and effort, you may end up working harder than you need to and carrying more than your share of the load. Remember to relax too!

Expenditures with which you are most comfortable are those which advance your career or assist and improve your health. Either of those goals can serve to rationalize even expensive purchases. Enhancement of productivity and efficient functioning appeal highly to you.

Letter 7: Sharing the Wealth

Finances, in your book, are joint. You are likely to earn your income through relating with other people. This could include personnel work, consulting, counseling or other careers involving a professional relationship to people. Business partnerships are quite possible. At times, a partner (business, marriage, live-in) could provide some or all of your income. Or, you may be the financial support to a partner.

Aesthetic talents are another potential source of income. Skill in interior decorating, photography, design, architecture, fashion, painting or other "visual" fields is quite possible. Of course, you may simply enjoy purchasing beautiful things to appreciate. It is quite likely that you have exquisite taste.

You are less inclined than most people to "go it alone" in making a financial decision. You prefer to bounce ideas off someone else first. Even if you argue with the other person, that form of decision making seems to work the best for you.

Letter 8: The Power of Money

Your feelings about finances are deep and intense. You have a tremendous drive to be in control of that area of your life. Consequently, you may sometimes interpret people's actions as manipulative or intrusive, even when they did not mean to be so. Withdrawal is one of your forms of defense, so when you feel threatened (especially in the pocketbook), you tend to simply cut yourself off and refuse to relate. Secrecy is often a form of protection for you; if others do not know anything about your monetary situation, they have no way to hurt you.

You can be quite intuitive and perceptive about money matters and are often drawn to financial or economic fields. Because you are naturally closemouthed, you can be a superb accountant, banker or investor of other's resources. Deeply analytical and investigative, you will ferret out all the facts and examine the situation thoroughly before reaching a decision. In fact, you can be a bit obsessive at times! Money, for you, is power, and you tend to focus on getting more of both.

Letter 9: Hey, Big Spender!

The eternal optimist, your motto is sometimes, "When my ship comes in...." Somewhat extravagant, you tend to have grand schemes and great dreams. Gambling, speculation, sweepstakes and other means of making a "quick buck" may appeal. However, unless they are grounded, you can end up with a head in the clouds and feet in the poorhouse! Your expansionist tendencies can create many potential money-making projects, but beware of taking on too much!

Your faith in life and money are tied up with one another. This can range from making money your ultimate value (and then how can you ever have enough?) to seeing money as a means to the grand philosophy that is your highest goal. Endless resources may be your vision of utopia, or you might spend great amounts in trying to create your utopia here on Earth.

Depending on how you express this blend, you could be 1) exceptionally rich — with seemingly limitless resources; 2) constantly dreaming about getting rich — but waiting for the Universe to drop it in your lap; 3) spending many of your resources on the pursuit of a vision — religious, philosophical, spiritual, educational; 4) a con artist who believes the world owes him/her a living; 5) a hedonist who values all the physical pleasures of life.

Your enthusiasm, energy and faith can be great assets to you financially — as long as they are not overdone.

Letter 10: Cautious and Conservative

All the puritan virtues could apply to you: conscientious, hardworking, stable, responsible, thrifty, careful, cautious, modest, unassuming, etc. You tend to expect life to demand hard work. Thus, you end up often doing more than your fair share on the job. Or, you may sometimes just give up on doing anything because you feel overwhelmed by all that you see before you. A tendency to feel overly responsible can contribute to you giving up on tasks. Concentrate on distinguishing what is truly your responsibility and doing that well. Then let other people do **their** jobs!

You are inclined to play it safe, financially. Money in the bank or in the safest, most secure investments helps you sleep soundly at night. A bit of a pinch-penny, you want to be sure you get your money's worth — whatever the purchase. Old things often appeal — especially when you expect them to go up in value. You often exhibit a strong business sense and your practicality is one of your best assets. Just remember to play too!

Letter 11: Fluctuating Finances

Your relationship to money and possessions tend to be erratic. You would prefer to be independent in your earnings and spending. Sometimes this means you are self-employed in fields with widely fluctuating income. Sometimes, this means you get fired periodically — again with ups and downs in your income. Even if your earnings are relatively stable, you prefer to deal with money in your own, unique way. You are not likely to follow the crowd. You will look for different forms of investments and spending — often preferring the progressive and avant-garde.

Expenditures could involve group activities, humanitarian causes, astrology, new technology (e.g., computers), friends or anything on the cutting edge of change. If something is unusual, that gives it added appeal in your eyes. You do not want to be typecast.

Letter 12: Financial Faith

Sometimes you seem to operate under the assumption that "God will balance the checkbook." Your faith in life can lead to extremes. Though this combination can indicate someone who is truly protected and taken care of financially (by money from others), it can also symbolize a lack of clarity about resources and money. Options can range from having seemingly infinite resources to wishing and dreaming for vast riches with little action. You might simply be confused about your financial situation and deceive yourself that things are rosier than they actually are.

There is a tendency toward wish fulfillment: "If I think it, it must be so." This can lead to being a sucker for what seems a worthy cause, or for trying to "save" people financially. If the need to help is overdone, you can end up the victim. Preferring to focus on what is beautiful and appealing, you may occasionally succumb to the idea that "If I ignore it, it will go away." Only it doesn't!

You can also put your imagination and dreams to work for you — earning money through beauty and artistic creations, films, advertising, sales — anything which involves a little illusion. Often, this combination shows tremendous aesthetic talents and an instinctive sense of beauty.

ALPHABET COMBINATIONS BY TWOS
Refer to Chapter 6 (Identity) and read the appropriate **Combinations by Two**, (pages 115-119), thinking in terms of money specifically.

POLARITIES

1-7: ♂-♀ or ♀ or ⚥, ♈-♎, 1st-7th houses

You probably feel torn between managing your own finances totally versus sharing accounts with someone else. On the one hand, you want to do it your way. On the other hand, you enjoy the give-and-take of interacting with another person and discussions can help clarify your position. Negotiation and compromise are called for. Competition could be an issue. Do not turn the relationship into a contest of who earns more or who is the more sensible purchaser. Enjoy one another's ideas and reach a middle position that allows you both power.

Often having a joint checking account (for household expenses, basic costs) **and** an individual account (for "mad" money) for each person is a helpful approach.

2-8: ♀-♇, ♉-♏, 2nd-8th houses

You are dealing with inner tension between spending versus saving and between earning your own way versus depending on someone else. Since you are probably ambivalent, it is likely you will attract other people who are also ambivalent. Then, you can adopt opposite ends of the seesaw and fight about who is right.

You could be hard for other people to read financially as you are likely to spend very easily for certain indulgences and hang onto every cent in other cases. You may act the part of the spendthrift with one friend and the penny-pincher with a different friend. Reaching an internal sense of balance is important. If you can accept both sides of who you are, there is no difficulty. Simply enjoy your behavior in the moment. Try to avoid doing one behavior and wishing you were doing the other. When you are spending, enjoy it. When you are saving, enjoy that. The more at ease you are with your internal balance, the easier it will be to reach a middle ground in your external relationships.

3-9: ☿-♃ or ⚷, ♊-♐, 3rd-9th houses

Thinking, talking, discussing and theorizing about money are likely. Tension between grand dreams and long-range scheme versus the everyday reality of people and necessities around you can occur. Keep in touch with consensual reality, but do not give up on your visions.

You have the capacity to relate to finances with a light touch. Indeed, you can even be a comedian in this area. Being able to step back and laugh at the situation helps to keep us from taking it too seriously.

You probably believe in the intellect where handling resources is concerned and are usually ready to improve your mind. You may study informally, discuss with knowledgeable people or even take classes and seminars and read books in order to become more skilled in dealing with money.

4-10: ☽-♄, ♋-♑, 4th-10th houses

Your attitudes and actions where finances are concerned could be influenced by one or both parents. Their behavior is likely to be a standard of comparison for yours — either what you want to do or the exact opposite. Their attitudes about money probably had a strong impact on your attitudes. Make sure you're not still "proving" something to Mom or Dad with the way you handle money.

Another option could be parents who are directly involved in your finances through inheritance or dependency from you to them or them to you. Often, the whole family is tied together financially.

Usually, safety needs are strong and you tend to hang on to what you have materially. Just be sure your feelings and approaches to monetary issues are satisfying for you as an individual. You probably look to a firm, financial base to feel safe in life. Traditional, conservative sources and protection of income may have the most appeal. Generally, you want money; it helps you feel safe. You are likely to be skilled at saving money. Protecting your finances is important.

You may feel torn between an ambitious, hardworking pursuit of resources versus a receptive waiting and acceptance from others. You will be balancing your emotional reactions to money (a deep, inner neediness) with your practical, rational business skills.

5-11: ☉-♅, ♌-♒, 5th-11th houses

The speculator at heart, yours is the impulse to spend money in order to make money. With the thrill of a gamble firing your ability to use logical analysis, you could be a successful investor. One question is how much you are able to balance passion and excitement with intellect and rationality in your monetary decisions.

Friends, lovers and children can be sources of income as well as sources of outgo. You may be involved in a business with your kids or find income through friends. It is also likely that you will easily spend money on children, lovers and friends.

You tend to have a good time and other people enjoy being with you where money is concerned because you make it fun!

6-12: ☿ or ♃ or ♆-♅, ♏-♓, 6th-12th houses

Realism and idealism may clash in your bank account. You are coming to terms with the conflict between your need for something ideal to believe in and your desire to be practical, efficient and face the real world. Avoiding the extremes of space cadet or Scrooge where money is concerned is the first step.

You need to find a way of handling your resources that gives you a sense of connection to something Higher. This can range from making the best (most ideal) financial decisions possible to turning money into a god and always seeking more. It can include utilizing your resources to search for meaning in life, through classes, study groups, gurus, books and other sources of inspiration. Don't give all your money to the church or some other worthy cause/ideal/person, but do have some source for feeling lifted up with how you are handling your money.

You must also retain some basic pragmatism in your financial situation and not just be starry-eyed and hope for the best. Excessive critical judgment can lead to a mean, parsimonious outlook of little help to you or anyone else. Be cautious and reasonable, but not unceasingly rational. Part of life is intuition and feelings — even where financial decisions are concerned. Combine your inner wisdom with your practical mind.

NODES OF THE MOON
The following nodal placements are particularly relevant in the area of money.

Across Taurus/Scorpio or 2nd/8th Houses

The handling of money in your life might require a bit of balancing. This configuration can point to some ambivalence around finances. You might feel torn between spending money versus saving it (or be very extravagant in some respects and extremely thrifty in others). You may experience ambivalence between being financially self-sufficient versus accepting support from other people (especially partners). You could range from demanding total control over your financial situation, to turning the books over to another party.

The more ambivalent you are, the more likely you will attract other people who share that ambivalence. Then, each of you could identify with one end of a financial seesaw (you with spending; a partner with saving or vice versa). You might fall into power struggles over money, with each of you mirroring an opposite side, so the two of you can learn to meet in the middle and compromise.

Typically, the more extreme our position is, the more extreme is the position of another person who becomes involved with us over the issue of money.

Feelings of inadequacy can complicate the picture, with either person unsure if s/he can really handle money properly, or perhaps doubting his/her ability to make a living. Because both sides of a polarity are present, you may find yourself always wanting what you don't have. For example, when you spend you might feel guilty and tell yourself you should save more, but when you save, you feel deprived and wish you could spend more. Finding an inner sense of balance and cultivating the ability to enjoy whichever side you express **in the moment** will help to resolve these issues.

Because you have two opposites extremes, you may sometimes flip from one to the other, or confuse people with your ''inconsistency.'' However, the more you acknowledge and allow expression of **both** sides in your life, the more likely you can enjoy spending **and** saving, earning your own way **and** receiving from other, indulgence **and** self-control. Greater inner balance also means more balance in your relationships, with both parties more able to give, receive and share in the financial realm.

ELEMENT EMPHASIS

Fire

♂, ☉, ♃, ⚷, ♈, ♌, ♐, 1st, 5th, 9th houses

You tend to seek excitement in your handling of resources. Sometimes money burns the proverbial hole in your pocket. Extravagance comes naturally. Impulsive spending is quite possible. Optimistic, you tend to assume that you can always get more or earn more and you may be quite generous to others. Grand schemes may appeal. Energetic and active in your pursuit of material goods, you can be impatient and prefer the ''quick buck'' to slow, steady gains. Gambling , speculation and investments often attract you.

It is important for you to have your finances under your own control. Depending on someone else to support you is an uncomfortable position; you like to be able to do as you please.

Earth

♀, ☿, ⚳, ⚶, ♄, ♉, ♍, ♑, 2nd, 6th, 10th houses

Practicality is your focus where finances are concerned. You are looking for long-term stability and security. You will choose to make money in sometimes boring or unexciting ways as long as they are dependable. Taking chances with money is usually anathema to you. You are willing to pay your dues, as long as you get your just rewards in the end.

You tend to work hard at earning money and sometimes fall into a ''poverty script'' (''If I don't have to really work for it, I haven't earned it!''). Your dedication and perseverance usually lead to productive accomplishments. The physical world is quite important to you. Having things on a concrete level makes sense to you.

Air
☿, ♀, ♀, ⚳, ♅, ♊, ♎, ♒, 3rd, 7th, 11th houses

Your approach to finances is cerebral. You tend to analyze situations logically and can be quite detached. Your forte is theoretical rather than practical; you may fall for ideas that sound great on paper but have no solid grounding.

Generally your money situation is involved with other people. This can range from family businesses, to a partner who supports you, to a career in personnel or some form of relating to others. You often earn money through ideas. You can be casual about money; you do not have to get emotionally involved.

Water
☽, ♇, ♆, ♋, ♏, ♓, 4th, 8th, 12th houses

Your *modus operandi* around money is intuitive and oriented toward security. You feel safest always keeping a little something tucked away for that "rainy day." Inclined to worry and brood if you feel vulnerable, you will do your best to keep yourself in a secure position financially.

Sometimes you rely on hunches around money. Be sure you can discern between a "right on" feeling and wishful thinking. Your purchases are often based on emotional reactions. Your feelings can sometimes be manipulated for financial gain, especially if your need for security is involved.

Fire-Earth
♂, ☉, ♃, ⚷, ♈, ♌, ♐, 1st, 5th, 9th houses &
♀, ☿, ♀, ⚳, ♄, ♉, ♍, ♑, 2nd, 6th, 10th houses

You will control your own finances and do it your way! You tend to know what you want and go after it. Having both initiative and practicality, you can usually blend them for the optimum result of aggressive success. However, if you set your confidence and pragmatism at odds with each other, you could swing from optimism to pessimism in finances, from impulsive spending to penny pinching. Most of the time, this combination shows great ability in handling resources and money.

Fire-Air
♂, ☉, ♃, ⚷, ♈, ♌, ♐, 1st, 5th, 9th houses &
☿, ♀, ♀, ⚳, ♅, ♊, ♎, ♒, 3rd, 7th, 11th houses

The general approach suggested to finances is free and easy. You may sometimes spend on impulse but are not usually a complete spendthrift. Usually, you do some thinking before deciding to give in to your impulse or not. The general theme is that money is fun! You expect to enjoy handling finances and do not want it to become a chore. This can indicate people who do not want to work hard at making or dealing with money. Sometimes this points to a lack of discipline where finances are concerned.

Usually, you are optimistic about money and trust that you will be able to manage. You are not inclined to take the whole thing too seriously anyway. You can easily joke and poke fun at other people who do. You are able to play with money.

Fire-Water
♂, ☉, ♃, ♄, ♈, ♌, ♐, 1st, 5th, 9th houses &
☽, ♇, ♆, ♋, ♏, ♓, 4th, 8th, 12th houses

You feel very strongly about money and can have intense emotional reactions to the state of your finances. However, you are dealing with an inner ambivalence where finances are concerned. On the one hand, you have strong desires to "blow" money periodically on some kind of a spending spree. On the other hand, you have strong security needs and feel the urge to keep a little savings around all the time — just in case.

You could confuse friends by alternating between these two approaches or by appearing a total spendthrift in one area only to pinch pennies unbearably in another area. Alternating styles does not have to be a problem. If you can enjoy your free-spending habits when you feel the urge and appreciate your caution and foresightedness when you are into being thrifty, you are simply versatile. But if you are bemoaning your lack of foresight when you make an impulsive purchase or if you feel confined and frustrated when you are into a saving mode, then integration is lacking. Enjoy your current handling of finances, knowing that the other side is likely to emerge before too long.

Earth-Air
♀, ☿, ?, ⚷, ♄, ♉, ♍, ♑, 2nd, 6th, 10th houses &
☿, ♀, ♀, ✳, ♅, ♊, ♎, ♒, 3rd, 7th, 11th houses

Your approach to money is solid and practical. You know how to get to the bottom of a ledger sheet and your 2 + 2 **always** makes 4. Relying on logic and pragmatism, you eschew an emotional approach where money is concerned. You examine your purchasing plans with care and reach a decision based on a rational dissection of needs and consequences. Coolheaded and sensible, you can be a whiz at budgeting if you choose.

You often work hard for what you earn and do not wish to blow it carelessly. Excellent at problem-solving, you can usually figure a better way to handle resources and may be a real efficiency expert where money management is concerned.

Earth-Water

♀, ☿, ⚳, ⚶, ♄, ♉, ♍, ♑, 2nd, 6th, 10th houses &
☽, ♇, ♆, ♋, ♏, ♓, 4th, 8th, 12th houses

Cautious and conservative, you choose not to rock the boat where finances are concerned. You want to have a secure foundation which usually means money in the bank and some safe (preferably blue chip) investments if you can manage it! Your style is traditional; you will not take chances with your money. You choose the most secure forms of investment and savings which you can find. You've worked too hard and take money too seriously to play games with it. It is possible that you are sharing your resources with others and/or gaining some income through other people (including inheritances). Stability and safety are what you look to for your income protection.

Air-Water

☿, ♀, ⚴, ⚵, ♅, ♊, ♎, ♒, 3rd, 7th, 11th houses &
☽, ♇, ♆, ♋, ♏, ♓, 4th, 8th, 12th houses

You are a great theoretician where money is concerned and it can be a favorite topic of conversation for you. Full of dreams, schemes and ideas, you may spend a lot of time in your inner world working out your version of "If I win the lottery, I'll. . . ." Often, the imaginative play and castles in the air are more satisfying than the real thing, so you may not do a lot of actual investment or speculation. But you can enjoy thinking about it and discussing options with other people.

If you choose to act, you have the potential of blending your rational understanding with your intuitive insight where finances are concerned. This can be a winning combination. Just be sure you can separate facts from fancy and psychic impressions from wish fulfillment.

QUALITY EMPHASIS

Cardinal

♂, ☽, ♀, ⚴, ⚵, ♄, ♈, ♋, ♎, ♑, 1st, 4th, 7th, 10th houses

Your handling of finances tends to be onc of balancing differing needs. At one moment, you may be convinced that your home is deserving of financial support; the next moment you are sure you must spend money on the kids and then you decide that furthering your self-development really needs to be a financial priority. Making choices between the various facets of your life is not always easy.

You often learn through experience, so your patterns of making, spending and saving money are subject to change as you gather new information. It means more to you to go through something directly than to read about it or try to learn by watching someone else. You may make some financial mistakes, but you do not repeat them. Unlike people who stick to one approach in handling money, you are willing to change your patterns when events suggest that is a wise move.

Fixed
♀, ☉, ♇, ♅, ♂, ♌, ♐, ♒, 2nd, 5th, 8th, 11th houses

Determined to control your own resources, you are likely to resolutely pursue your own course where money and possessions are concerned. Your assets include tremendous strength of will and constant desire to maintain mastery of the physical arena.

Resources and finances could be a source of ambivalence as you often have contradictory feelings. Security is usually important to you, but extravagance and risk-taking also appeal. Until you reach a comfortable compromise, there is a tendency to live life out as a series of seesaws: from one extreme to the other. This can range from spending versus saving conflicts; to feeling torn about earning your own income versus relying on someone else; to balancing self indulgence versus self-mastery issues around possessions and pleasures.

You resist the influences of other people, determined to run your finances **your** way. When pushed, you tend to dig in your heels. You are adamant about running monetary matters your own way.

Mutable
☿, ⚷, ⚶, ♃, ♄, ♆, ♊, ♍, ♐, ♓, 3rd, 6th, 9th, 12th houses

Flexibility and adaptability are your keynotes around finances. Relying on your powers of analysis and perhaps some intuition, you figure out the best action under any given circumstances. You are able to learn from the experiences of others and do not have to undergo disaster directly in order to avoid it the next time around. You are willing to listen to advice, read and gain knowledge about how to handle your possessions and money.

Intellectual activities, such as seminars, books, travel, may be major expenditures for you. Feeding the mind is very important to you.

THEMES

Freedom
♂, ♃, ♄, ♅, ♈, ♐, ♒, 1st, 9th, 11th houses

Your approach to finances is one of openness and optimism. You are unwilling to confine yourself unduly in order to earn a living. You want to feel free to do your own thing in terms of amassing monetary returns. Similarly, you refuse to feel tied down by any money you do possess. You tend to spend easily, partly because you have the faith and confidence that you can always get more. Although you can be impulsive, you generally use your head in purchasing. But central to your approach is doing what you want. You refuse to follow other people's rules in the area of finances.

Closeness or Interpersonal

☽, ☉, ♀, ⚵, ⚶, ♇, ♋, ♌, ♎, ♏, 4th, 5th, 7th, 8th houses

Other people are intimately involved with your financial picture. Whether they depend on you for income, or you depend on them, or some sort of shared business is an issue, you do not stand alone where money is concerned. You may work in a field involving relating to others.

Your approach to finances tends to be more emotional than objective. Your feelings often run deep and may sway you toward certain monetary choices. Other people, especially those you love, are likely to have a very strong influence on your decisions about money.

Purchases are likely to be joint and to satisfy others as well as yourself. Family and loved ones often benefit from your expenditures.

Artistic

♀, ⚵, ⚶, ☉, ♆, ♉, ♌, ♎, ♓, 2nd, 5th, 7th, 12th houses

You can be very laid-back and relaxed in your approach to earning a living. Often, you would prefer a situation that is comfortable and easygoing. Earning your bread by the sweat of your brow does not appeal. Charm and sweetness may be more your style. Aesthetic talent may also be a source of earning power.

You would rather life flow easily and smoothly where finances are concerned; you prefer not to argue or get into unpleasantness. If not kept in check, your desire to avoid confrontations could lead you to being taken advantage of.

When you do spend money, it is likely to be on items which will enhance your personal appearance or your surrounding environment. Beauty is likely to be important to you, as well as comfort, ease and pleasure.

Idealistic

♃, ⚷, ♆, ♐, ♓, 9th, 12th houses

Your relationship to money is tied to the theme of infinity. This can manifest as two very different extremes. One potential is the extremely rich individual, with seemingly infinite resources. Sometimes, in such cases, money is like a god. Whatever we turn into an idol, we tend to pursue wholeheartedly. And, if we believe something is good, we often feel "more is better" so can get carried away. This can indicate someone who sees financial success as an ultimate value.

Another potential is the person who, unconsciously, turns the handling of their resources and finances over to the Universe. Often, faith is excessive. They trust that somehow everything will all work out. Sometimes it does, but not always! Such individuals may be very poor and simply not in touch with the state of their finances.

One key here is expectations. Where we seek the infinite, we can easily be disappointed when "real life" does not match up to our vision of what it could or should. This can indicate people who feel very disillusioned or dissatisfied with their monetary situations. They may want more than is possible. They may be caught in unrealistic dreams and visions of great wealth. They may seek something grandiose in an impractical manner.

Another form of integration is seeing money as a channel to the spiritual or the ideal. Such people spend lots of their resources on books, education, travels, seminars, spiritual pursuits or causes — anything which they feel will uplift them, connect them to something Higher, assist their sense of purpose in life. Look to your faith around finances; you need enough — but not too much.

Obsessive-Compulsive
☿, ?, ♅, ♇, ♄, ♍, ♏, ♑, 6th, 8th, 10th houses

Organization is your forte and your checkbook balances (unless, of course, the bank made the mistake). Conscientious, dedicated, thorough and exacting, you may love to track the changing fortunes of dollars and cents. Thrift is another potential ability. You may seek out sales and track down the best bargains in order to get the most for your money. Skilled with details, you can research anyone's monetary situation with incredible thoroughness. Budgeting could be one of your skills.

When you choose to save, you can be very cautious and careful, amassing increased amounts of money through patient management. Your assets grow, not necessarily in a spectacular fashion, but in a regular, planned manner.

Sometimes your concern with figuring out the exact path of a mislaid penny, or getting the cheapest item available, or maintaining a realistic attitude about finances can drive other people up the wall. You might be obsessive in your concern with getting all the details right. Your compulsivity is an asset, however, where discipline and efficiency pay off. Control of your resources is vital where you are concerned and you are prone to power struggles if other people try to meddle in this area of your life. Sharing may not come easily and smoothly but takes time and trust. You do not like financial dependence, unless it comes with absolutely no strings. You wish to make your own decisions about spending and saving. And, you may enjoy giving to others, but would probably feel disapproving if they "wasted" the money on things you felt were foolish, impractical, unhealthy or silly. Deep down inside, you are prone to believing that no one else will manage the finances as well as you do. Unfortunately, that is often true.

Competence
☿, ?, ♅, ♄, ♍, ♑, 6th, 10th houses

You are probably a realist where finances are concerned. Practical and pragmatic, you depend on 2 and 2 to always equal 4. Your approach to money is likely to be sensible and structured. You could be skilled at budgeting or other forms of financial planning. Thriftiness could be one of your talents.

Often, you work hard for what you make, partly because you expect life to demand a good job from you. Just be sure this is not overdone into a "poverty script" which keeps you continually overworked and underpaid.

Your expenditures tend to be pragmatic. You will buy whatever is useful and functional. Often, purchases are work-related, something that will further your career. Or, they are necessary in your life — but seldom fripperies. You tend to be very sensible and realistic in your handling of money.

Mental Stimulation

☿, ⚳, ⚶, ⚴, ♃, ⚷, ♅, ♆, ♊, ♍, ♎, ♐, ♒, ♓, 3rd, 6th, 7th, 9th, 11th, 12th houses

You can be very intellectual in your approach to money. In fact, you probably enjoy reading, thinking and talking about finances. You may be a whiz at following the stocks, analyzing trends or otherwise dissecting our financial system. Or, you may simply be curious and open to learning all you can in this area. Possibilities range from the economist to the office gossip who knows everybody's salaries.

Often, your purchases are mind-related. Books, magazines, classes, seminars, travel and any form of mind expansion or mental stimulation can be a potential expenditure. Since your income often comes through your mind, this just keeps the spiral going upward.

Relationships

♀, ⚴, ⚵, ♇, ♎, ♏, 7th, 8th houses

Your income is likely to be joint in some way. This could mean work which involves other people (e.g., counseling, consulting, etc.). Another possibility is you supporting a partner financially or being supported by a partner. The likelihood is of other people being intimately involved with your monetary and other resources.

Sharing may be an issue. Many people have trouble balancing giving and receiving; they find it easier to do one side or the other. Sometimes, there are fierce arguments, competition and jockeying for power around money. Whether your challenge is to give more, receive more or simply be more equal in the sharing of finances, it is likely to be faced through interactions with other people, especially in committed relationships.

Security

♀, ☽, ☿, ⚳, ⚶, ♇, ♄, ♆, ♉, ♋, ♍, ♏, ♑, ♓, 2nd, 4th, 6th, 8th, 10th, 12th houses

You believe in playing it safe. Money and possessions provide you much of your security in life and you are not likely to risk them foolishly. Your financial decisions are usually carefully weighed. You prefer a conservative, protective road to one offering possible gain but much risk. Traditional routes to amassing more resources are just fine with you.

Risk/Creativity/Change
♂, ☉, ♃, ♀, ♅, ♈, ♌, ♐, ♒, 1st, 5th, 9th, 11th houses

A speculator at heart, you are willing to take a flyer if you feel the payoff would be great enough. Somewhat impatient, you would rather see a quick return on your money. Security means less to you than the thrill of attempting to get an even greater return on something (as you risk it all). Independence of action in your handling of material resources is vital.

You could be gifted creatively in the area of money. This can include making money by pouring out from your own center (whether in artistic, entertaining, persuasive or other channels). Stocks, gambling, other investments, all can appeal to your desire for expansion of resources. You know it usually takes money to make money and are willing to lay your finances on the line in the hopes of garnering a large reward.

Parents
☽, ♄, ?, ♋, ♑, 4th, 10th houses

Your basic financial attitude tends to be conservative — oriented toward safety and protection. You want to hang on to what you have and prefer secure, long-term investments to risky quickies that promise a big return, but may end up with little. You may sometimes feel a sense of tension between your desire to spend money on the home or family versus desire to spend money on items that will enhance your career or status in the world. A balance is necessary.

Your feelings about money are likely to be strongly influenced by one or both parents. They could be positive or negative models (how you want to be or the opposite). Clarify any old issues to be sure you are not reacting in patterns no longer in your best interests.

Power
☉, ♇, ♄, ♌, ♏, ♑, 5th, 8th, 10th houses

You may view money as a source of power and control. If so, its value for you lies in what you can accomplish with the weight of many dollars behind you. Pure financial gain is secondary to having an impact on the world. Control over your own resources is likely to be important to you. Managing your own life is a central theme, and financial independence helps to insure that.

If misdirected, this drive could lead you into power struggles with other people over the handling of resources and finances. But channeled appropriately, the ambitious motivation could lead you to success in the world.

Personal
♂, ♀, ☿, ☽, ♈, ♉, ♊, ♋, 1st, 2nd, 3rd, 4th houses

Making and spending money are forms of self-expression for you. Part of your identity is found through the handling of resources. Thus, a threat to them can seem like a personal threat to you. Your expenditures are usually purchases that satisfy some basic drives within your life. You are most concerned with here and now needs — what you can directly put to use. You make money and spend it primarily to please yourself. Less interested in other people's ideas, you tend to make your own financial decisions.

Transpersonal
♃, ⚷, ♄, ♅, ♆, ♐, ♑, ♒, ♓, 9th, 10th, 11th, 12th houses

The long-range view is important to you. Future planning is part of your makeup and you look ahead when making financial plans. The interconnectedness of the world is an established fact for you. Trying to figure out which trends in resources are most important is an activity which could appeal to you.

Causes (political, social, environmental, personal) of all sorts are often recipients of some of your funds. Perhaps because you feel group action has more impact than individual, you may be willing to subsidize certain movements.

ASPECTS

Harmony to Letter...

1: Your handling of money is potentially in harmony with your ability to assert yourself. Directness is a likely financial approach with you; you are probably clear about what you want, in terms of monetary resources and rewards, and able to express yourself easily. Your own personal action is your best source of financial gain, and you generally prefer having finances under your control anyway, so resist dependency. Following your own instincts about money usually works best.

2: There is relative harmony in the area of money, pleasures, possessions and beauty. This suggests a good potential for being comfortable. You can enjoy what you have materially and sensually. Some indulgence is possible, but generally this is an easygoing approach to finances, appreciating security but not inclined to push too hard. You enjoy the good things in life, but are less likely to break your back trying to get them. Being laid-back in your attitude about finances is most helpful.

3: Your handling of money is potentially in harmony with your ability to think and communicate. This implies you can be very articulate and clear where finances are concerned. It also suggests the mind as a potential source of income and a good ability to be logical, rational and detached in terms of monetary and other resources. Using your head in financial decisions is your best bet.

4: Your handling of money is potentially in harmony with your desire for emotional security and safety. This implies desire for a "nest egg" tucked away — just in case. You are likely to be protective around finances, but the comfortable flow suggests a good, solid foundation of emotional and physical security. Females, including your mother or mother figure, and/or the general public could contribute to your resources. Some intuitive abilities are present; use feelings as well as rationality in making your financial decisions.

5: Your handling of money is potentially in harmony with your desire for a response from the world. You may gain the limelight through financial speculations (e.g., investments, gambling) or earn some of your resources through avenues involving a "starring" quality (e.g., selling, promotion, advertising, teaching, entertainment). Children and other creative outlets are potential sources of income and outgo. Your generosity can be a decided asset as giving usually leads to receiving in return.

6: Your handling of money is potentially in harmony with your practical, pragmatic and productive side. Your resources tend to be well-earned; you work hard for them. Practical realism is your best asset for making financial decisions.

7: Your handling of money is potentially in harmony with your desire for balance, harmony and a one-to-one relationship. Other people (including spouses) can contribute to your income. So could aesthetic or beauty-oriented activities. You are likely to have a strong sense of justice and fair play around the handling of finances and wish things to be even. For best results, bounce financial decisions around with other people, rather than judging situations on your own.

8: Your handling of money is potentially in harmony with your ability to give, receive and share pleasures with others. This denotes potential financial support from others (including inheritance, government grants, royalties, return on speculation) and/or providing for others. Your capacity for depth analysis and ferreting out all the facts can be a decided asset in financial decisions. Use your native shrewdness.

9: Your handling of money is potentially in harmony with your optimism, faith and reach for more in life. Your trust that things **will** improve monetarily tends to set up a self-fulfilling prophecy. Your belief in "luck" seems to draw it into your life. The law of prosperity is likely to work well for you.

10: Your handling of money is potentially in harmony with your responsible, achieving, disciplined side. You can make money because you are willing to work hard for it. Sometimes your awareness of realistic limits can be carried too far, and you may experience deprivation (real or subjective) by focusing exclusively on the flaws of your financial picture rather than the assets. Hard work and experience will pay off for you; just don't overdo it.

11: Your handling of money is potentially in harmony with your unique, individualistic side. You can make money through innovative, unusual, progressive or eccentric channels. Or, you may simply value your freedom so much, you are not tied down by much money or many possessions. Coming from your own center and being inventive are your best bets in financial decision making.

12: Your handling of money is potentially in harmony with your visionary, idealistic side. You could gain resources through artistic, healing (or victim) routes. Your inner wisdom, used with discretion, can aid you in financial decisions; your intuition can be a real asset in some circumstances. Your unconscious faith is a likely source of support and can operate as an invisible "guardian angel," making sure that your interests are protected.

Conflict to Letter...

1: Your handling of money is potentially in conflict with your desire to do what you want and act freely. Your instinctive impulse may not be in your best interests financially; stop and think it over. One extreme to be avoided is extravagant spending — just because you feel like it. The other extreme is feeling deprived — that lack of resources stops you from doing what you want. Find ways and means to assert yourself in the world and enjoy doing your thing without feeling blocked and without getting carried away.

2: There is a potential conflict in the area of money, resources, possessions and pleasure. This could range from overindulgence to depriving yourself of sources of enjoyment that are perfectly okay. You may feel torn in deciding what to enjoy, how much and when. The challenge is to have a variety of fulfilling channels for pleasure without overdoing any one path.

3: Your handling of money is potentially in conflict with your desire to know, understand, communicate and exchange information. Perhaps the issue is a lack of detachment and the need for a more logical, rational approach to monetary issues. Another possibility is not collecting enough information, insufficient discussion on which to make financial decisions — or taking in **so much** information that you feel overwhelmed by bits of information. Use your mental faculties in balance with your material needs.

4: Your handling of money is potentially in conflict with your desire for emotional closeness and security. You could overvalue or undervalue a sense of safety where finances are concerned. If the first, you may be too timid, unwilling to take reasonable risks. If the latter, you could try avenues that are threatening to your secure base. Just be sure your basic needs are taken care of and maintain a middle position.

5: Your handling of money is potentially in conflict with your desire for taking a risk and garnering a rewarding return. This could indicate excessive or insufficient speculation. You may be too willing or too hesitant to take chances in your investments. Pride or ego could also be a factor in financial decisions — to your detriment. Self-esteem is important, but don't let it get tied to your level of financial success.

6: Your handling of money is potentially in conflict with your desire to do a good job and be productive. One potential extreme is a "poverty script" where you work hard for everything you get and could easily be overworked and underpaid because you value doing something well and are less concerned with the rewards. Another possibility is a reluctance to pay your dues in the sense of not wanting to deal with the (sometimes boring, but essential) duties and details of being an effective worker. Your practicality can be an asset if in balance with your material needs.

7: Your handling of money is potentially in conflict with your desire for balance, harmony and one-to-one relationships. This could indicate ambivalence over spending resources on personal or joint pleasures. Your relationship could be a source of outgo or there might be conflicts with a partner over finances. Differing ideas about what is fair, just and equitable in the area of resources are possible. Compromise.

8: There is the potential of conflict in the area of joint finances, pleasures and possessions. This could manifest as power struggles over money, sex or possessions. Control is often an issue and you need to find a way to maintain a sense of some (**not** all) control in these areas, while still being able to share. Giving and/or receiving could be issues. Make sure you can do both comfortably, with a reasonable balance between.

9: Your handling of money is potentially in conflict with your sense of faith, optimism and seeking of something more in life. This could indicate moral, ethical or religious conflicts around finances. It could also indicate excessive faith (and falling for "get rich quick" schemes or other ploys which sound wonderful) — or a lack of faith which leads to a sense of deprivation. Sufficient confidence is essential and visualization **does** help to bring rewards — as long as it is balanced by practicality.

10: Your handling of money is potentially in conflict with your awareness of the realistic limits of the world. This could indicate an excessive sense of responsibility, a tendency to shoulder more than your share of financial burdens. The opposite extreme is a desire to eschew all responsibility and an unwillingness to face facts about money. Realism is important for your financial success; keep a practical outlook. Just don't overdo (or underdo) your pragmatic attitude.

11: Your handling of money is potentially in conflict with your desire for freedom, uniqueness and individuality. One option is choosing to be erratic in your approach to finances, which can result in fluctuations of income even to the point of owning almost nothing (which means you are not tied down by possessions). Another option is not trusting your own inventiveness, avoiding unconventional avenues to financial success. Balance security needs with your sense of openness to alternative possibilities.

12: Your handling of money is potentially in conflict with your seeking of infinite love and beauty. Your idealism, if excessive, could lead your astray. Wearing rose-colored glasses could result in financial disillusionment, disappointment and even victimization if carried too far. The opposite extreme is a total lack of trust (in others, in the universe) around money which could lead to difficulties as the world is very interdependent. Find a middle ground between believing too much and believing too little around money.

CHAPTER THIRTEEN
SENSUALITY AND SEXUALITY

Sexuality and sensuality are life areas involving such intimate and highly charged contact with others that it is often particularly difficult to see them clearly and objectively. The horoscope helps understanding by providing insight into patterns of behavior which are often entirely or primarily subconscious. Once we become conscious of a behavior pattern, we can observe it clearly and initiate changes whereby we can express our needs lucidly and directly, rather than via projection or via subtle game playing. Recognizing and successfully communicating our own needs has the wonderful side effect of enabling us to open and respond to the needs of others at a very deep level.

A common behavior is to bestow (project) one's own motivation and decision-making on a partner. We may even deny certain vital needs and potential talents their natural expression because we instinctively bow to opposing personal, social and/or cultural conditioning, or because other needs take predominance. We might find ourselves overwhelmed by worshipful awe of a sexual partner who seems to express these needs in the most masterful wonderful manner. S/he seems to be the epitome of what we wish to become, at least in that particular area of life.

Well and good, **if** we can then begin to emulate the partner and to take the first baby steps toward expressing that need overtly for ourselves. Very often, however, we choose to intimidate ourselves by the contrast in competency between his/her skills and our own, and we continue our hero/heroine worship from afar, albeit with perhaps the first seeds of resentment sown. Over a remarkably short span of time, an inevitable twist of fate illuminates the partner as an unappealing, inconsiderate human specimen who indulges in such an exaggerated expression of that particular area of life that we can only conclude that we have somehow made a dreadful error. At this point, the last thing we would desire is to take this individual to bed.

If we find ourselves in the position of the person receiving adulation, we may count it as a mixed blessing. Suddenly a talent that has been a normal part of our daily activity is thrust into the limelight. Although pleasant enough at first, how do we deal with all this praise and attention? If the partner continues to admire us without attempting to develop the talent or characteristic for him/herself, we may begin to feel awkward about the situation, or to resent being the only half of the partnership responsible for this particular activity. It is possible to become ego-invested in keeping the center stage. It is also possible to withdraw coldly, even bitterly, in order to get some peace. If our lover does begin to work in this area, we may initially try hard to help but soon start to feel used, or we may be threatened by the rapid progress of the partner in an activity that was just yester-day our exclusive domain.

The sexual revolution has helped us to bring a great number of hidden feel-ings and urges out into the light, but now that we have opened Pandora's Box, we may not be convinced that it was such a great idea. Sexual and sensual rela-tionships have perhaps a higher failure rate than any other of our pursuits. Yet our desires and needs remain so strong that we continue to seek the means to satisfy them.

Role models in sexual relationships have truly run the gauntlet in the last few decades. Women and men have faced changes, which many times seemed threatening. With all of this to work on, is it any wonder that we struggle so often? Of course, a few ideas that should remain on the conscious level inevitably slide back down into subconscious realms, there to stir up trouble. We repress and have sexually related physical ailments. We project and invite power struggles. We become so confused and hurt that we give up on the whole idea altogether — at least temporarily.

Awareness does help. By regularly checking up and in on ourselves, we can become aware of those patterns through which we are currently working. And we can initiate progressive, dynamic changes. Sexual and sensual experiences can become the truly beautiful, ecstatic exchanges they were designed to be.

Some people do not currently have an active sex life. In such a case, read this chapter as showing potentials — issues and themes of future or past importance with lovers. Consider it also in terms of the individual's handling of sensuality (e.g., eating, drinking, smoking, spending money and other physical pleasures). But, most of all, sex is related to creativity.

If you are not utilizing the potentials in this section for sexual pleasure, con-sider what they imply about your creative abilities and your capacity to take risks. Apply the themes which emerge here also to Chapter 10 (Children and Creativity).

The Factors

Sensuality and sexuality are strongly connected to the first three of the fixed let-ters of our astrological alphabet (**2, 5 and 8**). In addition, most astrologers would consider the planet **Mars**, a key to basic energy and vitality, also indicative of sexual drive.[1] Thus, we would include:

GROUP I
Conjunctions to Venus, the Sun, Pluto and Mars
Conjunctions to rulers of the 2nd, 5th and 8th cusps
Conjunctions to rulers of other signs in the 2nd, 5th and 8th houses

GROUP II
Planets in the 2nd, 5th and 8th houses
Planets within two degrees of the 2nd, 5th and 8th houses, even though occupy-
ing the 1st, 3rd, 4th, 6th, 7th or 9th houses

GROUP III
Parallels to Venus, the Sun, Pluto and Mars
Parallels to the rulers of the 2nd, 5th or 8th cusps
House placements of Venus, the Sun, Pluto and Mars
House placements of rulers of the 2nd, 5th and 8th cusps
House placements of rulers of any other signs in the 2nd, 5th and 8th houses
Houses ruled by any planets in the 2nd, 5th and 8th houses
Houses ruled by planets forming any conjunctions to Venus, the Sun, Pluto, Mars,
or rulers of the 2nd, 5th or 8th cusps
Planets occupying Taurus, Leo or Scorpio
Houses occupied by planets in Taurus, Leo or Scorpio

GROUP IV
Sign placements of Venus, the Sun, Pluto and Mars
Sign placements of the rulers of the 2nd, 5th and 8th cusps
Houses with Taurus, Leo and Scorpio on cusps
Sign placements of rulers of any other signs in the 2nd, 5th and 8th houses
Signs occupied by planets in the 2nd, 5th and 8th houses
Unoccupied signs in the 2nd, 5th and 8th houses

---

1. If you prefer **not** to search for repeated themes yourself, you can order the "PP BOOK" option from Astro Computing Services (PO Box 16430, San Diego, Ca 92116), which allows you to use this book to make complete, synthesizing delineations of horoscopes without figuring out which themes are emphasized.

Available for $3.00 each, the "PP BOOK" report calculates the emphasis on all the letters of the alphabet, themes and aspects in each horoscope for which you provide the data. The report lists each significant focus (e.g., "There is a Letter 11 theme in "Sensuality and Sexuality," and gives the appropriate page numbers for you to read in this book ("See pages 360-361 in the *Complete Horoscope Interpretation* book.")

The computer will not **always** arrive at the same results as you might, as certain steps are ambiguous (e.g., how much weight to give a planet making a conjunction, based on the orb). However, the majority of the time, the computer answers will concur with those derived from use of the worksheets — or the recommended quick scan of a horoscope. Thus it provides an excellent teaching tool.

The "PP BOOK" does **not** provide a listing of **each and every** astrological factor making up the significant themes. For that, you would order "PP WEIGHTS" (discussed in next footnote).

How to Weight the Factors

Please note that these factors are rank ordered (in chunks) according to their weighting. If you want to use exact figures, a suggested weighting scale is given in the appendix — with worksheets for sexuality and the other various life areas.[2]

A SHORT CUT

For quickness and ease of use, especially for people just learning to use the alphabet, I suggest initially limiting your examination to factors in Groups I and II.

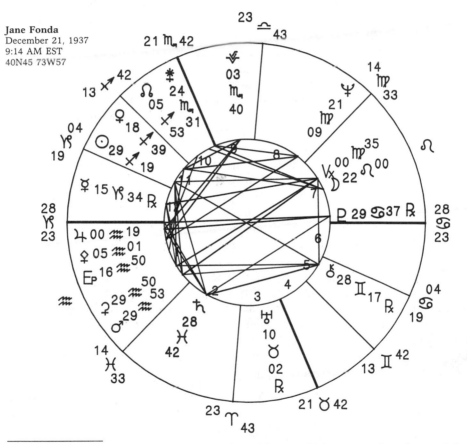

Jane Fonda
December 21, 1937
9:14 AM EST
40N45 73W57

2. You can also obtain a listing of **all** the astrological factors which compose those letters of the Zip Code determined to be significant in a horoscope. This makes an excellent teaching tool and a valuable resource to check yourself against when practicing with the Zip Code.

Astro Computing Services, PO Box 16430, San Diego, CA 92116, has calculated 28,000 horoscopes and established averages and standard deviations for the scores of each letter of the astrological alphabet, each theme, and the conflict and harmony aspects to each life area.

Astro's report, called "PP WEIGHTS," will list those letters of the astrological alphabet which
(footnote continued on next page)

If any letter of the alphabet is represented once in Group I or II, consider it as probably significant and read the interpretation for that letter. (If the letter occurs twice or more in Groups I and II, it is definitely significant.)

For example, in Jane Fonda's horoscope, Mars has a conjunction to Ceres, so we would include a tentative (half-weight) count for Letter 6 in this "Sexuality/Sensuality" section. Also, the 2nd, 5th and 8th houses are all occupied — by Saturn (Letter 10), Chiron (9 with overtones of 11) and Neptune (Letter 12). We would tentatively consider those letters as significant.

Once you are very familiar with the factors in Groups I and II, you can examine Groups III and IV, seeking a repetition of letters implied by Groups I and II. In the case of Ms. Fonda, the Letter 12 theme is repeated by Saturn (in 2nd) ruling the 12th (12), 2nd house occupied by Pisces (12), 5th cusp ruler (Mercury) in the 12th (12) and 8th cusp ruler (Mercury) in the 12th (12).

Letter 9 also gets a fair number of repetitions. Besides Chiron in the 5th, we see: the Sun in Sagittarius (9), Venus in Sagittarius (9), the 8th house Libra ruler (Venus) in Sagittarius (9), Scorpio occupied in the 9th house (9) and Jupiter in a Gauquelin sector. (Planets found in the Gauquelin "zones of power" seem to indicate highly significant themes in the personality. Jupiter and Saturn, especially, I count as Letter 9 or 10 in the areas of identity, work, sexuality and money.)

The focus on Letters 9 and 12 suggests an idealistic overtone to sex. This can manifest in a variety of forms (including from the extreme of "sex is too holy to indulge in except under perfect conditions" to the opposite extreme of "sex is among my highest values to be enjoyed as often as possible"). One potential, however, is a romantic/idealistic overtone to the sexuality. This can encompass the ability to cast a seductive spell, to act as a sex symbol for the public. Ms. Fonda's career (Letter 10), especially while she was married to Roger Vadim, cast her in the role of sex symbol and her personal attractiveness (and sexiness) is a persuasive selling point for her workout tapes and books!

Letter 10 can often be a challenge in the area of sensuality and sexuality. Sometimes there is a self-critical or judgmental focus. The need for control can be overdone. Ms. Fonda recently admitted to being bulimic for quite a few years — when she was younger. (Bulimia occurs when individuals induce vomiting after overeating as a form of weight control. If carried too far, the vomiting reaction can become automatic and beyond personal control. One therapist who works

---

2. (continued from previous page)
    are one standard deviation or more above the mean — and list **all** the astrological factors which point to each significant letter of the alphabet. These weightings will also compare each individual's score on the various themes (e.g., risk-taking, artistic) to the means and standard deviations to determine which themes are significant. Averages are established for aspects as well in order to note conflict or harmony in the different life areas.

    The results obtained by Astro's "PP WEIGHTS" will not **always** coincide with those you determine by a quick scan and intuitive judgment, or by use of the worksheets. Certain of the steps (e.g., how much to weight a planet based on orb) are ambiguous, so different results can occur. However, most of the time, Astro's answers will confirm those you could obtain in working with the Zip Code. Furthermore, the **complete** listing of relevant factors is an excellent teaching tool.

    Ask for "PP Weights." The price, as of December 1985 is $5.00.

with bulimics regularly suggests that they are perfectionistic, with high standards, (9-12) and they seek to take control (10) through their bulimia.

In examining Groups III and IV, also look for any letters of the alphabet which occur five or more times. Consider them as probably significant and read the appropriate interpretations (pages 352-362). For example, Letter 11 is repeated with: Sun in the 11th (11), Venus in the 11th (11), 2nd house Aries ruler (Mars) in Aquarius (11), 8th house Libra ruler (Venus) in 11th (11), Taurus occupied by Uranus (11), and Mars (in its own nature and as ruler of the Aries in the 2nd) makes a conjunction (to Ceres) in the sign of Aquarius (11). Letters which occur fairly often in Groups III and IV as well as in I and II include: 9, 10, 11 and 12.

Themes

Themes can be ascertained in two ways. The simplest is to simply note the emphasized letters of the alphabet (as above) and determine which form other themes. For example, the transpersonal theme is the total of scores from Letter 9, 10, 11 and 12. In the case of Jane Fonda, all four are strongly suggested as important, so we could suspect transpersonal theme in the area of sexuality.

The second method of spotting themes involves some rough arithmetic, or getting an intuitive impression. If a theme involves four (out of twelve) letters of the astrological alphabet, you would expect it to have about ⅓ of the total score. So, if the amount for those letters seems appreciably more than ⅓ of the total, count that as a theme — and read the appropriate section (page 376).

In addition, when searching for themes, give more weight to like planets in aspect to one another. Aspects between Jupiter, Saturn, Uranus and Neptune add to the focus on a broad perspective as far as sexuality, or the potential of one's sexual/sensual approach affecting the world. Ms. Fonda's personal workout approach has been widely disseminated and Roger Vadim's newest "kiss and tell" work about his ex-wives may reveal personal details to the world. Also give extra weight transpersonal planets occupying transpersonal houses or signs.

Aspects

Quickly scan all aspects other than conjunctions or parallels, grouping them according to harmony (sextile, trine, semisextile) and conflict (octile, tri-octile, square, opposition and quincunx). In considering each aspect, weight the nature of the planet most heavily, followed by the house and the sign. Count both the house occupied and the cusp ruled by each aspected planet.

For example, in Jane Fonda's horoscope, we would examine Mars as one key to sexuality. Mars makes the following **close** harmony aspects:
• sextile the Sun (5) in the 11th (11) in Sagittarius; Sun rules the 7th (7)
• semisextile Jupiter (9) in the 1st (1) in Aquarius (11); Jupiter rules the 11th (11)
• trine Vesta (6) in 9th (9) in Scorpio (8)
• trine Chiron (9) in 5th (5) in Gemini (3)

Mars makes the following **close** conflict aspects:
• sextile the Sun (5) in the 11th (11) in Sagittarius (9); the Sun rules the 7th (7)
• octile Mercury (3 — or perhaps 6 here) in the 12th (12) in Capricorn (10); Mercury rules the 5th (5) and the 8th (8)
• quincunx Pluto (8) in the 7th (7) in Cancer (4); Pluto rules the 10th (10)

Make an intuitive judgment as to whether any letters of the alphabet have lots of conflict to them or have quite a bit of harmony. If you feel any group of aspects has an emphasis on one or more letters of the alphabet, read the appropriate interpretation (pages 376-379).

Interpretations: Sensuality and Sexuality
(written primarily by Jalien Shandler)

ALPHABET THEMES

Letter 1: The Active Lover

You are like a firecracker shooting into the sky. Excitement drives you, and sex can be a prime motivator. Easily aroused, but also quickly turned off, you want action or you'll move on. Passionate, but often impatient, you may fall in and out of love in the time it takes most people to introduce themselves.

The thrill of pursuit is part of your pleasure and you may not fully appreciate a relationship too easily attained. However, much as you enjoy a conquest, you will not pursue forever. If your partner plays coy too long, you may seek someone more immediately responsive. Like a fire, you burn fiercely but can die rapidly if the flames are not fed.

Your sexual style is active and exciting. The bench mark is to do anything **once**. You abhor repetition. You will try each position, one time, and then look for a new approach. You may be quite athletic in lovemaking, as you enjoy motion, action, and physical exertion. Your energy level is very high. Your patience, however, is often low, and partners could have trouble keeping up with you when you go into your perpetual motion mode. You can be highly sensual but also enjoy occasional "quickies" due to your fast reaction time. Sports are sometimes a turn-on. Pumping iron may pump up your libido. Physical fitness and firmly muscled bodies often appeal. Risk-taking activities may excite you. When your adrenaline rises, so does your sex drive!

As a lover, you need a leash so long you don't even know it's there. You demand personal independence. Possessiveness is a no-no! You are inclined to take off, doing your own thing, periodically. Other people have to learn to put up with periodic absences. There is a loner streak in you. Sometimes you just do **not** want to relate.

Sexuality may be mixed with anger, aggression and power for you. Sex can be a way of asserting yourself, declaring your existence. If you are out of touch with your own power and needs for assertion, you could attract self-centered, aggressive, even violent people. Either of you might be selfish, rash, careless or even physically violent. Fights and arguments are negative ways to get the exciting "highs" that people want. Learn to utilize your strength in a positive fashion. You need a lover who values independence and freedom as do you, someone as strong as you are, someone to share your seeking of excitement!

If these qualities are projected, lovers can be too impetuous and totally lacking in responsibility, i.e., the ability to respond. They may seek self-gratification to the extreme so that you feel used and abused in sexual acts but definitely not satisfied and well loved. A traveling or truant partner may be your lot — someone who checks in occasionally, perhaps primarily for some action but is generally noted for his/her absence.

A harmonious connection promotes giving and receiving, space for individual projects and a willingness to play together. You can share the fun, love life and one another together!

Letter 2: The Sensualist

Slow, sensuous, savoring is your style. Able to appreciate all the material pleasures, a loving experience with you tends to include good food and/or wine, fine music, soft carpets, a comfortable bed, a physically attractive lover and skilled massages. Very tactilely oriented, you react to surfaces and how things feel. Visual and auditory turn-ons are fine, but most important is that the situation involve your sense of touch. Sometimes it takes you a little while to "warm up," and a lover who is in a hurry will not be appreciated.

You generally prefer to be comfortable so are less inclined to do acrobatics or highly strenuous lovemaking. Once you know what you like, you may prefer to stick to it rather than risking the letdown of something new. This stable approach is considered too conservative by some but merely shows your determination to enjoy what you know gives you pleasure.

You can indulge others as much as yourself and could slip into rampant materialism or hedonism as a life style if you let yourself go. Fortunately, there are other facets to your personality to balance this. You are often willing to spend money on things to make yourself and others more comfortable. And, you may gain a sense of pleasure, security and reassurance from taking stock of your material goods — knowing they are there. Beauty is another potential source of pleasure — whether through owning beautiful objects, relating to attractive people or creating beautiful things yourself.

You have a real flair for pleasure through the senses and are capable of sharing a sensual exchange more intense than most people. You can reach the peaks of pleasure!

If any of these themes are overdone in your intimate relationships, you may feel that you or your lover is getting excessively money-oriented, possessive, stodgy, self-indulgent, pleasure-loving or materialistic. Keep your options for fulfillment varied, so that many avenues can lead to enjoyment and no one path is carried to excess. Then you can serve as an example of the heights one can reach.

Letter 3: Mind Games

You are well aware that the most erotic part of the human body is the brain: sexual pleasure is 80% mentally created and 20% physical. This intellectual/verbal approach means that sometimes you would rather **talk** or **think** about making love than actually **do** it! And you can certainly make it sound exciting. When you are in the mood for action as well as speech, you may utilize your quick thinking to come up with inventive forms of stimulation for your partner or turning one another on partly through language. Oral sex has a whole new meaning for you.

Your nervous system may be quite sensitive and reactive. What is adequate stimulation for others can be an overload for you. At times, you will have to teach your lover to develop a light touch. Versatile and adaptable, you often have a number of erogenous zones and are best pleased with pleasure from many sources. Focusing too long on one area may feel harsh to you or just plain boring. Routines do not appeal. You seek variations on a theme. Your best bet is to involve all parts of your body in your lovemaking, to discover the many and varied reactions you can experience while making love.

Fantasies may be an important part of your love life. If sufficient trust and desire to share is there, you may wish to reveal some of your particular fantasy turn-ons to your lover. But be sure that is really in the best interests of both of you. Sometimes keeping your thoughts to yourself really is the wisest course. However, you would prefer someone with whom communication — and sex — is easy, playful and fun. Your spontaneity and flexibility are tremendous assets in the pursuit of ecstasy.

If the detached, objective, curious mind is carried too far in your love relationships, you may feel that you or a lover is excessively cool, emotionally distant, intellectual and rationalizing rather than emotional and feeling, superficial and scattered due to multitudinous interests and attractions. The mental and communication world needs to be shared easily between you.

Letter 4: The Caring Lover

Sex, for you, is tied to closeness and emotional security. You are not likely to view it as a purely physical act. Rather, you experience yourself as leaving a part of yourself with anyone you make love to (and they leave a part of themselves with you). This intimate connection can be an ultimately satisfying experience, or you can feel repelled that you shared something so basic with someone for whom you did not care deeply.

The tendency is to get to the gut level with someone else. You may instinctively seek their areas of weakness. Then you have the choice of nurturing the other person, supporting them where you are stronger — or using their vulnerabilities to protect your own weak spots. Mutual support and esteem are quite possible, with each of you doing some mothering of the other. There is often a deep, nonverbal connection between you, where you intuitively sense what the other is feeling. Security and trust are based partially on time, and memory becomes important. You are reassured when your lover also recalls "your" song, or where you first met, or what you favorite color is, or remembers the anniversary and your birthday.

Breasts are often a major erogenous zone for both men and women. Soft skin and someone comfortable to cuddle with probably appeal. Touch is very important and tactile stimulation vital. Sensuality is usually marked, with a preference for extended foreplay, building to a truly satisfying union.

Food may play a significant role in lovemaking rituals. You are seeking a sense of sustenance through relationships (giving and receiving nourishment) and eating together symbolizes that exchange on the material plane. Cuddling, sharing warmth and reassuring each other are as important as the merging of your bodies. You are seeking a sense of union with someone who will love you unconditionally — someone who will **be there** for you, someone you can depend upon to meet your needs.

If these themes are overdone, sex can be used for emotional reassurance, needing security to be reaffirmed again and again. You or your lover could be excessively needy, clutching, clinging, dependent or nurturing. Your relationship could seem more like that of a mother and child than two peers. The challenge is to share the warmth, caring, protectiveness and concern in a mutually satisfying manner.

Letter 5: The Exciting Lover

Sex is majestic, exciting and monumental. Part of your basic life drive is to climax. Your sense of vitality and aliveness may be central during lovemaking. Naturally charismatic and passionate, you seek a lover to share that intensity and ecstasy with you. No halfway measures for you; you fully expect bells to ring and lightning to flash.

You have a need to be onstage, and love relationships are one arena for satisfying your drive for attention, admiration and love. The theater, charades, sales, advertising and promotion are also possible avenues. For you, sex and power may be intertwined and intermingled. You may experience the fullest sense of vitality, strength, self-expression and joy through the sexual act. Just be sure your need to pour out into the world is not twisted into a drive to control others sexually.

Because you seek a response and applause from others, you can be ego-vulnerable in this area. Beware of needing other people's approval too much. It is important to love yourself as well as being able to receive love from others and give love to others. Occasionally, you may use a facade of pride, arrogance or self-sufficiency to cover the inner concern that people might not appreciate and value you. The more you love yourself, the more lovable you are to others.

An instinctive risk-taker and gambler, this may spill over into your intimate associations. Perhaps the lure of an affair promises an excitement you find hard to resist. Perhaps the "cool, calm" type incites your desires for a conquest. Perhaps the forbidden fruit seems to taste the sweetest. You need to expand, to do more than you have done before, to explore areas not yet chartered, but keep your speculating instincts under reasonable control — so they do not create havoc. If you meet these qualities initially through a lover, s/he could be arrogant, self-centered, childish, dominating, inclined to grandstand or apt to play the field.

More than most people, you need to love and be loved. Share your tremendous warmth, enthusiasm, inspiration and skill at turning people on (in many areas — not just sexually) with appreciative people!

Letter 6: The Sensible Lover

Practical and pragmatic, you are capable of being more levelheaded than most where love is concerned. A motto might be: "If it is worth doing, it is worth doing well." This can lead to an attitude of discipline, dedication and a determination to be the best of all possible lovers. When this performance orientation is carried too far, there could be sensual/sexual blocks. You might feel critical of your or your lover's performance. You might freeze up for fear of "making a mistake." If you unconsciously assign your lover the role of "making it right," you could feel s/he is too critical, practical, cool, etc.

Sex is not meant to be a job (although you could use your sensuality in your career or meet partners through your work). Focusing on flaws and how to do it better usually just stops us from enjoying the present moment. Your discipline and dedication can be used to create the optimal environment, the best situation. Then — just relax and enjoy it!

You may be inclined to overvalue cleanliness. Others joke that you shower before **and** after. But it is true that you sometimes notice and are bothered by what others see as petty, little details. For example, you may notice, in the middle of making love, that your lover's nails are dirty. This triggers your association of dirt with germs and you may get turned off. If fastidiousness is important to you, try to choose a lover who shares the same level of meticulousness as you do! (And avoid finding faults with each other's shortcomings. Turn your analytical, flaw-finding spirit into your work or tasks in the world.) If these qualities are projected into lovers, they will overdo the above tendencies.

Since being healthy and productive appeals to you, you may be attracted to diets or bodily disciplines which promote well being and sexual success. You are usually willing to do whatever is necessary to improve the situation. You thrive on accomplishment and doing something well. On its highest level, you are like a sexual craftsperson — subtly creating the most attractive style of lovemaking. Just don't let the technician side of you overwhelm the ability to have fun!

Letter 7: The Lover of Beauty

Lovemaking, with you, is like a work of art. Colors, sounds, surroundings, appearance and appeals are all orchestrated to create a harmonious whole. Grace and balance are sought. Beauty is a key. The right mood for you may include a lovely environment, an attractive lover, beautiful music or other aesthetic aids. You expect a smooth, easy flow. There are no rocks, in your opinion, in the River of Love.

Sometimes you value the appearance too much over the heart of the matter. Don't be misled by a lover with a pretty face, and do not depend on your own attractiveness alone to hold a relationship together. Remember to utilize your native tact, skill at pleasing people and affectionate nature as well.

A harmonious and beautiful environment is more important to you than to some people in making love. Disagreements may upset you and turn you off (unless you are into being competitive). A messy bedroom may also be less than exciting for you. Furnishings in the best of taste, exquisite and beautiful things, harmonious and melodic music, are likely turn-ons for you. You may have some difficulties in facing and dealing with what you see as ugliness in yourself or others. Remember to value the beauty of the soul and the essences of the world — not just outer appearances.

You appreciate the comradeship of love and truly want a partner with whom to share your life. You are oriented toward a "couple" mentality where love is concerned. Although often skilled socially, affable and adept at entertaining people, you like to have your "other half" around. You are a natural "people person" — learning more about yourself through your interactions with others.

You tend to put a high value on fairness which can lead to a very cooperative, giving attitude in making love — caring about your partner's pleasure as much as your own. Wanting things even can also lead to competitiveness if you start keeping score about who had more gratification. Enjoy the give and take of the dance of love without getting hung up in exactly who made the first move or who gained what.

Letter 8: The Passionate Possessor

Intense and passionate, you seek an equal depth of response in your love life. Oriented toward the deepest of emotional commitments, you will rarely settle for something superficial. Indeed, "all or nothing" can be your approach to making love: let's have either an incredibly moving, psyche-shaking experience or skip it! You want someone to touch you on the deepest levels of your being or it is not worth it. (And, sometimes the thought of being touched in your inner depths is too scary to let people get close enough!)

Sex, for you, is power — the power to reach the inner recesses of your soul. Ideally, this power is channeled inward for self-insight and self-control. Less ideally, the power can be channeled into efforts to control others — directly through intimidation or indirectly through manipulation. If this is an issue in your love relationships, you may be on the giving or receiving end of the power plays and/or emotional blackmail. The quest is to share the power over the physical/sensual/ sexual world — to enjoy giving, receiving and sharing pleasures and possessions. There is often a psychic connection with lovers — tuning into one another. But this can be used to figure out the chinks in each other's armor — or to help one another grow in understanding, love and power.

One theme here is a depth analysis and understanding of your own nature through seeing another person reflect some of your potentials. By observing certain characteristics of a mate, we learn to know, understand and master ourselves more fully. That process of inner searching through a relationship is intensely emotional, stirring our deepest passions and opening the door to incredible transformations. Often, what we most love (and most hate) in that other person, we carry in small, seed formation within us. By watching how a mate handles a certain drive, we can choose what to do and what not to do in terms of our expression of that basic motivational drive.

Sex can be experienced as a true merging — a sense of soul mates. The union may seem total — on the mental, emotional and spiritual levels as well as physical. But such an incredible union can also seem a threat to individuality so there are probably times when you cut yourself off sexually (consciously or unconsciously). If we do it deliberately, we are aware of the choice. If the choice is an unconscious one, we may attract a lover who cuts off from us or is incapable of physical intimacy — or some other blocks which give us space. The need here is for some alone, separate time to explore your inner depths, to gain self-mastery. But there is an equally intense need for a mate — someone with whom you can be truly intimate, someone who can know, understand and accept the deepest layers of your being, live with your most secret of secrets and share with you on all levels of their being as well.

Letter 9: The World's Greatest Lover

Joyous, jovial and fun-loving, you may often feel that sex is one of the best things in life. A common motto for you is "If this is good, more is better" — which can lead to an extremely active love life. Other people might see this as self-indulgent, but making love is a way for you to share the wondrousness of being alive. It is an expressive, expansive act which can lift you and your lover to the greatest of heights. Together, you feel vital, exciting and intimately connected to the pulse of the Universe. Physical intimacy can lead to a spiritual communion with a Higher meaning and purpose in life. And — **fun**! You know how to laugh and be playful in bed, as well as being inspired.

A part of your potential is being drawn to spiritual quests. If you choose certain paths, you may curtail your lovemaking except under ideal conditions. You may be drawn to Tantric Yoga or other forms of illumination which stress the use of sexual energies for inspirational purposes. Sometimes this results in a feeling that sex is too holy to be practiced under mundane conditions, so that you only indulge under very special conditions, with a very special person. You might spend a long time waiting for the "perfect" lover and the "perfect" moment (or attract lovers seeking perfection from you).

Generally exuberant and outgoing in your sexual style, you know how to give and receive tremendous enjoyment. Usually open and fairly uninhibited, your natural and spontaneous approach is very appealing. Occasionally you may fall into trying to make everything ideal, which could cause anxieties on your part or on the part of your lover. However, you are usually able to be relaxed and have a great time!

Sometimes the great outdoors is a source of refreshment for you. Just remember, if you get a sudden urge to make love off in the bushes from the hiking trail, try to pick a soft spot for the sake of your lover! Pictures of nature at her best, in the comfort of home, may be just as satisfying. Part of the pull within your nature is to go further with sex than most people, to expand your sensual horizons. This can be expressed as making love in a variety of locales, choosing foreigners as lovers, making love on trips, turning the sexual act into a search for God, trying a number of different positions, being open to new ideas and any other variations on this theme. A general thread is great gusto for life and love!

Letter 10: The Responsible Lover

Control is an important issue for you in making love. You need the security of feeling that you have things in hand. This can lead to a strong sense of responsibility for the other person as well. If your sense of safety is threatened, you are likely to withdraw or cut yourself off through criticism and fault-finding.

Careful and cautious, you do not usually commit yourself to love quickly. The tendency is to scout out the situation, think things over and then reach a considered decision. "Falling in love" may seem a bit impractical to you. Rather are you likely to view the love relationship as one which is built and created over time.

Similarly, you are not inclined to fall into bed with just anyone. Certain pragmatic parameters have to be satisfied. Usually you are seeking a lover with whom you will feel safe. Your definition of safety could range from someone with a good income, someone in a position of power and authority, someone whose behavior is predictable, someone strong and capable, someone responsible and mature. In a sense, there is a tendency to pick lovers who are father figures in some way (older, more powerful, responsible, achievement-oriented, etc.) or lovers who expect you to play the role of father figure (carrying the load, being capable, productive, accomplishing).

Since your sense of security in the relationship is involved, you may be quite willing to wait and delay having a love relationship until you feel you have found a situation that is safe. Part of the issue is one of power — a concern that the other party might dominate, reject, criticize, control or in some way put you down or hurt you. As long as you fear the power of the other person, there is a tendency to inhibit, hold back — not get involved. Once you feel secure in your own strength and abilities to cope, you are willing to become involved — but not before.

In some cases, this combination will indicate a career involved with sex. The control and mastery aspect is present since the individual is operating from a professional level. A few people have also been known to use a cool, "technically expert" attitude as a way to maintain distance and control in relationships. They may be able to sexually interact with a number of people, but are not truly emotionally involved with any.

This focus on control and performance can inhibit sexual pleasure if it is allowed to get in the way. Few things are more of a turn-off than the fear of criticism, rejection, put downs or domination. (This fear could operate from you to your lover or your lover to you.) The sense of strength and competence must be shared, with each of you contributing to the relationship in your own areas of ability. Similarly, the judgmental, practical attitude must not be allowed into the sensual realm where it tends to block pleasure. Keep the flaw-finding lens for the outside world and career accomplishments. Use your pragmatism to build the most solid and lasting of foundations and know when to kick back, not be serious and just enjoy!

Letter 11: The Freewheeling Lover

Making love is an arena for expressing your individuality and uniqueness. This can mean that you are willing to experiment, open to trying different avenues of expression to discover what fits you the best. At times, you may act (or simply talk) in an unconventional manner — partly to prove to people that you cannot be put into a mold or stereotype. You might even go so far as to deliberately shock people with your behavior or language — to show them that you are not bound by their rules and roles.

You need a love relationship which allows you independence and freedom. You can deliberately choose a lover who is open, tolerant, into his/her own thing and desirous of having lots of liberty. Or, you might unconsciously be drawn to "free souls" — people who are not really available (married, unwilling to make a commitment, living quite a distance away...) — thus gaining the space and freedom you are not fully aware of wanting. If you do not allow room for your own uniqueness and individuality to emerge, you may attract lovers who will overdo those qualities — to the point of chaos, rebelliousness, irresponsibility and thumbing the nose at the world.

When both you and your lover are in touch with your needs for self-expression and an equal sharing with mutual respect, tolerance and space between, your relationship is first and foremost a friendship. You accept one another without trying to change each other. You are you and s/he is s/he; that is enough. Together, you can communicate easily and enjoy the exchange of ideas.

You are open to exploring varied avenues of pleasures and would not condemn any source outright as "abnormal" or "strange." If anything, you are more willing to explore the new and different, to see if you can discover something of value. Sometimes your experimental approach is more of a head trip than it is exhibited in your behavior. That is, you can tolerate anything intellectually and believe "To each, his/her own" but would not participate in certain behaviors. But, in general, there is a great talent for inventiveness, relating as a peer and truly enjoying each other's ideas and the uniqueness of yourself and your lover.

One possibility is an attraction to new technology of all kinds, and you may enjoy livening up your love life with electronic and other gadgetry — or simply keep a computer beside your bed! Because you are usually relaxed and casual, it is easy for lovers to be the same, and together you generally enjoy the sensual/sexual world with relatively few, if any, hang-ups. You hate boredom, so set your love life up to be full of changes. Sometimes both you and your lover may not know what is coming next. The anticipation and uncertainty keeps your lovemaking exciting, electric and alive!

Letter 12: The Dream Lover

Sex, for you, can be a cosmic experience. You seek a merging of souls as much as bodies and a sense of union with the entire Universe on one level of your being. One potential is an incredibly joyous experience, with each wave of ecstasy lifting you higher and higher. Because you are capable of making an intuitive connection with a lover, you may participate in a mental/emotional blending as well as a physical sharing. Your sensitivity allows you to tune in and join with the other person.

If your need for submergence is carried too far, you may become lost in illusions and delusions. Because you **want** an ecstatic, incredible connection, you may fantasize that it is happening before enough discipline has been put out to create it. You could talk yourself into a fairy tale image which does not exist, only to be disillusioned later. You **can** make beautiful music together, but keep your eyes open along the way!

Another potential is falling into the roles of savior/victim with lovers. You may attract people who expect you to play God for them — make their world perfect, make everything loving and lovely. Or, you may be looking for inhuman perfection and idealism in your lovers, expecting them to supply the ecstasy on demand rather than learning to co-create it. The reach for something higher through your lovemaking is a very valid expression for you. Just be sure both parties are contributing to the emergence of an ideal vision.

Other possibilities include the seeking of a love so holy and inspired that no one measures up. You may declare sexuality as sacrosanct and refuse to share with anyone less than ideal (godlike). Or, you can look for an infinitely beautiful experience through artistic expression. Sharing aesthetic feelings with a lover then becomes very important.

The potential for pleasure is immense! Your rich imagination, sensitive perception, intuitive understanding, idealistic seeking and need for communion can blend together to create with another visionary person the most intense, ecstatic and uplifting of lovemaking sessions. Truly can you be swept away by the utter perfection of life and love!

ALPHABET COMBINATIONS BY TWOS

Refer to Chapters 6 (pages 115-119) and 8 (pages 189-197) and read the appropriate **Combinations by Two**, thinking in terms of sensuality potentials and possible sexual partners.

POLARITIES

1-7: ♂-♀ or ⚴ or ⚵, ♈-♎, 1st-7th houses

The opposites you are striving to balance are a quick, fiery, urgent approach to sex versus a laid-back, luxury-loving style. You are dealing with the compromise between asserting your wants, needs and desires versus trying to please the other person.

2-8: ♀-♇, ♉-♏, 2nd-8th houses

The opposites you are striving to balance are an indulgent, sensuous, slow style open to all pleasures versus a determined, powerful, disciplined approach which maintains a sense of control. Extremes of overindulgence or overcontrol (to the point of asceticism or withdrawal) are possible until you reach the middle ground of mutual giving, receiving and sharing of pleasure from the sensual/ sexual world. You may unconsciously set your life up to alternate between periods of great sexual involvement and celibacy. Attracting lovers who engage in power struggles over sexual or financial matters is another option. Once you gain a solid sense of inner balance (between hedonism and self-mastery), the outer balance with a lover flows easily.

3-9: ☿-♃, or ⚷, ♊-♐, 3rd-9th houses

You may be struggling between a desire to take matters of the heart casually and a desire to fall madly, totally in love. Your fiery exuberance could battle your objective ability to step back and not get involved.

Variety could be the spice of life where your love life is concerned. You may have a number of different partners, learning from each one. You could also limit yourself to one emotional commitment, but keep such an open, inquiring mind that you are continually expanding your sexual horizons. Communicating about your mutual pleasures can be a great help. Sometimes, you may even prefer the discussion and imagination to the actual experience!

Restless and eager to discover multiple sources of stimulation, you function better with a lover who is not hung up on routine. Quickly bored, you are best off with someone who is willing to change the scene, change positions and even change his/her appearance. Sometimes trading fantasies is a mutual turn-on too.

4-10: ☽-♄, ♋-♑, 4th-10th houses

The opposites you are striving to balance are a cuddly, warm, supportive, compassionate approach versus a practical, realistic assessment. Cold hard facts about the who, what, when and where of making love vie with emotional needs and gut-level desires.

5-11: ☉-♅, ♌-♒, 5th-11th houses

You may feel torn between letting it all hang out with an intense, driving passion and a spontaneous *joie de vivre* versus an intellectual approach which analyzes everything objectively to figure out the stimulation that will be most rewarding. You may swing from a powerful, loving commitment to the urge to run away because things are getting "too heavy." Your needs for freedom could seem at odds with your desire for sexual excitement, until you make room in your life for both.

6-12: ☿ or ♃ or ♆-♆, ♍-♓, 6th-12th houses

You are striving to make a balance between the heavy-handed critic approach in making love (focus on all the flaws to improve performance) and the utopian idealist (everything will be just perfect if you imagine it that way). Your practical side must be blended with your visionary side lest you find yourself mercilessly critiqued on your bedroom performance; left high and dry by a lover who preferred dreaming to doing; driving sexual partners away with your desire to get every detail just right; having trouble making a connection because you are so lost in imaginary pleasures, you are out of touch with physical sensations. By blending these seeming opposites you get the best of this physical world as well as the most inspiring of other (mystical) experiences!

NODES OF THE MOON
The nodal placements which are particularly relevant to the area of sexuality are 2-8 (Taurus/Scorpio or 2nd/8th houses) and 5-11 (Leo/Aquarius or 5th/11th houses). If your chart has any of those combinations, read the appropriate section in "Polarities" (above) with special care.

ELEMENT EMPHASIS
Fire
♂, ☉, ♃, ♄, ♈, ♌, ♐, 1st, 5th, 9th houses

Spontaneity is the name of the game. Vital, vibrant and vivacious, you can be turned on almost instantly (and turned off equally quickly). Whether it is the sight of an attractive body, appreciation of a finely honed mind or response to an act of warmth and feeling, you can feel desire rising at a swift rate. Your responsiveness is a tremendous turn-on to your partner, and people may adore making love with you because it is so exciting.

You approach sexuality with confident optimism, expecting to share pure, exalted highs with people for whom you feel a magnetic attraction. You love to exude charisma and charm in social settings. Even if devoted to one partner, you like to keep a bit of that magnetic and sexual energy in the air, just to make life interesting.

You probably dress and move in a fashion which catches the eye and hopefully arouses a bit of passion. Boredom is to be avoided at all costs; hence, your ears are always perked for news of sensuous massage oils, new positions to try, and — of course — who's new in town.

Light is often supportive of your sexual drive. The heat and beauty of a fire can be a great ploy to get you in the mood. Sunny days, basking on the beach or in the meadow and general soaking up of sunlight usually feeds your libido.

Your energy level is supported by activity. The more you do, the more you become capable of doing. Sitting around is not in your best interests. When making love, you need a sense of excitement, drama and high stimulation. Sometimes impatience can be a problem, if you feel held back by your partner. You may respond more quickly than the individual with whom you make love. A naturally "hot" number, you usually have strong physical needs and should seek lovers who can share that sense of aliveness that the sexual act can reinforce.

Fighting over power might drive you away from your lover, and — in anger — you could be unkind. But heated arguments can also be a turn-on, because there is the fun of "making up" to anticipate. Usually your blasts are over quickly anyway. When projected, your fire energy could attract a Don Juan or Salome, or someone who is just plain kinky. You might find yourself with a partner addicted to being the center of everyone's attention or, at least, the center of your universe, jealous of time you spend on other activities or other people. Perhaps your love will be a habitual party-goer, bar cruiser or gambler.

If shared, fiery love energy can take you to unprecedented heights, add zest to life, heal any hurt.

Earth
♀, ☿, ?, ♆, ♄, ♂, ♍, ♑, 2nd, 6th, 10th houses

You can be amazingly practical where affairs of the heart are concerned. You tend to take lovemaking very seriously. If you are going to do it, you want to do it **right**! Some people may feel you go so far as to make a career out of sex, with a real performance orientation. One potential is work involving sensuality — which can range from the massage therapist, to the advertiser using sex to sell products to a sex symbol of the cinema. Another option is finding a sexual partner(s) through your career. But this combinations can also simply show more pragmatism than the average person has in the emotional realm of sex and sensuality.

If practice makes perfect, you have been known to try again and again. If you have not fallen into excessive inhibition (due to a critical attitude), your technical skills are likely to be quite extensive. You make sure you are well trained. Deliberate and studied, you are unlikely to rush into something you might regret later. You will figure it all out beforehand — making sure you really want to do it. Despite some instinctive hesitancy, you are likely to have a very sensual nature, responding especially to hugs, caresses, back rubs and other forms of tactile stimulation. You might associate and enjoy food, drink, massage, music, candles or incense with lovemaking.

Comfort ranks high on your list of priorities; you will leave the flagpole intimacy or other high-risk shenanigans to more adventurous (foolhardy?) souls. Sometimes you can be a bit stuck-in-the-mud with your focus on security, but usually your desire to make love **well** leads to a satisfied partner.

Unrealistic expectations of performance levels for yourself or for your mate might create difficulties. Tedious analysis can spell certain death to a promising affair. Leave work at the job site along with acute, critical abilities. Distaste for anything messy could inhibit sexual/sensual needs.

If you project your earth energy, a partner can make any of these errors for you. A lover might be so wrapped up in material pursuits or so dedicated to work as to be no lover at all. S/he may want total authority and control over the whens, wheres and hows of making love. Your significant other could be too lethargic, monotonous, vapid, jaded, prosaic or hedonistic.

A flaw-finding attitude can interfere with pleasure, whether directed toward you by a lover or from you toward a lover. The desire for efficiency is useful for some beforehand preparations, but spontaneity is your best course once the scene is set!

Air
☿, ♀, ♀, ⚳, ♅, ♊, ♎, ♒, 3rd, 7th, 11th houses

Articulate and expressive, you can certainly explain the birds and the bees to anyone. Your skill with concepts and language may be useful in persuading a lover into your bed, but don't get so carried away with the discussion that you lose out on the action! Head trips can get in the way of having fun. Of course, you can also use your verbal talents to turn on yourself and your partner. The right words can work wonders!

Your decisions regarding with whom you make love, where and when are likely to be based on intellect as well as emotions. Your logic and rationality will be utilized. You may also read lots of books on the subject, always listen and learn or simply have a very open mind about different sources of pleasure.

It is not imperative that you and your partner agree on everything, but it is essential that you two can talk about anything, that you feel you are equals and very good friends. Sometimes to capture the essence of an experience in a few well-put phrases is more satisfying than the experience itself; it seems to give it new dimension. But, then again there are times when nervous chatter obliterates the emergence of the experience altogether.

If projected, your airy energy may attract a person who makes you feel intellectually inferior or who never gives you a chance to get a word in edgewise. S/he may be a comedian whose humor very shortly begins to wear thin. Your lover could be so coolly objective and detached as to be downright chilly. If overdone by you or a partner, excessive intellectualism can be a sure drag on sensual enjoyment. Think, communicate and share — but retain your ability to react in the moment, with excitement and ecstasy.

If mutually expressed, air energy defuses the intensity of sexual and sensual encounters, adding mirth and forgiving detachment, allowing imperfections and room to grow together.

Water
☽, ♇, ♆, ♋, ♏, ♓, 4th, 8th, 12th houses

For you, the sensuous dance of intimate contact reverberates best through the smooth and ever-deepening flow of feelings. Initial encounters go well when a leisurely sharing of activities enables you to get a psychic imprint of the other person and a first reading on how comfortably your energies can merge. You need a lover who can appreciate your sensitivity and who can plunge with you to great emotional depths. You might like to be able to lean on your partners sometimes, to drop your burden of responsibilities for awhile, and you may be willing to allow them a similar respite.

Sexual activity is tied to feelings where you are concerned. Though certainly a physical interaction, you realize that your emotions are also involved. Intuitive and empathic, you may pick up more than you wish from the exchange.

Your desires run very deeply and intensely. Casual quickies are definitely not your style. You seek a strong, feeling connection with the other person and the emotional security that comes with trust.

Water scenes may help relax you and tune you in to the other person — be it looking at the ocean, having a fountain or simply a painting of the sea. Walking or swimming in beautiful, natural surroundings, mutual aesthetic appreciation experiences, common meditative, spiritual and religious practices are all potential aphrodisiacs. The safer you feel, the easier it is for you to merge with another.

If you project your water energy, you may attract a partner who is so sensitive that you are afraid anything you say or do may be taken amiss. This could extend to a hypersensitivity to touch that you find restrictive. Flip the coin and you might be burdened by someone who cannot bear not to be touching you. Your lover could be overly dependent in other ways and never consent to walk a few miles in your shoes. There is also the possibility of a partner who is totally ungrounded and illogical, relying solely on intuition to see him/her through.

In power struggles, there could be floods of tears, from either or both of you. Many battles might be fought with never a word spoken due to extensive use of body language, facial expressions and general ambience. Negative feelings can be held in for long periods of time, and heaven help anyone who is accidentally in the way when the dam breaks.

When water energy is shared, unfathomable depths await your exploration. Understanding and communication on nonverbal levels are often experienced and such a merging occurs that two beings truly become one.

Fire-Earth

♂, ☉, ♃, ⚷, ♈, ♌, ♐, 1st, 5th, 9th houses &
♀, ☿, ⚳, ⚶, ♄, ♉, ♍, ♑, 2nd, 6th, 10th houses

With you, the earth may indeed move under someone's feet! Your high vitality and strong sexual drive is backed by real staying power and endurance. A sexual achiever, you can be courageous, initiating and start the whole thing off with a bang! Yet you also have a great capacity for hanging in there. Dynamic yet dependable, exciting and reassuring, many people would declare you the best of lovers if they had the opportunity to experience your abilities.

Because you have tremendous power and drive, you can sometimes push too hard. You probably present an almost undeterrable campaign on a person who has captured your fancy. If persistence coupled with charm will not work, what will?

Yet, you may occasionally bulldoze your way into a situation you later regret. If this quality is being projected into your lovers, you are likely to attract overwhelming individuals with whom you have a hard time coping. They could bowl you over with their incentive and momentum; their ambitions and need for public status could alienate you. Tunnel vision might cause friction as you regret other interests that have been left behind. Recognizing your own power is the first step to sharing power with another person. Sexual intimacy is a wondrous opportunity for learning give and take.

When integrated, mutual or parallel targets and a shared need for results and action augment your physical relationships.

Fire-Air

♂, ☉, ♃, ⚷, ♈, ♌, ♐, 1st, 5th, 9th houses &
☿, ♀, ⚴, ⚵, ♅, ♊, ♎, ♒, 3rd, 7th, 11th houses

Making love with you is likely to include a lot of laughs. You have a natural sparkle and a zest and enthusiasm for life backed up with a talent for witticisms. Whether you play the lighthearted lover, the classic comedian, the practical joker or some other entertaining role, you help keep the atmosphere fun-loving. This is not to say you cannot make love without bursting into giggles, but rather affirming that one of your greatest gifts is the ability to help other people enjoy life! You can be deeply philosophical as well, but assuredly despise sameness and staleness.

Of course, if you let the desire for "fun" take over too much, your partners may be frustrated. Like a butterfly, you tend to be here and there and not always easy to pin down. Oriented toward variety, you have been known to change partners if you felt someone was getting "too serious." If you are projecting this quality into a lover, you are likely to attract someone who is into having a good time, but perhaps not tremendously stable. Such people could be shallow and unsympathetic, fickle and never serious. They might be scattered and foolhardy, senselessly hopeful and irrational.

As long as you can share the casual approach — when appropriate — you leave room for both of you to be responsible and dependable as well. Together, you can solve any problem via fruitful communication, laugh wholeheartedly and love joyously.

Fire-Water

♂, ☉, ♃, ⚷, ♈, ♌, ♐, 1st, 5th, 9th houses &
☽, ♇, ♆, ♋, ♏, ♓, 4th, 8th, 12th houses

Making love for you is to experience incredible ups and downs in your emotions. Rarely in that safe, neutral zone, you tend to be euphoric and ecstatic or down and depressed. Sometimes your lovers may feel like you are two people: a confident, outgoing, eager lover and a shy, withdrawing, timid soul who needs to be coaxed and talked into making love. You can be incredibly spontaneous and impulsive in bed and then turn around, absolutely clamming up and shutting down.

If you are projecting some of these qualities, your lovers are likely to present you with the same kind of contradictory images. Their moods could range from incredible "*joie de vivre*" to rock bottom hopelessness. Either of you might bottle up emotions only to explode in a tirade or rage and frustration against others — or implode, becoming ill or involved in a series of accidents or surgeries. The challenge is to moderate your energy so that it is neither too self-contained nor too outwardly directed.

Once you recognize and make a place for both your sensitive, inward side and your risk-taking, outward side, lovemaking is likely to be more universally satisfying. You are amazingly intense; that is not likely to change. The issue is feeling a balance in your emotional life between outward expression and inward processing. Sexual interactions can assist developing that balance as you move between an inner experience of your pleasure and the other person's reactions to an outer involvement in the process of mutual gratification, and back.

You need to give to and receive encouragement and reassurance from a lover, who can be an invaluable anchor if s/he is sensitive and level. Finding partners can seem a bit frightening, because you tend to swing between great self-assurance and tremendous self-doubt. Seeking people who are willing to cooperate in a mutual support system can be beneficial and successful.

Earth-Air

♀, ☿, ⚳, ⚶, ♄, ♉, ♍, ♑, 2nd, 6th, 10th houses &
☿, ♀, ⚴, ⚵, ♅, ♊, ♎, ♒, 3rd, 7th, 11th houses

You are likely to instinctively use many of your practical and analytical skills in the bedroom, and they may not always be the most satisfying path. You truly want to do it **right**, and this concern with performance can create blocks in your own pleasure and that of your partner. Sometimes criticism becomes an issue with either one or both of you feeling fearful of being judged, of being inadequate according to some standard of "proper" sexual interactions.

If carried to an extreme by either you or your partner, the objective and pragmatic attitudes can interfere with pure, natural pleasure. Your capacity for abstraction can be utilized to detach from a judgmental attitude. Rather than getting caught up in what is wrong, allow yourself to mentally float above it. Your need for practical results can help to ground you in the physical world of sensations if you begin to get lost in a world of intellectualization and rationalizations.

Often intellectual and pragmatic in your approach, you can get right down into forthright discussions about common sensual and sexual preferences and techniques. This practical approach probably seems the sanest weeding out process both for finding a lover and preparing for intimate contact. Why waste time that could be better spent in bed?

If you are projecting part of your own nature, you could attract a cold, inhibited or blocked lover. Your partner could drag a pleasurable affair into the workshop or the bleak, pristine laboratory. You may tire of having to categorize and intellectualize about every feeling and long to just feel for the sheer joy of it!

You are capable of being an excellent lover and enjoying sensual exchanges tremendously. Just be sure to give as much time to emotions and sensations as to thoughts and practicalities. This shared energy can lead to levelheaded friends who are also sexual partners with no need to indulge in frivolous game playing. You both know what you want from a sexual relationship and can communicate about and work toward it companionably.

Earth-Water

♀, ☿, ⚳, ⚶, ♄, ♉, ♍, ♑, 2nd, 6th, 10th houses &
☽, ♇, ♆, ♋, ♏, ♓, 4th, 8th, 12th houses

Security is a watchword in your experience of making love. Whether you seek someone to provide it for you — that sense of safety and being able to rely on the other person to be supportive, or whether you attract people who look to you for that feeling of protection, the issue is there in your love relationships.

Ease, stability and commitment matter to you. You are unlikely to take sex casually. Making love is making a pledge where you are concerned. Fidelity is important to you; dependability a virtue. A natural cuddler, you enjoy the emotional support that comes of being close and caring with another person as well as the physical excitement of a climax. Caresses and contact are essential for your comfort.

Your tendency toward seriousness and responsibility could deprive you of some of the fun and laughter to be had in sensual and sexual encounters. You might also feel too bound by social and cultural mores that are outdated and unnecessarily restrictive. You may suffer from an overly active conscience. But when the frivolities are over, you are the caring, nurturant person who stays around to pick up the pieces and heal the wounded.

When these attributes are projected, you could attract a lover who is trying to carry the entire world and has few reserves left for you. Or, your partner could be concentrating on changing, improving or saving you from yourself. If you would only cut your hair, have a vasectomy or tubal ligation, bathe more often, earn more money (etc.), the relationship would work out perfectly. Or, the partner may be so unconditionally supportive that you think s/he would praise you if you committed murder and you begin to wonder if s/he ever really listens to you or seriously thinks about what you say or do.

When shared, mutual nurturance and support benefit both of you and you know that you and your partner are truly committed lovers — there when needed.

Air-Water

☿, ♀, ⚴, ⚵, ♅, ♊, ♎, ♒, 3rd, 7th, 11th houses &
☽, ♇, ♆, ♋, ♏, ♓, 4th, 8th, 12th houses

You can create your own inner world for making love, and fortunate is the lucky mortal selected to share it with you. Sometimes it seems you are inhabiting the landscape of a fantasy or dream more than the real world. This magical quality adds much to your lovemaking. When carried too far, however, the element of unreality can lead to a feeling that the envisioned experience was more satisfying than the actual act! The internal and external worlds must be brought together in a satisfying symphony of sensation and imagination, perception and romance.

If you manifest this combination first through a lover, s/he may spend too much time talking about feelings and accomplish little, including sexually. S/he might seem to live in outer (or inner) space and descend to the earth plane very rarely. Your partners could be uncomfortably psychic or resemble too well the probing psychoanalyst. Or they might be so empathic that they seem to be living everyone else's (or your) life instead of their own.

When a balanced expression is attained, you and your lover can make optimal use of both right and left hemispheres, logic and intuition in your sexual and sensual liaisons. You may share and/or enact fantasies, delight in romance, enjoy instinctive pleasures and cement bonds with intense, heartfelt conversations.

QUALITY EMPHASIS

Cardinal
♂, ☽, ♀, ♀, ⚷, ♄, ♈, ♋, ♎, ♑, 1st, 4th, 7th, 10th houses

You learn best through experience, and what a rewarding area to gain experience in! Not for you are the numerous sex manuals in this world. Actually making love teaches you more about yourself and your partner than any informational tome could.

You may feel torn in your sexual approach at times, being able to play many different roles. You can be the dominating, controlling lover who runs the show from start to finish with a firm hand. You can be the gentle, soft, cuddly lover who wants to sink into the experience like a bubble bath. You can be the direct, impatient, driving lover who does not want to wait! You can be the graceful, attractive, tactful lover who naturally draws admiration and response.

Finding a partner who also has a varied repertoire helps immensely. Then you merely work on getting your timing together so that you have similar or compatible roles going on at the same time.

Fixed
♀, ☉, ♇, ♅, ♉, ♌, ♏, ♒, 2nd, 5th, 8th, 11th houses

A naturally sensuous person, your desire nature is likely to be strong. With a large appetite for life, you could engage in eating, drinking, making love and making money with equal gusto. The material world is an important focus of learning for you. Torn between indulgence and control of the appetites, you get numerous opportunities to practice balance in your life.

It is likely that any lover you attract will be working on the same issues. Until you integrate your own internal ambivalences, you and a lover may fight about money (spending versus saving, who earns it, who controls it); sex (who enjoys what, when to make love, where, how); drinking; eating or other material pleasures. The issues of power and control (who has it?) are likely to surface often in your love relationships.

Through your interactions — in bed and elsewhere — you are learning to give, receive and share pleasures comfortably with another person. The physical world is meant to be enjoyed and your potential for sensual satisfaction is tremendous.

Mutable
☿, ⚵, ⚴, ♃, ⚶, ♆, ♊, ♍, ♐, ♓, 3rd, 6th, 9th, 12th houses

Flexible and adaptable, you are more willing than many to learn about making love from books, seminars or listening to other people. Open to ideas from any source, you will often try out (at least mentally) a number of different positions, placements and pleasures. Because your appetites are partially developed through thinking and imagining rather than action, you sometimes expect more than is reasonable. You may dream about infinitely ecstatic exchanges that are simply not feasible in our limited, human world. On the other hand, your visions sometimes spur you and a partner to previously unreachable heights!

Routines bore you, so a lover needs to remain stimulating, lest you be tempted to move on. New experiences are the spice in your life and you get no thrills if you know what happens next. Often highly mental, you have been known to get off on just **talking** about making love on occasion. Your mind must be involved enough to keep you interested, but not so active you lose touch (literally) with the physical.

You can be an extremely talented lover as you are able to master almost any technique. A natural student, you pick up fresh ideas and new information like a sponge and lovers find your openness rewarding.

THEMES

Freedom

♂, ♃, ⚷, ♅, ♈, ♐, ♒, 1st, 9th, 11th houses

Free and uninhibited, you can be very open in your sexual expression. Willing to experiment, you will try almost anything once. Spontaneity is your forte and you thrive on the excitement of pioneering spirit. Independence is essential to you; the partner who tries to tie you down is likely to be disappointed. A free soul, you can range far and wide in your sensual escapades and might keep several partners on a string simultaneously. You can be faithful to one partner if you choose — but abhor someone who tries to possess you and tie you down.

You can fall in and out of lust quickly and are susceptible to the old theme of "If I'm not near the one I love, I love the one I'm near." But your instinct for liberty may keep you wary of becoming too committed.

If this potential is projected, you are likely to attract lovers who overdo the need for space, self-expression, breaking new ground and sensual exploration. Best bet: see yourselves as two sensual explorers, constantly discovering new territory.

Closeness or Interpersonal

☽, ☉, ♀, ⚵, ⚶, ♇, ♋, ♌, ♎, ♏, 4th, 5th, 7th, 8th houses

Concerned and caring, you become deeply emotionally attached to lovers. Not comfortable with casual affairs, you tend to seek an intense commitment. Intimacy, for you, involves shared feelings as well as shared bodies. Because making love is a very meaningful act for you, it is hard for you to relate to people for whom that is not the case.

If this need for an emotional connection is projected, you are likely to attract lovers you experience as clinging, dependent, too absorbed in the relationship between you and overly intense. A depth of feeling is probable in your relationships, whether more through your focus or the other person's.

Artistic
♀, ♀, ⚷, ☉, ♅, ♂, ♌, ♎, ♓, 2nd, 5th, 7th, 12th houses

Beauty is central in your lovemaking schemes — but that is beauty by your definitions. That could range from a partner with a body that's a "perfect 10" to a bedroom decorated in the most exquisite of tastes. If you find modern, futuristic hard-edged glass or ruffly, fluffy, overstuffed furniture attractive — that is what you will strive to surround yourself with. The mood created by your physical setting is more important to you than most people.

Similarly, your appearance and that of your partner are likely to be very significant factors in whether or not (and how enthusiastically) you make love. Since you prefer sexual encounters to be smooth and flawless, someone who gives the impression of contentiousness will quickly be crossed off your list. The last thing you want is a struggle in bed. You are looking for a lovely, mutually satisfying, pleasing experience. Any hint of unpleasantness, disagreements, conflicts, is more likely to turn you off than on.

Idealistic
♃, ⚷, ♆, ♐, ♓, 9th, 12th houses

You want your sexual experiences to flow like a beautiful dream. Your vision is of infinite ecstasy. This might lead you to feeling sex is too pure and holy to be wasted on just anyone. You could wait for that optimal experience, that ideal person (who may never arrive). The opposite extreme is also possible, where sexual interchanges become a form of ultimate pleasure, one of your highest values. Then, it is hard to get enough. When sex is a "greatest good" in life, the tendency is to overdo.

You might also get involved with people that are seeking a sense of meaning, purpose, understanding in life — those on religious, spiritual or idealistic paths. You could fall into a savior/victim relationship with someone, thinking they would provide all meaning to you or striving to make their world perfect. Making love with a saint may not be the most satisfying experience in the world. Sharing the pursuit of ideal sexual exchanges can be quite rewarding.

Obsessive-Compulsive
☿, ?, ⚷, ♇, ♄, ♍, ♏, ♑, 6th, 8th, 10th houses

You feel that practice makes perfect and are willing to keep on practicing until you get it great! You may even exhaust your bed partners at times. Your flair for organization and thoroughness is extreme, and you may have a whole regime worked out for the "proper" (i.e., efficient) way to make love. Your concern with getting all the details just so could interfere with the exchange of pleasure. Your critical eye can help create an optimum environment, but do not allow it to inhibit the fun part of making love!

Intense, focused and concentrated, you are often known for your endurance and ability to sustain.

If these qualities are projected, you are likely to attract lovers who are too absorbed in certain physical details to really let loose and enjoy, critical or judgmental, focused on flaws and areas to improve.

You may meet potential sexual partners through your work, or use your sensual nature in your career. Just remember not to turn lovemaking into a "job" by working too hard at it and losing the sense of joy. You can be quite sensual when relaxed and not concentrating on getting things just right.

Competence

☿, ⚳, ⚶, ♄, ♍, ♑, 6th, 10th houses

You are dedicated to being an effective lover and are willing to work at it, to do whatever is necessary to improve your performance. This practicality can assist you in figuring out what is essential, but the judgmental attitude may block instinctive reactions or create inhibitions if carried too far.

Because you can be a pragmatist where sex is concerned, some people feel your attitude is too cold. You may come across, at times, more as a technician than as a lover. You can also work in the field, e.g., as a sex therapist, or meet lovemaking partners through your career. Your natural drive is to improve this area so that people's sexual exchanges are even better.

Mental Stimulation

☿, ⚳, ⚶, ⚴, ♃, ⚷, ♅, ♆, ♊, ♍, ♎, ♐, ♒, ♓, 3rd, 6th, 7th, 9th, 11th, 12th houses

You probably like to talk in bed. Mental stimulation, information exchange and the generation of ideas through sex and with sex are important to you. Ever eager to learn more about your or your partner's capacity for pleasure, there is an openness and eagerness to learn within you. You will probably seek out bright, articulate lovers who can share the world of the mind with you. If you project those qualities, you may deny your own intellectual capacities, experiencing them only through a lover. Such a lover would probably think too much, rationalize, talk too much or be scattered through multiple interests, overdoing a head trip.

Shared ideas and interests can help keep your love life stimulating.

Relationships

♀, ⚴, ⚵, ♇, ♎, ♏, 7th, 8th houses

You are probably very aware of your partner's responses when making love. You may be too concerned with his/her pleasure and not enough with your own, or you could be in a competitive framework, keeping track of who did what to whom and who enjoyed themselves the most. You are likely to emphasize the interaction between you. Just be sure you are sharing the fun in an equal manner. If you feel too vulnerable, you might withdraw or push the other person away in self-protection. Sexual pleasure is intended to be joint, but allow room for spontaneity and some reasonable self-centeredness (on both your parts) as well.

Security
♀, ☽, ☿, ?, ⚵, ♇, ♄, ♆, ♉, ♋, ♍, ♏, ♑, ♓, 2nd, 4th, 6th, 8th, 10th, 12th houses

You seek a sense of safety when making love. This can be through selecting partners who are stable, dependable and predictable. It could be through setting a very secure environment. You are likely to prefer the known pleasures to new experiments.

Risk/Creativity/Change
♂, ☉, ♃, ⚴, ♅, ♈, ♌, ♐, ♒, 1st, 5th, 9th, 11th houses

You are willing to take risks and seek freedom in your lovemaking. This can be through selecting partners who may not hang around or are into more unusual forms of pleasure. It could be through a pattern of more than one lover, or affairs or some other risk-taking activity where there may be a price to pay for discovery. Experimental in your approach, you are usually open to any new, sensual experience. You may express your creativity in the sexual arena (and/or channel your sexuality into creative expression).

Parents
☽, ♄, ?, ♋, ♑, 4th, 10th houses

Your experience of your parents had a strong impact on your sexual nature. What you see as appropriate to enjoy, what turns you on and off, are very influenced by their example. You may want to be like them, or just the opposite, but their sexual attitudes and actions set the standard (pro or con) by which you judge your own. You may want to release some old reactions and feelings so you can be truly in the present and not replaying patterns from the past.

   You may also attract lovers who end up playing child to your parent role or parent to your child role. You may even enjoy dominance/submission games with a sexual partner. Mutual support and security are usually sought.

Power
☉, ♇, ♄, ♌, ♏, ♑, 5th, 8th, 10th houses

Power needs may be an issue in your sexual experiences. Your need for control in this area could lead to power struggles if not handled with a bit of care. Or, if you project your drive for authority onto partners, you could attract very controlling, dominating individuals as lovers.

   Mutual respect will sidestep a lot of problems. Just as you are determined not to be told what to do by others, so you need to respect their rights and pleasures. The art of compromise where sensuality is involved is essential. It is quite possible that you (and/or your sexual partner) could feel that **your** approach to sex is the only right one. If you can remain open to each other's experiences, exciting new vistas may emerge!

If dominance/submission games happen to appeal (which is possible), let your good sense and self-protection be your guide in deciding how far to go. This configuration suggests strong sensuality, but ambivalence about indulging it. Don't punish yourself for imagined sins or withhold the erotic side of life from a misdirected desire for control.

Personal
♂, ♀, ☿, ☽, ♈, ♉, ♊, ♋, 1st, 2nd, 3rd, 4th houses

Your sexual approach is going to be strongly based on your personal likes and dislikes. You are clear about what you want and disinclined to compromise. Often, you would rather do without than have an encounter that is unlikely to include what you want. Occasionally, you may have difficulty appreciating the other person's point of view or sexual preferences because what you like seems so normal and natural to you. It is important to please yourself, but maintain tolerance for other approaches as well.

Transpersonal
♃, ⚷, ♄, ♅, ♆, ♐, ♑, ♒, ♓, 9th, 10th, 11th, 12th houses

Your sexual style is likely to be more free-ranging than most. Less tied to conventional ideas or current prejudices, you are more inclined to come from a broad perspective. Often able to appreciate a variety of approaches and points of view, your preferences tend to be somewhat eclectic. You are rarely locked into only one path to pleasure. As a lover, you might sometimes cite cross-cultural studies about differing patterns in sexual behavior or speculate about the habits of extraterrestrials. Your point of view is wide enough to encompass much. Your objectivity can come across as excessive detachment on occasion, but generally the openness to explore in many directions which you can express is an asset to you and your sexual partner(s).

ASPECTS

Harmony to Letters...

1: There is potential harmony in your balancing of sexual needs and self-assertion. This emphasizes passion in your nature, but suggests the likelihood of ease in directly expressing what you want sexually. You can be yourself and do what comes naturally in making love.

2: There is potential harmony in your handling of sensual and sexual needs. You can balance passion and comfort. You have the capacity for pleasure from all kinds of tactile involvements and physical indulgences as well as from sexual interactions. Your capacity for enjoyment is marked.

3: There is potential harmony in your handling of communication and sexual desires. You can balance logic and passion; lighthearted exchanges with heavy breathing. Your ability to think and exchange ideas can enhance your sexual satisfaction.

4: There is potential harmony in your handling of emotional attachments and your sexual desires. Your close, feelings connections to other people give depth and scope to your sensual interchanges. Your capacity to take care of (and be taken care of) strengthens the commitments between you and your lover(s). Nurturance can feed passion.

5: There is potential harmony between your ability to be significant, important, noticed and your sexual interactions. Your natural charm, magnetism and dynamism add excitement to your lovemaking. Mutual admiration and applause become sources of firing one another up — inspiring you and a lover to greater heights of passion.

6: There is potential harmony between your pragmatic, practical side and your passionate, sexual side. This suggests you have a good balance between being realistic and being passionately involved. You can work when appropriate and play — rewardingly — when appropriate.

7: There is potential harmony between your needs for partnership and your sexual desires. One possibility is easily combining the role of partner and lover in one person. Another option is friendly camaraderie with those who share passion with you. Competition might also add a little spice to your love life. Fair play and equality comes naturally to you in making love.

8: There is potential harmony in your desire for an intense, passionate involvement. Your desire for depth and commitment inclines you toward sexual relationships which are meaningful and go far beyond superficialities. You and your lover(s) may feel transformed by your shared experiences. You are capable of a greater level of intimacy than many people.

9: There is potential harmony between your search for something more in life and your sexual desires. Your loving involvements could be enhanced by your native optimism and faith. Your idealism could lead to very meaningful interchanges. Your intensity and depth of sexual response could feed your truth-seeking and inspire you to reach for more.

10: There is potential harmony between your responsible, cautious, disciplined side and your passionate, exciting side. You can work successfully, carrying out necessary duties as well as enjoying the rewards of satisfying sexual exchanges. You can be painstaking and dedicated as well as having a fulfilling, mutually pleasurable time in bed.

11: There is potential harmony between your pursuit of freedom, uniqueness, individuality and your enjoyment of sexual pleasures. Your openness and ability to consider alternatives can enhance your lovemaking experiences. Your passion and sexual drive can fuel your desire to go beyond the old to new and unusual creations and approaches.

12: There is potential harmony between your search for ecstasy through a cosmic connection and your search for ecstasy within a human, sexual sharing. Your ability to tune into the Infinite (through art, beauty, nature, spiritual paths, etc.) feeds your passion on the physical level. Your lovemaking can reach levels of such deep connection and communion, that you experience a blending with the other person and the Universe.

Conflict to Letter...

1: There is potential conflict sexually around areas of assertion, self-expression and anger. Either you or a lover could be too assertive, angry or self-centered. Directness and spontaneity can be helpful in sorting out sexual desires so everyone is satisfied; just be sure neither of you is too demanding in wanting it his/her way.

2: There is potential conflict sexually around comfort, ease and sensuality. Either you or a lover might be too indulgent, hedonistic, complacent or stolid. Stability and security are great, but don't overdo it. Mutual pleasure can be very rewarding; know also when to call a halt.

3: There is potential conflict sexually around communication, thinking and detachment. Either you or a lover might have difficulties in saying what you think or expressing what you want in bed. One of you might be excessively objective and rational — interfering with the passion of the situation. Be able to talk things over, but don't get stuck in the intellectual mode. Some situations call for **feeling** more than thinking.

4: There is potential conflict sexually around nurturance issues. You or a lover might overdo taking care of the other party (or wanting to be taken care of by the other party). Balance nurturing and dependency. Unexpressed feelings could be an issue; be sure you and your partner can bring things to the surface — don't brood. Mutual support works wonders.

5: There is potential conflict sexually around self-esteem needs, pride and ego. Either you or a lover might be inclined to get into grandstanding, boasting or excessive seeking of center stage. All of us need applause and admiration. Just be sure there is room for both of you to feel significant, important and valued in your interactions with one another.

6: There is potential conflict sexually around issues of practicality, hard work and doing things right. Criticism (toward yourself or others) could be an issue with you or a lover. Turning lovemaking into a job or a task (where you try to do it better and focus on what is wrong) is a sure way to get rid of spontaneity and pleasure. Pragmatism is fine for figuring things out beforehand and taking precautions, but remember to relax and enjoy it once you are in process!

7: There is potential conflict sexually around issues of sharing, equality, cooperation or competition. Either you or a lover might turn making love into a contest — a one-up/one-down game. Either of you might experience a lack of fairness or justice in your interactions. Exploring each others needs and expectations and finding mutually satisfying compromises is your best bet for mutual fulfillment.

8: There is potential conflict sexually around issues of control, letting go, intensity and depth understanding. Either you or a lover might be excessively concerned about maintaining control when making love. You could get obsessively focused on certain issues or forms of pleasure. Sometimes resentment festers; releasing emotions could be important for either or both of you. You are capable of much passion; use your intensity to bring out the best in one another.

9: There is potential conflict sexually around themes of idealism, ethics, truth, or the quest for more. This could manifest as excessively high standards for lovers or lovemaking, or moral/ethical issues in the sexual area. Sometimes excesses are a problem; a tendency to overdo is possible (on your part or by partners). Your sexual experiences can be inspired; keep your expectations and ideals high — but not **too** high.

10: There is potential conflict sexually around themes of responsibility, limits, practicality and dominance. Either you or a lover could take sex too seriously and be excessively hard on yourselves (or your partner). Criticism or trying to dominate (as a self-protective mechanism) could be a problem. Sometimes one or both partners experiences sexual blocks or inhibitions — which can be a combination of self-criticism, desire to maintain control and fear of letting go. Sensible precautions in who you choose, when you choose and what you choose to do sexually are reasonable, but do not restrict yourself unnecessarily with guilt, anxiety or fear.

11: There is potential conflict sexually around issues of freedom, individuality and uniqueness. Either you or a lover could be a bit **too** chaotic, weird or into unusual sexual expressions; one or both of you might express your rebelliousness through a sexual mode. An alternative is not trusting your own needs for freedom and unique self-expression. Openness, willingness to experiment and freedom of action can add much pleasure to your sexual repertoire; just don't overdo it.

12: There is potential conflict sexually around issues of yearning for cosmic beauty, grace and harmony. This can lead to you or a lover donning rose-colored glasses with subsequent disillusionment and disappointment. Either of you could talk yourselves (or the other person) into walking down the garden path, to eventual regret. Romance is wonderful and a marvelous component for satisfying sexual exchanges; just do not depend on romance alone!

CHAPTER FOURTEEN

HEALTH

Introduction

Health is the natural state of the human organism. Good health is best maintained by a positive attitude, minimal stress, a proper diet, loving relationships, systematic exercise, a sense of faith and the necessary rest and relaxation. All of these supportive activities supplement and reinforce one another. To some extent, factors such as a positive attitude can counterbalance junk foods, pollution, etc. But, the less we fulfill all the needed ingredients for good health, the more chance that we might succumb to illness.

Diet and exercise are very individual. There is no one diet that is best for everyone, nor is there an "optimum" system of exercise. Listen to the wisdom of your own body and consult your preferred doctor, holistic health practitioner, etc., in order to ascertain the best eating and moving habits for yourself. Similarly, the amount of sleep, rest and general relaxation needed varies tremendously from one person to another and also can change over time and circumstances. Pay attention to your own inner cycles and rhythms and be willing to listen to qualified experts.

A sense of faith (in God, in the ultimate goodness of Life...) can work wonders. Whether you look to God, traditional religion, nature, art, beauty, spiritual quests, meditation or other forms of seeking that sense of merging with something Higher, the connection to the Infinite can assist mightily in maintaining a healthy body. Prayer can contribute to cures as much, if not more than, many drugs. The spirit supports the body as well as vice versa.

I will not predict illness. This is too often destructive, setting up a self-fulfilling prophecy in the mind of the receiver. But astrology can help us to see the psychological roots of certain illnesses and physical problems in life. The person who is suffering can then work on the emotional and psychological level to **change** the patterns that contribute to the suffering. Of course, people will be healthiest if they work on **all** levels — physical (with medical assistance if appropriate), emotional, mental and spiritual.

The Factors

Traditionally, **Letter 6** is associated with maintaining good health — efficient functioning. **Letter 1** also has a lot to do with the physical body and our basic energy and vitality. However, health problems — or strengths — are not limited to only those areas of the chart. To some extent, any **water** (which is unconscious) is a candidate for repression. Water also rules the autonomic nervous system and has much to do with the day-to-day maintenance of our bodies. Water is connected to unconscious habit patterns — things we need not think about to accomplish, which includes keeping our hearts beating, etc. If carried too far, repression can lead to illness. This can be indicated by water planets, houses and/or signs. In addition, any extreme **imbalance** — over or under emphasis — could, potentially, be worked out on a physical level — or on an emotional, mental or spiritual level. Thus T-squares, grand crosses or other conflict aspects may point to an area requiring attention. Stelliums could indicate potential overdevelopment of an area. The possibilities are many.

Approach to Healing

To predict problems is not helpful and may encourage negativity among clients. But astrology can be helpful in pointing out the likely roots of various physical problems. This provides clients with tools for regaining their health, by enabling them to counter ill health with physical, emotional, mental and spiritual measures.

The following is a general guide for your use, to help in maintaining the natural state of health. We shall work our way from the top of the head to the feet. The assumption is that frustrated drives, inner conflicts and ambivalence contribute to the stress on the organism. By becoming aware of such conflicts and resolving them, we pave the way to good health (also supporting our bodies on all the other levels).

The approach here is to work back from the physical problem, to the associated astrological keys, to the indicated inner drives and issues. We can then express those inner needs more positively, while also treating the physical problem on the physical level. By working on **all** levels — physical, emotional, mental and spiritual — we are most likely to be successful. By treating underlying causes (psychological dynamics) as well as physical symptoms, we are most likely to create an actual cure, to ensure that those symptoms need not recur in our lives. We make good health a normal state of being for ourselves!

♂ 1st house ♈

Cuts, burns, accidents, headaches, head injuries, colds, surgery and violence all imply issues around anger, free self-expression, independence, space and one's sense of identity. Sometimes the issue is too much; more often the issue is too little. Headaches and sinus colds are commonly symptoms of blocked anger. (One of the most harmful forms of anger and resentment is self-directed. Somehow, people often find it most difficult to forgive themselves.) Violence directed toward others is often an overassertion of our rights and needs. Violence directed toward us is generally a sign that we do not value our own ability to be ourselves, to assert ourselves sufficiently. We may be holding back, projecting our own power, strength, abilities. Unfortunately, this can result in unconsciously attracting others who abuse power. (They provide a negative role model for us — teaching us about how to use power, but in an uncomfortable manner.)

Naturally, sickness can also be used (unconsciously) as a tool for anger or to meet personal needs. For example, the person who inevitably gets sick when it is his/her turn to car pool for the group (or carry out some other agreed-upon obligation) may very well have unresolved resentment about those duties.

When these problems come up, besides treating them on the physical and spiritual level, look also to what is going on in your mind and emotions. Are you angry with someone and not expressing it? (You don't have to punch them out. Perhaps writing a letter will work; perhaps telling someone; perhaps just acknowledging your frustration **to yourself** will be enough. But if some action which is not destructive will help — by all means **act**.) Are you feeling confined, frustrated, held in, unable to be who you feel you are, afraid to assert yourself? Figure out ways to do more of what you **want** to do. An excess of responsibilities is possible. Perhaps you do not **really** "have" to do all those things you have been telling yourself you "must" do. Can you loosen up and lighten up a bit? Even if you cannot change what you are doing, you can always change your **attitude** about it. Find something in the situation you can enjoy — something that is for **you**.

♀ 2nd house ♂

Problems with the throat often relate to our pursuit of pleasure in life. Also involved is the handling of sugar in the body and mild overweight. Sweets, carbohydrates and other fattening foods are a major source of pleasure for many people. When we overindulge, one potential consequence is overweight. An excess of sugar can also contribute to sore throats and colds in general. Sugar tends to lower the body's resistance to illness.

The best psychological solution to weight problems is to find satisfying substitute pleasures. Besides the sensual indulgence of food, we also have drink, money, possessions, sex and sensual gratifications of all kinds, including the artistic — pleasure from beauty. So, when we want to eat less, one way to help ourselves is to surround ourselves with more beauty — whether through gardening, dancing, painting, sculpting — or enjoying the creations of others. We can also spend more money, collect a few more possessions. We can make love more often, treat ourselves to a regular massage, lie in a hot tub daily or do whatever will feel good. The key is to satisfy the need for sensual pleasure through an avenue other than food.

Our society has tended to overvalue thinness (especially in women). Studies now suggest that **mild** overweight (or underweight) is not a problem. What is hardest on the body is bouncing up and down, changing weight frequently. Other research also supports the fact that the best, most effective way to lose weight and **keep it off** is through systematic exercise — again tailored to your individual needs. Without exercise, the body adopts a "famine" mentality and takes less and less calories (i.e., food) to maintain the organism. It "shuts down" to a large degree. By contrast, regular exercise tends to encourage the metabolism to operate at a higher rate and burn more calories — not just from the exercise, but keying the metabolism to that higher rate permanently.

Of course, if we are feeling a little bit deprived, getting sick may be a route to a little pampering (from ourselves or others). We may allow ourselves special treats, extra comfort, more relaxation, than we normally would. It is a way of indulging ourselves.

Throat issues can also involve communication — tied to "swallowing" your words instead of expressing them — and assertion. Holding back and holding in over a period of time leads to resentment and anger. That contributes to headaches and colds. Since colds often drain into the throat, the two are tied together. The ability to express one's self is also connected to our willingness to go after what we want — the pursuit of pleasure. The ability to enjoy the sense world is a natural, healthy part of life.

☿ 3rd house ♊

Problems with the hands, arms, shoulders, lungs and allergies in general often involve communication issues. How we learn, how we think and our early peer relationships (especially brothers, sisters, other relatives) can be a part of the picture. (For example, some people hold back on their verbal expression because they grew up with an exceptionally articulate sibling and they feel they could never compete anyway.)

Our hands, arms and shoulders are particularly useful in manipulating the physical world, handling ideas and reaching out to other people. So, social or intellectual issues can be a part of the picture. One necessary quality is detachment — the ability to take things lightly, to laugh at life and not be overwhelmed by it. Of course, if that is overdone, we become the perpetual spectator, the chronic observer who watches the world go by but refuses to get involved. A middle ground is usually best. A sense of comfort with our ability to talk, to share ideas, to relate casually with anyone, is helpful.

Allergies are usually a mixture of issues. Many allergies are an oversensitivity to substances that are usually harmless. This can be connected to people who are "open to the universe." They are often interested in anything and everything, wanting to know and learn it all. They tend to be scattered. It is as if they try to take in **so much** of the world, they sometimes get overwhelmed by it. For such people, focus and concentration can help. Sometimes just making lists or approaching a situation in a very linear (1,2,3) fashion will work wonders. Establishing priorities and value hierarchies are other options, so the person can make discriminations in importance rather than trying to absorb it all at once.

Breathing and lung difficulties can be related to a holding back of expression and communication. Some people with asthma have found that getting in touch with what they wanted to say — but were withholding — and **saying** it, could stop an oncoming asthma attack. So assertion is again a part of the issue, especially around relating to others and the use of the mind, tongue and ideas.

☽ 4th house ♋

Unrecognized, unmet dependency needs can set us up for illness. When people play the strong, invulnerable,"I don't need anyone" type of role, they often bury and refuse to admit any feelings of neediness. Then, illness may be the only route the unconscious finds to get TLC (tender, loving care). When people are sick, they usually expect to get some nurturance, to have some of the burdens removed from them. If an individual does not consciously allow any emotional closeness or concern, having physical problems becomes a socially acceptable path to some succor and concern by others.

Also, some people feel extremely dependent, that they **must** have others looking after them. In such a case, illness can become an unconscious mechanism for not being independent, perhaps for not working. Leaning on other people when one is not well is still a societally approved action.

Dependency and nurturance issues are also often involved with stomach difficulties, e.g., ulcers, colitis, "butterflies" in the stomach, and so on. The inner stress can range from wanting to be nurtured, supported, held, looked after (with ulcers, we drink milk, stay in bed and play at being a baby again), to feeling our emotional security is threatened ("butterflies" in the stomach when we face threatening situations). Literal homesickness — missing the warmth and closeness of the nest — can manifest as an upset stomach, problems with eating.

Serious dysfunctions around eating (e.g., *anorexia nervosa*, starving the self for unrealistic thinness — or extreme overweight) are also connected to our experience of nurturing and conditional love and support from the world. Where such heavy, intense feelings are involved (food tied to emotional security) and early familial relationships are often a part of the situation, psychotherapy can be very helpful as part of the treatment. Deeply felt issues, especially when partially unconscious, are difficult to resolve on one's own; detachment and objectivity present a challenge.

In general, one key is to be sure we have a balance in our lives between dependency and nurturance. We need to be able to be vulnerable, to lean on others, but also to be caring, concerned and able to support and assist other people.

☉ 5th house ♌

Heart problems are very related to the personality. Research has demonstrated that "Type A" behavior — driving, ambitious, in a hurry, feeling under pressure — is strongly connected to heart attacks. A more healthy life-style includes the ability to relax, to play, to have goals and ambitions, but not be obsessed by them. As with many illnesses, systematic exercise can be a great preventive of heart attacks, and diet is extremely important. Cholesterol is still strongly implicated in contributing to cardiovascular difficulties.

Sometimes it appears that heart attacks follow the loss of someone's "heart's desire." That could be a loved one, a cherished promotion, a career development, etc. If we put all our emotional eggs in one basket, we risk a large upset when that basket tips. The dynamics seem to involve self-esteem. We all need to feel proud of ourselves, good about who we are, have a sense of being important and significant in the world. If we gain most or all of our sense of self-esteem through another person (e.g., a spouse) or through a certain level of work success, we risk feeling very rotten when we lose that person or do not achieve that level of success. Or, even if we do achieve our "heart's desire," we can still worry, put stress on the system, about whether or not we can keep it!

A sensible exercise program, good eating habits and reasonable, reachable ambitions will help promote a healthy heart. Having a variety of paths and satisfactions to achieve a sense of self-esteem and self-worth is also very helpful. For a few people, the only road they have learned to gaining attention is to be sick. Perhaps it started when they were young and they discovered that Mommy and Daddy paid more attention and were more loving when one was laid up. Perhaps they feel inadequate, do not trust their talents and abilities to shine in any other ways, so they seek the limelight, the center stage through real or imagined ills. Such people can recite a catalog of their various ailments, operations, etc. The solution is for them to find alternative arenas of self-esteem, different options for receiving attention, love, affection, support from others. We all need love; we all need admiration and approval. How we gain it is up to us.

☿ ♀ ⚶ 6th house ♍

It is no accident that the same area of the chart rules both health and job. How we feel about our work has a profound effect on our health. (Work is our task in the world, our responsibilities, our need to contribute, whether or not we are paid with money to perform it.) People who **detest** their work can unconsciously get sick, in order to escape from the job they cannot stand. If we are feeling overburdened, under pressure, that there is too much to do, or fear we will not be adequate enough to do it well, illness becomes an escape. If we are sick, we do not have to feel guilty about not working! And, for typical workaholics, getting sick may be the only way they "know" to take a vacation!

This area of the chart symbolizes our need for efficient functioning — both in tasks and in our physical bodies. The more we deny our need to be effective, productive, practical and contributing, the more guilty we are likely to feel. This just puts more stress on the system and adds to the problem. If we are truly unhappy with our work, we have choices. We can find a new position. We can stay where we are and be unhappy. We can stay where we are and change our **attitude** about what we do by discovering things about our job we **like**. We can accentuate the positive rather than the negative.

Another common area of the body that often points to issues around productivity, analysis, discrimination and critical judgment is the intestines. Illnesses such as diverticulitis where the intestines are in an uproar usually reflect some psychological conflict about our role as a worker — our ability to be pragmatic, functional, to do a good job. In some cases, the problem may be a workaholic approach: the individual is **too** focused on the job, overemphasizing practicality and taking care of business. Such people need to learn to relax, to not be working or work-oriented all the time. Other cases involve people who feel unable or unwilling to work, so illness becomes their escape from feeling guilty for not doing what they feel they "ought" to do.

A sense of accomplishment is a necessary and normal part of life. We all need that feeling of carrying tasks to a productive end. The key is to be able to work effectively without making work our whole world.

♀ ☿ ⚷ 7th house ♎

One essential ingredient in life is intimacy. Almost everyone needs other people. Usually this includes a desire for some kind of one-to-one relating, an equal sharing with someone (friend, partner, mate, spouse) at or near our level. Where this is not happening, or we are dissatisfied with the way it is occurring, there is the potential of problems with the kidneys, the sugar balance in the body (diabetes, hypoglycemia), skin problems and a craving for sweets. Many of us substitute sweets for love and overindulge when we are feeling a little neglected. Other pleasures (dancing, artistic creation, gardening, art appreciation, spending money) are safer in the long run than excessive sugar consumption (or alcohol or smoking — two other sensual indulgences which are hard on the body).

When such difficulties occur, besides treating them on the physical and spiritual level, we can look to our handling of partnership and human relationships. Perhaps we have been pushing people away with excessively high standards or critical judgments. Perhaps we have been choosing other people who criticize, dominate or idealize us so that true equality is hard to achieve. Perhaps we are withdrawing for fear of being hurt or disappointed. Perhaps we have projected our own power and attract overly assertive or even violent people; or we are out of touch with our freedom needs and fall in love with people who do not want to make a commitment. Whatever the issue, we need to look at our handling of sharing in our life, at the potential of equality. Perhaps some changes in our support system will be necessary.

Equality can be reached through competitive as well as cooperative relationships. When we compete with someone, we build our own strength (and theirs) through a mutual testing and striving. And for a true contest (where both win sometimes and lose sometimes), the people have to be peers, or near-equals. But remember to keep a game-playing attitude. Don't take competition too seriously! The drive here is for a sense of connection, a sense of likeness, a sharing through communication, interaction and exchange.

Another need indicated here is the desire for balance, harmony, ease and beauty. Sometimes the above physical problems can be related to a simple desire to avoid confrontations. That is, unconsciously the individual does not want to deal directly with a certain issue, so s/he gets sick — knowing that sick people are not expected to fight or to have to deal with unpleasant, uncomfortable issues. Sometimes the illness is just an unconscious way of achieving a little peace and putting off dealing with nonharmonious or ugly facts.

Grace, beauty, harmony and equality are essential parts of life, but none of us can have them all the time. The challenge is to create as much as is possible and reasonable under the given circumstances.

♇ 8th house ♏

A part of true intimacy is sharing the physical, sensual world with someone else. The balance of power in a relationship is often tested with such questions as "Who earns it? Who spends it? For what? Who enjoys what?" Possessions and pleasures are a focus as people test their abilities to give, receive and share with another human being. A part of the process is knowing when to let go, when a situation or a relationship is finished and needs to be released (especially on the emotional level), so we can move on to something more growthful.

Conflicts in any of the above areas can manifest as problems with the bowels, bladder or sexual organs. Hanging on too long emotionally may be reflected by constipation or hemorrhoids on the physical level. Or, pockets of buried guilt, anger or resentment may be mirrored by cysts — physical pockets of liquids. In severe cases, surgery may be necessary. Surgery implies some difficulties around assertion and the handling of self-will, but particularly in the contexts of intimate relating. The deeper levels of our psyches are not always easy to deal with; sometimes withdrawal or secrecy seems less threatening than open confrontation. But, in the end, what is hidden will be revealed. We must all face our own shadows, our inner conflicts and ambivalences eventually. People will sometimes seek power through indirect routes. Illness can become a form of manipulation, with the sick person unconsciously using a physical problem to control those around him/her.

Integration of these themes means we can gracefully receive pleasures and physical assistance from others when appropriate. We can also spontaneously and naturally give to others. And, we know how to share equally, especially where sex, money and possessions are concerned, with those we are closest to for truly mutual gratification and satisfaction. We are able to recognize our deepest emotions, communicate as needed, and utilize the energy and intensity of our feelings to transform ourselves to more and more masterful people.

Our mate is a major mirror for us — reflecting back parts of our own potential. The more quickly, clearly and honestly we face our projections — the sides of ourselves we would rather give away — the more whole we can become, the more we can reach our highest potential. The ultimate learning ground is loving someone else. This gives us the opportunity to truly share power over the physical world, to honestly care for one another, to openly learn from one another.

♃ ☍ 9th house ♐

Living is based on assumptions. Some are fairly safe — like assuming that the Sun will rise again tomorrow. Some are more questionable — like assuming that there is, or is not, a deity. People make choices in life according to their basic assumptions or belief systems. An individual coming from the belief system of a certain religion will act in a different manner than an individual coming from the belief system called "scientific materialism." Ultimately, all belief systems are acts of faith; the fundamental underpinnings of any choices we make are based on a leap of faith because we do not have all the data. So, we choose to act in a certain fashion, knowing we are unlikely to obtain the full information.

Belief systems also provide faith and inspiration. They are the foundation of most ethics and moral principles. If we believe that people are basically good, that life is basically improving, we are more ready to go into the world and attempt a number of things than if we feel that people are basically evil and the world is basically degenerating. Assumptions also save time. If we can interact with someone based on the fact that he wears a police uniform without having to get to know him as a person or an individual, we may be able to get exactly what we want in a very short period of time. However, if some of our assumptions about the roles of an individual in a police uniform differ dramatically from **his** assumptions about the role of a police officer, trouble is likely to ensue. And there are few things people defend more rigidly than their basic beliefs and assumptions about truth, morality, reality and life.

Conflicts in this area can reflect in problems with the liver, hips and thighs, or the handling of fats in the body. This could range from too much faith — a sort of Pollyanna approach to life — to too little faith, afraid to try, fearful of risking anything. It could include faith in the wrong areas — expecting human beings to play God, rather than seeking the Infinite through art, nature, religion, philosophy, spiritual quests or other open-ended avenues. We may feel ambivalent about certain moral or ethical issues in our lives. We may be prone to excessive idealism and/or perfectionism.

All of us need enough faith in ourselves to act, to risk, to move forward, but also enough faith in a something beyond us so that we do not feel responsible for the whole world. We need ideals high enough to stretch our souls in reaching these ideals, but not so high that we feel we can never succeed. We need a sense of purpose, something to which we can aspire, a mountain top to climb.

The basic quest here is for answers about the meaning of the universe — the old, existential dilemma "Why are we here? Is there a reason? And, if so, what is it?" Each of us seeks the truth in our own, unique way.

♄ 10th house ♑

A number of potential difficulties can be related to the issue of structure: bone problems (including the bones of the inner ear, so hearing), teeth, knees, any premature crystallization (gout, arteriosclerosis, arthritis, stones in the body). Any of these can be indications of conflicts around duty, responsibility, practicality, following the rules and living within the limits of life and society. People can live out either extreme: too much structure, excessively holding themselves back and holding themselves in; or too little structure, fighting against the limits of what is possible in a physical world with expectations from others who share our world.

Part of one's ability to handle life and deal with the real world involves maintaining some kind of career, place in the world, contribution to society. A sense of work satisfaction and career achievement is a part of being healthy. However, like anything else, it can be overdone. If we carry practicality and order to extremes, rigidity on the physical level through these premature crystallizations is one potential. Back problems are another common ailment — for the "Atlas" type — who is, emotionally if not physically, carrying the "world on the back." Or, the workaholic may simply find that getting sick is the only way s/he "knows" to take a vacation!

The middle ground suggests a realistic appraisal of the world and our position in it, avoiding both excessive worry, responsibility and structure but also eschewing the opposite extremes of irresponsibility, chaos and a flippant refusal to face life's practicalities. If we figure out what is necessary for us to do, and then do it in a way that gives us satisfaction, there is no problem. If we carry more than our share of the load or try to avoid what is truly our duty, we are likely to set ourselves up for unpleasant consequences. Satisfaction lies in doing all that we can do within the reasonable limits and expectations of other people and the structure of the world.

♅ 11th house ♒

Of course, at times, rules need to be broken and structures need to be changed. At such moments, an inner ability to rebel, to be different, to try a novel approach, to seek a new experience, to pioneer an unusual area, can be very helpful. Our capacity for inventiveness and originality can be a marvelous gift. It can also create anarchy, disassociation and careless irresponsibility if carried to an extreme. This free and unconventional potential within each of us seems connected to the ankles, the electrical system within the body, the nervous system and potentially, accidents.

Some accidents are mostly the result of pent-up anger and frustration which has no other outlet. Some are mostly the result of haste and carelessness, where someone is simply acting impulsively, without sufficient intelligence, concern or forethought. Other accidents have large components of frustrated needs for independence and space. So, instead of breaking loose, breaking out, and breaking free, we sometimes break a leg (or at least an ankle). Dealing early on with our desire for liberty can help avoid such occurrences.

A sense of independence can be connected to free flow within the body. Circulatory blocks, problems in transporting within the body, may reflect psychological blocks and barriers. Discovering positive ways to express our uniqueness, to assert our individuality, and to demonstrate our openness and tolerance to new ideas and the wide sweep of humanity can help to keep openness and free flow on the physical level as well. Flexibility on one level can translate to flexibility on other levels.

Ψ 12th house ℋ

Most people acknowledge an inner yearning for a sense of connection to something Higher. Some seek the experience through religion, some through art, some through idealistic activities. These are different paths to that sense of being a part of something ultimate, something absolute and potentially very beautiful and/or loving. Another route includes the role of victim. Both the healer and the victim share a vision of something more, something beautiful. The difference is that the healer is working to bring that dream down to earth, to manifest a more ideal world. The victim is running away from the fact that the world is **not** beautiful, **not** ideal and that the victim is not doing anything to change it. Victims can retreat into drugs, alcohol, sleeping all the time, fantasy, psychosis or any other form of escapism, including physical or mental/emotional illness.

Ambivalence in the above areas can be associated with the following physical problems: poisons in the body, infections, mysterious ailments, cysts, tumors, dissolving ailments (e.g., *lupus erythematosus* is an extreme form) and anything involving the feet. Liquids can be involved and oversensitivity to drugs is possible.

We need a sense of inspiration, a sense of something to reach for, the ultimate experience of cosmic consciousness. The sense of merging that goes beyond words, beyond description, is one that pulls many people. The quest for infinite love and beauty is not to be forsworn, but we need to remember to be practical and not ignore physical realities while searching for something more, something profound and uplifting. The twin extremes of wanting more than is possible (from ourselves, other people, life in general) or settling for a sterile, dull existence because we deny the potential of something infinite, can be sidestepped. We can choose the paths which will lead toward the Light, toward a connection to all of Life, to goodness, purity, beauty, truth and love.

Summary

The horoscope pictures for us a number of basic human needs and drives. All are necessary; all are potentially positive and useful. But, sometimes they conflict with one another. If we do not face that inner conflict, we may end up with physical symptoms of the inner ambivalence. Illness can be treated on the emotional and mental levels, as well as the physical and spiritual. The above are some possible guidelines to spark ideas and possible roads to travel in regaining and maintaining the best of health.

If we meet our various needs in our lives and how we relate to our bodies, we do not have to have physical ailments. If we repress or project a part of ourselves, we often do receive a warning through the physical system. The longer we ignore such warnings, usually, the more serious they become. The sooner we confront any "wars" within and make peace, the easier the integration and the cure. Cures are most successful when we treat the problem on **all** levels: physical, mental, emotional and spiritual.

Good Health to all of you!

CHAPTER FIFTEEN

PARENTS

This chapter considers the life area of parents. Remember, a horoscope does **not** show the clients' parents. Rather, it reflects the issues they faced with their parents. The chart mirrors the experiences **that person** had/has with his/her parents. If a client has siblings, they may experience the same set of parents very differently. That difference will be reflected in their charts. Each of us is unique, and children **elicit** behavior from parents just as much as they **respond** to parental actions. No one else has quite the same relationship to your parents as you do. The horoscope reveals the opportunities for learning available in the interaction of each person and his/her parents. It does not determine that these associations were positive or negative. (For most of us, it is a mixture of positive and negative, anyway.) But it reveals what our parents were teaching us — either through doing it well (showing us what **to** do) or doing it so poorly (showing us what **not** to do) that we, hopefully, did better.

Projection is often an issue with parents (as with anyone we are close to). Because parents **are** generally role models, their job is to teach us about certain potentials, to demonstrate for us some of our own inner qualities, often before we have fully developed them. The danger is that we may experience those qualities as existing **only** in our parents and deny their potential within us. Particularly if we believe our parents are manifesting certain traits in a negative way, we are less likely to acknowledge the possibility of those traits within us (until we can appreciate the positive potential also carried).

If, for instance, parents are extremely dominating and controlling, they are setting a role model for their children in handling power drives. One child may react by fighting with the parents, striving to constantly beat them at their own game. Such a child is likely to grow up to be dominating and controlling. That child has learned to do what the parents do, but without much awareness or examination as to whether it is particularly positive. Another child may decide that "Power is bad; I am never going to be like Mommy and Daddy." That child is likely to grow up a patsy, constantly attracting people who use power against him/her. The more someone's strength and ability to use it are denied, the more likely that others will have no qualms about bulldozing them. Such a child has learned to do **the exact opposite** of what the parents do, but without much awareness or examination as to whether it is particularly positive. Another child may decide that there are helpful and harmful ways to utilize power and control. That child may grow into an adult who knows when to take charge and when to cooperate with others. It is likely that on the path to adulthood, that child will have some power struggles and probably do some bouncing between too much accommodation and too much control, but the potential for integration is there. That child has learned from the example of the parents — be it positive or negative — by incorporating his/her own thinking and considering, not just blindly reacting.

While reading, remember that the "parent" you learned (interacted with) the most, could have been an actual parent, a grandparent, elder sibling, long-term baby-sitter, nanny, impressive neighbor or other individual. The "parent" in your horoscope is not necessarily the birth parent.

One must also remember that even after our parents are no longer physically present, we all have an internalized parent. This is part of our conscience. Too often, we react blindly to that internal parent, still replaying old tapes, old reactions, old ways of being with our parents — long after they are gone. Part of the discrimination of adulthood is determining what we wish to keep of our parents and what is not useful for us.

Adoptive Versus Blood Parents

An issue often raised is whether the chart shows the adoptive parents or the blood parents. As usual, the answer is not really either/or. The horoscope reflects the parenting experience of the individual who owns it. Thus, a chart primarily mirrors the person's experience of his/her parental figures. In cases of adoption or foster children, the adoptive parents — as the ones who are truly caring for the child — will be most fully depicted in the chart.

However, most adopted children understand at some point that they **are** adopted. This often leads to dreams, fantasies and images of what the blood parents might have been like. There is generally at least a small element of mystery. Thus, it is quite common to find Letters 9 (idealization, high expectations) and/or 12 (fantasy, imagination, absence) involved with the parental area when adoption is the case. The themes of Letters 9 and 12 seem to relate to the absent or missing parents, who can (usually) only be met through imagination.

Naturally, there are other parental situations which can involve extreme idealism and/or absence. In such cases, Letters 9 and 12 would be configured in the parental arena. Thus, do **not** assume that 9 or 12 automatically point to adoption or missing parents. That is one of the possibilities, but not the only one.

Where the family situation is complicated, you will often have a complicated chart in regards to parents. This can include situations where grandparents are parental figures as well as parents, or take over for parents after death or divorce. It can include families in which there are numerous stepchildren and half-brothers and sisters due to numerous marriages and divorces. It can point to a communal kind of upbringing with a number of different authority figures. It can represent early environments where another relative (sibling, aunt, friend, etc.) did some of the parenting along with the actual parents. And so on.

A complicated picture in terms of parents is implied when there is a strong mixture of themes which do not easily blend. In such cases, the most common options are: (1) more than one parental role or (2) a parent who was extremely ambivalent and dealing with much inner conflict. It is not necessary that a large number of planets be involved in the parental area to indicate conflict and the potential of mixed parental figures. This **can** occur with a number of planets, but it can also occur even with empty 4th and 10th houses. Suppose, for example, the placements of Saturn and the Sun (usually keys to father) suggest a strong fire/earth father (dynamic, productive, energetic but enduring) and the Moon and Ceres (usually keys to mother) suggest a fiery mother (exuberant, expressive, extroverted). Suppose the 4th and 10th houses are unoccupied, but the rulers (of the signs on the cusps) strongly point to air/water parents (dreamy, imaginative, inwardly rather than outwardly-oriented). This is quite a contrast. We would suspect that either there was a third parental figure involved, or one or both parents were torn between their extroverted and introverted sides, and were teaching the child either how to (or how not to) balance this ambivalence.

Other Parental Figures

In many families, people other than just Mom and Dad play a parental role. The **potential** of this shows up in the horoscope, although we can never say it **had** to happen. But we can see it as a possibility.

The reason for wanting to identify the individuals playing parental roles is that those people strongly impact the child's handling of issues of unconditional love, nurturance, dependency, responsibility and control. For most people, the early home life is like a crucible which "sets" the mold of our personalities. We tend to keep on reacting, in ways which we learned at a young age — in order to survive. The behaviors are probably no longer necessary for survival, but they **feel** as if they are, because when we were very young and powerless, that was the impression we got. Many of us develop certain ways of reacting and behaving based on family patterns, which are no longer in our best interest. If we can identify those patterns, see the context in which we developed them (including the other people involved), it becomes easier for us to separate the past from the present and move on to new behaviors.

As you might expect, mixtures of the parental letters (4 and 10) of the Zip Code with parts of the astrological alphabet which apply to other people show the potential of these other individuals playing a parental role — or, of us playing a parental role to these other people. It works both ways!

Letter 3 mixed with 4 and/or 10 is a parent/sibling mixture. This can indicate that a brother or sister played a nurturing or responsible role in our life — or that we ended up parenting our siblings. It can also be a clue to an aunt, uncle or other relative taking that role. It does not **have** to be additional parental figures. The Letter 3 theme can simply point to parents who are bright, articulate, curious and eager to keep on the move — or gossipy, superficial and fickle. The parental experience is mixed with our learning to learn and learning to communicate. This **may — but does not have to** — include learning partially through other relatives, not just the parents.

Letters 1 and/or 7[1] mixed with 4 and/or 10 are a grandparent/parent mixture. This can indicate that a grandparent played a parental role. (It can also simply point to parents who are teaching us — through a positive or negative example — about balancing self assertion with accommodation.)

Communal living situations are often reflected by a mixture of the transpersonal (Letters 9, 10, 11 and 12) with 4 and 10, but especially with Letter 4 (the home environment). Letter 11 (community) and 12 (utopian ideals) seem to be the most common. It is as if these people feel "The world is my home and my home is open to the world." Or, less comfortably, "My home was open to the world growing up and it was disruptive and disappointing." or "My parents were so busy saving the world (or being victims of it), they had no time or inclination to take care of me." With such mixtures, the need is to make room for both a sense of roots and emotional security (Letter 4) and the reach for the transpersonal, the urge for making a difference to humanity (Letters 11 and 12).

Distinguishing Mom and Dad

An area which still attracts major contention in astrology is the question of "Which parent goes in which house?" As with many polarizing questions, the answer is not "either/or," but "and" or "it depends on the circumstances." With some charts, there seems to be a clear-cut distinction, with the mother clearly described in one house and the father well depicted by the other house. Often, it is not so simple. Sometimes, the picture is thoroughly mixed, and it appears that both parents are

---

1. Traditionally, the 1st and 7th houses are associated with grandparents. This is based on "derivative" houses. Derivative houses trace relationships, by counting houses, beginning in the house which symbolizes the base relationship. For example, parents in the horoscope are the 4th and 10th houses. Grandparents are "parents of parents." Thus, the system of derivative houses counts the fourth and the tenth houses **from** the 4th and the 10th to get to "parents of parents" or grandparents. In such cases, you count the house in which you begin as "one," the next house is "two," etc. Thus, the fourth house from the 4th is the 7th (the 4th is one; 5th is two; 6th is three and 7th is four). The tenth house from the 4th house is the 1st. The fourth house from the 10th is the 1st and the tenth house from the 10th is the 7th.

Using the derivative house system, grandchildren fall in the 9th house (the fifth from the 5th for "children of children"). Brothers-in-law and sisters-in-law also fall in the 9th (seventh from the 3rd for "partners of siblings"). A number of relationships can be assigned, but one must be wary of stretching the system too far. Batya Stark has spoken hilariously on the subject of tracing such items as: "my brother's wife's psychiatrist's dog groomer" and so on!

symbolized by the both houses. Or, it may be that one parent is denoted by **both** houses — common in cases where the second parent is absent through death, divorce or emotional withdrawal. Sometimes other figures (e.g., grandparents, siblings) are involved, playing parental roles. Deciding whether to assign the 4th (or 10th) house to Mom, Dad, both or someone else entirely may take a bit of time!

My experience is that the 4th house generally reflects the parent(s) who played (or was supposed to play) a nurturing, supportive role, while the 10th house generally reflects the parent(s) who played (or was supposed to play) a responsible, realistic, performance-oriented role. In terms of traditional roles, that associates Mom with the 4th house and Dad with the 10th. This assignment does occur relatively often, but not as often as you might suspect. (According to our census bureau, the "traditional" textbook family of father as the sole breadwinner and mother as a housewife with children, exists for only 10% of American families currently. More and more women work outside the home, earning a salary. The added economic clout often translates to more power and responsibility in the home as well. Other factors are changing sex roles as well.)

In choosing the house for a parent, my first step is to describe parents on the basis of the planetary keys. I find the Moon almost always a key to mother, with Ceres a valuable backup. I find Saturn almost always a key to father, with the Sun as a backup. An easy case would be where Moon and Ceres are in fire/water by house and sign, while Saturn and the Sun are in earth/air by house and sign. I then examine the houses. Suppose I find Venus and Mercury in Virgo in the 10th, an empty fourth, with Neptune (ruler of the Pisces cusp) in Leo in the 9th. I would strongly suspect a 4th house mother because the Neptune, the ruler, is emphasizing fire as do the Moon and Ceres. A 10th house father seems likely because Venus and Mercury occupy the 10th and are earth/air by sign and in terms of their own natures. In this case, if I found the Venus/Mercury in Virgo in the 4th, with Neptune in Leo in the 3rd, I would assume a 4th house (earth/air) father and a 10th house (fire-water) mother.

The key is a search for themes as always. I try to determine which house seems more similar to the planetary keys for each parent. I may match by element, quality, letter of the astrological alphabet or other themes (such as a freedom-oriented mother and an intellectual father), etc.

Of course, not all horoscopes offer nice, neat decisions for us. Many times, the clues are quite entangled and the picture seems totally mixed. As mentioned, a very intermingled picture may suggest several parental figures are involved in the picture, or that the parents had much inner ambivalence, a wide variety of talents and abilities to pursue. In cases where the two parental letters of the astrological alphabet (4 and 10) are strongly mixed with one another, there are several possibilities:

(1) the parents are somewhat alike, sharing qualities and sharing roles to some extent,

(2) there is a single, major parental role model. The other parent is literally missing

or strongly disconnected from the family, even if physically present.

(3) the parents have switched "traditional" roles. That is, father is more the nurturing figure; mother is more the authority figure.

(4) the child may have felt s/he had to "parent" his/her own parents, as if the child had to be supportive, strong and responsible for the parent(s) — even at a young age.

Please note that these factors as **not** mutually exclusive. It is quite possible that one parent played both roles, **and** the child felt as if s/he had to "parent" that parent. Or, the parents may have switched roles for a time and then one parent disappeared. Do not assume that only one of these options will occur.

Astrological factors which indicate a "mixture" of the mothering and fathering archetypes include:

1) Moon conjunct or parallel Saturn
2) Ruler(s)of the 4th house conjunct Saturn
3) Ceres conjunct or parallel Saturn
4) Ruler(s)of the 10th house conjunct Moon
5) Ruler(s)of the 10th house conjunct Ceres
6) Moon conjunct or parallel Sun
7) Ruler(s) of the 4th house conjunct the Sun
8) Ceres conjunct or parallel Sun
9) Moon in the 10th house
10) Ruler(s) of the 10th occupying the 4th
11) Ruler(s) of the 4th occupying the 10th
12) Ceres in the 10th house
13) Saturn in the 4th house
14) Sun in the 4th house
15) Cancer planets occupying the 10th house
16) Capricorn planets occupying the 4th house
17) Capricorn on the IC and Cancer on the MC

It is not possible to say that **only** this or that option will occur, but certain possibilities are more likely in certain cases. In the situation of a single parent playing **both** roles, a common configuration involves one parental house (4th **or** 10th) empty, with the ruler(s) of that house placed **inside** the other parental house. It is as if the one house "takes over" for both — just as the one parent has to "take over" and be "both" in a sense. This is **not** the only option here — but a bit more likely than the others.

If Letters 9 and/or 12 are also involved in the picture, the possibility of a missing or absent parent is again a focus. That parent may well be a dream or fantasy figure for the child. Further confirmations can be shown by separative aspects (oppositions and/or quincunxes) between keys to the parents — or between keys to the child and to either of the parents. (Examples of the former would be Moon,

Ceres or rulers of the appropriate house opposite or quincunx Saturn, Sun or rulers of the appropriate house. Example of the latter would be Ascendant, any 1st house planets, Mars or rulers of the 1st quincunx or opposite the Moon, Saturn, Sun or Ceres.) Jane Fonda lost her birth mother through death — a separation from both Jane and Henry Fonda (Jane's father). Note that Pluto rules the Scorpio MC (10th house parent) and opposes Ms. Fonda's Capricorn Ascendant (self) and Jupiter in the 1st. Pluto (key to 10th house parent) also quincunxes Mars (Jane Fonda) and Ceres (mother). Although I consider the orbs too wide, some astrologers would include the Moon (mother) opposite Mars (self) and quincunx Saturn (father).

Please do **not** jump to any conclusions based on one or two aspects! An important theme will be repeated in the chart. Also, please do **not** assume that such aspects mean there **must** be a painful or physical separation. They can also point to families that travel and thus are separated, psychological distance rather than actual absence by anyone, or simply people with very different styles and ways of being in the world.

As with any theme, the more times it is repeated by the horoscope, the more significant it is likely to be.

In cases where the chart shows very distinctive pictures for the two parents, yet still a blend of mother/father themes, the most likely possibility is that the parents have switched roles: mother is more the authority figure and dad is more the softie. An example would be where Saturn and the Sun strongly suggest an air/water father while the Moon and Ceres strongly imply a fire/earth mother, but Saturn occupies the 4th and the Moon occupies the 10th. This looks like parents who are very different, but mother in the role of reality figure and dad in the role of emotional and supportive caregiver.

In horoscopes where almost all of the parental keys seem totally blended with each other, it is likely that one cannot really assign **one** house to **either** parent. In such cases, both parents are represented by **both** houses and the chart is indicating a lot of similarity between the parents, tending to react like one another. An example might be a chart with Virgo on the IC and Pisces on the MC. Neptune in Virgo occupies the 4th, while the Moon, Mercury and Saturn (all in Pisces) occupy the 10th. They may even be conjunct one another. This would imply a strong 6/12 polarity for **both** parents.

Any of the above mixtures (where parental letters are blended) can show the potential of a child who feels s/he had to parent his/her own parents. And none of these possibilities eliminate the others. Remember to consider multiple options. There is often more than one ''right'' answer.

This text will not differentiate between the parents. You can read ''mother'' or ''father'' rather than ''parents'' in anything which follows. Or, substitute ''reality parent'' or ''unconditional parent'' or other key phrases for the parental figure with whom you are concerned. Remember that the ultimate goal is for each individual to become comfortable with his/her own, inner mother and father, to accept and express positively those authority and nurturing potentials.

The Factors

In considering the potentials as far as parents, as indicated by the horoscope, we would include **Letter 4** (the unconditional love parent) and **Letter 10** (the conditional love parent or reality parent), plus Ceres as an additional key to the mother figure and the Sun as an additional key to the fathering principle.[2]

Astrologically, this means we would examine:

GROUP I

Any conjunctions to the Moon, Sun and Saturn, plus Ceres (the Earth Mother) if we use asteroids (We would consider the nature of the planets making the conjunctions.)

Any conjunctions to the MC (the nature of the planet making the conjunction)

Any conjunctions to the IC (the nature of the planets)

Any conjunctions to the ruler of the Midheaven

Any conjunctions to the ruler of the IC

Any conjunctions to the rulers of other signs in the 4th or 10th houses

GROUP II

Any planets in the 4th and 10th houses (nature of the planets)

The signs on the MC and IC

Planets within two degrees of the 4th or 10th houses, even though occupying the 3rd, 5th, 9th or 11th

GROUP III

The Midheaven sign

The sign on the IC

Any parallels to Saturn, the Sun, Moon, Ceres, the MC, the IC, or the rulers of

---

2. If you prefer **not** to search for repeated themes yourself, you can order the "PP BOOK" option from Astro Computing Services (PO Box 16430, San Diego, Ca 92116), which allows you to use this book to make complete, synthesizing delineations of horoscopes without figuring out which themes are emphasized.

   Available for $3.00 each, the "PP BOOK" report calculates the emphasis on all the letters of the alphabet, themes and aspects in each horoscope for which you provide the data. The report lists each significant focus (e.g., "There is a Letter 9 theme in "Parents," and gives the appropriate page numbers for you to read in this book ("See pages 407-408 in the *Complete Horoscope Interpretation* book.")

   The computer will not **always** arrive at the same results as you might, as certain steps are ambiguous (e.g., how much weight to give a planet making a conjunction, based on the orb). However, the majority of the time, the computer answers will concur with those derived from use of the worksheets — or the recommended quick scan of a horoscope. Thus it provides an excellent teaching tool.

   The "PP BOOK" does **not** provide a listing of **each and every** astrological factor making up the significant themes. For that, you would order "PP WEIGHTS" (discussed in next footnote).

the 4th and 10th, including all signs within those houses
The placement of the Moon, Sun, Saturn and Ceres by house
The placement (by house) of the rulers of the 4th and 10th cusps
The house placement of the rulers of any additional signs in the 4th and 10th houses
The house cusp(s) ruled by any planet(s) in the 4th and 10th houses, e.g., if Mars in in the 4th, on what house cusp(s) does Aries fall?
The houses ruled by planets forming any conjunctions to Saturn, the Moon, the Sun, Ceres, the rulers of the 4th and 10th houses
Any planets in Cancer or Capricorn (the nature of the planets)
House(s) occupied by planet(s) in Cancer or Capricorn

GROUP IV
The Midheaven sign
The sign on the IC
The signs of the Moon, the Sun, Saturn and Ceres
The sign of the rulers of the 4th and 10th cusps
The signs of the rulers of any additional signs in the 4th and 10th houses
Any signs in the 4th and 10th houses which are occupied by a planet (the nature of the sign)
Cancer and Capricorn on any house cusp(s) — the nature of the house
Any additional (unoccupied) signs in the 4th and 10th houses

How to Weight the Factors

Please note that these factors are rank ordered (in chunks) according to their weighting. That is, planets (and angles) are most significant, so we first consider any conjunctions to the Moon or Saturn. Then we consider rulers of the 4th and 10th houses. Houses come next in weighting, so we look to the nature of the planets in the 4th and 10th and then house placements for important factors. Last, we consider signs.

If you want to use exact figures, a suggested weighting scale is given in the appendix — with worksheets for parents and the other life areas.[3]

3. You can also obtain a listing of **all** the astrological factors which compose those letters of the Zip Code determined to be significant in a horoscope. This makes an excellent teaching tool and a valuable resource to check yourself against when practicing with the Zip Code.
   Astro Computing Services, PO Box 16430, San Diego, CA 92116, has calculated 28,000 horoscopes and established averages and standard deviations for the scores of each letter of the astrological alphabet, each theme, and the conflict and harmony aspects to each life area.
   Astro's report, called "PP WEIGHTS," will list those letters of the astrological alphabet which are one standard deviation or more above the mean — and list **all** the astrological factors which point to each significant letter of the alphabet. These weightings will also compare each individual's score on the various themes (e.g., risk-taking, artistic) to the means and standard deviations to determine which themes are significant.
   (footnote continued on next page)

A SHORT CUT

For quickness and ease of use, especially for people just learning to use the Zip Code, I suggest the focusing initially on factors in Groups I and II.

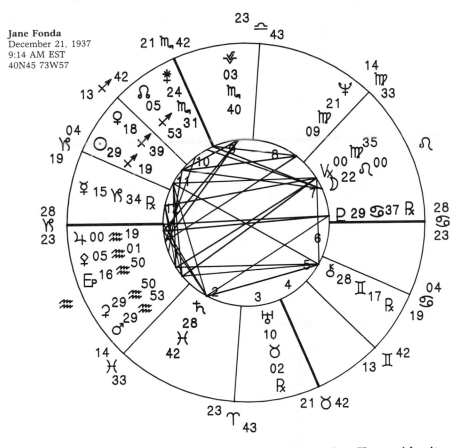

Jane Fonda
December 21, 1937
9:14 AM EST
40N45 73W57

If any letter of the alphabet is represented in Group I or II, consider it as probably significant. (If a letter of the alphabet is repeated in Groups I and II, it is definitely significant. Read the appropriate interpretation.) For example, since Mars closely conjuncts Ceres in the chart of Jane Fonda, you would suspect a Letter

---

3. (continued from previous page)
    Averages are established for aspects as well in order to note conflict or harmony in the different life areas.
    The results obtained by Astro's "PP WEIGHTS" will not **always** coincide with those you determine by a quick scan and intuitive judgment, or by use of the worksheets. Certain of the steps (e.g., how much to weight a planet based on orb) are ambiguous, so differe. ' results can occur. However, most of the time, Astro's answers will confirm those you could obtain in working with the Zip Code. Furthermore, the **complete** listing of relevant factors is an excellent teaching tool.
    Ask for "PP Weights." The price, as of December 1985 is $5.00

1 focus in terms of her parents, most likely her mother. In addition, we have the 10th house occupied by Juno (Letter 7 — ½ weight) and the north node of the Moon (not assigned to the Zip Code, but having overtones of Letter 4, since it relates back to the Moon).

Once you are familiar with factors in Groups I and II, add Groups III and IV. You can check to see if any of the letters from Groups I and II are repeated by the factors in Groups III or IV. For example, Ms. Fonda's Letter 1 theme for parents is repeated with Ceres in the 1st (1), 10th house Sagittarius ruler (Jupiter) in the 1st (1), Capricorn on the Ascendant (1), Ceres parallel the Ascendant (1), 10th house Sagittarius ruler (Jupiter) conjunct and parallel the Ascendant plus making another conjunction (to Pallas) in the 1st (1). Letter 7 as a key to parents is another repeated theme: 10th house Juno (7), Moon in the 7th (7), 10th cusp Scorpio ruler (Pluto) falls in the 7th (7), Cancer is occupied in the 7th (7), Cancer falls on the Descendant (7), 10th cusp Scorpio ruler (Pluto) conjuncts the Descendant (7), 10th house Sagittarius ruler (Jupiter) conjuncts Pallas (7).

In assessing Groups III and IV, also look for any letters of the alphabet which occur three or more times. Consider them significant and read the appropriate (pages 404-409) interpretations. For example, Letter 11 is repeated as a theme several times: Ceres in Aquarius (11), 4th cusp Taurus ruler (Venus) in the 11th (11), 10th house Sagittarius ruler (Jupiter) in Aquarius (11), Capricorn falls in the 11th (11), Ceres makes a conjunction (to Mars) in the sign of Aquarius (11) and 10th house Sagittarius ruler (Jupiter) makes a conjunction (to Pallas) in the sign of Aquarius (11).

We might also note that the nodes of the Moon fall across the 4th and 10th houses, pointing to the issue of conditional versus unconditional love in the childhood. The 4th/10th nodes **can** indicate tension between or separations between the parents (although that placement can also just point to balancing the polarity of compassion versus pragmatism). Many times, the south node in the 4th house points to tension surrounding the issues of dependency, nurturance and emotional support. It is not uncommon for people to feel a lack of unconditional support. There may even be a subjective sense of missing nurturance or of emotional deprivation in the early home. Ms. Fonda has indicated that her childhood was not easy and part of the reason she delayed having children was to become more sure she would be a good mother.

Ms. Fonda's parental experience was mixed. Her mother committed suicide when Jane was 12 years old. Her father was a role-model to some extent (Capricorn rising), but self-doubts held her back from fully following in his footsteps. Apparently Jane Fonda had a good relationship with her stepmother Susan Blanchard, who is described as a role model (Letter 1) for clothes, hair and make-up. Jane's relationship to Susan was reputed to be more sisterly or equalitarian (Letter 7) than parental. The fire and air focus which comes through for parents does also fit Frances Seymour Brokaw, Jane Fonda's mother, who was described as vivacious, party-loving and extroverted with an opinion on everything.

Themes

Themes can be ascertained by two methods. One approach is to look at only the letters emphasized by the above examination. Determine which themes are made up of various combinations of the emphasized letters. In the case of Jane Fonda, the emphasized Letters 1, 7 and 11 could contribute to a theme of air (3, 7, 11), freedom (1, 9, 11) or relationships/partnerships (7 and 8).

Both Jane Fonda's mother and her first stepmother are described as lively, outgoing, social people fitting the fire and air emphasis. Her father seemed to live out the freedom theme (often off doing his own thing, not always there emotionally for Jane). "On Golden Pond" presented the opportunity for father and daughter to accept one another as independent human beings — with different ideas and interests — who still loved and cared about one another.

A second approach to spotting themes is to look at the totals for **all** the letters of the alphabet and estimate which ones have more than their "average" share of the totals. For example, the relationship/partnership theme is the total of scores from Letters 7 and 8. You will need to do some rough arithmetic here or get an intuitive impression. If a theme involves two (out of twelve) letters of the astrological alphabet, you would expect it to have about 1/6 of the total score. So, if the amount for those letters seems appreciably more than 1/6 of the total, count that as a theme — and read the appropriate section (page 419).

In addition, when searching for themes, give more weight to like planets in aspect to one another. For example, Venus and Pluto are both partnership planets (plus the asteroids Pallas and Juno). Thus, aspects between them would add weight to a theme of relating within the chart. (Pallas is octile Venus in Ms. Fonda's chart. Pluto is contra-parallel Venus. Pluto is very widely opposite Pallas and very widely trine Juno.) Also give extra weight to like houses and like signs. Thus, Venus, Pluto, Pallas or Juno in the 7th or 8th houses or in Libra or Scorpio gives more emphasis to the theme of sharing equally. (In Ms. Fonda's case, Pluto occupies the 7th and Juno occupies Scorpio.)

Remember that each emphasized theme must be connected to that life area in order to be significant there. Ms. Fonda's chart has a strong focus on fire, due to the close aspects between all three of the fire planets plus two fire planets (Jupiter and Mars) occupying a fire house (the 1st) and the third fire planet (the Sun) in a fire sign (Sagittarius). However, this fire focus is not **necessarily** significant in **all** areas of her life — only in those arenas to which it is connected by placements of fire factors and rulership by fire factors. Her horoscope does connect fire principles to parents, but not, for example, to money.

Aspects

Quickly scan all aspects other than conjunctions, grouping them according to harmony (sexisextile, sextile, trine) and conflict (octile, tri-octile, square, opposition

and quincunx). In considering each aspect, weight the nature of the planet most heavily, followed by the house and the sign. Count both the house occupied and the cusp ruled by planets being aspected. For example, Jane Fonda has the following **close** harmony aspects to her Moon:
- trine the Venus (2) in the 11th (11) in Sagittarius (9); Venus rules the 4th and 9th (4)(9)
- semisextile Neptune (12) in the 8th (8) in Virgo (6); Neptune rules the 2nd (2)

She has the following **close** conflict aspects to her Moon:
- square the MC (10) in Scorpio (8)
- square Juno (7) in the 10th (10) in Scorpio (8)

If you feel any group of aspects has an emphasis on one or more letters of the alphabet, read the appropriate interpretation (pages 422-429).

  Harmony aspects show potential ease of flow — both between the individual and parental figures where those issues are concerned, but more importantly between the individual's **internal** mother and father images and other parts of his/her nature. Conflict aspects show potential stress between parental themes (nurturance, responsibility, authority, dependency) and other sides of life. For example, the squares from the Moon (4) to the MC (10) and Juno in the 10th can suggest tension or conflict **between** the parents (as do the nodes across the 4th/10th). However, those same aspects point to Ms. Fonda's inner need to balance dependency and dominance, home and family versus career, and unconditional versus conditional love. Remember to also think in terms of the individual's own **internal** parent (capacity to nurture the self, ability to be practical and responsible) and not just in terms of early caretakers.

Interpretations: Parents

ALPHABET THEMES

Letter 1: Parental Role Model(s)

Your parents probably had a strong impact on how you see yourself and how you express yourself. This combination shows strong parenting instincts within you and usually there is a desire for children. Sometimes, the need to nurture or be responsible for others is **so** strong, the individual ends up "playing parent" from a very young age. This can include the possibility of feeling as though you had to nurture yourself, take care of yourself, and maybe even look after a parent who was not competent.

  Assertion, expression and aggression were likely issues for you to face through one of your parents. You may have experienced your parent(s) as spontaneous, strong and able to do what they wanted. If they overdid this theme, you may have felt they were too self-centered, independent, even violent. Anger is sometimes a problem issue in such environments. You may have felt everyone around you was angry. It could have seemed that anger was **not** okay (at least for you) or that anger was the **only** allowable emotion at home. But learning to express anger without hurting others is often a lesson with such configurations.

Generally, one parent is a strong role model for you. (Sometimes it is a grand-parent rather than a parent.) Role models can be positive or negative. When we like the parents, we try to imitate them and be like them. When we do not get along with that parent, we strive to be the opposite of what they are and tend to quash any similarities within us to that detested parent. Whether you took your parents as positive or negative examples of who you wanted to be, the major learn-ing revolved around independence, self-expression, handling of anger and being able to be yourself and do what you want in the world.

Letter 2: Parents and Pleasure

Material comforts, security and pleasures were likely focuses in your relation-ship with your parents. The range could include parents you felt very comfort-able with; they were predictable, stable and inclined to indulge you. Food could have been used to express love. Other possibilities would be parents who were self-indulgent — perhaps too much so with eating, drinking, smoking, amassing money, spending or other forms of material acquisition and enjoyment. They may have seemed too money-oriented, overly focused on work, too concerned with the physical sense world, or simply boring and stuck in a rut. You could have experienced them as stubborn, self-satisfied and unwilling to put themselves out for anyone else, acting only for their personal pleasure. They could also have been quite artistic, enjoying the gratification of beauty through any number of art forms.

Whether the model they provided was helpful or harmful, the issues being faced revolved around pleasure from the material world: food, alcohol, money, possessions and beauty. The focus revolved around stability, comfort, ease, security and pleasures.

Letter 3: Facing the Mental World

The mind, communication and social interaction were likely areas of focus for you with your parents. They were probably bright and might have been very ar-ticulate and verbal. They could also have been scattered, gossipy and superficial. Part of what you were facing through them was the quality of detachment. That could have been developed through shared ideas and an objective attitude. If your parents carried it to an extreme, you may have experienced them as cold and aloof rather than warm and loving.

If you felt a sense of confidence in your own intellect and ability to share the mental world, an equalitarian relationship with your parents was likely; you felt on the same level as them. It is also possible that you played a parental role to other relatives (especially brothers and sisters) or had relatives who were sur-rogate parents to you (e.g., an aunt, uncle, cousin could have been a substitute mother or father). But the focus with all the people around you was learning to learn and learning to communicate, hopefully in an easy, give-and-take context.

Letter 4: Family Ties

At least one parent was teaching about emotional closeness and attachment. That parent could have been extremely nurturant or very dependent. If the former, you may have experienced your parent as warm, sensitive, caring and been very involved with that parent. If the latter (dependent) option was expressed, one or both parents could have seemed childlike, clingy, demanding and possibly smothering and overly possessive. If your parental figure overdid the dependency side, you could have felt that you ended up being a parent to your own parent, taking care of and being responsible for them. The focus was learning about being vulnerable and able to care and be cared for through the example (positive or negative) of that parent or parents.

Letter 5: Family Pride

Charisma, dynamism, excitement and a starring role were in some way a focus with one of your parents. This can range from a parent who was always "onstage," seeking attention, admiration and applause, to a parent who was a wonderful fan club, approving of all you did and encouraging you to constantly surpass yourself. When exaggerated, one potential is a self-centered parent who seemed unable to share the spotlight with anyone else, who was childish in their determination to have fun and achieve adulation the way they wanted it. When this theme is shared, both you and the parent are able to be important, have your place in the sun and enjoy the response and appreciation of others.

This theme puts a major focus on the need to love and be loved. Often there is a very deep bond between parents and children, plus a strong instinct within you to establish a family of your own. The need to give and receive love is strong.

Letter 6: Parents and Productivity

Work, practicality, realism and achievement were in some way exemplified by one of your parents. The theme was efficient functioning — both in some kind of work in the world and in the physical body. Your parent could have been a hard worker and possessed of many puritan virtues — duty, thoroughness, attention to details and analytical. Sometimes criticism is a problem — from parents toward you and/or vice versa. A focus on the flaws can be overdone.

Another potential is a family business or a home environment where everyone was expected to work and contribute to the household. Sometimes this indicates a parent whose work takes them away from home; it can also show an ill parent where the child learns to be realistic at a young age by having to do tasks normally performed by that ill parent. Whatever the circumstances, the focus ranges around pragmatism and efficiency.

Letter 7: Parents/Partners

This theme involves a mixture of parenting energy with partnership energy. One potential is a parent like a partner — a parent who accepted you as an equal, met you on the same level, regarded you as a peer. In such cases, there is often an ease of communication and equality between the parent and child. Sometimes the likeness is so much, there is competition between the parent and child. Being a partner (to the spouse) might also be very significant in the parent's life, with the goal of always presenting a "united front" to the children.

   This configuration suggests that your ability to relate and share is strongly tied to your relationship with a parent. If there is "unfinished business" with that parent — old, unresolved feelings, things you are still feeling resentful, guilty about, something you are still trying to "prove" to that parent — you are likely to attract partners who will elicit the same kinds of feelings from you. You will "meet" that parent, in a sense, through your close partners. Until you come to terms with whatever is being mirrored back to you and integrate it, the same old issues repeat; the same old feelings emerge again and again.

Letter 8: Parents and Power

Power, especially over the emotions and over the physical sense world, is a focus through one or both parents. This parent could be involved in seeking self-mastery and self-control, even through occult or other hidden areas. A parent might be learning to master the physical appetites, with conflicts around eating, drinking, smoking, money, sex or other physical pleasures. Or, the parent could be manipulative, power hungry and controlling. There is often a good ability to "psyche" each other out and tune into one another, but this is not always pleasant. Either or both of you may, at times, feel smothered and as if you have no privacy.

   Issues revolve around getting to the bottom of things, understanding them on the deepest levels and channeling that probing, investigative bent into arenas of self-control rather than abusing or using others (or letting them abuse or use us). Knowing when to let go, when a situation is finished, and being able to finish is often a challenge for parents and children. Resentment may be a challenging emotion for both of you. Being able to forgive and forget is a talent you are learning from one another.

Letter 9: Facing Ideals and Expectations

One or both parents are role models in the search for the truth or for something more in life. This can be a parent who is highly religious, spiritual or dedicated to science, education and searching for answers. Another option is a parent who believes s/he is perfect and has a right to whatever s/he wants in life.

   Freedom needs are often important to one or both parents. Such a parent may simply be gone a lot, perhaps traveling. The parent may come across as detached and not really involved, so the child creates his/her idealized version of how that parent should be — or what the parent would be like if s/he had actually been around.

Another alternative is a mutually idealistic relationship — where you each look up to and admire the other — **or** a mutually disillusioning relationship — where you both feel hurt and let down when the other party turns out **not** to be perfect, to have flaws, to be less than godlike. You may expect more than is reasonable from this parent and the parent may never be satisfied with you.

Of course, sharing the quest for ultimate answers is another option. Together, with this parent, you could travel, attend classes, teach, study, seek the meaning of the Universe.

The theme is dealing with expectations, goals, values and belief systems through your relationships with your parent(s).

Letter 10: Balancing Emotional and Physical Caretaking

This is a mother/father blend. It can manifest in several ways in the external sense. One potential is a parent who played both roles: a mother who was both nurturing and dominant; a father who was both responsible and warm; a parent who was responsible for being both mother and father to you. Another possibility is parents who were alike, both sharing qualities, with no sharp distinctions between them. Their roles could have overlapped. Mother did some of the outer world work, responsibility and realism; father did some of the nurturance, support and emotional caretaking. In some way, the parental archetypes are being blended.

The combination of conditional with unconditional love can manifest in several ways. One potential is parents that overdid the conditional side; they were harsh, judgmental, critical more than warm and caring. Sometimes this is simply a difficult childhood, where everyone had to work, where everyone was realistic, effective, etc. One variation is parenting your own parents, feeling you had to be the strong, responsible one, that everything rested on your shoulders. Another potential is parents that overdid the unconditional love side; they were extremely nurturing and protective, doing so much for their children that the children never had to develop much strength or responsibility on their own. Mommy or Daddy always did it. Yet another possibility is parents that were able to be unconditional in their expression of love when you were young — to build up your trust in the world and your sense of self-esteem — and the parents made the transition to conditional love as you got older. With age, you expected to meet certain demands, follow certain rules and regulations of society, deal with people's roles.

Letter 11: Unusual Parent(s)

Freedom, uniqueness, detachment and originality are role modeled — in some way — by a parent. This can range from a parent who has truly mastered the knack of being one's own person while still caring for and being involved with others to a weird, flaky and freaky parent who is expressing individualism and uniqueness in some very strange ways. Often, the parent seems more of a friend, an equal, than a parent. Communication may be very good. Or, the parent is simply off doing their own thing, too detached to really be involved, too busy with social causes, humanitarian principles, clubs and associations to really share emotionally. With openness and tolerance, much can be worked out, as long as people do not carry the principle of detachment **too** far.

Letter 12: "Perfect" Parent(s)?

The search for infinite love and beauty is being experienced through a parent. This can include a parent who plays the roles of artist, savior and victim. The artistic parent is involved with creating a more beautiful, lovely world. We can take that example and extend upon it, or deny the potential within ourselves and see the talent as "only" belonging to our parent. The savior parent is busy seeking a more perfect, a more ideal, world. Such parents may be very idealistic and involved in the healing arts, either professionally or on an informal basis. Their goal in life is to succor, to rescue, to take care of and make it all better. The victim parent also has a beautiful dream but is unable or unwilling to pursue it in life. So, the victim cops out and looks for an escape — through drugs, alcohol, fantasy, psychosis, illness, sleeping all the time, daydreaming, etc. — from the fact that the world is ugly (not beautiful), flawed (not ideal) and that s/he is not doing anything to change or improve all that!

We can also play the roles of artist, helper or victim. Sometimes we start early in life, feeling victimized by parents, or seeing them as victims and trying to rescue them. (One form of the "victim" parent is the absent or disappearing parent whom the child can only dream about and fantasize what "might" have been. Of course, such children can also identify themselves as "victims" for lacking a parent, if they so choose. A parent may also be emotionally absent even if physically present.) Attitude has a lot to do with rescuer/victim roles.

Sometimes the idealism is not too extreme, in which case parents and children tend to idolize one another, but not too excessively. They look up to one another, each may think the other is perfect, each may believe the other is almost godlike. Problems only ensue when they **demand** perfection from one another. Then disillusionment and disappointment is the inevitable denouement. Sharing a search for infinite love and beauty (through art, nature, spiritual/religious quests, etc.) is usually safer.

ALPHABET COMBINATIONS BY TWOS

Refer to Chapter 8 (Relationships) and read the appropriate **Combinations by Two** in terms of parents rather than partners (beginning page 189).

NODES OF THE MOON

The following nodal placements are particularly revelant for the life area of parents. For other polarities, read pages 198-200 in Chapter 8, thinking in terms of parents rather than partners.

Across Cancer/Capricorn or 4th/10th Houses

The polarity you are facing deals with conditional versus unconditional love. You may have experienced this opposition through your parents as they worked on balancing a performance orientation ("I appreciate you when you are good") with pure support ("I care about you because you are you"). Your parents could have gone to an extreme — or found a middle ground. One extreme is parents who teach a child to face reality at a very young age. This can range from a home focused on work, where everybody contributes even at a tender age. Sometimes there is poverty in the background or a farm family where physical labor starts early. The parents can be harsh, judgmental, punitive, where the child feels s/he can never do enough. The parents can be incompetent so that the child ends up parenting his/her own parents and having to be responsible very early in life.

Another extreme is parents who do too much for the child. Such parents are so supportive, so willing to help, the child does very little, even when relatively old. Such children may have difficulties finding their own strength and trusting their personal abilities because they are so used to having everything done by Mommy or Daddy. The child can be smothered or weakened by an excess of care.

The middle ground is parents who love the child unconditionally when s/he is young and provide more and more realism and reasonable expectations as the child grows. The child has a basic core of security, feeling cherished, but also the experience in coping with life to know s/he is capable and can be responsible and get things done.

It is important to remember that no matter how our parents act in terms of some outside, "objective" standard, what matters is how we feel about it. If other people saw our father as sweet and reasonable, but we experienced him as judgmental and hard to please, that is the reality for us. Our challenge is to develop a balance between emotions and pragmatism, acceptance and performance demands. We cannot change what our parents did, but we can change our feelings about it, our reactions to it and our future choices. We all have an internal "father" and "mother" striving to balance conditional and unconditional love. In the end, the internal balance is the one that truly matters.

ELEMENT EMPHASIS

Fire
♂, ☉, ♃, ♄, ♈, ♌, ♐, 1st, 5th, 9th houses

Vibrant, alive, exciting, spontaneous and extraverted, your parents could have been a dynamic handful! If the energy was shared, you probably enjoyed being active together. Sports could have been a connection or risky, pioneering, freedom-oriented activities. Creativity (of one or both parents) could have been quite high.

If your parents carried these qualities to an extreme, you may have experienced them as self-centered, intent on their own desires, restless, hyper or flamboyant.

The more you can own the positive potential within yourself, the less you need to replay any of the negative potentials (with parents or other people).

Earth
♀, ♄, ?, ⚷, ♉, ♍, ♑, 2nd, 6th, 10th houses

Your parents probably focused on the material world — either in terms of working, with a strong, practical focus, or in terms of pleasures, with a sensual, indulgent or materialistic focus.

If the energy was shared, you learned with them to enjoy the material world as well as being able to manipulate it for tangible results. You learned to work and play, to be effective as well as gaining satisfaction from physical pleasures.

If your parents overdid any of these qualities, they may have seemed materialistic, spoiled, indulgent (of you or themselves), workaholics, concrete, boring, only concerned with the "real" world.

Air
☿, ♀, ⚷, ?, ♅, ♊, ♎, ♒, 3rd, 7th, 11th houses

Your parents were likely to be bright, interested in communication, detached, casual and capable of being objective. If you shared that energy with them, your home was likely to be full of intellectual exchanges, discussions and communication of all kinds. You all could express logic and an objective viewpoint. You might enjoy one another's ideas.

If your parents carried any of these potentials too far, you may have doubted your own mind because you kept on comparing yourself to their "brilliance." Or, if they were exceptionally articulate (or just chatterboxes), you may have been more silent than necessary to compensate. Or, you may have experienced them as excessively detached — too cool, aloof and distant where you wanted emotional closeness. They may have been intellectual, but not very feeling.

Sometimes the role model is totally negative — that is, you developed your own mind in reaction to feeling your parents did **not** utilize their intellectual capacities. But whether positive or negative, the focus is on issues of thinking, communication and equality being faced through your relationship with your parents.

Water
☽, ♇, ♆, ♋, ♏, ♓, 4th, 8th, 12th houses

Your parents were likely to be sensitive, intuitive and deeply feeling. But they probably did not reveal much of their emotionality on the surface. They may very well have delved into a number of hidden depths, including their own psyches, looking for deeper answers. They may have operated more in an unconscious than a conscious realm. They could have felt a strong connection to Life, a sense of oneness with the Universe. They were likely to be either strongly dependent or nurturant (or both).

If the energy was shared, you and your parents could have had a very deep, psychic, nonverbal bond, instinctively tuning into one another. (Depending on what you tune into, that could feel very good or very bad.) Mutually sensitive, you could have had an interdependency, a sharing and caring for one another.

If the energy was not shared, you could have experienced your parents as suffocating and smothering in their need to care for you (overdoing nurturance). Or, you could have felt like you had to parent your own parents — being warm and comforting to them (if they overdid dependency). One option is that both parents and children retreated into their own little, internal worlds and did not interact much.

The issue being faced is learning about your own depths through close relationships, dealing with dependency and nurturing needs.

Fire-Earth
♂, ☉, ♃, ♗, ♈, ♌, ♐, 1st, 5th, 9th houses &
♀, ♄, ♇, ⚷, ♉, ♍, ♑, 2nd, 6th, 10th houses

Your parents were potential "bulldozers" — knowing what they wanted and going after it emphatically in the world. If you saw that as positive, they gave you a good example for practical achievements, for carrying through on your initiatives. If you experienced them as bulldozers or Mack trucks who simply swept away anything in their path, you may have had to work through some blocks to actualize your own creative, productive capacities. If their high degree of productivity struck you as negative, you may have taken some time and growing to reach an appreciation of your own capabilities. Perseverance blended with confidence can be a marvelous combination, as long as you maintain some sensitivity as well!

Fire-Air
♂, ☉, ♃, ♗, ♈, ♌, ♐, 1st, 5th, 9th houses &
☿, ♀, ♯, ♀, ♅, ♊, ♎, ♒; 3rd, 7th, 11th houses

Your parents were likely to be very restless and on the optimistic side. They could have had a marvelous sense of humor and been real "party" types. Probably articulate and persuasive, they may have lived life from "flower to flower" seeking constant activity.

If that energy was shared, you and your parents had a lot of laughs together. Some energetic discussions (even arguments) are likely, but this is a combination unlikely to bear grudges. A zest for life and a wish to experience it all would lead you onward in life.

If your parents carried this theme too far, they may have seemed foolish and extravagant in their dreams and schemes. They may have perennially searched for that pot of gold at the end of the rainbow. They may have been fun while life was easy, but tended to disappear if the going got rough. They could have been **too** persuasive with a bit of the con artist potential. You may have sometimes felt that you got stuck cleaning up their messes.

Fire-Water
♂, ☉, ♃, ♮, ♈, ♌, ♐, 1st, 5th, 9th houses &
☽, ♇, ♆, ♋, ♏, ♓, 4th, 8th, 12th houses

Intense, emotional and volatile, your parents probably had strong feelings about almost everything. Quite possibly very warm and caring, they could have given a lot of emotional support. An inner ambivalence between spontaneity and playing it safe may have plagued them. Choosing when to express one's emotions and when to lie back and make sure it will be okay is not always easy. Mood swings are a potential — from elation to depression. It is possible that you could express one end (either spontaneity or holding back; optimism or pessimism) of the emotional yo-yo in the relationship. Then it would be likely that you would overdo one side while your parents overdid the other.

If this energy was shared, you could have had a very close bond with your parents. The relationship may have been extremely intense. There is a capacity for fun as well as emotional commitment between you. Shared action as well as shared caretaking is suggested.

Earth-Air
♀, ♄, ♮, ♯, ♉, ♍, ♑, 2nd, 6th, 10th houses &
☿, ♀, ♯, ♀, ♅, ♊, ♎, ♒, 3rd, 7th, 11th houses

Your parents could have been quite logical and rational. They would have focused on the practical or intellectual world rather than the emotional. They might have appeared a bit dry, but you could depend on them to be predictable. They were the sort of people who would always give you the "correct" answer — even if it wasn't the "right" one (in terms of what you wanted).

If they overdid those qualities, you probably felt they were cold and aloof when you wanted warmth and closeness. You may have felt they could only deal with thoughts while you wanted to encompass feelings. You may have experienced them as too stolid and boring — not sufficiently spontaneous.

Earth-Water
♀, ♄, ?, ⚶, ♉, ♍, ♑, 2nd, 6th, 10th houses &
☽, ♇, ♆, ♋, ♏, ♓, 4th, 8th, 12th houses

Your parents were likely to be taking care of the world in some way or wanting the world to take care of them. They could have been professional helpers, or simply had the personality that encouraged others to cry on their shoulders. They were likely to be oriented toward security — both materially and emotionally. The dependence is more on status quo than change. They may have had a tendency to take themselves and life too seriously. They could even have been prone to depression and looked to others to succor them if they lacked inner security.

If you experienced them as carrying this to an extreme, you probably felt they didn't have enough fun, being too concerned with taking care of everybody. Or, you may have felt they didn't take enough chances in life. Perhaps they were so concerned about you that you felt confined and smothered — or so demanding and worried about their own emotional and physical needs, they could not care much for others. Issues of security and protection were being faced through your parents.

Air-Water
☿, ♀, ⚷, ♀, ♅, ♊, ♎, ♒, 3rd, 7th, 11th houses &
☽, ♇, ♆, ♋, ♏, ♓, 4th, 8th, 12th houses

Your parents could have been extremely imaginative with a rich inner world of ideas and impressions. But they may have been very internal people, not revealing much on the surface. They could have even been drifters and dreamers, who floated through life without making much of an impact. The spectator role may have appealed to them.

If your parents carried this too far, they could have seemed the typical "space cadets" — off in their own little world, hardly connected to physical reality. They might have watched the world go by without ever really getting involved. They could have had wonderful ideas and great, creative inspirations but lacked the grounding, realism or follow through to do anything with their visions.

QUALITY EMPHASIS

Cardinal
♂, ☽, ♀, ⚷, ♀, ♄, ♈, ♋, ♎, ♑, 1st, 4th, 7th, 10th houses

Your parents were teaching you about the struggle t ϶ balance needs for freedom, equality, closeness and control.

If your parents were able to provide a positive example, they made room in their lives for liberty and open pursuit of their own personal wants and needs; emotional sharing and attachments with significant others (such as home and family); equalitarian relationships where one-to-one interactions are on the same level;

and a position (often through a career or work in the world) of authority, control and power where it was done **their** way.

Negative examples include repressing any of the potentials (eventually leading to illness), projecting any corner (and attracting other people who overdo the energy), flipping from one extreme to another, always wanting whatever side they were not expressing at the moment. It is also possible that your parents identified with different ones of these various potentials with the danger of each parent overdoing the corner(s) s/he had chosen. Thus, if one parent identified with closeness and the other with freedom, each would be likely to carry their close — or free — behavior a bit too far. Whether you received a negative or positive example from your parents, you still have an opportunity to learn the balance in your own life.

This pattern in a horoscope often indicates changes in the basic life structure, many events and crises. The key is to make room in your life for everything you want and then deliberately support and nurture each potential.

Fixed

♀, ☉, ♇, ♏, ♉, ♌, ♏, ♒, 2nd, 5th, 8th, 11th houses

Your parents were teaching you about handling the physical, material, sensual world and learning to share power with other people. Part of the issue is balancing self-indulgence (in food, sex, drink, making and spending money, and other pleasures) with self-control (mastery of the appetites). Part of the issue is compromising between needs for security (physical and emotional) versus needs for risk (taking a chance, gambling, trying for the new). And part of the learning revolves around balancing the giving, receiving and sharing of sensual pleasures.

Your parents could have taken opposite ends of the issue (e.g., one parent identified with security, the other with risk and then they fought about it). Or, they could have nagged each other about weight, smoking, drinking, sex, etc. (opposite ends of the self-indulgence/self-control seesaw). They might both have overindulged or both overcontrolled themselves. The issue is how much you have learned from their examples. Until you make the inner balance, the likelihood is of attracting other people with the same conflicts. Then you and the other parties could easily fall into power struggles, each determined to show that **you** are right! Once you attain a relative balance within, you no longer need the experience of the external conflict to come to terms with your various sides. You have achieved an integration.

Mutable

☿, ⚳, ⚶, ♃, ⚷, ♆, ♊, ♍, ♐, ♓, 3rd, 6th, 9th, 11th houses

Your parents could have been quite mental and had a multitude of interests. They may have been somewhat scattered in attempts to cover the waterfronts in studies, hobbies, activities or careers. It is also possible that they were simply inconsistent, unpredictable and vacillated. You may have felt their standards and expectations were constantly changing. You could have experienced them as confusing because you could not read a consistent attitude from them.

Overextension may have been a problem. Perfectionism is also a common issue — wanting more than is humanly possible in some area — perhaps of themselves, perhaps in relationships, perhaps of their children, etc. Their ideal vision of how life should or could be might very well conflict with the reality of what is possible in this limited physical existence. Either could have played the victim or martyr role — bemoaning life's shortcomings.

If they adopted opposite ends of the seesaw, one of your parents might have played the realist and cynic while the other played the idealist and visionary. One could have played "God" — having it all together — or expected the other to be godlike in lack of flaws. They could have sought the Ultimate together — through traveling, studying, or through philosophical, scientific or religious endeavors. One could have had the other up on a pedestal.

Part of the issue is your accepting them as human — and their accepting you as human. Anyone who expects a person to be "God" is destined for disappointment sooner or later. Savior/victim games are also possible, with one person playing the all-powerful, all-healing savior and the other the victim who needs help. That does not last forever, though. Sooner or later the victim comes to resent having no power, or the savior comes to resent carrying all the load. Through the examples (positive and/or negative) of your parents, you could learn to balance vision with pragmatism, intellectual understanding with intuitive knowing. You had an opportunity to appreciate seeking something Higher in life — through art, nature, religion, spiritual quests or other channels to the Infinite — but not seeking perfection in human beings.

THEMES

Freedom
♂, ♃, ⚷, ♅, ♈, ♐, ♒, 1st, 9th, 11th houses

Independence was probably one of the issues with your parents. They could have expressed a love of liberty directly, spontaneously going their own way and doing their own thing. Or, you may have felt that gaining your own independence and freedom of action was particularly difficult. You could have experienced them as stifling or confining in regards to your needs for liberty.

If either parent repressed their need for space and assertion, typical problems could include lots of headaches, accidents, surgeries and colds. The extreme form of not dealing with one's own strength and power is attracting violence from the world. If either or both parents were negative role models, you might have come to emphasize your own independence in reaction to their inhibitions in this area.

A sense of openness and not being confined was likely to be an issue for them. If they carried this to an extreme, you may have experienced them as too busy meeting their own needs to nurture and care for you. Perhaps you even felt they were self-centered. Their activities in the outer world could have taken them away from home and family responsibilities.

If they set a positive, balanced example, they taught you to be true to yourself and your own needs, while still caring and involved with others.

Closeness or Interpersonal

☽, ☉, ♀, ⚵, ⚴, ♇, ♋, ♌, ♎, ♏, 4th, 5th, 7th, 8th houses

Emotional attachments were a likely focus in your home. You might have felt a very deep connection with your parent(s). If this theme was carried too far, you may have experienced your parents as suffocating and smothering. They could have seemed overly protective, emotional, sensitive or dependent. A very deep, nonverbal bond might have existed — between your parents and from them to you — but this is not always positive. You might have intuitively keyed into the worst in each other at times.

A very loving home is possible, but it could have been so intense and so overwhelmingly **close** that you felt stifled and had to get away. The focus in learning (through positive or negative examples) was around feelings and intimacy — the ability to share deeply with other human beings.

Artistic

♀, ☉, ♆, ⚵, ⚴, ♉, ♌, ♎, ♓, 2nd, 5th, 7th, 12th houses

Your parents were teaching you about the search for beauty in this life. They could have been actual artists with a talent for the aesthetic. They could have had a strong appreciation for beauty, grace and harmony in life. They might have valued harmony, balance, ease and comfort. If they manifested this theme in excess, they could have been overly concerned with appearance, looking good or appeasement to keep things "nice." If you experienced their example as a positive one, you learned through their attitudes and actions an appreciation of your own potential for enjoying and creating beauty, pleasure and ease in life.

Idealistic

♃, ⚷, ♆, ♐, ♓, 9th houses, 12th houses

Expectations were a learning ground in your family. Part of the issue was where you and your parents put your faith. One can look for the infinite in nature, God, art or other potentially ultimate areas. One can also look for infinite (total love, wisdom, understanding, etc.) from human beings and relationships. In such a case, we are usually disappointed.

With this theme, one positive option is parents and children who idealize and look up to one another while still allowing each other to be human with real faults and failings. Another option is parents who expect "perfect" children — to always do everything right, never make a mistake, etc. Such parents seem impossible to please, because no matter what you do, it is never enough. Another potential is children who expect their parents to be perfect — all-knowing, all-loving, all-powerful — and are disappointed, hurt and let down when the parents reveal their human shortcomings. Sometimes the parents idolize the children (or the children idolize the parents) and simply do not see what is there. They keep the other person up on a pedestal, determined to see only what they want to see in the relationship.

Parents and children can also seek God together, sharing a religious, spiritual, educational framework that gives meaning to their lives. The task is to have something to reach for, believe in and strive for, without seeking more than is humanly possible from those we are close to.

Obsessive-Compulsive
ħ, ♇, ?, ⚴, ♍, ♏, ♑, 6th, 8th, 10th houses

Your parents were teaching you about obsessive-compulsive behavior. On the positive side, they could have been very careful, painstaking, hard workers with a penchant for details, organization and thoroughness. On the negative side, they could have seemed picky, judgmental, critical and obsessed with unimportant items.

Whether you saw them as a negative or positive example in this area, they were teaching you about thoroughness, practicality, perseverance, putting everything in its place and exactitude. Such skills can be very helpful in the business world, in any area requiring some organization and efficiency — as long as they are not overdone.

Competence
(☿), ħ, ?, ⚴, ♍, ♑, 6th, 10th houses

Your parental relationships were a learning ground for work, responsibility, realism and doing a good job. This could be faced through a family where everybody worked — either because the parents valued the work ethic, or because the family was poor or circumstances dictated that everyone contribute. It could also be faced in a family where one or more parents were ill, so that you had to learn early on to cope, to manage, to be responsible. It could also be faced where parents were workaholics — carrying the desire for efficient functioning to an extreme. Or, the parents might have been very critical, harsh, judgmental and performance-oriented. No matter what you did, they seemed to feel it was never enough. They focused excessively on the flaws.

Regardless of the circumstances, the central issue was learning about productivity, efficiency, doing something well and the ability to work in the world.

Mental Stimulation

☿, ⚳, ⚶, ⚴, ♃, ⚷, ♅, ♆, ♊, ♍, ♐, ♒, ♓, 3rd, 6th, 7th, 9th, 11th, 12th houses

The development of the mind and communication skills was probably an issue in your home. The range of expressions can vary from very bright, articulate parents to cool, aloof, detached parents. Whether your parents set a positive role model of encouraging thinking, questioning and exploring the intellectual world, or set a negative role model of valuing rationality over emotions or detachment over caring, the learning opportunity was there.

Sometimes, when parents have developed certain qualities very strongly, children feel it is hard to compete and may give up in that area. If your parents were especially intelligent or fluent, you may have inhibited your own capacities in those areas for fear of never measuring up. Or, if they overdid some qualities, e.g., **too** talkative, **too** abstract, **too** detached, you may have reacted by condemning such qualities and denying them within yourself.

The goal is learning how to utilize the qualities of thinking, intellectual understanding and communication (verbal and written) in positive channels in your life.

Relationships

♀, ⚵, ⚴, ♇, ♎, ♏, 7th, 8th houses

Relationships were a focus for your parents, especially the one-to-one interactions with equals. This can indicate parents who were very equalitarian in their approach, encouraging you to relate to them on the same level. (If this is done at a reasonable age, it can be quite satisfying to the child. If it is done when the child is too young, it is simply a cop-out on responsibility by the parents.) They may also have valued their relationship to one another very highly. This can be the parents who try to always present a "united front" to the children, insisting on acting as a couple rather than individually. It can indicate very competitive or cooperative parents — and often some of both. Part of the question is whether they know when to compete and when to work together. Often beauty, harmony, ease and comfort are issues in the relationships.

Parents can teach us about these things by being attractive themselves and valuing that — or overemphasizing appearance in themselves and others. They could work to create a harmonious, comfortable, loving home, or they might expect others to provide it for them and feel disgruntled when it is not forthcoming.

These configurations point to parents as role models for our later love relationships. We tend to repeat the same issues with later partners. So, learning to share comfortably and equally the first time around makes later relating easier. But even if we got a negative role model initially, it teaches us what we do **not** want to do. So, we learn from our parents' handling of one-to-one relating what we will seek in our later associations. And, unfinished business with our parents is likely to emerge once more in our partnerships. A spouse or lover may not look like Mom or Dad, but s/he presses the same buttons, elicits the same responses and plays the same tapes as we went through with Mom and Dad until we grow, evolve and know better.

Security
♀, ☽, ?, ⚳, ☿, ♇, ♄, ♆, ♉, ♋, ♍, ♏, ♑, ♓, 2nd, 4th, 6th, 8th, 10th, 12th houses

Both emotional and physical security were likely focuses in your home. Your parents may have put an emphasis on dealing with the real world and on maintaining a safe position. They were more likely to support the status quo than to rock the boat. A sense of predictability may have appealed. If this was carried to an extreme, you could have done some freewheeling activities (perhaps even rash behaviors) to break loose, break free and break out of the familial mold.

The most positive potential is parents who provided a sense of safety, a sense of caring, a firm foundation from which you could venture into your own self-discovery and self-expression. Negative potentials include stodgy, stuck-in-the-mud, boring parents; parents who tried to keep you following their standard operating procedures; parents too materialistic or needing of reassurance and safety. Whatever the model, the learning ground was around issues of comfort, stability and a secure physical and emotional base in life.

Risk/Creativity/Change
♂, ☉, ♃, ⚵, ♅, ♈, ♌, ♐, ♒, 1st, 5th, 9th, 11th houses

Through your experiences with your parents, you learned about risk, courage, creativity and the ability to make changes. This could have ranged from real physical threats, running away, to encouragement to be and become all you are capable of. Your parents could have exhibited tremendous bravery and pursuit of their heart's desires. They could also have been foolish, foolhardy, carried their gambling instincts to a ridiculous extreme or insisted on having things **their** way.

Through positive and/or negative examples, your parents taught about laying it on the line and wholehearted commitment to expressing your creativity. Change and instability could have been common experiences, but the goal was development of your ability to take risks and alter the course of your life and actions in rewarding, exciting ways.

Parental Parents
☽, ☉, ♄, ?, ♋, ♑, 4th, 10th houses

Your parents were, in some way, mixing the traditional mothering archetype with the traditional fathering archetype. This can range from parents who are able to play both roles (mother strong and responsible as well as nurturing; father warm and caring as well as realistic and practical) to one parent playing both roles, whether due to death, divorce or absence of the other.

This polarity is the pull between unconditional acceptance support and caretaking versus a conditional judgment and approval based on the child's behavior. The tension is between compassion and emotional warmth versus pragmatism and cool assessment of performance. Your parent(s) could have gone to either extreme (or both) — overdoing the protection and caretaking or overdoing the critical judgment. They might also have manifested the happy medium of loving you unconditionally when you were young with increasing emphasis on facing facts and doing well as you got older.

Parents who overdo the supportive, caring role can raise spoiled children or simply people unsure of their own strength. If Mommy or Daddy always did everything for you, it is hard to develop confidence in your own ability to cope. Parents who overemphasize doing a good job can be experienced by the child as harsh, punitive, critical and impossible to please. Sometimes there is a poor or physically arduous childhood where the individual had to face reality at a relatively young age because everyone in the home had to work and contribute to making it. One option here is the child who is like a parent to his/her own parents. When the parent(s) simply cannot cope, the child may take over the responsible role and end up being the one carrying the burdens of the home — emotionally and often physically as well.

Parents who make a comfortable synthesis of this polarity are able to be caring and practical, emotional and realistic, loving and productive. But even parents who carry either side to an extreme offer the child an opportunity to learn about these themes, to choose what to do and what not to do in the future in trying to blend conditional and unconditional love.

Power
⊙, ♇, ♄, ♌, ♏, ♑, 5th, 8th, 10th houses

You were learning about issues of power, control and authority through your relationships with your parents. The challenge is to find positive outlets for a power drive (e.g., sports, games, business, worthy causes) without succumbing to the temptation of power struggles, confrontations and manipulation of those nearest and dearest to you. Your parents offered role models for the (positive or negative) handling of power.

Personal
♂, ♀, ☿, ☽, ♈, ♉, ♊, ♋, 1st, 2nd, 3rd, 4th houses

Your relationship with your parents was teaching you about personal needs and desires. This can include parents who encouraged you to realize and satisfy your own drives. It can also include parents who went overboard in meeting their own personal needs and were self-centered and selfish. You could have felt that everything had to be on their terms. The key is to realize that a certain amount of self-orientation is necessary and positive without carrying it to an extreme.

Transpersonal
♃, ⚷, ♄, ♅, ♆, ♐, ♑, ♒, ♓, 9th, 10th, 11th, 12th houses

Your parents were teaching you about appreciation of the wide perspective, the long-range view. In some way, their example offered learning to you around transpersonal issues — society as a whole, the establishment, people in large numbers. One possibility is parents who were strongly involved in large-scale issues. They could have been politically active, involved in social causes, concerned with broad, societal issues. They could have even been so caught up in the outside world that you felt they neglected the family to some extent. It is quite possible that your home was a forum in some way — for ideas, for people. Your parents could have easily brought the world into your home (discussions, arguments, books, ideas, visitors) as well as taking their home into the world with outer involvements.

Their focus could have been religious or spiritual more than political or concerned with some basic belief or cause. The thrust is toward something larger, more significant, something infinite. They could also have just dreamed of doing something highly important and meaningful without actually achieving anything. They could have come across more as victims of the system than people making a difference. But the basic theme is learning about larger questions, gaining a sense of history, seeing life from an expanded perspective.

ASPECTS
In this section, aspects are divided between mother (figure) and father (figure) or nurturing and responsibility themes. With each horoscope, you will have to determine if one parent seems to fit the 4th or the 10th house better, if the parents seem to "share" both houses, or if one parent seems to have taken over, playing both roles and indicated by both houses. Mixed parental figures (e.g., grandparents, other relatives, friends, etc.) can also be considered rather than the standard "mom or dad" choices. Remember to think in terms of balancing your internal "mother" and "father."

Harmony to Letter 4 (and Ceres)

1: There is a good possibility of harmony with your mother or mother figure. That early relationship gave you clues about balancing dependency and nurturance needs with the desire to be your own person. You have the potential of integrating your emotional security needs with your desire for free self-expression. Able to express both warm caring and independence of action, you can have close ties to others while still maintaining a sense of personal freedom.

2: There is potential harmony between your nurturing/dependency experiences and your ability to enjoy the physical, material world. Your mother (or mother figure) could have encouraged your capacity to earn money and/or enjoy beauty, eating, drinking or other sensual indulgences. Security, both physical and emotional, could have been emphasized in your early environment.

3: There is potential harmony between your nurturing/dependency experiences and your ability to think and communicate. Your mother (or mother figure) could have encouraged your intellect, your handling of the mental world. Ease of communication and interaction in the early environment is likely.

4: There is the potential of harmony in your handling of your nurturing and dependency needs. Your mother (or mother figure) could have encouraged your ability to care for others and to be cared for by others. Your early environment probably helped develop your warmth, compassion and ability to be emotionally committed to others.

5: There is the potential of harmony between your nurturing/dependency experiences and your ability to take the center stage. Your mother (or mother figure) could have encouraged your ability to shine, to be significant, to be noticed. Your early environment helped you to develop charisma, magnetism, sparkle and self-esteem. You learned to value and appreciate yourself as well as the positive response of others.

6: There is the potential of harmony between your nurturing/dependency experiences and your ability to be competent and productive. Your mother (or mother figure) could have encouraged your skill in getting the job done and being disciplined. Your early environment helped you to develop practicality, a focus on details, a desire for efficient functioning with health and work.

7: There is the potential of harmony between your nurturing/dependency experiences and your ability to be a partner. Your mother (or mother figure) could have encouraged your ability to share, to be an equal and to relate on the same level. Your early environment helped you to develop a sense of harmony, balance, aesthetic appreciation and/or competition.

8: There is the potential of harmony between your nurturing/dependency experiences and your desire for depth understanding. Your mother (or mother figure) could have encouraged your pursuit of fundamental answers, your desire to probe beneath the surface. Your early environment probably helped you to develop a sense of self-mastery and self-control.

9: There is the potential of harmony between your nurturing/dependency experiences and your desire to understand the meaning of the universe. Your mother (or mother figure) could have encouraged your pursuit of the truth, your search for answers. Your early environment probably helped you to develop a sense of ethics, morality and a belief system concerned with spiritual/religious/philosophical/scientific issues.

10: There is the potential of harmony between your nurturing/dependency experiences and your need to be practical and responsible. This can indicate harmony between your parents. It also represents your ability to be both warm and pragmatic; compassionate and realistic. Your early environment probably helped you in learning to balance outer world achievements with close, human interactions. You are likely to value both the caring of a family or nest and the satisfaction of accomplishments outside the home.

11: There is the potential of harmony between your nurturing/dependency experiences and your need to be a unique individual. Your mother (or mother figure) could have encouraged your sense of freedom and your need to find your own path. Your early environment probably helped you to develop your originality and inventiveness.

12: There is the potential of harmony between your nurturing/dependency experiences and your yearning to experience ultimate union. Your mother (or mother figure) could have encouraged you to seek a sense of merging with something higher through art, beauty, idealistic endeavors, healing activities or other forms of connecting to the infinite. Playing victim is one possible role. Your early environment probably helped you to develop a sense of faith and trust in the universe.

Conflict to Letter 4 (and Ceres)

1: There is the potential of contention between your nurturing/dependency experiences and your desire for personal freedom and self-expression. You could have experienced conflict with your mother (or mother figure) over issues of self-expression and doing your own thing. Perhaps you felt she stifled you; perhaps you felt she was too independent and not supportive enough when you needed her — or other options. The challenge is to integrate your desire for liberty and action as a single human being with your wish for close, caring interactions.

2: There is the potential of a struggle between your nurturing/dependency experiences and your desire for physical possessions and pleasures. You could have experienced conflict with your mother (or mother figure) over issues of money, sensual indulgences or comfort. Perhaps one of you saw the other as spoiled, self-indulgent or materialistic. The challenge is to integrate your desire for resources and enjoyment with your need to care and be cared for by others.

3: There is the potential of a struggle between your nurturing/dependency experiences and your intellectual understanding and communication. You could have experienced conflict with your mother (or mother figure) over issues of thinking, speaking, information and idea exchanges. Perhaps one of you saw the other as too flippant, lighthearted, talkative or cool, intellectual and aloof. The challenge is to integrate your mental and emotional sides, to have your thoughts and feelings reinforcing one another — not fighting.

4: There is the suggestion of an inner struggle — both within your own mother (or mother figure) and within you in terms of how you wish to care for others and be cared for by them. Ambivalence around the nurturing role is suggested and and potential conflict concerning dependency. Learning through the example of of your mother, you can choose a mode of emotional relating that is satisfactory to you. Select a style of nurturance and dependency that satisfies your needs.

5: There is the potential of a struggle between your nurturing/dependency experiences and your desire for self-esteem, admiration and response from others. You could have experienced conflict with your mother (or mother figure) over issues of being in the limelight, applause and needing to be important. Either of you could have tried to play the star too much. The challenge is to integrate your expressive, dramatic, dynamic side with your inward, sensitive and caring side.

6: There is the potential of a struggle between your nurturing/dependency experiences and your need to be competent, efficient and productive. You could have experienced conflicts with your mother (or mother figure) over issues of critical judgment (feeling put down), proper performance, discipline and hard work. The challenge is to integrate your practical, capable side with your warm, compassionate, protective side.

7: There is the potential of a struggle between your nurturing/dependency experiences and your desire for a committed, equalitarian relationship. You could have experienced conflicts with your mother (or mother figure) over issues of balance, harmony, aesthetics, competition or equality. You may feel torn between time and energy commitments to a home, nest and/or family versus attention spent on creating a satisfying partnership. The challenge is to integrate your differing relationships needs, creating space to be parental, dependent, vulnerable and a peer — perhaps at differing times and places in your life.

8: There is the potential of a struggle between your nurturing/dependency experiences and your desire for a depth exploration of self and basic needs. You could have experienced conflicts with your mother (or mother figure) over issues of power, appetite control, sensual and sexual resources, self-mastery and letting go. You may feel torn between relating as an equal versus playing parent to others or being parented by others. You may feel ambivalent about your dependency needs; you want closeness and intimacy, yet you do not want to give up control of your life. The challenge is to manifest your deeper feelings in fulfilling ways, achieving intimacy as a peer, as a protector and as a receiver.

9: There is the potential of a struggle between your nurturing/dependency experiences and your quest for ultimate answers. You could have experienced conflicts with your mother (or mother figure) over values, ethics, moral principles or religious/philosophical/spiritual ideals. You may feel torn between your need for a nest and your desire to search for the truth, wherever that takes you. The challenge is to seek your dreams while still maintaining close ties to people who matter.

10: There is the potential of a struggle between your nurturing/dependency experiences and your need to achieve in and control the external world. You may feel torn between dominance and dependency; vulnerability and power; emotions and pragmatism. You could have seen this inner struggle played out in conflicts between your parents. You must balance your own internal "mother" and "father" to create space in life for both caring and realism, emotional attachments and physical accomplishments. Seek compromises involving both compassion and the bottom line (practicalities).

11: There is the potential of a struggle between your nurturing/dependency experiences and your essential uniqueness. You could have experienced conflicts with your mother (or mother figure) over independence, the new or unusual, unconventionality and friendships. Whether you saw her as too free and easy (and not warm enough) or too possessive (and trying to hem you in), the challenge is to balance liberty and intimacy. Your sentimental attachments must be balanced with your thrust toward the future and progress. Both closeness needs and freedom needs must be met.

12: There is the potential of a struggle between your nurturing/dependency experiences and your yearning for ecstasy. You could have experienced conflicts with your mother (or mother figure) over areas of faith, trust, dreams, imagination, fantasy, art, beauty or beliefs. You may feel torn between uniting more with the people close to you (e.g., home, family) versus seeking a sense of Union with the universe.

Harmony to Letter 10 (and Sun)

1: There is potential harmony between your father (or authority figures) and yourself. This indicates inner agreement between your desire for self-assertion and your awareness of the rules of the game of life. You have the capacity to achieve a great deal, working sensibly and doing what is possible. If out of balance, you could succumb to giving up too soon or trying more than is reasonable, but generally you are a practical achiever.

2: There is potential harmony between your father (or authority figures) and your sensual, physical side. Your dad could have helped you to develop the capacity to make money, enjoy physical pleasures and appreciate beauty. You know how to blend hard work with indulgence and achieve a satisfying result.

3: There is potential harmony between your father (or authority figures) and your ability to think and communicate. Your dad could have helped you to develop your intellectual skills. You know how to blend the light, casual touch with a serious, productive effort.

4: There is the potential of harmony between your nurturing/dependency experiences and your need to be practical and responsible. This can indicate harmony between your parents. It also represents your ability to be both warm and pragmatic; compassionate and realistic. Your early environment probably helped you in learning to balance outer world achievements with close, human interactions. You are likely to value both the caring of a family or nest and the satisfaction of accomplishments outside the home.

5: There is potential harmony between your father (or authority figures) and your need to be dynamic, applauded and appreciated. Your dad could have helped you to develop your ability to shine and be center stage. Your sense of personal power and prominence could have been enhanced by his responsibility and pragmatism. You have the ability to make a significant impact on others and the world.

6: There is potential harmony between your father (or authority figures) and your need to be competent, capable and productive. Your dad could have encouraged your hardworking, practical side. He may have been supportive of your desire to do things well. You have the ability to achieve much through concentrated efforts, discipline and a determination to perform well.

7: There is potential harmony between your father (or authority figures) and your need to maintain lasting, one-to-one relationships. Your dad could have encouraged you to develop a firm sense of equality and the ability to meet others on their level. His support might have furthered your aesthetic talents, competitive spirit and/or sense of balance and harmony.

8: There is potential harmony between your father (or authority figures) and your need to dig beneath the surface of life for insight and understanding. Your dad could have encouraged you to develop a penchant for incisive questions, thorough analysis, probing of motivations and need for self-control. Giving, receiving and sharing material resources and pleasures would be learned partly through your relationship to him.

9: There is potential harmony between your father (or authority figures) and your search for ultimate answers. Your dad could have encouraged your quest for the meaning of life — through travel, education, philosophy, religion, spiritual paths or other forms of looking for answers. His expectations and ideals probably had a strong impact on you.

10: There is potential harmony in your handling of power, responsibility, authority and control issues. Your father (or authority figures) could have encouraged you to develop realism, practicality, ambition and a focus on performance. Your career achievements could be supported by him. You know how to sensibly achieve your ambitions.

11: There is potential harmony between your father (or authority figures) and you need for personal uniqueness and individuality. You dad could have encouraged you to be original, inventive and avant garde. He may have been supportive of your innovative, rebellious side. You can be yourself, yet still be effective within the structure of society.

12: There is potential harmony between your father (or authority figures) and your yearning for an emotional absolute. Your dad could have encouraged you to seek a sense of connection to the cosmos through religion, alcohol, helping activities, beauty or other forms of merging with the universe. You probably have some caretaking instincts.

Conflict to Letter 10 (and Sun)

1: There is the potential of conflict between you and your father (or authority figures). You are learning to balance self-will with the limits of what is possible and authorities are the first external manifestations of limits. Pushing too hard is not a solution, nor is giving up and not trying. The middle ground is to figure out what is possible, in the given situation, and do all that you can.

2: There is the potential of conflict between your needs for authority, control, power and your desire for physical possessions, pleasure and comfort. This could manifest as contention with your father (or authority figures) over issues of money, appetite indulgence or ease. You may experience inner tension between the drive to work hard and achieve versus the desire to kick back and enjoy life. Keep room for both.

3: There is the potential of conflict between your desire for authority, control, power and your intellectual, communicative needs. This could express as struggles with your father (or authority figures) over issues of information, discussion, communication or the mental world. Your (or his) standards of performance could inhibit easy communication and/or learning or you might express in a critical, judgmental manner. Your mind can back up your power and vice versa, once integrated.

4: There is the potential of a struggle between your nurturing/dependency experiences and your need to achieve in and control the external world. You may feel torn between dominance and dependency; vulnerability and power; emotions and pragmatism. You could have seen this inner struggle played out in conflicts between your parents. You must balance your own internal "mother" and "father" to create space in life for both caring and realism, emotional attachments and physical accomplishments. Seek compromises involving both compassion and the bottom line (practicalities).

5: There is the potential of conflict between your drive for responsibility practicality and realistic achievements versus your desire to shine and be significant in the world. You may have power struggles with your father (or authority figures) over issues of control, importance and dominance. You are learning to integrate two different routes to power: through charisma, persuasion and magnetism as well as through hard work, perseverance and discipline.

6: There is the potential of conflict between your desire for authority, control, power and your need to get the job done well. You could engage in struggles with your father (or authority figures) over issues of competence, discipline and practicality. You might end up working too hard, carrying more than your share of the workload as you do not trust other people to perform as well as you do. You might also end up feeling blocked and inhibited, judging that your performance will be inadequate before you even try. Health problems could result from overwork or as an unconscious escape from feeling guilty about not doing as much as you feel you ought. The challenge is to be realistic without being excessively pessimistic or too hard on yourself.

7: There is the potential of conflict between your desire for authority, control, power and your drive for a committed, long-term relationship. This could surface in disagreements with your father (or authority figures) over issues of equality, competition, relationships or balance and harmony. You may feel that your career and achievement needs are at odds with your wish for a significant, sharing relationship. You are learning to balance partnership with work; equality with control.

8: There is the potential of conflict between your desire for authority, control, power with your drive for a depth understanding of underlying motivations. One option is power struggles with your father (or authority figures) over issues of analysis, probing questions, joint resources, sexuality and emotionally letting go of situations. You are learning to use discipline and self-control wisely — neither too much nor too little.

9: There is the potential of conflict between your desire for authority, control, power and your quest for ultimate answers to the meaning of life. You could experience contention with your father (or authority figures) around issues of ethics, morality, world views, principles and long-range goals. You are learning to bring your dreams to earth and make them real. Balance optimism and pessimism. Keep dreams to reach for without selling yourself short, but also without demanding more than is reasonable.

10: There is the potential of an inner conflict within your own father (or authority figures) and within yourself in terms of the handling of power, responsibility, authority, control and realism. Your career aspirations may be at odds with one another. You may be torn between different paths to success. Reality testing is essential. Avoid stopping yourself with excessive criticism or judgment. Likewise bypass opportunities to push too hard, trying more than is reasonable. Do all that you can to achieve concrete, measurable results in the world.

11: There is the potential of a conflict between your desire for authority, control, power and your desire to be humanitarian, equalitarian and friends with everybody. You may feel torn between conventionality and unconventionality; traditions and the new. This could also express as contention with your father (or authority figures) around issues of personal freedom, uniqueness, social causes, progressive ideas, friends and new age principles.

12: There is the potential of a conflict between your desire for authority, control, power and your yearning to merge with the Infinite. This might manifest as disagreements with your father (or authority figures) over issues of beauty, idealism, religion, faith, healing, fantasy and imagination. You are learning to blend inspiration with plain, old hard work for optimum results.

CHAPTER SIXTEEN

GROWTH AREAS

Growth areas refer to issues which we find difficult to ignore this lifetime. The themes involved are important for us to face, but often point to areas where we experience personal discomfort. The tendency is, where our growth areas are involved, to overdo or underdo. We may exaggerate the energy involved and carry it to an extreme. We also may sit on our potential, repressing our abilities and perhaps attracting other people who will do to excess what we do not allow within ourselves. Sometimes we are dealing inappropriately with a potential learning experience by overdoing the energy in one part of our life and underdoing it in another.

While reading this section, keep in mind a few questions:

Am I expressing this potential in a balanced way?
Am I carrying this theme too far in any area of my life?
Am I refusing to acknowledge this potential within myself?
How can I express the possibilities indicated here most positively?

The potential life experiences indicated by these areas are called "*karmic* lessons" by some astrologers. Basically, *karma* simply means consequences — the principle of "As ye sow, so shall ye reap." *Karma* can point to established patterns, and growth sometimes necessitates changing our set patterns. Evolution and development on all levels — physical, mental, emotional and spiritual — requires some effort, attention and discipline from us. This chapter points to issues requiring our attention.

It is important to remember that *karma* is "positive" as well as "negative." Skills we have built in the past are as *karmic* as lessons we are still learning. Any task which we master currently becomes a solid foundation for us to depend upon and from which we can assist others.

The challenge of our *karmic* lesson(s) is to master the themes involved, and then share our understanding with others. Once we gain a positive manifestation of a lesson area, it becomes something we can teach to others. Growth is contagious. As you spiral upwards, you inspire others to join you.

If you have already balanced the themes involved here, the growth goal is sharing that integration with others.

The Factors

Saturn and the south node of the Moon are considered, by many astrologers, *karmic* points. Thus, themes in common between them would represent potential challenges or growth areas. All forms of Letter 10, including Capricorn and the 10th house, could be considered if you wished, not limiting the focus to Saturn. (You could also argue that all of water — planets, houses and signs — is also *"karmic"* inasmuch as it involves the past, presumably including past lives. As a reader, you are free to change the list of factors you consider, if you feel another definition is more apt.) Here, we will consider:[1]

GROUP I
Planets conjuncting Saturn and the south node

GROUP II
Planets parallel Saturn and the south node
House placements of Saturn and the south node
Sign placements of Saturn and the south node
House(s) ruled by Saturn

GROUP III
Aspects (other than conjunction or parallel) to Saturn and the south node broken
  down into planet, house and sign making the aspect

---

1. If you prefer **not** to search for repeated themes yourself, you can order the "PP BOOK" option from Astro Computing Services (PO Box 16430, San Diego, Ca 92116), which allows you to use this book to make complete, synthesizing delineations of horoscopes without figuring out which themes are emphasized.

Available for $3.00 each, the "PP BOOK" report calculates the emphasis on all the letters of the alphabet, themes and aspects in each horoscope for which you provide the data. The report lists each significant focus (e.g., "There is a Letter 12 theme in "Growth Areas," and gives the appropriate page numbers for you to read in this book ("See pages 436-437 in the *Complete Horoscope Interpretation* book.")

The computer will not **always** arrive at the same results as you might, as certain steps are ambiguous (e.g., how much weight to give a planet making a conjunction, based on the orb). However, the majority of the time, the computer answers will concur with those derived from use of the worksheets — or the recommended quick scan of a horoscope. Thus it provides an excellent teaching tool.

The "PP BOOK" does **not** provide a listing of **each and every** astrological factor making up the significant themes. For that, you would order "PP WEIGHTS" (discussed in next footnote).

How to Weight the Factors

The factors are rank ordered according to their weight, broken into chunks. The basic assumption here is that any alphabet or other theme which appears more than once (other than conjunctions) is significant. Conjunctions, in and of themselves, are enough to qualify as a theme.[2]

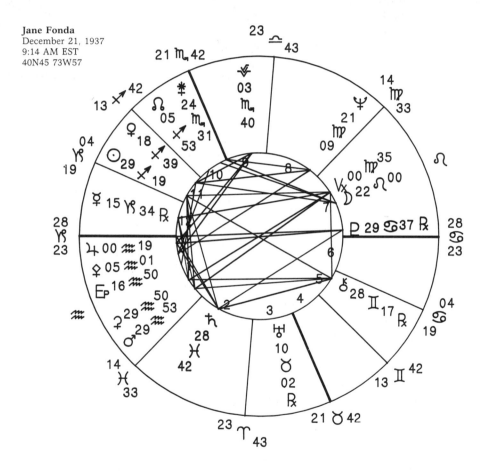

Jane Fonda
December 21, 1937
9:14 AM EST
40N45 73W57

2. You can also obtain a listing of **all** the astrological factors which compose those letters of the Zip Code determined to be significant in a horoscope. This makes an excellent teaching tool and a valuable resource to check yourself against when practicing with the Zip Code.

Astro Computing Services, PO Box 16430, San Diego, CA 92116, has calculated 28,000 horoscopes and established averages and standard deviations for the scores of each letter of the astrological alphabet, each theme, and the conflict and harmony aspects to each life area.

Astro's report, called "PP WEIGHTS," will list those letters of the astrological alphabet which are one standard deviation or more above the mean — and list **all** the astrological factors which (footnote continued on next page)

A SHORT CUT

If an instance of Group I occurs, read the appropriate paragraphs below, bearing in mind the above questions regarding overdoing, underdoing or displacing the energy involved with the issues being faced. You may also wish to refer back to the discussions in Chapters 3 and 4 of the alphabet and the various themes, in considering whether you have integrated these issues as yet or not. (The Fonda chart has no instances of a theme with Group I.)

For Group II, if there is a letter of the alphabet or theme which is repeated (occurring two or more times), read that interpretation below (and in Chapters 3 or 4). In the case of Jane Fonda's chart, Letter 12 repeats: Saturn in Pisces (12) and Saturn ruling the 12th (12). Letters 1, 2, 3 and 4 all occur once.

Themes

Even though there may not be a repeated theme for one letter of the astrological alphabet, other themes commonly exist. The theme of mutability repeats in Jane Fonda's case, as both Saturn and the south node occupy mutable signs. You would read the description of the mutable quality below (and in Chapter 4), weighing whether that theme is integrated, or might be insufficiently expressed or overdone.

Ms. Fonda's life affirms that she has expressed some of the multiple talents implied by a mutable focus, but she has had to pull back from the overextension which can be a problem. Her ideals remain an ongoing issue in her life, with tension between the way she would like the world to be and the way it actually is. She appears to have found a compromise position which allows her to work successfully, while funneling money into causes which she supports. She seems to have avoided the extremes of excessive cynicism (forsaking ideals) and excessive idealism (too starry-eyed to face reality). Hopefully, she has an excellent balance between her enthusiasm, faith and optimism versus her practicality, caution and pessimism.

Any theme whose letters occur three or more times through Group II placements should be included in the analysis.

---

2. (continued from previous page)
point to each significant letter of the alphabet. These weightings will also compare each individual's score on the various themes (e.g., risk-taking, artistic) to the means and standard deviations to determine which themes are significant.

Averages are established for aspects as well in order to note conflict or harmony in the different life areas.

The results obtained by Astro's "PP WEIGHTS" will not **always** coincide with those you determine by a quick scan and intuitive judgment, or by use of the worksheets. Certain of the steps (e.g., how much to weight a planet based on orb) are ambiguous, so different results can occur. However, most of the time, Astro's answers will confirm those you could obtain in working with the Zip Code. Furthermore, the **complete** listing of relevant factors is an excellent teaching tool.

Ask for "PP Weights." The price, as of December 1985 is $5.00

Aspects

For the aspects, scan the aspects (other than conjunctions) to Saturn and the south node, weighting planets most, then houses then signs. You can get an intuitive feel for whether any factor in the Zip Code is emphasized by aspects.

If you prefer to use numbers: count the nature of the planet making the aspect 3 points, the house that planet is in 2 points and the sign occupied by the planet 1 point. Give two points to the house on whose cusp a sign ruled by that planet falls. Total the points from all aspects for each letter of the astrological alphabet. If any total is five points or more, read the appropriate interpretation.

As an example, Jane Fonda's Saturn:

- squares the Sun (3 points for Letter 5) in the 11 (2 points for Letter 11) in Sagittarius (1 point for Letter 9)
- squares Chiron (1-1/2 points for Letter 9) in the 5th (2 points for Letter 5) in Gemini (1 point for Letter 3)

Ms. Fonda had to come to terms with the idealized image of her father (Saturn in Pisces and Sun in Sagittarius) as an actor and her own self-critical tendencies before she allowed her natural dynamism, magnetism and creativity (Letter 5) full flower. (Since Letters 5, 9 and 11 are all involved and include three of our four risk-taking letters, we might also suspect that Ms. Fonda faces issues around taking chances — knowing when it is appropriate to push, to risk, to fly toward the future, and when it is appropriate to be more conservative.)

Aspects are not counted in a separate section for "Growth Areas." If there is a repeated theme among the aspects to Saturn and/or the south node, that is a *karmic* lesson. Simply read the appropriate section here (and in Chapters 3 or 4).

Interpretations: Growth Areas

ALPHABET THEMES

Letter 1: Being Yourself

The themes revolve around assertion, independence, courage and self-expression. Whether the lesson is a case of too much or too little, the challenge is to **appropriately** manifest your basic potential — without running roughshod over others, but also without allowing others to overpower you. Courage, strength, freedom and self-will are all part of the focus — being able to express them in fulfilling ways in life.

Letter 2: Enjoying Yourself

Themes revolve around sensuality, indulgence, physical appetites, possessions, pleasures, money and security. The challenge is to be able to enjoy the sense world without being ruled by it — to handle money and pleasures in a reasonable, sensible manner — without overindulgence or excessive denial. Balanced attitudes toward money and material goods are being called for.

Letter 3: Objectivity Without Aloofness

Issues include the light touch, detachment, interest in a variety of areas, communication and the mind. The challenge could revolve around your mental or communicative capacities. Perhaps you talk **too** much, perhaps too little. It might be that you are afraid to utilize your mind, or do not really trust it. You may be excessively objective or be learning to cultivate the ability to be detached and uninvolved.

Letter 4: Emotional Needs

The themes here range around dependency, nurturance, emotional security, caretaking and the home. You might be learning how to **be** dependent — or how **not** to be dependent. Perhaps nurturance is a focus — faced through family, friends, pets or other sources. Your home environment can be a place of much growth and development.

Letter 5: Self-Esteem

The fascination is with charisma, ambition, power, loving and being loved, emotional feedback and self-esteem. Whether the instance is one of an excess of pride, drama, self-aggrandizement or other forms of hogging the limelight, **or** a case of needing to appreciate oneself more, the challenge is to build self-esteem, to allow one's natural magnetism to flourish. Growth and evolution comes through confronting the issue of being center stage, doing more than has been done before in life and gaining adulation for it.

Letter 6: Getting the Job Done (But Not Overdone)

The challenge is to successfully face the need to be efficient and productive — both in work and in health. Whether the issue revolves around working **too** hard or not hard enough, the theme is learning to deal with productivity, effectiveness and taking care of business. Sometimes the issue revolves around maintaining a healthy body — paying proper attention to rest, diet, exercise, etc. A challenge may be to keep the work attitude (critical, judgmental) from spilling over into more personal, emotional sides of life (e.g., love relationships).

Letter 7: Justice, Fair Play and Beauty

Themes include equality, balance, harmony, aesthetics and one-to-one interactions. Challenges can range from excessive competitiveness, to a tendency toward appeasement to a lack of balance. Issues around beauty and appearance may be central (e.g., too much concern with the appearance of things and/or people, discomfort with disharmony, lack of appreciation for aesthetics, etc.).

Letter 8: Intimacy Issues

The principles involved concern self-mastery and self-control, especially in relationship matters. The arenas of shared resources, possessions and pleasures can be a focus of learning. The lesson is to be able to give, receive and share money, sex and pleasures with other human beings in comfortable, appropriate ways. Excessive manipulation, power plays or self-denial are all various sides of a challenge in this area.

Letter 9: Faith, Trust and Beliefs

Goals, ideals, visions, philosophies and belief systems are the focus or concentration. The lesson often revolves around faith — too much, too little, or in the wrong area (such as worshipping another human being instead of God). The search for life's meaning is central here. Meeting the challenge includes achieving a reachable sense of faith and purpose in life without demanding more than is possible from ourselves, the world or other people. It includes having something to strive for, but being able to enjoy the journey **toward** our goals.

Letter 10: Limits Without Limitation

Pragmatism, power, responsibility, authority, the structures of society and the world are a part of this challenge. Finding our own internal power, strength and authority is the goal — without succumbing to a sense of worthlessness (because we never do "enough") but also without falling into a need to control anything and everything in our life. We need enough structure and order to make practical decisions, but enough flexibility to change when appropriate.

Letter 11: Innovation Without Anarchy

Themes revolve around uniqueness, rebellion, progress, the new, the different, the unusual, technology and the widest reach of humanity. We can overdo or underdo our need for individual self-expression, to be exactly who we are without fitting anyone else's molds, roles or preconceptions. The new needs to be fit into our lives in an appropriate manner — neither too much nor too little. Technology is a tool to be used wisely. Openness and tolerance are healthy qualities. However, like anything, they can be carried too far — into putting up with weird, flaky, irresponsible behavior that is not constructive. Discover your unique essence and express it.

Letter 12: Cosmic Consciousness

A sense of Oneness with the Universe is the calling here. Faith on an unconscious level is part of the challenge. We may have too much (like expecting God to balance the checkbook), too little (afraid to trust) or faith in the wrong areas (trying to play savior to another human being). A sense of mystical connection may be sought through limited avenues such as drugs, alcohol, psychosis. Spiritual studies and religious pursuits are another option. The lesson is to develop a satisfying sense of connection with the Infinite, a supportive feeling of meaning and purpose in life.

ALPHABET COMBINATIONS BY TWOS
Refer to Chapters 6 and 9 and read the appropriate **Combinations by Two**, thinking in terms of potential overdoing or underdoing and how you can contribute this theme to the world if you have integrated the area.

POLARITIES

The Self/Other Polarity
1-7: ♂-♀ or ♀ or ⚸, ♈-♎, 1st-7th houses

The lesson is to balance self-will with the need for relationships. Avoiding the extremes of too much aggression or assertion or too much giving in and giving up to "make peace" is important. Compromise is an issue. Learn to negotiate fairly, to reach a middle ground satisfying to both parties. Do not give up all your own needs and wants, nor trample too heavily on the desires and needs of the other person. Share. Cooperate.

Indulgence/Self-Mastery Polarity
2-8: ♀-♇, ♉-♏, 2nd-8th houses

The challenge is to balance appetite indulgence with appetite control and the battle grounds could range from sex to money to food to alcohol or other sensual pleasures. Total withdrawal, abstinence and asceticism is not a balanced path; neither is a reckless, self-centered hedonism. Relationships could draw you into power struggles around spending versus saving money, who has control of the finances, differing modes of sexual pleasure, etc. The goal is to be able to give, receive and share pleasures and resources with another person in a context of intimacy and equality. The more you are balanced internally — able to enjoy the physical world without being controlled by it — the more balanced your relationships are likely to be.

Short-term/Long-term Polarity
3-9: ☿-♃ or ♄, ♊-♐, 3rd-9th houses

A balance sought is between the present and the future, the long-range view and short range needs. The consensual reality of other people must be balanced with your dreams, visions and hopes for the future. Communication must be on a common level, despite our own internal hopes and aspirations. Keeping the mind too focused on either end (concepts, ideas, people right around us versus future goals, ideals and the pull from above) can result in imbalance. Both contribute to a full life. Both enjoy the mind, learning, studying, teaching, traveling and sharing information.

Closeness/Control Polarity
4-10: ☽-♄, ♋-♑, 4th-10th houses

The balance sought is between caring, compassion and concern versus pragmatism, achievement needs and realism. Emotions must be balanced with results. An integration is sought between the task orientation and the emotional, supportive role. Neither one by itself is sufficient. They need each other for optimum teamwork.

Emotions/Intellect Polarity
5-11: ☉-♅, ♌-♒, 5th-11th houses

A blend is needed between the passions and the intellect. The calls of the heart must be mixed with the inclinations of the head. Intensity and detachment can both contribute to a useful end result if they do not fight one another. The need to feel special and "better than" in some fashion must confront the sense of everyone being equal and deserving of equal opportunity. Equality and special privileges vie for recognition as we make choices. Love relationships and friendships are arenas to face these issues as we learn to make peace between freedom and closeness; fiery emotions and intellectual objectivity; specialness and equality.

Real/Ideal Polarity
6-12: ☿ or ♀ or ♆-♆, ♍-♓, 6th-12th houses

The arena for integration here is your great, beautiful dream versus the reality of what is possible in the physical world. Bringing your visions into concrete manifestation is part of the challenge. Succumbing to the extreme of staying lost in the clouds, or your own internal world and daydreams is no solution. But neither is a locked-in, workaholic, excessively "practical" attitude an answer. Both inspiration and hard work are necessary.

ELEMENT EMPHASIS

Fire
♂, ☉, ♃, ♃, ♈, ♌, ♐,1st, 5th, 9th houses

The theme revolves around confidence, spontaneity, courage, risk-taking and action. If underdone, you may feel insecure, afraid to try, inhibited, unwilling to act naturally, threatened and fearful of doing your own thing. Exercises to encourage self-esteem, faith, zest, enthusiasm and assertiveness can all be helpful. Pay attention to the times in your life when you get positive feedback for being strong, quick, vibrant and active. Reward yourself for those behaviors.

If overdone, you may be prone to hasty, rash, impulsive and foolish behaviors. Your courage may outweigh your caution and common sense. Your determination to live life on your own terms, doing things **your** way may hurt other people. Your faith may be excessive. Practicing patience, follow through and empathy can help to balance your rapid-fire approach to life.

Earth
♀, ♄, ?, ⚵, ♂, ♍, ♑, 2nd, 6th, 10th houses

The theme involves pragmatism, focus, ability to work and dealing with the "real" (physical) world. If underdone, you may feel a lack of grounding. Abstractions and imaginative ventures may easily sweep you into grandiose schemes and dreams with little reality. Plain, old hard work may have little appeal. The nitty-gritty details may turn you off. Earthly matters could appear much less significant than spiritual issues. Practicality may be your weakest suit. Literal contact with the earth can be helpful in such cases: gardening, feeling the soil with your feet, being in the outdoors. Learning to focus and concentrate, dealing with details one at a time in a linear fashion can also encourage the development of your earthy side.

If overdone, you could feel stolid, heavy, and be a typical "salt of the earth" individual — hardworking, capable, reasonable, respectable — and probably not feeling very exciting or excited. Remember that all of life is not practical; not everything can be measured and quantified in a physical manner. Appreciate your artistic, aesthetic, abstract and divine qualities as well as your ability to calculate the bottom line and deal with it sensibly.

Air
☿, ♀, ✴, ♀, ♅, ♊, ♎, ♒, 3rd, 7th, 11th houses

The theme revolves around the mind, communication, intellect and detachment. If underdone, you may feel sadly lacking in any of these areas. You could doubt your mental capacities; feel blocked as a communicator; be intensely emotionally involved in everything in your life. In such a case, the challenge is to learn how to just float sometimes — watching the world go by. The need is to learn to appreciate your own mental style and understanding of life without criticizing, judging, denying or comparing to other people.

If you are carrying this theme too far, you are a rationalizer par excellence. Whatever happens, you can come up with a reason and an excuse on a moment's notice. You can explain away almost everything and are often quite glib. People may experience you as someone easy to talk to, but difficult to get close to, because you share lots of words but few feelings. You can change **if** you decide that emotions are as important as rationality; that caring is as significant as logic. If you continue to overvalue ''knowing'' everything (on an intellectual level), your heart will continue to be denied while the head reigns supreme.

Water
☽, ♇, ♆, ♋, ♏, ♓, 4th, 8th, 12th houses

Deep feelings, the watery realm of emotions is the issue. How do you deal with buffeting waves of emotions? Do you run away and try to deny that you have reactions? Are you hiding behind a rational/logical front that claims nothing phases you? Do you stay with surface meanings because you fear the depths of feelings could end up drowning you? Do you allow your sensitivity, empathy and intuition to enrich your life — or flee from them lest you be hurt?

If overdone, you may be wallowing in a swamp of intense emotions. You may feel the slightest interpersonal jars as severe affronts and personal put downs. You may experience the world as overwhelming in its impact on your feeling nature. You may be caught in a wheels-within-wheels sensation, like a whirlpool feeding itself as various reactions coalesce and combine within you. How can you put your sensitivity, empathy and psychic understanding to use helping yourself and others?

Fire-Earth
♂, ☉, ♃, ♆, ♈, ♌, ♐, 1st, 5th, 9th houses
♀, ♄, ?, ♇, ♉, ♍, ♑, 2nd, 6th, 10th houses

The key here is confidence with capability.

If overdone, you are likely to overwhelm other people, as you determinedly pursue whatever your goals are with ambition and endurance. You may sometimes regret the end results of your actions, because you were too focused on getting something done to question whether you really **wanted** what the likely outcome would be.

If underdone, you may tend to drift through life, to react rather than act, to allow others to do the initiating. You may prefer a rich inner life to an active outer one. Learning to master the outside world and accomplish some dreams is an important part of your work this lifetime.

Fire-Air
♂, ☉, ♃, ♆, ♈, ♌, ♐, 1st, 5th, 9th houses
☿, ♀, *, ♀, ♅, ♊, ♎, ♒, 3rd, 7th, 11th houses

The key here is liveliness and conviviality.

If overdone, you are the life of the party, the original rolling stone, the happy-go-lucky, hail-well-met individual who never meets a person that s/he cannot like. Optimistic and active, you tend to flit from flower to flower in many areas of your life and may have to learn to make commitments and to deal with the less fun sides of life.

If underdone, you are likely to be overly serious, self-conscious, afraid of how you come across to others. You may be studied and step-by-step, holding back your spontaneous reactions. Your "realistic" attitude is sometimes just a justification of inner pessimism. Learning to "lighten up" is part of your lesson. The other part is really **liking** yourself — both when you are serious and when you are fun!

Fire-Water
♂, ☉, ♃, ♅, ♈, ♌, ♐, 1st, 5th, 9th houses
☽, ♇, ♆, ♋, ♏, ♓, 4th, 8th, 12th houses

The issues here are intensity and emotionality.

If overdone, you may come across as erratic, blowing hot and cold, up and down, happy and depressed, spontaneous and clinging to security. You are likely to have extraordinarily intense emotional reactions to life and other people. You are not a halfhearted person; you tend to love and hate with equal fervor. Capable of tremendous warmth and caring, you relate most often on a feeling level.

If underdone, you may shun the morass of emotions. Perceiving feelings as a quicksand or quagmire, you will stay on the safe, dry land of rationality and intellectualization. Fearful of being swept away by intense emotions, you may avoid the feeling side of your nature. Learning to appreciate and utilize the driving, energizing powers of your emotional reactions is an important lesson.

Earth-Air
♀, ♄, ?, ♇, ♉, ♍, ♑, 2nd, 6th, 10th houses
☿, ♀, ✷, ?, ♅, ♊, ♎, ♒, 3rd, 7th, 11th houses

The issues here are logic and practicality.

If overdone, you can come across as unflappable. You could be so logical, rational, careful, cautious and sensible, people may wonder if you ever cry, ever laugh, ever act on impulse. Calm, cool, collected, you believe that the mind can handle just about anything and emotions may strike you as disorganized, foolish and just a wee bit nasty!

If underdone, extreme emotionality is likely. Detachment may be a challenge and learning to be logical a lesson.

Earth-Water
♀, ♄, ?, ♇, ♉, ♍, ♑, 2nd, 6th, 10th houses
☽, ♇, ♆, ♋, ♏, ♓, 4th, 8th, 12th houses

The themes involve nurturance, productivity and stability.

If overdone, a likely result is that you are carrying the world on your back — doing more than your share of everything, trying to take care of everyone. Extreme compassion is likely and you may be highly effective, but inclined to take on too much responsibility. You may take yourself and life too seriously at times. You may resist needed changes. You may be too busy seeking your own security to be concerned with anyone else. You could be centered on protecting yourself and gaining material goods.

If underdone, you could be learning to develop perseverance and steadiness. Accustomed to flitting from one thing to another (or one person to another), you may resist settling down to finish up a job or to deal with a relationship. You might prefer playing to working and a casual, carefree approach to a careful, considered one. Following through and completing projects may be a challenge. Learning to be nurturant might be a lesson.

Air-Water

☿, ♀, ⚵, ⚶, ♅, ♊, ♎, ♒, 3rd, 7th, 11th houses
☽, ♇, ♆, ♋, ♏, ♓, 4th, 8th, 12th houses

The issues revolve around an inner perspective — thinking and feeling.

If overdone, others could perceive you as nebulous, misty-headed and unclear. Usually engrossed in a rich inner life with a creative imagination, you may not relate well in the outer, physical reality. Perhaps you prefer your own realms of wonder to consensual reality. Perhaps you prefer dreaming to doing.

If underdone, external reality may be your primary focus. Acting and affecting the world may take precedence over thinking and imagining. Developing your intuition, knowing when to float and just observe the world, allowing life to happen, without feeling a need to always push may be challenges.

QUALITY EMPHASIS

Cardinal

♂, ☽, ♀, ⚵, ⚶, ♄, ♈, ♋, ♎, ♑, 1st, 4th, 7th, 10th houses

The issues revolve around balancing major life sectors and handling overt, structural changes in the course of your life. The major areas which you are striving to integrate include personal self-expression and development, home and family, partnership needs and career aspirations. You could slip into emphasizing any of these areas at the expense of any of the others. For you, a complete life requires involvement with all four.

This struggle is often felt on the inner level as tension between self-assertion, dependency and nurturance needs, a drive for equality and a drive for power and authority. Each of these basic motivations needs an outlet in your life. Trying to fit it all together often results in major life shifts. You may experience a number of changes of residence, job, relationships, health or personal actions and attitudes. Some are likely to be directly sought by you; others will come through unconscious attraction. (For example, when we despise the job we have, we can act — unconsciously — in such a manner as to get fired.)

Balance allows you to include these major life sectors with time and energy for each. You can harmonize them, so they support one another. Integration also includes an awareness of the importance of learning through experience. You tend to attract events and changes into your life so that you can understand the issues. You learn best through doing, through the actual experience of what is happening. Crises become opportunities for growth and evolution.

Fixed

♀, ☉, ♇, ⚷, ♉, ♌, ♏, ♒, 2nd, 5th, 8th, 11th houses

The issues revolve around the handling of power, especially in sharing the material, physical, sensual and sexual world. Appetite indulgence and appetite control may be important focuses.

The challenge is being able to give, to receive and to share comfortably where money, resources and pleasures are concerned. If out of balance, you could have difficulties in any of these areas. Some people find giving easy, but are inhibited from receiving. Some people happily accept, but may experience challenges in giving to others. Some individuals can both give and receive, but tend to turn the situation into a power struggle, keeping score in a competitive manner and not easily meeting another person on the same level.

Using sex, money or possessions as a weapon; trying to control the other person for one's own gratification are negative forms of this challenge. Similarly, you could attract people into your life who are power-hungry and inclined to use intimidation, power plays and/or tears, threats or other forms of emotional blackmail.

Learning to compromise and cooperate; valuing your pleasures and those of a partner equally; making room to enjoy the physical world without being ruled by it, can all contribute to a comfortable expression of this theme. Denial and asceticism is not an answer. Neither is overindulgence (be it in food, sex, alcohol, making money, spending money or other physical outlets). The urge is toward intimacy — truly meeting another human being on a peer level and being able to share resources and the sensual/sexual realm for mutual satisfaction.

Mutable

☿, ⚳, ⚵, ♃, ⚷, ⚷, ♊, ♍, ♐, ♓, 3rd, 6th, 9th, 11th houses

The themes revolve around thinking, communicating, consensual reality and ideals. Flexibility, adaptability and versatility are highlighted. If these qualities are carried to an extreme, you may be learning to be more focused, to establish priorities, to choose among your many interests and talents which one(s) to pursue at a given moment. Expectations can be an issue. Excessive idealism may be a challenge, the tendency to want more than is possible — from life in general, relationships, work, yourself or other areas. Realism must balance your visions. Another potential focus is to make peace between your inner dreams and consensual reality — not to value one over the other, but being able to blend and combine.

If this is a theme you are learning to express, the emphasis is on developing the ability to bend, to adapt, to learn vicariously. Thinking, theorizing and planning ahead, can be more helpful than charging into life. Information gleaned from observing others, reading and studying may enable you to sidestep the traumas direct experience can bring. Openness is being called for, an awareness of the multiplicity of options that lie before you at any given moment.

THEMES

Freedom
♂, ♃, ♅, ♅, ♈, ♐, ♒, 1st, 9th, 11th houses

A major focus is on personal freedom and independence. If the question is one of excess, you are likely to be too concerned with your own liberty, intent on maintaining space, unwilling to commit to others, determined to keep your options open and yourself fancy free. You may go so far as to split when you feel emotional entanglements are in the offing.

If the issue is that you need to be developing this ability, you are probably constrained and restrained in some way in your life. Whether through the dictates of duty and conscience, the needs of other people, your concern for convention or other pressures, you probably feel you do not get to do much of what you want to do. Rather, you do what you have to, what is necessary, what will please others. Learning to act as a free soul can be a challenge. This can include independence of emotions, the ability to love freely and openly without getting enmeshed in security needs. The necessary freedoms include the ability to know what you want and to act upon it, the ability to pursue the truth wherever it takes you and an appreciation of your own uniqueness with the pursuit of new ideas, approaches and avenues in life.

Closeness or Interpersonal
☽, ☉, ♀, ⚹, ♀, ♇, ♋, ♌, ♎, ♏, 4th, 5th, 7th, 8th houses

These themes revolve around sharing, intimacy and one-to-one exchanges. Issues include equality, competition, nurturance, support and vulnerability, the ability to receive. Any side of these potentials could be excessively developed with concomitant excesses in fighting to always "win," dependency, caretaking, "smothering mothering," sensitivity, etc.

The opposite side is a discomfort with the feeling side of life, with the desire for closeness. This could express as fear of intimacy, avoidance of getting emotionally involved, withdrawal from relating. Your needs for an emotional connection must be met in some positive fashion.

Artistic

♀, ☉, ♆, ⚵, ⚴, ♉, ♌, ♎, ♓, 2nd, 5th, 7th, 12th houses

The theme revolves around beauty and aesthetics. This could range from an over appreciation of beauty to an excessive focus on appearance. You might be so invested in having everything lovely, attractive and flowing that you have difficulties in coping with life when it is not smooth and easy. Or, you could be too concerned with your own appearance, the physical looks of other people, or how situations seem.

Another option is that you might be denying yourself certain beauty outlets that are very natural and worthwhile. From feelings of inadequacy, inferiority, harsh judgments or other blocks, you might be afraid to express your feelings for beauty, or resist your aesthetic impulses.

Idealistic

♃, ⚷, ♆, ♐, ♓, 9th, 12th houses

The theme revolves around idealism and expectations. One danger is expecting more than is reasonable — whether from yourself, other people, a situation, a job or life in general. Making discriminations as to what is truly achievable is helpful. Extending your time table for success can also be an excellent move. Remembering you are human never hurts. Being able to accept and learn from your mistakes (not chastising or punishing yourself) is very important.

Another side is denying your reach for something more, something higher. You could blindfold yourself to your aspirations, ignore the inner reaching, deny your dreams. You could draw in other people to express this side for you, but they would be likely to carry it to extremes such as too much idealism, martyrdom or talking themselves into believing everything is wonderful even when it isn't. Having dreams is vital; pursuing them in a realistic manner is also essential.

Obsessive-Compulsive

♄, ♇, ⚳, ⚶, ♍, ♏, ♑, 6th, 8th, 10th houses

The theme revolves around a focus on the nitty-gritty, details, perseverance, thoroughness and organization.

If you have carried this to an extreme, you are probably driving yourself and everyone around you crazy with your need for precision and efficiency. You can truly get lost in a morass of details and miss the overview. Your obsessive focus on one small area and concern with it being "right" could lead to overlooking alternatives and other options. You could be persnickety and overly critical. Remember that "right" and "wrong" are often subjective judgments. Use any talent for organization where it is useful; avoid trying to systematize areas which are not suited to such action.

If this theme is one you are learning to develop, the lesson could be to deal with the details successfully, to work hard, to be disciplined, to finish up, to probe and research issues thoroughly, to endure and be efficient or any combination of the above.

Competence

(☿), ♄, ⚳, ⚶, ♍, ♑, 6th, 10th houses

The challenge revolves around work, practicality, getting the job done and being efficient.

If it is a case of too much, you are learning to work **less**, to be able to take vacations, to relax, to be less concerned with physical outcomes, to let other people carry some of the load, shoulder some of the responsibility.

If it is a case of too little, you are learning to be disciplined, to work hard, to be able to stay focused and get the job done. You are learning to deal with the real, physical world in a practical, productive manner that gets results.

Mental Stimulation

☿, ⚳, ⚶, ⚴, ♃, ⚷, ♅, ♆, ♊, ♍, ♐, ♒, ♓, 3rd, 6th, 7th, 9th, 11th, 12th houses

The theme revolves around the mind and communication. It could be a case of excessive emphasis, such as an overly intellectual approach, rationalizing everything. Or, the tendency might be to believe that thinking can solve any problem or to see communication as the answer to any ills. Objectivity may be overrated and the mind put on a pedestal.

Another possibility is a denial of your mental focus, a tendency to experience it through other people, a discomfort with your verbal, communicative and logical skills. Your inner standards could inhibit you in this area, or you could be comparing yourself to other people's accomplishments in an exaggerated fashion.

Relationships

♀, ⚵, ⚴, ♇, ♎, ♏, 7th, 8th houses

The theme revolves around close, one-to-one, personal interactions. You may be very concerned with cooperation, sharing and harmony. You could also be quite involved in competitive activities. The issue being emphasized is peer relationships, meeting other people on an equal level. If you overdo this quality, you might carry competitiveness to an extreme, be overly accommodating to others or sacrifice too much for your relationships. You are seeking a balance between your needs and those of another human being.

If this quality is one you are learning to develop, the challenge is to make a place in your life for an equalitarian relationship, a face-to-face sharing with another human. Competition and cooperation can both be manifested, but be sure you are not fighting the people on your team. Keep a sensible place for each. Sharing can feel uncomfortable, especially if you are used to doing your own thing, or just relating to people at large.

Retreat from relationships is not a solution, but neither is giving up all your power in an attempt to please and appease the other party. The goal is to be able to maintain committed, deep, caring relationships with other people in a comfortable exchange. Learning the subtle give-and-take involved in the dance of a committed relationship takes time and energy.

Security
♀, ☽, ?, ⚷, ☿, ♇, ♄, ♆, ♉, ♋, ♍, ♏, ♑, ♓, 2nd, 4th, 6th, 8th, 10th, 12th houses

The issue revolves around the search for security — both on the emotional and the physical level. This can be overdone as a stodgy, grasping, conservative attitude towards life, afraid to ever reach out, risk or try anything new, out of the ordinary or beyond standard rules and roles. Or, if you are learning to express this drive, you may be out of touch with your need for something solid, dependable to lean on. You may resist receiving from others because you dislike the feelings of vulnerability. You could seek control as a way to maintain security or look to money and possessions to give you the safety you seek.

Risk/Creativity/Change
♂, ☉, ♃, ♁, ♅, ♈, ♌, ♐, ♒, 1st, 5th, 9th, 11th houses

Risk-taking is the issue and courage one of the central hallmarks. Independence and creativity are part of the picture. If overdone, you could be rash, an impulsive gambler, with an instinct for "laying it on the line." Playing the odds could be done financially, with speculation, in love, in work or other arenas. Zest, confidence, freedom, expressiveness or native optimism could be overdone.

If this is a quality you are learning to develop this lifetime, the need is to encourage your brave, initiating, forward-going side. Such attributes are best learned through doing. The more chances you take which have successful payoffs, the easier it will become to continue risking. The more you allow yourself to pour out from your own center, the more your creative instincts will flourish.

Parents
☽, ☉, ♄, ?, ♋, ♑, 4th and 10th houses

Some of the major tensions of this lifetime could have been experienced through your home life and relationship with your parent(s). This is an area for great learning, to develop a balance between your need for emotional protection and warmth with your need for achievement and amounting to something in the world. Your parents could have overdone either side with you sometimes reacting to the opposite extreme. The goal is to reach a middle ground synthesis between pragmatic realism and compassionate support.

Power
☉, ♇, ♄, ♌, ♏, ♑, 5th, 8th, 10th houses

The theme revolves around authority, control and having an impact on the world. Power drives can be channeled into sports, competitive business, fighting for causes or any area where we fight to win, including power struggles with those near and dear to us. When this is a karmic lesson, the issue of power is important in the life.

You may be avoiding your power drive and attracting other people who use and abuse power (perhaps even against you). You may be overdoing your need to be in control, running the show, making things happen. The goal is to create optimum situations for feeling and expressing your strength to have a meaningful impact in the world. Use your force wisely, in contexts which will have satisfying results.

Personal
♂, ♀, ☿, ☽, ♈, ♉, ♊, ♋, 1st, 2nd, 3rd, 4th houses

The theme revolves around personal needs. An excessive development can come across as self-centered, too concerned with doing what you want and pleasing yourself.

An underdevelopment points to a challenge in learning to focus on what you wish for (independent of the desires of other people or pressures of society). A goal is being able to pursue and obtain most of what you crave in life.

Transpersonal
♃, ♨, ♄, ♅, ♆, ♐, ♑, ♒, ♓, 9th, 10th, 11th, 12th houses

The theme revolves around large-scale issues and concerns, whether political, economic, social, etc. The focus is on the long-range view, the wide perspective, the greatest good for the greatest number. Excessive development implies you may be too concerned with a historical perspective. You could emphasize societal issues at the expense of one-to-one relationships or meeting your own needs.

Underdevelopment points to a need for a broader world view in your life. You may need to deliberately consider the long-range point of view more often. It could be helpful to try to visualize the issues from a global perspective. Thinking in larger terms is essential.

CHAPTER SEVENTEEN

FUTURE

People come into life with certain tendencies and habit patterns already developed. This includes issues likely to emerge in the future. Human development does follow logical sequences, and some themes can be predicted. What this chapter discusses is how to judge issues, feelings and concerns that are likely to emerge with age and maturity.

Each of us changes as we grow and gain experience in life. Certain sides of our nature are more emphatic when we are younger; some emerge more strongly as we get older. This chapter considers parts of your own nature which are likely to move into higher focus in years ahead.

We cannot detail everything. A more complete look would require current patterns (not just a natal or birth chart), but a few themes do emerge.

The Factors

There are four major letters of our astrological alphabet associated with the future:
Letter 5 (includes our procreative capacity, traditionally not active until after puberty)
Letter 9 (includes long-term goals, dreams, values which help to create our future)
Letter 11 (hopes, wishes and future orientation, our yearning for what lies ahead)
Letter 12 (dreams, visions, utopian ideals and aspirations).

In addition, using secondary (day-for-a-year) progressions, we can determine whether a major stellium (by house or sign) will occur in the next five years of the life and include that focus in the "Future" section.[1]

---

1. If you prefer **not** to search for repeated themes yourself, you can order the "PP BOOK" option from Astro Computing Services (PO Box 16430, San Diego, Ca 92116), which allows you to use (footnote continued on next page)

Astrologically, we would examine:

GROUP I
Conjunctions to the Sun, Jupiter, Uranus, Neptune and Chiron (since it is associated
   with Letters 9 and 11)
Conjunctions to rulers of the 5th, 9th, 11th and 12th cusps
Conjunctions to rulers of other signs in the 5th, 9th, 11th and 12th houses
Any stellia by house forming in secondary progressions in the next 5 years.
Any stellia by sign forming in secondary progressions in the next 5 years

GROUP II
Planets in the 5th, 9th, 11th and 12th houses
Planets within two degrees of occupying the 5th, 9th, 11th and 12th houses even
   if in the 4th, 6th, 8th, 10th or 1st houses

GROUP III
Parallels to Sun, Jupiter, Uranus, Neptune and Chiron
Parallels to any rulers of the 5th, 9th, 11th or 12th houses
House placements of the Sun, Jupiter, Uranus, Neptune and Chiron.
House placements of the rulers of the 5th, 9th, 11th and 12th cusps
House placements of the rulers of other signs in the 5th, 9th, 11th and 12th houses
Houses ruled by planets occupying the 5th, 9th, 11th and 12th houses

GROUP IV
Sign placements of the Sun, Jupiter, Uranus, Neptune and Chiron
Sign placements of the rulers of the 5th, 9th, 11th and 12th cusps
Sign placements of the rulers of other signs in the 5th, 9th, 11th and 12th houses
Signs occupied by planets in the 5th, 9th, 11th and 12th houses
Unoccupied signs in the 5th, 9th, 11th and 12th houses

---

1. (continued from previous page)
this book to make complete, synthesizing delineations of horoscopes without figuring out which themes
   are emphasized.
   Available for $3.00 each, the "PP BOOK" report calculates the emphasis on all the letters of
the alphabet, themes and aspects in each horoscope for which you provide the data. The report
lists each significant focus (e.g., "There is a Letter 3 theme in "Identity," and gives the appropriate
page numbers for you to read in this book ("See pages 107-108 in the Complete Horoscope Interpretation book.")
   The computer will not **always** arrive at the same results as you might, as certain steps are ambiguous (e.g., how much weight to give a planet making a conjunction, based on the orb). However,
the majority of the time, the computer answers will concur with those derived from use of the
worksheets — or the recommended quick scan of a horoscope. Thus it provides an excellent teaching
tool.
   The "PP BOOK" does **not** provide a listing of **each and every** astrological factor making up
the significant themes. For that, you would order "PP WEIGHTS" (discussed in next footnote).

How to Weight the Factors

Please note that the factors are rank ordered (in chunks) according to their weighting. If you want to use exact figures, a suggested weighting scale is given in the appendix — with worksheets for the various areas.[2]

A SHORT CUT
For quickness and ease of use, especially for people just learning to use the Zip Code, I suggest the following system:

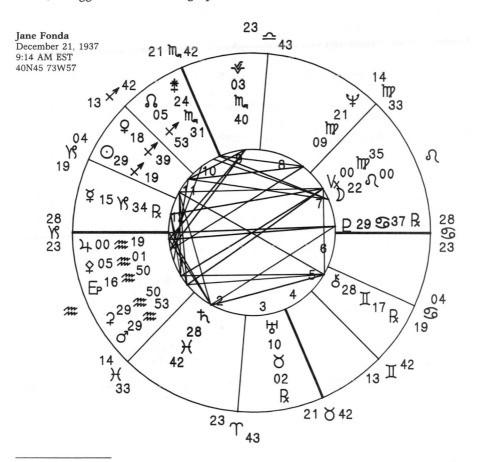

Jane Fonda
December 21, 1937
9:14 AM EST
40N45 73W57

---

2. You can also obtain a listing of **all** the astrological factors which compose those letters of the Zip Code determined to be significant in a horoscope. This makes an excellent teaching tool and a valuable resource to check yourself against when practicing with the Zip Code.

Astro Computing Services, PO Box 16430, San Diego, CA 92116, has calculated 28,000 horoscopes and established averages and standard deviations for the scores of each letter of the astrological alphabet, each theme, and the conflict and harmony aspects to each life area.
(footnote continued on next page)

If any letter of the alphabet is represented in Group I or II, consider it as probably significant. Repetitions are definitely significant. For example, Jane Fonda's Jupiter (one future key) closely conjuncts Pallas (Letter 7) and we count Jupiter twice (once for its own nature and once as the ruler of the 11th house cusp), so we might read the interpretation for Letter 7 (in Chapters 3 and 6) from the viewpoint of future trends. Three of her planets (Sun, Venus and Jupiter) will be occupying the sign of Aquarius by secondary progressions,[3] so we also read the interpretations for Letter 11.

Check to see if an emphasis in Groups I and II is repeated in Groups III and IV. In terms of Letter 7 we note that: the 11th house Sun rules the 7th (7), the 9th house cusp is Libra (7), the 9th house Scorpio ruler (Pluto) is in the 7th (7), the 5th house Cancer ruler (Moon) is in the 7th (7), Leo is occupied in the 7th (7), Aquarius is occupied by Pallas (7) and the 9th house Scorpio ruler (Pluto) conjuncts the Descendant (7).

In examining Groups III and IV, also look for any letters of the alphabet which occur several times. For example, Jane Fonda's Jupiter occupies the 1st (1), Aquarius is occupied by Mars (1), Aquarius is occupied by five different factors (Jupiter, Pallas, East Point, Ceres and Mars) in the 1st (1) (1) (1) (1) (1), Jupiter parallels the Ascendant (1), Jupiter conjuncts the Ascendant (1), 11th house Sagittarius ruler (Jupiter) conjuncts and parallels the Ascendant (1) (1). This suggests a letter 1 theme for her future.

The 1-7 polarity suggests an ongoing balancing act for Ms. Fonda — between self-assertion and the needs of other people. This could be tension between freedom needs (1) and the desire for emotional closeness and partnerships (7). It could be time and energy demands for personal activities and interests (1) compete with the needs of a partner (7). Individuality may vie with couple interests. Accommodation of others must be balanced with self-expression. This is a common polarity with counselors, consultants, people in personnel or anyone whose job involves relating to people. There is usually a lot of activity in interpersonal relations, constantly meeting new people, ending old relationships and beginning new ones.

---

2. (continued from previous page)
    Astro's report, called "PP WEIGHTS," will list those letters of the astrological alphabet which are one standard deviation or more above the mean — and list **all** the astrological factors which point to each significant letter of the alphabet. These weightings will also compare each individual's score on the various themes (e.g., risk-taking, artistic) to the means and standard deviations to determine which themes are significant. Averages are established for aspects as well in order to note conflict or harmony in the different life areas.
    The results obtained by Astro's "PP WEIGHTS" will not **always** coincide with those you determine by a quick scan and intuitive judgment, or by use of the worksheets. Certain of the steps (e.g., how much to weight a planet based on orb) are ambiguous, so different results can occur. However, most of the time, Astro's answers will confirm those you could obtain in working with the Zip Code. Furthermore, the **complete** listing of relevant factors is an excellent teaching tool.
    Ask for "PP Weights." The price, as of December 1985 is $5.00
3. For a rough approximation of secondary progressions, add the age of the person to the birth date and look up the planetary positions for the new date. For example, Jane Fonda will be 49 in 1986. Adding 49 days to her birthday (December 21, 1937) brings us to February 8, 1938. The positions of the planets that day include the Sun at 18 of Aquarius, Venus at 19 of Aquarius and Jupiter at 11 Aquarius.

Themes

Themes can be ascertained by two methods. One approach is to examine **only** those letters of the alphabet which were significant in the above scans. In the case of Jane Fonda, the focus on Letters 1 and 7 emphasizes the polarity theme (balancing opposites).

An alternative way to seek themes is to combine the totals for **all** the letters of the alphabet and see which factors seem to have an above average focus. You need to do some rough arithmetic here or get an intuitive impression. If a theme involves three (out of twelve) letters of the astrological alphabet, you would expect it to have about ¼ of the total score. So, if the amount for those letters seems appreciably more than ¼ of the total, count that as a theme — and read the appropriate section. (By this system, Ms. Fonda emerges with themes of fire, freedom, risk-taking and relationships for her future.)

When searching for themes, give additional weighting to like planets in aspect to one another. For example, the Sun, Pluto and Saturn are the three power planets. Any aspects between the Sun, Pluto and Saturn add to the power theme. (Note that all three of Ms. Fonda's power planets are in **close** aspect to each other. Also give extra weight to like houses and like signs. Thus, the Sun, Pluto or Saturn occupying the 5th, 8th or 10th houses or Leo, Scorpio or Capricorn would give extra weight to the power theme for each occurrence.

Aspects

Quickly scan all aspects other than conjunctions or parallels, grouping them according to harmony (sextile, trine, semisextile) and conflict (octile, tri-octile, square, opposition and quincunx). In considering each aspect, weight the nature of the planet most heavily, followed by the house and the sign. Note both the house occupied and the cusp ruled by each planet being aspected. For example, Uranus is one of the future factors. Jane Fonda's Uranus makes **no** close aspects — conflict or harmony. (It has a few wide aspects.) Her Chiron (another future factor) makes the following **close** harmony aspects:

- trine Ceres (6) in the 1st (1) in Aquarius (11)
- trine Mars (1) in the 1st (1) in Aquarius (11); Mars rules the 3rd (3)

Her Chiron makes the following conflict aspects:
- quincunx the Ascendant (1) in Capricorn (10)
- opposite the Sun (5) in the 11th (11) in Sagittarius (9); the Sun rules the 7th (7)
- quincunx Jupiter (9) in the 1st (1) in Aquarius (11); Jupiter rules the 11th (11)
- square Saturn (10) in the 2nd (2) in Pisces (12); Saturn rules the 12th and 1st (12)(1)

You can get an intuitive sense by glancing through, which letters (if any) have lots of conflict to them and which have quite a bit of harmony. If you feel any group of aspects has an emphasis on one or more letters of the alphabet, read the appropriate interpretations in Chapter 3 and 6, in terms of issues easy to blend (harmony aspects) or challenging to integrate (conflict aspects) with future developments. In Ms. Fonda's case, we might suspect a theme involving freedom (with Letters 1 and 11 repeated). Ms. Fonda has moved toward more and more independence (as in her control over her films) and getting involved with books and video cassettes that do things **her** way.

Interpretations: Future

After ascertaining which issues and themes are emphasized, use the discussions in Chapters 3, 4 and 6. Remember, that the emphasis is forward. These are themes which are emerging in the future, issues that become more significant as the person ages and progresses in life.

For example, a shorthand description of a future emphasis on the element of fire might be:

A movement in your life is toward increased extraversion, confidence, zest, enthusiasm and spontaneity. You may experience a sense of greater vitality and energy in your later years. Your sparkle and dynamism are likely to grow along with you. You will do more and more in time.

With maturity comes increased awareness of your own needs and desires. Less tied to what other people think and value, you are truer to yourself. More direct and spontaneous, you have less patience for game playing. Life, you feel, is meant to be lived to the full. You devote yourself to a wholehearted pursuit of excitement, activity and drama.

Read the appropriate alphabet and other emphasized themes in Chapters 4 and 6, **thinking in terms of characteristics you are manifesting more and more** in your life. Titles for the alphabet sections might include:

Letter 1:	**To Thine Own Self Be True**	(see also page 107)
Letter 2:	**If It Feels Good, Do It!**	(see also page 107)
Letter 3:	**Mind Your Mind**	(see also page 107)
Letter 4:	**Feelings**	(see also page 108)
Letter 5:	**Go For It**	(see also page 109)
Letter 6:	**The Efficiency Expert**	(see also page 109)
Letter 7:	**Both Sides Now**	(see also page 110)
Letter 8:	**Depth Understanding**	(see also page 111)
Letter 9:	**Truth Seeking**	(see also page 111)
Letter 10:	**Facing the "Real World"**	(see also page 112)
Letter 11:	**Doing Your Thing**	(see also page 113)
Letter 12:	**Cosmic Connections**	(see also page 114)

CHAPTER EIGHTEEN

OVERVIEW OF THE WHOLE CHART

Analyze each entire chart by looking for repeated themes. What is most important in the nature will be repeated in the horoscope in several different ways. In looking at factors in the previous twelve chapters, you will have already noticed cases in which certain themes popped up again and again (in a variety of life areas) for one chart (such as the freedom theme for Jane Fonda). You **know** those themes are important! But, if you wish a systematic approach, you can follow the outline given below until you develop your own style. (Interpretations of the issues pinpointed by this outline begin on page 463.)

Outline for Analysis of Chart as a Whole

1. Is there a major stellium by house or sign?

A major stellium (three or more planets or two planets and two asteroids occupying a single sign or a single house) is probably the most visually obvious statement of a theme. Stelliums indicate a focus, a concentration in a given area. This can be a very great talent, something that comes easily and naturally to that person, something quite familiar. It can also be experienced as an area of problems or tension, often like an overload where the fuse has blown. Wherever the stellium is (by house or sign) shows an issue.

For example, someone with three or more planets in Aquarius (like Jane Fonda) is likely to have strong freedom needs, desire for uniqueness, individuality and originality. Such a person may be very interested in new-age ideas, technology and on the cutting edge of change. Friends could be very important in the life as could groups or political action.

Sometimes even our greatest talents become problems because we tend to overdo whatever we are good at. Take, for example, the individual with a stellium in Aquarius. This indicates potential objectivity, tolerance, openness, uniqueness, individuality, affinity for the new/different/unusual, desire for change and innovation. Sounds great, doesn't it? But look what happens if the person overdoes that talent. Such people can rationalize or intellectualize everything. They may be detached (because it **is** a talent) and try to use it even when inappropriate (as when the other party wants a feeling response). People with Aquarian stelliums may be chronic rebels, always fighting the old. They can be weird, flaky and strange — carrying their penchant for eccentricity and individuality too far. In short, anything can be overdone! It is a real temptation for people with stelliums to be expressing that part of their potential **all over** their lives — even in areas where it is inappropriate.

Remember, you will also find stelliums among people who do not seem to be able to handle that part of life at all — like the overload. One collection of charts of children with Down's Syndrome, for example, often had stelliums in the mental houses. The chart shows an issue: that this mental theme is of major concern for the individual. It does **not** tell us how the person will handle it. Ideally, of course, we use our talents wisely, but also remember life is growth and we need to work in areas less familiar and comfortable in order to develop in new directions.

A similar process is applied to stelliums by house or sign.

Interpretations for stellia begin on page 463.

2. Is one element particularly emphasized?

In making this judgment, it is vital to consider occupied houses (and not just signs) and planets with close, tight aspects. For example, a chart with all the water planets (Moon, Pluto, Neptune) aspecting one another within 1° plus several planets in the water houses (4th, 8th and 12th) has an emphasis on water **even if there are no water signs occupied.** Too often people are taught to count only occupied signs, which will lead you astray; you will miss important themes. Pay attention to strongly aspected planets and occupied houses. They are **more** significant than occupied signs.

I suggest you practice scanning the chart for a quick sense of element balance or imbalance. The objective is gaining an overall impression quickly, not getting hung up in precise numbers or relationships. (If you want numbers to play with, count one point for every occupied house, one for every occupied sign and one for every close aspect to a planet. Thus, four close aspects to the Sun adds four points to your total for fire. However, I feel your delineation skills will progress faster if you concentrate on seeking an intuitive overview, rather than trying to come up with precise figures.)

Elements which reinforce one another have extra importance as well. That is, if the water planets all aspect one another (rather than aspecting other planets), or if water planets fall in water houses or water signs, there is an extra focus on that element.

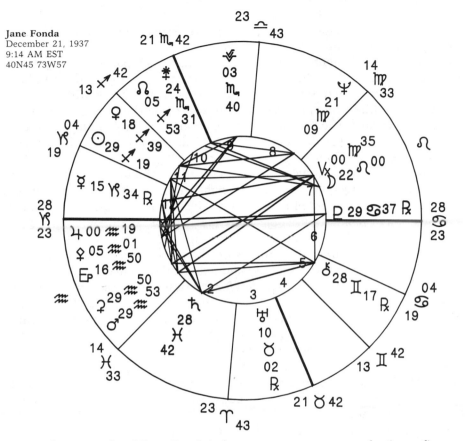

Jane Fonda
December 21, 1937
9:14 AM EST
40N45 73W57

In the example of Jane Fonda's horoscope, a strong emphasis on fire comes through. Fire houses are occupied by two planets and four asteroids; fire signs are occupied by three planets and the north node. The fire planets (Mars, the Sun and Jupiter) make 7, 6 and 6 close (3° orb) longitude aspects, respectively, to other planets, asteroids and angles in the horoscope, for a total of 19 fire aspects (counting asteroids at half-weight). Even more significant is the fact that all three fire planets are aspecting one another — within an orb of **one degree**! This is a very strong fire statement.

Earth houses are occupied by one planet, one asteroid and the north node. Earth signs are occupied by three planets. Earth planets and asteroids (counting half-weight for aspects to asteroids) make 2 (Venus), 4 (Ceres), 3 (Vesta) and 6½ (Saturn) close aspects, for a total of 15½ earth aspects.

In contrast, Jane Fonda has five planets in air houses, two planets, three asteroids and the south node in air signs, and her air factors make 1½ (Mercury), 2 (Pallas), 1 (Juno) and 0 (Uranus) close aspects, for a total of 4½ air aspects. Water houses are occupied by two planets and the south node. Water signs are occupied by two planets and two asteroids, while water factors make 2½ (Moon), 6 (Pluto) and 4 (Neptune) close aspects, for a total of 12½ watery aspects.

Ms. Fonda is famous for her energy (fire) — in terms of her workout regime, her acting career, her political activism and more.

When analyzing elements, notice also if the emphasis is particularly centered around certain areas within the horoscope. For example, most of the air in Jane Fonda's chart is connected to fire. Aquarius (air) occupies the 1st (fire), Gemini (air) is in the 5th (fire), Leo (fire) is placed in the 7th (air) and Sagittarius (fire) occupies the 11th (air). The fire planets fall in an air sign (Jupiter and Mars) and an air house (the Sun). The air asteroid (Pallas) falls in a fire house (the 1st) and conjuncts a fire planet (Jupiter).

The fire/air combination suggests that Ms. Fonda's thinking and communicating (air) tends to be direct, expressive, forthright and sometimes impulsive (fire). Fire/air suggests a good sense of humor, and skills at entertaining people and in sales, promotion or politics. Pure objectivity (pure air) is less likely. Strong emotions (fire) will sway the perceptions and descriptions (air).

In general, fire and air tend more toward the present and future. Earth and water are more concerned with security and may denote someone who clings to the past. Ms. Fonda definitely has a vision for the future of our society, and feels there is much room for improvement. In a recent interview, she said: "I'm scared. I think that we're in a position that people can't understand and it threatens them." (*Los Angeles Herald-Examiner*, September 13, 1985, p.9). Her message is that people need to act (fire) — that change is needed!

With much of her air focus in the area of personal identity (Letter 1), we again return to Jane Fonda as the communicator. In each chapter, remember to seek the themes present, but also **where** in the person's life those themes are most likely to be expressed.

Interpretation for emphasized elements can be gleaned from Chapter 4, beginning on page 71.

3. Is one quality particularly emphasized?

Be sure to consider the angularity of planets and number of tight, close aspects they have, plus occupied houses as well as occupied signs. (You can use a tentative weighting similar to the one suggested for elements as a beginning point — or design your own.)

In the case of Jane Fonda's chart, I would not characterize the horoscope as predominantly cardinal, fixed or mutable. There is a **relative** balance, with no quality being strongly under- or overemphasized. Note, for example, that three of her angles have bodies closely (within 3°) conjunct: Jupiter (mutable) on the Ascendant, Juno (cardinal) on the MC and Pluto (fixed) on the Descendant.

Quality emphasis can be delineated through information in Chapter 4, beginning on page 76.

4. Are certain elements nearly always in combination?

Consider planets aspecting one another, planets in houses or signs, and signs (which are occupied) in houses. For example, in the Fonda chart, Neptune in the 8th house shows the water/earth combination in terms of planet/house, Saturn in Pisces is earth/water by planet/sign, and Capricorn occupied in the 12th house is earth/water by sign/house. Aspects between water and earth planets (e.g., Neptune square Venus) can also add to the theme.

Interpretations for emphasized elements, qualities and element combinations are available in Chapters 4 and 6 beginning on pages 71 and 120.

5. Is a certain letter of the astrological alphabet emphasized?

Repeated themes can come through planets (and aspects), houses and signs. Even though Jane Fonda has no planets in Aries, Letter 1 comes through emphatically in her horoscope, with the strongly occupied 1st house, the prominent placement of Mars (closely conjunct the Antivertex, a secondary angle) and the many close aspects to Mars (conjunct Ceres, semisextile Jupiter, sextile the Sun, semisextile Saturn, trine Chiron, quincunx Pluto and octile Mercury). These placements reflect her self-assertion, focus on a healthy body, high energy and drive for independence of action. They also point to the potential of excessive focus on what she wants and possible rashness or misplaced courage.

When a letter of the alphabet is emphasized, read the meaning of that letter in Chapter 3 or Chapter 6.

6. What is the relationship of occupied signs to houses?

That is, thinking of the houses in terms of the natural zodiac, what aspect would the house (in the natural zodiac) make to the sign which is in that house? Look at signs which are occupied by planets — not just the signs on the cusp of the house. Occupied signs are a more emphatic statement, although you can also consider the relationship of the cusp signs to the houses on which they fall.

Aries occupying the 1st house forms the natural zodiac. Taurus or Pisces planets occupying the 1st house make a semisextile relationship. Gemini or Aquarius planets occupying the 1st house make a natural sextile. Cancer or Capricorn planets in the 1st have a square relationship to the house. Leo or Sagittarius planets occupying the 1st house have a trine relationship. Virgo or Scorpio occupying the 1st house is a natural quincunx. Planets in Libra in the 1st house make a natural opposition.

Many charts will have a mixed pattern and cannot be categorized with one major theme of house/sign relationships. Consider it a theme when three-quarters (or more) of the planets occupy signs which have the same relationship (e.g., square, trine, etc.) to the house occupied. In the case of Ms. Fonda, her chart is **mostly** a natural sextile: Aquarius occupied in the 1st, Pisces in the 2nd, Gemini in the 5th, etc. (Thirteen of her fifteen planets and asteroids occupy signs which are naturally sextile the house they are in. The other two factors occupy signs naturally semisextile their houses.) Those many sextile combinations show the potential of much inner agreement, with houses and signs backing each other up. The person can have good energy for what s/he wants, but may be inclined to go overboard — especially when strong fire is involved, as in the case of Jane Fonda. If several sides of her nature all support one course, she is less likely to consider other options. When there is strong inner agreement, we may go to an extreme (as in Ms. Fonda's strong convictions).

Interpretations for house/sign blends begin on page 467.

7. Do certain alphabet combinations repeat often?

Jane Fonda's horoscope has a repeated 1-11 theme: Mars (1) is in Aquarius (11), the East Point (1) is in Aquarius (11), five placements (Jupiter, Pallas, East Point, Ceres, Mars) occupy the 1st house (1) (1) (1) (1) (1) in Aquarius (11) (11) (11) (11) (11), a planet, Jupiter, in the 1st house (1) rules the 11th cusp (11) and several conjunctions take place involving the 1st house (1) and Aquarius (11). This puts an emphasis on her identity tied to being individualistic, unique, progressive, forward-looking, liberal, concerned with humanitarian causes and groups, and potentially rebellious or overly eccentric. She also has a repeated theme of 9-11: Sagittarius (9) on the cusp of the 11th (11), two planets, the Sun and Venus, occupy Sagittarius (9) (9) in the 11th (11) (11), the ruler of the 9th cusp (9) is in the 11th house (11) and Jupiter (9) occupies Aquarius (11). This theme further points to risk-taking, a futuristic orientation, restlessness, strong freedom needs, concern with truth, justice, equal opportunity and our judiciary (9) and legislative bodies (11). Ms. Fonda has expressed the courage, independence and inventiveness of these combinations in a number of ways. She has also exhibited some of the impulsivity, rebelliousness and fighting for causes.

Different combinations by twos (of the alphabet) are discussed in Chapters 6, 7, 8 and 9.

8. Are there any other repeated themes?

When analyzing a chart life area by life area (as in previous chapters), certain themes will often come up again and again, emerging for many life areas. (In the case of Jane Fonda, we often found themes of fire, freedom, mind/communication and relationships.) These repeated themes are obviously very important in the nature of the individual.

You can check the horoscope systematically for any of the themes described in Chapter 4 and read the descriptions in Chapter 6. The themes would be noted when there is an emphasis — by many aspects to the planets, houses and/or signs or by house or sign stellia. For example, the **relationships/partnership** theme emerges with several planets in houses 7 and 8 or signs Libra and Scorpio. It can also be highlighted by many close aspects to Pluto, Pallas and Juno (or Venus), especially to each other. Aspects emphasizing planets in or ruling the 7th or 8th or in Libra or Scorpio also add to the theme. And, when the "relationship" planets fall in each other's houses and/or signs, that is more emphasis on sharing the life with other people.

Jane Fonda's horoscope has such a "relationships" theme with Pluto, the Moon and Neptune in the 7th and 8th, two asteroids in Scorpio, and aspects linking Pluto, Pallas and Juno. (Pluto opposes Pallas and trines Juno.) In addition Pluto in the 7th and Juno in Scorpio are examples of "partnership" keys backing each other up. The prominent placements of Juno and Pluto (both conjuncting angles of the chart) repeat the "relationships" theme yet again. All of this shows a strong need for involvement with people. (It is also at odds with the strong theme of freedom which repeats for Ms. Fonda. One of her tasks is to positively balance her need for independence with her desire for emotional involvements and interactions with others.)

The following themes are available (plus any more you choose to invent):

1. **Freedom**: ♂, ♃, ⚷, ♅, ♈, ♐, ♒, 1st, 9th, 11th houses
2. **Closeness**: ☽, ☉, ♀, ⚴, ⚵, ♇, ♋, ♌, ♎, ♏, 4th, 5th, 7th, 8th houses
3. **Freedom versus Closeness**: ♂, ♃, ⚷, ♅, ♈, ♐, ♒, 1st, 9th, 11th houses, versus ☽, ☉, ♀, ⚴, ⚵, ♇, ♋, ♌, ♎, ♏, 4th, 5th, 7th, 8th houses
4. **Artistic**: ♀, ⚴, ⚵, ☉, ♆, ♉, ♌, ♎, ♓, 2nd, 5th, 7th, 12th houses
5. **Idealistic ("Great Expectations")**: ♃, ⚷, ♆, ♐, ♓, 9th, 12th houses
6. **Obsessive-compulsive**: ☿, ⚳, ⚶, ♇, ♄, ♍, ♏, ♑, 6th, 8th, 10th houses
7. **Competence/Work**: ☿, ⚳, ⚶, ♄, ♍, ♑, 6th, 10th houses
8. **Mind/Communication**: ☿, ⚳, ⚶, ⚴, ♃, ⚷, ♅, ♆, ♊, ♍, ♎, ♐, ♒, ♓, 3rd, 6th, 7th, 9th, 11th, 12th houses
9. **Relationships**: ♀, ⚴, ⚵, ♇, ♎, ♏, 7th, 8th houses
10. **Security**: ♀, ☽, ☿, ⚳, ⚶, ♇, ♄, ♆, ♉, ♋, ♍, ♏, ♑, ♓, 2nd, 4th, 6th, 8th, 10th, 12th houses
11. **Risk/Creativity/Change**: ♂, ☉, ♃, ⚷, ♅, ♈, ♌, ♐, ♒, 1st, 5th, 9th, 11th houses
12. **Parents**: ☽, ♄, ⚳, ♋, ♑, 4th, 10th houses
13. **Power**: ☉, ♇, ♄, ♌, ♏, ♑, 5th, 8th, 10th houses
14. **Personal**: ♂, ♀, ☿, ☽, ♈, ♉, ♊, ♋, 1st, 2nd, 3rd, 4th houses
15. **Transpersonal**: ♃, ⚷, ♄, ♅, ♆, ♐, ♑, ♒, ♓, 9th, 10th, 11th, 12th houses
16. **Polarities**

Refer back to Chapter 4 for the interpretation of these themes. You can also read the descriptions in Chapter 6. Be willing to combine and contrast themes, as in the "Ideal" (Letters 9 and 12) versus the "Real" or Work/Competence (Letters 6 and 10).

9. What qualities are suggested by planets in the Gauquelin sectors or planets making close (4 degrees or less) conjunctions to the Ascendant, Descendant, Midheaven or IC?

Michel and Francoise Gauquelin found certain key words strongly associated with individuals having some of the planets in what the Gauquelins call "zones of power." Highly successful individuals with the planets in these key sectors of the chart tended to have certain descriptions in their biographies — in odds many times against chance.

The areas of the chart noted by the Gauquelins are roughly equivalent to the 9th and 12th houses in the Placidian system, plus the first ten degrees of the 10th and 1st houses. Jane Fonda's Jupiter occupies the "zone of power" and the Gauquelins found actors and politicians had such a Jupiter placement more often than chance would suggest. Associated key words for the Gauquelin work begin on page 469.

Astrologers have noted that planets closely conjunct the angles of the horoscope are often keys to major drives within the nature of the person, to basic personality characteristics. When a planet is tightly conjunct an angle, think of it as a strong focus on that letter of the alphabet. In Jane Fonda's chart, as mentioned, the close conjunction (1°56') of Jupiter to the Ascendant emphasizes the Letter 9 theme in Ms. Fonda's nature: concern with truth, justice, education.

The close conjunction of Pluto to the Descendant (1°14') emphasizes a theme of intensity, power and self-mastery in her relationships. The close conjunction of Juno to her MC (2°49') suggest working with people, including the possibility of contgributing to a marriage partner's career or a partner contributing to her career. Juno also ties beauty and aesthetics into the job area.

10. Are there any strong aspect configurations, e.g., grand cross, T-square, grand trine, etc.?

Such patterns point to major issues, talents, abilities and challenges within the nature. Be sure to weight planets most heavily, followed by houses and then signs. Aspects configurations may be categorized as primarily one quality, a mixture of two mostly, or all three — depending on the horoscope. For instance, Jane Fonda has a very close T-square between the Sun, Saturn and Chiron. It involves mutable signs and fixed houses. The planets are fixed, cardinal and mutable. This configuration would be a mixture of all three qualities. Interpretations for configurations begin on page 470.

You will have to decide whether you wish to include the asteroids, nodes of the Moon or auxiliary angles (East Point and Antivertex) in your search for configurations. One option is to use a smaller orb for such factors. Another option is to exclude them.

Orb is still a matter of opinion. For configurations (grand crosses, grand trines, T-squares), I tend to use a **maximum** orb of 6°, but feel closer aspects are much more significant. Use your judgment and be flexible from case to case in determining orbs.

Once you have determined the major themes involved in a horoscope, discuss them with the client. Remember that any motif can be expressed both positively and negatively. Discuss the options with the individual.

Interpretations: Overview

STELLIA
In addition to the delineations give here you can read the appropriate letter theme (e.g. Aries or 1st house is Letter 1) in Chapters 3 and 6 (identity).

First House

You are very aware of yourself and your own needs. Sometimes that can result in extreme self-consciousness. You may swing from excessive assertion to keeping a lot inside — partly because your feelings are so complicated and intermixed, you are not sure what to express. Your personality is complex; you can be many different people.

Second House

You enjoy material comforts: food, drink, money, possessions and all forms of sensual pleasure. You may have a strong feeling for beauty and the ability to create it. Practical, you prefer seeing results in the physical world rather than abstractions. You may be a bit stubborn, but are generally easygoing and pleasant.

Third House

The mental world is important to you. Whether you emphasize thinking, learning, teaching, communicating, or simply socializing with relatives and neighbors, you are involved with people and ideas. Your focus is wide and you may be inclined to scatter a bit, since you want to know something about everything. You usually learn a lot informally — from talking with and observing others.

Fourth House

Home and family are important to you. You probably look to your nest for a feeling of security and to "recharge your batteries." Emotional closeness and attachment are fundamental in your life, whether experienced through family, pets or other sources of emotional support. If food becomes your source of reassurance, overweight can be a problem. Your relationship to the parent you felt was nurturing (or was supposed to be) has a strong impact on who you are. Be sure you are comfortable now with both nurturing and being nurtured.

Fifth House

You have a great deal of potential magnetism and charisma. Your inner need is to be a star in some way. You may gravitate to teaching, entertainment, selling, promotion or other avenues of taking center stage. You are willing to gamble and take risks, but you sometimes hold back for fear of not being appreciated or because you hate to lose. Children may be important in your life — or other creative outlets.

Sixth House

You need a feeling of efficiency and productivity in your life. You are likely to be very hardworking with a tendency to feel: "If you want it done right, do it yourself." Proper functioning (on the job and in the body) is important to you. If your work in the world does not satisfy your need to do something well, you could be ill or obsessed with your health. Whether or not you have an actual "career" or paying job, you need to feel you are contributing to society.

Seventh House

Other people, especially partners and close friends, are very important in your life. It is as if you find yourself partially through relating to others. This can feel vulnerable at times and you may be inclined to give in too much, fight to get back your power or retreat from the whole thing. The best course is to cooperate in appropriate areas, compete where acceptable and help some people (who are weaker) to reinforce your own feelings of strength.

Eighth House

There is a lot going on beneath the surface that you do not always share with people. You tend to probe the motivations of people — your own and others. You are a natural psychotherapist, but may be drawn to any hidden areas — occult, detective work, research, etc. Sharing is commonly a major issue in your life — whether shared sensuality, sexuality, or money and possessions.

Ninth House

Your life is a perpetual quest for **more**. That could be more fun, more parties, more education, more knowledge, more wisdom, more travel. ... Your instinctive sense is to expand on what you have, to search for the ultimate. That search could carry you to the ends of the Earth literally or on perennial spiritual, religious, philosophical, educational forays.

Tenth House

You are dealing with the realistic limits of the world. If you have mastered the ability to work within the rules in life, you are likely to be in a position of authority and power. If you still experience the power of the world as external, you may feel very blocked, inhibited, helpless. Your relationship to authority figures gives some clues. Use your pragmatic capacity to figure out all you can do and then do it!

Eleventh House

Friends are likely to be very important to you. New-age activities may attract you — or anything on the cutting edge of change, from new technology (space, computers, lasers) to avant-garde or even revolutionary ideas. You are inclined to break the rules of life periodically — sometimes just to shock people. You are likely to be quite bright and original. One of your skills is problem-solving.

Twelfth House

Your faith in life is crucial here. If you trust in yourself and a Higher Power, you are likely to be extremely effective, living out most of your potential. If you are trying to carry the whole load yourself (playing God) or expecting others to make everything perfect for you, disillusionment and disappointment lie ahead. Beauty and spiritual, idealistic or religious activities offer support.

Aries ♈

Action is important to you. You may be physically restless and need a sense of openness in your life. Sports or other vigorous activity can be a good outlet for your need to move. You are usually direct, spontaneous and forthright. Psychologically, you need to feel free and independent and are likely to fight against anything or anyone you see as confining. Doing your "own thing" is essential.

Taurus ♉

You really just want to be comfortable. The status quo is okay, especially if it includes some physical indulgence such as back rubs, fine wine, good food, excellent art and lots of money. You tend to seek security. You are practical but inclined to be a bit lazy at times. People usually find you easy to get along with; you rarely make waves.

Gemini ♊

Insatiably curious, you go searching for new ideas, new people, new forms of stimulation from the world. You have the butterfly mind — flying from flower to flower as each looks more interesting than the last. You may be physically as well as mentally restless, enjoying travel. You need to communicate, especially with the people right around you.

Cancer ♋

Security is what you want: emotional and physical. You look for people you can care for and receive nurturance from, although pets and even plants can also serve as sources of emotional support. You tend to need to be needed. Cautious, you are inclined to keep a nest egg stored away for a rainy day. Sometimes weight is a problem, when you use food as a security blanket. You are often just naturally "motherly" and supportive. Sensitive and caring, your feelings run deep.

Leo ♌

Excitement draws you; you seek that adrenaline high. You may look to physically risky activities such as motorcycling or taking chances financially through speculation and gambling. With an urge to pour out from your own center, doing more than has been done before, you can be highly creative in many areas. Positive feedback (love, admiration, attention, applause) is important to you. Sometimes, you may decline to try things because you fear being laughed at and cannot stand losing. A natural leader, you would prefer to be onstage, swaying people emotionally — as long as you are assured of a positive response.

Virgo ♍

Health and/or work are important focuses for you. You may combine them in fields of nutrition, medicine, holistic health or even professional hypochondria. You have marvelous abilities to analyze, discriminate and find the flaws. This can make you a super employee, a marvelously productive person or a critical pain in the neck, depending on where you channel your desire to improve life and make it more efficient.

Libra ♎

Peer relationships are important to you. One-to-one interchanges with other people are the spice of life. But you may enjoy competitive as well as cooperative relationships. Just be sure you keep the competition where you want it and are able to harmonize with those near and dear to you. Artistic talent, particularly the visual arts, is possible. Grace, harmony, balance, justice, fair play and equality can be essential parts of your life.

Scorpio ♏

Concentrated focus is one of your skills. You want to go to **the end** with whatever you are doing. With a bulldog tenacity, you are determined to accomplish what you set out to do. Learning when to let go, especially emotionally, may be a challenge. Passionate commitment is your style — whether to a lover, spouse, friend, job or hobby. Intense and deeply emotional, sharing with others is not always easy. Finances or sexuality could be arenas for power struggles. Probing and concerned with root causes, your interest is in what lies beneath the surface; superficialities bore you.

Sagittarius ♐

Jovial and fun-loving, you are inclined to play the wise professor (guru) role or the joking entertainer. Ideas excite you, but you may prefer talking to listening. Although you may act out the playboy or playgirl role when young, generally maturity brings an interest in philosophy, religion, spirituality or other roads to explore the question of "What is the meaning of life?" You may explore that question through travel, books, seminars or various paths which offer answers. Expansive and optimistic, you tend to look for (and often get) more and more out of life.

Capricorn ♑

Standing in the community, a career and a sense of power are probably important to you. You are likely to feel quite responsible and may have difficulty delegating authority. If you are not yet secure in your own power, you may feel blocked and limited by others. You are capable of tremendous achievement and can work your way to the top in whatever you do. A key issue is dealing with structure and order — figuring out the rules and then working within them.

Aquarius ♒

Original and creative, you are coming from your own unique center. Sometimes that may strike others as weird and eccentric, but you care more about breaking new ground than what people think. You are drawn to the unusual, the different, the progressive. Detachment is one of your skills and you are likely to place a high value on your independence.

Pisces ♓

Sensitive and feeling, you are seeking channels to make your world more beautiful or more ideal. You may operate as an artist or as a helper/healer of others. If you do not trust your abilities, you may be a victim — through drugs, alcohol, fantasy, illness — searching for the more ideal world you are afraid to try and create. Art, nature, beauty and God offer potential support.

ELEMENT EMPHASIS AND COMBINATIONS

See appropriate interpretations in Chapter 4 and Chapter 6.

HOUSE/SIGN RELATIONSHIP

Natural Zodiac: ♈ in 1st house, ♉ in 2nd, etc.

Your orientation to life is more intense and pure. Where others tend to have mixed feelings and reactions, you have a doubled-up situation. Thus, you tend to experience things more fully, be more emphatic in your approach. This can be an advantage in many cases, but obviously could be a drawback when you need to be aware of alternatives.

Semisextile ⚹: ♓ or ♉ in 1st house, etc.

Your life is a process of building on the foundations of what has gone before. Cultivate a sense of stepping stones. If a situation seems conflicted, search your history for roots which can be melded comfortably with part of what is happening. Then make a positive connection. Part of your pattern is to understand how each "new" occurrence and experience builds on the old.

Sextile ✶: ♒ or ♊ in 1st house, etc.

You have the advantage of some inner harmony. Your expressive side tends to back up your spontaneous side. Your need for security is supportive of your desires for stability. Generally, when you are in one mode, you agree with yourself. Thus, when you are oriented toward the future, that feels right, and when you are confronting past issues, that also feels correct. These issues may conflict sometimes, but much of the time you tend to focus on one approach or the other.

Square ☐: ♋ or ♑ in 1st house, etc.

You are working with some inherent, built-in conflict. You have a natural ambivalence operating. No matter what you want, you tend to simultaneously be aware of a conflicting desire and also want it. You may sometimes feel as though you always want what you do not have. Learning to compromise between your various needs and drives will probably take time and attention. But once you have been able to make the integration, to create room in your life for all your various ways of being, you will be very versatile and talented.

Trine △: ♌ or ♐ in 1st house, etc.

Your inner agreement tends to be strong. When you are confident, you are very confident; when you are practical, you are extremely pragmatic. The tendency is to express yourself to the hilt in whatever you are currently involved. This can lead to extremes at times, when you get carried away with what you feel is "right." Deliberate examination of the various options can help to avoid a tendency to go "whole hog" in one direction or another.

Quincunx ⚻: ♍ or ♏ in 1st house, etc.

You are facing an innate ambivalence and may feel sometimes that your life just won't get together. Whenever you confront one aspect of your being, another side is likely to pop up which has very different motivations. Healing old scars in your psyche and making the effort to tend to the sometimes tedious details in establishing a practical outlet for some form of self-expression might be preoccupations. Finding a middle ground is not always easy, but with time and discipline, you will be able to make peace between the warring factions.

Once you have room in your life for all that you can be, you may be surprised at how helpful the old adversaries can be to one another. You can be many different people, depending on the environment in which you find yourself.

Opposition ♌: ♎ in 1st house, etc.

Your life is likely to be full of polarities. You make a good devil's advocate because you can see both sides of most issues. You rarely experience one viewpoint without also going to the opposite one. Though you may sometimes feel like you are on a nonstop seesaw, or just flip-flopping from one extreme to the other, you are actually in a constant process of synthesis. You are taking what is optional from both sides and finding that magic, golden mean in the center which combines the best of both worlds!

THEMES
See Chapter 4 for a description of the various themes. Also read the descriptions of themes in Chapter 6.

GAUQUELIN SECTORS[1]
Moon: charitable, comical, a dreamer, has facility, funny, gay (as in merry), generous, hot tempered, often in a group, humorous, has lightness, loves nature, lyrical, mystical, naive, poetic, religious, sentimental, susceptible to influences, witty, worldly, youthful.

Venus: benevolent, a dandy, has facility, gracious, greathearted, great beauty, often in love, scandalous, successful, youthful.

Mars: active, animates others, ardent, audacious, bold, combative, courageous, a director, dynamic, efficacious, energetic, heroic, a leader, lively, realistic, resolute, self-willed, stubborn, tenacious, unyielding, vigorous, has vitality.

Jupiter: abundant, admirable, ambitious, has authority, bantering, bohemian, brilliant, charming, a dandy, at ease, expressive, gay (merry), harsh, impetuous, influences others, ironic, liked, lively, masterful, merry, mordant, original, popular, powerful, self-willed, smiling, sparkling, successful, has verve, has vitality, warm, witty.

Saturn: amiable, calm, careful, cold, has common sense, conscientious, deep, dignified, discreet, distant, esteemed, experimenter, likes family, not financially motivated, good, good fellow, hardworking, intellectual, meditative, methodical, minute, modest, observant, patient, precise, prudent, pure, reflective, reserved, a research worker, respectful, retiring, scrupulous, secretive, serene, severe, silent, simple, solemn, solitary, straight, a teacher, timid, trustworthy, unsociable.

PLANETS CONJUNCT ANGLES
Consider any planet conjuncting an angle (within four degrees) as a major focus on the letter of the alphabet represented by that planet. Read the appropriate section in Chapter 3. If the angle is the Ascendant, read about that letter also in Chapter 6 (identity). If the angle is the Descendant, read also in Chapter 8

---

1. See also *The Psychology of the Planets* by Francoise Gauquelin published by ACS Publications, 1982.

(relationships). If the angle is the Midheaven, read also in Chapters 7 (career) and 15 (parents). If the angle is the IC, read also in Chapter 15 (parents).

ASPECT CONFIGURATIONS

T-squares and Grand Crosses

Cardinal: This configuration symbolizes inner ambivalence. You are trying to balance: 1) the need to be free and independent, 2) a desire for emotional closeness and vulnerability, 3) comfortable and equal associations and 4) control and power in the world. Juggling needs for liberty, dependence, peer relationships and authority is not always easy. It takes discipline and attention to make a place in life for each of these.

On another level, this is the struggle to divide your time and energy between personal self-development, a home and family, a commitment to a mate and a career or position of dominance in the outside world. All are important to you and all are necessary for a fulfilling life. The challenge is to structure your life in order to make room for each, not sacrificing any one for the others.

Fixed: This configuration indicates inner ambivalence. The struggle is between a focus on personal pleasures and possessions, the urge to do something more which will gain an emotional response from others, the desire to share an intimate, mutually pleasurable relationship and the drive to be independent, free from any ties.

The battleground is often over sexual/sensual/financial issues. You may have an internal struggle between self-indulgence versus self-control and swing from feast to famine styles (whether over food, sex, drinking, spending money or other physical pleasures). The inner conflict could be externalized so that you end up in power struggles with the people closest to you — usually over issues of the control of finances and pleasures.

The challenge is to balance your own, inner needs. Then the outer relationships come more into tune. Choices must be made between security versus risk or stability versus change in your handling of love, money, sex and indulgences. Intimacy must be balanced against freedom and independence of action. All have a place in your life. You must choose when and where.

Mutable: This configuration symbolizes inner ambivalence in areas of faith, trust, values and goals. You are likely to be multitalented and initially experience difficulty in settling down to one or two options. You may be scattered for a time, trying to keep up with a multiplicity of interests. Perfectionism may very well be a challenge. Whether directed toward yourself (wanting to never make a mistake) or other people (searching for the perfect parent, partner, child, etc.), demanding more than is possible from human beings sets us up for disillusionment and disappointment.

Faith and values are often an important area to examine. Unless your priorities are clear, it is easy to feel scattered or overextended with your fingers in too many pies. You may experience a lack of faith, needing to develop confidence in yourself or trust in a Higher Power. You may exhibit too much faith — grandiose or simply rash in your actions. This placement points to the need to develop clear priorities, a firm and grounded belief system and goals which are reachable.

Grand Trines

Fire: This configuration indicates much potential confidence, directness and spontaneity. You are likely to have a higher level of physical vitality and energy than other people and recuperate more rapidly than most. Zest, creativity, enthusiasm and love of life are all high. With a native optimism, you tend to trust that things will work out — and they usually do. Warm, exuberant and expressive, you are generally clear about what you want and able to go for it!

Earth: This configuration indicates the potential of great ability in handling the physical/material world. This includes the capacity to enjoy the senses and also to work successfully. Skills at working effectively and well are likely. A sense of dedication is usually strong. Discipline, effort, pragmatism, a practical assessment of necessities, all come naturally to you. Grounded and thorough, you know how to get the job done and have the patience to keep on until you complete your projects. Capable and competent, you realistically assess the world and carry out your responsibilities (and often more).

Air: This configuration shows a mental emphasis, an involvement with the world of ideas. Often, an active and articulate tongue is suggested as well. People and social interactions are a part of the focus. The suggestion is that you are an individual who needs a lot of mental stimulation, information exchange and interactions with others. Detachment, logic, rationality and a lighthearted approach are all likely talents of yours. Theorizing and dealing with abstractions come naturally to you. You thrive in an intellectual atmosphere.

Water: This configuration suggests a deep sensitivity and potentially very strong empathy for others. With the capacity to tune into your own depths as well as those of other people, much can be learned on the intuitive, nonverbal level. Feelings are paramount as you seek to unravel wish fulfillment from a true inner knowing. With such a protective combination, you may very well receive assistance from others, or give succor to them (or both).

CHAPTER NINETEEN

THE ART OF ASTROLOGICAL COUNSELING

The astrological counselor is operating in a helping role. Though there are no absolute rules about "how" to be a counselor, there are some common themes which emerge from skilled healers. (More specific details about counseling techniques and research in the area of effective strategies for helping people is provided in my book *Healing with the Horoscope*.)

The process of **turning negatives into positives** is a major hallmark of all the great psychotherapists from Jung to Perls to Satir. The successful healer knows how to set limits; s/he does not rush in immediately to make everything better, but rather encourages clients to help themselves, to develop their own strengths. Therapists who are highly effective tend to be flexible and utilize whatever tools seem appropriate at a given moment in counseling. Empathic and open, expert counselors are able to enter the world views of their clients. And the talented therapist knows that there can be more than one "right" answer to any given question or "problem." They are open to alternatives.

Some potential pitfalls of counseling can be illustrated with an example of one "combination of two" (letters of the astrological alphabet). A chart could emphasize the 1/10 issues in at least 14 different ways:

1) A conjunction between Mars and Saturn (or **any** aspect between Mars and Saturn).
2) Saturn in the 1st house.
3) Mars in the 10th house.
4) Saturn in Aries.
5) Mars in Capricorn.
6) Saturn in aspect to any planet in the 1st house, any planet ruling the 1st, or Saturn in aspect to the Ascendant (or East Point or Antivertex if you use them).
7) Mars in aspect to any planet in the 10th, any planet ruling the 10th, or Mars in aspect to the MC.

8) Any ruler of the 1st in the 10th or in Capricorn.
9) Any ruler of the 10th in the 1st or in Aries.
10) Any planet in Capricorn occupying the 1st house.
11) Any planet in Aries occupying the 10th house.
12) Any ruler of the 1st in aspect to any ruler of the 10th.
13) Any planet in the 1st aspecting a planet in the 10th.
14) Any planet in Aries aspecting a planet in Capricorn.

In a given chart, a 1-10 (or other) theme might never appear, or it might appear 16 or more times. Clearly, the more important the theme in the nature of the person, the more times that theme is repeated in the horoscope! This makes our task much easier. We know what is **most** significant will be emphasized by the chart also!

How then do we read such a theme in our astrological alphabet? Take the example of a Mars/Saturn conjunction. Many of the old, traditional books will tell you that this means you will be blocked, inhibited, held back from personal action. (The world will get you.) Other books will accuse the person with such a conjunction of being hard, ruthless, ambitious, willing to step on people to get to the top. More modern texts will tell you that you are potentially very capable, have tremendous drive and endurance and can achieve almost anything in life.

Who is right? They all are. (And they are all wrong too!) **Some** people at **some** periods in their lives will feel blocked, inhibited and held back. At other times, they may be ruthless, ambitious and hard. And they are likely to have periods of great achievement. To limit any client to one form of the potential expressions of any 1/10 combination is shortsighted and rarely helpful.

What are we combining? Letter 1 (in any form) symbolizes self-will — the drive, energy, vitality, physical health and strength to go for what you want in life. It indicates assertion and (potentially) aggression, the pursuit of one's own, personal desires. The basic theme is: "I want to do what I want to do and I want to do it **now**!" Letter 10 (in any form) symbolizes the rules of the game, the limits that are bigger than a single human being, the multiple restrictions placed by societal rules and regulations, physical laws (such as gravity) and social expectations (such as "appropriate" behavior). Letter 10 is a key to all the "shoulds" and "shouldn'ts" of life, including our internal monitor — the conscience.

So, what can happen when we put together self-will with the limits to self-will? Three general outcomes are possible, with many variations on a theme within each general group.
(1) The individual may overdo the limits side of life and give up. Such people are afraid to even try. They give up, convinced they would just fail and fall short anyway. Expecting to be blocked, criticized, inhibited or otherwise limited in their endeavors, they stop before starting and do not even try for what they want. Dr. Dobyns calls them self-blockers.
(2) The individual may overdo the self-assertion side and be constantly pushing the world. Such people are trying to do more than is possible and continually

hit the stone wall of reality, having to confront the fact that there **are** certain rules of the game of life; we cannot live solely on our own terms. Until they learn to live within the limits, such people may break the laws of society (criminals), the regulations of social behavior and expectations, the physical laws of the universe (for example, endangering their health through Type A behavior or other actions which ignore the basic limitations of a physical body). Dr. Dobyns calls them overdrivers.

(3) The individual may reach a reasonable compromise between assertion and reality. Such people accomplish a great deal, working within the limits of the world. They figure out the rules of the game and do all that they can, to get what they want, from within a pragmatic framework.

Is there a way to make a judgment between these three general potentials? Yes and no. The first clue is that the planets are the strongest statement. So, all other things being equal, Saturn in the 1st is more likely to indicate self-blocking while Mars in the 10th is more likely to symbolize overdrive. (However, all other things are seldom equal.) Houses are also vital. A strongly occupied 10th house shows a strong inner focus on limits, rules and roles, regulations and doing something right. This can lead to self-blocking if carried too far.

Generally, the more fire in a chart (counting planets strongly aspected and occupied houses as well as occupied signs), the more potential overdrive. The more water and often earth, the more caution, conservatism and, potentially, self-blocking. Cultural expectations are significant. Certain cultural groups (such as the Japanese) are much less likely to express overdrive through criminal behavior (although they may do it in business). Women are traditionally socialized to be less in touch with the Martian side of their nature, so are more prone to depression and potentially self-blocking.

Early experiences can be influential and offer clues. For example, a self-blocker may have had a difficult childhood with a critical parental figure. However, it is also quite possible that the overdrive individual is trying to "prove" something to Mommy or Daddy by making it to the top; the overdrive individual also could have experienced a childhood that was difficult. What is important is not so much **what** happened when we were young (or at any age), but **how we feel about it**! Our interpretations of our experience, our perspectives on events are much more significant than the actual happenings. Two people can have the same outer event and react in diametrically opposed fashions.

And, it gets even more complicated. So far, we have just discussed three general categories of behavior for the 1/10 mixture in a horoscope. Within these three general possibilities, there are as many variations as there are human beings. Self-blockers can include the true paranoid who is afraid to try anything because he "knows" the FBI, CIA, KGB or some other conspiracy will just step in and "get him" if he attempts to do what he wants. Another self-blocker might have had parents (especially a father figure) who were impossible to please. No matter what she did, it was never enough, never measured up, always could have been better. So, after a time, she simply stopped trying to do anything. Sadly, even after the parents died, the person could have so internalized that critical parent image, that she continued to put herself down. Another individual might have had an extremely difficult childhood, with many traumatic events, lacking opportunities to develop many skills or strengths. That person might simply lack the experience to trust his/her abilities, never having had the option of trying things on for size. And so on, with many other possibilities.

In terms of the overdrive option, the variations are still myriad. One person might be a criminal, choosing anything from robbery to rape to embezzlement to other forms of putting his own personal needs, aggression, desires far ahead of any societal standards or considerations of the humanity of all of us. Another person might be subject to periodic health breakdowns. Unwilling to accept the limitations of 24 hours in a day and certain basic physical needs for nutrition, rest and relaxation, she could simply live life at a high stress level, with her body becoming ill and **forcing** her to slow down periodically and take it easy. In terms of the middle ground, achievement can occur in many different areas — from the successful artist to the capable zoo keeper. The blend merely indicates talent for combining energy and practicality; assertion and realism; action and endurance.

Herein lies the trap for the unwary astrologer who believes that astrology should be able to "predict" which path the client will take. If you see ten clients, each one containing a strong, repeated theme of 1/10 in the horoscope, how do you decide which one is a criminal, which one is a successful business executive, which one is a frustrated, inhibited artist, which one is an unhappy, inadequate, unemployed individual, etc.?

I fervently hope you **don't**!

Let's look at the options. You can be right. You can be wrong and you can be partially right and partially wrong. If you are wrong, you look silly; astrology looks silly and you may end up with a libel suit (for implying someone could be a criminal) or worse.

Suppose you are right. Your psyche is right on that day and you tell a client (correctly) that she is a dynamite person, the president of her company, earning $800,000 a year and already listed in several *Who's Whos*. What have you accomplished? Well, you probably feel great. Being "right" is a wonderful sensation; I love it myself. How does the client feel? She probably feels a sense of awe (though she may also wonder if you simply recognized her from those *Who's Who* articles). She is also likely to feel, "Oh, I guess it had to be this way. I guess I was destined to be successful. After all, that's what the horoscope says and that is what happened." So, where does she go from here?

Let us suppose she is a fairly together person and she decides, "This is incredible and amazing that an astrologer could pick up all that about me, but I am still going to do my part regardless of what the stars say." She may continue on her road to the top. She could also decide, "The stars guarantee me success; I can do what I want!" and slip into overdrive, stepping on people and being too ruthless and self-centered in her drive for success. She might also decide, "Gee, if it's all foreordained anyway, there isn't much fun to it. Guess I'll just let life happen, since it doesn't matter what I do; fate will determine it anyway!" and fall into self-blocking.

The above example is working with a client who has had a successful, productive life. How much more damage might be done with a client who feels naturally inadequate, unable to cope, who identifies himself as a failure if the astrologer were to "confirm" that "Yes, your horoscope indicates that you have had a hard life and are likely to encounter many roadblocks and much difficulty in this life. You have many challenges ahead!" In an extreme situation, such a client might even choose suicide rather than continue what he saw as an "inevitable" downward trend.

The point is not that astrologers are supposed to be Pollyannas and seek only the positive in the horoscope. **Unremitting sweetness is as poisonous as unmitigated gloom**. The point is that **if** we are successful in guessing the right details of a client's life, we usually contribute to that client feeling "locked in" — it "had" to happen that way! As modern psychological research demonstrates, one of the most important factors in people handling their lives is a sense of personal responsibility and personal power. "Right on" predictions take that away from the client.

And what of the times when the astrologer is partially right and partially wrong? Take, for example, our successful lady executive. By concentrating on her current achievements, I may take the focus away from other options and other experiences. If I blow her away by predicting her exact salary, or the precise field of business she occupies, we may never get around to discussing how inadequate she felt as a child, how she could never please her father and believed,until age 30, that she would never amount to anything! You may never discover that she **has** experienced at least two of the different paths of blending 1 and 10 in her chart and in her nature. Similarly, with the man who feels totally blocked, inadequate and unhappy, if you focus only on his current pain and lack of success (as he defines it), you may never discover that ten years ago, he was a high achiever, the top of his field, pushing himself to the limit. Then, he overdid the stress and ended up in a serious accident with subsequent health problems that led to his current difficulties and feelings of failure. So, he has experienced overdrive and realistic accomplishments as well as self-blocking. But if you reaffirm his self-blocking stance with "correct" predictions, there is little support for other options in his life!

When working with people, being "right" can also mean being very "wrong." The truth is many-sided and often not that simple.

Let's look at another example. The partnership letters of our astrological alphabet, for example, are 7 and 8. Letter 7 has to do with face-to-face interactions, partnerships and regular, ongoing relationships. Letter 8 has to do with intimacy, joint resources and finances, and the ability to share pleasures, passions and money with another human being in a mate relationship. Both 7 and 8 are involved in reading the partnership picture.

Letters 9 and 12, by contrast, are connected to our search for the Infinite, our looking for God in some form. This search can be through religion, science, education, travel, mysticism, the occult or other forms of inspiration and seeking a sense of meaning and purpose for life. Often, the person is drawn to nature, art, beauty in some form as a channel for experiencing the connection to something Higher. The reach is toward the Infinite and consequently, expectations are often infinitely high. We may dream and yearn for more than is possible, expecting that part of life to be ultimately meaningful and ecstatic on a cosmic level.

So, what happens if we mix 7 and 8 with 9 and 12? We have the search for God mixed with human relationship. Logically, we can see a number of possibilities. Some people will literally marry God (go into the church). Some people will search forever for the perfect partner, never finding him or her. No one will ever measure up to the impossibly high standard. Others will have multiple relationships, wanting **so much** to have the beautiful dream that they talk themselves into believing everything is ideal. When they wake up to the reality of a human relationship that is not perfect, they may give it up and try again with a new Prince of Princess Charming. Each time, they fall for the fantasy. Another option is attracting partners who believe they **are** perfect, ideal and expect to be placed on a pedestal! Savior/victim relationships can also occur, where one party plays God to the other, trying to save him/her — whether from alcoholism, drug addiction, illness or some other form of escapism. The victim is avoiding facing an imperfect world. The savior has succumbed to the illusion that s/he can make everything perfect for the other person.

Another option is to project that search for beauty and choose partners that are exceptionally attractive, or artistically talented. If we select someone mostly on the basis of outside appearance, we are likely to be disappointed and disillusioned later. If we attract someone who is artistic and has a talent for creating beauty, we need to also recognize our own aesthetic side, lest we fall into extremes in the relationship. (A typical division by projection, for example, is the spacey, talented, impractical artist and the hardworking, disciplined, critical realist.)

Some people will simply have incredibly high standards for relating and sharing — almost a spiritual sense where unless it is pure and ideal, they do not want to be involved. Some people will make their relationships an ultimate value and constantly strive to create a more perfect environment, a more ideal sharing. Other people will seek God together. Rather than expecting one person to provide the truth and meaning for the other, **together** they can study, read, take a spiritual path, travel or otherwise seek that sense of meaning and inspiration in life. That last couple is still blending 9 and 12 with 7 and 8 — but in a very different way than the earlier examples.

All these are options for the individual with some combination of 9 and/or 12 with 7 and/or 8. Again, picking on the old traditional books, they will warn the individual with Neptune in the 7th that s/he will marry an alcoholic. Certainly that is one option. But how helpful — as a counselor — is it to say, "You could marry an alcoholic"? How does that help the person in any way to deal with the issue?

If individuals can realize that their search for meaning and something higher in life is connected to their desire for a sharing, human relationship, they have the opportunity to make some choices. They can deal with their idealism and build a positive channel for it. Whether they choose to create beauty, or adopt a healing role on a professional level or seek a partner to share their religious/philosophical/spiritual quest — it does not matter. The key is that the client is now empowered. The client can learn to **share** the reach for the Infinite with a partner — neither party expecting the other to do or be all, or to provide infinite love and beauty **for** him/her. By recognizing the underlying motivations, clients can develop satisfying channels for meeting their needs to replace old, frustrating conflicts.

Please note here again, there is absolutely nothing wrong with the search for the Infinite. We all need that sense of meaning and purpose, inspiration in our lives. We all need something to reach for, something to yearn toward. And, there is nothing wrong or "bad" or "malefic" about wanting a partnership, an equal give and take. What requires a little work is figuring out a way to live our lives that will satisfy both those needs, in some reasonable blend. (Our role is to assist the client in turning perceived "negatives" into positives.)

My goal, as an astrological counselor, is to truly see the inherent good in the **whole** horoscope and the whole person. The more I can be accepting and see the potential for every theme to be expressed in a fulfilling way, the more likely my clients will discover that satisfaction themselves!

CHAPTER TWENTY

PUTTING ALL THE PIECES TOGETHER: A SUMMARY

Many students and even semiprofessional astrologers end up feeling that the horoscope is a jigsaw puzzle — with a myriad of small pieces needing to be interlocked. The use of the Zip Code makes the search for themes in a horoscope much easier.

The technical steps of this process can be summarized as:
1) Memorize the Zip Code.
2) Conceptualize themes listed here — and invent your own — which involve combinations of letters of the alphabet.
3) Pinpoint different life areas in the horoscope (identity, career, etc.) by logical analysis of the different factors of the Zip Code.
4) Analyze the chart as a whole, and each life area individually, in terms of **repeated themes**.
5) In weighting different letters of the alphabet and themes, consider planets the strongest statement, followed by aspects, houses and signs in that order.
6) Read the interpretations given in this book, and expand upon them with your own thinking, intuition and experience.

The philosophical premises of this approach can be summarized as:
1) Life is learning and everything offers potential growth in understanding.
2) Everything in the horoscope and in the life has **potentially** positive manifestations.
3) The role of the astrological counselor is to assist personal empowerment and the assumption of personal responsibility.
4) Healers help people turn perceived "negatives" into positives.

5) Life is a balancing act — to make a place for each of our various sides, to make peace between warring factions, and to allow positive expression of the different parts of ourselves and our horoscopes.
6) There is often more than one "right" answer to a given question, more than one meaning in a given experience.

These twelve principles, along with the twelve-letter alphabet of astrology, can open the door to a richer, fuller, more satisfying life!

May the best in Life and Love and Light be yours!

WORKSHEETS

Following are worksheets for the various life areas described in a horoscope (identity, career, relationships, etc.). Their inclusion here is for three purposes:

(1) for the enjoyment of those people in this world who just love numbers and lists
(2) for the reassurance of individuals practicing the rapid scanning method of spotting themes who want something specific against which to check their results
(3) for those individuals interested in the question of weighting various factors — my tentative contributions (which may change over time).

   I again **strongly urge** that these worksheets be used only as a handy review of factors to be scanned in delineating various options. You will gain a quicker and easier use of the astrological alphabet if you do not tie yourself down to exact lists and numbers. Allow yourself to get an "impression" of a horoscope based on a rapid scan. You can then check your impression a few times by using these worksheets. You are likely to find that a quick scan gains the same conclusions as completing these worksheets thoroughly — with much less time and effort.

IDENTITY

FACTOR	WEIGHTING POINTS	LETTER OF ALPHABET	WEIGHT
♂♂ - 8° orb	12 → 2 (depending on orb)		
♂ Asc. - 8° orb	12 → 2 (depending on orb)		
♂ Asc. ruler - 8° orb	12 → 2 (depending on orb)		
♂ Ruler of other signs in 1st house - 8° orb	6 → 1 (depending on orb)		
♂ AV - 3° orb	8 → 4 (depending on orb)		
♂ EP - 3° orb	8 → 4 (depending on orb)		
Houses ruled by planets forming any of the above conjunctions	2 pts. for sign on the cusp		2
	2 pts. if that sign is occupied in a house		2
	1 pt. if that sign is unoccupied in a house		1
Planet(s) in 1st house	10		10
Planet(s) within 2° of 1st house, but in 2nd	3		3
Asc. sign	6		6
∥ ♂ - 1° orb	2		2
∥ Asc. - 1° orb	2		2
∥ Asc. ruler - 1° orb	2		2
∥ Ruler of other sign(s) in 1st house - 1° orb	1		1
∥ AV - 1° orb	2		
∥ EP - 1° orb	2		2
House of ♂	2		2
House of Asc. ruler	2		2
House of ruler of other sign(s) in 1st	1		1
House of AV	2		2
House of EP	2		2
House cusp(s) ruled by planet(s) in 1st	2		2
House(s) with sign(s) ruled by planet(s) in 1st	2 pts. if sign is occupied		2
	1 pt. if sign is unoccupied		1
	2		2
Planet(s) in ♈	2		2
House occupied by planet(s) in ♈	2		2
	2		2

IDENTITY (CONTINUED)

FACTOR		WEIGHTING POINTS	LETTER OF ALPHABET	WEIGHT
_____	Sign of ♂	1	_____	1
_____	Sign of Asc. ruler	1	_____	1
_____	Sign of ruler of other sign(s) in 1st house	½	_____	½
_____	Sign of AV	1	_____	1
_____	Sign of EP		_____	1
_____	Sign occupied by planet(s) in 1st	1	_____	1
_____	House with ♈ on cusp	1	_____	1
_____	Unoccupied sign(s) in 1st	½	_____	½

TOTALS

Letter 1: ____   Letter 4: ____   Letter 7: ____   Letter 10: ____
Letter 2: ____   Letter 5: ____   Letter 8: ____   Letter 11: ____
Letter 3: ____   Letter 6: ____   Letter 9: ____   Letter 12: ____

Emphasized element(s) if any _____   Emphasized quality if any _____
Nodal polarity by house ____ by sign ____   Significant theme(s) _____
Harmony aspects to Letter(s) _____   Conflict aspects to Letter(s) _____

WORK

FACTOR		WEIGHTING POINTS	LETTER OF ALPHABET	WEIGHT
_____	♂ ♀ - 8° orb	12 →2 (depending on orb)	_____	_____
_____	♂ ♄ - 8° orb	12 →2 (depending on orb)	_____	_____
_____	♂☿ - 8° orb	12 → 2 (depending on orb)	_____	_____
_____	♂♃ - 8° orb	6 →2 (depending on orb)	_____	_____
_____	♂♅ - 8° orb	6 →2 (depending on orb)	_____	_____
_____	♂ MC - 8° orb	12 →2 (depending on orb)	_____	_____
_____	♂ MC ruler - 8° orb	12 →2 (depending on orb)	_____	_____
_____	♂ 2nd cusp ruler - 8° orb	12 →2 (depending on orb)	_____	_____
_____	♂ 6th cusp ruler - 8° orb	12 →2 (depending on orb)	_____	_____
_____	♂ Ruler of other signs in 2nd house - 8° orb	6 →1 (depending on orb)	_____	_____
_____	♂ Ruler of other signs in 6th house - 8° orb	6 →1 (depending on orb)	_____	_____
_____	♂ Ruler of other signs in 10th house - 8° orb	6 →1 (depending on orb)	_____	_____
_____	Houses ruled by planets forming any of the above conjunctions	2 pts. if sign is on a cusp	_____	2
_____		2 pts. if sign is occupied in the house	_____	2
_____		1 pt. if sign is unoccupied in house	_____	1
_____	Planets within 2° of 2nd, 6th or 10th but occupying 1st, 3rd, 5th, 7th or 11th	3	_____	3
_____	Planet(s) in 2nd house	10	_____	10
_____	Planet(s) in 6th house	10	_____	10
_____	Planet(s) in 10th house	10	_____	10
_____	MC sign	6	_____	6

WORK

FACTOR		WEIGHTING POINTS	LETTER OF ALPHABET	WEIGHT
_____	‖ ♀ - 1° orb	2	_____	2
_____	‖ ♂ - 1° orb	2	_____	2
_____	‖ ♄ - 1° orb	2	_____	
_____	‖ ♃ - 1° orb	1	_____	1
_____	‖ ♅ - 1° orb	1	_____	1
_____	‖ MC - 1° orb	2	_____	2
_____	‖ MC ruler - 1° orb	2	_____	2
_____	‖ 2nd cusp ruler - 1° orb	2	_____	2
_____	‖ 6th cusp ruler - 1° orb	2	_____	2
_____	‖ Ruler of other sign(s) in 2nd house - 1° orb	1	_____	1
_____	‖ Ruler of other sign(s) in 6th house - 1° orb	1	_____	1
_____	‖ Ruler of other sign(s) in 10th house - 1° orb	1	_____	1
_____	House of ♀	2	_____	2
_____	House of ♄	2	_____	2
_____	House of ♂	2	_____	2
_____	House of ♃	1	_____	1
_____	House of ♅	1	_____	1
_____	House of MC ruler	2	_____	2
_____	House of ruler of 6th cusp	2	_____	2
_____	House of ruler of 2nd cusp	2	_____	2
_____	House of ruler of other sign(s) in 2nd	1	_____	1
_____	House of ruler of other sign(s) in 6th	1	_____	1
_____	House of ruler of other sign(s) in 10th	1	_____	1
_____	House cusp(s) ruled by planet(s) in 2nd	2	_____	2
_____		2	_____	2
_____	House cusp(s) ruled by planet(s) in 6th	2	_____	2
_____		2	_____	2
_____	House cusp(s) ruled by planet(s) in 10th	2	_____	2
_____	Houses with signs ruled by planet(s) in 2nd, 6th or 10th	2 pts. if sign is occupied	_____	2
_____		1 pt. if sign is unoccupied	_____	1
_____		2	_____	2
_____	House(s) occupied by planet(s) in ♉, ♍ or ♑	2	_____	2
_____	Planet(s) in ♉	2	_____	2
_____		2	_____	2
_____		2	_____	2
_____	Planet(s) in ♍	2	_____	2
_____		2	_____	2
_____		2	_____	2

WORK   (CONTINUED)

FACTOR	WEIGHTING POINTS	LETTER OF ALPHABET	WEIGHT
_____ Planet(s) in ♑	2	_____	2
_____	2	_____	2
_____	2	_____	2
_____ Sign of ☿	1	_____	1
_____ Sign of ♀	1	_____	1
_____ Sign of ♄	1	_____	1
_____ Sign of ♃	½	_____	½
_____ Sign of ♅	½	_____	½
_____ Sign of MC ruler	1	_____	1
_____ Sign of ruler of 6th cusp	1	_____	1
_____ Sign of ruler of 2nd cusp	1	_____	1
_____ Sign of ruler of other sign(s) in 2nd house	½	_____	½
_____ Sign of ruler of other sign(s) in 6th house	½	_____	½
_____ Sign of ruler of other sign(s) in 10th house	½	_____	½
_____ Sign occupied by planet(s) in 2nd	1	_____	1
_____ Sign occupied by planet(s) in 6th	1	_____	1
_____ Sign occupied by planet(s) in 10th	1	_____	1
_____ House with ♉ on cusp	1	_____	1
_____ House with ♍ on cusp	1	_____	1
_____ House with ♑ on cusp	1	_____	1
_____ Unoccupied sign(s) in 2nd	½	_____	½
_____ Unoccupied sign(s) in 6th	½	_____	½
_____ Unoccupied sign(s) in 10th	½	_____	½

TOTALS

Letter 1: ____   Letter 4: ____   Letter 7: ____   Letter 10: ____
Letter 2: ____   Letter 5: ____   Letter 8: ____   Letter 11: ____
Letter 3: ____   Letter 6: ____   Letter 9: ____   Letter 12: ____

Emphasized element(s) if any _____   Emphasized quality if any _____
Nodal polarity by house ____ by sign ____   Significant theme(s) _____
Harmony aspects to Letter(s) _____   Conflict aspects to Letter(s) _____

RELATIONSHIPS

FACTOR		WEIGHTING POINTS	LETTER OF ALPHABET	WEIGHT
_____ _____	♂ ♀ - 8° orb	12→2 (depending on orb)	_____ _____	_____ _____
_____ _____	♂ ♇ - 8° orb	12→2 (depending on orb)	_____ _____	_____ _____
_____ _____	♂ ☿ - 8° orb	6→1 (depending on orb)	_____ _____	_____ _____
_____ _____	♂ ⚹ - 8° orb	6→1 (depending on orb)	_____ _____	_____ _____
_____ _____	♂ Descendant - 8° orb	12→2 (depending on orb)	_____ _____	_____ _____
_____ _____ _____	♂ Vertex - 3° orb	8→4 (depending on orb)	_____ _____	_____ _____
_____ _____	♂ West Point - 3° orb	8→4 (depending on orb)	_____ _____	_____ _____
_____ _____	♂ Descendant ruler - 8° orb	12→2 (depending on orb)	_____ _____	_____ _____
_____ _____	♂ 8th cusp ruler - 8° orb	12→2 (depending on orb)	_____ _____	_____ _____
_____ _____	♂ Ruler of other signs in 7th house - 8° orb	6→1 (depending on orb)	_____ _____	_____ _____
_____ _____	♂ Ruler of other signs in 8th house - 8° orb	6→1 (depending on orb)	_____ _____	_____ _____
_____ _____ _____ _____ _____ _____	Houses ruled by planets forming any of the above conjunctions	2 pts. if sign is on a cusp 2 pts. if sign is occupied in the house 1 pt. if sign is unoccupied in the house	_____ _____ _____ _____	2 2 1
_____ _____ _____ _____	Planet(s) in 7th house	10	_____ _____ _____	10
_____ _____	Planet(s) in 8th house	10	_____ _____	10
_____ _____	Planets within 2° of 7th or 8th, but in 6th or 9th	3	_____	3
_____	Descendant sign	6	_____	6
_____	∥ ♀ - 1° orb	2		2

RELATIONSHIPS (CONTINUED)

FACTOR		WEIGHTING POINTS	LETTER OF ALPHABET	WEIGHT
_____	‖ ♇ - 1° orb	2	_____	2
_____	‖ ♀ - 1° orb	1	_____	1
_____	‖ ✳ - 1° orb	1	_____	1
_____	‖ Descendant - 1° orb	2	_____	2
_____	‖ Descendant ruler - 1° orb	2	_____	2
_____	‖ Vertex - 1° orb	2	_____	2
_____	‖ West Point - 1° orb	2	_____	2
_____	‖ 8th cusp ruler - 1° orb	2	_____	2
_____	‖ Ruler of other sign(s) in 7th house - 1° orb	2	_____	2
_____	‖ Ruler of other sign(s) in 8th house - 1° orb	2	_____	2
_____	House of ♀	2	_____	2
_____	House of ♇	2	_____	2
_____	House of ♀	1	_____	1
_____	House of ✳	1	_____	1
_____	House of Descendant ruler	2	_____	2
_____	House of 8th cusp ruler	2	_____	2
_____	House of Vertex	2	_____	2
_____	House of West Point	2	_____	2
_____	House of ruler of other sign(s) in 7th	1	_____	1
_____	House of ruler of other sign(s) in 8th	1	_____	1
_____	House cusp(s) ruled by planet(s) in 7th	2	_____	2
		2	_____	2
_____	House cusp(s) ruled by planet(s) in 8th	2	_____	2
		2	_____	2
_____	House(s) with sign(s) ruled by planet(s) in 7th or 8th	2 pts. if signs are occupied	_____	2
_____		1 pt. if signs are occupied	_____	1
_____	House(s) occupied by planet(s) in ♎ or ♏	2	_____	2
_____		2	_____	2
_____	Planet(s) in ♎	2	_____	2
_____		2	_____	2
_____	Planet(s) in ♏	2	_____	2
_____		2	_____	2
_____		2	_____	2
_____	Sign of ♀	1	_____	1
_____	Sign of ♇	1	_____	1
_____	Sign of ♀	½	_____	½
_____	Sign of ✳	½	_____	½
_____	Sign of Descendant	1	_____	1
_____	Sign of 8th cusp	1	_____	1
_____	Sign of Vertex	1	_____	1
_____	Sign of West Point	1	_____	1

RELATIONSHIPS (CONTINUED)

FACTOR		WEIGHTING POINTS	LETTER OF ALPHABET	WEIGHT
_____	Sign of Descendant ruler	1	_____	1
_____	Sign of 8th cusp ruler	1	_____	1
_____	Sign of ruler of other sign(s) in 7th house	½	_____	½
_____	Sign of ruler of other sign(s) in 8th house	½	_____	½
_____	Sign occupied by planet(s) in 7th	1	_____	1
_____	Sign occupied by planet(s) in 8th	1	_____	1
_____	House with ♎ on cusp	1	_____	1
_____	House with ♏ on cusp	1	_____	1
_____	Unoccupied sign(s) in 7th	½	_____	½
_____	Unoccupied sign(s) in 8th	½	_____	½

TOTALS

Letter 1: ____   Letter 4: ____   Letter 7: ____   Letter 10: ____
Letter 2: ____   Letter 5: ____   Letter 8: ____   Letter 11: ____
Letter 3: ____   Letter 6: ____   Letter 9: ____   Letter 12: ____

Emphasized element(s) if any _____   Emphasized quality if any _____
Nodal polarity by house ____ by sign ____   Significant theme(s) _____
Harmony aspects to Letter(s) _____   Conflict aspects to Letter(s) _____

MIND

FACTOR		WEIGHTING POINTS	LETTER OF ALPHABET	WEIGHT
_____ _____	♂ ☿ - 8° orb	12→2 (depending on orb)	_____ _____	_____ _____
_____ _____	♂ ♃ - 8° orb	12→2 (depending on orb)	_____ _____	_____ _____
_____ _____	♂ ♅ - 8° orb	12→2 (depending on orb)	_____ _____	_____ _____
_____ _____	♂ ? - 8° orb	6→1 (depending on orb)	_____ _____	_____ _____
_____ _____	♂ ⚵ - 8° orb	6→1 (depending on orb)	_____ _____	_____ _____
_____ _____	♂ ♀ - 8° orb	3→1 (depending on orb)	_____ _____	_____ _____
_____ _____	♂ ♆ - 8° orb	6→1 (depending on orb)	_____ _____	_____ _____
_____ _____	♂ 3rd cusp ruler - 8° orb	12→2 (depending on orb)	_____ _____	_____ _____
_____ _____	♂ 6th cusp ruler - 8° orb	12→2 (depending on orb)	_____ _____	_____ _____
_____ _____	♂ 9th cusp ruler - 8° orb	12→2 (depending on orb)	_____ _____	_____ _____
_____ _____	♂ 11th cusp ruler - 8° orb	12→2 (depending on orb)	_____ _____	_____ _____
_____ _____	♂ 7th cusp ruler - 8° orb	6→1 (depending on orb)	_____ _____	_____ _____
_____ _____	♂ 12 cusp ruler - 8° orb	6→1 (depending on orb)	_____ _____	_____ _____
_____ _____	♂ Ruler of other signs in 3rd house - 8° orb	6→1 (depending on orb)	_____ _____	_____ _____
_____ _____	♂ Ruler of other signs in 6th house - 8° orb	6→1 (depending on orb)	_____ _____	_____ _____
_____ _____	♂ Ruler of other signs in 9th house - 8° orb	6→1 (depending on orb)	_____ _____	_____ _____
_____ _____	♂ Ruler of other signs in 11th house - 8° orb	6→1 (depending on orb)	_____ _____	_____ _____

MIND (CONTINUED)

FACTOR		WEIGHTING POINTS	LETTER OF ALPHABET	WEIGHT
_____ _____	♂ Ruler of other signs in 7th house - 8° orb	3→1 (depending on orb)	_____ _____	_____ _____
_____ _____	♂ Ruler of other signs in 12th house - 8° orb	3→1 (depending on orb)	_____ _____	_____ _____
_____ _____ _____ _____ _____	Houses ruled by planets forming any of the above conjunctions	2 pts. if signs is on cusp 2 pts. if signs is occupied in house 1 pt. if sign is unoccupied in house	_____ _____ _____ _____ _____	2 2 1
_____ _____ _____ _____	Planet(s) in 3rd house	10	_____ _____ _____	10
_____ _____ _____ _____	Planet(s) in 6th house	10	_____ _____ _____	10
_____ _____ _____	Planet(s) in 9th house	10	_____ _____ _____	10
_____ _____ _____	Planet(s) in 11th house	10	_____ _____ _____	10
_____ _____ _____	Planet(s) in 7th house	5	_____ _____ _____	5
_____ _____ _____	Planet(s) in 12th house	5	_____ _____ _____	5
_____ _____ _____	Planet(s) within 2° of 3rd, 6th, 9th or 11th, but in 2nd, 4th, 5th, 8th or 10th	3 3	_____ _____ _____	3 3
_____	‖ ☿ - 1° orb	2	_____	2
_____	‖ ♃ - 1° orb	2	_____	
_____	‖ ♅ - 1° orb	2	_____	2
_____	‖ ♄ - 1° orb	1	_____	1
_____	‖ ♆ - 1° orb	1	_____	1
_____	‖ ♀ - 1° orb	½	_____	½
_____	‖ ♇ - 1° orb	1	_____	1
_____	‖ 3rd cusp ruler - 1° orb	2	_____	2
_____	‖ 6th cusp ruler - 1° orb	2	_____	2

MIND (CONTINUED)

FACTOR		WEIGHTING POINTS	LETTER OF ALPHABET	WEIGHT
_____	‖ 9th cusp ruler - 1° orb	2	_____	2
_____	‖ 11th cusp ruler - 1° orb	2	_____	2
_____	‖ 7th cusp ruler - 1° orb	1	_____	1
_____	‖ 12th cusp ruler - 1° orb	1	_____	1
_____	‖ Ruler of other sign(s) in 3rd house - 1° orb	1	_____	1
_____	‖ Ruler of other sign(s) in 6th house - 1° orb	1	_____	1
_____	‖ Ruler of other sign(s) in 9th house - 1° orb	1	_____	1
_____	‖ Ruler of other sign(s) in 11th house - 1° orb	1	_____	1
_____	‖ Ruler of other sign(s) in 7th house - 1° orb	½	_____	½
_____	‖ Ruler of other sign(s) in 12th house - 1° orb	½	_____	½
_____	House of ☿	2	_____	2
_____	House of ♃	2	_____	2
_____	House of ♅	2	_____	2
_____	House of ☊	1	_____	1
_____	House of ☋	1	_____	1
_____	House of ♀	½	_____	½
_____	House of ♆	1	_____	1
_____	House of ruler of 3rd cusp	2	_____	2
_____	House of ruler of 6th cusp	2	_____	2
_____	House of ruler of 9th cusp	2	_____	2
_____	House of ruler of 11th cusp	2	_____	2
_____	House of ruler of 7th cusp	1	_____	1
_____	House of ruler of 12th cusp	1	_____	2
_____	House of ruler of other sign(s) in 3rd	1	_____	1
_____	House of ruler of other sign(s) in 6th	1	_____	1
_____	House of ruler of other sign(s) in 9th	1	_____	1
_____	House of ruler of other sign(s) in 11th	1	_____	1
_____	House of ruler of other sign(s) in 7th	½	_____	½
_____	House of ruler of other sign(s) in 12th	½	_____	½
_____	House cusp(s) ruled by planet(s) in 3rd	2	_____	2
_____		2	_____	2
_____	House cusp(s) ruled by planet(s) in 6th	2	_____	2
_____		2	_____	2
_____	House cusp(s) ruled by planet(s) in 9th	2	_____	2
_____	House cusp(s) ruled by planet(s) in 11th	2	_____	2

MIND (CONTINUED)

FACTOR		WEIGHTING POINTS	LETTER OF ALPHABET	WEIGHT
_____	House cusp(s) ruled by planet(s) in 7th	1	_____	1
_____	House cusp(s) ruled by planet(s) in 12th	1	_____	1
_____	House with sign ruled by planet(s) in 3rd, 6th, 9th or 11th	2 pts. if sign is occupied	_____	2
_____		1 pt. if sign is unoccupied	_____	1
_____				
_____	House with sign ruled by planet(s) in 7th or 12th	1 pt. if sign is occupied	_____	1
_____		½ pt. if sign is unoccupied	_____	½
_____			_____	
_____		2	_____	2
_____	Planet(s) in ♊	2	_____	2
_____		2	_____	2
_____		2	_____	2
_____	Planet(s) in ♍	2	_____	2
_____		2	_____	2
_____		2	_____	2
_____	Planet(s) in ♐	2	_____	2
_____		2	_____	2
_____		2	_____	2
_____	Planet(s) in ♒	2	_____	2
_____		2	_____	2
_____		2	_____	2
_____	Planet(s) in ♎	1	_____	1
_____		1	_____	1
_____		1	_____	1
_____	Planet(s) in ♓	1	_____	1
_____		1	_____	1
_____		1	_____	1
_____	Sign of ☿	1	_____	1
_____	Sign of ♃	1	_____	1
_____	Sign of ♅	1	_____	1
_____	Sign of ♆	½	_____	½
_____	Sign of ?	½	_____	½
_____	Sign of ⚴	½	_____	½
_____	Sign of ♀	¼	_____	¼
_____	Sign of ruler of 3rd cusp	1	_____	1
_____	Sign of ruler of 6th cusp	1	_____	1
_____	Sign of ruler of 9th cusp	1	_____	1
_____	Sign of ruler of 11th cusp	1	_____	1
_____	Sign of ruler of 7th cusp	½	_____	½
_____	Sign of ruler of 12th cusp	½	_____	½
_____	Sign of ruler of other sign(s) in 3rd house	½	_____	½
_____	Sign of ruler of other sign(s) in 6th house	½	_____	½
_____	Sign of ruler of other sign(s) in 9th house	½	_____	½

MIND

(CONTINUED)

FACTOR		WEIGHTING POINTS	LETTER OF ALPHABET	WEIGHT
_____	Sign of ruler of other sign(s) in 11th house	½	_____	½
_____	Sign of ruler of other sign(s) in 7th house	¼	_____	¼
_____	Sign of ruler of other sign(s) in 12th house	¼	_____	¼
_____	Sign occupied by planet(s) in 3rd	1	_____	1
_____	Sign occupied by planet(s) in 6th	1	_____	1
_____	Sign occupied by planet(s) in 9th	1	_____	1
_____	Sign occupied by planet(s) in 11th	1	_____	1
_____	Sign occupied by planet(s) in 7th	½	_____	½
_____	Sign occupied by planet(s) in 12th	½	_____	½
_____	House with ♊ on cusp	1	_____	1
_____	House with ♍ on cusp	1	_____	1
_____	House with ♐ on cusp	1	_____	1
_____	House with ♒ on cusp	1	_____	1
_____	House with ♎ on cusp	½	_____	½
_____	House with ♓ on cusp	½	_____	½
_____	Unoccupied sign(s) in 3rd	½	_____	½
_____	Unoccupied sign(s) in 6th	½	_____	½
_____	Unoccupied sign(s) in 9th	½	_____	½
_____	Unoccupied sign(s) in 11th	½	_____	½
_____	Unoccupied sign(s) in 7th	¼	_____	¼
_____	Unoccupied sign(s) in 12th	¼	_____	¼

TOTALS

Letter 1: ____ Letter 4: ____ Letter 7: ____ Letter 10: ____
Letter 2: ____ Letter 5: ____ Letter 8: ____ Letter 11: ____
Letter 3: ____ Letter 6: ____ Letter 9: ____ Letter 12: ____

Emphasized element(s) if any _____ Emphasized quality if any _____
Nodal polarity by house ____ by sign ____ Significant theme(s) _____
Harmony aspects to Letter(s) _____ Conflict aspects to Letter(s) _____

CHILDREN

FACTOR		WEIGHTING POINTS	LETTER OF ALPHABET	WEIGHT
_____	♂☽ - 8° orb	12→2 (depending on orb)	_____	_____
_____	♂☉ - 8° orb	12→2 (depending on orb)	_____	_____
_____	♂♅ - 8° orb	6→1 (depending on orb)	_____	_____
_____	♂♃ - 8° orb	6→1 (depending on orb)	_____	_____
_____	♂? - 8° orb	6→1 (depending on orb)	_____	_____
_____	♂ Ascendant - 8° orb	6→1 (depending on orb)	_____	_____
_____	♂ 5th cusp ruler - 8° orb	12→2 (depending on orb)	_____	_____
_____	♂♂ - 8° orb	6→1 (depending on orb)	_____	_____
_____	♂ IC - 8° orb	12→2 (depending on orb)	_____	_____
_____	♂ Asc. ruler - 8° orb	6→1 (depending on orb)	_____	_____
_____	♂ IC ruler - 8° orb	12→2 (depending on orb)	_____	_____
_____	♂ 11th house ruler - 8° orb	6 → 1 (depending on orb)	_____	
_____	♂ Ruler of other signs in 4th house - 8° orb	6→1 (depending on orb)	_____	_____
_____	♂ Ruler of other signs in 5th house - 8° orb	6→1 (depending on orb)	_____	_____
_____	♂ Ruler of other signs in the 11th house - 8° orb	3 → 1 (depending on orb)	_____	
_____	Houses ruled by planets forming any of the above conjunctions	2 pts. if sign is on a cusp	_____	2
_____		2 pts. if sign is occupied in the house	_____	2
_____		1 pt. if sign is unoccupied in house	_____	1
_____	Planet(s) in 4th house	10	_____	10
_____	Planet(s) in 5th house	10	_____	10
_____	Planet(s) in 11th house	5	_____	5
_____	Planets within 2° of 4th or 5th, but in 3rd or 6th	3	_____	3

CHILDREN   (CONTINUED)

FACTOR		WEIGHTING POINTS	LETTER OF ALPHABET	WEIGHT
_____	IC sign	6	_____	6
_____	‖ ☽ - 1° orb	2	_____	2
_____	‖ ☉ - 1° orb	2	_____	2
_____	‖ ♅ - 1° orb	1	_____	1
_____	‖ ♃ - 1° orb	1	_____	1
_____	‖ ♂ - 1° orb	1	_____	1
_____	‖ Asc. - 1° orb	1	_____	1
_____	‖ Asc. ruler - 1° orb	1	_____	1
_____	‖ ? - 1° orb	1	_____	1
_____	‖ 5th house ruler - 1° orb	2	_____	2
_____	‖ IC - 1° orb	2	_____	2
_____	‖ IC ruler - 1° orb	2	_____	2
_____	‖ Ruler of other sign(s) in 4th house - 1° orb	1	_____	1
_____	‖ Ruler of other sign(s) in 5th house - 1° orb	1	_____	1
_____	‖ Ruler of other sign(s) in 11th house 1° orb	½	_____	½
_____	House of ☽	2	_____	2
_____	House of ♅	1	_____	1
_____	House of ♃	1	_____	1
_____	House of ♂	1	_____	1
_____	House of Asc. ruler	1	_____	1
_____	House of ?	1	_____	1
_____	House of 5th cusp ruler	2	_____	2
_____	House of IC ruler	2	_____	2
_____	House of ruler of other sign(s) in 4th	1	_____	1
_____	House of ruler of other sign(s) in 5th	1	_____	1
_____	House of ruler of other signs in 11th	½	_____	½
_____	House cusp(s) ruled by planet(s) in 4th	2	_____	2
_____	House cusp(s) ruled by planet(s) in 5th	2	_____	2
_____	House(s) with sign(s) ruled by planet(s) in 4th or 5th	2 pts. if occupied 1 pt. if unoccupied	_____	2 / 1
_____	House(s) with sign(s) ruled by planet(s) in 11th	1 pt. if occupied ½ pt. if unoccupied	_____	1 / ½
_____	House(s) occupied by planet(s) in ♋ or ♌	2 / 2	_____	2 / 2
_____	Planet(s) in ♋	2 / 2 / 2	_____	2 / 2 / 2
_____	Planet(s) in ♌	2 / 2 / 2	_____	2 / 2 / 2
_____	Sign of ☽	1	_____	1

CHILDREN (CONTINUED)

FACTOR		WEIGHTING POINTS	LETTER OF ALPHABET	WEIGHT
_____	Sign of ☉	1	_____	1
_____	Sign of ♅	½	_____	½
_____	Sign of ♃	½	_____	½
_____	Sign of ♂	½	_____	½
_____	Sign of Asc.	½	_____	½
_____	Sign of Asc. ruler	½	_____	½
_____	Sign of ♀	½	_____	½
_____	Sign of 5th cusp ruler	1	_____	1
_____	Sign of IC ruler	1	_____	1
_____	Sign of ruler of other sign(s) in 4th house	½	_____	½
_____	Sign of ruler of other sign(s) in 5th house	½	_____	½
_____	Sign occupied by planet(s) in 4th	1	_____	1
_____	Sign occupied by planet(s) in 5th	1	_____	1
_____	House with ♋ on cusp	1	_____	1
_____	House with ♑ on cusp	1	_____	1
_____	Unoccupied sign(s) in 4th	½	_____	½
_____	Unoccupied sign(s) in 5th	½	_____	½

TOTALS

Letter 1: ____   Letter 4: ____   Letter 7: ____   Letter 10: ____
Letter 2: ____   Letter 5: ____   Letter 8: ____   Letter 11: ____
Letter 3: ____   Letter 6: ____   Letter 9: ____   Letter 12: ____

Emphasized element(s) if any _____   Emphasized quality if any _____
Nodal polarity by house ____ by sign ____   Significant theme(s) _____
Harmony aspects to Letter(s) _____   Conflict aspects to Letter(s) _____

CREATIVITY

FACTOR		WEIGHTING POINTS	LETTER OF ALPHABET	WEIGHT
_____ _____	♂♂ - 8° orb	12→2 (depending on orb)	_____ _____	_____
_____ _____	♂☉ - 8° orb	12→2 (depending on orb)	_____ _____	_____
_____ _____	♂♃ - 8° orb	12→2 (depending on orb)	_____ _____	_____
_____ _____	♂♅ - 8° orb	12→2 (depending on orb)	_____ _____	_____
_____ _____	♂ Ascendant - 8° orb	12→2 (depending on orb)	_____ _____	_____
_____ _____	♂ Ascendant ruler- 8° orb	12→2 (depending on orb)	_____ _____	_____
_____ _____	♂ 5th cusp ruler - 8° orb	12→2 (depending on orb)	_____ _____	_____
_____ _____	♂ 9th cusp ruler - 8° orb	12→2 (depending on orb)	_____ _____	_____
_____ _____	♂ 11th cusp ruler - 8° orb	12→2 (depending on orb)	_____ _____	_____
_____ _____	♂ Ruler of other signs in 1st or 5th houses - 8° orb	6→1 (depending on orb)	_____ _____	_____
_____ _____	♂ Ruler of other signs in 9th or 11th house - 8° orb	6→1 (depending on orb)	_____ _____	_____
_____ _____ _____	Houses ruled by planets forming any of the above conjunctions	2 pts. if sign is on a cusp	_____ _____	2
_____ _____		2 pts. if sign is occupied in the house	_____	2
_____		1 pt. if sign is unoccupied in house	_____ _____	1
_____	Planet(s) in 1st house	10	_____	10
_____	Planet(s) in 5th house	10	_____	10
_____	Planet(s) in 9th house	10	_____ _____	10

CREATIVITY (CONTINUED)

FACTOR		WEIGHTING POINTS	LETTER OF ALPHABET	WEIGHT
_____	Planet(s) in 11th house	10	_____	10
_____			_____	
_____			_____	
_____	Planet(s) within 2° of 1st, 5th, 9th or 11th, but in 12th, 2nd, 4th, 6th, 8th or 10th houses	3	_____	3
_____	‖ ♂ - 1° orb	2	_____	2
_____	‖ ☉ - 1° orb	2	_____	
_____	‖ ♃ - 1° orb	2	_____	2
_____	‖ ♅ - 1° orb	2	_____	2
_____	‖ Ascendant - 1° orb	2	_____	
_____	‖ Ascendant ruler - 1° orb	2	_____	
_____	‖ 5th cusp ruler - 1° orb	2	_____	2
_____	‖ 9th cusp ruler - 1° orb	2	_____	2
_____	‖ 11th cusp ruler - 1° orb	2	_____	2
_____	‖ Ruler of other sign(s) in 1st or 5th houses - 1° orb	1	_____	1
_____	‖ Ruler of other sign(s) in 9th or 11th houses - 1° orb	1	_____	1
_____	House of ♂	2	_____	2
_____	House of ☉	2	_____	2
_____	House of ♃	2	_____	2
_____	House of ♅	1	_____	1
_____	House of Ascendant ruler	2	_____	2
_____	House of 5th cusp ruler	2	_____	2
_____	House of 9th cusp ruler	2	_____	2
_____	House of 11th cusp ruler	2	_____	2
_____	House of ruler of other sign(s) in 1st or 5th	1	_____	1
_____	House of ruler of other sign(s) in 9th or 11th	1	_____	1
_____	House cusp(s) ruled by planet(s) in 1st or 5th	2	_____	2
_____	House cusp(s) ruled by planet(s) in 9th or 11th	2	_____	2
_____	House(s) occupied by planet(s) in ♈, ♌, ♐ or ♒	2	_____	2
_____	Planet(s) in ♈	2	_____	2
_____	Planet(s) in ♌	2	_____	2
_____	Planet(s) in ♐	2	_____	2

CREATIVITY (CONTINUED)

FACTOR		WEIGHTING POINTS	LETTER OF ALPHABET	WEIGHT
_____	Planet(s) in ♒	2	_____	2
_____			_____	
_____	Sign of ♂	1	_____	1
_____	Sign of ☉	1	_____	1
_____	Sign of ♃	1	_____	1
_____	Sign of ♅	1	_____	1
_____	Sign of Ascendant	1	_____	1
_____	Sign of Ascendant ruler	1	_____	1
_____	Sign of 5th cusp ruler	1	_____	1
_____	Sign of 9th cusp ruler	1	_____	1
_____	Sign of 11th cusp ruler	1	_____	1
_____	Sign of ruler of other sign(s) in 1st or 5th houses	½	_____	½
_____	Sign of ruler of other sign(s) in 9th or 11th houses	½	_____	½
_____	Sign occupied by planet(s) in 1st or 5th	1	_____	1
_____	Sign occupied by planet(s) in 9th or 11th	1	_____	1
_____	House with ♈ on cusp	1	_____	1
_____	House with ♌ on cusp	1	_____	1
_____	House with ♐ on cusp	1	_____	1
_____	House with ♒ on cusp	1	_____	1
_____	Unoccupied sign(s) in 1st	½	_____	½
_____	Unoccupied sign(s) in 5th	½	_____	½
_____	Unoccupied sign(s) in 9th	½	_____	½
_____	Unoccupied sign(s) in 11th	½	_____	½

TOTALS

Letter 1: ____   Letter 4: ____   Letter 7: ____   Letter 10: ____
Letter 2: ____   Letter 5: ____   Letter 8: ____   Letter 11: ____
Letter 3: ____   Letter 6: ____   Letter 9: ____   Letter 12: ____

Emphasized element(s) if any _____   Emphasized quality if any _____
Nodal polarity by house ____ by sign ____   Significant theme(s) _____
Harmony aspects to Letter(s) _____   Conflict aspects to Letter(s) _____

BELIEFS AND VALUES

FACTOR	WEIGHTING POINTS	LETTER OF ALPHABET	WEIGHT
☌ ♃ - 8° orb	12 → 2 (depending on orb)		
☌ ♆ - 8° orb	12 → 2 (depending on orb)		
☌ ♅ - 8° orb	6 → 1 (depending on orb)		
☌ ⚷ - 8° orb	6 → 1 (depending on orb)		
☌ Ruler of 9th cusp - 8° orb	12 → 2 (depending on orb)		
☌ Ruler of 12th cusp - 8° orb	12 → 2 (depending on orb)		
☌ Ruler of 11th cusp - 8° orb	6 → 1 (depending on orb)		
☌ Rulers of other signs in 9th or 12th	12 → 2 (depending on orb)		
☌ Ruler of other signs in 11th	3 → 1 (depending on orb)		
Houses ruled by planets forming any of the above conjunctions	2 pts. if sign is on a cusp		2
	2 pts. if sign is occupied in the house		2
	1 pt. if sign is unoccupied in house		1
Planet(s) in 9th house	10		10
Planet(s) in 11th house	5		5
Planets in 12th house	10		10
Planets within 2° of 9th, 11th, and 12th houses, even if occupying 8th, 10th or 1st houses	3		3
∥ ♃ - 1° orb	2		2
∥ ♅ - 1° orb	1		1
∥ ♆ - 1° orb	2		2
∥ Ruler of 9th cusp - 1° orb	2		2
∥ Ruler of 11th cusp - 1° orb	1		1
∥ Ruler of 12th cusp - 1° orb	2		2
∥ ⚷ - 1° orb	1		1
House of ♃	2		2
House of ♅	1		1
House of ♆	2		2
House of ⚷	1		1

BELIEFS AND VALUES (CONTINUED)

FACTOR		WEIGHTING POINTS	LETTER OF ALPHABET	WEIGHT
_____ _____	House of rulers of 9th and 12th cusps	2	_____	2
_____	House of ruler of 11th cusp	1	_____	1
_____ _____	House cusp(s) ruled by planet(s) in 9th and 12th	2	_____	2
_____ _____	House cusp(s) ruled by planet(s) in 11th	1	_____	1
_____ _____	House(s) of ruler(s) of other signs in 9th and 12th	1	_____	1
_____ _____	House(s) of ruler(s) of other signs in the 11th	½	_____	½
_____	Planet(s) in ♐ or ♓	2	_____	2
_____	Planet(s) in ♒	1	_____	1
_____ _____	House(s) occupied by planet(s) in ♐ or ♓	2	_____	2
_____ _____	House(s) occupied by planet(s) in ♒	1	_____	1
_____	Sign of ♃	1	_____	1
_____	Sign of ♅	½	_____	½
_____	Sign of ♆	1	_____	1
_____	Sign of ♇	½	_____	½
_____ _____	Sign of rulers of 9th and 12th cusps	1	_____	1
_____	Sign of ruler of 11th cusp	½	_____	½
_____ _____	Sign of ruler of other signs in 9th and 12th	½	_____	½
_____ _____	Sign of ruler of other signs in 11th	¼	_____	¼
_____ _____	Sign(s) occupied by planet(s) in 9th or 12th	1	_____	1
_____ _____	Sign(s) occupied by planet(s) in the 11th	½	_____	½
_____ _____	Houses with ♐ or ♓ on cusp	1	_____	1
_____	Houses with ♒ on cusp	½	_____	½
_____ _____	Unoccupied signs in 9th or 12th	½	_____	½
_____	Unoccupied signs in 11th	¼	_____	¼

TOTALS

Letter 1: ____	Letter 4: ____	Letter 7: ____	Letter 10: ____
Letter 2: ____	Letter 5: ____	Letter 8: ____	Letter 11: ____
Letter 3: ____	Letter 6: ____	Letter 9: ____	Letter 12: ____

Emphasized element(s) if any _____   Emphasized quality if any _____
Nodal polarity by house ____ by sign ____   Significant theme(s) _____
Harmony aspects to Letter(s) _____   Conflict aspects to Letter(s) _____

MONEY

FACTOR		WEIGHTING POINTS	LETTER OF ALPHABET	WEIGHT
_____	♂♀ - 8° orb	12 → 2	_____	_____
_____		(depending on orb)	_____	_____
_____	♂♇ - 8° orb	12 → 2	_____	_____
_____		(depending on orb)	_____	_____
_____	♂ Ruler of 2nd cusp -	12 → 2	_____	_____
_____	8° orb	(depending on orb)	_____	_____
_____	♂ Ruler of other signs	6 → 1	_____	_____
_____	in 2nd house - 8° orb	(depending on orb)	_____	_____
_____			_____	_____
_____	♂ Ruler of 8th cusp - 8° orb	12 → 2	_____	_____
_____		(depending on orb)	_____	_____
	♂ Ruler of other signs	6 → 1	_____	_____
_____	in 8th house - 8° orb	(depending on orb)	_____	_____
_____			_____	
_____	Houses ruled by planets	2 pts. if sign is on a	_____	2
_____	forming any of the	cusp	_____	
_____	above conjunctions	2 pts. if sign is	_____	2
_____		occupied in the	_____	
_____		house		
_____		1 pt. if sign is		1
_____		unoccupied in	_____	
_____		house		
_____	Planet(s) in 2nd house	10	_____	10
_____			_____	
_____			_____	
_____	Planet(s) in 8th house	10	_____	10
_____			_____	
_____			_____	
_____	Planets within 2° of 2nd or	3	_____	3
_____	8th houses even though		_____	
_____	occupying 1st, 3rd, 7th,		_____	
_____	or 9th		_____	
_____	‖ ♀ - 1° orb	2	_____	2
_____	‖ ♇ - 1° orb	2	_____	2
_____	‖ Ruler of 2nd cusp- 1° orb	2	_____	2
_____	‖ Ruler of other sign(s)	1	_____	1
	in 2nd house - 1° orb			
_____	‖ Ruler of 8th cusp - 1° orb	2	_____	2
_____	‖ Ruler of other signs	1	_____	1
	in 8th - 1° orb		_____	
_____	House of ♀	2	_____	2
_____	House of ♇	2	_____	2
_____	House of ruler of	1	_____	1
	other sign(s) in 2nd or 8th			
_____	House of ruler of 2nd cusp	2	_____	2
_____	House of ruler of 8th cusp	2	_____	2
_____	House cusp(s) ruled	2	_____	2
	by planet(s) in 2nd or 8th			

MONEY (CONTINUED)

FACTOR		WEIGHTING POINTS	LETTER OF ALPHABET	WEIGHT
_____	Houses with signs ruled by planets in 2nd or 8th	2 pts. if sign is occupied	_____	2
_____		1 pt. if sign is unoccupied	_____	1
_____		2	_____	2
_____	Planet(s) in ♉ or ♏	2	_____	2
_____	House occupied by	2	_____	2
_____	planet(s) in ♉ or ♏	2	_____	2
_____	Sign of ♀	1	_____	1
_____	Sign of ♇	1	_____	1
_____	Sign of ruler of other sign(s) in 2nd or 8th house	½	_____	½
_____	Sign of ruler of 2nd cusp	1	_____	1
_____	Sign of ruler of 8th cusp		_____	1
_____	Sign occupied by planet(s) in 2nd or 8th	1	_____	1
_____	House with ♉ or ♏ on cusp	1	_____	1
_____	Unoccupied sign(s) in 2nd or 8th	½	_____	½
_____			_____	

TOTALS

Letter 1: ____   Letter 4: ____   Letter 7: ____   Letter 10: ____
Letter 2: ____   Letter 5: ____   Letter 8: ____   Letter 11: ____
Letter 3: ____   Letter 6: ____   Letter 9: ____   Letter 12: ____

Emphasized element(s) if any _____   Emphasized quality if any _____
Nodal polarity by house ____ by sign ____   Significant theme(s) _____
Harmony aspects to Letter(s) _____   Conflict aspects to Letter(s) _____

SEXUALITY

FACTOR		WEIGHTING POINTS	LETTER OF ALPHABET	WEIGHT
_____	♂♀ - 8° orb	12 → 2 (depending on orb)	_____	_____
_____	♂⊙ - 8° orb	12 → 2 (depending on orb)	_____	_____
_____	♂♇ - 8° orb	12 → 2 (depending on orb)	_____	_____
_____	♂♂ - 8° orb	12 → 2 (depending on orb)	_____	_____
_____	♂ Ruler of 2nd cusp - 8° orb		_____	_____
_____	♂ Ruler of 5th cusp - 8° orb	12 → 2 (depending on orb)	_____	_____
_____	♂ Ruler of 8th cusp - 8° orb	12 → 2 (depending on orb)	_____	_____
_____	♂ Rulers of other signs in the 2nd, 5th and 8th	6 → 1 (depending on orb)	_____	
_____	Houses ruled by planets forming any of the above conjunctions	2 pts. if sign is on a cusp	_____	2
_____		2 pts. if sign is occupied in the house	_____	2
_____		1 pt. if sign is unoccupied in house	_____	1
_____	Planet(s) in 2nd house	10	_____	10
_____	Planet(s) in 5th house	10	_____	10
_____	Planet(s) in 8th house	10	_____	10
_____	Planets within 2° of 2nd, 5th or 8th, but in 1st, 3rd, 4th, 6th, 7th or 9th	3	_____	3
_____	‖ ♂ - 1° orb	2	_____	2
_____	‖ ♀ - 1° orb	2	_____	2
_____	‖ ⊙ - 1° orb	2	_____	2
_____	‖ ♇ - 1° orb	2	_____	2
_____	‖ Ruler of 2nd, 5th or 8th cusps - 1° orb	2	_____	
_____	‖ Ruler of other signs in 2nd, 5th or 8th	1	_____	1
_____	House of ♂	2	_____	2
_____	House of ♀	2	_____	2
_____	House of ⊙	2	_____	2
_____	House of ♇	2	_____	2
_____	House of rulers of cusps of 2nd, 5th & 8th	2	_____	2

SEXUALITY (CONTINUED)

FACTOR		WEIGHTING POINTS	LETTER OF ALPHABET	WEIGHT
_____	House of ruler(s) of other sign(s) in 2nd, 5th or 8th	1	_____	1
_____	House cusp(s) ruled by planet(s) in 2nd, 5th or 8th	2	_____	2
_____	Houses with signs ruled by planets in 2nd, 5th or 8th	2 pts. if sign is occupied	_____	2
_____		1 pt. if sign is unoccupied	_____	1
_____		2	_____	2
_____	Planet(s) in ♉, ♌ or ♏	2	_____	2
_____	House occupied by	2	_____	2
_____	planet(s) in ♉, ♌ or ♏	2	_____	2
_____	Sign of ♂	1	_____	1
_____	Sign of ♀	1	_____	1
_____	Sign of ☉	1	_____	1
_____	Sign of ♇		_____	1
_____	Signs of rulers of 2nd, 5th and 8th cusps	1	_____	1
_____	Signs of rulers of other signs in 2nd, 5th or 8th houses	½	_____	½
_____	Signs occupied by planet(s) in 2nd, 5th or 8th	1	_____	1
_____	Houses with ♉, ♌ or ♏ on cusp	1	_____	1
_____	Unoccupied sign(s) in 2nd, 5th or 8th	½	_____	½

TOTALS

Letter 1: ____   Letter 4: ____   Letter 7: ____   Letter 10: ____
Letter 2: ____   Letter 5: ____   Letter 8: ____   Letter 11: ____
Letter 3: ____   Letter 6: ____   Letter 9: ____   Letter 12: ____

Emphasized element(s) if any _____   Emphasized quality if any _____
Nodal polarity by house ____ by sign ____   Significant theme(s) _____
Harmony aspects to Letter(s) _____   Conflict aspects to Letter(s) _____

PARENTS

FACTOR		WEIGHTING POINTS	LETTER OF ALPHABET	WEIGHT
_____	♂ ☽ - 8° orb	12→2 (depending on orb)	_____	_____
_____	♂ ♄ - 8° orb	12→2 (depending on orb)	_____	_____
_____	♂ ? - 8° orb	6→1 (depending on orb)	_____	_____
_____	♂ ☉ - 8° orb	6 → 1 (depending on orb)	_____	
_____	♂ MC - 8° orb	12→2 (depending on orb)	_____	
_____	♂ MC ruler - 8° orb	12→2 (depending on orb)	_____	━━━
_____	♂ IC - 8° orb	12→2 (depending on orb)	_____	_____
_____	♂ IC ruler - 8° orb	12→2 (depending on orb)	_____	_____
_____	♂ Ruler of other signs in 4th house - 8° orb	6→1 (depending on orb)	_____	_____
_____	♂ Ruler of other signs in 10th house - 8° orb	6→1 (depending on orb)	_____	_____
_____	Houses ruled by planets forming any of the above conjunctions	2 pts. if sign is on a cusp	_____	2
_____		2 pts. if sign is occupied in the house	_____	2
_____		1 pt. if sign is unoccupied in house	_____	1
_____	Planet(s) in 4th house	10	_____	10
_____	Planet(s) in 10th house	10	_____	10
_____	Planets within 2° of 4th or 10th but in 3rd, 5th, 9th or 11th	3	_____	3
_____	MC sign	6	_____	6
_____	IC sign	6	_____	6
_____	∥ ☽ - 1° orb	2	_____	2
_____	∥ ♄ - 1° orb	2	_____	2
_____	∥ ? - 1° orb	1	_____	1
_____	∥ ☉ - 1° orb	1	_____	1
_____	∥ MC - 1° orb	2	_____	2
_____	∥ MC ruler - 1° orb	2	_____	2
_____	∥ IC - 1° orb	2	_____	2
_____	∥ IC ruler - 1° orb	2	_____	2
_____	∥ Ruler of other sign(s) in 4th house - 1° orb	1	_____	1

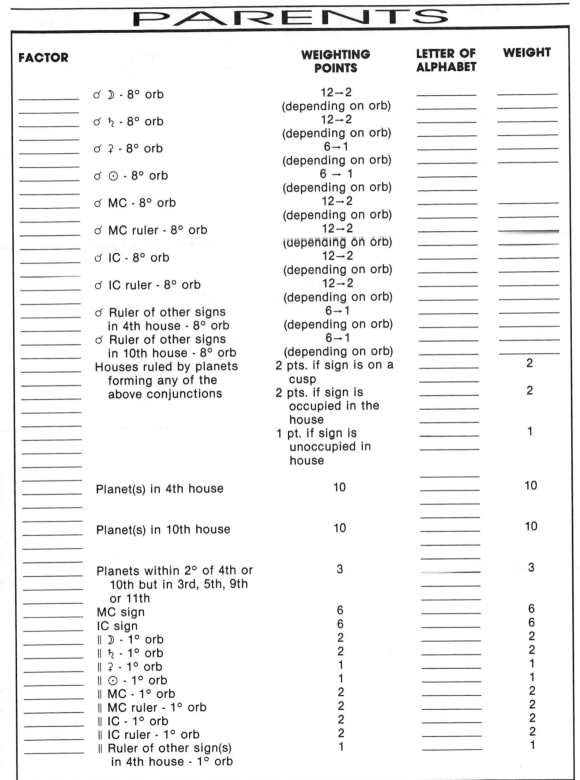

PARENTS   (CONTINUED)

FACTOR		WEIGHTING POINTS	LETTER OF ALPHABET	WEIGHT
_____	‖ Ruler of other sign(s) in 10th house - 1° orb	1	_____	1
_____	House of ☽	2	_____	2
_____	House of ♄	2	_____	2
_____	House of ♃	1	_____	1
_____	House of ☉	1	_____	1
_____	House of MC ruler	2	_____	2
_____	House of IC ruler	2	_____	2
_____	House of ruler of other sign(s) in 4th	1	_____	1
_____	House of ruler of other sign(s) in 10th	2	_____	2
_____	House cusp(s) ruled by planet(s) in 4th	2	_____	2
_____	House cusp(s) ruled by planet(s) in 10th	2	_____	2
_____ _____ _____ _____	House with sign ruled by planet(s) in 4th or 10th	2 pts. if sign is occupied 1 pt. if sign is unoccupied	_____ _____ _____ _____	2
_____	House(s) occupied by planet(s) in ♋ or ♑	2	_____	2
_____ _____ _____	Planet(s) in ♋	2	_____ _____	2
_____ _____ _____	Planet(s) in ♑	2	_____ _____	2
_____	Sign of ☽	1	_____	1
_____	Sign of ♄	1	_____	1
_____	Sign of ♃	½	_____	½
_____	Sign of ☉	½	_____	½
_____	Sign of MC ruler	1	_____	1
_____	Sign of IC ruler	1	_____	1
_____	Sign of ruler of other sign(s) in 4th house	1	_____	1
_____	Sign of ruler of other sign(s) in 10th house	1	_____	1
_____	Sign occupied by planet(s) in 4th	1	_____	1
_____	Sign occupied by planet(s) in 10th	1	_____	1
_____	House with ♋ on cusp	1	_____	1
_____	House with ♑ on cusp	1	_____	1
_____	Unoccupied sign(s) in 4th	½	_____	½
_____	Unoccupied sign(s) in 10th	½	_____	½

PARENTS (CONTINUED)

TOTALS

Letter 1: ____   Letter 4: ____   Letter 7: ____   Letter 10: ____
Letter 2: ____   Letter 5: ____   Letter 8: ____   Letter 11: ____
Letter 3: ____   Letter 6: ____   Letter 9: ____   Letter 12: ____

Emphasized element(s) if any _____   Emphasized quality if any _____
Nodal polarity by house ____ by sign ____   Significant theme(s) _____
Harmony aspects to Letter(s) _____   Conflict aspects to Letter(s) _____

KARMIC LESSONS

FACTOR		WEIGHTING POINTS	LETTER OF ALPHABET	WEIGHT
_____	♂ ♄ - 8° orb	12 → 2 (depending on orb)	_____	_____
_____	♂ ☋ - 8° orb	12 → 2 (depending on orb)	_____	_____
_____	Houses ruled by planets forming any of the above conjunctions	2 pts. if sign is on a cusp	_____	2
_____		2 pts. if sign is occupied in the house	_____	2
_____		1 pt. if sign is unoccupied in house	_____	1
_____	‖ ♄ - 1° orb	2	_____	2
_____	‖ ☋ - 1° orb	2	_____	2
_____	House of ♄	2	_____	2
_____	House of ☋	2	_____	2
_____	Sign of ♄	1	_____	1
_____	Sign of ☋	1	_____	1

OPTIONAL

	FACTOR	WEIGHTING POINTS	LETTER OF ALPHABET	WEIGHT
_____	♂ MC - 8° orb	12 → 2 (depending on orb)	_____	_____
_____	♂ Ruler of 10th cusp - 8° orb	12 → 2 (depending on orb)	_____	_____
_____	♂ Ruler of other signs in 10th - 8° orb	6 → 1 (depending on orb)	_____	
_____	Planet(s) in 10th house	10	_____	10
_____	Planets within 2° of 10th even though in 9th or 11th	3	_____	3
_____	House of ruler of MC	2	_____	2
_____	House of ruler of other signs in the 10th house	2	_____	2
_____	Planet(s) in ♑	2	_____	2
_____	House with ♑ on cusp	1	_____	1
_____	House with ♑ within (but not on cusp)	½	_____	½
_____	♂ ☽ - 8° orb	6 → 1 (depending on orb)	_____	_____
_____	♂ ♇ - 8° orb	6 → 1 (depending on orb)	_____	_____
_____	♂ ♆ - 8° orb	6 → 1 (depending on orb)	_____	_____
_____	♂ Rulers of 4th, 8th or 12th cusps	6 → 1 (depending on orb)	_____	_____

KARMIC LESSONS (CONTINUED)

FACTOR		WEIGHTING POINTS	LETTER OF ALPHABET	WEIGHT
_____	Planet(s) in the 4th house	5	_____	5
_____	Planet(s) in the 8th house		_____	
_____	Planet(s) in the 12th house		_____	
_____	‖ ☽ - 1° orb	1	_____	1
_____	‖ ♇ - 1° orb	1	_____	1
_____	‖ ♆ - 1° orb	1	_____	1
_____	‖ Rulers of 4th, 8th or 12 cusps	1	_____	1
_____	House of ☽	1	_____	1
_____	House of ♇	1	_____	1
_____	House of ♆	1	_____	1
_____	Houses of rulers of 4th, 8th and 12th cusps	1	_____	1
_____	Planet(s) in ♋	1	_____	1
_____	Planet(s) in ♏	1	_____	1
_____	Planet(s) in ♓	1	_____	1
_____	Sign of ☽	½	_____	½
_____	Sign of ♇	½	_____	½
_____	Sign of ♆	½	_____	½
_____	Sign of rulers of 4th, 8th and 12th cusps	½	_____	½

TOTALS

Letter 1: ____   Letter 4: ____   Letter 7: ____   Letter 10: ____
Letter 2: ____   Letter 5: ____   Letter 8: ____   Letter 11: ____
Letter 3: ____   Letter 6: ____   Letter 9: ____   Letter 12: ____

Emphasized element(s) if any _____   Emphasized quality if any _____
Significant theme(s) _____

FUTURE

FACTOR	WEIGHTING POINTS	LETTER OF ALPHABET	WEIGHT
_____ ♂ ☉ - 8° orb	12 → 2 (depending on orb)	_____	_____
_____ ♂ ♃ - 8° orb	12 → 2 (depending on orb)	_____	_____
_____ ♂ ♅ - 8° orb	12 → 2 (depending on orb)	_____	_____
_____ ♂ ♆ - 8° orb	12 → 2 (depending on orb)	_____	_____
_____ ♂ ♇ - 8° orb	6 → 1 (depending on orb)	_____	_____
_____ ♂ Rulers of 5th, 9th, 11th or 12th - 8° orb	12 → 2 (depending on orb)	_____	_____
_____ ♂ Rulers of other signs in 5th, 9th, 11th or 12th - 8° orb	6 → 1 (depending on orb)	_____	
_____ Houses ruled by planets forming any of the above conjunctions	2 pts. if sign is on cusp	_____	2
_____	2 pts. if sign is occupied in the house	_____	2
_____	1 pt. if sign is unoccupied in the house	_____	1
_____ Stellim by house or sign occurring in secondary progressions in next 5 years	10	_____	10
_____ Planet(s) in 5th house	10	_____	10
_____ Planet(s) in 9th house	10	_____	10
_____ Planet(s) in 11th house	10	_____	10
_____ Planet(s) in 12th house	10	_____	10
_____ Planets within 2° of 5th, 9th 11th or 12th, even if in 4th, 6th, 8th, 10th or 1st	3	_____	3
_____ ∥ ☉ - 1° orb	2	_____	2
_____ ∥ ♃ - 1° orb	2	_____	2
_____ ∥ ♅ - 1° orb	2	_____	2
_____ ∥ ♆ - 1° orb	2	_____	2
_____ ∥ ♇ - 1° orb	1	_____	1

FUTURE

FACTOR		WEIGHTING POINTS	LETTER OF ALPHABET	WEIGHT
_____	‖ Rulers of 5th, 9th, 11th and 12th cusps - 1° orb	2	_____	2
_____	‖ Rulers of other signs in 5th, 9th, 11th or 12th houses - 1° orb	1	_____	1
_____	House of ☉	2	_____	2
_____	House of ♃	2	_____	2
_____	House of ♅	2	_____	2
_____	House of ♀	1	_____	1
_____	House of rulers of 5th, 9th, 11th and 12th cusps	2	_____	2
_____ _____	Houses of rulers of other signs in 5th, 9th, 11th and 12th	1	_____	1
_____	House cusp(s) ruled by planet(s) in 5th, 9th, 11th or 12th	2	_____	2
_____	Houses with signs ruled by planet(s) in 5th, 9th, 11th or 12th	2 pts. if sign is occupied	_____	2
_____		1 pt. if sign is unoccupied	_____	1
_____		2	_____	2
_____	Planet(s) in ♌, ♐, ♒ or ♓	2	_____	2
_____	Houses ruled by planets in ♌, ♐, ♒ or ♓		_____	
_____	Sign of ☉	1	_____	1
_____	Sign of ♃	1	_____	1
_____	Sign of ♅	1	_____	1
_____	Sign of ♀	½	_____	½
_____	Sign of any ruler of 5th, 9th, 11th or 12th cusps	1	_____	1
_____	Sign occupied by planet(s) in 5th, 9th, 11th, or 12th	1	_____	1
_____	Houses with ♌, ♐, ♒ or ♓ on cusp	1	_____	1
_____	Unoccupied sign(s) in 5th, 9th, 11th or 12th	½	_____	½

TOTALS

Letter 1: ____   Letter 4: ____   Letter 7: ____   Letter 10: ____
Letter 2: ____   Letter 5: ____   Letter 8: ____   Letter 11: ____
Letter 3: ____   Letter 6: ____   Letter 9: ____   Letter 12: ____

Emphasized element(s) if any _____   Emphasized quality if any _____
Nodal polarity by house ____ by sign ____   Significant theme(s) _____
Harmony aspects to Letter(s) _____   Conflict aspects to Letter(s) _____

USING THIS BOOK AS A TRADITIONAL ASTROLOGICAL "COOKBOOK"

Some readers may not wish to plunge immediately into synthesis. For those readers who prefer to deal with the horoscope a single piece at a time, I offer guidelines by which this book can be utilized as a traditional "planets in signs," or "planets in houses" cookbook. This is **not** the recommended approach, but it will supply useful information (though more limited than what a search for repeated themes will reveal).

Simply use the following "cookbook" lists of planets in houses or signs to find the appropriate pages of interpretation within this text. Page numbers are also provided to interpret conjunctions, while other aspects are covered in a final section. Because traditional formats are being followed, the planets will be listed in their traditional order, rather than in the order of the astrological alphabet.

The Sun

IN HOUSES

Sun in the **1st** house: See Letter 5 in Identity (page 109), Letter 5 in Health (page 385), Letter 1 in Children (page 261), Letter 1 in Sexuality (page 352), Letter 1 (page 107) thinking in terms of Future Trends.

Sun in the **2nd** house: See Letter 5 in Work (page 143), Letter 5 in Money (page 326), Letter 5 in Sexuality (page 353), Letter 2 in Children (page 262), Letter 2 in Sexuality (page 353), Letter 2 (page 107) thinking in terms of Future Trends.

Sun in the **3rd** house: See Letter 5 in Mind (page 225), Letter 3 in Children (page 262), Letter 3 in Sexuality (page 354) and Letter 3 (page 107) thinking in terms of Future Trends.

Sun in the **4th** house: See Letter 5 in Children (page 263), Letter 5 in Parents (page 406), Letter 4 in Children (page 263), Letter 4 in Sexuality (page 354) and Letter 4 (page 108) thinking in terms of Future Trends.

Sun in the **5th** house: See Letter 5 in Children (page 264), Letter 5 in Sexuality (page 355), and Letter 5 (page 109) thinking in terms of Future Trends.

Sun in the **6th** house: See Letter 5 in Work (page 143), Letter 5 in Mind (page 225), Letter 5 in Health (page 385), Letter 6 in Children (page 265), Letter 6 in Sexuality (page 356), and Letter 6 (page 109) thinking in terms of Future Trends.

Sun in the **7th** house: See Letter 5 in Relationships (page 183), Letter 7 in Children (page 265), Letter 7 in Sexuality (page 357), and Letter 7 (page 110) thinking in terms of Future Trends.

Sun in the **8th** house: Letter 5 in Relationships (page 183), Letter 5 in Money (page 326), Letter 5 in Sexuality (page 357), Letter 8 in Children (page 266), Letter 8 in Sexuality (page 357), and Letter 8 (page 111) thinking in terms of Future Trends.

Sun in the **9th** house: Letter 5 in Mind (page 225), Letter 5 in Beliefs (page 303), Letter 5 (page 109) thinking in terms of Future Trends, Letter 9 in Children (page 267), Letter 9 in Sexuality (page 358) and Letter 9 (page 111) thinking in terms of Future Trends.

Sun in the **10th** house: Letter 5 in Work (page 143), Letter 5 in Parents (page 406), Letter 10 in Children (page 268), Letter 10 in Sexuality (page 359), and Letter 10 (page 112) thinking in terms of Future Trends.

Sun in the **11th** house: Letter 5 in Mind (page 225), Letter 5 in Beliefs (page 303), Letter 5 (page 109) thinking in terms of Future Trends, Letter 11 in Children (page 269), Letter 11 in Sexuality (page 360) and Letter 11 (page 113) thinking in terms of Future Trends.

Sun in the **12th** house: Letter 5 in Beliefs (page 303), Letter 5 (page 109) thinking in terms of Future Trends, Letter 12 in Children (page 269), Letter 12 in Sexuality (page 361) and Letter 12 (page 114) thinking in terms of Future Trends.

IN SIGNS

Sun in **Aries**: See Letter 5 in Identity (page 109), Letter 5 in Health (page 385), Letter 1 in Children (page 261), Letter 1 in Sexuality (page 352), Letter 1 (page 107) thinking in terms of Future Trends.

Sun in **Taurus**: See Letter 5 in Work (page 143), Letter 5 in Money (page 326), Letter 5 in Sexuality (page 353), Letter 2 in Children (page 262), Letter 2 in Sexuality (page 353), Letter 2 (page 107) thinking in terms of Future Trends.

Sun in **Gemini**: See Letter 5 in Mind (page 225), Letter 3 in Children (page 262), Letter 3 in Sexuality (page 354), Letter 3 (page 107) thinking in terms of Future Trends.

Sun in **Cancer**: See Letter 5 in Children (page 263), Letter 5 in Parents (page 406), Letter 4 in Children (page 263), Letter 4 in Sexuality (page 354), Letter 4 (page 108) thinking in terms of Future Trends.

Sun in **Leo**: See Letter 5 in Children (page 264), Letter 5 in Sexuality (page 355), Letter 5 (page 109) thinking in terms of Future Trends.

Sun in **Virgo**: See Letter 5 in Work (page 143), Letter 5 in Mind (page 225), Letter

5 in Health (page 385), Letter 6 in Children (page 265), Letter 6 in Sexuality (page 356), and Letter 6 (page 109) thinking in terms of Future Trends.

Sun in **Libra**: See Letter 5 in Relationships (page 183), Letter 7 in Children (page 265), Letter 7 in Sexuality (page 357), Letter 7 (page 110) thinking in terms of Future Trends.

Sun in **Scorpio**: Letter 5 in Relationships (page 183), Letter 5 in Money (page 326), Letter 5 in Sexuality (page 355), Letter 8 in Children (page 266), Letter 8 in Sexuality (page 357), Letter 8 (page 111) thinking in terms of Future Trends.

Sun in **Sagittarius**: Letter 5 in Mind (page 225), Letter 5 in Beliefs (page 303), Letter 5 (page 109) thinking in terms of Future Trends, Letter 9 in Children (page 267), Letter 9 in Sexuality (page 358), Letter 9 (page 111) thinking in terms of Future Trends.

Sun in **Capricorn**: Letter 5 in Work (page 143), Letter 5 in Parents (page 406), Letter 10 in Children (page 268), Letter 10 in Sexuality (page 359), Letter 10 (page 112) thinking in terms of Future Trends.

Sun in **Aquarius**: Letter 5 in Mind (page 225), Letter 5 in Beliefs (page 303), Letter 5 (page 109) thinking in terms of Future Trends, Letter 11 in Children (page 269), Letter 11 in Sexuality (page 360), Letter 11 (page 113) thinking in terms of Future Trends.

Sun in **Pisces**: Letter 5 in Beliefs (page 303), Letter 5 (page 109) thinking in terms of Future Trends, Letter 12 in Children (page 269), Letter 12 in Sexuality (page 361), Letter 12 (page 114) thinking in terms of Future Trends.

CONJUNCTIONS

Sun conjunct **Moon**: See Letter 5 in Children (page 264), Letter 5 in Parents (page 406), Letter 4 in Children (page 263), Letter 4 in Sexuality (page 354) and Letter 4 (page 108) thinking in terms of Future Trends.

Sun conjunct **Mercury**: See Letter 5 in Mind (page 225), Letter 3 in Children (page 262), Letter 3 in Sexuality (page 354) and Letter 3 (page 107) thinking in terms of Future Trends.

Sun conjunct **Venus**: See Letter 5 in Work (page 143), Letter 5 in Money (page 326), Letter 5 in Sexuality (page 355), Letter 2 in Children (page 262), Letter 2 in Sexuality (page 353), Letter 2 (page 107) thinking in terms of Future Trends.

Sun conjunct **Mars**: See Letter 5 in Identity (page 109), Letter 5 in Health (page 385), Letter 1 in Children (page 261), Letter 1 in Sexuality (page 352), Letter 1 (page 107) thinking in terms of Future Trends.

Sun conjunct **Ceres or Vesta**: See Letter 5 in Work (page 143), Letter 5 in Mind (page 225), Letter 5 in Health (page 385), Letter 6 in Children (page 265), Letter 6 in Sexuality (page 356), and Letter 6 (page 109) thinking in terms of Future Trends.

Sun conjunct **Pallas or Juno**: See Letter 5 in Relationships (page 183), Letter 7 in Children (page 265), Letter 7 in Sexuality (page 357), and Letter 7 (page 110) thinking in terms of Future Trends.

Sun conjunct **Jupiter** or **Chiron**: Letter 5 in Mind (page 225), Letter 5 in Beliefs page 303), Letter 5 (page 109) thinking in terms of Future Trends, Letter 9 in Children (page 267), Letter 9 in Sexuality (page 358), and Letter 9 (page 111) thinking in terms of Future Trends.

Sun conjunct **Saturn**: Letter 5 in Work (page 143), Letter 5 in Parents (page 406), Letter 10 in Children (page 268), Letter 10 in Sexuality (page 359), and Letter 10 (page 112) thinking in terms of Future Trends.

Sun conjunct **Uranus**: Letter 5 in Mind (page 225), Letter 5 in Beliefs (page 303), Letter 5 (page 109) thinking in terms of Future Trends, Letter 11 in Children (page 269), Letter 11 in Sexuality (page 360) and Letter 11 (page 113) thinking in terms of Future Trends.

Sun conjunct **Neptune**: Letter 5 in Beliefs (page 303), Letter 5 (page 109) thinking in terms of Future Trends, Letter 12 in Children (page 269), Letter 12 in Sexuality (page 361) and Letter 12 (page 114) thinking in terms of Future Trends.

Sun conjunct **Pluto**: Letter 5 in Relationships (page 183), Letter 5 in Money (page 326), Letter 5 in Sexuality (page 355), Letter 8 in Children (page 266), Letter 8 in Sexuality (page 357), and Letter 8 (page 111) thinking in terms of Future Trends.

The Moon

IN HOUSES

Moon in the **1st** house: Letter 4 in Identity (page 108), Letter 4 in Health (page 384), Letter 1 in Children (page 261), Letter 1 in Parents (page 404).

Moon in the **2nd** house: Letter 4 in Work (page 142), Letter 4 in Money (page 325), Letter 4 in Sexuality (page 354), Letter 2 in Children (page 262), Letter 2 in Parents (page 405).

Moon in the **3rd** house: Letter 4 in Mind (page 224), Letter 3 in Children (page 262), Letter 3 in Parents (page 405).

Moon in the **4th** house: Letter 4 in Children (page 263), Letter 4 in Parents (page 406).

Moon in the **5th** house: Letter 4 in Children (page 263), Letter 4 in Sexuality (page 354), Letter 4 (page 108) thinking in terms of Future Trends, Letter 5 in Children (page 264), Letter 5 in Parents (page 406).

Moon in the **6th** house: Letter 4 in Work (page 142), Letter 4 in Mind (page 224), Letter 4 in Health (page 384), Letter 6 in Children (page 265), Letter 6 in Parents (page 406).

Moon in the **7th** house: Letter 4 in Relationships (page 182), Letter 7 in Children (page 265), Letter 7 in Parents (page 407).

Moon in the **8th** house: Letter 4 in Relationships (page 182), Letter 4 in Money (page 325), Letter 4 in Sexuality (page 354), Letter 8 in Children (page 266), Letter 8 in Parents (page 407).

Moon in the **9th** house: Letter 4 in Mind (page 224), Letter 4 in Beliefs (page 302), Letter 4 (page 108) thinking in terms of Future Trends, Letter 9 in Children (page 267), Letter 9 in Parents (page 407).

Moon in the **10th** house: Letter 10 in Children (page 268), Letter 10 in Parents (page 408), Letter 4 in Work (page 142), Letter 4 in Parents (page 406).

Moon in the **11th** house: Letter 4 in Mind (page 224), Letter 4 in Beliefs (page 302), Letter 4 (page 108) thinking in terms of Future Trends, Letter 11 in Children (page 269), Letter 11 in Parents (page 408).

Moon in the **12th** house: Letter 4 in Beliefs (page 302), Letter 4 (page 108) thinking in terms of Future Trends, Letter 12 in Children (page 269), Letter 12 in Parents (page 409).

IN SIGNS

Moon in **Aries**: Letter 4 in Identity (page 108), Letter 4 in Health (page 384), Letter 1 in Children (page 261), Letter 1 in Parents (page 404).

Moon in **Taurus**: Letter 4 in Work (page 142), Letter 4 in Money (page 325), Letter 4 in Sexuality (page 354), Letter 2 in Children (page 262), Letter 2 in Parents (page 405).

Moon in **Gemini**: Letter 4 in Mind (page 224), Letter 3 in Children (page 262), Letter 3 in Parents (page 405).

Moon in **Cancer**: Letter 4 in Children (page 263), Letter 4 in Parents (page 406).

Moon in **Leo**: Letter 4 in Children (page 262), Letter 4 in Sexuality (page 354), Letter 4 (page 108) thinking in terms of Future Trends, Letter 5 in Children (page 264), Letter 5 in Parents (page 406).

Moon in **Virgo**: Letter 4 in Work (page 142), Letter 4 in Mind (page 224), Letter 4 in Health (page 384), Letter 6 in Children (page 265), Letter 6 in Parents (page 406).

Moon in **Libra**: Letter 4 in Relationships (page 182), Letter 7 in Children (page 265), Letter 7 in Parents (page 407).

Moon in **Scorpio**: Letter 4 in Relationships (page 182), Letter 4 in Money (page 325), Letter 4 in Sexuality (page 354), Letter 8 in Children (page 266), Letter 8 in Parents (page 407).

Moon in **Sagittarius**: Letter 4 in Mind (page 224), Letter 4 in Beliefs (page 302), Letter 4 (page 108) thinking in terms of Future Trends, Letter 9 in Children (page 267), Letter 9 in Parents (page 407).

Moon in **Capricorn**: Letter 10 in Children (page 268), Letter 10 in Parents (page 408), Letter 4 in Work (page 142), Letter 4 in Parents (page 406).

Moon in **Aquarius**: Letter 4 in Mind (page 224), Letter 4 in Beliefs (page 302), Letter 4 (page 108) thinking in terms of Future Trends, Letter 11 in Children (page 269), Letter 11 in Parents (page 408).

Moon in **Pisces**: Letter 4 in Beliefs (page 302), Letter 4 (page 108) thinking in terms of Future Trends, Letter 12 in Children (page 269), Letter 12 in Parents (page 409).

CONJUNCTIONS

Moon conjunct **Mercury**: Letter 4 in Mind (page 224), Letter 3 in Children (page 262), Letter 3 in Parents (page 405).

Moon conjunct **Venus**: Letter 4 in Work (page 142), Letter 4 in Money (page 325), Letter 4 in Sexuality (page 354), Letter 2 in Children (page 262), Letter 2 in Parents (page 405).

Moon conjunct **Mars**: Letter 4 in Identity (page 108), Letter 4 in Health (page 384), Letter 1 in Children (page 261), Letter 1 in Parents (page 404).

Moon conjunct **Ceres** or **Vesta**: Letter 4 in Work (page 142), Letter 4 in Mind (page 224), Letter 4 in Health (page 384), Letter 6 in Children (page 265), Letter 6 in Parents (page 406).

Moon conjunct **Pallas** or **Juno**: Letter 4 in Relationships (page 182), Letter 7 in Children (page 265), Letter 7 in Parents (page 407).

Moon conjunct **Jupiter** or **Chiron**: Letter 4 in Mind (page 224), Letter 4 in Beliefs (page 302), Letter 4 (page 108) thinking in terms of Future Trends, Letter 9 in Children (page 267), Letter 9 in Parents (page 407).

Moon conjunct **Saturn**: Letter 10 in Children (page 268), Letter 10 in Parents (page 408), Letter 4 in Work (page 142), Letter 4 in Parents (page 406).

Moon conjunct **Uranus**: Letter 4 in Mind (page 224), Letter 4 in Beliefs (page 302), Letter 4 (page 108) thinking in terms of Future Trends, Letter 11 in Children (page 269), Letter 11 in Parents (page 408).

Moon conjunct **Neptune**: Letter 4 in Beliefs (page 302), Letter 4 (page 108) thinking in terms of Future Trends, Letter 12 in Children (page 269), Letter 12 in Parents (page 409).

Moon conjunct **Pluto**: Letter 4 in Relationships (page 182), Letter 4 in Money (page 325), Letter 4 in Sexuality (page 354), Letter 8 in Children (page 266), Letter 8 in Parents (page 407).

Mercury

IN HOUSES

Mercury in the **1st** house: Letter 3 in Identity (page 107), Letter 3 in Health (page 383), Letter 1 in Mind (page 223).

Mercury in the **2nd** house: Letter 3 in Work (page 141), Letter 3 in Money (page 325), Letter 3 in Sexuality (page 354), Letter 2 in Mind (page 223).

Mercury in the **3rd** house: Letter 3 in Mind (page 224).

Mercury in the **4th** house: Letter 3 in Children (page 262), Letter 3 in Parents (page 405), Letter 4 in Mind (page 224).

Mercury in the **5th** house: Letter 3 in Children (page 262), Letter 3 in Sexuality (page 354), Letter 3 (page 107) thinking in terms of Future Trends, Letter 5 in Mind (page 225).

Mercury in the **6th** house: Letter 3 in Work (page 141), Letter 3 in Mind (page 224), Letter 3 in Health (page 383), Letter 6 in Mind (page 225).

Mercury in the **7th** house: Letter 3 in Relationships (page 182), Letter 7 in Mind (page 226).

Mercury in the **8th** house: Letter 3 in Relationships (page 182), Letter 3 in Money (page 325), Letter 3 in Sexuality (page 354), Letter 8 in Mind (page 227).

Mercury in the **9th** house: Letter 3 in Mind (page 224), Letter 3 in Beliefs (page 302), Letter 3 (page 107) thinking in terms of Future Trends, Letter 9 in Mind (page 227).

Mercury in the **10th** house: Letter 3 in Work (page 141), Letter 3 in Parents (page 405), Letter 10 in Mind (page 228).

Mercury in the **11th** house: Letter 3 in Mind (page 224), Letter 3 in Beliefs (page 302), Letter 3 (page 107) thinking in terms of Future Trends, Letter 11 in Mind (page 229).

Mercury in the **12th** house: Letter 3 in Beliefs (page 302), Letter 3 (page 107) thinking in terms of Future Trends, Letter 12 in Mind (page 229).

IN SIGNS

Mercury in **Aries**: Letter 3 in Identity (page 107), Letter 3 in Health (page 383), Letter 1 in Mind (page 223).

Mercury in **Taurus**: Letter 3 in Work (page 141), Letter 3 in Money (page 325), Letter 3 in Sexuality (page 354), Letter 2 in Mind (page 223).

Mercury in **Gemini**: Letter 3 in Mind (page 224).

Mercury in **Cancer**: Letter 3 in Children (page 262), Letter 3 in Parents (page 405), Letter 4 in Mind (page 224).

Mercury in **Leo**: Letter 3 in Children (page 262), Letter 3 in Sexuality (page 354), Letter 3 (page 107) thinking in terms of Future Trends, Letter 5 in Mind (page 225).

Mercury in **Virgo**: Letter 3 in Work (page 141), Letter 3 in Mind (page 224), Letter 3 in Health (page 383), Letter 6 in Mind (page 225).

Mercury in **Libra**: Letter 3 in Relationships (page 182), Letter 7 in Mind (page 226).

Mercury in **Scorpio**: Letter 3 in Relationships (page 182), Letter 3 in Money (page 325), Letter 3 in Sexuality (page 354), Letter 8 in Mind (page 227).

Mercury in **Sagittarius**: Letter 3 in Mind (page 224), Letter 3 in Beliefs (page 302), Letter 3 (page 107) thinking in terms of Future Trends, Letter 9 in Mind (page 227).

Mercury in **Capricorn**: Letter 3 in Work (page 141), Letter 3 in Parents (page 405), Letter 10 in Mind (page 228).

Mercury in **Aquarius**: Letter 3 in Mind (page 224), Letter 3 in Beliefs (page 302), Letter 3 (page 107) thinking in terms of Future Trends, Letter 11 in Mind (page 229).

Mercury in **Pisces**: Letter 3 in Beliefs (page 302), Letter 3 (page 107) thinking in terms of Future Trends, Letter 12 in Mind (page 229).

CONJUNCTIONS

Mercury conjunct **Venus**: Letter 3 in Work (page 141), Letter 3 in Money (page 325), Letter 3 in Sexuality (page 354), Letter 2 in Mind (page 223).

Mercury conjunct **Mars**: Letter 3 in Identity (page 107), Letter 3 in Health (page 383), Letter 1 in Mind (page 223).

Mercury conjunct **Ceres or Vesta**: Letter 3 in Work (page 141), Letter 3 in Mind (page 224), Letter 3 in Health (page 383), Letter 6 in Mind (page 225).

Mercury conjunct **Pallas or Juno**: Letter 3 in Relationships (page 182), Letter 7 in Mind (page 225).

Mercury conjunct **Jupiter** or **Chiron**: Letter 3 in Mind (page 224), Letter 3 in Beliefs (page 302), Letter 3 (page 107) thinking in terms of Future Trends, Letter 9 in Mind (page 227).

Mercury conjunct **Saturn**: Letter 3 in Work (page 141), Letter 3 in Parents (page 405), Letter 10 in Mind (page 228).

Mercury conjunct **Uranus**: Letter 3 in Mind (page 224), Letter 3 in Beliefs (page 302), Letter 3 (page 107) thinking in terms of Future Trends, Letter 11 in Mind (page 229).

Mercury conjunct **Neptune**: Letter 3 in Beliefs (page 302), Letter 3 (page 107) thinking in terms of Future Trends, Letter 12 in Mind (page 229).

Mercury conjunct **Pluto**: Letter 3 in Relationships (page 182), Letter 3 in Money (page 325), Letter 3 in Sexuality (page 354), Letter 8 in Mind (page 227).

Venus

IN HOUSES

Venus in the **1st** house: Letter 2 in Identity (page 107), Letter 2 in Health (page 382), Letter 1 in Work (page 140), Letter 1 in Money (page 324), Letter 1 in Sexuality (page 352).

Venus in the **2nd** house: Letter 2 in Work (page 141), Letter 2 in Money (page 325), Letter 2 in Sexuality (page 353).

Venus in the **3rd** house: Letter 2 in Mind (page 223), Letter 3 in Work (page 141), Letter 3 in Money (page 325), Letter 3 in Sexuality (page 354).

Venus in the **4th** house: Letter 2 in Children (page 262), Letter 2 in Parents (page 405), Letter 4 in Work (page 142), Letter 4 in Money (page 325), Letter 4 in Sexuality (page 354).

Venus in the **5th** house: Letter 2 in Children (page 262), Letter 2 in Sexuality (page 353), Letter 2 (page 107) thinking in terms of Future Trends, Letter 5 in Work (page 143), Letter 5 in Money (page 326), Letter 5 in Sexuality (page 355).

Venus in the **6th** house: Letter 2 in Work (page 141), Letter 2 in Health (page 382), Letter 2 in Mind (page 223), Letter 6 in Work (page 144), Letter 6 in Money (page 326), Letter 6 in Sexuality (page 356).

Venus in the **7th** house: Letter 2 in Relationships (page 181), Letter 7 in Work (page 145), Letter 7 in Money (page 326), Letter 7 in Sexuality (page 357).

Venus in the **8th** house: Letter 2 in Relationships (page 181), Letter 2 in Money (page 325), Letter 2 in Sexuality (page 353), Letter 8 in Work (page 145), Letter 8 in Money (page 327), Letter 8 in Sexuality (page 357).

Venus in the **9th** house: Letter 2 in Mind (page 223), Letter 2 in Beliefs (page 302), Letter 2 (page 107) thinking in terms of Future Trends, Letter 9 in Work (page 146), Letter 9 in Money (page 327), Letter 9 in Sexuality (page 358).

Venus in the **10th** house: Letter 2 in Work (page 141), Letter 2 in Parents (page

405), Letter 10 in Work (page 147), Letter 10 in Money (page 328), Letter 10 in Sexuality (page 359).

Venus in the **11th** house: Letter 2 in Mind (page 223), Letter 2 in Beliefs (page 302), Letter 2 (page 107) thinking in terms of Future Trends, Letter 11 in Work (page 148), Letter 11 in Money (page 328), Letter 11 in Sexuality (page 360).

Venus in the **12th** house: Letter 2 in Beliefs (page 302), Letter 2 (page 107) thinking in terms of Future Trends, Letter 12 in Work (page 149), Letter 12 in Money (page 328), Letter 12 in Sexuality (page 361).

IN SIGNS

Venus in **Aries**: Letter 2 in Identity (page 107), Letter 2 in Health (page 382), Letter 1 in Work (page 140), Letter 1 in Money (page 324), Letter 1 in Sexuality (page 352).

Venus in **Taurus**: Letter 2 in Work (page 141), Letter 2 in Money (page 325), Letter 2 in Sexuality (page 353).

Venus in **Gemini**: Letter 2 in Mind (page 223), Letter 3 in Work (page 141), Letter 3 in Money (page 325), Letter 3 in Sexuality (page 354).

Venus in **Cancer**: Letter 2 in Children (page 262), Letter 2 in Parents (page 405), Letter 4 in Work (page 142), Letter 4 in Money (page 325), Letter 4 in Sexuality (page 354).

Venus in **Leo**: Letter 2 in Children (page 262), Letter 2 in Sexuality (page 353), Letter 2 (page 107) thinking in terms of Future Trends, Letter 5 in Work (page 143), Letter 5 in Money (page 326), Letter 5 in Sexuality (page 355).

Venus in **Virgo**: Letter 2 in Work (page 141), Letter 2 in Health (page 382), Letter 2 in Mind (page 223), Letter 6 in Work (page 144), Letter 6 in Money (page 326), Letter 6 in Sexuality (page 356).

Venus in **Libra**: Letter 2 in Relationships (page 181), Letter 7 in Work (page 145), Letter 7 in Money (page 326), Letter 7 in Sexuality (page 357).

Venus in **Scorpio**: Letter 2 in Relationships (page 181), Letter 2 in Money (page 325), Letter 2 in Sexuality (page 353), Letter 8 in Work (page 145), Letter 8 in Money (page 327), Letter 8 in Sexuality (page 357).

Venus in **Sagittarius**: Letter 2 in Mind (page 223), Letter 2 in Beliefs (page 302), Letter 2 (page 107) thinking in terms of Future Trends, Letter 9 in Work (page 146), Letter 9 in Money (page 327), Letter 9 in Sexuality (page 358).

Venus in **Capricorn**: Letter 2 in Work (page 141), Letter 2 in Parents (page 405), Letter 10 in Work (page 147), Letter 10 in Money (page 328), Letter 10 in Sexuality (page 359).

Venus in **Aquarius**: Letter 2 in Mind (page 223), Letter 2 in Beliefs (page 302), Letter 2 (page 107) thinking in terms of Future Trends, Letter 11 in Work (page 148), Letter 11 in Money (page 328), Letter 11 in Sexuality (page 360).

Venus in **Pisces**: Letter 2 in Beliefs (page 302), Letter 2 (page 107) thinking in terms of Future Trends, Letter 12 in Work (page 149), Letter 12 in Money (page 328), Letter 12 in Sexuality (page 361).

CONJUNCTIONS

Venus conjunct **Mars**: Letter 2 in Identity (page 107), Letter 2 in Health (page 382), Letter 1 in Work (page 140), Letter 1 in Money (page 324), Letter 1 in Sexuality (page 352).

Venus conjunct **Ceres or Vesta**: Letter 2 in Work (page 141), Letter 2 in Health (page 382), Letter 2 in Mind (page 223), Letter 6 in Work (page 144), Letter 6 in Money (page 326), Letter 6 in Sexuality (page 356).

Venus conjunct **Pallas or Juno**: Letter 2 in Relationships (page 181), Letter 7 in Work (page 145), Letter 7 in Money (page 326), Letter 7 in Sexuality (page 357).

Venus conjunct **Jupiter** or **Chiron**: Letter 2 in Mind (page 223), Letter 2 in Beliefs (page 302), Letter 2 (page 107) thinking in terms of Future Trends, Letter 9 in Work (page 146), Letter 9 in Money (page 327), Letter 9 in Sexuality (page 358).

Venus conjunct **Saturn**: Letter 2 in Work (page 141), Letter 2 in Parents (page 405), Letter 10 in Work (page 147), Letter 10 in Money (page 328), Letter 10 in Sexuality (page 359).

Venus conjunct **Uranus**: Letter 2 in Mind (page 223), Letter 2 in Beliefs (page 302), Letter 2 (page 107) thinking in terms of Future Trends, Letter 11 in Work (page 148), Letter 11 in Money (page 328), Letter 11 in Sexuality (page 360).

Venus conjunct **Neptune**: Letter 2 in Beliefs (page 302), Letter 2 (page 107) thinking in terms of Future Trends, Letter 12 in Work (page 149), Letter 12 in Money (page 328), Letter 12 in Sexuality (page 361).

Venus conjunct **Pluto**: Letter 2 in Relationships (page 181), Letter 2 in Money (page 325), Letter 2 in Sexuality (page 353), Letter 8 in Work (page 145), Letter 8 in Money (page 327), Letter 8 in Sexuality (page 357).

Mars

IN HOUSES

Mars in the **1st** house: Letter 1 in Identity (page 107), Letter 1 in Health (page 381).

Mars in the **2nd** house: Letter 2 in Identity (page 107), Letter 2 in Health (page 382), Letter 1 in Work (page 140), Letter 1 in Money (page 324), Letter 1 in Sexuality (page 352).

Mars in the **3rd** house: Letter 3 in Identity (page 107), Letter 3 in Health (page 383), Letter 1 in Mind (page 223).

Mars in the **4th** house: Letter 4 in Identity (page 108), Letter 4 in Health (page 384), Letter 1 in Children (page 261), Letter 1 in Parents (page 404).

Mars in the **5th** house: Letter 5 in Identity (page 109), Letter 5 in Health (page 385), Letter 1 in Children (page 261), Letter 1 in Sexuality (page 352), Letter 1 (page 107) thinking in terms of Future Trends.

Mars in the **6th** house: Letter 6 in Identity (page 109), Letter 6 in Health (page 385), Letter 1 in Work (page 140), Letter 1 in Mind (page 223), Letter 1 in Health (page 381).

Mars in the **7th** house: Letter 7 in Identity (page 110), Letter 7 in Health (page 386), Letter 1 in Relationships (page 179).

Mars in the **8th** house: Letter 8 in Identity (page 111), Letter 8 in Health (page 387), Letter 1 in Relationships (page 179), Letter 1 in Money (page 324), Letter 1 in Sexuality (page 352).

Mars in the **9th** house: Letter 9 in Identity (page 111), Letter 9 in Health (page 388), Letter 1 in Mind (page 223), Letter 1 in Beliefs (page 301), Letter 1 (page 107) thinking in terms of Future Trends.

Mars in the **10th** house: Letter 10 in Identity (page 112), Letter 10 in Health (page 389), Letter 1 in Work (page 140), Letter 1 in Parents (page 404).

Mars in the **11th** house: Letter 11 in Identity (page 113), Letter 11 in Health (page 389), Letter 1 in Mind (page 223), Letter 1 in Beliefs (page 301), Letter 1 (page 107) thinking in terms of Future Trends.

Mars in the **12th** house: Letter 12 in Identity (page 114), Letter 12 in Health (page 390), Letter 1 in Beliefs (page 301), Letter 1 (page 107) thinking in terms of Future Trends.

IN SIGNS

Mars in **Aries**: Letter 1 in Identity (page 107), Letter 1 in Health (page 381).

Mars in **Taurus**: Letter 2 in Identity (page 107), Letter 2 in Health (page 382), Letter 1 in Work (page 140), Letter 1 in Money (page 324), Letter 1 in Sexuality (page 352).

Mars in **Gemini**: Letter 3 in Identity (page 107), Letter 3 in Health (page 383), Letter 1 in Mind (page 223).

Mars in **Cancer**: Letter 4 in Identity (page 108), Letter 4 in Health (page 384), Letter 1 in Children (page 261), Letter 1 in Parents (page 404).

Mars in **Leo**: Letter 5 in Identity (page 109), Letter 5 in Health (page 385), Letter 1 in Children (page 261), Letter 1 in Sexuality (page 352), Letter 1 (page 107) thinking in terms of Future Trends.

Mars in **Virgo**: Letter 6 in Identity (page 109), Letter 6 in Health (page 385), Letter 1 in Work (page 140), Letter 1 in Mind (page 223), Letter 1 in Health (page 381).

Mars in **Libra**: Letter 7 in Identity (page 110), Letter 7 in Health (page 386), Letter 1 in Relationships (page 179).

Mars in **Scorpio**: Letter 8 in Identity (page 111), Letter 8 in Health (page 387), Letter 1 in Relationships (page 179), Letter 1 in Money (page 324), Letter 1 in Sexuality (page 352).

Mars in **Sagittarius**: Letter 9 in Identity (page 111), Letter 9 in Health (page 388), Letter 1 in Mind (page 223), Letter 1 in Beliefs (page 301), Letter 1 (page 107) thinking in terms of Future Trends.

Mars in **Capricorn**: Letter 10 in Identity (page 112), Letter 10 in Health (page 389), Letter 1 in Work (page 140), Letter 1 in Parents (page 404).

Mars in **Aquarius**: Letter 11 in Identity (page 113), Letter 11 in Health (page 389), Letter 1 in Mind (page 223), Letter 1 in Beliefs (page 301), Letter 1 (page 107) thinking in terms of Future Trends.

Mars in **Pisces**: Letter 12 in Identity (page 114), Letter 12 in Health (page 390),

Letter 1 in Beliefs (page 301), Letter 1 (page 107) thinking in terms of Future Trends.

CONJUNCTIONS

Mars conjunct **Ceres or Vesta**: Letter 6 in Identity (page 109), Letter 6 in Health (page 385), Letter 1 in Work (page 140), Letter 1 in Mind (page 223), Letter 1 in Health (page 381).

Mars conjunct **Pallas or Juno**: Letter 7 in Identity (page 110), Letter 7 in Health (page 386), Letter 1 in Relationships (page 179).

Mars conjunct **Jupiter** or **Chiron**: Letter 9 in Identity (page 111), Letter 9 in Health (page 388), Letter 1 in Mind (page 223), Letter 1 in Beliefs (page 301), Letter 1 (page 107) thinking in terms of Future Trends.

Mars conjunct **Saturn**: Letter 10 in Identity (page 112), Letter 10 in Health (page 389), Letter 1 in Work (page 140), Letter 1 in Parents (page 404).

Mars conjunct **Uranus**: Letter 11 in Identity (page 113), Letter 11 in Health (page 389), Letter 1 in Mind (page 223), Letter 1 in Beliefs (page 301), Letter 1 (page 107) thinking in terms of Future Trends.

Mars conjunct **Neptune**: Letter 12 in Identity (page 114), Letter 12 in Health (page 390), Letter 1 in Beliefs (page 301), Letter 1 (page 107) thinking in terms of Future Trends.

Mars conjunct **Pluto**: Letter 8 in Identity (page 111), Letter 8 in Health (page 387), Letter 1 in Relationships (page 179), Letter 1 in Money (page 324), Letter 1 in Sexuality (page 352).

Jupiter or Chiron

IN HOUSES

Jupiter or **Chiron** in the **1st** house: Letter 9 in Identity (page 111), Letter 9 in Health (page 388), Letter 1 in Mind (page 223), Letter 1 in Beliefs (page 301), Letter 1 (page 107) thinking in terms of Future Trends.

Jupiter or **Chiron** in the **2nd** house: Letter 9 in Work (page 146), Letter 9 in Money (page 327), Letter 9 in Sexuality (page 358), Letter 2 in Mind (page 223), Letter 2 in Beliefs (page 301), Letter 2 (page 107) thinking in terms of Future Trends.

Jupiter or **Chiron** in the **3rd** house: Letter 9 in Mind (page 227), Letter 3 in Mind (page 224), Letter 3 in Beliefs (page 302), Letter 3 (page 107) thinking in terms of Future Trends.

Jupiter or **Chiron** in the **4th** house: Letter 9 in Children (page 267), Letter 9 in Parents (page 407), Letter 4 in Mind (page 324), Letter 4 in Beliefs (page 302), Letter 4 (page 108) thinking in terms of Future Trends.

Jupiter or **Chiron** in the **5th** house: Letter 9 in Children (page 267), Letter 9 in Sexuality (page 358), Letter 9 (page 111) thinking in terms of Future Trends, Letter 5 in Mind (page 225), Letter 5 in Beliefs (page 303), Letter 5 (page 109) thinking in terms of Future Trends.

Jupiter or **Chiron** in the **6th** house: Letter 9 in Work (page 146), Letter 9 in Mind (page 227), Letter 9 in Health (page 388), Letter 6 in Mind (page 225), Letter 6 in Beliefs (page 303), Letter 6 (page 109) thinking in terms of Future Trends.

Jupiter or **Chiron** in the **7th** house: Letter 9 in Relationships (page 186), Letter 7 in Mind (page 226), Letter 7 in Beliefs (page 304), Letter 7 (page 110) thinking in terms of Future Trends.

Jupiter or **Chiron** in the **8th** house: Letter 9 in Relationships (page 186), Letter 9 in Money (page 327), Letter 9 in Sexuality (page 358), Letter 8 in Mind (page 227), Letter 8 in Beliefs (page 304), Letter 8 (page 111) thinking in terms of Future Trends.

Jupiter or **Chiron** in the **9th** house: Letter 9 in Mind (page 227), Letter 9 in Beliefs (page 305), Letter 9 (page 111) thinking in terms of Future Trends.

Jupiter or **Chiron** in the **10th** house: Letter 9 in Work (page 146), Letter 9 in Parents (page 407), Letter 10 in Mind (page 228), Letter 10 in Beliefs (page 305), Letter 10 (page 112) thinking in terms of Future Trends.

Jupiter or **Chiron** in the **11th** house: Letter 9 in Mind (page 227), Letter 9 in Beliefs (page 305), Letter 9 (page 111) thinking in terms of Future Trends, Letter 11 in Mind (page 229), Letter 11 in Beliefs (page 306), Letter 11 (page 113) thinking in terms of Future Trends.

Jupiter or **Chiron** in the **12th** house: Letter 9 in Beliefs (page 305), Letter 9 (page 111) thinking in terms of Future Trends, Letter 12 in Mind (page 229), Letter 12 in Beliefs (page 306), Letter 12 (page 114) thinking in terms of Future Trends.

IN SIGNS

Jupiter or **Chiron** in **Aries**: Letter 9 in Identity (page 111), Letter 9 in Health (page 388), Letter 1 in Mind (page 223), Letter 1 in Beliefs (page 301), Letter 1 (page 107) thinking in terms of Future Trends.

Jupiter or **Chiron** in **Taurus**: Letter 9 in Work (page 146), Letter 9 in Money (page 327), Letter 9 in Sexuality (page 358), Letter 2 in Mind (page 223), Letter 2 in Beliefs (page 301), Letter 2 (page 107) thinking in terms of Future Trends.

Jupiter or **Chiron** in **Gemini**: Letter 9 in Mind (page 227), Letter 3 in Mind (page 224), Letter 3 in Beliefs (page 302), Letter 3 (page 107) thinking in terms of Future Trends.

Jupiter or **Chiron** in **Cancer**: Letter 9 in Children (page 267), Letter 9 in Parents (page 407), Letter 4 in Mind (page 224), Letter 4 in Beliefs (page 302), Letter 4 (page 108) thinking in terms of Future Trends.

Jupiter or **Chiron** in **Leo**: Letter 9 in Children (page 267), Letter 9 in Sexuality (page 358), Letter 9 (page 111) thinking in terms of Future Trends, Letter 5 in Mind (page 225), Letter 5 in Beliefs (page 303), Letter 5 (page 109) thinking in terms of Future Trends.

Jupiter or **Chiron** in **Virgo**: Letter 9 in Work (page 146), Letter 9 in Mind (page 227), Letter 9 in Health (page 388), Letter 6 in Mind (page 225), Letter 6 in Beliefs (page 303), Letter 6 (page 109) thinking in terms of Future Trends.

Jupiter or **Chiron** in **Libra**: Letter 9 in Relationships (page 186), Letter 7 in Mind (page 226), Letter 7 in Beliefs (page 304), Letter 7 (page 110) thinking in terms of Future Trends.

Jupiter or **Chiron** in **Scorpio**: Letter 9 in Relationships (page 186), Letter 9 in Money (page 327), Letter 9 in Sexuality (page 358), Letter 8 in Mind (page 227), Letter 8 in Beliefs (page 304), Letter 8 (page 111) thinking in terms of Future Trends.

Jupiter or **Chiron** in **Sagittarius**: Letter 9 in Mind (page 227), Letter 9 in Beliefs (page 305), Letter 9 (page 111) thinking in terms of Future Trends.

Jupiter or **Chiron** in **Capricorn**: Letter 9 in Work (page 146), Letter 9 in Parents (page 407), Letter 10 in Mind (page 228), Letter 10 in Beliefs (page 305), Letter 10 (page 112) thinking in terms of Future Trends.

Jupiter or **Chiron** in **Aquarius**: Letter 9 in Mind (page 227), Letter 9 in Beliefs (page 305), Letter 9 (page 111) thinking in terms of Future Trends, Letter 11 in Mind (page 229), Letter 11 in Beliefs (page 306), Letter 11 (page 113) thinking in terms of Future Trends.

Jupiter or **Chiron** in **Pisces**: Letter 9 in Beliefs (page 305), Letter 9 (page 111) thinking in terms of Future Trends, Letter 12 in Mind (page 229), Letter 12 in Beliefs (page 306), Letter 12 (page 114) thinking in terms of Future Trends.

CONJUNCTIONS

Jupiter or **Chiron** conjunct **Ceres or Vesta**: Letter 9 in Work (page 146), Letter 9 in Mind (page 227), Letter 9 in Health (page 388), Letter 6 in Mind (page 225), Letter 6 in Beliefs (page 303), Letter 6 (page 109) thinking in terms of Future Trends.

Jupiter or **Chiron** conjunct **Pallas or Juno**: Letter 9 in Relationships (page 186), Letter 7 in Mind (page 226), Letter 7 in Beliefs (page 304), Letter 7 (page 110) thinking in terms of Future Trends.

Jupiter or **Chiron** conjunct **Saturn**: Letter 9 in Work (page 146), Letter 9 in Parents (page 407), Letter 10 in Mind (page 228), Letter 10 in Beliefs (page 305), Letter 10 (page 112) thinking in terms of Future Trends.

Jupiter or **Chiron** conjunct **Uranus**: Letter 9 in Mind (page 227), Letter 9 in Beliefs (page 305), Letter 9 (page 111) thinking in terms of Future Trends, Letter 11 in Mind (page 229), Letter 11 in Beliefs (page 306), Letter 11 (page 113) thinking in terms of Future Trends.

Jupiter or **Chiron** conjunct **Neptune**: Letter 9 in Beliefs (page 305), Letter 9 (page 111) thinking in terms of Future Trends, Letter 12 in Mind (page 229), Letter 12 in Beliefs (page 306), Letter 12 (page 114) thinking in terms of Future Trends.

Jupiter or **Chiron** conjunct **Pluto**: Letter 9 in Relationships (page 186), Letter 9 in Money (page 327), Letter 9 in Sexuality (page 358), Letter 8 in Mind (page 227), Letter 8 in Beliefs (page 304), Letter 8 (page 111) thinking in terms of Future Trends.

Saturn

IN HOUSES

Saturn in the **1st** house: Letter 10 in Identity (page 112), Letter 10 in Health (page 389), Letter 1 in Work (page 140), Letter 1 in Parents (page 404).

Saturn in the **2nd** house: Letter 10 in Work (page 147), Letter 10 in Money (page 328), Letter 10 in Sexuality (page 359), Letter 2 in Work (page 141), Letter 2 in Parents (page 405).

Saturn in the **3rd** house: Letter 10 in Mind (page 228), Letter 3 in Work (page 141), Letter 3 in Parents (page 405).

Saturn in the **4th** house: Letter 10 in Children (page 268), Letter 10 in Parents (page 408), Letter 4 in Work (page 142), Letter 4 in Parents (page 406).

Saturn in the **5th** house: Letter 10 in Children (page 268), Letter 10 in Sexuality (page 359), Letter 10 (page 112) thinking in terms of Future Trends, Letter 5 in Work (page 143), Letter 5 in Parents (page 406).

Saturn in the **6th** house: Letter 10 in Work (page 147), Letter 10 in Mind (page 228), Letter 10 in Health (page 389), Letter 6 in Work (page 144), Letter 6 in Parents (page 406).

Saturn in the **7th** house: Letter 10 in Relationships (page 187), Letter 7 in Work (page 145), Letter 7 in Parents (page 407).

Saturn in the **8th** house: Letter 10 in Relationships (page 187), Letter 10 in Money (page 328), Letter 10 in Sexuality (page 359), Letter 8 in Work (page 145), Letter 8 in Parents (page 407).

Saturn in the **9th** house: Letter 10 in Mind (page 228), Letter 10 in Beliefs (page 305), Letter 10 (page 112) thinking in terms of Future Trends, Letter 9 in Work (page 146), Letter 9 in Parents (page 407).

Saturn in the **10th** house: Letter 10 in Work (page 147), Letter 10 in Parents (page 408).

Saturn in the **11th** house: Letter 10 in Mind (page 228), Letter 10 in Beliefs (page 305), Letter 10 (page 112) thinking in terms of Future Trends, Letter 11 in Work (page 148), Letter 11 in Parents (page 408).

Saturn in the **12th** house: Letter 10 in Beliefs (page 305), Letter 10 (page 112) thinking in terms of Future Trends, Letter 12 in Work (page 149), Letter 12 in Parents (page 409).

IN SIGNS

Saturn in **Aries**: Letter 10 in Identity (page 112), Letter 10 in Health (page 389), Letter 1 in Work (page 140), Letter 1 in Parents (page 404).

Saturn in **Taurus**: Letter 10 in Work (page 147), Letter 10 in Money (page 328), Letter 10 in Sexuality (page 359), Letter 2 in Work (page 141), Letter 2 in Parents (page 405).

Saturn in **Gemini**: Letter 10 in Mind (page 228), Letter 3 in Work (page 141), Letter 3 in Parents (page 405).

Saturn in **Cancer**: Letter 10 in Children (page 268), Letter 10 in Parents (page 408), Letter 4 in Work (page 142), Letter 4 in Parents (page 406).

Saturn in **Leo**: Letter 10 in Children (page 268), Letter 10 in Sexuality (page 359), Letter 10 (page 112) thinking in terms of Future Trends, Letter 5 in Work (page 143), Letter 5 in Parents (page 406).

Saturn in **Virgo**: Letter 10 in Work (page 147), Letter 10 in Mind (page 228), Letter 10 in Health (page 389), Letter 6 in Work (page 144), Letter 6 in Parents (page 406).

Saturn in **Libra**: Letter 10 in Relationships (page 187), Letter 7 in Work (page 145), Letter 7 in Parents (page 407).

Saturn in **Scorpio**: Letter 10 in Relationships (page 187), Letter 10 in Money (page 328), Letter 10 in Sexuality (page 359), Letter 8 in Work (page 145), Letter 8 in Parents (page 407).

Saturn in **Sagittarius**: Letter 10 in Mind (page 228), Letter 10 in Beliefs (page 305), Letter 10 (page 112) thinking in terms of Future Trends, Letter 9 in Work (page 146), Letter 9 in Parents (page 407).

Saturn in **Capricorn**: Letter 10 in Work (page 147), Letter 10 in Parents (page 408).

Saturn in **Aquarius**: Letter 10 in Mind (page 228), Letter 10 in Beliefs (page 305), Letter 10 (page 112) thinking in terms of Future Trends, Letter 11 in Work (page 148), Letter 11 in Parents (page 408).

Saturn in **Pisces**: Letter 10 in Beliefs (page 305), Letter 10 (page 112) thinking in terms of Future Trends, Letter 12 in Work (page 149), Letter 12 in Parents (page 409).

CONJUNCTIONS

Saturn conjunct **Ceres or Vesta**: Letter 10 in Work (page 147), Letter 10 in Mind (page 228), Letter 10 in Health (page 389), Letter 6 in Work (page 144), Letter 6 in Parents (page 406).

Saturn conjunct **Pallas or Juno**: Letter 10 in Relationships (page 187), Letter 7 in Work (page 145), Letter 7 in Parents (page 407).

Saturn conjunct **Uranus**: Letter 10 in Mind (page 228), Letter 10 in Beliefs (page 305), Letter 10 (page 112) thinking in terms of Future Trends, Letter 11 in Work (page 148), Letter 11 in Parents (page 408).

Saturn conjunct **Neptune**: Letter 10 in Beliefs (page 305), Letter 10 (page 112) thinking in terms of Future Trends, Letter 12 in Work (page 149), Letter 12 in Parents (page 409).

Saturn conjunct **Pluto**: Letter 10 in Relationships (page 187), Letter 10 in Money (page 328), Letter 10 in Sexuality (page 359), Letter 8 in Work (page 145), Letter 8 in Parents (page 407).

Uranus

IN HOUSES

Uranus in the **1st** house: Letter 11 in Identity (page 113), Letter 11 in Health (page 389), Letter 1 in Mind (page 223), Letter 1 in Beliefs (page 301), Letter 1 (page 107) thinking in terms of Future Trends.

Uranus in the **2nd** house: Letter 11 in Work (page 148), Letter 11 in Money (page 328), Letter 11 in Sexuality (page 360), Letter 2 in Mind (page 223), Letter 2 in Beliefs (page 301), Letter 2 (page 107) thinking in terms of Future Trends.

Uranus in the **3rd** house: Letter 11 in Mind (page 229), Letter 3 in Mind (page 223), Letter 3 in Beliefs (page 302), Letter 3 (page 107) thinking in terms of Future Trends.

Uranus in the **4th** house: Letter 11 in Children (page 269), Letter 11 in Parents (page 408), Letter 4 in Mind (page 224), Letter 4 in Beliefs (page 302), Letter 4 (page 108) thinking in terms of Future Trends.

Uranus in the **5th** house: Letter 11 in Children (page 269), Letter 11 in Sexuality (page 360), Letter 11 (page 113) thinking in terms of Future Trends, Letter 5 in Mind (page 225), Letter 5 in Beliefs (page 303), Letter 5 (page 109) thinking in terms of Future Trends.

Uranus in the **6th** house: Letter 11 in Work (page 148), Letter 11 in Mind (page 229), Letter 11 in Health (page 389), Letter 6 in Mind (page 225), Letter 6 in Beliefs (page 303), Letter 6 (page 109) thinking in terms of Future Trends.

Uranus in the **7th** house: Letter 11 in Relationships (page 188), Letter 7 in Mind (page 226), Letter 7 in Beliefs (page 304), Letter 7 (page 110) thinking in terms of Future Trends.

Uranus in the **8th** house: Letter 11 in Relationships (page 188), Letter 11 in Money (page 328), Letter 11 in Sexuality (page 360), Letter 8 in Mind (page 227), Letter 8 in Beliefs (page 304), Letter 8 (page 111) thinking in terms of Future Trends.

Uranus in the **9th** house: Letter 11 in Mind (page 229), Letter 11 in Beliefs (page 306), Letter 11 (page 113) thinking in terms of Future Trends, Letter 9 in Mind (page 227), Letter 9 in Beliefs (page 305), Letter 9 (page 111) thinking in terms of Future Trends.

Uranus in the **10th** house: Letter 11 in Work (page 148), Letter 11 in Parents (page 408), Letter 10 in Mind (page 228), Letter 10 in Beliefs (page 305), Letter 10 (page 112) thinking in terms of Future Trends.

Uranus in the **11th** house: Letter 11 in Mind (page 229), Letter 11 in Beliefs (page 306), Letter 11 (page 113) thinking in terms of Future Trends.

Uranus in the **12th** house: Letter 11 in Beliefs (page 306), Letter 11 (page 113) thinking in terms of Future Trends, Letter 12 in Mind (page 229), Letter 12 in Beliefs (page 306), Letter 12 (page 114) thinking in terms of Future Trends.

IN SIGNS

Uranus in **Aries**: Letter 11 in Identity (page 113), Letter 11 in Health (page 389), Letter 1 in Mind (page 223), Letter 1 in Beliefs (page 301), Letter 1 (page 107) thinking in terms of Future Trends.

Uranus in **Taurus**: Letter 11 in Work (page 148), Letter 11 in Money (page 328), Letter 11 in Sexuality (page 360), Letter 2 in Mind (page 223), Letter 2 in Beliefs (page 301), Letter 2 (page 107) thinking in terms of Future Trends.

Uranus in **Gemini**: Letter 11 in Mind (page 229), Letter 3 in Mind (page 224), Letter 3 in Beliefs (page 302), Letter 3 (page 107) thinking in terms of Future Trends.

Uranus in **Cancer**: Letter 11 in Children (page 269), Letter 11 in Parents (page 408), Letter 4 in Mind (page 224), Letter 4 in Beliefs (page 302), Letter 4 (page 108) thinking in terms of Future Trends.

Uranus in **Leo**: Letter 11 in Children (page 269), Letter 11 in Sexuality (page 360), Letter 11 (page 113) thinking in terms of Future Trends, Letter 5 in Mind (page 225), Letter 5 in Beliefs (page 303), Letter 5 (page 109) thinking in terms of Future Trends.

Uranus in **Virgo**: Letter 11 in Work (page 148), Letter 11 in Mind (page 229), Letter 11 in Health (page 389), Letter 6 in Mind (page 225), Letter 6 in Beliefs (page 303), Letter 6 (page 109) thinking in terms of Future Trends.

Uranus in **Libra**: Letter 11 in Relationships (page 188), Letter 7 in Mind (page 226), Letter 7 in Beliefs (page 304), Letter 7 (page 110) thinking in terms of Future Trends.

Uranus in **Scorpio**: Letter 11 in Relationships (page 188), Letter 11 in Money (page 328), Letter 11 in Sexuality (page 360), Letter 8 in Mind (page 227), Letter 8 in Beliefs (page 304), Letter 8 (page 111) thinking in terms of Future Trends.

Uranus in **Sagittarius**: Letter 11 in Mind (page 229), Letter 11 in Beliefs (page 306), Letter 11 (page 113) thinking in terms of Future Trends, Letter 9 in Mind (page 227), Letter 9 in Beliefs (page 305), Letter 9 (page 111) thinking in terms of Future Trends.

Uranus in **Capricorn**: Letter 11 in Work (page 148), Letter 11 in Parents (page 408), Letter 10 in Mind (page 228), Letter 10 in Beliefs (page 305), Letter 10 (page 112) thinking in terms of Future Trends.

Uranus in **Aquarius**: Letter 11 in Mind (page 229), Letter 11 in Beliefs (page 306), Letter 11 (page 113) thinking in terms of Future Trends.

Uranus in **Pisces**: Letter 11 in Beliefs (page 306), Letter 11 (page 113) thinking in terms of Future Trends, Letter 12 in Mind (page 229), Letter 12 in Beliefs (page 306), Letter 12 (page 114) thinking in terms of Future Trends.

CONJUNCTIONS

Uranus conjunct **Ceres or Vesta**: Letter 11 in Work (page 148), Letter 11 in Mind (page 229), Letter 11 in Health (page 389), Letter 6 in Mind (page 225), Letter 6 in Beliefs (page 303), Letter 6 (page 109) thinking in terms of Future Trends.

Uranus conjunct **Pallas or Juno**: Letter 11 in Relationships (page 188), Letter

7 in Mind (page 226), Letter 7 in Beliefs (page 304), Letter 7 (page 110) thinking in terms of Future Trends.

Uranus conjunct **Neptune**: Letter 11 in Beliefs (page 306), Letter 11 (page 113) thinking in terms of Future Trends, Letter 12 in Mind (page 229), Letter 12 in Beliefs (page 306), Letter 12 (page 114) thinking in terms of Future Trends.

Uranus conjunct **Pluto**: Letter 11 in Relationships (page 188), Letter 11 in Money (page 328), Letter 11 in Sexuality (page 360), Letter 8 in Mind (page 227), Letter 8 in Beliefs (page 304), Letter 8 (page 111) thinking in terms of Future Trends.

Neptune

IN HOUSES

Neptune in the **1st** house: Letter 12 in Identity (page 114), Letter 12 in Health (page 390), Letter 1 in Beliefs (page 301), Letters 1 (page 107) thinking in terms of Future Trends.

Neptune in the **2nd** house: Letter 12 in Work (page 149), Letter 12 in Money (page 328), Letter 12 in Sexuality (page 361), Letter 2 in Beliefs (page 301), Letter 2 (page 107) thinking in terms of Future Trends.

Neptune in the **3rd** house: Letter 12 in Mind (page 229), Letter 3 in Beliefs (page 302), Letter 3 (page 107) thinking in terms of Future Trends.

Neptune in the **4th** house: Letter 12 in Children (page 269), Letter 12 in Parents (page 409), Letter 4 in Beliefs (page 302), Letter 4 (page 108) thinking in terms of Future Trends.

Neptune in the **5th** house: Letter 12 in Children (page 269), Letter 12 in Sexuality (page 361), Letter 12 (page 114) thinking in terms of Future Trends, Letter 5 in Beliefs (page 303), Letter 5 (page 109) thinking in terms of Future Trends.

Neptune in the **6th** house: Letter 12 in Work (page 149), Letter 12 in Mind (page 229), Letter 12 in Health (page 390), Letter 6 in Beliefs (page 303), Letter 6 (page 109) thinking in terms of Future Trends.

Neptune in the **7th** house: Letter 12 in Relationships (page 188), Letter 7 in Beliefs (page 304), Letter 7 (page 110) thinking in terms of Future Trends.

Neptune in the **8th** house: Letter 12 in Relationships (page 188), Letter 12 in Money (page 328), Letter 12 in Sexuality (page 361), Letter 8 in Beliefs (page 304), Letters 8 (page 111) thinking in terms of Future Trends.

Neptune in the **9th** house: Letter 12 in Mind (page 229), Letter 12 in Beliefs (page 306), Letter 12 (page 114) thinking in terms of Future Trends, Letter 9 in Beliefs (page 305), Letter 9 (page 111) thinking in terms of Future Trends.

Neptune in the **10th** house: Letter 12 in Work (page 149), Letter 12 in Parents (page 409), Letter 10 in Beliefs (page 305), Letter 10 (page 112) thinking in terms of Future Trends.

Neptune in the **11th** house: Letter 12 in Mind (page 229), Letter 12 in Beliefs (page 306), Letter 12 (page 114) thinking in terms of Future Trends, Letter 11 in Beliefs (page 306), Letter 11 (page 113) thinking in terms of Future Trends.

Neptune in the **12th** house: Letter 12 in Beliefs (page 306), Letter 12 (page 114) thinking in terms of Future Trends.

IN SIGNS

Neptune in **Aries**: Letter 12 in Identity (page 114), Letter 12 in Health (page 390), Letter 1 in Beliefs (page 301), Letters 1 (page 107) thinking in terms of Future Trends.

Neptune in **Taurus**: Letter 12 in Work (page 149), Letter 12 in Money (page 328), Letter 12 in Sexuality (page 361), Letter 2 in Beliefs (page 301), Letter 2 (page 107) thinking in terms of Future Trends.

Neptune in **Gemini**: Letter 12 in Mind (page 229), Letter 3 in Beliefs (page 302), Letter 3 (page 107) thinking in terms of Future Trends.

Neptune in **Cancer**: Letter 12 in Children (page 269), Letter 12 in Parents (page 409), Letter 4 in Beliefs (page 302), Letter 4 (page 108) thinking in terms of Future Trends.

Neptune in **Leo**: Letter 12 in Children (page 269), Letter 12 in Sexuality (page 361), Letter 12 (page 114) thinking in terms of Future Trends, Letter 5 in Beliefs (page 303), Letter 5 (page 109) thinking in terms of Future Trends.

Neptune in **Virgo**: Letter 12 in Work (page 149), Letter 12 in Mind (page 229), Letter 12 in Health (page 390), Letter 6 in Beliefs (page 303), Letter 6 (page 109) thinking in terms of Future Trends.

Neptune in **Libra**: Letter 12 in Relationships (page 188), Letter 7 in Beliefs (page 304), Letter 7 (page 110) thinking in terms of Future Trends.

Neptune in **Scorpio**: Letter 12 in Relationships (page 188), Letter 12 in Money (page 328), Letter 12 in Sexuality (page 361), Letter 8 in Beliefs (page 304), Letters 8 (page 111) thinking in terms of Future Trends.

Neptune in **Sagittarius**: Letter 12 in Mind (page 229), Letter 12 in Beliefs (page 306), Letter 12 (page 114) thinking in terms of Future Trends, Letter 9 in Beliefs (page 305), Letter 9 (page 111) thinking in terms of Future Trends.

Neptune in **Capricorn**: Letter 12 in Work (page 149), Letter 12 in Parents (page 409), Letter 10 in Beliefs (page 305), Letter 10 (page 112) thinking in terms of Future Trends.

Neptune in **Aquarius**: Letter 12 in Mind (page 229), Letter 12 in Beliefs (page 306), Letter 12 (page 114) thinking in terms of Future Trends, Letter 11 in Beliefs (page 306), Letter 11 (page 113) thinking in terms of Future Trends.

Neptune in **Pisces**: Letter 12 in Beliefs (page 306), Letter 12 (page 114) thinking in terms of Future Trends.

CONJUNCTIONS

Neptune conjunct **Ceres or Vesta**: Letter 12 in Work (page 149), Letter 12 in Mind (page 229), Letter 12 in Health (page 390), Letter 6 in Beliefs (page 303), Letter 6 (page 109) thinking in terms of Future Trends.

Neptune conjunct **Pallas or Juno**: Letter 12 in Relationships (page 188), Letter 7 in Beliefs (page 304), Letter 7 (page 110) thinking in terms of Future Trends.

Neptune conjunct **Pluto**: Letter 12 in Relationships (page 188), Letter 12 in Money (page 328), Letter 12 in Sexuality (page 361), Letter 8 in Beliefs (page 304), Letter 8 (page 111) thinking in terms of Future Trends.

Pluto

IN HOUSES

Pluto in the **1st** house: Letter 8 in Identity (page 111), Letter 8 in Health (page 387), Letter 1 in Relationships (page 179), Letter 1 in Money (page 324), Letter 1 in Sexuality (page 352).

Pluto in the **2nd** house: Letter 8 in Work (page 145), Letter 8 in Money (page 327), Letter 8 in Sexuality; Letter 2 in Relationships (page 181), Letter 2 in Money (page 325), Letter 2 in Sexuality (page 353).

Pluto in the **3rd** house: Letter 8 in Mind (page 227), Letter 3 in Relationships (page 182), Letter 3 in Money (page 325), Letter 3 in Sexuality (page 354).

Pluto in the **4th** house: Letter 8 in Children (page 266), Letter 8 in Parents (page 407), Letter 4 in Relationships (page 182), Letter 4 in Money (page 325), Letter 4 in Sexuality (page 354).

Pluto in the **5th** house: Letter 8 in Children (page 266), Letter 8 in Sexuality (page 357), Letter 8 (page 111) thinking in terms of Future Trends, Letter 5 in Relationships (page 183), Letter 5 in Money (page 326), Letter 5 in Sexuality (page 355).

Pluto in the **6th** house: Letter 8 in Work (page 145), Letter 8 in Mind (page 227), Letter 8 in Health (page 387), Letter 6 in Relationships (page 184), Letter 6 in Money (page 326), Letter 6 in Sexuality (page 356).

Pluto in the **7th** house: Letter 8 in Relationships (page 186), Letter 7 in Relationships (page 185), Letter 7 in Money (page 326), Letter 7 in Sexuality (page 357).

Pluto in the **8th** house: Letter 8 in Relationships (page 186), Letter 8 in Money (page 327), Letter 8 in Sexuality (page 357).

Pluto in the **9th** house: Letter 8 in Mind (page 227), Letter 8 in Beliefs (page 304), Letter 8 (page 111) thinking in terms of Future Trends, Letter 9 in Relationships (page 186), Letter 9 in Money (page 327), Letter 9 in Sexuality (page 358).

Pluto in the **10th** house: Letter 8 in Work (page 145), Letter 8 in Parents (page 407), Letter 10 in Relationships (page 187), Letter 10 in Money (page 328), Letter 10 in Sexuality (page 359).

Pluto in the **11th** house: Letter 8 in Mind (page 227), Letter 8 in Beliefs (page 304), Letter 8 (page 111) thinking in terms of Future Trends, Letter 11 in Relationships (page 188), Letter 11 in Money (page 328), Letter 11 in Sexuality (page 360).

Pluto in the **12th** house: Letter 8 in Beliefs (page 304), Letter 8 (page 111) thinking in terms of Future Trends, Letter 12 in Relationships (page 188), Letter 12 in Money (page 328), Letter 12 in Sexuality (page 361).

IN SIGNS

Pluto in **Aries**: Letter 8 in Identity (page 111), Letter 8 in Health (page 387), Letter 1 in Relationships (page 179), Letter 1 in Money (page 324), Letter 1 in Sexuality (page 352).

Pluto in **Taurus**: Letter 8 in Work (page 145), Letter 8 in Money (page 327), Letter 8 in Sexuality (page 357), Letter 2 in Relationships (page 181), Letter 2 in Money (page 325), Letter 2 in Sexuality (page 353).

Pluto in **Gemini**: Letter 8 in Mind (page 227), Letter 3 in Relationships (page 182), Letter 3 in Money (page 325), Letter 3 in Sexuality (page 354).

Pluto in **Cancer**: Letter 8 in Children (page 266), Letter 8 in Parents (page 407), Letter 4 in Relationships (page 182), Letter 4 in Money (page 325), Letter 4 in Sexuality (page 354).

Pluto in **Leo**: Letter 8 in Children (page 266), Letter 8 in Sexuality (page 357), Letter 8 (page 111) thinking in terms of Future Trends, Letter 5 in Relationships (page 183), Letter 5 in Money (page 326), Letter 5 in Sexuality (page 355).

Pluto in **Virgo**: Letter 8 in Work (page 145), Letter 8 in Mind (page 227), Letter 8 in Health (page 387), Letter 6 in Relationships (page 184), Letter 6 in Money (page 326), Letter 6 in Sexuality (page 356).

Pluto in **Libra**: Letter 8 in Relationships (page 186), Letter 7 in Relationships (page 185), Letter 7 in Money (page 326), Letter 7 in Sexuality (page 357).

Pluto in **Scorpio**: Letter 8 in Relationships (page 186), Letter 8 in Money (page 327), Letter 8 in Sexuality (page 357).

Pluto in **Sagittarius**: Letter 8 in Mind (page 227), Letter 8 in Beliefs (page 304), Letter 8 (page 111) thinking in terms of Future Trends, Letter 9 in Relationships (page 186), Letter 9 in Money (page 327), Letter 9 in Sexuality (page 358).

Pluto in **Capricorn**: Letter 8 in Work (page 145), Letter 8 in Parents (page 407), Letter 10 in Relationships (page 187), Letter 10 in Money (page 328), Letter 10 in Sexuality (page 359).

Pluto in **Aquarius**: Letter 8 in Mind (page 227), Letter 8 in Beliefs (page 304), Letter 8 (page 111) thinking in terms of Future Trends, Letter 11 in Relationships (page 188), Letter 11 in Money (page 328), Letter 11 in Sexuality (page 360).

Pluto in **Pisces**: Letter 8 in Beliefs (page 304), Letter 8 (page 111) thinking in terms of Future Trends, Letter 12 in Relationships (page 188), Letter 12 in Money (page 328), Letter 12 in Sexuality (page 361).

CONJUNCTIONS

Pluto conjunct **Ceres or Vesta**: Letter 8 in Work (page 145), Letter 8 in Mind (page 227), Letter 8 in Health (page 387), Letter 6 in Relationships (page 184), Letter 6 in Money (page 326), Letter 6 in Sexuality (page 356).

Pluto conjunct **Pallas or Juno**: Letter 8 in Relationships (page 186), Letter 7 in Relationships (page 185), Letter 7 in Money (page 326), Letter 7 in Sexuality (page 357).

Ceres and Vesta

IN HOUSES

Ceres or **Vesta** in the **1st** house: Letter 6 in Identity (page 109), Letter 6 in Health (page 385), Letter 1 in Work (page 140), Letter 1 in Mind (page 223), Letter 1 in Health (page 381).

Ceres or **Vesta** in the **2nd** house: Letter 6 in Work (page 144), Letter 6 in Money (page 326), Letter 6 in Sexuality (page 356), Letter 2 in Work (page 141), Letter 2 in Mind (page 223), Letter 2 in Health (page 382).

Ceres or **Vesta** in the **3rd** house: Letter 6 in Mind (page 225), Letter 3 in Work (page 141), Letter 3 in Mind (page 224), Letter 3 in Health (page 383).

Ceres or **Vesta** in the **4th** house: Letter 6 in Children (page 265), Letter 6 in Parents (page 406), Letter 4 in Work (page 142), Letter 4 in Mind (page 224), Letter 4 in Health (page 384).

Ceres or **Vesta** in the **5th** house: Letter 6 in Children (page 265), Letter 6 in Sexuality (page 356), Letter 6 (page 109) thinking in terms of Future Trends, Letter 5 in Work (page 143), Letter 5 in Mind (page 225), Letter 5 in Health (page 385).

Ceres or **Vesta** in the **6th** house: Letter 6 in Work (page 144), Letter 6 in Mind (page 225), Letter 6 in Health (page 385).

Ceres or **Vesta** in the **7th** house: Letter 6 in Relationships (page 184), Letter 7 in Work (page 145), Letter 7 in Mind (page 226), Letter 7 in Health (page 386).

Ceres or **Vesta** in the **8th** house: Letter 6 in Relationships (page 184), Letter 6 in Money (page 326), Letter 6 in Sexuality (page 356), Letter 8 in Work (page 145), Letter 8 in Mind (page 227), Letter 8 in Health (page 387).

Ceres or **Vesta** in the **9th** house: Letter 6 in Mind (page 225), Letter 6 in Beliefs (page 303), Letter 6 (page 109) thinking in terms of Future Trends, Letter 9 in Work (page 146), Letter 9 in Mind (page 227), Letter 9 in Health (page 388).

Ceres or **Vesta** in the **10th** house: Letter 6 in Work (page 144), Letter 6 in Parents (page 406), Letter 10 in Work (page 147), Letter 10 in Mind (page 228), Letter 10 in Health (page 389).

Ceres or **Vesta** in the **11th** house: Letter 6 in Mind (page 225), Letter 6 in Beliefs (page 303), Letter 6 (page 109) thinking in terms of Future Trends, Letter 11 in Work (page 148), Letter 11 in Mind (page 229), Letter 11 in Health (page 389).

Ceres or **Vesta** in the **12th** house: Letter 6 in Beliefs (page 303), Letter 6 (page 109) thinking in terms of Future Trends, Letter 12 in Work (page 149), Letter 12 in Mind (page 229), Letter 12 in Health (page 390).

IN SIGNS

Ceres or **Vesta** in **Aries**: Letter 6 in Identity (page 109), Letter 6 in Health (page 385), Letter 1 in Work (page 140), Letter 1 in Mind (page 223), Letter 1 in Health (page 381).

Ceres or **Vesta** in **Taurus**: Letter 6 in Work (page 144), Letter 6 in Money (page 326), Letter 6 in Sexuality (page 356), Letter 2 in Work (page 141), Letter 2 in Mind (page 223), Letter 2 in Health (page 382).

Ceres or **Vesta** in **Gemini**: Letter 6 in Mind (page 225), Letter 3 in Work (page 141), Letter 3 in Mind (page 224), Letter 3 in Health (page 383).

Ceres or **Vesta** in **Cancer**: Letter 6 in Children (page 265), Letter 6 in Parents (page 406), Letter 4 in Work (page 142), Letter 4 in Mind (page 224), Letter 4 in Health (page 384).

Ceres or **Vesta** in **Leo**: Letter 6 in Children (page 265), Letter 6 in Sexuality (page 356), Letter 6 (page 109) thinking in terms of Future Trends, Letter 5 in Work (page 143), Letter 5 in Mind (page 225), Letter 5 in Health (page 385).

Ceres or **Vesta** in **Virgo**: Letter 6 in Work (page 144), Letter 6 in Mind (page 225), Letter 6 in Health (page 385).

Ceres or **Vesta** in **Libra**: Letter 6 in Relationships (page 184), Letter 7 in Work (page 145), Letter 7 in Mind (page 226), Letter 7 in Health (page 386).

Ceres or **Vesta** in **Scorpio**: Letter 6 in Relationships (page 184), Letter 6 in Money (page 326), Letter 6 in Sexuality (page 356), Letter 8 in Work (page 145), Letter 8 in Mind (page 227), Letter 8 in Health (page 387).

Ceres or **Vesta** in **Sagittarius**: Letter 6 in Mind (page 225), Letter 6 in Beliefs (page 303), Letter 6 (page 109) thinking in terms of Future Trends, Letter 9 in Work (page 146), Letter 9 in Mind (page 227), Letter 9 in Health (page 388).

Ceres or **Vesta** in **Capricorn**: Letter 6 in Work (page 144), Letter 6 in Parents (page 406), Letter 10 in Work (page 147), Letter 10 in Mind (page 228), Letter 10 in Health (page 389).

Ceres or **Vesta** in **Aquarius**: Letter 6 in Mind (page 225), Letter 6 in Beliefs (page 303), Letter 6 (page 109) thinking in terms of Future Trends, Letter 11 in Work (page 148), Letter 11 in Mind (page 229), Letter 11 in Health (page 389).

Ceres or **Vesta** in **Pisces**: Letter 6 in Beliefs (page 303), Letter 6 (page 109) thinking in terms of Future Trends, Letter 12 in Work (page 149), Letter 12 in Mind (page 229), Letter 12 in Health (page 390).

CONJUNCTIONS

Ceres or **Vesta** conjunct **Pallas** or **Juno**: Letter 6 in Relationships (page 184), Letter 7 in Work (page 145), Letter 7 in Health (page 386), Letter 7 in Mind (page 226).

Pallas and Juno

IN HOUSES

Pallas or **Juno** in the **1st** house: Letter 7 in Identity (page 110), Letter 7 in Health (page 386), Letter 1 in Relationships (page 179).

Pallas or **Juno** in the **2nd** house: Letter 7 in Work (page 145), Letter 7 in Money (page 326), Letter 7 in Sexuality (page 357), Letter 2 in Relationships (page 181).

Pallas or **Juno** in the **3rd** house: Letter 7 in Mind (page 226), Letter 3 in Relationships (page 182).

Pallas or **Juno** in the **4th** house: Letter 7 in Children (page 265), Letter 7 in Parents (page 407), Letter 4 in Relationships (page 182).

Pallas or **Juno** in the **5th** house: Letter 7 in Children (page 265), Letter 7 in Sexuality (page 357), Letter 7 (page 110) thinking in terms of Future Trends, Letter 5 in Relationships (page 183).

Pallas or **Juno** in the **6th** house: Letter 7 in Work (page 145), Letter 7 in Mind (page 226), Letter 7 in Health (page 386), Letter 6 in Relationships (page 184).

Pallas or **Juno** in the **7th** house: Letter 7 in Relationships (page 185).

Pallas or **Juno** in the **8th** house: Letter 7 in Relationships (page 185), Letter 7 in Money (page 326), Letter 7 in Sexuality (page 357), Letter 8 in Relationship (page 186).

Pallas or **Juno** in the **9th** house: Letter 7 in Mind (page 226), Letter 7 in Beliefs (page 304), Letter 7 (page 110) thinking in terms of Future Trends, Letter 9 in Relationship (page 186).

Pallas or **Juno** in the **10th** house: Letter 7 in Work (page 145), Letter 7 in Parents (page 407), Letter 10 in Relationships (page 187).

Pallas or **Juno** in the **11th** house: Letter 7 in Mind (page 226), Letter 7 in Beliefs (page 304), Letter 7 (page 110) thinking in terms of Future Trends, Letter 11 in Relationships (page 188).

Pallas or **Juno** in the **12th** house: Letter 7 in Beliefs (page 304), Letter 7 (page 110) thinking in terms of Future Trends, Letter 12 in Relationships (page 188).

IN SIGNS

Pallas or **Juno** in **Aries**: Letter 7 in Identity (page 110), Letter 7 in Health (page 386), Letter 1 in Relationships (page 179).

Pallas or **Juno** in **Taurus**: Letter 7 in Work (page 145), Letter 7 in Money (page 326), Letter 7 in Sexuality (page 357), Letter 2 in Relationships (page 181).

Pallas or **Juno** in **Gemini**: Letter 7 in Mind (page 226), Letter 3 in Relationships (page 182).

Pallas or **Juno** in **Cancer**: Letter 7 in Children (page 265), Letter 7 in Parents (page 407), Letter 4 in Relationships (page 182).

Pallas or **Juno** in **Leo**: Letter 7 in Children (page 265), Letter 7 in Sexuality (page 357), Letter 7 (page 110) thinking in terms of Future Trends, Letter 5 in Relationships (page 183).

Pallas or **Juno** in **Virgo**: Letter 7 in Work (page 145), Letter 7 in Mind (page 226), Letter 7 in Health (page 386), Letter 6 in Relationships (page 184).

Pallas or **Juno** in **Libra**: Letter 7 in Relationships (page 185).

Pallas or **Juno** in **Scorpio**: Letter 7 in Relationships (page 185), Letter 7 in Money (page 326), Letter 7 in Sexuality (page 357), Letter 8 in Relationship (page 186).

Pallas or **Juno** in **Sagittarius**: Letter 7 in Mind (page 226), Letter 7 in Beliefs (page 304), Letter 7 (page 110) thinking in terms of Future Trends, Letter 9 in Relationship (page 186).

Pallas or **Juno** in **Capricorn**: Letter 7 in Work (page 145), Letter 7 in Parents (page 407), Letter 10 in Relationships (page 187).

Pallas or **Juno** in **Aquarius**: Letter 7 in Mind (page 226), Letter 7 in Beliefs (page 304), Letter 7 (page 110) thinking in terms of Future Trends, Letter 11 in Relationships (page 188).

Pallas or **Juno** in **Pisces**: Letter 7 in Beliefs (page 304), Letter 7 (page 110) thinking in terms of Future Trends, Letter 12 in Relationships (page 188).

Rulerships

It would be more complete to also consider the placement of the rulers of every cusp in a horoscope. Think in terms of the natural zodiac. Thus, use the listings for Mars to find the placements for the ruler of the Ascendant for house and sign. That is, if the ruler of the Ascendant is in Aries, go to Letter 1 in Identity (page 107) and Letter 1 in Health (page 381) — just as with Mars in Aries. Repeat the process for the house the ruler occupies. Check the page numbers for Venus which match the placements of the ruler of the 2nd cusp, etc.

Other Aspects

It is possible to use this material to gain a quick grasp of other aspects. Remember that harmony aspects (trine, sextile, semisextile) indicate inner agreement (where we may overdo), while conflict aspects point to drives we must integrate, where there is inner ambivalence and peace must be made between fighting factions.

The following summary lists the planets associated with each of the themes discussed in Chapter 4. (A theme has more than one planet associated with it.) Harmony aspects point to the likelihood of relative ease in blending themes, while challenge aspects point to probable conflict, and the need to make room in life for contradictory themes.

To get the essence of any aspect quickly, simply locate both planets in the list below and scan the summary of themes (and simple key words) associated with each planet. Then compare and contrast the themes for the planets involved in the aspect, recalling that harmony aspects show easier blending and conflict aspects the need to take turns or find different times and places for the varying drives in life. (If you wish to include more factors, you can also consider the themes of the houses and signs involved in each aspect. The themes listed below for the planets can also be assigned to the sign each planet rules and the house associated with it in the natural zodiac.)

For more details on any theme, read the complete descriptions (in Chapter Four) of the themes involved.

As an example, a Sun/Moon harmony aspect would imply a strong focus on closeness and interpersonal issues. Love and family could be quite important. Caring comes naturally. A conflict aspect would suggest a need to balance fire spontaneity and excitement with water sensitivity and inwardness, the desire to take risks with the need for security, artistic/creative needs with parental demands, etc. The basic themes are listed below.

SUN: closeness, artistic, risk/creativity, power, fire (excitement), fixed (willpower).
MOON: closeness, parents, security, personal, water (feelings), cardinal (event-oriented).

MERCURY: mind, personal, air (intellect/communication), mutable (flexible, vicarious).

[Note: if you do not use the asteroids, the themes listed for Vesta should be added to Mercury, as should the themes listed for Ceres, with the exception of the parental theme. The themes listed for Juno should be added to the themes for Venus, as should the themes for Pallas, with the exception of the mental (mind) theme.]

VENUS: security, artistic, personal, earth (physical results), fixed (willpower).

MARS: freedom, risk/creativity, personal, fire (excitement), cardinal (event-oriented).

JUPITER or **CHIRON**: freedom, idealistic, risk/creativity, mind, transpersonal, fire (excitement), mutable (flexible, vicarious).

SATURN: parents, work, obsessive-compulsive, security, power, transpersonal, earth (physical results), cardinal (event-oriented).

URANUS: freedom, risk/creativity, mind, transpersonal, air (intellect/communication), fixed (willpower).

NEPTUNE: idealistic, artistic, transpersonal, water (feelings), mutable (flexible, vicarious).

PLUTO: closeness, obsessive-compulsive, security, power, relationships, water (feelings), fixed (willpower).

CERES: parents, work, obsessive-compulsive, security, mind, interpersonal, earth (physical results), mutable (flexible, vicarious).

VESTA: work, obsessive-compulsive, security, mind, interpersonal, earth (physical results), mutable (flexible, vicarious).

PALLAS: closeness, artistic, mind, relationships, air (intellect/communication), cardinal (event-oriented).

JUNO: closeness, artistic, relationships, air (intellect/communication), cardinal (event-oriented).

Index

Boldface indicates areas of major discussion.